THE BOOK OF THE TWELVE AND THE NEW FORM CRITICISM

Society of Biblical Literature

Ancient Near East Monographs

General Editors
Ehud Ben Zvi
Roxana Flammini
Alan Lenzi
Juan Manuel Tebes

Editorial Board:
Reinhard Achenbach
Esther J. Hamori
Steven W. Holloway
René Krüger
Steven L. McKenzie
Martti Nissinen
Graciela Gestoso Singer

Number 10

THE BOOK OF THE TWELVE AND THE NEW FORM CRITICISM

Edited by
Mark J. Boda, Michael H. Floyd, and Colin M. Toffelmire

SBL Press
Atlanta

Copyright © 2015 by SBL Press

All rights reserved. No part of this work may be reproduced or transmitted in any form or by any means, electronic or mechanical, including photocopying and recording, or by means of any information storage or retrieval system, except as may be expressly permitted by the 1976 Copyright Act or in writing from the publisher. Requests for permission should be addressed in writing to the Rights and Permissions Office, SBL Press, 825 Houston Mill Road, Atlanta, GA 30329 USA.

Library of Congress Cataloging-in-Publication Data

The Book of the Twelve and the new form criticism / edited by Mark J. Boda, Michael H. Floyd, and Colin M. Toffelmire.
   pages cm. -- (Ancient Near East monographs ; volume 10)
   Includes bibliographical references and indexes.
   Summary: "Contributors to this volume explore the theoretical issues at stake in recent changes in form criticism and the practical outcomes of applying the results of these theoretical shifts to the Book of the Twelve. This volume combines self-conscious methodological reflection with practical examination of specific texts in an effort to demonstrate the practical consequences of theoretical decisions and the value of certain methodological stances"-- Provided by publisher.
   ISBN 978-1-62837-060-7 (pbk. : alk. paper) -- ISBN 978-1-62837-062-1 (hardback : alk. paper) -- ISBN 978-1-62837-061-4 (electronic)
   1. Bible. Minor Prophets--Criticism, Form. I. Boda, Mark J., editor. II. Floyd, Michael H., editor. III. Toffelmire, Colin M., editor.

BS1560.B575 2015
224'.90663--dc23   2015014546

Printed on acid-free paper.

Contents

Abbreviations	vii
Introduction *Michael H. Floyd*	1
New Form Criticism and Beyond: The Historicity of Prophetic Literature Revisited *Michael H. Floyd*	17
"I Will Make Her Like a Desert": Intertextual Allusion and Feminine and Agricultural Metaphors in the Book of the Twelve *Beth M. Stovell*	37
Reading the "Prophetic Lawsuit" Genre in the Persian Period *James M. Trotter*	63
The Vision Report Genre between Form-Criticism and Redaction-Criticism: An Investigation of Amos 7–9 and Zechariah 1–6 *Lena-Sofia Tiemeyer*	75
Harrowing Woes and Comforting Promises in the Book of the Twelve *Carol J. Dempsey*	97
Twelve (and More) Anonyms: A Biblical Book without Authors *Erhard S. Gerstenberger*	119
Form and Eschatology in the Book of the Twelve Prophets *Marvin A. Sweeney*	137
Where *Are* the Prophets in the Book of the Twelve? *James D. Nogalski*	163

A Deafening Call to Silence: The Rhetorical "End" of Human Address to the
Deity in the Book of the Twelve   183
   Mark J. Boda

The Book of Amos as "Prophetic Fiction": Describing the Genre of a Written
Work that Reinvigorates Older Oral Speech Forms   205
   Tim Bulkeley

Sitz im What? Context and the Prophetic Book of Obadiah   221
   Colin M. Toffelmire

The Non-Israelite Nations in Zephaniah: Conceptual Coherence and the
Relationship of the Parts to the Whole   245
   D. C. Timmer

Form Criticism in Haggai, Zechariah, and Malachi: From Oral Sayings to
Literature   265
   Paul L. Redditt

A New Form-Critical Approach to Zechariah's Crowning of the High Priest
Joshua and the Identity of "Shoot" (Zechariah 6:9–15)   285
   Anthony R. Petterson

Goals and Processes of the "New" Form Criticism   305
   Martin J. Buss

New Form Criticism and the Prophetic Literature: The Unfinished Agenda   311
   Robert R. Wilson

Bibliography   323
Ancient Sources Index   347
Modern Authors Index   361

Abbreviations

AB	Anchor Bible
ABR	*Australian Biblical Review*
AcBib	Academia Biblica
AIL	Ancient Israel and Its Literature
ANEM	Ancient Near East Monographs
AOAT	Alter Orient und Altes Testament
ApOTC	Apollos Old Testament Commentary
ARM	Archives royales de Mari
ATD	Das Alte Testament Deutsch
AzTh	Arbeiten zur Theologie
BBR	*Bulletin for Biblical Research*
BEATAJ	Beiträge zur Erforschung des Alten Testaments und des antiken Judentum
BETL	Bibliotheca Ephemeridum Theologicarum Lovaniensium
BHQ	*Biblia Hebraica Quinta*. Edited by Adrian Schenker et al. Stuttgart: Deutsch Bibelgesellschaft, 2004–
Bib	*Biblica*
BJS	Brown Judaic Studies
BKAT	Biblischer Kommentar, Altes Testament
BLS	Bible and Literature Series
BSac	*Bibliotheca Sacra*
BSOAS	*Bulletin of the School of Oriental and African Studies*
BZAW	Beihefte zur Zeitschrift für die alttestamentliche Wissenschaft
CBET	Contributions to Biblical Exegesis and Theology
CBQ	*Catholic Biblical Quarterly*
CC	Continental Commentaries
CHANE	Culture and History of the Ancient Near East
Colloq	*Colloquium*
COS	*The Context of Scripture*. Edited by William W. Hallo. 3 vols. Leiden: Brill, 1997–2002
CTR	*Criswell Theological Review*
DJD	Discoveries in the Judaean Desert
EvT	*Evangelische Theologie*

ExAud	*Ex Auditu*
FAT	Forschungen zum Alten Testament
FOTL	Forms of the Old Testament Literature
FRLANT	Forschungen zur Religion und Literatur des Alten und Neuen Testaments
GMTR	Guides to the Mesopotamian Textual Record
HBAI	*Hebrew Bible and Ancient Israel*
HBM	Hebrew Bible Monographs
HBS	History of Biblical Studies
HCOT	Historical Commentary on the Old Testament
HdO	Handbuch der Orientalistik
HS	*Hebrew Studies*
HSM	Harvard Semitic Monographs
HThKAT	Herders Theologischer Kommentar zum Alten Testament
HTS	*HTS Teologiese Studies/Theological Studies*
HUCA	*Hebrew Union College Annual*
IBS	*Irish Biblical Studies*
IBT	Interpreting Biblical Texts
ICC	International Critical Commentary
IECOT	International Exegetical Commentary on the Old Testament
Int	*Interpretation*
JANESCU	*Journal of the Ancient Near Eastern Society of Columbia University*
JAOS	*Journal of the American Oriental Society*
JBL	*Journal of Biblical Literature*
JETS	*Journal of the Evangelical Theological Society*
JHebS	*Journal of Hebrew Scriptures*
JNES	*Journal of Near Eastern Studies*
JNSL	*Journal of Northwest Semitic Languages*
JSNT	*Journal of the Study of the New Testament*
JSNTSup	Journal for the Study of the New Testament Supplement Series
JSOT	*Journal for the Study of the Old Testament*
JSOTSup	Journal for the Study of the Old Testament Supplement Series
JSS	*Journal of Semitic Studies*
JTS	*Journal of Theological Studies*
KAT	Kommentar zum Alten Testament
LAI	Library of Ancient Israel
LBS	Linguistic Biblical Studies
LCBI	Literary Currents in Biblical Interpretation
LHBOTS	The Library of Hebrew Bible/Old Testament Studies
LSAWS	Linguistic Studies in Ancient West Semitic
LSTS	The Library of Second Temple Studies
MGWJ	*Monatschrift für Geschichte und Wissenschaft des Judentums*

NAC	New American Commentary
NCB	New Century Bible
NICOT	New International Commentary on the Old Testament
NIVAC	The NIV Application Commentary
OBO	Oribis Biblicus et Orientalis
OTG	Old Testament Guides
OTL	Old Testament Library
OTM	Oxford Theology and Religion Monographs
OTT	Old Testament Theology
RBL	*Review of Biblical Literature*
RBS	Resources for Biblical Studies
ResQ	*Restoration Quarterly*
RNBC	Readings: A New Biblical Commentary
RSR	Recherches de science religieuse
SAA	State Archives of Assyria
SBB	Stuttgarter biblische Beiträge
SBLDS	Society of Biblical Literature Dissertation Series
SBS	Stuttgarter Bibelstudien
SGBC	The Story of God Commentary Series
SemeiaST	Semeia Studies
SHBC	Smyth & Helwys Bible Commentary
SJOT	*Scandinavian Journal of the Old Testament*
SR	*Studies in Religion*
SSN	Studia Semitica Neerlandica
StBibLit	Studies in Biblical Literature (Lang)
SymS	Symposium Series
TAD	*Textbook of Aramaic Documents from Ancient Egypt.* Edited by B. Porten and A. Yardeni. 4 vols. Winona Lake, IN: Eisenbraun, 1986–1999
TDOT	*Theological Dictionary of the Old Testament.* Edited by G. Johannes Botterweck and Helmer Ringgren. Translated by John T. Willis et al. 8 vols. Grand Rapids: Eerdmans, 1974–2006.
TOTC	Tyndale Old Testament Commentaries
TUMSR	Trinity University Monograph Series in Religion
USQR	*Union Seminary Quarterly Reviews*
VT	*Vetus Testamentum*
VTSup	Supplements to Vetus Testamentum
WAW	Writings from the Ancient World
WBC	Word Bible Commentary
WUNT	Wissenschaftliche Untersuchungenzum Neuen Testament
ZAW	*Zeitschrift für die altestamentliche Wissenschaft*
ZTK	*Zeitschrift für Theologie und Kirche*

Introduction

Michael H. Floyd

This collection of essays addresses new developments in form criticism in relation to the Minor Prophets. Martin Buss and Robert Wilson, who were invited to give their responses to the collection, both trace many of these new developments, and the individual articles all touch on them in one way or another. It would therefore be redundant to recount here at the outset all that is new in these examples of form-critical method as it is currently being practiced. For present purposes suffice it to summarize the evolution of the discipline in terms of a major shift from treating prophetic books as a means of accessing the prophets for whom they were named to treating prophetic literature as the primary object of investigation in its own right. The main goal of interpretation is no longer to recover the original messages of the prophets from the heavily edited prophetic texts. Now the main goal is to discern the messages being sent by the scribes who wrote these texts long after the prophets for whom they are named.

The essays in the present collection explore the kinds of questions that arise when form criticism's ongoing concerns with genre, setting, and intention are recast in light of this methodological shift. Buss views the interpretive work done here from the perspective of intellectual history in general, and Wilson views it from the perspective of biblical studies in particular. In this introduction I will plot where the various contributions fit within the current scene and also identify the points at which the differences among them call for further discussion.

A "Book of the Twelve"?

The essays gathered here confine themselves to the corpus of prophetic literature that the title of this volume calls The Book of the Twelve. This nomenclature reflects the idea that the twelve Minor Prophets constitute an entity which is in some sense unified. Some authors—particularly Mark Boda and Marvin Sweeney and to a lesser extent Paul Redditt—accept this assumption and base their work on it. However most of the authors use cases from one or more of the Minor Prophets as examples of issues germane to prophetic literature in general, without necessarily entailing any particular presuppositions about the Twelve as a whole. Some in this latter group—particularly James Nogalski—express their agreement with the hypothesis of a Book of the Twelve even though they do not depend upon it here. Thus this collection generally reflects the present state of affairs with regard to this still open question, which is to agree to disagree.[1]

The present strategy seems to be a pragmatic one. Rather than argue about the hypothesis itself—whether each of the twelve is to be read as a discrete prophetic book, or the twelve are to be read collectively as a single document—studies taking a holistic approach are conducted to see whether the hypothesis can generate interesting and plausible insights. "The proof is in the pudding." Boda's and Sweeney's articles are good examples of this trend. Both advocate reading the Twelve individually as well as collectively[2]—and they indeed do so in their articles—but they are mainly interested in the way each book contributes to a pattern that characterizes the Twelve as a whole.

Boda shows that, as one moves through the Masoretic order of the Twelve, direct address to God consistently decreases, reflecting a growing sense of the theological inappropriateness of complaint resulting from Israel's historical experience of defeat, exile, and restoration. The message which those who put together this form of the Book of the Twelve addressed to their postexilic contemporaries was thus, both in effect and literally (Hab 2:20; Zeph 1:7; Zech 2:17), a call to silence before God. Such studies suggest that there is indeed some rhyme or reason in the way the Twelve have been edited and ordered in relation to one another.

Sweeney, using the example of eschatology, and calling attention to the fact that the Twelve are ordered differently in MT and LXX, shows that each book has its own take on the new future which YHWH has in store for his people and that these individual eschatological perspectives collectively take on different connotations when they are configured differently in the MT and LXX.

Sweeney's point is well taken because it grows out of observations regarding the distinctive form(s) of the Twelve. It points toward the need for further work on the genre of the Book of the Twelve. It is obviously not a single prophetic book in the same sense as Isaiah or Jeremiah. Nor is it just a collection of totally unrelated documents. Studies conducted thus far, such as Boda's and Sweeney's

---

[1] Ehud Ben Zvi and James D. Nogalski, *Two Sides of A Coin: Juxtaposing Views on Interpreting the Book of the Twelve/The Twelve Prophetic Books*, Analecta Gorgiana 201 (Piscataway, NJ: Gorgias, 2009).

[2] Nogalski takes the same position as Boda and Sweeney on this point, but his article is not mainly concerned with demonstrating it.

here as well as others elsewhere,[3] show various affinities and levels of affinity among the prophetic books that make up the collection. Could the results of these studies be synthesized in a way that would better describe the Twelve as prophetic literature *sui generis* and more closely define the possibilities and limits for reading the Twelve holistically?

GENRES IN PROPHETIC LITERATURE

When scholarly investigation was focused primarily on reconstructing the hypothetical original form of prophetic literature, rooted in the oral proclamations of the prophets themselves, much effort was expended—and considerable progress was made—in defining "the basic forms of prophetic speech."[4] Now that scholarly investigation focuses primarily on prophetic literature as we presently have it, rather than any hypothetical original form, questions arise about these formerly operative genre categories. Are they applicable to prophetic literature as well as prophetic speech? And if so, to what extent? Several articles in this collection reflect the range of opinion that is evident in recent scholarship.

At one end of the spectrum we might locate the work of Ehud Ben Zvi, who is not a contributor to this volume but has had a big influence on the approach that is represented here. He maintains that prophetic literature has its own genres, in which the genres of prophetic speech are occasionally echoed but largely effaced. For example, one of his main categories is the *prophetic reading*, a rhetorically distinct section of a prophetic book designed to be read and reread so as to evoke associations with other such readings.[5]

In the present collection the article of James Trotter reaches a conclusion that comes pretty close to Ben Zvi's position. From the earliest days of form criticism, the *prophetic lawsuit* was one of the staple genre categories used in the analysis of prophetic texts, thought to have originated from prophets confronting unfaithful Israelites in a way that imitated an offender being brought to trial. Trotter takes three texts that have been considered parade examples of this genre—Hos 2:3–25, Hos 4:1–3, and Mic 6:1–8—and asks whether those who produced and read these prophetic books in the Persian Period would have understood them in such legal terms. After surveying Neo-Assyrian, Neo-Babylonian, and Achaemenid legal genres and practices, he reaches a negative

---

[3] E.g., Paul L. Redditt and Aaron Schart, eds., *Thematic Threads in the Book of the Twelve*, BZAW 325 (Berlin: de Gruyter, 2003); also James Nogalski, "Recurring Themes in the Book of the Twelve: Creating Points of Contact for a Theological Reading," *Int* 61 (2007): 125–36.
[4] The classic work is Claus Westermann, *Basic Forms of Prophetic Speech*, trans. Hugh C. White (Louisville: Westminster John Knox, 1991).
[5] Ehud Ben Zvi, *Micah*, FOTL 21b (Grand Rapids: Eerdmans, 2000); idem, *Hosea*, FOTL 21a.1 (Grand Rapids: Eerdmans, 2005).

conclusion. These texts would not be understood as reflecting any particular legal procedure. Trotter only intends to show how one of "old" form criticism's classical genre categories can become unraveled when texts are read as writings about prophecies rather than speeches once made by prophets. Thus he does not venture any definition of the genres of literary prophecy to which his example texts might belong. He does say that Persian Period readers would have understood all three as having a common theme—YHWH and Israel having a dispute (*rîb*)—but not as belonging to the same genre.

At the other end of the spectrum we might locate Paul Redditt's essay. He recognizes that prophetic books are literary creations, but he affirms that recorded prophetic speeches were the raw material with which scribes worked to produce them. Readers of prophetic literature can thus still "hear the prophetic voices" that underlie the text. As he works through Haggai, Zechariah, and Malachi he finds cases in which the standard forms of prophetic speech appear full-fledged and cases in which they have been transformed but not completely effaced by scribal editors, as well as one extended passage (Zech 9–14) which he believes to have had a largely literary origin. Even in this largely literary text, however, he finds echoes of oral prophetic speech. From Redditt's perspective the genres of prophetic speech are still evident in prophetic literature and still serviceable in its analysis, even when focusing primarily on prophetic literature as such.

Lena-Sofia Tiemeyer takes a position similar to Redditt as she investigates a particular genre, the *vision report*, in terms of how its function as prophetic speech relates to its function as prophetic literature. Like earlier form critics, she argues that it is possible to distinguish earlier textual material rooted in prophetic proclamation from textual material resulting from later redactional additions. However, she does not assume—as earlier form critics tended to—that the earlier material was necessarily cast in a static and relatively pristine form.

Pericopes that contain vision reports usually have explanatory oracular speech accompanying the account of what was seen in the vision per se. Scholars have debated whether this oracular speech belonged to the original version of the report or whether it was a secondary addition. After examining closely the vision reports in Amos and Zechariah, Tiemeyer finds that there can be no hard and fast rule in this regard. The vision report genre cannot be defined in terms of a form that invariably includes or does not include oracular speech, and oracular speech cannot automatically be relegated to the status of primary or secondary material. One must consider the function of the oracular speech in relation to the account of what was seen. Does it provide an explanation of the image, without which its basic meaning would be incomprehensible? If so, it was probably part of the original form of the report. Or does it give a *re*interpretation of the image, modifying or adding to its basic meaning? If so, it was probably a redactional addition. Knowing the difference is useful for understanding whether the writers of prophetic literature transmitted the vision reports they inherited without much modification, thus leaving their readers free to understand them in a variety of ways, or whether they intended to direct their readers' understanding through editorializing additions.

Carol Dempsey's essay falls somewhere between the extremes represented by Trotter and Redditt. She uses broad genre categories based on those of classical form criticism to analyze how the writers of prophetic books characterized the function of prophecy in the past, and thereby addressed theological messages to their postexilic readers. Within the category she calls *prophecies of woe* she subsumes various genres of prophetic speech used in connection with proclamations of divine judgment, including those that earlier form critics termed *oracles of doom*, *woe oracles*, *laments*, and *disputation speeches*, et cetera. Within the category that she calls *prophecies of weal*, she subsumes various genres of prophetic speech used in connection with proclamations of salvation, including those that earlier form critics termed *oracles of salvation*, *exhortations*, and *calls to rejoicing*, et cetera. She gives a book-by-book analysis, comparing passages that consist solely of prophecies of woe, passages that consist solely of prophecies of weal, and passages that mix the two. She sees these broad genre categories as a point of entry into each book, in order to see the distinctive ways in which the writers of each book used them to address their own particular messages of warning and hope to their contemporaries—and to subsequent readers as well.

Dempsey's approach resembles Redditt's in that she finds traces of prophetic speech forms in prophetic literature, but unlike him she does not assume that this necessarily reveals anything about whatever prophetic speech may have once underlain prophetic literature as it now stands. Instead, she sees the generic structures still evident in prophetic literature as evidence that its writers appropriated traditional prophetic rhetoric in addressing their readers. Dempsey's approach resembles Trotter's in that she keeps the focus on how readers would have understood the writers of prophetic literature, without venturing to consider how any earlier versions of prophecies might have been understood by earlier audiences. For Dempsey, however, this does not result in a radical questioning of any genres identified by earlier form critics, as it does for Trotter.

With regard to the basic forms of prophetic speech, the above-mentioned contributors to this volume affirm that they are still relevant to the form-critical analysis of prophetic literature. However, as we can see, there is a wide variety of working assumptions about the ways in which oral genres might have informed the writing of prophetic literature. This calls for further discussion, as well as interaction with the discussion—covered in the following group of essays—about how prophetic books were produced. How closely were they tied to earlier prophetic proclamation, and what was the nature of those ties?

THE FORMATION OF PROPHETIC BOOKS

Most scholars believe that prophetic books were not entirely invented by those who wrote them in their present form and that they were somehow related to previous prophetic activity. There are widely differing opinions, however, regarding the nature of that previous prophetic activity and how much we can know about it. Three of the essays in this collection address this issue.

Erhard Gerstenberger argues that our perspective has been anachronistically skewed by the modern assumption that books are written by authors for the edification of individual readers. He sees the prophetic books in the Twelve as the result of a different sort of process with a different end. The beginning of the process was prophetic proclamation, but that is no longer recoverable as such from prophetic literature. The earliest stage that can be detected is the recording and collection of anonymous prophecies, which were then augmented and adapted for liturgical use. The first of these two textual layers is evident in the short, pithy oracular sayings addressed to particular situations, which are now often found clustered together in series. The second layer is evident in accusatory, exhortative, and hymnic language that draws out the didactic implications of the oracles, generalizing and applying them to the common life of a community gathered for worship. Gerstenberger views a liturgical setting, in which prophetic writings are read in order to renew and strengthen the relationship between the community and YHWH, as the formative matrix for prophetic literature, and he emphasizes the anonymity of the overall process. The original oracular sayings themselves came from anonymous speakers of YHWH's word, and they were compiled and augmented for liturgical use by anonymous scribes and cultic functionaries. The identification of each book of the Twelve with a particular historical figure, by means of a superscription naming it after a supposedly great prophet from the past, was the last stage in the process of literary production, coincident with its being incorporated into the Book of the Twelve. The data in the superscriptions—including the names of the prophets themselves—thus have no real biographical implications, and no substantial bearing on either the contents or the formation of these books.

James Nogalski takes as his starting point the same anonymity emphasized by Gerstenberger, and ends up taking a position very similar to Gerstenberger's. Nogalski works in reaction to a theory of Karl Budde about the lack of biographical information concerning the prophets named among the Twelve. Budde argued that more biographical material, especially narrative material, had once been included, but most of it—except Amos 7:10–17, Hos 1 and 3, and Mic 3:1—was removed in a redaction of the entire Book of the Twelve, intended to make its contents more generally applicable to later readers. Nogalski finds little to commend this theory, but he finds the questions with which Budde wrestled still worthy of attention. What is the nature of the redactional processes that shaped each of the books of the Twelve, as well as the collection as a whole? And why have the books in this collection included so little biographical information in their present form?

Nogalski accepts the traditional assumption that, at least in most cases, prophetic literature was ultimately rooted in prophetic proclamation, perhaps on the part of the prophets for whom the books in the Twelve were named. In any case, however, all that can now be recovered from prophetic literature are the rhetorical elements with which its writers worked. Like Gerstenberger, Nogalski attempts to identify these elements and describe the patterns of their interrelationships, but he gives a somewhat different inventory: headings, anthologies and small collections, source blocks, longer redactional compositions, and shorter editorial comments. Source blocks have a variety of functions: They can be used as building blocks for extended passages or entire books, as complementary enhancements of already existing anthologies and collections, and as intertwined textual threads. When one considers how such elements are interrelated in the formation of the various books that comprise the Twelve, a reason for the absence of biographical information becomes evident. The writers of these prophetic books were primarily interested in the liveliness of YHWH's word, not the lives of the prophets.

Nogalski does not say much about the setting of this redactional activity, but one of his general conclusions leaves him very much open to the kind of liturgical context described in detail by Gerstenberger:

> Significantly, the function of the source texts that are involved in the compilation and framing of the writings reflect more cultic associations than biographical material.... This cultic flavor has been underappreciated in prophetic studies and it requires more consideration in the development of the Twelve since it probably sheds more light upon the process of editing than the biographies of the prophets.[6]

Thus Gerstenberger and Nogalski come by different routes to much the same place, and I find myself in substantial agreement with much of what they say. In one particular respect, however, the position that I take in my essay is diametrically opposed to theirs. It is an obvious fact that the biographical information given in the Twelve is next to none. It is also evident that the writers of these prophetic books were more interested in the liveliness of YHWH's word than in the lives of the prophets. I question, though, whether this means that they had no biographical interest whatsoever. Gerstenberger and Nogalski are primarily concerned with the redactional process into which oral prophecies were incorporated after having been recorded and collected. They are certainly correct in noting that the scribes who were the agents of this redactional activity and thus also the creators of prophetic literature—and who also may have been

---

[6] P. 182.

cultic functionaries, as Gerstenberger argues—were anonymous. I am more interested in the initial stage of the process, in which oral prophecies were recorded and collected. I would question whether these oracular sayings were also anonymous to begin with.

Although the original oral prophecies are no longer recoverable as such—and most scholars now seem to be pretty much agreed on this point—I would argue that in at least some cases we can nevertheless know something about them on the basis of external comparative evidence as well as internal textual evidence. First of all, comparative evidence does not altogether support the theory that scribes recorded anonymous prophetic sayings. In many examples of recorded prophecies from Mari, Nineveh, and elsewhere in the ancient world, the name of the prophet who received a revelation is often noted as an integral part of the record. With regard to the recorded prophecies on which biblical prophetic literature was based we might therefore suppose that they were not necessarily anonymous to begin with. Second, the writers of prophetic books often invite their readers to make typological connections with prophecies that were fulfilled long before these books were written. The word of YHWH articulated by the writers of prophetic literature had implications for readers in general, in their various situations, because it was rooted in the fulfillment of prophecies once addressed by particular prophets to particular audiences in particular crisis situations. The rhetorical persuasiveness of prophetic literature's message lies largely in its being warranted by previous prophecies already fulfilled. This is at least the case with regard to Mic 1:1–16, the example text that I have used in my essay, and this is arguably the case with regard to many other prophetic texts too.

As I see it, the main impetus for prophecies being written down and subjected to reinterpretation was the fact that they were spoken by a prophet whose prophecies had come to pass. Association with a known prophet from a particular time and place—however tentative—was an important aspect of the basis for assuming that a prophecy had general implications above and beyond its original circumstances. The attribution characteristic of the superscription that heads each book of the Twelve, which associates the contents of each book with a particular prophetic figure, is thus a key element in the formation of the book, indicative of a genuine—though obviously quite limited—historical interest on the part of its writer. Prophetic books do not pretend that they are, in their entirety, the work of the prophets for whom they are named; but they do claim to be ultimately based on the revelations once made to those prophets, however little may be additionally known about them. The writers of prophetic literature were indeed more interested in the liveliness of the word of YHWH than in the lives of the prophets, but they nevertheless wanted to affirm that the word of YHWH had originally been incarnate in the lives of particular prophets.

Nogalski recognizes that there may have been some underlying historical connection between the prophets for whom the Twelve were named and the recorded oracles that were elaborated in the process of forming prophetic books, but he does not see this connection as the impetus for their formation. Gerstenberger seems to imply that the impetus for recording and collecting anonymous prophetic sayings would have been their potential for present liturgical use, not their connections with the past. I would argue that their connections with past prophets were precisely what made prophetic sayings adaptable for the uses to which their redactors may have wanted to put them. Gerstenberger believes that the ostensibly biographical connections of the Twelve with past prophets were late, superficial inventions because the superscriptions, in which the biographical connections are largely made, were added late in the redaction of the Twelve. But even if the superscriptions were added last—and Gerstenberger may well be right about this—it does not necessarily follow that the biographical connections came late in the development of the tradition. These sharp differences of opinion show the need for more discussion of the formation of prophetic books.

HOLISTIC SYNCHRONIC READINGS OF PROPHETIC LITERATURE

Along with new form criticism's insistence on beginning with the text in its present form comes the assumption that it is not a hodge-podge, but rather an entity whose writers gave it this form in order to communicate a particular, comprehensible message. The initial challenge is to discern on the basis of synchronic analysis what the writers of prophetic texts wanted to communicate to their contemporary readers, before considering whether there is any reason to believe that they drew on previously existing records or traditions, in which case it may also be appropriate to undertake diachronic analysis.

It is hard for biblical scholars to break the habit of giving priority to diachronic concerns, so two of the essays in the present volume set out to show the advantages of doing so. Anthony Petterson argues that major differences in the interpretation of Zech 6:9–15 stem from the methodologically mistaken approach of first considering diachronically what this prophecy might have meant for the prophet in relation to his contemporaries instead of first considering synchronically what it might mean for the writer in relation to his contemporaries. D. C. Timmer argues that ostensible discrepancies in Zephaniah are understandable if they are read synchronically in terms of the message of the book as a whole, rather than diachronically in terms of different redactional layers. Because Timmer draws on linguistic theory his essay will be treated below, along with others that similarly employ concepts from linguistic and literary theory. Here we will consider Petterson's thesis.

Does the prophecy concerning צמח in Zech 6:9–15 refer to Zerubbabel and the completion of the Second Temple, or does it refer to a future messianic figure and the completion of another more glorious, even eschatological temple? In addition to the problem of who צמח is, this text contains several cruxes that must somehow be resolved in the course of its overall interpretation, all of which Petterson takes up in his survey of opinion. Here we are mainly interested in his argument about the central question—*a* messiah, Zerubbabel, or *the* Messiah? He says that the answer depends largely on two things: (1) Is the text read as if addressed to the prophet's contemporaries, or to the writer's contemporaries? (2) Is the text read as having a message that is coherent with the message of Zechariah as a whole, and also coherent with the royal ideology of the wider prophetic corpus? Those who regard Zech 6:9–15 as a prophecy addressed to the prophet's contemporaries tend to take it as a legitimation of Zerubbabel's messianic status because he completed the Second Temple. Such a reading raises the question of whether this is not then a failed prophecy—for Zerubbabel nevertheless failed to attain a kingly crown—and what ongoing significance it could possibly have as such. It also creates a discrepancy between the way צמח is used as royal terminology here and elsewhere in other prophetic literature (i.e., Jer 23:5; 33:15–18), as well as a discrepancy between the way kingship is conceived here and elsewhere in Zechariah (e.g., Zech 9:9–10). Those who regard Zech 6:9–15 as a prophecy addressed by the writers of Zechariah to their readers tend to take it as foretelling the advent of a future king—a prophecy yet to be fulfilled—in a way that is consistent with other messianic prophecies. Petterson prefers the latter alternative as less problematic.

Petterson's analysis raises the question of just what the synchronic reading of a prophetic book entails. Some advocates of new form criticism assume, as he does, that it means treating the text as temporally one-dimensional, as if it addresses its readers only with respect to their present circumstances and as if it projects the future only with respect to their time. It is correspondingly assumed that any diachronic analysis is an imposition of modern historical criticism that has no warrant in the text itself. But what if the text itself expresses a historical perspective on its own prophetic past? In that case, wouldn't a synchronic reading of the text involve a consideration of how the book as a whole reconstructs the past—as opposed to the historical-critical practice, often abetted by earlier form criticism, of dismembering the text in order to read it in relation to the way modern scholars reconstruct the past? Some unexplored issues seem to be lurking in the approach represented by Petterson.

Form Criticism Meets Literary and Linguistic Theory

Earlier form critics had literary as well as historical interests. Hermann Gunkel, in particular, showed a profound aesthetic appreciation for as well as a historical interest in biblical texts. Because of the analytical practices that their historical interests entailed, however, the pioneers of form criticism often did not have an opportunity to take their literary interests very far. In the quest for original layers of material, the text had to be dissected in search of small, self-contained, conceptually homogenous, and historically datable units. The only literary features taken seriously into account were those on which such dissection was based. With the text so dismembered, many of its other literary features were often lost from view. This state of affairs led James Muilenburg in 1969 to call for going beyond form criticism into what he called rhetorical criticism, making room in the analysis of texts for a fuller delineation of their aesthetic dimensions.[7] Newer form criticism makes it possible to take this call all the more seriously, particularly in its insistence that any type of analysis must begin with a comprehensive view of the text as a whole in its present state. This opens up the possibility of a fruitful cross-fertilization, in which the categories of literary and form-critical analysis are allowed to interact.

Just when form criticism began opening up to literary-critical concerns, literary criticism itself was taking a linguistic turn. Structuralism provided the theoretical framework for this trend, but the usefulness of linguistic categories for purposes of literary analysis has proved itself pragmatically without necessarily resorting to any particular ideological justification. It should thus be possible for form-critical concerns to be addressed in creative ways using analytical practices developed by linguists as well as literary critics.

Four of the essays in this collection illustrate the various ways in which form criticism can interact with literary and linguistic analysis. Beth Stovell allows the literary-critical concept of metaphor to interact with the form-critical concept of genre in order to better understand how similar metaphorical imagery can have different connotations in different generic contexts. Using Amos as an example, Tim Bulkeley seeks to refine the genre category of prophetic books by analyzing the rhetorical flow of the book as a whole in relation to its redactionally identifiable components, synthesizing the results in terms of the literary-critical distinction between fictionalized history and historicized fiction. D. C. Timmer uses the linguistic distinction between semantic coherence and semantic cohesion to resolve a long-standing crux in the form- and redaction-critical analysis of Zephaniah. And Colin Toffelmire draws upon Systemic Functional Linguistics (SFL) to refine the conventional form-critical notion of *Sitz im Leben* or setting.

Stovell's starting point is the realization that the definition of generic and metaphorical structures is not an end in itself. The usefulness of identifying a recurring verbal generic structure, such as a prophetic lament, lies in noting the diverse and variable ways it can figure in particular instances. Similarly, the usefulness of identifying a recurring metaphor, such as God compared with a shepherd, lies in noting the diverse and variable ways it can figure in particular instances. Moreover, genres and metaphors—in all their diversity—are interactive. Stovell attempts to map out the ways in which particular genres and metaphors can vary in relation to their context, as well as the ways they can affect one another in the process.

---

[7] James Muilenburg, "Form Criticism and Beyond," *JBL* 88 (1969): 1–18.

Stovell focuses on the metaphor of Israel as adulterous wife in Hos 2 and Mic 1, and the metaphor of Israel as a woman in labor in Hos 9 and Mic 4. She devises an analytical grid consisting of four factors that condition the use of both genres and metaphors: (1) *Cultural and historical context*. Genre and metaphor have currency and meaning in relation to their own time and place. (2) *Partiality and blending*. The ideal forms of genres and metaphors are seldom fully realized, and in any given instance they are typically found in combination with (an)other genre(s) and metaphor(s). (3) *Linguistic context*. Genre and metaphor function within particular frames of both intra- and intertextual discourse. And (4) *theological context*. Biblical genres and metaphors are often used in the service of some particular theological position, such as the Deuteronomistic or Priestly perspective. The result of Stovell's analysis is a highly nuanced description of how these same metaphors express different ideas in different contexts, and how these four passages improvise with various genre forms, thus enabling the metaphors to have such diverse meanings.

Bulkeley begins by signaling the practical importance, from a literary-critical viewpoint, of understanding the genre of prophetic books as a whole—in contrast with the earlier form-critical goal of understanding only the genres of individual units of prophetic speech. He notes the attempts of Marvin Sweeney and Ehud Ben Zvi to define *prophetic book* as a literary genre, evaluating these as major steps forward but also identifying some shortcomings. In particular, he argues that these definitions do not do justice to the way prophetic books conjure up a literary world in which a prophetic character speaks with a distinctive voice—not to be confused with a biographical account of what any prophet may have once prophesied. A prophetic book presents a literary image of a prophetic speaker that was perhaps initially inspired by an actual prophet from the historical past, but this literary image no longer refers to things that this prophet may have actually done or said. Bulkeley searches for terminology that adequately captures this phenomenon and, drawing on Robert Alter's distinction between fictionalized history and historicized fiction, he settles on *prophetic fiction*.

Bulkeley's conclusion intersects with the issue left dangling by the essays concerning the formation of prophetic books. Like Gerstenberger and Nogalski, he emphasizes the extent to which the production of prophetic literature is removed from the prophetic proclamation that it imitates, thus losing historical referentiality to what a prophet from the past may have actually said. He does not go as far as Gerstenberger, who argues that any traces of prophetic proclamation still evident in prophetic literature must have originally come from anonymous mediators of YHWH's word. Like Nogalski, he recognizes that a prophetic book's presentation of its message may have been inspired by the example of the historical prophet for whom it is named, although it does not intend to give a systematic account of what he did and said. Bulkeley does not address the issue raised in my essay, whether a biographical connection with a prophecy once spoken by the prophet for whom a book is named might substantially affect the way in which the admittedly non-biographical book—as a prophetic fiction—rhetorically functions.

D. C. Timmer starts with a tension in Zephaniah's description of the nations. Throughout that book they are generally portrayed in a negative light, as the object of YHWH's punishment. However there are two references, in Zeph 2:11 and 3:9, which portray them favorably as having become devotees of YHWH. Because of this tension scholars have long regarded these verses as the result of secondary additions and theorized about the kind of redactional process that might explain how they came to be where they presently are. Timmer proposes that instead of jumping immediately to such diachronic conclusions the text might be approached in line with the new form-critical principle of first attempting to read it as comprehensively as possible, on the assumption that the writer was attempting to communicate a comprehensible message to readers by shaping the text into whatever form it now has. Can inconsistencies like those that are evident in Zephaniah's description of the nations be understood as part of the total message of a text, rather than as incomprehensible disruptions? How can you tell the difference?

Timmer resorts to a distinction made in semantics between *coherence* and *cohesion*. Cohesion refers to the harmony of a text's surface features like vocabulary, grammar, and syntax, et cetera. Coherence refers to the infratextual conceptual system that informs readers' understanding of the text as a whole. In terms of this distinction it is not problematic if a single text includes more than one perspective on a subject, thus stretching its cohesiveness, as long as there exists a unifying conceptual basis that accommodates the particularities of the various occurrences of that subject in the text. In the case of Zephaniah, is there a unifying conceptual basis that coherently accommodates both the negative and the favorable perspectives on the nations? Or are these differences still best understood as incohesive inconsistencies indicating secondary redactional layers?

Timmer finds a unifying conceptual framework that encompasses Zephaniah's contrasting perspectives on the nations. The book opens with YHWH's cosmic judgment of the whole world, including Judah and the nations. This sets in motion a process in which contrasting perspectives on Judah also become readily apparent. First YHWH will destroy Judah, then he will save a faithful remnant, and finally he will use them to restore Judah. Within the context of worldwide judgment Timmer finds a similar progression in the destiny of the nations. First YHWH will destroy them, then he will save a righteous remnant, and finally he will use them to create a gentile community faithful to YHWH. The perspectives on the nations are different because they describe different stages in this process. Timmer's article thus provides a good example of how the new form-critical approach can draw on linguistic theory in a way that affects the interface between form and redaction criticism.

Petterson's essay, discussed above, also invokes the criterion of *coherence*. In contrast with Timmer, who defines coherence as capable of comprehending certain kinds of inconsistency, Petterson defines it as uniformity. In view of form criticism's present emphasis on reading the present form of the text as a coherent message, it would be helpful to clarify the difference between these two approaches in further discussion.

Colin Toffelmire's essay is concerned with the form-critical concept of *Sitz im Leben*, or setting. This was one of Hermann Gunkel's key concepts, which at first seemed very productive. He thought that certain types of social situations invariably called for certain fixed forms of expression, and that in the ancient world these forms of expression were primarily oral. Gunkel was hardly incorrect, and in many cases this hypothesis served well, but problems emerged in the attempt to apply this concept of setting across the board. As it turned out, all texts were not necessarily rooted in one of the typically recurring situations of ancient society, the forms of expression called forth by similar social situations were not invariably fixed, and all forms of expression did not necessarily originate as oral traditions. As form criticism has shifted its focus from a reconstruction of the oral traditions lying behind biblical literature to a better understanding of scripture as literature, the need for a more flexible concept of setting has become apparent. Attention has become focused on a cadre of scribes in early Persian Yehud as the setting in which biblical books as such began to be produced. But since we have no direct information about this group, we are limited to what is known about scribes in general, and to what can be inferred about them from the documents they created.[8]

The question is whether the attempt to infer the setting from the documents themselves can be systematized, and Toffelmire argues that Systemic Functional Linguistics (SFL) offers a promising possibility in this regard. SFL is a sub-field of linguistics distinguished by its inclusion of social context, along with phonology, grammar, and semantics, as one of the essential levels of language analysis. Using a wide range of variable factors it asks of texts what their patterns of language disclose about the possible settings in which they were used. As Toffelmire demonstrates, using Obadiah as an example, SFL analysis covers aspects of texts that have often been noted by biblical scholars, but it makes use of this and other data in a more purposeful and organized way. The result is a description of Obadiah's "context of situation" (in SFL jargon) that brings together the historical specificity of Edom's role in the overthrow of Jerusalem, the use of this historical memory by highly literate scribes to engender in their readers both a feeling of betrayal and a hope of vindication, and the wider applicability of the theme of brotherly betrayal to a variety of circumstances, et cetera.

---

[8] For a *tour de force* in this regard, see Ehud Ben Zvi, *Signs of Jonah: Reading and Rereading in Ancient Yehud*, JSOTSup 367 (Sheffield: Sheffield Academic, 2003).

As a result of the complications encountered by Gunkel's concept of setting form criticism might be tempted to downplay its interest in social context, but this would be counter to one of the main contemporary trends in linguistics, which places increasing emphasis on the need to understand language in its social context. If form criticism wishes to continue its historic concern with setting, and if it finds generalizations about scribes in ancient society less than totally satisfying in this regard, SFL would seem to offer a promising way forward.

As noted at the outset, the responses by Wilson and Buss put into larger perspectives the particular issues raised by comparison of the articles in this collection. Wilson emphasizes that many questions are still left unanswered in the shift from focusing on the original words of the prophets to focusing on prophetic literature in its present form. Not nearly enough is known about the scribal elite that produced this literature, and Wilson observes that describing these scribes and their ways is just as much a project of historical reconstruction as was the "old" form-critical project of supplying data for historical criticism's biographies of the prophets. Buss locates the genius of form criticism in its sometimes unrealized potential for relating particular expressions of language and thought in their sociohistorical contexts to general issues of human life and faith in similar sociohistorical contexts. He challenges those of us who continue to practice form criticism to stand firm in this stream of scholarly tradition descended from Gunkel.

1

New Form Criticism and Beyond: The Historicity of Prophetic Literature Revisited

Michael H. Floyd

INTRODUCTION

Over the last couple of decades there has been a decisive shift in the form-critical study of prophetic literature. The discipline of form criticism, which focuses on questions of genre and social location, emerged in the modern era as a means of interpreting what the prophets said to their contemporaries. As that quest proved elusive, the goal has now shifted to interpreting what the authors of prophetic books wrote for their contemporaries.[1] Scholars are recognizing that the Bible's prophetic literature, as well as other types of canonical scriptures, resulted primarily from the formative role played by a small scribal elite in the emergent Judaism of the Persian period. These scribes were endeavoring to mediate "the word of YHWH" to their colleagues through the creation, continual study, and expository interpretation of prophetic books.[2]

---

[1] Ferdinand E. Deist, "The Prophets: Are We Heading for a Paradigm Switch?" in *Prophet und Prophetenbuch: Festschrift für Otto Kaiser zum 65. Geburtstag*, ed. Volkmar Fritz, Karl-Friedrich Pohlman, and Hans-Christoph Schmitt, BZAW 185 (Berlin: de Gruyter, 1989), 1–18; Michael H. Floyd, "Basic Trends in the Form-Critical Study of Prophetic Texts," in *The Changing Face of Form Criticism for the Twenty-First Century*, ed. Marvin A. Sweeney and Ehud Ben Zvi (Grand Rapids: Eerdmans, 2001), 298–311; Colin M. Toffelmire, "Form Criticism," in *Dictionary of the Old Testament: Prophets*, ed. Mark J. Boda and J. Gordon McConville (Downers Grove, IL: InterVarsity and IVP Academic, 2012), 257–71.

[2] Ehud Ben Zvi, "The Prophetic Book: A Key Form of Prophetic Literature," in Sweeney and Ben Zvi, *Changing Face of Form Criticism*, 276–97; Ehud Ben Zvi, "The Concept of

In this essay I wish to probe this emerging consensus at one particular point: the eclipse of the prophet.[3] Earlier form-critical scholarship emphasized the original prophetic message at the expense of the scribes who produced the prophetic books. I believe that some current scholarship similarly emphasizes the work of these scribes at the expense of the original prophetic message. I am not advocating a return to form criticism as it was formerly practiced, using it to reconstruct the supposed *ipsissima verba* of the prophets. That project has clearly reached the point of diminishing returns. Nor am I challenging the basic insight of form criticism as it is currently practiced, that our primary focus has to be first of all on the evidence that we actually have in front of us, namely, the prophetic books themselves and, by direct implication, the scribes that produced them.[4] I propose here that we affirm this insight as the only way forward and attempt to go beyond it by raising the question of whether these scribes were not making historical claims about the prophets who preceded them, of whom they wrote. In other words, were the writers of the prophetic books in some sense historiographers?[5]

The new form-critical study of prophecy finds itself in the midst of a scholarly trend which asserts that we have no direct access to the prophets as such, and which doubts the historical veracity of the biographical incidents narrated in the prophetic books. According to this view, the biblical prophets are not historical personages in their own right, but only characters in the books that scribes wrote about them. Moreover, the scribes have told their readers precious

---

Prophetic Books and Its Historical Setting," in *The Production of Prophecy: Constructing Prophecy and Prophets in Yehud*, ed. Diana V. Edelman and Ehud Ben Zvi (London: Equinox, 2009), 73–95; Michael H. Floyd, "The *Maśśā'* as a Type of Prophetic Book," *JBL* 121 (2002): 401–22; Floyd, "The Production of Prophetic Books in the Early Second Temple Period," in *Prophets, Prophecy and Prophetic Texts in Second Temple Judaism*, ed. Michael H. Floyd and Robert D. Haak, LHBOTS 427 (New York: T&T Clark, 2006), 276–97.

[3] As foreseen by James M. Ward, "The Eclipse of the Prophet in Contemporary Prophetic Studies," *USQR* 41 (1988): 97–104.

[4] Odil Hannes Steck (*Die Prophetenbücher und ihr theologisches Zeugnis: Wege der Nachfrage un Fährten zur Antwort* [Tübingen: Mohr Siebeck, 1996], 9–10): "Unser Beitrag in dieser Studie redet nicht dem Defätismus das Wort, als blieben die ursprünglichen Prophetengestalten und ihr Wirken under der Last der Tradition in Jedem Fall unauffindbar verborgen. Und ebensowenig ist ihm am Verzicht auf die Nachfrage nach dem Propheten selbst gelegen.... Sind die ursprünglichen Propheten nur in der gegebenen Überlieferung von Prophetenbüchern anzutreffen, dann muß man mit der Untersuchung dieser gegebenen Quellen einsetzen."

[5] "I would like to see some argument ... about the historiographic intentions of the biblical writers as well as some evidence against alternative suggestions that they might have been writing for ideological or propagandist purposes (not to mention inventive literary or epigonic commentary reasons)." Robert P. Carroll, "Whose Prophet, Whose History? Troubling the Interpretive Community Again: Notes to a Response to T. W. Overholt's Critique," *JSOT* 48 (1990): 41.

little about the prophets for whom their books are named, making only cursory references to a few biographical data and relating very few prophecies to specific historical contexts of the prophets' own lifetimes. The scribes have left us no clues as to how they might have known anything about prophets who lived centuries earlier and, in any case, judging from the scant information they have passed on to their readers, they seem not to have known very much. The naming of particular prophets in the introductions to prophetic books thus appears to be merely a *pro forma* gesture having little to do with the contents of the book itself, and the few stories that we have about biblical prophets appear to be largely the inventions of later writers.[6]

These are points more or less well taken, but they stand in need of qualification. The assertion that the prophets are literary characters is certainly true as far as it goes. As this assertion is usually stated, however, it often entails a false either/or that results in a questionable conclusion. It is typically assumed that being a literary character implies being fictional, and that a truly historical figure would be represented in some more "real" way. This assumption is a vestigial remnant of the "old" form-critical method, based on the principle that true history involves making direct contact with persons from the past. This idea was presupposed in the project of attempting to recover the original speeches of the prophets. It was thought that by means of identifying their own words we could, as it were, put ourselves in the real presence of these men. Having recognized that this is not what the prophetic books do, some scholars have now conversely jumped to the conclusion that these texts are therefore ahistorical.

However, contemporary historiographical theory has reminded us that history and fiction are not antithetical in this sense. We have no direct access to any figures from the past. We know them only as they are characterized by historians in narration. In some cases we have artifacts or documents that are directly connected with persons who lived ages ago—Julius Caesar's account of his exploits in *The Gallic Wars*, Bolívar's sword, Mozart's manuscripts,

---

[6] Robert P. Carroll has been the main advocate for this view in, e.g., "Inventing the Prophets," *IBS* 10 (1988): 24–36; Carroll, "Prophecy and Society," in *The World of Ancient Israel: Social, Anthropological and Political Perspectives*, ed. R. E. Clements (Cambridge: Cambridge University Press, 1989), 203–25; and Carroll, "Whose Prophet, Whose History," 33–49. See also Roy F. Melugin, "Prophetic Books and the Problem of Historical Reconstruction," in *Prophets and Paradigms: Essays in Honor of Gene M. Tucker*, ed. Stephen Breck Reid, JSOTSup 229 (Sheffield: Sheffield Academic, 1996), 63–78; Martti Nissinen, "The Historical Dilemma of Biblical Prophetic Studies," in *Prophecy in the Book of Jeremiah*, ed. Hans M. Barstad and Reinhard G. Katz, BZAW 388 (Berlin: de Gruyter, 2009), 103–20; Philip R. Davies, "The Audiences of Prophetic Scrolls: Some Suggestions," in Reid, *Prophets and Paradigms*, 48–62; Davies, "Why Do We Know about Amos?" in Edelman and Ben Zvi, *The Production of Prophecy*, 55–72; and James M. Bos, *Reconsidering the Date and Provenance of the Book of Hosea: The Case for Persian-Period Yehud*, LHBOTS 580 (London: Bloomsbury, 2013).

Columbus's diaries, et cetera. However, such remains do not put us in contact with these persons in any meaningful sense until they are used by historians to produce narrative characterizations of them. The difference between historical figures—insofar as we know them at all—and fictional figures is not that the latter are literary characters and the former are not. Both are literary characters. The difference is that the characterization of fictional figures is based solely or largely on the writer's imagination. In contrast the characterization of historical figures is based on, and also constrained by, the actually available sources of information.[7]

Historical literary characterizations depend upon how writers evaluate the reliability of their sources and how they imaginatively interpret them. Because Carl Sandberg and David Herbert Donald weigh and interpret the sources of information about Abraham Lincoln somewhat differently, their literary characterizations of him differ in many respects—but this does not make Abraham Lincoln a fictional figure.[8] Similarly, the mere fact that the biblical prophets are literary characters in prophetic books does not necessarily imply that they are fictional figures. It all depends on whether or not the writers of the prophetic books were basing their characterizations of the prophets on what could be reasonably imagined about them from reliable sources of information.

What sources of information might the writers of the prophetic books have used? Since they have left no explicit clues, we have to look at the few biblical data in light of ancient Near Eastern culture at large, to get some idea of what sort of records were typically kept about prophecy. Resorting to this sort of comparison does not necessarily imply that biblical prophecy was directly connected with or imitated any of the other ancient prophetic traditions that have left sporadic traces in the ancient Near Eastern archaeological record. It only claims that biblical prophecy is a manifestation of the same phenomenon of divinatory intermediation that pervaded antiquity as a whole.[9] The ways in

---

[7] Hans M. Barstadt, "What Prophets Do: Reflections on Past Reality in the Book of Jeremiah," in Barstad and Katz, *Prophecy in the Book of Jeremiah*, 10–32.

[8] Carl Sandburg, *Abraham Lincoln: The Prairie Years and the War Years* (New York: Harcourt Brace Jovanovich, 1970), and David Herbert Donald, *Lincoln* (New York: Simon & Schuster, 1995).

[9] There is no need to enter here into the debate about whether the term *prophecy* properly applies to forms of divination that existed in preexilic times. (See A. Graeme Auld, "Prophets through the Looking Glass: Between Writings and Moses," *JSOT* 27[1983]: 27–42; repr. along with responding articles by Robert P. Carroll, H. G. M. Williamson, and Thomas Overholt in *The Prophets*, ed. Philip R. Davies, Biblical Seminar 42 [Sheffield: Sheffield Academic, 1996]). For present purposes it is sufficient to recognize that although *prophecy* came to be used at a relatively late date to synthesize and critique the traditions concerning various theologically diverse forms of divination that had been practiced earlier, these forms of divination—insofar as we can reconstruct them—all seem related in some way to the phenomenon that contemporary anthropology calls

which this phenomenon was expressed in other times and places may thus shed some light on the possible ways it was expressed in the prophetic traditions inherited by postexilic Yehud. Such comparison must be attentive to differences as well as similarities, and there must be some telling indication in the present biblical text of dependence on the kinds of sources that are hypothesized by means of the comparison.

With regard to the biblical data, for present purposes it does not matter whether they come from texts of doubtful historicity because the comparative evidence shows them to be generally verisimilar, realistically reflecting the ways in which prophecy and writing were interrelated in the ancient Near Eastern context.[10]

WRITTEN RECORDS OF PROPHECY

The comparative evidence comes mostly from the Mesopotamian cities of Mari and Nineveh and from classical Greece, with a few scattered sources from other times and places.[11] In the vast majority of cases the texts are evidently written reports or transcriptions of oracles that were originally spoken. It is conceivable that a prophet could have also been a scribe and could thus have written the revelations that he himself received. In the case of Jeremiah, however, he complied with YHWH's command to "write!" his oracles (Jer 30:2) by dictating them to a scribe (Jer 36).[12] Some scholars have proposed that oracles were transmitted orally by "disciples" of the prophet until they were eventually recorded, but there is little evidence of this.[13] It appears that whenever

---

intermediation. In addition to the articles by Overholt in the Biblical Seminar volume cited above, see Robert R. Wilson, *Prophecy and Society in Ancient Israel* (Philadelphia: Fortress, 1980), and David L. Petersen, *The Roles of Israel's Prophets*, JSOTSup 17 (Sheffield: JSOT Press, 1981).

[10] Barstadt, "What Prophets Do."

[11] The ancient Near Eastern texts are conveniently gathered in Martti Nissinen, *Prophets and Prophecy in the Ancient Near East*, WAW 12 (Atlanta: Society of Biblical Literature, 2003). For the Greek sources, see Armin Lange, "Literary Prophecy and Oracle Collection: A Comparison between Judah and Greece in Persian Times," in Floyd and Haak, *Prophets, Prophecy, and Prophetic Texts*, 248–75.

[12] In Isa 30:8 and Hab 2:2 the prophet is also commanded to write the revelations received. Cf. ARM 26 no. 414:29–42 (Nissinen, *Prophets and Prophecy*, 75).

[13] Most notably Sigmund Mowinckel, *Prophecy and Tradition: The Prophetic Books in the Light of the Study of the Growth and History of the Tradition* (Oslo: Dybwad, 1946), esp. 36–71. Isaiah 8:16 is often cited as a reference to prophetic disciples, but see Casbah Balogh, "Isaiah's Prophetic Instruction and the Disciples in Isaiah 8:16," *VT* 63 (2013): 1–18. James L. Crenshaw ("Transmitting Prophecy across Generations," in *Writings and Speech in Israelite and Ancient Near Eastern Prophecy*, ed. Ehud Ben Zvi and Michael H. Floyd, SBLSymS 10 (Atlanta: Society of Biblical Literature, 2000], 44) and Karel van der Toorn (*Scribal Culture and the Making of the Hebrew Bible* [Cambridge: Harvard University Press, 2007], 195) have

prophecies were preserved in writing, this was primarily due to the more or less immediate intervention of scribes, which could be instigated by the prophet himself or by others.

There were various reasons for transcribing prophecies: to deliver them to intended recipients who were absent;[14] to document that the message had indeed been delivered even when the recipient was present;[15] to preserve oracles that were thought to have unresolved implications for the future, et cetera.[16] Only

---

recently revived the theory of the oral transmission of prophetic traditions. Van der Toorn does not argue—as Mowinckel and some other early form critics did—that prophetic oracles were transmitted in an exclusively oral form, but rather that "recollections about the prophet ... were shared among his followers and admirers" in a way that complemented written transmission. Neither he nor Crenshaw offer any evidence, however, of any setting in which what they propose could happen, nor any explicit examples of the oral transmission of prophetic oracles being practiced in other cultures. For a more extensive critique see Marti Nissinen, "How Prophecy Became Literature," *SJOT* 19 (2005): 170–72.

[14] ARM 26 no. 414:29–42 (Nissinen, *Prophets and Prophecy*, 75) and Jer 29.

[15] E.g., SAA 9 3.2, i 27–ii 9 (Nissinen, *Prophets and Prophecy*, 119), describes a prophet addressing to an assembly an oracle occasioned by a royal victory and then depositing a written copy of it before the image of a god. Similarly in Isa 8:1–4 the inscription onto a tablet of the name Maher-Shalal-Hash-Baz seems to attest the delivery of the oracular message, "the spoil speeds, the prey hastens," through the prophetic sign of giving this name to the prophet's son.

[16] Isaiah and Jeremiah were motivated to record their oracles because of the popular rejection of their as yet unfulfilled predictions of disaster. Similarly Habakkuk is to "write the revelation" (Hab 2:2b), because it will take time to be fulfilled. In the meantime its promise will be communicated through ongoing study and interpretation of the text in view of unfolding events. Joachim Schaper argues that the purpose clause in Hab 2:2bβ indicates that the written text is to be read aloud in a public place by a town crier ("Exilic and Post-exilic Prophecy and the Orality/Literacy Problem," *VT* 55 (2005): 330, 331; Schaper, "On Writing and Reciting in Jeremiah 36," in Barstadt and Katz, *Prophecy in the Book of Jeremiah*, 143–45). I agree with his grammatical analysis (the participle קורא is the subject and ירוץ בו is the predicate (see Michael H. Floyd, "Prophecy and Writing in Habakkuk 2,1–5," *ZAW* 105 [1993], 471–81), but I find the semantic analysis problematic. Biblical Hebrew has several terms for functionaries whose role is to orally publicize noteworthy information. The צפה is stationed at a vantage point to keep watch and report what he sees (2 Sam 18:24–28; 2 Kgs 8:17–20; Isa 7:8; cf. Isa 21:6). The שמר is stationed at gates and doorways (Jer 35:4; 1 Kgs. 14:27; Neh 13:22) and at other key points around the city (Isa 62:6; Ps 127:1; Cant 3:3, 5:7), and it is also his job to keep people informed about current developments (Isa 21:11–12). The מבשר is a messenger who comes bringing good news (Isa 40:9; 41:27; 52:7; Nah 2:1). All of these functionaries typically give their reports orally, and none is described as reading anything from tablets. The verb קרא is one of the verbs used to describe their oral reporting, but the participle is nowhere used as a substantive that denotes someone doing this sort of thing. In 2 Chr 30:1–12 "runners" (רצים) take written documents announcing Hezekiah's Passover

those prophecies that were deemed to have significance above and beyond the immediate situation in which they originated were archived for preservation, and some of these were selected for recopying in a more substantial library format.[17] Archives were concentrated in two institutional contexts, royal courts and temples. Household libraries also existed in the homes of some wealthy persons and scribal families.[18] Transcribed prophecies could have been collected in any and all of these settings.

If much of biblical prophetic literature was based on records of prophetic activity in monarchic times, the question arises as to how such records could have been preserved despite the overthrow of Judah's monarchy in 586 BCE. Such a great social dislocation would have brought an end to most of the institutional contexts in which documents could have been archived. However, a limited number of texts could have been taken to Babylon by the entourage of the deported King Jehoiachin[19] or stored in the household libraries of scribal families outside Jerusalem. As the Qumran discoveries show, the region's climate made it possible to keep treasured manuscripts in desert caves in a time of crisis, in hope of retrieving them at some later date. With regard to the preservation of possible written sources for biblical books, we have no specific evidence one way or the other, but in any case the fall of Jerusalem need not be considered a disruption that would necessarily have obliterated all means of preserving documents.

---

celebration throughout the land, and this announcement is proclaimed, presumably by being read aloud, but it is not clear that these runners are also the ones who do the public reading (cf. Est 3:12–14; 8:9–10). In any case it is difficult to imagine that the oracle in Hab 2:3–5 would be treated like the royal decree in 2 Chr 30:6–9. I would argue that Schaper has mistakenly taken a metaphorical expression literally. In Hab 2:1 the recipient of the revelation in vv. 2–5 figuratively describes himself as assuming the role of a צפה, stationing himself on a watchtower to see what will happen (cf. Jer 6:17; Ezek 3:17; 33:7; Hos 9:8). In the same vein, the reader of the written oracle—the קורא—does not literally "run" with it but rather subjects it to further mantic interpretation. Prophetic activity can figuratively be described as "running" (e.g., Jer. 23:21).

[17] The vertical *ṭuppu* format, in contrast with the horizontal *u'iltu* format used for disposable documents not necessarily intended for long-term preservation (Martti Nissinen, "Spoken, Written, Quoted, and Invented: Orality and Writtenness in Ancient Near Eastern Prophecy," in Ben Zvi and Floyd, *Writings and Speech*, 247–48).

[18] J. Andrew Dearman, "My Servants the Scribes: Composition and Context in Jeremiah 36," *JBL* 109 (1990): 403–20; David M. Carr, *Writing on the Tablet of the Heart: Origins of Scripture and Literature* (New York: Oxford University Press, 2005), 111–42 and passim.

[19] As maintained, e.g., by William M. Schniedewind, *How the Bible Became a Book* (Cambridge: Cambridge University Press, 2004), esp. 138–64. He also argues that many biblical books were written or began to be written at the royal court of Jehoiachin in exile, but the preservation of older records there would not necessarily entail the production of biblical books there. See Ben Zvi, "Concept of Prophetic Books," 78–85.

Once archived, oracular texts could be cited in other writings and studied for their deeper meanings. If a controversial prophecy came to pass, this would make it particularly worthy of preservation and intensive study. In ancient scribal culture reflective analysis was primarily expressed in the form of compiling lists—lists of signs, words, natural phenomena, proverbs, omens, et cetera.[20] By means of lists items were juxtaposed in a series so as to show their affinities and differences, thus implying an underlying connection. In the case of prophecies, too, oracles were compiled and listed on the basis of traits that were perceived to show some commonality—thematic links, similar rhetorical patterns, correspondences to ritual sequences, and so on. Prophecies delivered by the same prophet were also compiled and listed in series on this basis.[21] By virtue of their interconnections listed prophecies came to have implications transcending the situations to which they were initially addressed, a surplus of meaning that scribal interpreters learned to apply to their own situations. The collection and listing of oracles created the potential for them to become what Armin Lange calls *literary* as opposed to merely *written* prophecy. Because such prophecies are thus recontextualized they can be understood in new ways, above and beyond what they meant in their original context.[22]

The potential for collected prophecies to interact with one another and generate new insights is evident in letters from Mari that contain several oracles along with comments of the persons sending these letters to the king. Such comments are based on connections that become apparent only when the oracles are juxtaposed.[23] Generally, however, Mesopotamian scribes do not seem to have been interested in the systematic reinterpretation of the prophecies they archived. Although they typically annotated the lists they compiled with commentary of various kinds,[24] particularly the lists of omens,[25] such annotations

---

[20] Wolfram von Soden, *The Ancient Orient: An Introduction to the Study of the Ancient Near East*, trans. Donald G. Schley (Grand Rapids: Eerdmans, 1994), 145–72.

[21] The Neo-Assyrian texts include three oracle collections, SAA 9, nos. 1, 2, and 3 (Nissinen, *Prophets and Prophecy*, 101–24). The oracles in one of these, no. 3, are all by the same prophet. The Deir 'Alla inscription provides another sort of example (Nissinen, *Prophets and Prophecy*, 207–12), as does Jer 36.

[22] Lange, "Literary Prophecy and Oracle Collection," 248–75. Nissinen maintains that the kind of recontextualization which characterizes literary prophecy is evident in the Mesopotamian texts ("Spoken, Written, Quoted and Invented," 254), but Lange argues that Mesopotamian prophecy, in contrast with biblical and Greek prophecy, remains merely written.

[23] E.g., A. 1121 + A. 2731 (Nissinen, *Prophets and Prophecy*, 17–21); ARM 26, nos. 199 and 237 (Nissinen, *Prophets and Prophecy*, 30–32 and 67–69). See further Aaron Schart, "Combining Prophetic Oracles in Mari Letters and Jeremiah 36," *JANESCU* 23 (1995): 77–88.

[24] Joachim Krecher, "Kommentare," *Reallexikon der Assyriologie und Vorderasiatischen Archäologie*, ed. Erich Ebeling et al. (Berlin: de Gruyter, 1980–1983), 6:188–91.

scarcely appear in their lists of oracles.²⁶ In contrast, the biblical prophetic books show not only the annotation of collected oracles with scribal additions, but also the integration of such interpretive commentary within the text of compiled prophecies—a phenomenon paralleled only in Greek rather than Mesopotamian oracle collections.²⁷

THE PHENOMENON OF ORACLE LISTING

In the hypothetical trajectory just sketched, describing the process by which prophetic speech could have been turned into prophetic literature, there is one aspect of that process which has not been sufficiently explored. In recent discussion nothing much has been made of the fact that compilations of prophetic oracles take the form of a list.²⁸ The listing of oracles has sometimes been seen in relation to the larger phenomenon of list-making in ancient scribal culture, as the basis for reinterpretations transcending their original historical context.²⁹ As far as I know, however, no further implications of oracle-listing have been drawn out. I believe that this factor deserves greater attention.

In its understanding of the phenomenon of lists—such as the lists of sayings that make up the book of Proverbs—Old Testament scholarship has generally adopted Wolfram von Soden's concept of *Listenwissenschaft*. Von Soden (1908–1996) interpreted the extensive corpora of ancient Near Eastern list-texts as manifestations of primitive science, implying rudimentary systems of classification based on principles that their compilers were incapable of explicitly articulating. This concept has recently been critiqued because it entails the ethnocentric assumption that only modern Western culture—based on its classical Greek philosophical heritage—is fully capable of reason and logic.³⁰ There is now a body of research on the list as a form of communication that has persisted for millennia, ever since the invention of writing, ranging from the mundane lists that facilitate the routine tasks of daily living to such baroque

---

25 René Labat, *Commentaires Assyro-Babyloniens sur les Présages* (Bordeaux: Imprimerie-Librairie de l'Université, 1933).

26 SAA 9, no. 3, is a compilation that intersperses oracles with ritual rubrics, which may reflect a kind of recontextualization—reusing oracles attesting the divine favor shown the king in his enthronement ritual.

27 Lange, "Literary Prophecy and Oracle Collection," 250–75.

28 For example, neither Philip Davies ("'Pen of Iron, Point of Diamond' [Jer 17:1]: Prophecy as Writing," in Ben Zvi and Floyd, *Writings and Speech*, 65–81) nor Martti Nissinen ("How Prophecy Became Literature") mention the listing of oracles as a significant factor in their similar sketches of such a trajectory.

29 E.g., van der Toorn, *Scribal Culture*, 118–24.

30 Markus Hilgert, "Von 'Listenwissenschaft' und 'epistemischen Dingen': Konzeptuelle Annäherungen an altorientalische Wissenspraktiken," *Journal for General Philosophy of Science* 40 (2009): 277–309.

literary examples as the medieval florilegia. There is a growing consensus that lists represent a way of knowing that, although obviously less propositional than Western science, is no less rational and logical.[31]

Among the various traits of lists that have figured in recent scholarly discussion, there are four that seem to me particularly germane to a theory of how lists of oracles might have morphed into the biblical prophetic books: (1) lists are closed series of items, but at the same time they are, in a sense, open-ended; (2) lists are a non-narrative, non-linear way of relating various items to one another; (3) the juxtaposition of items in a list generates a complex web of different sorts of ideational relationships; and (4) lists generally presuppose and embody some way of exercising power in the contexts that give rise to them. Let us consider in turn each of these characteristics of lists.

LISTS ARE CLOSED SERIES OF ITEMS, BUT AT THE SAME TIME THEY ARE, IN A SENSE, OPEN-ENDED

The word *list* is etymologically descended from an old Germanic root-meaning *border*, *edge*, or *boundary*. Lists are bounded in the sense that they contain just certain items and not others. However, because the relationships among these items are not made explicit, a list naturally gives rise to the question of what other items might (or might not) also be included. Lists thus lend themselves to getting a provisional hold on immense matters about which not enough is known, and may never be known. The compiler of a list gives some examples or specimens that are evocative of a large, unfathomable totality, and leaves it to readers to imagine the rest.

With regard to the biblical corpus of prophetic books, the unfathomable totality in question was something like this: What does prophecy as a whole teach about exile and restoration? Looking back from a postexilic perspective, what divinatory insights should be considered truly prophetic, and how do they illuminate the collective experience of several centuries? The introduction to the book of Zechariah poses this question (1:1–6), noting that former prophets had called former generations to repent, but they did not heed the prophets' call, and thus YHWH fulfilled their predictions of downfall. Now that the present generation is learning the lessons of this past history and responding more

---

[31] In particular, see Jack Goody, *The Domestication of the Savage Mind* (Cambridge: Cambridge University Press, 1977), 74–111; Liam Cole Young, "Un-Black Boxing the List: Knowledge, Materiality, and Form," *Canadian Journal of Communication* 38 (2013): 497–516; Young, "On Lists and Networks: An Archaeology of Form," Amodern 2: Network Archaeology, http://amodern.net/article/on-lists-and-networks/, and the works cited in these two articles by Young. More generally see Umberto Eco, *The Infinity of Lists*, trans. Alastair McEwen (New York: Rizzoli, 2009); and Robert E. Belknap, *The List: The Uses and Pleasures of Cataloguing* (New Haven: Yale University Press, 2004), esp. 1–35.

positively to prophetic direction, YHWH promises to restore their fortunes. How do the people begin to grasp what this present historical turning point demands of them?

Getting a provisional hold on this immense matter involved lists of two sorts. On the one hand there had to be compiled, out of all the possibilities, a representative list of prophets who had something truly revelatory to say about the historical process of exile and restoration—some aspect of the international situation leading up to the fall of the northern kingdom of Israel in the eighth century BCE, the fall of the southern kingdom of Judah in the early sixth century BCE, and the restoration of Yehud as an imperial province in the late sixth to fifth centuries BCE. On the other hand, there also had to be compiled lists of the authenticated oracles of these prophets, in which they expressed their inspired views regarding these events. Fulfillment was the criterion determining which prophets were true (Deut 18:22), and authentic oracles were those that had come to pass, or oracles based on those that had come to pass.[32] None of these lists were exhaustive, for even comprehensive lists—because they too give rise to the question of whether there is anything else that might (or might not) be included—are never completely exhaustive. The resulting corpus of prophetic books, based on list upon list, nevertheless appears to have been sufficiently comprehensive to serve its purpose.[33]

LISTS ARE A NONNARRATIVE, NONLINEAR WAY OF RELATING VARIOUS ITEMS TO ONE ANOTHER

Even if items are listed in chronological order—which is sometimes but not necessarily the case—they are not linked by any narrative sequences or grammatical structures. Thus listed items usually do not have to be considered in any particular order, and the list invites consideration of the many ways in which various items might be related to one another regardless of where they come in the series. This does not mean that lists express no sense of historical time. On the contrary, they can sometimes be a means of organizing past experience, but without locking the past into any particular narrative sequence. One scholar describes this as "a folding of time, in which different epochs are made to touch and resonate with one another."[34]

This trait of lists is relevant to the question of how prophetic books are organized. Prophetic literature is notorious for its overall lack of narrative sequence, and in a single section of text there can be a kaleidoscopic shifting of

---

[32] This Deuteronomic criterion obviously can only be employed retrospectively.
[33] Jonathan Z. Smith, "Sacred Persistence: Towards a Redescription of Canon," in *Imagining Religion: From Babylon to Jonestown* (Chicago: University of Chicago Press, 1982), 36–52.
[34] Young, "On Lists and Networks," 16.

temporal perspectives. Earlier form critics generally attempted to disassemble the text, chronologically sort the resulting parts, and then impose a narrative sequence on them. More recent critics, noting the resistance of the text to such treatment, have conversely concluded that prophetic literature is essentially ahistorical. If we take seriously the possibility that prophetic books grew out of oracle lists, we are not reduced to this either/or. In the nonchronological interplay of temporal differences that is characteristic of listing, those differences are not necessarily effaced.

THE JUXTAPOSITION OF ITEMS IN A LIST GENERATES A COMPLEX WEB OF DIFFERENT SORTS OF IDEATIONAL RELATIONSHIPS

According to von Soden's concept of *Listenwissenschaft* ancient list texts tacitly expressed primitive forms of the same sorts of taxonomic systems that are assumed by Western science to be normative—incomplete and underdeveloped versions of hierarchical taxonomies that, like the Linnaean system, can be represented by branched tree diagrams. It is now recognized that the ideational relationships expressed in lists are far more complex because they operate on different levels of meaning simultaneously. Items in a list can be tacitly related to one another by varying degrees of affinity and difference with respect to semantics, rhetoric, etymology, social status, philosophical principles, historical circumstances, material composition, ethical obligations, alliteration, visual appearance, word play, emotional connotations, and the like—just about anything. In contrast with a one-dimensional relational system that can be represented by the branches of a *tree* diagram, such a multidimensional set of ideational relationships can be metaphorically compared instead with the tangled web of a *root* system. The taxonomies that are implicit in lists revel in generous polysemy rather than reductive abstraction.

This characteristic of lists has implications for the way in which prophetic books were produced, assuming that the raw materials for them were lists of oracles, and also for the way in which the resulting prophetic books were designed to be read. Once prophecies had been compiled into a list on the basis of some perceived affinity, such as their having been proclaimed at various times and places by the same prophet, their reinterpretation involved looking for the ways in which they might be related to one another, not necessarily in the order in which the oracles were uttered or listed. Oracles at various places in the series could be interrelated in terms of their metaphorical similarities and differences in any and all sorts of ways. This was recognized by Ben Sira (39:1–3) in saying that scribes plumb the "mysteries" (αἰνίγματα) of recorded prophecies by means of metaphorical "similitudes" or "analogies" (παραβολαί). In other words, compilations of oracles invite reinterpretation that is *typological* in the broadest sense of that word.

The search for typological relationships among prophecies from the past was motivated by a desire to discover prophetic insights into the present and future. If connections could be seen among the various ways in which a prophet had truly discerned YHWH's involvement in past situations, this could enable the scribal interpreter to see connections among the ways in which YHWH had been involved then and the ways in which YHWH might be involved in subsequent situations, whether in the more recent past, the present, or the future. By drawing out such analogies, the scribal interpreters of prophecies were attempting to play in their day a divinatory role similar to the one that their prophetic predecessors had played in their day, which makes their scribal interpretations, in effect, prophetic too (Sir 24:32–33).[35]

If lists of oracles were indeed the raw materials from which prophetic books were fashioned, these lists have been substantially transformed in the finished product. Assuming that prophetic books emerged from compilations of oracles, it appears that what we have in the present texts are the initial attempts of mantic scribal interpreters to make practical sense of these oracular deposits through interpretive commentary, showing their readers how "the word of YHWH" calls to them in their own time.

In their reinterpretation of the oracles of their prophetic predecessors, the writers of prophetic books were modeling for their readers the way in which to approach such prophetic literature. Just as the scribal authors found typological connections among the collected oracles, which suggest typological connections with their present situation, readers of prophetic texts were to look for typological connections among the various sections of prophetic books that suggest typological connections with their present situation. Just as the scribal authors of prophetic books were not constrained to read the oracles they were interpreting in any particular sequence, the readers of prophetic books are not constrained to read them in a linear way. One passage might resonate with another found much later in the text, in which case the reader might well jump over the intervening material in order to make the connection. Ehud Ben Zvi has advanced the notion of "branched modes of reading" as an implication of what he calls the "general web-like construction of the repertoire and knowledge of ancient literati":

> The very concept of rereading, the presence of multiple allusions, sign-posts, cross-references, and at time overlapping structure suggests that prophetic books were likely meant to be read by their intended readerships (and likely

---

[35] Steck, *Die Prophetenbücher und ihr theologisches Zeugnis*, 127–204; Armin Lange, "Interpretation als Offenbarung: Zum Verhältnis von Schriftauslegung und Offenbarung in apokalyptischer und nichtapokalyptischer Literatur," in *Wisdom and Apocalypticism in the Dead Sea Scrolls and in the Biblical Tradition*, ed. F. García Martínez, BETL 168 (Leuven: Peeters, 2003), 17–33.

their primary readerships) not necessarily, and not always in a narrow linear manner.[36]

In light of the foregoing discussion, I would describe Ben Zvi's "branched modes of reading" as readers looking for typological connections *in* the text in order to make typological connections *with* the text, and note that this approach is rooted in the phenomenon of listing prophetic oracles.

LISTS GENERALLY PRESUPPOSE AND EMBODY SOME WAY OF EXERCISING POWER IN THE CONTEXTS THAT GIVE RISE TO THEM

A list is not only a strategy for getting ahold of a vast and unwieldy subject. It is also a strategy for defining the authoritative approach to such a subject. The particular ideational network generated by a list implies a particular social network that makes use of the list in a particular way. In the production of prophetic books we see a multifaceted attempt by Yehud's scribal elite to assert their power in the context of the early Persian period. They redefined prophecy in terms of the records of past revelations rather than oracles currently being spoken, and they reshaped the prophetic tradition by delimiting the prophets and oracles that make up the prophetic canon.[37] In the way that they integrated interpretive commentary with the oracle collections that provided the raw material for the prophetic books, they also modeled and thus defined the right way of interpreting this canon. Only if just these books were read in just this way would the authentic "word of YHWH" be revealed for the present time. In claiming such authority, the writers of the prophetic books were initially backed by the power of Yehud's civic and religious institutions, but as emergent Judaism expanded beyond the bounds of provincial Yehud the authority of their claims came to depend upon the persuasiveness of the literature they had produced.

That lists of oracles were the literary raw material for prophetic books is thus not just a hypothetical possibility that should be considered only because such collections happen to exist in other ancient sources. It is also a hypothesis that helps to explain major definitive characteristics of the finished product: prophetic literature's lack of narrative sequence; its webs of textual interconnections based on all sorts of ideational similarities, differences, and ambiguities; its scrambled temporal perspectives; and its integration of

---

[36] Ehud Ben Zvi, "Is the Twelve Hypothesis Likely from an Ancient Readers' Perspective?" in Ehud Ben Zvi and James D. Nogalski, *Two Sides of A Coin: Juxtaposing Views on Interpreting the Book of the Twelve/The Twelve Prophetic Books*, Analecta Gorgiana 201 (Piscataway, NJ: Gorgias, 2009), 93.

[37] Armin Lange argues that this was done in an attempt to resolve "inter-prophetic conflict" (*Vom prophetischen Wort zur prophetischen Tradition: Studien zur Traditions- und Redaktionsgeschichte innerprophetischer Konflikte in der Hebräischen Bibel*, FAT 34 [Tübingen: Mohr Siebeck, 2002]).

typological interpretive commentary into the finished text. Precisely because of these particular definitive characteristics there is no reason to suppose that oracles from the original collections are recoverable as such, but there is also no reason to doubt that they existed—quite the contrary.

A Case Study: Micah 1:1–16

How might these generalizations about the formation of prophetic books play out in the analysis of a particular text? Let us take, for example, Mic 1:1–16, entering into dialogue with Ehud Ben Zvi whose treatment of this text is representative of the approach of the new form criticism that this essay generally affirms, but also questions with respect to the prophet's historicity.[38] Ben Zvi observes that this passage systematically plays upon ambiguities with respect to such factors as the role of the nations (Mic 1:22), the identity of Israel (Mic 1:5, 13, 14, and 15), who is addressed, and who is speaking, most notably blurring the distinction between the voice of the reporter/writer and the voice of the prophetic figure. Such ambiguities are reinforced by the presence of word play, sound repetitions, and other sorts of thematic associations that link the constituent sections of the passage in sequence, and conversely by the absence of the sorts of markers that could clear up the uncertainties. He concludes that these are characteristics of a fictive, literary world, and that there is no direct historical referentiality here, neither with regard to any particular events nor to any actual prophet. Thus the figure of the prophet Micah is a once-upon-a-time pretext used by the writer to convey his own notion of "the word of YHWH" to his readers. I would agree with most of Ben Zvi's observations but question whether they necessarily lead to this conclusion.

Let us review the passage in question with this possibility in mind, beginning with the superscription in 1:1. It heads the entire book and thus necessarily frames how we read 1:2–16. From this heading we learn that this document purports to be "the word of YHWH"; that it is somehow related to a prophetic figure named Micah from the town of Moresheth, who prophesied during the reigns of the three Judahite kings, Jotham, Ahaz, and Hezekiah; and that his revelations concerned both Samaria and Jerusalem. This introduction clearly distinguishes between the writer of the book, who presents it to his readers as "the word of YHWH," and the prophet Micah about whom he writes. It therefore confronts us with the question of how the writer is related to this prophetic figure. In light of the forgoing discussion we can assume that the writer is not a reporter who has simply compiled and arranged for his readers the records of various prophetic speeches that this Micah once made. This leaves

---

[38] Ehud Ben Zvi, "Micah 1:2–16: Observations and Possible Implications," *JSOT* 77 (1998): 103–20; Ben Zvi, *Micah*, FOTL 21B (Grand Rapids: Eerdmans, 2000), 1–41; for others who hold similar views about the prophetic books in general, see n. 5 above.

two possibilities: (1) Is he a purely creative author who has invented a fictional prophetic figure named Micah, or perhaps adapted legendary references to the existence of such a prophet, so as to address his own prophetic message to his readers in the guise of revelations received by a prophet of long ago? Or (2) is he an imaginatively collaborative writer who has taken records of Micah's prophecies and elaborated on them, presenting his own divinatory insights as extensions of those first seen by the former prophet? In the latter case we might further ask, if the writer was indeed working with records of Micah's prophecies, how was he dependent on them?

Now let us take a look at 1:2–16 to see if the text provides us with any reasons to opt for either of these two possibilities. There is obviously no narrative sequence but, as Ben Zvi has observed, there are thematic sequences that give an overall coherence to this passage. First, there is a progression from a cosmic perspective to a local perspective. The reference to "the earth and all that fills it," including all the peoples (v. 2a), together with the description of YHWH's groundbreaking theophanic appearance (v. 3–4) puts the ensuing description of YHWH's judgments on specific cities of Israel and Judah into the context of a global crisis in which the world order is being violently transformed both geologically and geopolitically. In the following chapters subsequent references to the international context (especially 4:1–5 and 7:16–17, and also 4:11–12 and 5:7–9 [Eng. 6–8]), seen as connected to one another in terms of Ben Zvi's "branched mode of reading," make this the dominant frame of reference for the book as a whole. Other thematic sequences in this particular passage include a progression that is typical of the prophecy of punishment, from accusation (v. 5) to announcement of punishment (v. 6–7), and also a progression from a description of YHWH's judgment (v. 2–7) to various descriptions of lamenting response (v. 8–16).

As these sequences unfold there is the kaleidoscopic shifting of temporal perspectives that has previously been noted as a common characteristic of prophetic literature. From the standpoint of the announcement of punishment in verses 6–7 the downfall of Samaria lies in the future. When the lamentation gets underway (v. 8), however, it is not because this has come to pass. The lamentation is a response to the fact that the same fate now threatens Jerusalem (v. 9 and 12b) because "she" is guilty of the same transgressions that brought judgment on Samaria (v. 13b). Then comes a series of Judahite towns that are anticipating the negative effect on them of the adversity befalling Jerusalem (v. 10–15). Within this series there are more references to "Israel" (cf. v. 5) which presuppose that the northern kingdom still exists—references to "kings of Israel" being "deceived" (v. 14b) and to "the glory of Israel" (v. 15b). Such terminology is vague and highly ambiguous, but its range of possible connotations may be somewhat narrowed by the global-international dimensions of the book's overall frame of reference (mentioned above with respect to v. 2–4). When viewed in this context the kings in question could be those that followed one another in rapid succession as the northern kingdom was approaching its end, and the deception in question could be the political and diplomatic treachery in which they were chaotically embroiled, both among themselves and with Assyria (2 Kgs 15–17). Israel's "glory" (*kābōd*) could be its wealth, its prestige, its army, its strength, or even its relationship with its god YHWH.[39] The coming of any one of these things to the ill-fated Judahite city of Adullam (v. 15b) would portend that thing's demise (1 Sam 4:21; cf. Isa 16:14, 21:16). In any case, in verses 6–15 passages reflecting the temporal perspective of the northern kingdom under threat of destruction are intertwined with passages reflecting the temporal perspective of the southern kingdom under threat of destruction, thus presenting these two chronologically distinct situations as analogous developments within one and the same historical process.

The conclusion in verse 16 is ambiguous as to which of these situations it applies. An unidentified feminine singular figure is addressed, calling on her to lament because her children have gone into exile. This is consistent with the mode of address used throughout the passage, according to which each city and/or its inhabitants are personified as female individuals. Thus it is not possible to tell which city is addressed here—Samaria, or Jerusalem, or maybe even one of the other Judahite towns? In light of Ben Zvi's observations regarding the ambiguities that pervade this text on every level, it is probable that this conclusion intentionally applies to any and all of the cities mentioned in 1:2–15 and is operative in relation to both of the temporal perspectives that are evident in verses 6–15.[40]

At this point another thematic sequence becomes evident, one which underlies and is more fundamental than the others mentioned above, the progression from prophecy to fulfillment. This progression, in turn, points to a typological comparison on which the entire passage is based: YHWH's judgment upon Jerusalem and the fall of Judah happened in much the same way, and for much the same reasons, as YHWH's judgment upon Samaria and the fall of Israel.[41] Ben Zvi claims that "the text does not provide its readers with any clear marker to anchor it to any historical event."[42] This is true in the limited technical sense that there are no dates or other specific chronological indicators, nor even any explicit references to the identity of the forces that are executing YHWH's judgment, et cetera. However, when one considers the gist of this passage as a whole, namely, that Jerusalem has been defeated just as Samaria was defeated, in the midst of YHWH's reconfiguration of the world order, the text clearly points to the conclusive demise that wiped first the northern and then

---

[39] Ben Zvi, *Micah*, 36.
[40] Ibid., 37.
[41] "A folding of time, in which different epochs are made to touch and resonate with one another." See n. 37 above.
[42] Ben Zvi, *Micah*, 34.

the southern kingdom off the map. As the text unfolds, readers might be prompted by the ambiguous description at any one point to recall previous similar but less extreme crisis situations—as Ben Zvi says the text would allow them to—but in the end such events would be seen as having happened on the way to the final destruction of "Israel."[43]

With regard to the typology that informs the text there are two salient points related to our present concerns: (1) It is predicated on the fulfillment of a prophecy. If the prophetic prediction of the fall of Samaria had not come to pass, there would have been no basis on which to construct the typology in the first place. And (2) with respect to YHWH's condemnation of Samaria the typology is formulated *prospectively*, while with respect to the destruction of Jerusalem it is formulated *retrospectively*. Thus the typology spans about 150 years. It had to have been constructed by someone who knew that, like Samaria, Jerusalem had fallen—an event that the person who made the original prediction could not have witnessed.

On the basis of these observations we can now revisit the two alternatives posed above, between a purely creative writer who has created a fictional prophetic figure and a collaborative writer who has imaginatively elaborated on the records of a prophet from the past. We can eliminate the first possibility. If the writer had wanted to invent a fictive Micah out of whole cloth, the literary culture of Second Temple Yehud and of the ancient Near East in general would have offered him various ways of writing pseudepigraphical *vaticinia ex eventu*, and none of them look anything like what we have in this passage from Micah.[44] In fact, in its preoccupation with narration in chronological sequence most of the ancient literature featuring *vaticinia ex eventu* is exactly the opposite of the biblical prophetic books.[45] Rather, it appears that we have here a text which presupposes collaboration between a prophet, whose oracles were compiled and preserved because they included predictions that were fulfilled, and a later writer who elaborated on those oracles, making comparisons with subsequent events so as to draw out the portentous implications for himself and his readers in their own time.

---

[43] Ben Zvi ("Observations," 116–18; *Micah*, 30–31) notes that the references to "Israel" in this passage can refer to the northern kingdom and at the same time to Judah understood theologically as the successor to what the northern kingdom once represented in its complementary relationship with Judah. Such double entendre is rooted precisely in the typological analogy that informs the passage as a whole.

[44] Matthew Neujahr, *Predicting the Past in the Ancient Near East: Mantic Historiography in Ancient Mesopotamia, Judah, and the Mediterranean World*, BJS 354 (Providence, RI: Brown Judaic Studies, 2012).

[45] Jonah is, of course, the major exception to such generalizations. For its place in the prophetic corpus, see Ehud Ben Zvi, *The Signs of Jonah: Reading and Rereading in Ancient Yehud*, JSOTSup 367 (Sheffield: Sheffield Academic, 2003).

Thus the "contract" of the author of Micah with his readers, as it is expressed in the superscription that heads the book, is that he is addressing to them a "word of YHWH," that has a basis in historical reality. It is derived from what a real prophet once claimed about YHWH's involvement in real events, which was authenticated in the way those events turned out. The readers also fully understand that the author has put his own spin on whatever materials were handed down to him, reformulating them and adding to them in ways that show their implications for subsequent events, and in ways that show readers how to discern their implications for any situation—showing readers how to look for typological connections *in* the text in order to make typological connections *with* the text, as this way of rereading was summarily described above. This rereading strategy does not entail distinguishing the words of Micah himself from the words of the anonymous author—which in any case, as we have now discovered, cannot be done—but it does presuppose that the words of this "former" prophet stand behind the book.[46]

Did the writer actually draw upon the recorded oracles of a prophet named Micah from Moresheth who lived in the days of Jotham, Ahaz, and Hezekiah, kings of Judah? The composition of the book of Micah is predicated on this fact, but we have no way of independently verifying it. We can say that if someone of that sort did not prophesy that Samaria would be destroyed because of its infidelity to YHWH, and perhaps also that Jerusalem was heading in the same direction, it would be difficult to explain why the book is as it is. We can also say that the cultural milieu makes it altogether conceivable that the oracles of such a prophet could have been preserved in writing until they were reworked by scribes from Yehud in the early Persian period. The book gives us no reason to undertake a quest for the historical Micah, but it also gives us no reason to doubt that he existed. We have to be content with what little we can know about him because the writer and readers of this prophetic book were content with so little. The only biographical information that they cared much about—which was also perhaps the main piece of biographical information that they had—was the fact that Micah rightly discerned "the word of YHWH" in his day, because they felt that this had something to teach them about what YHWH was doing in their day.

---

[46] I see this conclusion as compatible with Ben Zvi's observation that there is "a blurring of the differentiation between direct and indirect modes in the presentation of speeches assigned to different characters in the text. This confusion of modes of representation associates the voice *reporting* a speaker (a character in the book) said so and so with the *speaker* himself (or herself), while at the same time acknowledging their separate existence" ("Observations," 111–12).

Conclusion

The results of this one case study can hardly be generalized to apply to the entire biblical prophetic corpus, but such a view of how this prophetic text was produced could arguably be extended, *mutatis mutandis*, to include several if not most of the prophetic books, particularly those named for prophets from the monarchic era. On that basis we can give a partial, tentatively positive answer to the question posed at the outset: Were the writers of the prophetic books in some sense historiographers? In the case of Micah and several other such books, yes, but only in a limited sense. They appear to have worked with reliable documentation of what was once said by the prophets of whom they wrote, but they reworked and amplified this documentation to fashion for their readers a richly typological literary world. Ben Zvi and those who take a similar approach have rightly seen that prophetic texts are characterized by all-pervasive metaphor and ambiguity, but it does not necessarily follow that these texts have therefore lost all historical referentiality. Prophetic literature is not historical in the way that earlier form critics assumed, as they attempted to segment the text and date each segment in relation to a specific event. We must think, not in terms of pieces of text referring to separate events, but in terms of the text as a whole referring to a historical process happening over a span of time. And the text can be referential in this way precisely because of its metaphorical nature, not in spite of it. When viewed comparatively in light of the broader cultural milieu in which they worked, the literary achievement of the scribes who wrote prophetic books like Micah appears highly original and creative, but they could not have produced such literature if they were not building on the recorded insights of real prophets who in earlier crisis situations prophesied things that really happened.

2

"I Will Make Her Like a Desert": Intertextual Allusion and Feminine and Agricultural Metaphors in the Book of the Twelve

Beth M. Stovell

Among the major issues facing form criticism throughout its development is the relationship between the definitions of "form" and "genre." Using linguistic terminology, one may differentiate these two concepts as "instance" vs. "system."[1] This topic has been a common one among new form critics. In *The Changing Face of Form Criticism*, Antony Campbell distinguishes between literary genre (or type) as "the typical, the matrix for a text" and literary form (or structure), which is the text itself "in all its individuality." As Campbell notes,

> matrixes are all very well, but the biblical texts are the only certain realities we have. It may be important to know the class or type to which a text belongs. It is equally or more important to know what the communication is that this text, of this particular class or type, is articulating.... The communication of a

---

[1] Colin Toffelmire suggested this distinction in personal correspondence October 12, 2012 based on the categories of M. A. K. Halliday and Ruqaiya Hasan. See Halliday, *Language as Social Semiotic: The Social Interpretation of Language and Meaning* (Baltimore: University Park Press, 1978); Halliday, *An Introduction to Functional Grammar*, 2nd ed. (New York: Edward Arnold, 1985); Halliday and Ruqaiya Hasan, *Cohesion in English* (London: Longman, 1976); Halliday and Hasan, *Language, Context, and Text: Aspects of Language in a Social-Semiotic Perspective* (Geelong, Australia: Deakin University Press, 1985).

particular text may be typical ... but as a particular text it will have its own particular communication to make.²

These notions of the typical and the particular are especially valuable as one addresses the issue of intratextual allusion. When one text utilizes another text, the second text may both build on preexistent types or classes from that original text and also create elements unique to the secondary text, because "it will have its own particular communication to make."³

These concepts of particularity versus generality and specific instance versus system have a similar evaluative function in cognitive theories of metaphor: Cognitive approaches assume, on the one hand, that scholars can describe concepts in terms of large systems.⁴ When speaking of conceptual metaphors, scholars can articulate a general description of the given metaphor (e.g., Israel as woman, God as Shepherd, etc.) that they could identify as present throughout the Hebrew Bible, or throughout a particular corpus like the Book of the Twelve. On the other hand, scholars must also examine specific instances of these concepts/metaphors and note how they are used within a particular framework in new and unique ways (e.g., how Israel as woman is depicted in Hosea compared to Jeremiah or how God as Shepherd is depicted in Isaiah compared to Ezekiel, etc.). This second step of analysis highlights the "instance" and "particular" side of the form/genre equation. The theories of Giles Fauconnier and Mark Turner (among others) demonstrate how typical metaphors may be joined together ("blended") to create something new and innovative that did not occur previously.⁵ Thus, an examination of the way

---

² See Antony F. Campbell, "Form Criticism's Future," in *The Changing Face of Form Criticism for the Twenty-First Century*, ed. Marvin A. Sweeney and Ehud Ben Zvi (Grand Rapids: Eerdmans, 2003), 29.

³ Like Campbell, Buss speaks of this as particularity versus generality. See Martin J. Buss, *The Changing Shape of Form Criticism: A Relational Approach*, HBM 18 (Sheffield: Sheffield Phoenix, 2010). Similarly Melugin speaks of the relationship between the "typical" and the "unique" in Roy Frank Melugin, "Recent Form Criticism Revisited in an Age of Reader Response," in Sweeney and Ben Zvi, *Changing Face of Form Criticism*, 47. See also Melugin's list of his previous works exploring this subject in Melugin, "Recent Form Criticism Revisited," 48, n.7.

⁴ This is evidenced in cognitive approaches such as George Lakoff's work. See George Lakoff, *Women, Fire, and Dangerous Things: What Categories Reveal About the Mind* (Chicago: University of Chicago Press, 1987); Lakoff, "Conceptual Metaphor: The Contemporary Theory of Metaphor," in *Cognitive Linguistics: Basic Readings*, ed. Dirk Geeraerts, Cognitive Linguistics Research 34 (Berlin: de Gruyter; New York: Mouton, 2006); George Lakoff and Mark Johnson, *Metaphors We Live By* (Chicago: University of Chicago Press, 1980); George Lakoff and Mark Turner, *More Than Cool Reason: A Field Guide to Poetic Metaphor* (Chicago: University of Chicago Press, 1989).

⁵ This idea is evidenced throughout Gilles Fauconnier and Mark Turner, *The Way We Think: Conceptual Blending and the Mind's Hidden Complexities* (New York: Basic Books, 2002).

metaphors are constrained in their particularity and how this relates to their generality—in other words, how any particular instance of metaphor works within the broader system of metaphors—also allows one to think carefully about how instance and system work in terms of form and genre. Thus, the constraints placed on metaphorical analysis prove valuable for categories common to form criticism. Further, such an analysis can prove particularly helpful when applied to intratextual allusion as this chapter will demonstrate through an analysis of the use of agricultural and feminine metaphors within the generic structures of the books of Hosea and Micah.

For these reasons, this chapter discusses the relationship between genre analysis within new form-critical approaches and modern metaphor theories. Rethinking issues of instance and system, or form and genre, in light of conceptual metaphor theory provides new insight on the constraints that impact a specific instance of metaphor or a specific use of "form" as compared to a wider system or genre. This chapter identifies four ways that genres and metaphors are constrained: (1) cultural and temporal constraints, (2) the partiality of any use of metaphor or genre and the desire for innovation creating constraints on "system" descriptions, (3) linguistic constraints based on the particular needs of a given passage or discourse, and (4) theological constraints stemming from adjustments of theological concerns from one context to another. After describing the utility of such a comparison between constraints in genre and metaphor analysis, the subsequent section of this chapter will demonstrate the direct impact this approach has on texts like those found in the Book of the Twelve. To illustrate the value of this approach, the final section of this chapter demonstrates these four kinds of constraints on metaphors and genres by analyzing the intratextual allusions found in Hosea and Micah in their respective uses of feminine and agricultural metaphors.

Past Theories on Genre and Metaphor in the Twelve

Prior to discussing the utility of comparisons of metaphor and genre constraints, it is necessary to establish how past theories have understood the relationship between genre and metaphor. In past studies of the Book of the Twelve, and the Hebrew Bible more generally,[6] scholars have often assumed that certain kinds of

---

[6] Hyun Chul Paul Kim examines the value of ancient Near Eastern texts to genre studies of form criticism. See Hyun Chul Paul Kim, "Form Criticism in Dialogue with Other Criticisms: Building the Multidimensional Structures of Texts and Concepts," in Sweeney and Ben Zvi, *Changing Face of Form Criticism*, 90–91. He notes other scholars in the volume using similar texts including Tremper Longman, III, "Israelite Genres in Their Ancient Near Eastern Context"; Martin Rösel, "Inscriptional Evidence and the Question of Genre," and Margaret S. Odell, "Ezekiel Saw What He Said He Saw: Genres, Forms, and the Vision of Ezekiel 1," in Sweeney and Ben Zvi, *Changing Face of Form Criticism*, 177–95, 107–21, and 162–76 respectively.

metaphors are integral to genre forms. Specifically in the case of Hosea and Micah, scholars have made assumptions about how genre forms in Hosea and Micah related to their metaphors. For example, when considering genre questions in Hosea related to the allegory of the promiscuous wife as idolatrous nation, many scholars have identified idolatry rituals behind the metaphors, suggesting that some elements that may appear as figurative were actually non-figurative and implicitly linked to ritual practices.[7] In this sense, *Religionsgeschichte* approaches and form-critical approaches that focus on cultic practice provide one way of examining the passage that allows for insight into cultural systems and diachronic development. However, this approach can be aided by synchronic readings that allow for a careful awareness of the metaphors at hand and how they function across the book as a literary whole.

Genre studies in Hosea and Micah provide concrete examples of the strengths and weaknesses implicit in linking genre directly to metaphor without a solid approach to the instance in comparison to the system. Analysis of ancient Near Eastern legal documents, marriage contracts, and other ancient Near Eastern texts related to childbirth have proved helpful to genre studies in Hosea and Micah and their relation to metaphors (particularly feminine metaphors). As noted by some scholars, the feminine and agricultural metaphors in Hos 1 and 2 are impacted by ancient Near Eastern marriage contracts, where agricultural goods are explicitly part of the marriage contract.[8] This creates a link between agricultural goods and marital relations.[9] Some scholars have further drawn a link between covenant language, such as is found elsewhere in Hosea, and marriage contracts.[10] Thus, the genre of marriage contracts creates a partial explanation for how metaphor works in Hosea. However, both the *Religionsgeschichte* and traditional *Formgeschichte* approaches demonstrate their limitations in this analysis as they only allow one to compare and contrast within the system, but not to delineate a way of differentiating the form from the genre

---

[7] For example, there have long been scholarly disputes over what role grain, wine, etc. play in Hosea and to what degree Gomer should be considered a literal example of a temple prostitute or some other kind of adulterous or unfaithful wife. For discussions on the role of grain, etc. in ancient Near Eastern sources in relation to Hos 2, see Brad E. Kelle, *Hosea 2: Metaphor and Rhetoric in Historical Perspective*, AcBib 20 (Leiden: Brill, 2005), 67–69. For debates on Gomer as temple prostitute or adulterous wife, see Sharon Moughtin-Mumby, *Sexual and Marital Metaphors in Hosea, Jeremiah, Isaiah and Ezekiel*, OTM (Oxford: Oxford University Press, 2008), 49–79, 206–68.

[8] Kelle provides a helpful survey of these ANE sources. See Kelle, *Hosea*, 67–69.

[9] See the section on Hos 1–2 in Beth M. Stovell, *Minor Prophets I (Hosea–Micah)*, SGBC 21 (Grand Rapids: Zondervan, forthcoming). See also Gerline Baumann, *Love and Violence: Marriage as Metaphor for the Relationship between YHWH and Israel in the Prophetic Books* (Collegeville, MN: Liturgical Press, 2003), 59–67.

[10] See Gordon Paul Hugenberger, *Marriage as a Covenant: A Study of Biblical Law and Ethics Governing Marriage, Developed from the Perspective of Malachi*, VTSup 52 (Leiden: Brill, 1993).

and instance from the system as one examines Hosea's metaphors and genre. This becomes particularly evident when one moves from study of Hosea to study of intratextual allusion with Micah.

What one finds if one examines Micah's use of Hosea closely is something akin to Bakhtin's definitions of genre as sameness yet change.[11] In Micah one might argue that the same metaphorical blending of feminine and agricultural metaphors occurs as in Hosea, which lends as much to the structure of Micah as it does to Hosea. Yet, while these metaphors are the same in their basic blending, they are also modified in unique ways in this new setting when shifted from Hosea to Micah. These metaphors also exist within different frameworks of genre within Micah compared to Hosea. These changes appear to have historical and contextual moorings and these metaphors appear to move toward development and innovation as they move from Hosea to Micah.

CONSTRAINTS ON GENRE AND METAPHOR

This awareness of the limitations of past approaches suggests that a new way of thinking of genre and form may be helpful to continuing recent trajectories of new form criticism and as a way of better understanding the relationship of intrabiblical allusions such as Micah's use of Hosea. Recent shifts in form criticism provides the first steps in this direction. For example, scholars like Hyun Chul Paul Kim have provided new approaches including integrating literary and linguistic approaches to answer "form" and "genre" questions in new ways.[12] The use of conceptual metaphor theories may provide another synchronic approach that can be used alongside past literary and linguistic approaches to find better refinements of the meaning of "form" and "genre."

Similar to some of the weaknesses of traditional types of form criticism, early approaches to conceptual metaphor theory demonstrated a tendency to over generalize positions on systems of thought surrounding metaphor or concepts. For example, in the early work of Lakoff, there is frequently the suggestion that

---

[11] See M. M. Bakhtin, *Speech Genres and Other Late Essays*, ed. Michael Holquist and Caryl Emerson, University of Texas Press Slavic Series 8 (Austin: University of Texas Press, 1986). For further discussion on the impact of Bakhtin in biblical studies, see Roland Boer, *Bakhtin and Genre Theory in Biblical Studies*, SemeiaSt 63 (Atlanta: Society of Biblical Literature, 2007); Barbara Green, *Mikhail Bakhtin and Biblical Scholarship: An Introduction* (SemeiaSt 38; Atlanta: Society of Biblical Literature, 2000); William R. Millar, "A Bakhtinian Reading of Narrative Space and Its Relationship to Social Space," in *Constructions of Space I: Theory, Geography, and Narrative*, ed. Jon L. Berquist and Claudia V. Camp, LHBOTS 481 (New York: T&T Clark, 2007); Carol A. Newsom, "Bakhtin," in *Handbook of Postmodern Biblical Interpretation*, ed. A. K. M Adam (Atlanta: Chalice, 2000); Seth Sykes, *Time and Space in Haggai–Zechariah 1–8: A Bakhtinian Analysis of a Prophetic Chronicle*, StBibLit 24 (New York: Peter Lang, 2002).

[12] See Kim, "Form Criticism in Dialogue with Other Criticisms."

particular views of metaphor are based on ways that human brains work, with little differentiation based on culture, time period, or other aspects of context. Subsequent to these initial attempts at developing theories of conceptual metaphor in the 1980s, scholars have critiqued this overgeneralizing or overtly "system" focus by creating more data driven and culturally specific analyses.[13] These corrections to conceptual metaphor theory in terms of instance in relation to the overall system provide a helpful analogy for the analysis of form and genre. This section will highlight four constraints on metaphor coming from recent metaphor analysis that provide helpful parallels with genre analysis in new form criticism and will end with a suggestion for how this may impact the examination of intratextual allusion.

METAPHORS AND GENRES ARE CULTURALLY AND TEMPORALLY CONDITIONED

Location in culture and in time impacts shifting understandings of metaphor and genre. Some initial studies of metaphors tended to speak of metaphor as though it were fixed and stable from culture to culture. Studies of metaphor that based concepts of metaphor on Platonic or Neoplatonic philosophy in particular show these tendencies.[14] Recent studies of metaphor have emphasized the importance of locating metaphor in its cultural and temporal context in order to understand how a particular metaphor is understood within that culture and time with its particular nuances.[15] With metaphors in ancient literature, the complexities of

---

[13] See Terrell Carver and Jernej Pikalo, *Political Language and Metaphor: Interpreting and Changing the World*, Routledge Innovations in Political Theory (New York: Routledge, 2008); J. Charteris-Black, *Corpus Approaches to Critical Metaphor Analysis* (New York: Palgrave Macmillan, 2004); Gilles Fauconnier and Mark Turner, "Rethinking Metaphor," in *The Cambridge Handbook of Metaphor and Thought*, ed. Raymond W. Gibbs (New York: Cambridge University Press, 2008), 53–66; Raymond W. Gibbs, "Taking Metaphor Out of Our Heads and Putting It into the Cultural World," in *Metaphor in Cognitive Linguistics*, ed. Raymond W Gibbs and Gerard Steen, Current Issues in Linguistic Theory 4 (Philadelphia: J. Benjamins, 1999), 145–66; Zoltan Kövecses, *Metaphor in Culture: Universality and Variation* (Cambridge: Cambridge University Press, 2005); Neil Smith and Cindi Katz, "Grounding Metaphor: Toward a Spatialized Politics," in *Place and the Politics of Identity*, ed. Michael Keith and Steve Pile (London: Routledge, 1993), 66–81; Anatol Stefanowitsch and Stefan Thomas Gries, *Corpus-Based Approaches to Metaphor and Metonymy* (Berlin: de Gruyter, 2006).

[14] These kinds of studies exist both in cognitive linguistics, in ancient metaphor studies, as well as in literary metaphor studies and have been widely critiqued by scholars such as Janet Martin Soskice, *Metaphor and Religious Language* (Oxford: Clarendon, 1985); Stefanowitsch and Gries, *Corpus-Based Approaches*, Trends in Linguistics 171 (Berlin: de Gruyter, 2006).

[15] For an overview of many of these approaches and for a developed theory of metaphor and culture, see Kövecses, *Metaphor and Culture*. Recent work on the impact of culture on metaphors in the Hebrew Bible include P. van Hecke, *Metaphor in the Hebrew Bible*, BETL

locating a particular metaphor within its specific culture and time is often augmented by exploring the metaphors in neighboring cultures as a means of greater illumination. However, as with the critique of a fixed or stable view of metaphor as if it were universal, there are necessary constraints on examining surrounding cultures to the Hebrew Bible in an analysis of their metaphors. Among the constraints to consider are as follows: (1) There will be similarities and differences between metaphors in other surrounding cultures and metaphors within the biblical text. (2) Establishing the original cultural context of a metaphor is key prior to comparisons with other cultures. (3) Temporal similarities to other metaphors create a higher likelihood of similarity. (4) Geographical and linguistic proximity allows for greater likelihood of similarity between metaphors in surrounding cultures.

Scholars like Tremper Longman have demonstrated that genres are not "pure or fixed" as Gunkel suggested with his neoclassical approach. Rather, genres have a great level of fluidity that is in part impacted by cultural and temporal factors.[16] Longman argues that the methods used to describe comparisons with ancient Near Eastern literature play a key role as one analyzes biblical texts. The cultural factors impacting genre in comparisons between the ancient Near Eastern literature and the biblical text are both similar and dissimilar. Longman pushes for the necessity of methodological controls in comparative genre study as a means to create more sound and fruitful comparative analysis. Several of the methodological controls that Longman suggests parallel the constraints on metaphor described above. For example, contrasts and similarities must be noted in comparing cultures. "The genres being compared must be understood as thoroughly as possible in their original cultural context before being compared," just as metaphors must be understood within their original cultural context before they are compared to those within other cultures. Longman asserts that that temporal, geographical, and linguistic proximity create a greater likelihood for influence of genre from one culture to another.[17]

When applying this to the relationship between Hosea and Micah, one finds that when looking at the overall shape of the Book of the Twelve one can see that whether we look at the MT ordering or the LXX ordering, Hosea is always read prior to Micah in the scrolls. It is thus canonically prior. This priority of Hosea may provide us with a clue toward how other books of the

---

187 (Leuven: Peeters, 2005); Paul A. Kruger, "A Cognitive Interpretation of the Emotion of Anger in the Hebrew Bible," *JNSL* 26 (2000): 181–93; Zacharais Kotzé, "A Cognitive Linguistic Approach to the Emotion of Anger in the Old Testament," *HTS* 60 (2004): 843–63.
[16] Longman, "Israelite Genres in their Ancient Near Eastern Contexts," 183.
[17] Ibid., 193–95.

Book of the Twelve were intended to be read in relation to Hosea. Examining Micah's use of Hosea provides a helpful step in this direction.

METAPHORS AND GENRES ARE PARTIAL AND BLENDED

Scholars who study how metaphor works often speak of the concept of metaphorical entailments. Entailments are the specific elements used to connect A to B in a particular metaphor. For example, in Mic 4:9–10 when Micah describes Israel ("Daughter Zion") as a woman who is a mother in labor, he is focusing on particular aspects of mothers and not other aspects to describe Israel's experience. The entailments he chooses to highlight are the sounds of groaning and the pain associated with a mother giving birth in order to emphasize the crisis that is occurring to Daughter Zion.[18]

Entailments demonstrate that metaphors are never creating a full or complete link between the target and the source in the metaphor. Israel is not like a mother in every possible facet, but rather Mic 4 is highlighting particular entailments of motherhood to connect to Israel. This is evidenced by a comparison of the reuse of the metaphor of Israel as birthing mother in Mic 5:2. Whereas Mic 4 focuses only on entailments related to the sounds and experience of the pain associated with childbirth, Mic 5:2 focuses on the hope of new life associated with childbirth.[19] Thus, the relationship is necessarily partial for the analogy between the target and source to work.[20]

Understanding how metaphors function partially and can be taken apart also allows us to focus on ways that these metaphorical entailments can be blended in unique ways.[21] For example, in Mic 4:10 the entailments related to the sounds and pain of childbirth follow the description of the people crying out in Mic 4:9. The sounds of crying out due to grief and crying out due to pain provide a place for blending the idea of exile with the idea of childbirth.[22]

---

[18] Claudia Bergmann explores the metaphor of childbearing as it exists throughout the Hebrew Bible in Claudia D. Bergmann, *Childbirth as a Metaphor for Crisis: Evidence from the Ancient Near East, the Hebrew Bible, and 1QH XI, 1–18*, BZAW 382 (Berlin: de Gruyter, 2008). For Bergmann's examination of Mic 4:9–10 specifically, see Bergmann, *Childbirth as a Metaphor for Crisis*, 109–11.

[19] See Bergmann, *Childbirth as a Metaphor for Crisis*, 111. For discussion of this metaphor in relation to the larger theme of Zion in Micah, see Rick R. Marrs, "'Back to the Future': Zion in the Book of Micah," in *David and Zion: Biblical Studies in Honor of J. J. M. Roberts*, ed. Kathryn L. Roberts and J. J. M. Roberts (Winona Lake, IN: Eisenbrauns, 2004), 93.

[20] Lakoff provides helpful explanation of entailments in Lakoff and Johnson, *Metaphors We Live By*, 93–96.

[21] See Fauconnier and Turner's theories of conceptual blending in Fauconnier and Turner, *Way We Think*.

[22] Katheryn Darr notes a similar blending of the sounds of distress in war and the sounds of distress in childbirth in her work on Isa 42. See Katheryn Pfisterer Darr, "Like

Claudia Bergmann has argued that these kinds of conceptual blends allow childbirth to become a metaphor related to distress in the Hebrew Bible.[23]

Similarly, it is helpful to describe partial and blended genre structures. Longman explains that genre exists at different levels of abstraction. What scholars describe as typical genres are eclectic in their very nature because they are drawn from a variety of different sources.[24] Thus it is reasonable to speak of genre entailments, or the specific parts of the "ideal" or prototypical genre structure, that one may see instantiated in a particular text. One may also speak of genre blending, where these partial genre elements are blended in new ways to create new generic structures. Melugin's study of Jeremiah demonstrates this blending of partial genre elements to create an innovative and artistic new literary form. Speaking of Jer 2, Melugin states, "the combining of the trial speech in the mouth of YHWH (v. 2–3) and a woe utterance as a human voice (vv. 4–9) shows how artistically reshaped conventional speech forms can be juxtaposed for creative purposes.... Two different linguistic conventions are artfully juxtaposed by creatively combining similar themes and by the skillful use of poetic imagery."[25] In this chapter, we will see similar blending of genres in Hosea and Micah to create artistic and rhetorical effect.

METAPHORS AND GENRES EXIST IN DISCOURSE AND ARE LINGUISTICALLY CONTEXTUALIZED

The location of metaphor within its linguistic context deeply impacts its meaning. Unfortunately, there has long been a tendency among many scholars to disconnect metaphor from its linguistic context in many studies as a way of connecting it to other cultures or to other parts of Scripture. While many metaphors in the Bible are allusions to prior uses of a similar metaphor elsewhere in the Scriptures, these metaphors by their very nature are never the *same* metaphor, but are given new meaning in their new linguistic setting. Several recent studies have worked to reintegrate metaphors into their linguistic context, affirming the absolute necessity of metaphorical interpretation within a context.[26]

Warrior, Like Woman: Destruction and Deliverance in Isaiah 42:10–17," *CBQ* 49 (1987): 560–71.
[23] See Bergmann, *Childbirth as a Metaphor for Crisis*, 109–11.
[24] Longman, "Israelite Genres in their Ancient Near Eastern Contexts," 183.
[25] Melugin, "Recent Form Criticism Revisited," 50.
[26] Some recent studies have demonstrated the relationship between linguistic structures and metaphorical analysis including Beth M. Stovell, *Mapping Metaphorical Discourse in the Fourth Gospel: John's Eternal King*, LBS 5 (Leiden: Brill, 2012); Beth M. Stovell, "Seeing the Kingdom of God, Seeing Eternal Life: Comparing Cohesion and Prominence in John 3 and the Apocryphal Gospels in Terms of Metaphor Use," in *The Language of the New Testament: Context, History and Development*, ed. Stanley Porter and Andrew Pitts, LBS 6

Similarly genre structures are impacted not only by their culture, time, and the partial nature of structure itself, but are also constrained by linguistic contexts. Genre does not exist separately from linguistic contexts, but is always contextualized by linguistic frameworks that provide clarity on genre's meaning in a given passage. Recent shifts in genre analysis have started to acknowledge the need for linguistic contextualization as part of genre theory.[27] Specifically, Antony Campbell identifies this awareness as part of the future of form criticism.[28] In subsequent sections, this chapter will demonstrate how both genre and metaphor in Hosea and Micah are constrained by their linguistic context.

METAPHORS AND GENRES ARE THEOLOGICALLY CONTEXTUALIZED AND ADAPTATIONS TO METAPHORS AND GENRES MAY HAVE THEOLOGICAL PURPOSES

Another constraint on the metaphors within a given biblical text is theological understandings and themes important to the particular author of the text. On the one hand, theological conceptions can allow for great diversity in metaphorical and generic expression. On the other hand, certain assumed theologies or desires to convey a given theology may create constraints on what a given metaphor might mean, or how a particular genre will be used in a particular passage.[29] Study of metaphors in the Old Testament frequently demonstrates that metaphors are constrained by assumptions around how God can be described based on preexisting theological traditions. For example, when an author is standing within the Deuteronomic tradition, metaphors describing God are often constrained by the theological underpinnings of this tradition.[30] Similarly, it is logical that one may find uses of genre that stand within a

---

(Leiden: Brill, 2013), 439–67; Beth M. Stovell, "Yahweh as Shepherd-King in Ezekiel 34: Linguistic-Literary Analysis of Metaphors of Shepherding," in *Modeling Biblical Language: Papers from the McMaster Divinity College Linguistics Circle*, ed. Stanley Porter, Christopher Land, and Gregory Fewster, LBS (Leiden: Brill, forthcoming).

[27] Sweeney and Ben Zvi describe the impact of text linguistics on the writings of Wolfgang Richter and Klaus Koch as examples of recent shifts in Form Criticism, noting the focus on syntax and semantics in their work. See Sweeney and Ben Zvi, "Introduction," in Sweeney and Ben Zvi, *Changing Face of Form Criticism*, 3, n.7.

[28] While Campbell does not use the language of "linguistics" specifically, he does note the need to see genre and form as located in the context of their specific biblical passage and repeatedly states that the future of Form Criticism lies in examining what exists before us rather than the hypothetical. See Campbell, "Form Criticism's Future," 15–31.

[29] See Roy Frank Melugin, "Muilenburg, Form Criticism, and Theological Exegesis," in *Encounter with the Text: Form and History in the Hebrew Bible*, ed. Martin J. Buss (Philadelphia: Fortress, 1979), 91–100.

[30] See Moshe Weinfeld, *Deuteronomy and the Deuteronomic School*, (Oxford: Clarendon, 1972; repr. Winona Lake, IN: Eisenbrauns, 1992).

particular theological tradition. The Book of the Twelve shows varied connections to this Deuteronomic tradition that impact the metaphors and genres present in the specific books and their intratextual allusions to one another.[31]

Scholars have often noted particular themes and theological tendencies within the Book of the Twelve. For example, Nogalski's work demonstrates the impact of literary development and theology that constrain metaphors and genres in the Book of the Twelve. Nogalski points to four key themes in the Book of the Twelve, which "show signs of editorial activity, literary development, and/or diverse theological perspectives. These themes intersect with one another in places, but they also each tell portions of a story of their own." He lists these themes as "the Day of YHWH, fertility of the land, the fate of God's people, and the theodicy problem."[32] Of these four themes, this chapter focuses on two: fertility of the land and the fate of God's people. These two themes play an important role in shaping and constraining the metaphors and genres present in Hosea and Micah.

INTRATEXTUAL ALLUSIONS IN THE BOOK OF THE TWELVE AND METAPHOR AND GENRE THEORIES

Studies of metaphor and genre are also impacted directly when one text alludes to another text as part of its development. In the past form criticism tended toward examining the role of allusion primarily to answer diachronic questions related to the Book of the Twelve.[33] However, some recent studies within New form criticism have begun to identify key themes developed within the Book of the Twelve through intratextual allusion among the books.[34] As with the other

---

[31] Moshe Weinfeld, *Deuteronomy and the Deuteronomic School*, 366–70.

[32] James Nogalski, "Recurring Themes in the Book of the Twelve: Creating Points of Contact for a Theological Reading," *Int* 61 (2007): 126.

[33] For extensive discussion of past approaches related to intertextuality in the Book of the Twelve, see ch. 4 of Marvin A. Sweeney, *Form and Intertextuality in Prophetic and Apocalyptic Literature*, FAT 45 (Tübingen: Mohr Siebeck, 2005), 173–236; Myrto Theocharous, *Lexical Dependence and Intertextual Allusion in the Septuagint of the Twelve Prophets: Studies in Hosea, Amos and Micah*, LHBOTS 570 (New York: Bloomsbury T&T Clark, 2012). The relative role of Amos or Hosea in other parts of the Book of the Twelve has also been a place of exploration of intertextual and intra-textual allusion in works like Tchavdar Hadjiev, *The Composition and Redaction of the Book of Amos*, BZAW 393 (Berlin: de Gruyter, 2009); Tchavdar Hadjiev, "Zephaniah and the 'Book of the Twelve' Hypothesis," in *Prophecy and Prophets in Ancient Israel: Proceedings of the Oxford Old Testament Seminar*, ed. John Day, LHBOTS 531 (New York: T&T Clark, 2010), 325–38; and James Nogalski, *Redactional Processes in the Book of the Twelve*, BZAW 218 (Berlin: de Gruyter, 1993).

[34] See the discussion of intertextuality in the Book of the Twelve in Marvin A. Sweeney, "Zechariah's Debate with Isaiah," in Sweeney and Ben Zvi, *Changing Face of Form Criticism*, 335–50. Examples of intertextuality and new form-critical approaches include Sweeney,

constraints placed on metaphor discussed above, the use of metaphor within intratextual allusion also works within a particular set of constraints based on the relationship between the first text and second text (which alludes to the first). The secondary text is always constrained in some way by some of the conventions of the earlier use of the metaphor in the first text, but is also always re-creating the metaphor in some ways based on its new temporal, cultural, and linguistic location in a new text. Similarly, the use of genre can function as a form of intratextual allusion. Conventional structures of genre may play a role in the development of genre in a secondary text, which alludes to a previous use in other texts and social contexts. Thus, the methodological constraints on genre and metaphor analysis analyzed in this chapter provide a means to examine the many facets of intratextual allusion in ways consistent with recent shifts in form criticism. This chapter will observe the impact of intratextual allusion on the different constraints on metaphor and genre as Micah alludes to Hosea. Using intratextual allusion provides a means to highlight the changes we find between these two books, which both show striking continuity and discontinuity in their examples of metaphorical and generic allusions.

APPLYING THIS THEORY TO HOSEA'S AND MICAH'S FEMININE AND AGRICULTURAL METAPHORS

This section demonstrates how the four major constraints discussed in metaphor and in genre are present and impact Hosea's and Micah's use of feminine and agricultural metaphors. To provide focus for this study, this chapter will analyze on the depictions of feminine and agricultural metaphors in Hos 2 and 9 and draw connections with Mic 1 and 4, grouping together Hos 2 and Mic 1 as depictions of Israel as adulterous wife/prostitute and Hos 9 and Mic 4 as depictions of Israel as mother.[35] First, comparing Hosea's depiction of Israel as adulterous wife/barren mother in relation to Israel as a land of loss and waste to Micah's depiction of Israel as prostitute/mother and Israel as land in its

---

Form and Intertextuality in Prophetic and Apocalyptic Literature; Richard L. Schultz, "The Ties That Bind: Intertextuality, the Identification of Verbal Parallels, and Reading Strategies in the Book of the Twelve," in *Thematic Threads in the Book of the Twelve*, ed. Paul L. Redditt and Aaron Schart, BZAW 325 (Berlin: de Gruyter, 2003).

[35] The metaphors of Israel as wife and mother run throughout Hosea. For more on Israel as wife in Hosea, see Richtsje Abma, *Bonds of Love: Methodic Studies of Prophetic Texts with Marriage Imagery, Isaiah 50:1–3 and 54:1–10, Hosea 1–3, Jeremiah 2–3*, SSN 40 (Assen, Netherlands: Van Gorcum, 1999); Baumann, *Love and Violence*; F. Charles Fensham, "The Marriage Metaphor in Hosea for the Covenant Relationship between the Lord and His People (Hos 1:2–9)," *JNSL* 12 (1984): 71–78; J. Gerald Janzen, "Metaphor and Reality in Hosea 11," *Semeia* 24 (1982): 7–44; Joy Philip Kakkanattu, *God's Enduring Love in the Book of Hosea: A Synchronic and Diachronic Analysis of Hosea 11,1–11*, FAT 2.14 (Tübingen: Mohr Siebeck, 2006).

experience of judgment allows us to explore how constraints on metaphors and genres are related to culture and temporality. Second, examining the feminine and agricultural metaphors in Hosea and Micah in terms of the differing specific entailments used in each case and examining the partial generic structures used in both books allows us to analyze how metaphors and genres are partial and blended in Hosea and Micah. Third, locating the metaphors and genres in Hosea and Micah within their linguistic contexts demonstrates the constraints that linguistic contextualization places on feminine and agricultural metaphors in these books as well as on generic structures. Finally, in Hosea metaphors of loss, unfaithfulness, and a lack of fecundity will be explored in contrast to the positive metaphors of fruition and God's relationship of love with Israel. Micah uses very similar metaphors to Hosea, likely built upon Hosea's metaphors via intrabiblical allusion. However, Micah's theological purposes differ, which is reflected in Micah's use of generic structures. Analysis of the theological constraints on each passage allows for a greater awareness of how theology constrains metaphor and genre.

METAPHORS AND GENRES IN HOSEA AND MICAH ARE CULTURALLY AND TEMPORALLY CONDITIONED

Both Hos 2 and Mic 1 describe Israel as a promiscuous wife and/or a prostitute and relate these feminine metaphors to the depiction of Israel in terms of agricultural metaphors. These depictions are deeply impacted by the cultural and temporal context of the Hebrew people broadly and specifically within the context of each book. Analysis of these metaphors and the genres will follow the steps laid out in the earlier section of this chapter.

Hosea 1 sets up the metaphor of Gomer as adulterous wife to her husband Hosea as parallel to Israel as an idolatrous and unfaithful wife to her husband YHWH. In Hos 2 this metaphor is dramatically described in detail as the narrative genre of Hos 1 shifts to the prophetic genre of Hos 2.[36] In Hos 2, the first half of the chapter describes Israel's unfaithfulness to YHWH, her husband, and YHWH's response to her unfaithfulness. The second half of Hos 2 focuses on YHWH's desire to draw Israel as wife back to himself. In both sections of Hos 2, agricultural metaphors are interwoven with feminine metaphors. In the first section, Israel in her unfaithfulness is "made like a wilderness ... like a land of drought" (Hos 2:5 [Eng. 2:3]).[37] To block her way, YHWH uses a hedge of

---

[36] Many have located the shift from Hos 1 to Hos 2 as a marked change, but they usually locate this change as part of the unit beginning at Hos 2:4. In contrast to the majority of scholars, Kelle argues for reading Hos 2 in its entirety as a single unit, see Kelle, *Hosea 2*, 169–200.

[37] The language of Israel becoming like a desert incorporates agricultural metaphors with marriage metaphors as a means of demonstrating the totality of YHWH's potential judgment and its impact on the land. See Gert Kwakkel, "The Land in the Book of

thorns (Hos 2:8 [Eng. 2:6]). When YHWH puts an end to her idolatrous and unfaithful practices, it is described not only in terms of the practices themselves, but as laying waste to her vines and her fig trees. These vines and fig trees are also described as the wages of Israel's prostitution, which YHWH will make into a forest that wild animals shall devour (Hos 2:14 [Eng. 2:12]).

As the emphasis shifts from judgment on Israel for her actions to a restored relationship with Israel, the metaphors of agriculture move from images of loss and destruction to positive images echoing the creation story itself. In an intertextual journey back into the wilderness that echoes the Exodus account, Israel's vineyards are returned to her (vv. 16–17 [Eng. vv. 14–15]) as YHWH allures her back into relationship with him. Using an allusion to Genesis, YHWH makes a covenant with Israel that involves all of the natural world (v. 20 [Eng. v. 18]) including the heavens and earth joining in a chorus (vv. 23–24 [Eng. v. 21–22]). This vision culminates in sowing Israel in the land (v. 25 [Eng. v. 23]).

Micah 1 appears to build on the feminine and agricultural metaphors established by Hosea. Micah 1 describes the idolatry of Samaria. In Mic 1:7, the means of Samaria's idolatry will be destroyed. Idols, temple gifts, and images (of false gods) will be broken and burned. Following in the metaphors of Hosea, Micah describes these in terms of prostitution. Picking up on the language of Israel's wages as a prostitute in Hos 2:14 (Eng. 2:12) and desolation of the vines that were her pay, Mic 1:7 speaks of the wages of prostitution and the desolation of her images.[38] In both Hos 2 and Mic 1, YHWH lays waste the items that were associated with the pay of Israel for her unfaithfulness,[39] yet in Hos 2 this action of desolation is followed relatively shortly in verse 14 with YHWH's seeking restoration of his relationship with Israel. In contrast, Mic 1 follows this depiction of prostitution and desolation with the weeping, wailing, howling, and moaning of a lament.

Two questions arise from these blendings of agricultural and feminine metaphors: (1) What is the cultural and temporal background for these metaphors? and (2) How does this cultural and temporal background shape one's understanding of Hosea? These questions lead to a subsequent question

---

Hosea," in *The Land of Israel in Bible, History, and Theology: Studies in Honour of Ed Noort*, ed. Jacques Ruiten Edward Noort and Jacobus Cornelis De Vos, VTSup 124 (Leiden: Brill, 2009), 169–71.

[38] Ben Zvi notes that this language "activates (among other things) the 'traditional' yet problematic biblical topos of the unfaithful city/woman, the polemic associations of prostitution and cult in Samaria (e.g., Hosea)." Ehud Ben Zvi, *Micah*, FOTL 21B (Grand Rapids: Eerdmans, 2000), 32.

[39] Several scholars have noted that Micah's language is reminiscent of Hosea in this passage. See Jan A. Wagenaar, *Judgement and Salvation: The Composition and Redaction of Micah 2–5*, VTSup 85 (Leiden: Brill, 2001), 56; Ben Zvi, *Micah*, 32.

that is crucial for this study: How do cultural and temporal shifts in turn impact the genres represented in Hos 2 and Mic 1?

As noted previously, rather than beginning with metaphors from other cultures, it is helpful to begin by establishing the original cultural context of a metaphor prior to making comparisons to other cultures. The blending of agricultural and feminine metaphors found in Hos 2 is able to occur because of the cultural assumptions developed among the Hebrew people found in prior sections of the Hebrew Bible. These conceptions develop in several ways. First, God's covenant with Abraham to give a particular land to the people of Israel ultimately leads the land itself to become associated with the name "Israel." This creates a dynamic in which "Israel" is used to refer to both a people and a land. For this reason, it is not surprising to find this concept of covenant as a key theme throughout Hosea. For example, Hos 1:10 alludes to God's covenant with Abraham in Gen 22:17, repeated to Jacob in Gen 32:12, that Israel's promise will still be fulfilled and she will still be "like sand on the seashore, which cannot be measured." By echoing the promises given to their ancestors, Hosea is tapping into the entire tradition of the Old Testament and to God's faithfulness to his promises to his chosen people.[40]

When this association between Israel as a people and as a land is depicted in metaphorical terms, Israel becomes depicted as a wife to God and as a woman defiled by her unfaithfulness. This defiling has two extensions: Israel are a people who defile their land and Israel are a people who defile themselves by their idolatrous actions.[41] This locates Israel metaphorically as both Israel a land defiled and Israel a people defiled, blending the people-focused metaphor of a woman with the land-focused metaphor of agriculture, blurring the lines of people- and land-focus.

These concepts of land defilement and human defilement as metaphors of Israel's unfaithfulness come from another metaphorical link between covenantal contracts and marital contracts. There were stipulations for the vassal king and the wife, respectively, in both covenantal and marriage contracts.[42] Both the vassal king and the wife in these contracts must swear loyalty to maintain their contractual relationship with the suzerain or the husband. If they violate this loyalty—whether by foreign military alliances in the case of the covenantal contract or by marital infidelity in the case of the marriage contract—the forged relationship could end either in dissolution of the contract or in public

---

[40] See Kwakkel, "Land in the Book of Hosea," 167–81.

[41] There are similar links that may be noted in Jeremiah's use of the metaphors of Israel as land and Israel as people connected to feminine and agricultural metaphors. Beth M. Stovell, "Mother and Whore, Vine and Water: Rhetorical Violence and Comfort through the Blended Metaphors of Jeremiah" (paper presented at the annual meeting for the Society of Biblical Literature, Chicago, Illinois, November 17–20, 2012).

[42] Hugenberger, *Marriage as a Covenant*, 168–85.

humiliation.⁴³ Thus, cultural conceptions of marriage and political relationships impact the creation and development of the metaphors in Hos 1–2, demonstrating the impact of cultural and temporal constraints on these metaphors.

The relationship between the metaphors in Hos 2 and Baal worship in the ancient Near East demonstrate another way that Hosea's metaphors are constrained by their cultural and temporal context. Yet this is an area of some current debate in part due to the principles related to the issue of temporal constraints discussed earlier in this chapter. The major issue related to Baal worship practices and Hos 2 is the question of whether the ancient Near Eastern practices that have long been associated with Hos 2, particularly in relation to temple prostitution to the worship of Baal, have any evidence dating to the time period of Hosea's initial creation. Several scholars have challenged these assumptions by way of non-Hosean texts.⁴⁴ Most notably, Tigay has argued this based on onomastic and inscriptional evidence.⁴⁵ If Tigay's critique of the typical scholarly approaches to Baal worship and the use of metaphors in Hos 2 is correct, then this would suggest that Baal worship as the most likely referent for either metaphors or genre is less likely than scholars have long thought. Such a shift in the assumptions of Hosean scholarship would also demonstrate the constraints related to temporal and cultural similarities. This further illustrates that temporal similarities to other metaphors and genres need to be considered before assuming a parallel between sources.

Similar issues arise as we examine the cultural and temporal constraints on genre in Hosea and Micah. Beginning with the original cultural context of the texts first implies the need to begin by analyzing the two texts in light of their relationship within the Book of the Twelve prior to examining external cultural contexts. Tracing the cultural and temporal differences between the metaphors of Hosea and Micah provides insight into the mixed nature of the genres found in Hos 2 and Mic 1. First, while Hosea and Micah use similar metaphors, they use different genres to convey their messages. Hosea 2 appears to model itself on a combination of genres,⁴⁶ using the formal language of covenant and marriage contracts nestled in the structures of prophetic speech.⁴⁷ Some have argued that

---

⁴³ Baumann, *Love and Violence*, 59–67.

⁴⁴ Scholars who have challenged this position include Gale A. Yee, *Poor Banished Children of Eve: Woman as Evil in the Hebrew Bible* (Minneapolis: Fortress, 2003), 85–92, and see also the introduction to Alice A. Keefe, *Woman's Body and the Social Body in Hosea 1–2*, Gender, Culture, Theory, JSOTSup 338 (New York: Sheffield Academic, 2001).

⁴⁵ Jeffrey H. Tigay, *You Shall Have No Other Gods: Israelite Religion in the Light of Hebrew Inscriptions*, HSS 31 (Atlanta: Scholars Press, 1986).

⁴⁶ For a detailed discussion of genre in Hos 2, see Kelle, *Hosea 2*, 169–79, and J. Andrew Dearman, *Hosea*, NICOT (Grand Rapids: Eerdmans, 2010), 56.

⁴⁷ Many scholars have noted, however, that Hosea is hard to categorize, because it does not have a clear inner structure and does not use prophetic formulas like "thus says the

Hos 2 contains a court scene,[48] but several have demonstrated that if such a scene exists it is latent or partial rather than consistent throughout the chapter.[49]

In contrast, Micah extends Hosea's initial set of genres by integrating the genres of trial and lament alongside the developed metaphor of Israel as unfaithful wife.[50] If one argues that Hos 2 is a partial court scene, then Mic 1 may be developing this genre in more detail along with Hosea's primary metaphor of Israel as unfaithful wife. Micah's uses of genre create a noticeable shift from the covenant renewal found in the second half of Hos 2 to the call to lament found in the second half of Mic 1. Even Micah's initial call for the earth to witness the charge against Israel possibly alludes to Hosea's call for heaven and earth to sing in chorus at the rejoining of Israel to her husband God. If this is the case then the use of genre in Mic 1 deviates in important ways from Hos 2.

METAPHORS AND GENRES IN HOSEA AND MICAH ARE PARTIAL AND BLENDED

The metaphors of motherhood and agriculture and the use of complex genres in Hos 9 and in Mic 4 demonstrate the partial and blended quality of metaphors and genres. Both Hos 9 and Mic 4 emphasize judgment through metaphors related to childbirth and to agriculture. Hosea 9 describes Ephraim's judgment in terms of an inability to give birth and destruction of what is birthed. Hosea 9 focuses on the inability to conceive, the loss of a child, and the inability to care for a child once delivered. Hosea 9:11 begins with the bird metaphors found in Hos 8 of Ephraim's glory "fly[ing] away like a bird," but how this occurs is through a series of metaphors associated with motherhood: Ephraim will experience "no birth, no pregnancy, no conception." Where the normal order of motherhood is conception, pregnancy, birth, the infertility of Israel is so complete that the normal structure of becoming a mother is reversed in its negation. The depiction of the Lord taking away children from Israel (Hos 9:12) inflicts the final plague of the exodus on Israel. Their sin is so great they have brought the penalties of the Egyptians upon them. This theme is found in the description in Hos 8 of being sent back into Egypt. Hosea 9:13 demonstrates that Ephraim causes the death of his children by choosing to "bring out their

---

Lord" as found in other prophetic works. See Buss, *The Prophetic Word of Hosea: A Morphological Study*, 35–36. Wolff argues in many cases that Hosea is a complex mixing of genres. For example, see Wolff's discussion of Hos 2 in Hans Walter Wolff, *Hosea*, Hermeneia (Philadelphia: Fortress, 1974), 47.

[48] William D. Whitt, "The Divorce of Yahweh and Asherah in Hos 2:4–7,12ff," *SJOT* 6 (1992): 31–67.

[49] Kelle demonstrates the problems with arguments surrounding a divorce court scene as the primary genre in Hos 2. See Kelle, *Hosea 2*, 172–73.

[50] Several scholars have noted the blended genres in Mic 1. See Ben Zvi, *Micah*, 31–33; Wagenaar, *Judgement and Salvation*, 54–57; Charles S. Shaw, *The Speeches of Micah: A Rhetorical-Historical Analysis*, JSOTSup 145 (Sheffield: Sheffield Academic, 1993), 33–41.

children to the slayer." The result of this action is the expectation of what the Lord will give them: "wombs that miscarry and breasts that are dry." Again, Hosea is using the metaphors associated with mothering. Instead of bodies that do not become pregnant, this description in verse 14 focuses on the potential for life (via giving birth) and the nurturing of life (via nursing) that is instead emptied of its ability to complete these actions. Their wombs cannot hold the children they try to birth, their breasts cannot provide the milk that they are biologically supposed to provide. These descriptions utilize only some of the possible entailments of childbirth or motherhood. Notably they do not focus on the possibilities of life and fruition that can also be associated with childbirth and motherhood.

These negative depictions of childbirth and motherhood can thus be blended with metaphors related to agriculture that focuses on the potential for growth that ultimately ends in loss. The hope that the Lord had of Israel and its ancestors described in verse 10, as like "finding grapes in the desert," "like seeing the early fruit on the fig tree" are quenched when they consecrated themselves to an idol.[51] Similarly in verse 13, Ephraim was "planted in a pleasant place," but they brought their children to the slayer and caused their potential as planted ones to be removed, not only for themselves, but for their next generation as well. Because of the sin described in verse 15, in verse 16 the judgment of Ephraim is described in terms of both agricultural loss and the loss of children: Ephraim is described like a diseased plant whose roots are withered and cannot bear fruit. Parallel to this description are the deaths of Ephraim's beloved offspring of their wombs.

Micah 4 also uses metaphors related to childbirth to describe the experience of judgment, but unlike in Hos 9, this judgment is placed in the context of the hope of restoration. As noted above in Mic 4:10 it is the sound of the mother's birthing and the pain of childbirth that are the primary entailments rather than conception, pregnancy, miscarriage, and the death of children as in Hos 9. The difference in the entailments related to the metaphors of mothering and childbirth allows for different metaphorical blends. Whereas in Hos 9 Israel is the childless mother and thus is the plant that had the potential to grow, but instead could not bear fruit, in Mic 4, the moment of pain in childbirth anticipates a hopeful conclusion of a new birth, which allows for the agricultural metaphors to likewise focus on restoration and new life as "everyone will sit under their own vine and under their own fig tree" (Mic 4:4). Micah 4 also

---

[51] Macintosh has noted how this description of YHWH catching sight of Israel in v. 10 emphasizes the intimate relationship between Israel and YHWH. This intimacy is destroyed in the subsequent verses. Thus, Macintosh links these agricultural metaphors with the feminine metaphors found in Hos 2 of Israel as YHWH's unfaithful wife as well as the mothering metaphors found in this passage. See A. A. Macintosh, *A Critical and Exegetical Commentary on Hosea*, ICC (Edinburgh: T&T Clark, 1997), 362–63.

locates itself within the larger tradition of describing Israel in terms of Daughter Jerusalem and Daughter Zion.[52] In comparison, Hosea makes no direct reference to Daughter Zion or Daughter Jerusalem, despite the many associations by scholars to the contrary.[53] Discussion of Daughter Zion and Jerusalem draw additional metaphorical links between the mothering metaphor and the experience of the people leaving the city to their exile in Babylon in verse 10.

Metaphors are not the only element blended in Hosea and Micah; genres are also blended in notable ways based on their partial entailments/structures. Many scholars have commented that Hosea itself seems more like a mixture of several genre forms interspersed than following particular set patterns throughout.[54] Scholars have debated the genres comprising Hos 9. Many scholars have seen Hos 9 to be comprised of at least two units. These scholars often locate Hos 9:1–9 dating back to the prophet Hosea addressing his community related to the Sukkot festivals, separating this from the divine speech in Hos 9:10–17.[55] Davies suggests the first unit in verses 1–9 is a prophetic diatribe, while verses 10–17 are a prophetic oracle.[56] Ben Zvi argues for reading Hos 9:1–17 as a single unified prophetic reading, arguing against an oral component to this unit. However, to deal with the complexities of genres present in Hos 9, Ben Zvi explains that "prophetic readings are fluid units, and that the intended and primary readerships are allowed to develop different but complementary structures of the book, each with its own set of slightly different 'prophetic readings.'"[57] Scholars generally note the shifts between Hos 9:9 and 9:10. The reason for this acknowledgement lies in the shift in time, person, and tone in verse 10 compared to what proceeds it.[58] Scholars have identified

---

[52] For more on the debates surrounding the figure of Daughter Zion, see Carleen Mandolfo, *Daughter Zion Talks Back to the Prophets: A Dialogic Theology of the Book of Lamentations*, SemeiaSt 38 (Atlanta: Society of Biblical Literature, 2007); Mark J. Boda, Carol Dempsey, and LeAnn Snow Flesher, eds., *Daughter Zion: Her Portrait, Her Response*, AIL 13 (Atlanta: Society of Biblical Literature, 2012); Christl Maier, *Daughter Zion, Mother Zion: Gender, Space, and the Sacred in Ancient Israel* (Minneapolis: Fortress, 2008).

[53] Scholars like Cheryl Kirk-Duggan and Carleen Mandolfo refer to the woman/Gomer in Hosea as Daughter Zion when putting together their depiction of Daughter Zion despite the prophet's lack of utilization of this title. Cheryl A. Kirk-Duggan, "Demonized Children and Traumatized, Battered Wives: Daughter Zion as Biblical Metaphor of Domestic and Sexual Violence," in Mark J. Boda, Carol Dempsey, and LeAnn Snow Flesher, eds., *Daughter Zion*, 243–68; Mandolfo, *Daughter Zion Talks Back*, 31–36.

[54] See n. 47 above.

[55] Marvin A. Sweeney, *The Twelve Prophets*, vol. 1, Berit Olam (Collegeville, MN: Liturgical Press, 2000), 93–98; Wolff, *Hosea*, 152–53.

[56] Graham I. Davies, *Hosea*, NCB (Grand Rapids; Eerdmans, 1992), 211.

[57] Ehud Ben Zvi, *Hosea*, FOTL 21a (Grand Rapids: Eerdmans, 2005), 195.

[58] See Wolff, *Hosea*, 161.

structures in Hos 9:1–9 resembling a prophetic announcement of threats and judgment, pointing to the use of direct address in verse 1 as "disrupt[ing] the jubilant rejoicing of an important harvest festival," which Wolff identifies with the Autumn Festival based on references to festivals within these verses.[59]

Many scholars have noted that Hos 9:10 appears to contain a different set of attributes than verses 1–9. Hosea 9:10 shifts to a retrospective of YHWH's relationship with Israel in the wilderness and conquest periods, "which marked the beginning of Israel's apostasy to the Baal cult and was constitutive of her present situation."[60] Compared to the prior section, there is no debate between the prophet and the people and instead this passage is primarily couched in the language of divine speech.[61] For the majority of Hos 9:10–17, YHWH speaks directly to Israel about their unfaithfulness and ultimate judgment, rather than through his messenger. If one approaches these differences as generic entailments that parallel metaphorical entailments, one could argue that the final arrangement of these genres comes out of the ability to blend the entailments of these two genres.[62] While the linguistic shifts in verse 10 move the text from prophetic to divine speech, the theme of judgment provides links that blend the different portions of Hos 9. In both Hos 9:1–9 and 9:10–17 the language of wine/grapes and harvest/plants provide links between the harvest festivals of verses 1–9 and the judgment against Ephraim in verses 10–17. Further, 9:10–17 is not purely in the form of divine speech, but is interspersed with interjections in verses 13–14, 17 that appear to come from the prophet, blending the prophetic speech of verses 1–9 with the divine speech in verses 10–17.[63]

Like the prophetic diatribe and oracle genres of Hos 9, the structure of Mic 4 is widely debated.[64] Despite these debates, one can state that generally Mic 4 is described as a liturgical formula in verses 1–5[65] followed by a series of oracles of

---

[59] Ibid., 153. See also Mays who locates this specifically in Bethel in James Luther Mays, *Hosea: A Commentary*, OTL (Philadelphia: Westminster, 1969), 125.

[60] Wolff, *Hosea*, 161. See also Douglas Stuart, *Hosea–Jonah*, WBC 31 (Waco, TX: Word Books, 1987), 150–51.

[61] For distinctions between divine speech and prophetic speech in Hos 9, see Wolff, *Hosea*, 161; Mays, *Hosea*, 132; Stuart, *Hosea–Jonah*, 150–51.

[62] Ben Zvi's assumption that textuality explains the complexity of genre forms in what he calls "prophetic readings" would tend to lend itself to agreeing with my position. Ben Zvi, *Hosea*, 195.

[63] Because of these interspersing of interjections, Mays divides the passage into four sections rather than two. See Mays, *Hosea*, 124–37.

[64] See Ben Zvi, *Micah*, 92.

[65] Decisions regarding the genre of Mic 4:1–5 are often determined in part by how one deals with the intertextual allusion to Isa 2:2–5. See Wagenaar, *Judgement and Salvation*, 262.

salvation in verses 6–7(8)[66] and of restoration in 4:(8)9–5:4.[67] These shifts in genre in Micah are based on particular genre structures in each of these three main sections. The liturgical formula is marked by a style mirroring forms of worship including a response from the congregation in 4:5, while the oracle of salvation focuses on YHWH's salvation of Israel. In 4:8–5:4, there is a message of YHWH's restoration of those who have been sent into exile. Yet in each case, the genres found in Mic 4 do not use all of the expected structures that their prototypical genre might include, but rather focus on particular entailments of these genres that are blended in their final form.

METAPHORS AND GENRES EXIST IN THE DISCOURSE OF HOSEA AND MICAH AND ARE LINGUISTICALLY CONTEXTUALIZED

Besides being constrained by their cultural and temporal contexts and by their own partial structures, metaphors and genres are also constrained by their location within a particular linguistic context. To demonstrate the impact of these linguistic constraints on Hosea and Micah, this section will analyze the metaphors and genres of Hos 9 and Mic 4 in terms of their linguistic structures. Due to spatial constraints, it is not possible to examine all the linguistic aspects impacting Hos 9 and Mic 4, but rather I will focus specifically on the contexts where mothering/childbirth and agricultural metaphors are found as well as the major sections where genre structures are displayed.

As noted, Hos 9:9 and 9:10 mark a critical shift in linguistic structure within Hos 9. This change is initiated by a change in syntax alongside a change in register. Whereas Hos 9:1–9 uses primarily a verb at the start of each of its phrases, verse 10 shifts to locate the verb at or near the end of each clause. Verse 10 also shifts person, aspect, and number from third person plural *qal* imperfect in verse 9 to first person singular *qal* perfect in verse 10. The result is a focus on the two similes in verse 10 beginning with the comparative preposition כְּ ("like, as"). This emphasis on these similes uses the metaphorical language of agriculture to highlight the past intimacy between Israel and YHWH that is quickly undone by Israel's idolatry.[68] By the time the reader reaches the כְּ ("like, as") in verse 11 the link with the similes in verse 10 becomes clear.

---

[66] Among those describing parts of this passage as an oracle of salvation or restoration, see Mays, *Hosea*, 94–95; Bernard Renaud, *La formation du livre de Michée: Tradition et actualisation* (Paris: J. Gabalda, 1977), 207–9; Hans Walter Wolff, *Micah: A Commentary*, CC (Minneapolis: Augsburg, 1990), 85, 88; Delbert R. Hillers, *Micah*, Hermeneia (Philadelphia: Fortress, 1984), 51; Wagenaar, *Judgement and Salvation*, 273; Marvin A. Sweeney, *King Josiah of Judah: The Lost Messiah of Israel* (New York: Oxford University Press, 2001), 291.
[67] See Mays, *Hosea*, 29.
[68] See Macintosh's discussion of language related to intimacy and rejection. See Macintosh, *Hosea*, 362–63.

Ephraim/Israel is the source of this metaphor, described like a bird flying away from a triple repeated form of words in the semantic range of childbirth. The potential posed in the *piel* imperfect of verse 12a is met with the bereavement of the *piel* perfect of verse 12b: what they might have obtained (third person plural) is taken away by YHWH (first person singular). Again YHWH stands in grammatical opposition to the "they" of Israel. This opposition recurs in verse 13. YHWH expresses a desire to see Ephraim be planted only to be met with Ephraim bringing sons to the slayer. This verbal opposition between YHWH's desires cast in the first person and Israel's actions cast in the third person reaches a head for the prophet, apparently observing, who speaks up in verse 14. The prophet's voice comes in the form of imperatives, asking the Lord to continue the course of action that Ephraim began in verse 11 and the Lord continued in verse 12: to remove the ability to procreate and the ability to tend to a baby. The loss of fecundity in childbirth is teamed with the loss of agricultural fecundity in verse 16 as Ephraim is blighted. No longer is YHWH the clear agent of this action as the verb changes to the *hophal* perfect third person singular. Similarly, the roots are dry and they cannot bear fruit, but the agent of this dryness and barrenness appears absent until the final clause. YHWH reappears as the one who puts to death their cherished ones, echoing the final plague on Egypt.[69]

The same linguistic structures that impact the use of metaphors in Hos 9 constrain the genres. As noted previously, it is the shift from prophetic voice in verse 9 to divine voice in verse 10 that creates the marked divide in this passage at times attributed to two genres. Yet the smaller linguistic shifts create troubles for suggesting a consistent genre covering all of verses 10–17. These shifts in focus from Israel's actions to YHWH's response, along with the response of the prophet in verse 14, create linguistic structures that break with the prototypical models of genre, suggesting a greater complexity than a single genre and creating a diversity of opinions of scholars wrestling with this passage.

The childbirth and agricultural metaphors and the genres in Mic 4 are constrained by their linguistic context. The agricultural metaphors of hope appear in Mic 4:4 amidst a description of a reinstitution of peace. This picture is drawn linguistically as well as metaphorically. The framing of person and number vary greatly within Mic 4 leading up to Mic 4:4. Micah 4:1 shifts from identifying the coming day and the actions of the Lord to reports of the people speaking of what they will do via first person plural forms in verse 2. The Lord's actions in verse 3 lead to Israel's weapons of war being dismantled via a series of repeated prepositional phrases. This leads to a more generalizing statement in Mic 4:4 that universalizes this experience of peace by describing what everyone will do with this peace once in place: because peace is restored, agricultural attainment endures. The land is returned to fruition and to the people. In Mic

---

[69] Thomas Jemielity, *Satire and the Hebrew Prophets*, Literary Currents in Biblical Interpretation (Louisville: Westminster John Knox, 1992), 116.

4:7, the Lord is depicted as king over Zion forever. Yet the metaphors in Mic 4:9 and the linguistic structure surrounding it suggest that this story of perfect peace has not yet been realized by the people of Israel. This sense of uncertainty and tension is depicted linguistically through the use of interrogatives and the repetition of the adverb עַתָּה "now").[70] The height of this crisis comes as Daughter Zion is commanded via an imperative to writhe and groan as in labor pains. Thus, the metaphors of childbirth used to depict the experience of crisis are layered upon a linguistic structure that echoes this crisis[71] providing a structure that promotes greater clarity to interpreting the metaphors themselves.

The genres of Mic 4 itself are also constrained by its linguistic structure. The liturgical style of Mic 4:1–5 is constrained by the movement back and forth between the use of the third person and first person, making the genre less like the prototypical understanding of the liturgical genre. Similarly, the evoking of the crisis of childbirth in verse 9 amidst the oracles of salvation through interrogatives creates some tension in the usual forms present in salvation oracles based on the universal models of such genres. This in part explains the complications over whether verse 8 should be located with verses 6–7 or verse 9 to the end of the chapter. The linguistic context provides the framework for locating the linking structures between the generic structures in the passage.

METAPHORS AND GENRES IN HOSEA AND MICAH ARE THEOLOGICALLY CONTEXTUALIZED AND ADAPTATIONS TO METAPHORS AND GENRES MAY HAVE THEOLOGICAL PURPOSES

The connection between Israel as people and Israel as land, which echoes in the blending of agricultural and feminine metaphors in Hosea and Micah, may be rooted in an intertextual allusion to Deut 28, which describes Israel's promise in terms of fruition of bodies as well as the land. The cursing of bearing fruit and bearing children in Hos 9 may be an inversion of the promises in Deut 28:4 and 11. In contrast, Mic 4 uses the metaphor of childbirth leading to new life to positively expect fruition of the land, which may echo this expectation in Deuteronomy. Many scholars have noted the use of Deuteronomy in the Book of the Twelve extensively and in Hosea and Micah specifically.[72] This includes drawing connections between particular themes, metaphors, and genres in

---

[70] Waltke points out this interrogation following Renaud and Wolff. See Bruce K. Waltke, *A Commentary on Micah* (Grand Rapids: Eerdmans, 2007), 238–39.

[71] See Bergmann, *Childbirth as a Metaphor for Crisis*, 109–11.

[72] For discussion of the scholars who have noted Hosea's use of Deuteronomy, see Gordon J. Wenham, "The Date of Deuteronomy: Linch-Pin of Old Testament Criticism," *Themelios* 10 (1985): 18–19; Gary Harlan Hall, *Deuteronomy*, College Press NIV Commentary (Joplin, MO: College Press, 2000), 21. For Micah's use of Deuteronomy, see Shaw, *The Speeches of Micah*, 80–81, 169–70; Renaud, *La formation*, 319–26; Jack R. Lundbom, *Deuteronomy: A Commentary* (Grand Rapids: Eerdmans, 2013), 35.

Hosea and Micah and the larger Deuteronomic tradition. Thus, the Deuteronomic tradition may function as theological pattern influencing Hos 9 and Mic 4 in different ways based on the unique theological message each book is intending to share with its audience, while more broadly one can also argue that the frequent allusions to Deuteronomy and its themes throughout the Book of the Twelve provides a level of theological cohesion.[73]

The covenant and new exodus are among the primary theological themes in Hosea alongside the obvious themes of Israel's return to God and God's faithfulness to Israel despite their recurring sin. In Hos 2, the promise of return and restoration that YHWH gives to Israel is dependent on the allusions to promises to Israel from the beginning of creation,[74] the continued faithfulness of YHWH in his liberation of Israel from Egypt,[75] and YHWH's purposeful time for Israel in the wilderness.[76] These theological themes constrain Hosea's use of the marital metaphor in Hos 2 in a different direction than Micah's use in Mic 1. In comparison, Mic 1 focuses on the coming destruction YHWH will carry out against Samaria because of their idolatry. Micah 1 calls the earth to judge against Israel and then expresses lament over the judgment that is at hand.[77] Thus, while Hosea uses a more developed relational metaphor to depict Israel's unfaithfulness and God's judgment as well as his eventual restorative love, Micah's use of these feminine and agricultural metaphors focuses more extensively on the destructive elements of this judgment by explicitly connecting these feminine and agricultural metaphors to metaphors of warfare and natural disaster. While these depictions differ in their respective emphases, the repeated blending of similar feminine and agricultural metaphors in Hosea and Micah demonstrates continuity between the metaphorical depictions of God's relationship to Israel in the Book of the Twelve. This continuity of metaphorical depiction may provide fruit for further exploration if expanded to a metaphorical study of the Twelve.

---

[73] Elizabeth Achtemeier notes the impact of Deuteronomy on Haggai, Malachi, and Obadiah in Elizabeth Achtemeier, *Preaching from the Minor Prophets: Texts and Sermon Suggestions* (Grand Rapids: Eerdmans, 1998), 52, 106, 127. John Barton locates parts of Deuteronomic tradition in the theology of Amos. See John Barton, *The Theology of the Book of Amos*, OTT (New York: Cambridge University Press, 2012). Weinfeld argues for a similar usage in Amos. See Weinfeld, *Deuteronomy and the Deuteronomic School*, 91. Similarly Sweeney notes the use of Deuteronomy in Hosea and Amos. See Sweeney, *Twelve Prophets*, 31–32, 45, 91, 256.

[74] Mark E. Rooker, "The Use of the Old Testament in the Book of Hosea," *CTR* 7 (1993): 52–53.

[75] Francis I. Anderson and David Noel Freedman, *Hosea: A New Translation with Introduction and Commentary*, AB 24 (New York: Doubleday, 1980), 269–70.

[76] For more on the Exodus metaphor throughout Hosea, see Steven L. McKenzie, "Exodus Typology in Hosea," *ResQ* 22 (1979): 100–108.

[77] Ben Zvi, *Micah*, 33.

Conclusions: Implications for the Book of the Twelve and New Form Criticism

Rethinking issues of instance and system/form and genre in light of conceptual metaphor theory sheds new light on the constraints that impact a specific instance of metaphor or a specific use of form as compared to a wider system or genre. This chapter has identified four ways that genres and metaphors are constrained: (1) cultural and temporal constraints, (2) constraints related to the partiality and the innovation in metaphor and genre use, (3) linguistic constraints within a given passage or discourse, and (4) theological constraints stemming from adjustments of theological concerns from one context to another. Examining Hosea and Micah as a representation of these constraints also provides fresh insight into the use of feminine and agricultural metaphors in Hosea and Micah. This analysis demonstrates that while Hosea and Micah both share metaphors of Israel as mother and as unfaithful wife that are blended with agricultural metaphors, Hosea's use of Israel as mother in Hos 9 focuses on images of loss, while Mic 4 focuses on the ultimate hope for new life that may come from birth. Meanwhile the genres of prophetic speech and divine speech in Hos 9 are better understood in light of their areas of structural blending and Mic 4 is both destabilized and more clearly linked when seen in terms of its linguistic ties.

Similarly, the image of Israel as unfaithful wife in Hos 2 focuses first on God's judgment and then his restoration of relationship with Israel, using agricultural metaphors to highlight this change. In contrast, Mic 1 develops Hosea's image of Israel's unfaithfulness to bring a charge against Samaria. These shifts in metaphor move alongside substantial shifts in genre as in Hos 2 covenant and marital contracts provide generic grounding for Hosea's message, while in Mic 1 the trial genre is developed, blending with elements of the lament genre.

These insights in modern metaphor theory provide the groundwork for thinking of genre in helpful new ways that provide for systems of genre, but also its individual forms, while they provide new ways of interpreting Hosea and Micah in light of these findings. Such analysis may provide future ways of examining the interrelationship between metaphors and genres in the Book of the Twelve more broadly and the frequent use of intratextual allusion from book to book within the Book of the Twelve.

3

Reading the "Prophetic Lawsuit" Genre in the Persian Period

James M. Trotter

The existence of a prophetic lawsuit genre has been a staple of form-critical analyses of the prophetic texts of ancient Israel from the earliest days of form criticism. The most commonly identified features of this genre have been: (1) a call to hear the word of Yahweh; (2) the presence of the term ריב; and (3) reference to the heavens and earth, with varying proposals regarding their role in the lawsuit. Since the 1980s, there has been substantial debate about whether or not it is possible to make a compelling case for the existence of this genre. Doubts have particularly been raised in articles by Michael de Roche and D. R. Daniels.[1]

While it will be necessary to deal with general matters regarding the existence and shape of the prophetic lawsuit genre, this analysis will focus specifically on those texts in the Book of the Twelve which have been identified as possible examples of this genre. In this regard, there are three texts which require consideration, Hos 2:3–25; 4:1–3, and Mic 6:1–8, all of which have been commonly identified as examples of the prophetic lawsuit genre.[2] The particular issue here will not be whether they were heard as prophetic lawsuits by the

---

[1] Michael de Roche, "Yahweh's Rîb against Israel: A Reassessment of the So-Called "Prophetic Lawsuit" in the Preexilic Prophets," *JBL* 102 (1983): 563–74; a good, brief summary of the history of the identification of the genre is provided in Dwight R. Daniels, "Is There a 'Prophetic Lawsuit' Genre," *ZAW* 99 3 (1987): 339–60.

[2] A number of other texts have been variously identified as prophetic lawsuits (see, for example, Claus Westermann, *Basic Forms of Prophetic Speech*, trans. Hugh C. White [Louisville: Westminster John Knox, 1967; 1991], 199–200), but these three are the most commonly proposed examples from the Book of the Twelve.

original oral audience of Hosea and Micah, but whether or not these texts would have been read as lawsuits by Persian period Yehudite readers.

Proposed Origins of the Genre

Since it lies outside the primary focus of this analysis, it is unnecessary to give a detailed account of the history of the old form-critical analyses of these texts.[3] A few key highlights concerning different proposed *Sitz im Leben* will suffice here. Following the lead of H. Gunkel, many scholars have located the origins of the genre in secular legal practice in ancient Israel. In this reading, there is a distinction between the original setting, which Gunkel interpreted as legal activities at the city gate, and the later, formal setting in the cult. E. Würthwein collapsed these two settings by proposing that the genre was not borrowed from secular legal practice, but had its origin in the cult as a judgement on the behaviour of nations, in the case of Israel, a judgment on the nation's covenant faithfulness.[4] H. Huffmon developed the insight of the connection with covenant traditions further in relation to the Hittite vassal treaty forms. In his view, these texts were covenant lawsuits that reflect some of the same elements found in vassal treaties. These elements can also be identified in other covenantal texts.[5] J. Harvey carried the insight of the connection with international treaty forms made by Huffmon further. Harvey proposed that the *Sitz im Leben* of these texts was the practice of international law connected with these treaty formulations.[6] There are significant difficulties with all of these proposed genre identifications and social settings in the context of eighth century Judah and Israel, as has been indicated by de Roche and Daniels.[7] The analyses of de Roche and Daniels, indicating the difficulties in identifying a prophetic lawsuit genre contemporary with the activities of the eighth century prophets, not only challenge the proposal that these oracles were heard in this way at the time, but also raise serious questions about the possibility that they were interpreted in this way in later periods as they circulated in oral and/or written form. That they should have been read as prophetic lawsuits once they had been incorporated into written prophetic books becomes an even more problematic assertion.

---

[3] A very good overview of that history has already been provided by: Kirsten Nielsen, *Yahweh as Prosecutor and Judge: An Investigation of the Prophetic Lawsuit*, JSOTSup 9 (Sheffield: University of Sheffield Press, 1978), 5–26.

[4] Ernst Würthwein, "Der Ursprung der prophetischen Gerichtsrede," *ZTK* 49 (1952): 1–16.

[5] Herbert B. Huffmon, "The Covenant Lawsuit in the Prophets," *JBL* 78 4 (1959): 285–95.

[6] Julien Harvey, "Le 'Rîb-Pattern,' réquisitoire prophétique sur la rupture de l'alliance," *Biblica* 43 2 (1962): 172–96.

[7] De Roche, "Yahweh's Rîb against Israel," 563–66.

Even if the problematic assertion that these texts represent a prophetic lawsuit genre in their original sociohistorical setting is granted, there is no extant evidence of the continued use of this proposed genre after the late sixth century, Jer 2:2–4 likely representing the latest possible example.[8] By the time these texts had become integrated into and read as portions of prophetic books in the Persian period, it is highly unlikely that Persian period readers would have read them in the same way as the individual, oral oracles were heard by the eighth century audiences of the prophets. As written texts, contextualized within larger written documents that were read in a later and dramatically different sociohistorical context, it is necessary to reflect on the way in which both the changed literary and sociological settings would have shaped the reception of these texts. Specifically, in regard to the question as to whether or not these texts would have been read as lawsuits, prophetic or otherwise, by Persian period readers, it is necessary to examine Persian period legal texts and practices. Is there sufficient correspondence between legal practices and genres from the Achaemenid period and the structure, language, and content of these texts to support the assertion that they would have been read as lawsuits by Persian period readers?

FIRST MILLENNIUM LEGAL PRACTICES IN THE ANCIENT NEAR EAST

The literate reading community of Achaemenid Yehud, those who produced and maintained texts and who read and reread texts, are the segment of the community most likely to have been involved in and familiar with the legal systems and institutions of the colony. They would have been the elites within the community that had regular contact with imperial administration, both as personified by imperial administrators and as enacted in imperial administrative procedures. Any investigation as to whether or not specific texts within the Book of the Twelve (or otherwise) would have been read as exemplars of legal genres must include consideration of the legal systems and institutions of imperial Persia and, in particular, those that were present in the Beyond the River satrapy. Given the lack of evidence from Yehud itself, the following examination will consider legal genres and practices from first millennium contexts across the Neo-Assyrian, Neo-Babylonian, and Achaemenid empires. The analysis of this material will be used to decide the likelihood as to whether or not Hos 2:3–25; 4:1–3, and Mic 6:1–8 would have been read as legal texts by Yehudite readers in the Achaemenid period.

---

[8] Julia M. O'Brien has presented a case for reading Malachi as an adapted (extended) version of the prophetic lawsuit genre which could represent a later adaptation of the genre. Since the argument depends on the identification of these earlier texts as prophetic lawsuits, the case for Malachi as an adaptation of the genre rests entirely on the judgment made about these earlier texts. See Julia M. O'Brien, *Priest and Levite in Malachi*, SBLDS 121 (Atlanta: Scholars Press, 1990), 63–81.

NEO-ASSYRIAN LEGAL PRACTICES

As S. Parpola notes, there was a progressive homogenization under Neo-Assyrian rule as a common imperial language, Aramaic, and a uniform imperial culture came to dominate most areas ruled by the empire.[9] As a result, there is a significant degree of continuity in legal practices, terminology, and genres across imperial-controlled territories. In Neo-Assyrian judicial practice, a number of different official titles are used to designate those deciding lawsuits. While there are appeals to the king, the role of the king appears to be more figurative than actual in Neo-Assyrian legal cases.[10] As S. Démare-Lafont observes, "While the usual term *dayyānum* 'judge' was no longer used for human judges in the Neo-Assyrian period, various high officials are attested in judicial roles (Radner 2003: 890)."[11] Significantly for the purposes of this analysis, she also notes that the same types of personnel are also found to be active in Neo-Babylonian law cases, demonstrating significant continuity in legal practices under Neo-Assyrian and Neo-Babylonian rule.

In terms of generic characteristics, Neo-Assyrian legal texts (*dēnu* texts) use the third person and rarely report direct speech from the trial. They are generally short documents containing a brief report of the cause of the trial with the verdict or agreement of the parties comprising the bulk of the text.[12] These texts end with the date and a list of (human) witnesses to the verdict or resolution. The roles of the gods are two-fold in these texts. In a small number, for example, *dēnu* texts 7, 10, and 11 analysed by Jas, a god, in these texts Adad, acts as the judge.[13] More commonly, gods are identified as adversaries or prosecutors of any party who might recontest the matter after the judgment or settlement has been finalized. In other words, the gods most often function as guarantors of the outcome, rather than judge or prosecutor in the legal proceeding itself. Similarly, human witnesses listed in lawsuit texts from the period function as a living repository of the judgment, so that they could be consulted as witnesses to the outcome should one of the litigants or one of their heirs raise the matter in the future.

---

[9] Simo Parpola, "International Law in the First Millennium," in *A History of Ancient Near Eastern Law*, ed. Raymond Westbrook (Leiden: Brill, 2003), 1051.

[10] Remko Jas, *Neo-Assyrian Judicial Procedures* (Helsinki: The Neo-Assyrian Text Corpus Project, 1996), 4–5.

[11] Sophie Démare-Lafont, "Judicial Decision-Making: Judges and Arbitrators," in *The Oxford Handbook of Cuneiform Culture*, ed. Karen Radner and Eleanor Robson (Oxford: Oxford University Press, 2011), 341.

[12] Jas, *Neo-Assyrian Judicial Procedures*, 5–6.

[13] Ibid., 17–18, 21–23.

NEO-BABYLONIAN AND ACHAEMENID LEGAL PRACTICES

In the Neo-Babylonian period, lawsuits were heard in the courts (*bīt dīni*). They were often tried before royal judges (*dayyānē ša* RN). Royal courts usually consisted of three to five judges. Local matters were handled by local courts that consisted of provincial officials and judges.[14] Depositions could be taken locally in preparation for trial at a higher court. These were recorded under the format: "These are the witnesses before whom (PN stated…)" (*annūti mukinnū ša ina pānīšunnu*).[15] Documents which record court proceedings generally have a tripartite structure: address by one of the parties to the judges, the judges' inquiries, and the judgment.[16] The recording of direct speech represents one significant variation as compared with the Neo-Assyrian legal texts discussed previously. After judgment, the judges could draft a document, sealed with their seals, that would be given to the successful litigant.[17]

In his recent book, *Neo-Babylonian Court Procedure*, S. E. Holtz offers a reconstruction of the "tablet trail" associated with legal proceedings in the period.[18] Due to the high degree of continuity in the legal textual record across the Neo-Babylonian and Achaemenid periods, Holtz defines the "Neo-Babylonian" of his title broadly to include texts from the time of Nebuchadnezzar II to the end of the reign of Darius II.[19] As a result, his reconstruction of legal practices and genres provides an excellent window into the way in which these matters would have been understood by the literate elites within these imperial systems.

Holtz proposes a "functional typology" that locates the various legal documents within the different phases of legal proceedings. His analysis provides a very good overview of the different types of extant legal texts from the period and their function within the legal processes. Decision records are those texts which record the details and outcomes of a particular case. Holtz identifies different styles of decision records, associated with different venues, but notes that the consistent function of these records is to prove the occurrence of the lawsuit and its outcome as a means of preventing further claims and/or changes to the ruling.[20] Holtz also discusses three additional text types that are related to resolution of disputes: conclusion of disputes, memoranda including decisions, and settlements. While serving somewhat different functions, each of these types

---

[14] Joachim Oelsner, Bruce Wells, and Cornelia Wunsch, "Neo-Babylonian Period," in *A History of Ancient Near Eastern Law*, ed. Raymond Westbrook (Leiden: Brill, 2003), 918–19.
[15] Ibid., 922.
[16] Michael Jursa, *Neo-Babylonian Legal and Administrative Documents: Typology, Contents and Archives*, GMTR 1 (Munster: Ugarit-Verlag, 2005), 16–17.
[17] Oelsner, Wells, and Wunsch, "Neo-Babylonian Period," 923.
[18] Shalom E. Holtz, *Neo-Babylonian Court Procedure*, CM 38 (Leiden: Brill, 2009).
[19] Ibid., 1–2.
[20] Ibid., 23–27.

shares in common with the decision records that they record the resolutions of disputes after the fact.[21] In addition to these text types which relate to the resolution of disputes, Holtz identifies preliminary protocols that describe the events that occurred before a trial and serve as memoranda of the actual proceedings. The protocols functioned as the scribe's record of events, rather than the official record and did not include an indication of the outcome of the proceedings.[22] All of these text types analysed by Holtz "narrate activities in court during the course of a trial."[23] They share common features: identification of the parties and the issue, address by one or both litigants, the judges' inquires, and, where appropriate to the genre, the resolution of the dispute in the form of a settlement or legal judgment. H. H. Figulla already identified all of these key elements in legal texts in his translation and discussion of a text recording legal action concerning the theft of temple property at Eanna during the second year of Cambyses.[24]

Holtz identifies a range of text types which function as summonses or guarantees for an individual(s) to argue a case, present evidence in a case, be present at a judicial proceeding, or guarantee the presence of someone else.[25] These text types include: *dabābu* summonses to argue a case, *quttû* summonses to end a case, summonses to establish (*kunnu*) a case, guarantees for testimony, summonses to present or bring (*abāku*) an individual, and guarantees for an individual's presence. In distinguishing between summonses and guarantees, Holtz notes, "Both summonses and guarantees may impose a penalty for failure to perform the action. The major difference between the two is that the guarantees explicitly use the phrase *pūta našû* ("to assume responsibility") while the summonses do not use this phrase."[26] These are all legal text types which relate to specific preparatory aspects of legal proceedings. They contain little in the way of information regarding the parties or the issue in dispute unless it is necessary to support the specific purpose of the document. As a result, these text types are certainly not relevant to the discussion of prophetic lawsuits. Holtz also identifies a small number of much less common text types, but those identified above represent the predominant components of the "tablet trail" in Neo-Babylonian and Achaemenid period legal processes. As will be noted further below, there are no strong parallels between any of these known legal texts of the period and the texts from the Hebrew Bible identified as prophetic lawsuits.

---

[21] Ibid., 69–83.
[22] Ibid., 85–116.
[23] Ibid., 117.
[24] H. H. Figulla, "Lawsuit concerning a Sacrilegious Theft at Erech," *Iraq* 13.2 (1951): 100.
[25] Holtz, *Neo-Babylonian Court Procedure*, 117–95.
[26] Ibid., 133.

As is the case with most of our knowledge about the ancient Near East, the quality and quantity of the evidence for legal practices under the Achaemenid Persians varies significantly both chronologically and geographically. There is, however, very substantial textual evidence of legal practices during the Neo-Babylonian and Achaemenid periods from Mesopotamia. In light of the fact that Judah had been a colony of the Neo-Babylonian empire for decades before its incorporation into the Achaemenid empire as part of the territory that would eventually become the satrapy, Babylon and Beyond the River (*Bābilu u ebir nāri*), the legal texts that have been preserved from the Mesopotamian cultural heartland of the satrapy are likely to provide the best insight into the legal practices and procedures that were in place in Achaemenid Yehud. As was indicated above, Holtz has provided significant evidence of continuity across the Neo-Babylonian and Achaemenid periods. In addition, J. Oelsner and others note that this continuity can be detected even into the Hellenistic period: "As regards the law, the traditional concept of ancient Near Eastern kingship embraced by Babylonian kings not only continued into these later empires but also held true for the Hellenistic kings."[27] This is particularly fortuitous, since this is a time from which there are very substantial textual resources. "The documentation is especially rich in the sixth and the early fifth centuries, making that period one of the best known in Mesopotamian history."[28] In fact, the influence of cuneiform legal traditions and formulae on cultural regions further to the West is already identified in an earlier historical period by Kwasman, who notes the major role of the Neo-Assyrian Empire "in the transformation of cuneiform legal formulary into Aramaic."[29]

The Achaemenid conquest of the Neo-Babylonian Empire resulted in very little immediate change to the normal functioning of the existing administrative and social institutions, including legal practices and texts. The creation in 535 BCE of the satrapy, Babylon and Beyond the River (*Bābilu u ebir nāri*), with a Persian governor, Gubaru, resulted in more direct Persian imperial oversight of and involvement in these institutions, but there were no major changes to their functions and operations.[30] "Sometime after 486 BC the enormous satrapy of Babylon and Across-the-River, comprising almost all the territory of the former Neo-Babylonian empire, was split in two.[31] In the Herodotus list (3.91–92) of the satrapies of the Achaemenid Empire these countries appear as different

---

[27] Oelsner, "Neo-Babylonian Period," 915.
[28] Ibid., 912.
[29] T. Kwasman, "Two Aramaic Legal Documents," *BSOAS* 63 2 (2000): 274.
[30] M. A. Dandamaev, "Achaemenid Mesopotamia: Traditions and Innovations," in *Continuity and Change*, ed. Heleen Sancisi-Weerdenburg, Amelie Kuhrt, and Margaret Cool Root, vol. 8 of *Achaemenid History* (Leiden: Nederlands Instituut voor het Nabije Oosten, 1994), 229.
[31] Matthew W. Stolper, "The Governor of Babylon and Across-the-River in 486 B.C." *JNES* 48.4 (1989): 288ff.

provinces, namely Babylonia and 'the rest of Assyria' which constituted the ninth satrapy, while the lands beyond the Euphrates formed the fifth satrapy."[32] Apart from this major geographical reorganization of the satrapies, there were mainly only gradual changes to the administrative system with an increasing use of Persian administrative and legal terms in Babylonian documents. The increasing use of Persian terms seems to have originated with the changes instituted by Darius I.[33] On the whole, however, the changes represent a gradual evolution resulting from Persian cultural influence, rather than a dramatic exchange of one system for another. In fact, there is far more continuity than difference in legal practices across the periods of Neo-Babylonian and Achaemenid rule. Dandamaev and Lukonin, for example, begin their discussion of legal systems and institutions in the Achaemenid Persian Empire by noting that some diversity existed across the empire, but they also highlight the continuity of legal practices before and after the arrival of the Persians in conquered territories.[34] In particular, they attribute this continuity to the central role of Mesopotamian legal traditions in the legal institutions and practices of the Achaemenid Empire. "Under the Achaemenids, Babylonian law reached its pinnacle. It was the model for the legal norms of the countries of the Near East and began to spread to the West."[35]

Dandamaev and Lukonin identify a wide range of evidence that indicates that the influence of Achaemenid imperial legal language and practice permeated the empire, including the western satrapies. Royal judges are mentioned by Herodotus (3.14) as being present in Egypt with Cambyses.[36] Satraps were the highest judicial officials in the satrapies, with substantial textual evidence from both Babylon and Egypt.[37] Persians were sent throughout the empire to function as judges, according to the Greek sources and supported by the evidence of the Babylonian legal documents.[38] Persian legal terms are also present in documents from across the empire. They note that across the empire, "Not infrequently during lawsuits the parties would give 'the oath of the king' or swear by the Babylonian gods or the Persian kings."[39] Although there was no centrally imposed uniformity in legal practices, there is evidence of centuries of common legal culture that can be found in Neo-Babylonian and Achaemenid sources.

---

[32] Ibid., 229–30.
[33] Ibid., 230–31.
[34] Muhammad A. Dandamaev, Vladimir G. Lukonin, and Philip L. Kohl, *The Culture and Social Institutions of Ancient Iran* (Cambridge: Cambridge University Press, 1989), 116.
[35] Ibid., 121.
[36] Ibid., 118.
[37] Ibid., 122, 125–26.
[38] Ibid., 122–23.
[39] Ibid., 123.

EGYPTIAN LEGAL PRACTICES DURING THE ACHAEMENID PERIOD

The other major source of information about legal practices and legal genres during the Achaemenid period is Egypt. Since much of this information derives from the ethnically Judahite garrison at Elephantine, it is a potentially highly valuable resource for this examination. Some legal matters at Elephantine were dealt with by a "court of the Jews" (*AP* 45).[40] Other matters, however, were considered by a royal court which consisted of at least two royal judges plus the commander of the garrison (*AP* 6).[41] B. Porten provides a useful summary of the range of individuals and groups who regularly heard cases at Elephantine: judges, the military commander with the judges (designated "judges of the king"), and either or both of these groups plus other local officials ("the judges of the province").[42]

In relation to litigation, Porten notes a few texts which exemplify the use of oaths in the names of different gods as evidence regarding the central matter in the dispute.[43] Specifically, there are three texts from Elephantine which clearly relate to legal disputes, all of which employ oaths (*TAD* B7.1–7.3). All of these texts date from the late fifth century BCE.[44] *TAD* B7.1 and 7.2 are similarly structured, noting the date, place, parties, accusation, interrogation, oath, and indication of consequences of not swearing the oath. B7.1 also contains the possibility of a counter-oath and consequences, the penalty that will result, and finishes with the name of the scribe and place. B7.2 is broken after the indication of consequences of not swearing the oath, so may have originally contained the additional elements. B7.3 is a brief text which indicates the parties, the point of contention and an oath by the defendant denying the claim in the contention. Holtz, in his discussion of oaths found in legal texts from Eanna, notes that they served two functions. Oaths could be used for evidentiary purposes to establish the basis for a decision in a case. In other instances, oaths had an exculpatory function by which individuals would attempt to clear themselves of charges.[45] B7.1 and 7.2 from Elephantine are best interpreted as examples of the latter function. Both of these texts record a formal proceeding that includes accusation and interrogation. The oaths in both texts function as an effort by the accused to be cleared of the accusation. The function in B7.3 is less clear due to the brevity of the text. It does, however, correspond more closely to the evidentiary

---

[40] Ibid., 128.
[41] Ibid., 128–29.
[42] Bezalel Porten, "Elephantine," in Westbrook and Beckman, *History of Ancient Near Eastern Law*, 869.
[43] Ibid., 869.
[44] Bezalel Porten and Ada Yardeni, *Textbook of Aramaic Documents from Ancient Egypt: Contracts*, vol. 2 (Winona Lake, IN: Eisenbrauns, 1989), 141.
[45] Holtz, *Neo-Babylonian Court Procedure*, 290.

function, providing evidence that might decide the case in favour of the oath taker.

A number of fragmentary court records have also been recovered from Saqqarah. These texts all date from the mid-fifth century. One of these records contains a summary of three cases written in three different hands.[46] "The formula seems to be 'PN spoke against PN as follows.... Afterwards, it was given to PN and his colleagues' (*TAD* B8.6)."[47] Another text records court proceedings in terms of the interrogation of the litigants, "'PN$_1$ was interrogated in light of the words of PN$_2$ and he said...' Two horizontal lines enclose this statement. There follows cross-examination: 'PN$_2$ was interrogated in light of the words of PN$_1$ and he said...' (*TAD* B8.7; cf. B8.8)."[48] The other legal texts in this collection are even more fragmentary. As a result, it is difficult to arrive at clear determinations of their genres and functions. The three summaries contained in *TAD* B8.6 are closest in form to the memoranda including decisions identified by Holtz.[49] They contain much less detail than the full decision records. The recording of decisions one after another in different hands on the same document may suggest the same function, proof of the occurrence of the lawsuit to prevent further claims, as the memoranda including decisions.

The limited and fragmentary nature of the documents requires a degree of caution in regard to conclusions. Overall, however, the evidence indicates similarity with the legal genres and practices of Mesopotamia in the same period. The texts indicate dates and participants, report statements on the litigated issue in the first person, and conclude with the outcome of the proceedings. There appears to be very few similarities between the content and form of these texts and the so-called prophetic lawsuits of the Hebrew Bible.

READING 'PROPHETIC LAWSUITS' FROM THE BOOK OF THE TWELVE IN THE PERSIAN PERIOD (HOS 2:3–25; 4:1–3; AND MIC 6:1–8)

So, in light of the available evidence regarding first millennium legal practices, particularly those found in areas dominated by the cultural and political influence of the Neo-Babylonian and Achaemenid Persian empires, is it likely that Hos 2:3–25; 4:1–3; and Mic 6:1–8 would have been read as prophetic lawsuits by Persian period Yehudite readers? Such a reading appears highly unlikely for a number of reasons.

It seems very unlikely that these three texts would have been read as a single genre by readers in this period. Of the three key features commonly proposed as markers of the prophetic lawsuit genre by modern interpreters, (1) a call to hear

---

[46] Porten and Yardeni, *Textbook of Aramaic Documents*, 149.
[47] Porten, "Elephantine," 870.
[48] Ibid., 870.
[49] Holtz, *Neo-Babylonian Court Procedure*, 74–78.

the word of Yahweh; (2) the presence of the term ריב; and (3) reference to the heavens and earth, only one of them, the presence of the term ריב, is found in all three texts. In fact, the similarities that these texts share revolve around the common theme of announcing divine judgment on the people of Israel and Judah, rather than the presence of any specialized legal language or structure. Persian period Yehudite readers would have perceived each of these texts as words of divine judgment on their ancestors, but are unlikely to have found more specific commonality across them.[50]

A call to the heavens and earth or other natural phenomena to function as participants in the events of the text is found only in Mic 6. This motif is entirely absent from Hos 2 and 4. In Mic 6, they may have a function broadly described as witnesses to the events in the text, but even there it is unclear whether or not this has any basis in legal traditions or international treaty law, as proposed by proponents of the prophetic lawsuit or covenant lawsuit genre.[51] In the legal texts of the Neo-Babylonian and Persian periods, witnesses, when they are present in the decision records, are found at the end of the texts rather than the beginning, as in Mic 6. Their function in these texts is to observe and bear witness to the outcome of the legal proceedings, so that they may be called upon should the matter ever be litigated again, or perhaps to prevent the matter ever being litigated again. There is no reason to expect that Yehudite readers familiar with the legal practices and genres of the period would have read the references to mountains, hills, and foundations of the earth in Mic 6 in light of the references to witnesses found in the contemporary legal texts.

Only two of these three texts, Hos 4 and Mic 6, contain a call to hear the word of Yahweh. Again, there seems to be little reason to expect that these texts would be read by Yehudite readers as examples of a common genre. In addition, such a call is common to a variety of texts in prophetic literature. There is certainly nothing about this motif that would tie it explicitly to legal genres or practices. There is also no identifiable parallel in the legal texts that derive from the Neo-Babylonian and Persian periods.

The only common element across all three of these texts is the presence of a form of the word ריב. On this point, the analysis of the significance of the term ריב by de Roche is particularly important. He demonstrates persuasively that this term is used to indicate the existence of a dispute between two parties, not the means of resolution, judicial or otherwise. "The difference between a *rib* and a lawsuit is that a *rib* is a contention, while a lawsuit is a particular way of solving a contention."[52] De Roche also examines several key texts in which the term ריב

---

[50] For a discussion of the historical particularity of Persian period readings of the prophetic texts see: James M. Trotter, *Reading Hosea in Achaemenid Yehud*, JSOTSup 328 (Sheffield: Sheffield Academic, 2001), 168–73.
[51] For example, Huffmon, "Covenant Lawsuit in the Prophets," 291–93.
[52] De Roche, "Yahweh's Rîb against Israel," 569.

occurs and which have been regarded as prophetic lawsuits by other interpreters, including Hos 2, Hos 4, and Mic 6. He establishes that they represent a contention or a dispute that Yahweh has with Israel, but that they each lack formal elements, such as witnesses or judges, that would be expected in a lawsuit.[53] In other words, the term ריב indicates a dispute between two or more parties, but does not inherently presume formal legal procedures. In relation to the legal texts from the Neo-Babylonian and Persian periods, there is no clear correspondence between the term ריב and any legal technical term used regularly in these texts. As a result, there is no reason to expect that a Yehudite reader of these texts would read them as exemplars of a lawsuit genre or any other legal genre on the basis of the presence of this term.

CONCLUSION

There is a substantive body of textual evidence regarding the legal genres and procedures in the geographical areas controlled by the Neo-Babylonian and Achaemenid Persian empires. These texts reflect a significant commonality in the legal texts and practices across this period in all the areas controlled by these empires, from Mesopotamia to Egypt. These texts provide an excellent insight into the likely expectations of a Persian period Yehudite reader regarding the form and content of legal texts in this period. On this basis, it is possible to conclude that such a reader would not have read Hos 2:3–25; 4:1–3; and Mic 6:1–8 as examples of a lawsuit or any other legal genre. In fact, the Neo-Assyrian evidence strongly indicates that earlier readers of these prophetic texts would not have read them as lawsuit genres either. The focus of the new form criticism on the reception of texts by readers in specific settings, particularly on the basis of the extant evidence regarding generic features and their use in the contemporary social contexts, provides extremely valuable insights for modern readers of these ancient texts.

---

[53] Ibid., 569–71.

4

The Vision Report Genre between Form-Criticism and Redaction-Criticism: An Investigation of Amos 7–9 and Zechariah 1–6

Lena-Sofia Tiemeyer

INTRODUCTION

The present article explores the genre category of vision report, with focus on the textual relationship within a pericope between the account of the visual impression and the accompanying divine oracles.

Five books in the Latter Prophets feature vision reports: Amos 7–9; Isa 6; Jer 1; 24; Ezek 1; 8–11; 37; 40–48, and Zech 1–6. In addition, there are vision reports in the Former Prophets (2 Kgs 22) and in the Writings (Dan 7; 8; 10, and 12). My investigation here is limited to the two sets of vision accounts in the Book of the Twelve, namely, the sequence of five vision reports in Amos 7:1–3; 7:4–6; 7:7–9; 8:1–3, and 9:1–4, and the eight vision reports in Zech 1:8–6:8.

Several scholars have used arguments that draw on form criticism in their attempt to (dis-)prove a matter related to redaction-criticism. In particular, they have argued that the form of the vision accounts in the book of Amos can shed light upon the redaction-critical formation of Zechariah's vision report.[1] As each of Amos's vision account ends with a divine word, the argument goes, so should

---

[1] Most recently, see Michael R. Stead, "The Interrelationship between Vision and Oracle in Zechariah 1–6," in *'I Lifted My Eyes and Saw': Reading Dream and Vision Reports in the Hebrew Bible*, ed. Elizabeth R. Hayes and Lena-Sofia Tiemeyer, LHBOTS 584 (London: T&T Clark, 2014), 149–68. See also Mark J. Boda, "Writing the Vision: Zechariah within the Visionary Traditions of the Hebrew Bible," in *'I Lifted My Eyes and Saw,'* 101–18, for a slightly different approach.

Zechariah's. It follows, these same scholars maintain, that the oracular material within Zech 1–6 is the natural and integral continuation of the preceding vision account, without which the vision account cannot be properly understood. In this article, I hope to demonstrate that this type of comparison is partly flawed. Form-critical and redaction-critical considerations must go hand-in-hand when seeking to determine the textual development of a given text. Form-critical considerations shed light upon the ways in which readers read the (final form of the) text, while redaction-critical concerns tell us about the gradual formation of the same text and the reasons behind the continuous textual growth. On this latter matter, I shall seek to show that the two sets of vision reports in Amos and Zechariah display the *same* type of relationship between vision and oracle. In both cases, the oracular material constitutes a later addition, which interprets and in some cases also redefines the message of the earlier account of the vision.

History of Research

This article builds upon the insights of a long list of scholars who have explored the form of the vision report genre in order to define (1) what parts constitute a vision report and (2) what rhetorical goals each part plays.[2] These scholars tend to be uninterested in the experience behind the scene and/or of any oral prophetic communication, and focus instead on the written reports. How are the reports constructed? What are their defining literary features? Moreover, exegetes have long sought to categorize the vision reports in the Hebrew Bible into subgroups. There is, however, no agreement as to the criteria employed for defining those subgroups. Should thematic or structural concerns carry the day?

Moses Sister's article from 1934 is one of the earliest studies. Sister's discussion revolves around questions such as: How are the visions structured? What kinds of literary-stylistic tools are used? What shared and distinct features do the different vision reports have in the different prophetic books?[3] Sister further compares the biblical vision reports with the biblical dream reports. Due to the form-critical similarities between the two genres, Sister postulates that the form of the dream report served as the prototype for the (later) form of the vision report.[4] On the basis of this conclusion, Sister detects three different types of vision reports:

---

[2] What follows is a survey of a selection of significant scholarly work. See also the studies by Christian Jeremias, *Die Nachtgesichte des Sacharja: Unters. zu ihrer Stellung im Zusammenhang d. Visions- berichte im Alten Testament u. zu ihrem Bildmaterial*, FRLANT 117 (Göttingen: Vandenhoeck & Ruprecht, 1977), 51–61, 100–108, and G. Heinzmann, "Formgeschichtliche Untersuchung der prophetischen Visionsberichte" (Ph.D. diss., University of Heidelberg, 1978).

[3] Moses Sister, "Die Typen der prophetischen Visionen in der Bible," *MGWJ* 78 (1934): 399.

[4] Ibid., 422–25.

1. Visions in the form of a dream, the content of which is an appearance of God or an angel (theophany) (e.g., Amos 9:1–4).
2. Visions in the form of a dream, the content of which is a picture which is immediately understandable (self-explanatory images) (e.g., Amos 7:1–3; 7:4–6; Zech 3:1–7).
3. Visions in the form of a dream, the content of which is a picture which needs to be interpreted (images demanding interpretation) (e.g., Amos 7:7–9; 8:1–3; most of Zechariah's eight vision accounts; cf. Jer 1:11–12; 1:13–16; 24:1–10).[5]

One weakness of Sister's model is that his typology is keyed exclusively to the hypothetical original literary model of dream reports.[6] Another weakness is that aspects of each type may overlap in any one vision. In addition, some of the decisions as to which vision report belongs in which groups appear to be rather subjective.[7]

Friedrich Horst's article from 1960 advanced the discussion in more than one aspect. Focusing on the interplay between word and image in the vision report, Horst differentiates between three types of visions:[8]

1. "Numinal or presence visions" (*Anwesenheitsvisionen*): The prophet is before God's throne or in the divine assembly, where he catches a glimpse of a numinous presence. The prophet is the one who sees and hears God's word (Amos 7:1–6; 9:1–4; Zechariah's first, fourth, and eighth vision, cf. also 1 Kgs 22:17, 19–22; Isa 6).[9]
2. "Word-symbol visions" (*Wortspiel- oder Wortsymbolvisionen*): In this type of vision, God sends an image which, through assonance, alludes to its meaning (Amos 7:7–9; 8:1–3; Zechariah's second, third, fifth, sixth, and seventh vision, cf. also Jer 1:11–14).
3. His last category, "Event visions" (*Ereignis- oder Geschehnisvisionen*) have no attested examples in Amos and Zechariah.[10]

Few scholars have adopted Horst's categorization. Niditch, for instance, points out that the substantial variation within each of Horst's categories makes it

---

[5] Ibid., 425–29.
[6] Burke O. Long, "Reports of Visions Among the Prophets," *JBL* 95 (1976): 353.
[7] Susan Niditch, *The Symbolic Vision in Biblical Tradition*, HSM 30 (Chico, CA: Scholars Press, 1980), 2–3.
[8] The English translations of Horst's German terminology follow those of Long, "Reports of Visions Among the Prophets," 354.
[9] Friedrich Horst, "Die Visionsschilderungen der alttestamentlichen Propheten," *Evangelische Theologie* 20 (1960): 194–200.
[10] Horst, "Visionsschilderungen," 202–4. According to Horst, the texts in Isa 21:1–10; Jer 4:5ff.; Nah 2:2–11; 3:1–3; Hab 1:5–11, constitute examples of this type of vision account.

doubtful that a definable form exists. In particular, Horst's second category actually contains two rather different types of reports. Niditch further argues that Horst's treatment of Zechariah's eight vision accounts appears to be arbitrary. Why, for instance, is the third account (Zech 2:5–9) a *Wortsymbolvision* and not an *Anwesenheitvisions*, even though Zechariah encounters two heavenly beings?[11] From a different perspective, Behrens notes that Horst's categories depend to a large extent on their content rather than on their structure.[12]

In his dissertation from 1976, Stephan Reimers seeks to demarcate the biblical vision report by determining its linguistic and formal characteristics vis-à-vis the surrounding material in the prophetic books.[13] Reimers focuses on the formal structure of the vision report and argues, *contra* Horst, that form-critical aspects have priority over matters of content when seeking to categorize the different reports.[14] Reimers detects a three-part-structure that is shared by all vision reports:[15]

1. "Preliminary Remark" (*Führungsnotiz / Vorbemerkung*). The first part consists only of general information: who is the seer and where did he see the vision? For instance, Zech 1:7 is a typical preliminary remark.[16]
2. "Description of the Image" (*Schaubeschreibung*).[17]
3. "Speech part" (*Redeteil*).[18]

Reimers's scheme is both too detailed and too rigid to be useful. The fact that the "speech part" of a single vision account may fall into several subcategories begs the questions as to whether these structures really are conscious literary patterns. For instance, Reimer categorizes Zech 2:6 as a "question dialogue" while Zech 2:8a constitutes a "commissioning speech."

In the same year, Burke O. Long wrote an influential article devoted to the structure of the vision reports in the Hebrew Bible. He suggests that most vision reports consist of three basic parts (Jer 38:21b–22 being a typical example thereof):

---

[11] Niditch, *Symbolic Vision*, 4–5.
[12] Achim Behrens, *Prophetische Visionsschilderungen im Alten Testament: Sprachliche Eigenarten, Funktion und Geschichte einer Gattung*, AOAT 292 (Münster: Ugarit-Verlag, 2002), 19.
[13] Stephan Reimers, "Formgeschichte der profetischen Visionsberichte" (Ph.D. diss., University of Hamburg, 1976), iii–iv.
[14] Ibid., 19.
[15] Ibid., 127–28 (table), 153 (conclusion). The first part is discussed in more detail on pp. 43–55. This part may contain, among other matters, chronological and geographical information about the vision.
[16] Ibid., 43–55.
[17] Ibid., 56–71, 127–28 (table), 131–32.
[18] Ibid., 72–107, 127–28 (table).

1. announcement (containing a verb from the root ראה)
2. transition (והנה)
3. vision sequence

Long divides the vision reports in the Hebrew Bible into three categories:

1. "Oracle-Vision": This type is dominated by a question-and-answer dialogue. God's final reply gives the report its characteristic quality, and, as such, determines its significance. In contrast, the description of the visionary imagery is sparse, and the images themselves are of little consequence for the interpretation of the pericope (Amos 7:7–8; 8:1–2; Zech 5:1–4, cf. also Jer 1:11–14; 24:1–10).[19]
2. "Dramatic Word-Vision": This type depicts a heavenly scene/dramatic action. Although the situation is otherworldly, it is taken as being a portent which presages a future event in the earthly realm. There may be a divine word, but it does not have the character of a public oracle. Rather, it is integral to the drama. It grows out of it and is addressed to it (Amos 7:1–6; Zech 1:8–17, cf. also 1 Kgs 22:17, 19–22; Isa 6; Ezek 1; 8–11; 40–48).[20]
3. "Revelatory-Mysteries-Vision": This type of vision conveys, in a veiled form, secrets of divine activity and future events. The question-and-answer pattern in this type is reminiscent of the two aforementioned categories, yet differs in that the seer's interlocutor is no longer YHWH but a mediator. Further, the questions do not lead to any elaboration of the images, but seek interpretation. "The vision-report intends to instruct the cognizant, while mystifying those lacking proper keys." (Zech 2:1–4; 4:1–14; 5:5–11 [in part], cf. also Dan 8; 10–12).[21]

As with the aforementioned attempts to categorize the biblical vision reports, Long's attempt has not gone without criticism.[22] Niditch, for instance, objects pertinently to the "lumping together" in the same category of such diverse reports as the initiation vision in Isa 6, the visions in Amos 7:1–6 where the symbolism is evident, and Zech 1:8–17. She also questions why, given the definition of the third category, Zech 1:8–17 and 6:1–8 are excluded.[23]

---

[19] Long, "Reports of Visions," 357–58. Long states further that "the association between image and oracle is casual and unpredictable.... The visionary image is merely the occasion for oracle, and the vision report is opportunity for proclamation.... Nor does the oracle interpret or explain the image, which otherwise would remain esoteric and mysterious. There is nothing to be explained, but everything to be proclaimed."
[20] Ibid., 359–63.
[21] Ibid., 363–64.
[22] Niditch, *Symbolic Vision*, 6.
[23] Ibid., 6.

In 1983, Susan Niditch published a full-length monograph on the symbolic vision in the biblical tradition. In line with Jeremias, Niditch takes a diachronic approach. Looking at twelve select reports of symbolic visions, she identifies three major stages of development, from the simple, early form in Amos and Jeremiah, via the more prose-like, yet also more mythologized, in Zechariah, to an even more baroque and narrative state in Daniel and later visions.[24]

As in the aforementioned cases, also Niditch's proposal has received its share of critique. Behrens questions her treatment of Amos 7:7–9; 8:1–3 as distinct from the preceding two vision accounts in Amos 7:1–3, 4–6. As there is a dramatic progression throughout the four accounts, it makes little sense to discuss them separately. Likewise, it also makes no sense to single out five of Zechariah's vision accounts.[25] It is also difficult to establish the chronological development of the *Gattung* of vision reports without taking the material in Ezekiel, as well as that in Isa 6 and Amos 7:1–6, into consideration.[26]

Most recently, Achim Behrens's form-critical investigation of the vision reports in the Hebrew Bible from 2002 is devoted solely to the form and the structure of the final literary accounts. He argues that the vision accounts remain constant in their outer form, yet allows for great variation in terms of theme and message. Behrens argues that every vision report consists of two basic parts:[27]

1. A description of the vision (*Visionsteil*): Following Reimers, Behrens argues that this part often begins with either a form of the verb ראה, the particle הנה, and a nominal clause, or, alternatively, the verbal construction ראה את and an object clause.
2. A speech part (dialogue or divine/angelic monologue) (*Redeteil / Dialogteil*): This part opens with a *wayyiqtol*-form of the root אמר (ויאמר). This speech is either a question or an imperative. This part always ends with the speech of either YHWH or the messenger. The exact identity of the speaker is unimportant for determining the literary genre. Behrens concludes that the message of this speech is supported by the preceding images.

Behrens postulates two lines of historical development of the vision report genre. The first line is located in Amos 7–8 and Jer 1; 24. At a later point, the vision of the scroll in Ezek 2:9–3:9 connected with this line of development. The second line is located in Isa 6 and 1 Kgs 22:17, 19–22, as well as in Amos 9:1–4. The vision report in Ezek 1:1–2:8, linked thematically to Isa 6 and 1 Kgs 22, is a later development of this line. Behrens further argues that the two lines of

---

[24] Ibid., 7–12, 243–48.
[25] Behrens, *Visionsschilderungen*, 29.
[26] Ibid., 30.
[27] Ibid., 32–60, 377–80.

tradition met and mutually influenced one another in Ezekiel. The current vision report in Ezek 1–3 is thus a redactional combination of two different traditions (Ezek 1:1–2:8 and 2:9–3:9). At an even later stage, the genre underwent further changes, the result of which we can see in Zech 1–6 and Dan 8–12.[28]

While there is much to commend Behren's proposed structure, I am not convinced by his two part structure. In the case of Zech 1:8–17, for instance, Behrens's distinction between the *Visionsteil* in verse 8 and the *Dialogteil* in verses 9–15 is not in line with the extant textual evidence (see below).[29] Further, we cannot put the divine oracles which, for example, end Zechariah's eighth vision (Zech 6:8) on par with the Interpreting Angel's concluding speech in 4:14 and 5:11.[30] They do not share the same literary form and they fill different rhetorical functions within the pericope. Finally, his claim that the message of the concluding speech is supported by the preceding images is only partly true. Again, as we shall discuss below, the concluding divine speech often singles out *one* meaning of the preceding visionary part.[31]

THE RELATIONSHIP BETWEEN VISION AND ORACLE: FORM-CRITICAL CONSIDERATIONS

In this section, we shall survey the structure of Amos's and Zechariah's vision reports in detail, with the aim of discovering whether or not they share the same overall structure.

The structures of Amos's vision accounts are relatively simple:[32]

---

[28] Ibid., 381–85.
[29] Ibid., 35.
[30] Ibid., 276.
[31] For additional critique of Behrens's proposal, see Martin Pröbstle, "Review of Achim Behrens, Prophetische Visionsschilderngen im Alten Testament," *RBL* 09 (2004). http://www.bookreviews.org/pdf/3984_4081.pdf. Pröbstle criticizes Behrens for circular reasoning. Behrens discounts Jer 4:23–26 and 38:21–23 from his discussion, because they lack a dialogue part. He likewise refrains from discussing Dan 7, because it does not conform to the proposed form of a prophetic vision report. Pröbstle further points out that Behrens ignores the possibility that the varying forms of vision reports are due to the prophetic visionaries' real experiences. A prophetic author might deviate from the literary conventions of the vision report genre because he wished to give as accurate a description as possible of what he had experienced.
[32] The division of the individual verses follows the Masoretic accents. So, v. Xa is always the text before the *ethnachta*, and v. Xb is always the text following the *ethnachta*.

Textual Unit	Visual Scene	Speech	Divine Action	Divine Speech
Amos 7:1–3	God shows the seer a scene (v. 1). God is part of this scene (v. 1aβ, הנה יוצר).	In response, Amos speaks to God (v. 2).	In response, God acts (v. 3a).	In response, God speaks (v. 3b).
Amos 7:4–6	God shows the seer a scene (v. 4). God acts in this scene (v. 4aβ, והנה קרא).	In response, Amos speaks to God (v. 5).	In response, God acts (v. 6a).	In response, God speaks (v. 6b).
Amos 7:7–9	God shows the seer a scene (v. 7). God acts in this scene (v. 7b, והנה אדני נצב).	Dialogue between God and the seer (8a).		God speaks (vv. 8b, 9).
Amos 8:1–3	God shows the seer an image (v. 1).	Dialogue between God and the seer (v. 2a).		God speaks (vv. 2b, 3).
Amos 9:1–4	The seer sees a scene. God is part of this scene (v. 1aα, אדני נצב).			God speaks (vv. 1aβ–4).[33]

---

[33] The first person divine speech ends in v. 4 and recommences in vv. 7–10, 11–15. The intermediate vv. 5–6 refer to YHWH in the third person and is therefore unlikely to be part of the divine speech. Instead, they form a doxology (cf. also 4:13; 5:8–9) which in all likelihood was attached secondarily to the vision report. See further Hans W. Wolff, *Joel and Amos*, trans. Waldemar Janzen, S. Dean McBride Jr., and Charles A. Muenchow, Hermeneia (Philadelphia: Fortress, 1977), 215–17, 341; Jason Radine, *The Book of Amos in Emergent Judah*, FAT 2/45 (Tübingen: Mohr Siebeck, 2010), 213, and Tchavdar S. Hadjiev, *The Composition and Redaction of the Book of Amos*, BZAW 393 (Berlin: de Gruyter, 2009), 131–33. As to the divine oracles in verses 7–10, 11–15, it is possible that they form a sequence of oracles which seek to extract insights from the visionary scene in verse 1aα and also to continue on from the oracular material in verses 1aβ–4. There are, however, no clear verbal or thematic connections between the visual scene in v. 1aα and the oracular material in verses 7–15. See further Hadjiev, *Composition and Redaction*, 68–73, 111–23.

The five accounts of Amos's visions share several key features:

1. Amos always sees one single scene. In the first, second, third, and fifth accounts, this scene features an action which is described by the use of a participle (7:1, 4, 7; 9:1). The exception is the fourth vision account which contains a static image.
2. God and the seer are the only actors/interlocutors.

In contrast, the relation between the visual scene and the divine speech changes and develops throughout the vision report sequence:

1. In the first two vision accounts, the divine oracle is intimately connected with the image. The seer sees scenes of destruction, he intercedes, and God responds in deeds and words to the seer's intercession.
2. In the third and the fourth vision accounts, the situation is more complicated. God's initial speech is immediately connected to the seen image via a word-pun (7:8 / 8:2). The following statement in 7:9 / 8:3 explicates in specific details what God's punishment will do. The link between the oracle and the immediately preceding vision account is vague. The concluding oracular material does not share any vocabulary with the vision account, and it never refers to its images.
3. The structure of the fifth vision account is distinct from the four preceding ones. There is no clear connection between the image of the altar in verse 1aα and the message of the ensuing oracle in verses 1aβ–4.

The structure of the individual vision accounts in Zech 1:8–6:8 (henceforth Zech 1–6) is significantly more complicated than in Amos 7–9, yet the relationship between visual scene and oral speech in Zech 1–6 is in many respects comparable to that in Amos 7–9.[34]

---

[34] I use the term "dialogue" in the following chart to indicate a discussion between two interlocutors. In contrast, I employ the term "speech" to denote the utterance of a single person that is not followed by an apparent reply.

Textual Unit	Visual Scene	Dialogue within Scene	Angelic Speech	Divine Speech
Zech 1:8–17	The seer sees a scene (v. 8).	Conversation between the seer, the Interpreting Angel, and the characters in the visionary scene (vv. 9–11).	The Angel of YHWH laments (v. 12).	God speaks (vv. 13, 14–17).
Zech 2:1–4	The seer sees a scene (vv. 1, 3).	Conversation between the seer and the Interpreting Angel / God (vv. 2, 4).		
Zech 2:5–9[35]	The seer sees a scene (vv. 5–8a).	Conversation between the seer and the different Angels (vv. 6, 8a).	An Angel speaks (v. 8b).	God speaks (v. 9).
Zech 3:1–10	The seer is shown a scene (vv. 1–5).	Conversation between the seer, the Adversary, and the Angel of YHWH.	The Angel of YHWH speaks (vv. 6–7)	God speaks (vv. 8–10).
Zech 4:1–14	The seer sees a scene (vv. 2–3).	Conversation between the seer and the Interpreting Angel (vv. 4–6aα, 10b–14).		God speaks (vv. 6aβ–10a).
Zech 5:1–4	The seer sees a scene (vv. 1–2).	Conversation between the seer and the Interpreting Angel (v. 2).	Additional speech by the Interpreting Angel (v. 3).	God speaks (v. 4).

---

[35] The oracular material in Zech 2:10–17 is not discussed here as it is only loosely connected to the preceding vision account(s). For the same reason, I have chosen not to interact with the material in Zech 6:9–15 here.

| Zech 5:5–11 | The seer sees a scene (vv. 6, 8aβ–9). | Conversation between the seer and the Interpreting Angel (vv. 5–6, 8aα, 10–11). | | |
| Zech 6:1–8 | The seer sees a scene (vv. 1–3, 7). | Conversation between the seer and the Interpreting Angel (vv. 4–6). | | God speaks (v. 8). |

When we compare the text in Zech 1–6 with that in Amos 7–9, we discover many shared features. First, the overarching structure of most of the individual accounts in Zech 1–6 account is similar to that found in the individual accounts in Amos 7–9.

1. In both sets of reports, the seer "sees" or someone else "shows him" a visual scene.
2. In both sets of reports, there is a conversation between the seer and another person about the scene.

At the same time, two sets of reports differ in important ways, both in terms of content and in terms of form:

1. In terms of content, while Amos communicates directly with God, Zechariah's main interlocutor is the Interpreting Angel.
2. Also in terms of content, several of Zechariah's accounts feature conversations which include characters within the visionary world.
3. In terms of form, Zechariah's conversations and Amos's conversations do not share the same structure. In particular, Zechariah's conversations are significantly longer and more elaborate.

Secondly, in both Zech 1–6 and Amos 7–9 the relation between the visual scene and the divine speech does not remain the same throughout the whole vision report sequence:

1. The angelic speeches in Zech 1:12 (first); 2:8b (third), and 5:3 (sixth) are to a large extent integral to the preceding scene. They relate closely to the preceding visionary scene and add a layer of interpretation to it. In this respect, they fill the same function as the divine speech in Amos 7:8 and 8:2.

2. In contrast, the divine speeches in Zech 1:13, 14–17 (first); 2:9 (third); 3:6–7, 8–10 (fourth); 4:6aβ–10a (fifth); 5:4 (sixth), and 6:8 (eighth) explicate the vision account to which they are attached. In some cases, they also reinterpret the scenery and also draw out possible practical consequences from them. As such, they have a supplementary role. In this respect, they fill the same function as the divine speech in Amos 7:9 and 8:3.

The Relationship Between Vision and Oracle: Redaction-Critical Considerations

After having established that (1) many of the oracular sayings in both Amos 7–9 and Zech 1–6 are at best tangential to the immediately preceding visionary scene, and that (2) in both sets of texts the oracles often fill an interpretative function, namely to tease out possible interpretations and practical implications from the visionary scene, we are in a position to explore the redaction-critical repercussions of these insights. On this issue, Stead has pointed out that many of those scholars who distinguish between vision and oracle in Zech 1–6 are inconsistent. Instead of treating all oracular material as later additions, they consider some oracles to be secondary (e.g., Zech 4:4–6aα, 10b–14) whilst treating others as integral to the vision report (e.g., Zech 5:4).[36] In view of Stead's apt critique, I shall endeavour to find a compatible model which treats equally all the oracular sayings in Amos 7–9 and Zech 1–6.

Amos

Beginning with Amos's five vision accounts, the oracular material imbedded into the first and the second vision account definitely must be an integral part of the earliest layer of the account. Without God's speech in 7:3b and 6b, neither vision account makes sense.

The situation in the third and the fourth vision account differs in this respect. As in the case of the first and the second account, God's speech in 7:8b and 8:2b is necessary for comprehending the third and the fourth account. In contrast, the divine speech in 7:9 and 8:3 respectively do not relate immediately to the imagery in the visionary scene, and they do not share significant vocabulary with the preceding account. It is thus, at least theoretically, possible that these two verses are later additions. They *explicate* the vision account to which they are attached, and they *draw out possible practical consequences* from them.

Many scholars have noted the explanatory character of 7:9 and 8:3. Mays, for example, notes that verse 7:9 and 8:3 form "an element which stands outside the common structure [of the four vision reports]." He is therefore open to the

---

[36] Stead, "Interrelationship between Vision and Oracle in Zechariah 1–6," 152–56.

possibility that these two verses were either written by Amos or by a later redactor, in order to "make clear the consequences of Yahweh's withdrawal of forbearance."[37] Soggin likewise assigns an interpretative quality to Amos 7:9, suggesting that it shows the consequences of the demolition, that is, the judgement.[38] Wolff develops this thought further, noting that Amos 7:9 is set off from its context by reason of its prosodic form as well as by its content. He concludes that the verse was inserted into its present context in order to facilitate the transition from 7:7–8 to 7:10–17.[39] As to the oracle in Amos 8:3, Wolff suggests that it was added by the same redactor who added 7:9. This verse serves to illustrate the preceding oracle as it conjures up a scene of mass dying, thus suggesting that the "end" envisioned in the preceding vision is the end of life.[40] Along similar lines, Anderson and Freedman treat the oracle in Amos 7:9 as a later added bridge which forms an enveloping structure together with verse 17bβ.[41] They further view 8:3a and 3b as separate exclamations or even fragments that do not belong in the present context at all. Although these two half-verses are connected thematically, their formal, logical, and syntactic connections to the preceding vision report are vague.[42] Jeremias even goes so far as to discuss Amos 7:7–8; 8:1–2[43] separately from 7:9 and 8:3. As the aforementioned scholars, he sees Amos 7:9 as a later addition.[44] He likewise views Amos 8:3 as a bridge between the fourth visionary account in Amos 8:1–2 and Amos 8:4–14. The latter offers a commentary on the fourth vision account,

---

[37] James Luther Mays, *Amos: A Commentary*, OTL (London: SCM, 1969), 124. Mays suggests that the narrative in Amos 7:10–17 was placed in its current place because of the similarity between the connection between 7:9 and 7:11 (p. 123).

[38] J. Alberto Soggin, *The Prophet Amos: A Translation and Commentary*, trans. John Bowden, OTL (London: SCM, 1987), 117. Soggins suggests that this verse forms a "Deuteronomistic-type addition, the aim of which seems to have been ... to provide a transition to vv. 10ff."

[39] Wolff, *Joel and Amos*, 295, 301.

[40] Ibid., 318–20.

[41] Francis I. Anderson and David Noel Freedman, *Amos: A New Translation with Introduction and Commentary*, AB 24A (New York: Doubleday, 1989), 794 (translation), 754–55 (commentary).

[42] Ibid., 797–99.

[43] Jörg Jeremias, *The Book of Amos: A Commentary*, trans. Douglas W. Scott, OTL (Louisville: Westminster John Knox, 1998), 124 (translation), 130–34 (exegesis). Jeremias points out that v. 9 contains unique vocabulary within the book of Amos while, at the same time, these unique features are shared with the book of Hosea. Based on this observation, Jeremias suggests that the tradents of the book of Amos established this connection between the books of Amos and Hosea in order to emphasize that the readers should read the two books together in order to comprehend fully the measure of Israel's sin, as well as the limits to God's patience with this people. As to the timeframe of the insertion, Jeremias points out that v. 9 appears to presuppose the fall of the Northern kingdom.

[44] Ibid., 142.

seeking "to make comprehensible for its readers the enigmatically brief, harsh announcement of the fourth vision."[45] Most other critical scholars, among them Bergler, Wöhrle, Riede, Hadjiev, Radine, and, somewhat surprisingly, Behrens follow suit.[46] Slightly differently, Clements notes that verse 9 "elaborates upon the initial interpretation of Amos's third vision" and "presents a fuller explanation of its meaning."[47] He postulates that in the earliest layer in 7:7–8, Amos predicted a nonspecific catastrophe. A later author, mindful of the instability caused by the overthrow of the Jehu dynasty, wrote 7:9 in an attempt to anchor the original vision account to a historical event and to draw out its fuller meaning.[48]

A scholarly minority treat Amos 7:7–9 and 8:1–3 as original textual units. Niditch, for example, sees no need to exclude 7:9 from the pericope on thematic or structural grounds or on grounds related to content. As a result, she interprets all of 7:8b–9 as one divine oracle which explains the object which Amos saw in his vision.[49] According to Niditch, God's word is revealed in verse 8b and reemphasized in verse 9.[50] The symbol of the plumb-line is reused and nuanced by the divine oracle in verse 8b in order to reveal its deeper meaning. The theme of judgement, in turn, is reemphasized in verse 9.[51] Likewise, she regards Amos 8:2b, 3 together as God's explanation of the objects seen by the seer in his vision.[52] Along similar lines, Gese argues that there is no thematic contradiction between 7:9 and 8:3 respectively and the preceding vision account. Rather they serve to put the threat in concrete terms.[53] Hayes states that in both Amos 7:9

---

[45] Ibid., 143–46.
[46] Siegfried Bergler, "'Auf der Mauer—auf dem Altar': Noch einmal die Visionen des Amos," *VT* 50 (2000): 448; Jakob Wöhrle, *Die frühen Sammlungen des Zwölfprophetenbuches: Entstehung und Komposition*, BZAW 360 (Berlin: de Gruyter, 2006), 102. Wöhrle singles out Amos 7:1–8 and 8:1–2 as the four original vision reports. He treats Amos 7:9 as a linking verse (pp. 110, 242–43), and argues that Amos 8:3 belongs with the following Amos 8:4–14 (p. 105). See also Peter Riede, *Vom Erbarmen zum Gericht: Die Visionen des Amosbuches (Am 7–9*) und ihr literatur- und traditionsgeschichtlicher Zusammenhang*, WMANT 120 (Neukirchen-Vluyn: Neukirchener Verlag, 2008), 157–68; Hadjiev, *Composition and Redaction*, 78–79, 97–98; Radine, *Amos in Emergent Judah*, 38–39, and Behrens, *Visionsschilderungen*, 78–88, 89, 102.
[47] Ronald E. Clements, "Amos and the Politics of Israel," in *Storia e tradizioni di Israeli. Festschrift J.A. Soggin*, ed. Daniele Garrone and Felice Israel (Brescia: Paideia, 1991), 49–64; repr. in *Old Testament Prophecy: From Oracles to Canon*, ed. Ronald E. Clements (Louisville: Westminster John Knox, 1996), 25.
[48] Ibid., 28, 32–34.
[49] Niditch, *Symbolic Vision*, 22–23.
[50] Ibid., 27.
[51] Ibid., 28.
[52] Ibid., 37.
[53] Hartmut Gese, "Komposition bei Amos," in *Congress Volume Vienna 1980*, ed. John A. Emerton, VTSup 32 (Leiden, Brill, 1981), 78–83.

and 8:3, YHWH "spells out the consequences of the vision's imagery," yet he treats 7:8b–9 and 8:2b–3 as internally coherent textual units.[54] Paul likewise maintains that the "poetic description" of the forthcoming destructive punishment in Amos 7:9 and 8:3 is integral to the text. Thus these verses are not later interpolations.[55] Along similar lines, Wood interprets 7:7–9 and 8:1–3 as two internally coherent pericopes[56]

In my view, it makes exegetical sense to distinguish between 7:7–8 and 9 and between 8:1–2 and 3 insofar as verses 9 and 3 each provides an additional layer of interpretation to the original vision account which precedes them. It is, however, not strictly necessary to postulate different authorship. We might rather be dealing with the same author. He originally saw and interpreted the third and the fourth vision. At a later point, he realized its full historical significance or, alternatively, wished to elaborate further on the repercussions of God's judgement, perhaps for rhetorical effect.

Turning to Amos's fifth vision account (9:1–4), we are actually dealing with the same, interpretative relationship between the visual image and the ensuing divine oracle. The link between the image of the altar in verse 1aα and the message of the ensuing oracle in verses 1aβ–4 is opaque. Notably, the words מזבח and נצב, central to the image in verse 1aα, are never mentioned in the subsequent oracle. We appear to have the report of what Amos saw, together with the report of God's words which sought to explicate the meaning of the image seen. It is significant to note, however, that the divine elucidation is *one possible* explanation of the visual imagery. It is definitely not the *only feasible one*. The image in itself is meaningless or, expressed more positively, multivalent. No reader would have batted an eye-lid, had God delivered a different oracle. At the same time, it is reasonable to assume that verse 1aα never existed independently from (at least parts of) the ensuing oracle.

As to the text-historical relationship between the fifth vision account and the preceding four ones, there is no scholarly consensus. For a recent discussion of the matter, see the survey by Hadjiev.[57] Hadjiev himself argues that Amos 9:1–4 forms a single textual unit,[58] and he demonstrates that there is no thematic discontinuity between the four preceding accounts and the one in Amos 9:1–4.

---

[54] John H. Hayes, *Amos the Eighth-Century Prophet: His Times and His Preaching* (Nashville, TN: Abingdon, 1988), 199, 206, 208. See also Aaron W. Park, *The Book of Amos as Composed and Read in Antiquity*, StBibLit 37 (New York: Lang, 2001), 95–96, who treats 7:8b–9 and 8:2b–3 as the speech part of the vision report, subdivided into two parts: punishment (vv. 8b / 2b) and substantiation of punishment (vv. 9 / 3).

[55] Shalom M. Paul, *A Commentary on the Book of Amos*, Hermeneia (Minneapolis: Fortress, 1991), 224 (including footnote 21).

[56] Joyce L. Rilett Wood, *Amos in Song and Book Culture*, JSOTSup 337 (Sheffield: Sheffield Academic, 2002), 38–43.

[57] Hadjiev, *Composition and Redaction*, 60–61.

[58] Ibid., 62–65.

In addition, although there are significant differences between the two sets of texts, nothing precludes shared authorship. He concludes that Amos 7–9 is based on an original five-part vision report found in Amos 7:1–8; 8:1–2; 9:1–4.[59] From a different perspective, Radine maintains that all the five vision accounts are integral to the earliest layer of the book of Amos.[60]

ZECHARIAH

As in the case of Amos's first two vision accounts, Zechariah's second account (2:1–4) must be read as a whole in order to make sense. Unless read in conjunction with verse 4, it is not possible to comprehend the message of the account. Further, from a syntactical perspective, it is preferable to treat this speech as being uttered by the Interpreting Angel and not by YHWH. As to the seventh vision account in Zech 5:5–11, it contains no divine speech and thus falls outside the parameters of this enquiry. In the remaining six accounts, however, there are two good reasons to distinguish between the visionary and the oracular material on redaction-critical grounds: (1) the vision report makes sense on its own, and (2) the oracular material reinterprets and modifies the message of the vision report. The message of the final text thus communicates a new message that is different from the message of its earliest layer.

First vision	There are good reasons to differentiate between the vision account (vv. 8–11), the initial angelic/divine words (vv. 12–13), and the later added oracular material. Read on its own, the first vision account provides a glimpse of the entrance to the Divine Council. YHWH's equine servants have just returned from their reconnaissance trips across the earth and they report to the Angel of YHWH that the whole earth is at peace. The material in vv. 12–13, 14–17 do not relate to the visual imagery of the vision at all. Instead they expand on and/or modify primarily the oral statement in v. 11. Verses 12–14aα (and probably also v. 17aβ–bβ)[61] *reinterpret* the last statement (v. 11) about the world-wide peace.[62] The divine oracles in Zech 1: 14–16 further build upon v. 11, as well as on the first layer of interpretation (vv. 12–14aα, 17aβ–bβ) and spell out their historical implications.

---

[59] Ibid., 65–77.
[60] Radine, *Amos in Emergent Judah*, 37–38.
[61] Cf. Wöhrle, *Frühe Sammlungen*, 326–32.
[62] Cf. Holger Delkurt, *Sacharjas Nachtgesichte: Zur Aufnahme und Abwandlung prophetischer Traditionen*, BZAW 302 (Berlin: de Gruyter, 2000), 55–56.

Third vision	There are good reasons to differentiate between the vision account (vv. 5–8a), the initial angelic/divine words (v. 8b), and the later added oracular material (v. 9). Read on its own, the third vision account speaks about measuring Jerusalem. The oracular material in vv. 8b and 9 provides *additional* information about the future situation in Jerusalem or, as Jeremias suggests, *corrects* the message of the vision account concerning his plans for Jerusalem. While the visionary impression in v. 6 betrays the hope of a steady plan and of safety behind walls, the oracle speaks of an increase of population and of future freedom and peace.[63]
Fourth vision	There are good reasons to differentiate between the vision account (vv. 1–5), the initial angelic/divine words (vv. 6–7), and the later added oracular material (vv. 8–10). Read on their own, vv. 1–5 describe how Joshua is made fit to perform the duties of the High Priest. The oral statement of the Angel of YHWH in vv. 6–7 *interprets* the preceding visual scene and, by assigning tasks to Joshua, seeks to give it practical relevance. The oracles in vv. 8a, 9 likewise *explain* the actions in vv. 1–5 as they connect Joshua's cleansing with the Day of Atonement. The even later material in vv. 8b and 10 transforms the original oracle from a political and cultic message into an eschatological prediction.[64]
Fifth vision	There are good reasons to differentiate between the vision account (vv. 1–6aα, 10b–14) and the later added oracular material (vv. 6aβ–10a). Read on its own, the fifth vision account speaks of God's omnipotence and omniscience, symbolized by the lamp-stand, the seven eyes (God's scouts), and the two olive trees (God's divine servants).[65] The two oracles in Zech 4:6aβ–10a *interpret* the surrounding vision account. In particular, they *identify* one of the "sons of oil" in v. 14 with Zerubbabel, and they encourage the reader to understand the image of the lamp-stand as symbolizing the temple.
Sixth vision	There are good reasons to differentiate between the vision account (vv. 1–2), the initial angelic explanation (v. 3), and the later added oracular material (v. 4). Read on their own, vv. 1–3 identify the scroll as the curse which is currently in the process of going out in order to deal with the thief and the perjurer who as yet are unpunished. The concluding oracle in v. 4 *changes the perspective* from present to past (הוצאתיה, perfect), it *adds details* about the divine origin of the scroll/curse (הוצאתיה, "I have sent it forth"), and it *clarifies* that "those swearing" (וכל הנשבע, v. 3) have in fact committed perjury (הנשבע בשמי לשקר, v. 4).

---

[63] Jeremias, *Nachtgesichte*, 167–69.
[64] Cf. Lena-Sofia Tiemeyer, "The Guilty Priesthood (Zech 3)," in *The Book of Zechariah and Its Influence*, ed. Christopher M. Tuckett (Aldershot: Ashgate, 2003), 1–19.
[65] Cf. Wolter H. Rose, *Zemah and Zerubbabel: Messianic Expectations in the Early Postexilic Period*, JSOTSup 304 (Sheffield: Sheffield Academic, 2000), 204–7.

| Eighth vision | There are good reasons to differentiate between the vision account (vv. 1–7), and the later added oracular material (v. 8). Read on their own, vv. 1–7 emphasize God's omnipotence and omniscience as he sends his executive servants along the north-south axis (v. 6). The concluding oracle in v. 8 *remodels* the horses' north-south movement into a mission only towards the north.[66] It is possible that this interpretative move was caused by the author's wish to assign a contemporaneous political significance to the horses' movement. |

COMPARISON

When we explore the relationship in Amos 7–8 and Zech 1–6 between (1) the account of the visual image, (2) the explanation of this imagery offered by the divine being responsible for showing the image, and (3) YHWH's concluding speech, we encounter significant affinity in terms of both structure and exegetical relationship. First, Amos's third and fourth vision account share the same form as Zechariah's first, third, fourth, and sixth vision account. In all six cases, we have a four-part structure:

1. The visual scene;
2. A dialogue between the seer and the one showing him the scene;
3. An initial explanation of the scene;
4. An additional statement, presented as YHWH's speech, which reinterprets either a select aspect of the visual scene or the initial explanation of that same scene.

This basic structure appears in modified forms also in Zechariah's fifth and eighth vision account. While these accounts do not contain any initial explanation of the visual scene, the imbedded (fifth account) and the concluding (eighth account) divine speeches reinterpret the visual scene to which they are attached.

These results, in turn, show that form-critical and redaction-critical considerations must go hand-in-hand. To note that most biblical vision reports in their final form contain a divine oracle and, on that basis, to conclude that the divine oracle forms an integral part of the vision report, or even that it is a defining feature of the genre of vision reports, does not show the whole picture. We need also to explore the *purpose* of this divine oracle. This divine oracle, in both Amos's and Zechariah's vision accounts, *reinterprets* either the visionary

---

[66] Cf. Michael H. Floyd, *Minor Prophets*, vol. 2, FOTL 22 (Grand Rapids: Eerdmans, 2000), 401, and Henning G. Reventlow, "Tradition und Aktualisierung in Sacharjas siebentem Nachtgesicht Sach 6,1–8," in *Alttestamentlicher Glaube und biblische Theologie: Festschrift für Horst Dietrich Preuß*, ed. Jutta Hausmann and Hans-Jürgen Zobel (Stuttgart: Kohlhammer, 1992), 188–89.

scene and/or the initial explanation of the scene. Furthermore, not every vision report contains a divine oracle, as attested by Amos's first and second account and by Zechariah's second and seventh account. We thus cannot speak of one *basic* vision-report-form that all vision reports in the Hebrew Bible share. Instead, there are multiple vision-report-forms, most of which feature one or more interpretative oracles but some of which do not.

JEREMIAH 1 AND 24

The three vision reports in Jeremiah (1; 24) present interesting comparative cases:

Textual Unit	Dialogue about the Visual Scene	Divine Speech
Jer 1:11–12	YHWH asks the seer what he sees and the seer describes the image (v. 11).	YHWH explains the meaning of the scene (v. 12).
Jer 1:13–19	YHWH asks the seer what he sees and the seer describes the image (v. 13).	YHWH explains the meaning of the scene (vv. 14, 15–16, 17–19).

Textual Unit	Visual Scene	Dialogue about the Visual Scene	Divine Speech
Jer 24:1–10	YHWH shows the seer an image (vv. 1–2).	YHWH asks the seer what he sees and the seer describes the image (v. 3).	YHWH speaks (vv. 4–10).

The first vision report in Jer 1:11–12 has a similar form to Amos's first and second account (Amos 7:1–3, 4–6). They present an image and the immediate explanation of that image.

The form of the second vision report in Jer 1:13–19 differs from the first one. Instead it resembles the form of Amos's third and fourth vision account in that there are multiple divine explanations of the same scene.[67] The image of the pot, the opening of which faces away from north (ופניו מפני צפונה, i.e. towards the south), emphasizes the threat of danger. In response, God offers several interpretations. The divine oracle in verse 14 declares, in line with the image, that evil will break out from the north upon all the inhabitants of land (i.e., Judah). The following verses 15–16 shift the focus slightly from Judah's fate to

---

[67] Behrens, *Visionsschilderungen*, 120–25, discusses the form-critical similarities between Jer 1:11–12 and 13–14, on the one hand, and Amos 7:7–8 and 8:1–2, on the other. Behrens's conclusion is different from mine because he refrains from including in his discussion Amos 7:9 and 8:3 and their relation to the immediately preceding vision account.

that of the kingdoms of the north. The focus shifts again in verses 17–19 to Jeremiah's prophetic role in this matter. In a sense, the oracular sayings in verses 15–16, 17–19 add information to God's initial speech in verse 14. This complementary character is not necessarily a sign of different and/or later authorship; rather it highlights the task of the oracles to exemplify, to render in concrete terms, and furthermore also to nuance the meaning of the initial visionary image. For instance, verse 15a, though its use of the term משפחות כל ממלכות צפונה, is suggestive of a threat from the northern kingdom Israel, while verse 16b makes it clear that the threat from the north in verses 13–14 in fact constitutes the attack of the Babylonians. It is possible that verse 15a forms one layer of interpretation of the visionary image, while verses 15b–16 form a second, later one, and verses 17–19 yet another one.[68]

The third vision report in Jer 24 attests to yet another type of vision-report-form. It features only one explanation of the visual imagery, yet this explanation stretched across six verses. In this respect, the vision report in Jer 24 brings Amos's fifth vision account to mind: one image and one extended and internally coherent explanation of that imagery. Verses 5–7 present the interpretation of the good grapes, while verses 8–10 present the corresponding interpretation of the bad grapes.[69]

Conclusion

After surveying the two sets of vision reports in the Book of the Twelve, and also comparing them with the set of three vision reports in Jeremiah, we are in a position to draw some conclusions.

1. A vision report nearly always includes some form of divine speech. YHWH utters this speech in most case; yet in a few cases this task is carried out by another divine being (Zech 1:12; 2:8a).
2. In several cases this initial divine speech is complemented by additional divine oracles. These oracles often do not relate to the visual imagery in the vision report, but instead elaborate on the interpretation given in the initial divine speech. These oracles further seek to specify, in concrete and historically anchored terms, the exact meaning of the vision. As such, these oracles often redefine and reinterpret the meaning of the original vision report. While the original report could support a wide variety of meanings, the oracles limit their inherent polyvalence.

---

[68] Cf. William L. Holladay, *Jeremiah*, vol. 1: *A Commentary on the Book of the Prophet Jeremiah: Chapters 1–25*, Hermeneia (Philadelphia: Fortress, 1986), 23–25.
[69] Ibid., 655–56.

3. In a few cases (Jer 1:13–19; Zech 1:12–17; 4:6aβ–10a) there are multiple oracles that each emphasizes a distinct interpretative angle of the preceding text.

From a form-critical perspective, it is incorrect to state that the biblical vision report has one overarching form where the divine oracle is a necessary and integral part. Rather, the biblical evidence displays at least four different constellations, characterized not only by their form but also by the interpretative relationship of the oracle to the visual image:

1. Vision reports without a divine oracle (Zech 5:5–11).
2. Vision reports with one short divine oracle.
   a. In some of these cases, the message of the oracle is intimately connected with the visual imagery (Jer 1:11–12; Amos 7:1–3, 4–6; Zech 2:1–4).
   b. In other cases, the link between the visual imagery and the message of the oracle is weak. The latter modifies and reinterprets the former (Zech 6:1–8).
3. Vision report with several divine oracles:
   a. Some cases feature an initial, short oracle with strong ties to the visual imagery, and subsequent longer oracles with weak ties to the visual image (Jer 1:13, 14, 15–16, 17–19; Amos 7:7–8a, 8b, 9; 9:1–2a, 2b, 3; Zech 1:8–11, 12–13 , 14–17; 2:5–8a, 8b, 9; 5:1–2, 3, 4).
   b. In one case (Zech 4), no oracle is closely connected with the visual imagery. The two existing oracles (4:6aβ–7, 8–10a) both display only weak ties to the visual imagery.
4. Visions with one long oracle:
   a. Jer 24:1–10 features one extended oracle, which is intimately connected to the visual imagery.
   b. Amos 9:1–4 features one extended oracle, which has only a weak link to the visual imagery.

There is no evidence to suggest that the vision-report-form without a concluding oracle is the earliest vision-report-form, which later developed into a more fully-fletched form with a (series of) concluding oracle(s). On the contrary, the data from the three textual corpora under examination demonstrate that both monarchic and post-monarchic texts attest to the same wide range of vision-report-forms. Moreover, the different forms co-exist in close textual proximity. Zech 1–6 employs four different forms, Amos 7–9 employs three, and Jer 1 employs two. In view of this "consistent variety" of vision-report-forms across time and literary collections, redaction-critical scholars need to tread carefully when appealing to form-critical arguments in order to determine the gradual growth of a given vision report. Rather, they need to focus more on the interpretative relationship between the visual imagery and the ensuing oracles.

On the positive side, form-critical considerations can shed significant light upon the impact that a vision report has upon its readers. The different types of vision-report-forms influence the readers of the final form in distinct ways. Put succinctly, a vision report without a concluding oracle will inevitably be read differently than a vision report with a concluding oracle. Fewer oracles will result in a more polyvalent final text, while a series of oracles will restrict the message of the final text to one or more interpretations and also anchor it to specific historical contexts.[70] For example, Zechariah's seventh vision account (Zech 5:5–11), which does not attest to a concluding oracle, is open-ended insofar as it can be interpreted in many different ways. A brief glance at the history of interpretation reveals a staggering lack of consensus. Does the seventh vision speak of social justice or idolatry? Is the *ephah* or the woman inside it its salient symbol? Does the *ephah* symbolize omniscience or guilt, and whose omniscience/guilt does it speak of? These are merely some of the many questions that exegetes have asked of Zechariah's seventh vision account.[71] In contrast, as discussed above, most readers of Zechariah's fifth vision account (Zech 4) will intuitively identify one of the two "sons of oil" (Zech 4:14) with Zerubbabel whom the oracular material in Zech 4:6aβ–10a refers to by name. Expressed differently, the two oracles in verses 6aβ–10a control the readers' interpretation of the images in the surrounding vision account and connect its message to the sixth century BCE. Moreover, the interpretations of the vision account found in the oracular material are treated as authoritative in the final form of the text. When readers approach a textual unit which consists of vision account + oracles, they expect a certain degree of cohesion.

Turning from the realm of readers to the realm of authors/redactors, the people responsible for the text had a choice whether to present the vision report on its own or accompanied by a series of oracles. Given the scarcity of the vision-report-form without an adjacent oracle, I suggest that the addition of an interpretative layer to any given vision accounts may have been a standard and accepted procedure. I might even go so far as to say that a later redactor would have understood it to be his obligation to add one or more interpretative oracles to any given vision account, in this way using the existing vision account as the hook upon which to hang the divine oracle that he wanted to convey.

---

[70] See further my discussion in "The Polyvalence of Zechariah's Vision Report," in Hayes and Tiemeyer, *"I Lifted My Eyes and Saw,"* 16–29.
[71] For a detailed discussion of these interpretative options, see Lena-Sofia Tiemeyer, *Zechariah and His Visions: An Exegetical Study of Zechariah's Vision Report*, LHBOTS 605 (London: T&T Clark, 2015).

5

Harrowing Woes and Comforting Promises in the Book of the Twelve

Carol J. Dempsey

INTRODUCTION: SETTING THE STAGE

Form criticism, one of several methods of biblical interpretation, enjoys a long history of scholarship, most notably from the time of Hermann Gunkel (1901) to the groundbreaking contributions of Ehud Ben Zvi (2003) and Martin Buss (2010).[1] This history of scholarship offers insights into the shifts taking place within the sphere of form criticism. With respect to prophetic literature, the focus of this article, classic form criticism focused on the historical milieu for the setting of a book, considered a prophet's life, pondered where proclamations took place, and looked at when a prophet was active and what position the prophet held in the community. This type of form criticism also tried to discern what texts were original units and what passages could be assigned to a specific prophet. Form criticism of this nature attempted to recreate both the general historical and social situation of the historical prophet. The approach to texts was often diachronic; the orientation to the texts was primarily historical.

---

[1] See Hermann Gunkel, *The Legends of Genesis*, trans. W. H. Carruth (Chicago: Open Court Publishing, 1901); Ehud Ben Zvi, "The Prophetic Book: A Key Form Of Prophetic Literature," in *The Changing Face of Form Criticism for the Twenty-First Century*, ed. Marvin A. Sweeney and Ehud Ben Zvi (Grand Rapids: Eerdmans, 2003), 276–97; and Martin J. Buss, *The Changing Face of Form Criticism: A Relational Approach*, ed. N. Stipe, HBM 18 (Sheffield: Sheffield Phoenix, 2010).

Unlike classic form criticism, the new form criticism takes as its starting point the text as it stands. This newer way has no interest in attempting to determine when various prophecies were originally written down. Newer form critics look at when a book was likely to have been collected and edited into a literary whole. Only then do these critics consider how a text or book functioned in relation to a theoretical community that, most likely, received, reread, and recopied a text. The new form criticism focuses on not only the readers and rereaders of the text but also the social settings in which texts would have been read.

Ben Zvi has chosen his rereaders of the text to be primarily those living during postexilic times, specifically during the Persian period, when the Judeans were resettling in the land. Ben Zvi, however, understands the texts' rereaders to be many different communities down through history such as the Early Church during the time of Paul, the church fathers and others during the Patristic Era, and also contemporary communities today who may tend to reread the texts from various postmodern perspectives which would include feminist, liberationist, and postcolonial perspectives, among others. With Ben Zvi, this study explores how the various woes and promises would have functioned among the ancient rereaders of these texts during the Persian Period, but then the study stretches the thought of Ben Zvi to include how the various texts function for contemporary rereaders today. The methodological approach to this study is holistic and synchronic; the orientation to the text is primarily literary.[2]

New form criticism takes into account the work of classic form criticism and moves it forward. One element common to classic and new form criticism is the study of genre, especially with regard to prophetic literature. Classic form criticism talked about the forms and genre of prophetic speech; new form criticism discusses the forms and genre of prophetic texts and prophetic literature. Classic form criticism focused on diachronic issues and thus identified woe proclamations as authentic prophecy and weal proclamations as later additions. This study stretches the traditional understanding of woe and weal and now understands woe to be anything that casts a judgment or a curse, and thus, anything that creates a negative and foreboding message that does or does not necessarily begin with הוי. Weal is anything that expresses promise and sheds a positive light on a situation. New form criticism looks at woe and weal

---

[2] For a full discussion on the development of form criticism see Colin M. Toffelmire, "Form Criticism" in *Dictionary of the Old Testament: Prophets*, ed. Mark J. Boda and J. Gordon McConville (Downers Grove, IL: InterVarsity and IVP Academic, 2012), 257–71; see also Ehud Ben Zvi, "Prophetic Book," 276–97; Michael H. Floyd, "Basic Trends in the Form-Critical Study of Prophetic texts," in Sweeney and Ben Zvi, *Changing Face of Form Criticism*, 298–311.

proclamations as they stand in a prophetic book as prophetic literature and then discerns their role and function not only in the book as a whole but also in the lives of various communities who read and reread these proclamations.

The Book of the Twelve contains many genres that help to give the various books their rich literary textures while shaping the books' profound theological statements. This essay examines the genres of woe[3] and promise (weal) as they appear in the texts of various minor prophets in order to shed light on (1) how these two genres contribute to the understanding of the various texts in which they appear; (2) how these two genres function rhetorically within their respective books; and (3) how these two genres contribute to the theological message of their respective books.

In the context of the Book of the Twelve, some books feature pericopes that are primarily woes as found in the books of Amos (5:18–27; 6:1–14) and Habakkuk (2:6–20). Other books feature pericopes that mix both woes and promises as in the books of Micah (2:1–13) and Nahum (1:12–15; 3:1–7). Although Zech 8:1–17 is primarily a pericope that features several promises, followed by a word of affirmation (8:20–23), the text is couched between a series of woeful pericopes that reflect Israel's past (7:1–14) and what will happen to Israel's enemies (9:1–8). Still other books feature pericopes that are just promises as found in the books of Hosea (1:10–11; 14:4–7), Joel (2:18–32), Zephaniah (3:14–20) and Haggai (2:10–19, 20–23). This study is structured so as to first look at the books that contain the aforementioned woe pericopes, then those books that mix woe and promise (weal) pericopes, and lastly those books that contain promise (weal) pericopes. Where the genres of woe and promise (weal) occur in the same book, the essay looks at the interplay of these two genres in a given book. Thus, this study is structured around woe pericopes, woe and promise (weal) pericopes, and promise (weal) pericopes as they appear in specific books within the Book of the Twelve. Given space constraints, this study is a selective one and not an exhaustive one; discussion on the various pericopes is, at times, uneven because of space constraints. Thus, pericopes chosen serve as models and are not the only examples of woe and promise (weal) contained in the Book of the Twelve.[4]

---

[3] For a more traditional and narrower discussion on the genre and function of woes in prophetic literature, see W. Janzen, *Mourning Cry and Woe Oracle*, BZAW 125 (Berlin: de Gruyter, 1972); Richard J. Clifford, "The Use of Hoy in the Prophets," CBQ 28 (1966): 458–64; James G. Williams, "The Alas-Oracles of the Eighth Century Prophets," HUCA 38 (1967) 75–91; and Erhard S. Gerstenberger, "The Woe-Oracles of the Prophets," *JBL* 81 (1962): 249–63 among others. These authors and texts consider woe pericopes to be only those that begin with הוי.

[4] A classic text that has not only influenced form criticism but also isolated some of the basic forms of prophetic speech in prophetic literature is the work by Claus Westermann, *Basic Forms of Prophetic Speech*, trans. Hugh C. White (Louisville: Westminster John Knox, 1991).

This study engages the thought of the new form criticism and takes as its starting point the texts as they stand in their "final form" of the prophetic books. With Ben Zvi, the study accepts that the texts are polyvalent, and that a very small intellectual elite group were involved in the composition, editing, reading, rereading, study, preservation, and transmission of these various prophetic texts and the books in which these texts appear. Ben Zvi identifies this elite group as the postexilic literati of Achaemenid Yehud who were probably living and working in Jerusalem.[5]

In addition to being culturally elite, this group would have had considerable religious and social authority. They produced documents, namely the prophetic books, that claimed to be "the word of YHWH" to enable themselves and later rereaders of the prophetic texts and books to understand their own past, present, and future in light of its divine revelation, this "word of YHWH."[6] Ben Zvi also makes clear that the basic genre of the prophetic books is revelation, an understanding that guides the study of the selected texts in this essay. This understanding of prophetic literature as "authoritative" served an important role in building and defining community and identity then and now.[7]

For the sake of making this essay accessible to a wide readership, the study uses the New Revised Standard translation of the Bible. Texts are approached synchronically and read holistically. In this way we discover that ancient prophetic texts that once informed and shaped ancient readers and communities still have the potential to be instructive and transformative for later and present day rereaders whose own insights and cultural realities pose new questions to the prophetic texts and books. This helps to move the entire prophetic tradition forward with new understandings that keep prophetic literature prophetic and revelatory today and deep into the future.

Harrowing Woes

Within the Book of the Twelve, a series of woes appears. These woes are directed not only toward Israel and Judah but also toward other nations as symbolized by the word against Nineveh. Collectively the woes reveal the people's various transgressions, their abuse of power, and nations' desire for supremacy on the geopolitical landscape. Life in ancient Israel and life lived in the context of the ancient Near Eastern world had its many challenges. The woes reflect and reveal some of Israel's past experiences. They teach invaluable lessons to Israel's postexilic communities who read and reread these texts while trying to reshape and redefine their lives after the trauma of the Exile. For later

---

[5] See Ben Zvi, "Prophetic Book," 294–95; Floyd, "Basic Trends," 303.
[6] Floyd, "Basic Trends," 303.
[7] Ben Zvi, "Prophetic Book," 296; Floyd, "Basic Trends," 304.

rereaders of the texts, the woes continue to generate new lessons as the texts are read in new social, political, and religious contexts and times. Thus, the woes function as warnings and lessons and provide readers with insights into how life should be lived in right relationship with God and with one another.

THE BOOK OF AMOS (AMOS 5:18–27; 6:1–14)

The book of Amos describes life in the first half of the eighth century BCE. Israel's king at that time was Jeroboam II (786–746 BCE). Judah's king was Uzziah (783–742 BCE). During Jeroboam II's reign, Egypt, Assyria, and Babylon were not yet formidable nations or threats to Israel. Jeroboam II had successfully subdued the Arameans who were Israel's most powerful enemy (2 Kgs 14:25–28). At this time, no strife existed between Israel and Judah. According to the world within the text, Israel during the first half of the eighth century BCE enjoyed a time of prosperity that brought with it, unfortunately, the exploitation of the poor and defenseless by the wealthy and the powerful. With a new economic order came excessive wealth for some Israelites, which, in turn, led to a leisured upper class, many of whom became involved in decadent lifestyles (2:8; 4:1; 6:1–6). Judicial corruption also took root (5:7–12) along with religious hypocrisy. Both woe proclamations capture the dynamic relationship that existed between God and God's people, and these proclamations teach invaluable lessons.

Two harrowing woe poems found in the book of Amos are Amos 5:18–27 and 6:1–14. Both proclamations speak of divine judgment that is about to befall the people of Israel because of their egregious injustices.

Amos 5:18–27, which focuses on the condemnation of the cultic leadership of Israel, is one of the most gut-wrenching texts in the entire book of Amos. Verses 18–20 describe the Day of the Lord[8] as a foreboding one filled with terror. The rhetorical question posed in verse 20 highlights the dreadful day. Verses 21–24 describe divine dissatisfaction with the Israelites' rituals (v. 21). Moreover, God rejects the people's burnt offerings, grain offerings, and well-being offerings (v. 22). God demands that all song and music to be silenced (v. 23) and then calls for justice and righteousness to roll down like waters and like an ever-flowing stream, respectively (v. 24). The speech concludes with a threat to exile the people to a place beyond Damascus. Because of their hypocrisy—their empty religious rituals that did not bespeak of right relationship and ethical

---

[8] The Day of the Lord (YHWH) is a motif that appears often throughout the prophetic literature (cf. Isa 2; Ezek 30: Joel 2; Zeph 1:14–18; 2:1–3). For further discussion on this motif, especially as it appears within Amos 5:18–27, see Marvin A. Sweeney, *The Twelve Prophets*, Berit Olam (Collegeville, MN: Liturgical Press, 2000), 238–39.

praxis on a daily basis—Amos's community will be made to suffer exile by the God of Israel.[9]

A second woe, Amos 6:1–14 features the prophet railing against those who are complacent in Zion and secure in Samaria (vv. 1–7). Although the text gives no mention of the economic status of these people, one could presume that the prophet is delivering a woe proclamation to the wealthy upper class of Israelite society (cf. 4:1, 4–7) that, by its complacent and self-indulgent attitude, allows violence to go unchecked (v. 3). Clearly, the elite have not used their power on behalf of justice (v. 4) and have made self-serving choices instead (vv. 5–6). Such choices will result in exile (v. 7) and the destruction of Jerusalem (v. 8). Verses 8–10 continue the sentiments of verses 1–7. The text features the prophet upbraiding the Israelites for their pride, a theme that continues in verses 11–14, where they stand condemned not only for turning justice into poison and righteousness into wormwood but also for taking pride in their own strength without due recognition of God's role in their recent successful military campaign (vv. 12b–13). Thus, the text portrays a group of Israelite people, most likely the political leadership of Israel and Judah, along with the elite, who are guilty of proud self-assertion and the perversion of justice who stand condemned by God and will fall prey to an enemy nation (v. 14).

GENRE, FUNCTION, AND INTENTION OF AMOS 5:18–27 AND 6:1–14. Amos 5:18–27 and 6:1–14 are two prophetic woes couched between a collection of proclamations concerning eight centers of Syria Palestine (1:3–2:16), three words to Israel (3:1–5:6, 8–9), five vision reports and two judgment speeches (7:1–9:10). These two woes serve as a warning to the Israelites of Amos' day. The woes foreshadow the horrific events about to befall the people if they do not change their ways. They point forward to a time of utter calamity (5:18–20) when Jerusalem will be delivered up (6:8), people will die (6:9), the wealthy elite will be toppled from their positions of privilege and power and then exiled (6:4–7), and an oppressive enemy nation, specifically the Assyrians (and then the Babylonians) will take control of the land (6:14).

The composers of these two woe texts, and other woe texts throughout the Book of the Twelve, were undoubtedly the literati who were addressing the elite among them. In the context of prophetic literature and the book of Amos as a whole, these two woes advance the book's central message that worship devoid of ethical praxis is meaningless and unacceptable, and that a lifestyle of self-

---

[9] In his article "'In God We Trust?' The Challenge of the Prophets" (*Ex Aud* 24 [2008]: 18–33), R. W. L. Moberly makes the point that "Integrity in public life is the *sine qua non* of true worship" (p. 22). Here, ethical praxis is linked to worship. Israel lacked not only ethical praxis in the social sphere but also fidelity to God in the religious sphere. Thus, the people stand condemned by their God.

indulgence and decadence on the part of a privileged few can lead to the demise of an entire community and everything that it holds as sacred. The woes also shed light on the function of a prophetic text and prophetic persona, both of which have the power (1) to awaken people out of their self-complacency; (2) to point out the corruption that exists within the human condition; and (3) to communicate YHWH's sentiments toward members of the community who are guilty of injustices. Finally, the two woes offer an instruction on the relationship that needs to exist between worship and ethical praxis, reveal the economic disparity that existed in the first half of the eighth century BCE make clear how the abuse of power and wealth can lead to the demise of a community, and underscore the point that Israel's God will not tolerate injustice. Consequences will occur for the failure to live in right relationship with God and with one another.

For those who would have read these texts in postexilic times when Israel was redefining itself as a community and reestablishing its relationship with God and with each other, Amos 5:18–27 and 6:1–14 point the way to a life of wholeness and holiness lived in right relationship. The day of the Lord is, then, a time when justice rolls down like waters and righteousness like an ever-flowing stream, when worship and ethical praxis go hand in hand, and when economic prosperity does not lead to self-indulgence and aggrandizement that turns justice into poison and the fruit of righteousness into wormwood (6:12). Thus, these two woes serve as a reminder to the elite within Israel's postexilic community (and later communities), that they have ethical responsibilities as members of a community called to be holy like the Holy One of Israel who desires justice and righteousness for all (5:24).

For contemporary rereaders of the text today, Amos 5:18–27 and 6:1–14 invite people to work for transformation of a global economy where the rich are getting richer and the poor getting poorer, and where some who are wealthy, with little concern for the needs of others, are becoming richer at the expense of the poor. Finally, these two texts reveal to readers then and now that the fate of the human community often rests in the hands of the community itself, especially in the hands of the powerful and wealthy who can either help transform the human condition or bring about its demise. One needs only to ponder the peril of the planet today to understand the full import of these two timeless texts that condemn the self-serving, self-centered lifestyles of the past that, unfortunately, continue to be part of today's global reality.

THE BOOK OF HABAKKUK (HAB 2:6–20)

The book of Habakkuk reflects the historical times of the seventh century BCE when the southern kingdom Judah and its inhabitants stood on the brink of ruin and exile and when the fall of Jerusalem and the destruction of the Temple were imminently on the horizon. During this time, Judah's greatest threat was the

Babylonians whom God, ironically, roused up against the Judahites (1:6). The Babylonians became God's means of chastising Judah for its injustices that included greed, extortion, theft, embezzlement, debauchery, and idolatry.

Habakkuk 2:6–20 contains five woes. Each of the woes offers a foreboding message. The recipients of these woes are not clear from the text. Possibilities include the Babylonians, Judahites, other foreign countries, or the wicked in general. The first four woes present a picture of how some people have used their power to benefit themselves at the expense of others (2:6–17). The fifth woe (2:18–20) condemns idolatry and is thus different from the other four woes.

The five woes appear in a taunt song (vv. 6b–20).[10] The first woe is a word of doom for robbers, thieves, embezzlers, and deceivers (vv. 6–8). The second woe is doom for exploiters and extortionists (vv. 9–11). The third woe condemns evil and violence (vv. 12–14). The fourth woe casts judgment on debauchery (vv. 15–17). Within this fourth woe, verse 16 uses a cup as a powerful metaphor. No doubt it is the cup of God's wrath (see Obadiah). Iniquity will not be the final word; justice will prevail. The fifth woe is different. People are upbraided for their trust in idols (vv. 18–20). Undergirding the expression of justice is the law of retaliation, *lex talionis*. Guilty parties will suffer the same harm they have incurred. The taunt song, in which these five woes appear, closes on an explanatory note: Israel's God is Lord of creation and history. This God is the ultimate power of the universe before whom all should remain silent in the presence of such awesomeness that resides in the Temple—in the heavenly abode and in Jerusalem, both of which are the "center" of all that exists.[11] Here silence is an expression of profound respect.

GENRE, FUNCTION AND INTENTION OF HAB 2:6–20. In the context of prophetic literature and the book of Habakkuk as a whole, this series of woes serves to inform those who have performed wicked deeds that, in fact, they will reap what they have sown. As they have acted wickedly, so shall they be the recipients of wicked deeds done to them as a form of restitution and divine chastisement. Harsh judgment will be meted out to those who have acted unjustly.

The five woes featured in the taunt song: (1) expose the graft that seems to have been a part of the fabric of life in the seventh century BCE; (2) point out that the unrestrained and abusive use of power is condemned; (3) make clear that the proud, the haughty, the wicked who achieve their status, wealth, and power at others' expense will themselves be brought low; and (4) reinforce the teaching that the crafting of and dependence upon idols is pointless since these

---

[10] The notion of a "taunt" (Hab 2:6a) usually refers to a song or poetic composition (see, e.g., Num 21:27–30; 1 Kgs 4:32; Ps 49:4; 78:2).

[11] The call for silence in the presence of God is also found in Ps 46:10; Zeph 1:7; and Zech 2:13.

gold and silver plated creations are devoid of Spirit and life and are thus nothing more than the mere artifacts made by human hands.

For those who would have read this text in postexilic times, Hab 2:6–20 clarifies how power and wealth are to be used, namely, for building up the common good which implies not taking advantage of other people or nations even when the opportunity arises or is with in one's power to do so. Readers are also encouraged and challenged to remain faithful to the God of Israel who remains at the center of all life—the still point that has the capacity to draw all into that abiding Presence which no other god can do.

For contemporary readers and rereaders of the text today, the five woes in Hab 2:6–20 serve as reminders that justice will prevail over injustice, that those who have achieved success through injustice will themselves become objects of derision. Rereaders learn that violence stands condemned down through the ages and that trusting in any kind of idols is foolish because in the end, all comes to naught.

HARROWING WOES AND COMFORTING PROMISES

Having looked at texts that feature harrowing woes in a pericope, focus now shifts to those passages that contain both a woe and a promise. Within the Book of the Twelve, and particularly in the books of Micah and Nahum, both the genres of woe and comfort are part of the books' literary fabric and help to flesh out the prophetic tradition. Even though a people may experience pain and suffering and live under threat, hope remains alive through divine promise. Restoration, liberation, and salvation are the final word and not destruction or annihilation. Harrowing woes give way to comforting promises that continue to unfold and move toward fulfillment down through the ages, in new times and circumstances, with new lessons still to be taught and learned by readers and rereaders of this ancient, ageless, and wondrous text.

THE BOOK OF MICAH (MIC 2:1–13)

As a literary work, the book of Micah can be divided into three sections: Mic 1–3, 4–5, and 6–7. The book describes the Israelite community during the latter half of the eighth century BCE during the reigns of Jotham (742–735 BCE), Ahaz (735–715 BCE), and Hezekiah (715–686 BCE). Even though the "story" of Mic 1–7 makes the prophet's career seem expansive, the prophet's activity was probably confined to the last quarter of the century during Hezekiah's reign. The book itself reflects a period in Israel's and Judah's history that was plagued by Assyrian military invasions. These invasions began with the Syro-Ephraimite War (734–732 BCE) and continued down through Sennacherib's invasion of Judah in 701 BCE. In the midst of such unrest, Judah did experience religious reforms and an economic revolution. These changes allowed the wealthy landowners to grow in prosperity at the expense of small peasant farmers. Thus, self-interest and self-serving endeavors on the part of the economically and socially powerful replaced concern for the common good.

The text of Mic 2:1–13, in which a woe is found (Mic 2:1–5), reflects the struggles and injustices of Micah's day (vv. 1–2, 8), asserts divine condemnation and judgment upon the abuse of power (vv. 3–7, 9–11), and features Israel's God as Lord of history taking charge of the situation to offer hope by means of divine power (vv. 12–13).

The woe in Mic 2:1–5 opens the second chapter of the book and forms the basic pattern of a prophetic judgment speech. Verses 1–2 lay out the crimes that some within the community are guilty of doing, and verses 3–5 describe the consequences for having committed such crimes. The main crime is the unjust confiscation of land. In ancient Israel, land ownership played a key role. It was foundational to people's security, wealth, and prosperity. Ancient Israelite law protected a person's or family's right to own and inherit land. Other laws governed the right to transfer land to people outside of the family. Sabbatical and jubilee laws also protected the land as well as debts that involved the land. Thus, to covet and seize another's field (v. 2) is a serious offense.[12] Verses 3–5 outline the consequences for having done such an egregious injustice. This announcement of judgment features a proclamation of intended chastisement (v. 3), a prediction of disaster (v. 4), and a threat (v. 5). Here the text depicts God as a schemer of actions that are going to take place to "get even" with those who have transgressed others. Those who have taken land will lose their fields (v. 4) and will be banned from any further acquisition of property (vv. 6–11).

Verses 6–11 are a disputation speech. The verses describe the strained relationship that exists between God and some Israelites because of their smug attitude (v. 6) and their deeds of injustice (vv. 8–9). Verse 8 adds a new transgression to the list already begun in verses 1–2. Some people are guilty of acting with hostility, like an enemy, against their own people. These guilty parties stand accused of stripping the robe from the peaceful. The act of taking another's cloak is also a serious offense and represents a violation of Israel's own social law and a disregard for God's commands (Exod 20:17; 22:26–27).[13] Verse 9 expands the crimes cited in verse 2. Now the powerful ones within the community evict women from their homes and deprive children of their "glory" which refers to their inheritance, a reference to land. Expulsion from the land is the punishment for such treachery. Hence, the people's ill-gotten land will

---

[12] For further discussion on Mic 2:1–2 and the topic of land, see Marvin A. Sweeney, "Micah," in *The Twelve Prophets*, 359–60. Additionally, the Torah forbids the coveting of land (see Exod 20:17; 34:24; Deut 5:21).

[13] According to Israelite social law, if a cloak is taken in pawn from a neighbor, then it must be restored before sunset since it would be needed as a covering during the night (see Exod 22:26–27).

provide no resting place for the guilty. The land has become unclean, defiled by the guilty party's wickedness (see Lev 18:24–25). The prophecy closes on a note of sarcasm, which is God's final response to the objection raised by the opponents in verse 6 who do not want to hear an honest word proclaimed.

The message changes in verses 12–13 which is a comforting promise, a word of future salvation. These verses promise divine care to the exiled ones of the remnant of "Jacob." Here "Jacob" does not refer to the northern kingdom; instead, "Jacob" refers to Judah as the remnant of Israel.

GENRE, FUNCTION, AND INTENTION OF MIC 2:1–13. Micah 2:1–13 is part of a larger unit—Mic 1–3—that, for the most part, outlines the transgressions and injustices of some members within the Israelite community. Micah 2:12–13 is a word of hope—a comforting promise—in the midst of a judgment speech (1:2–7), a dirge-lament (1:8–16), a woe (2:1–5), a disputation prophecy (2:6–11), a biting address to Israel's political leadership (3:1–4), a statement concerning Israel's prophets (3:5–7), a statement of confidence (3:8), and a second address to Israel's leadership (3:9–12). Thus, at the heart of the foreboding message presented in Mic 1–3 is this message of hope, this comforting promise (2:12–13).

In the context of prophetic literature and the book of Micah as a whole, and Mic 2:1–13, the woe of Mic 2:1–5 helps to solidify the book's central theme: injustice will not be tolerated; consequences will be meted out. The woe draws attention to the misuse and abuse of power on the part of those who are in positions of power within the community who, because of their injustices, are destined themselves to lose everything, and in particular, their own ill-gotten land to forces greater than themselves. Thus Mic 2:1–5 serves as an expression of support for social ethics within the community.

The promise in Mic 2:12–13 is couched between a disputation prophecy (Mic 2:6–11) and a biting address to Israel's political leadership (3:1–4). In the context of Mic 1–3, Mic 2:12–13 is the only passage that offers any sense of hope and comfort. In the context of the book as a whole, this comforting promise points forward to Mic 4–5, a proclamation of future restoration that features another promise (Mic 4:6–5:14) and anticipates one further promise in Mic 7:11–13. Together, the harrowing woe of Mic 2:1–5 and the comforting promise of Mic 2:12–13 capture the ebb and flow of the book's fabric that moves back and forth between judgment and hope, with promise being at the heart of the prophet's message (2:12–13 in Mic 1–3; 2:12–13 in relation to Mic 4:1–5:14 in Mic 1–7; and 2:12–13 in relation to Mic 7:11–13, the book's final chapter). The powerful who use their power for ill gain will be defeated; ruin and chaos will occur, giving way to promise and restoration by a God who will cast all sins into the depths of the sea, and who will show compassion, faithfulness, and unswerving loyalty to an Israelite community living under divine threat and divine promise like its ancestors of old (7:18–20).

For the literati composers of Mic 2:1–13, these two genres serve (1) to reveal to readers and later rereaders the function of the prophet and prophetic literature which was not only to expose transgression but also to provide hope; (2) to show that hope did and does exist for those who remain(ed) faithful; (3) to make known to primary and later readers that God is ultimately the one in power who, as king over all, did and will continue to lead the people out of exile (see Isa 45:1–7).

For those who would have read this text in postexilic times, Mic 2:1–13 and especially verses 1–5 and verses 12–13, functions as an instruction: if one chooses to use power inappropriately, then one more powerful, namely the God of Israel, will assert divine power to destroy all that has been gained unjustly. Readers, and especially those among the elite social and economic classes, are forewarned about retributive justice: what goes around comes around. Furthermore, they are instructed in the reliability of God's word and learn that injustice will not be tolerated. They are called to live a life of justice and righteousness—to respect what belongs to others in the community, and if they enjoy positions of power, then those positions are to be used to safeguard the property and well being of others in the community so that all may live securely in the land and in right relationship with their God whose promise to free those exiled has already been partially fulfilled. The postexilic community themselves are the living testament to the certainty of God's divine promise made centuries earlier. Finally, the woe and promise reveal the world of the past, one that has been mired by transgression, and the world of the future in the here and now, one that is full of hope with life being lived in the presence of God.

For contemporary readers and rereaders of Mic 2:1–13, the text becomes an instruction on human and divine power and how, in the end, justice on behalf of the disenfranchised, inclusive of women and children, will ultimately rule the day. Finally, the text reveals that divine promise of salvation and hope is meant for those who have suffered unjustly at the hands of others. God does and will act on behalf of those people who survive perilous situations. Israel's God is a God of liberation who is both pastoral and regal and who remains faithful to the divine word uttered.[14]

THE BOOK OF NAHUM (NAH 1:12–15; 3:1–7)

Like the book of Micah, the book of Nahum contains both a woe (3:1–7) and a promise (1:12–15). The promise, however, occurs before the woe. The promise concerns good news for Judah; the woe, part of a larger proclamation (3:1–17), describes what is about to befall Nineveh, the primary concern of the book. Nineveh falls to the Babylonians and the Medes in 612 BCE. The book as a

---

[14] For further discussion on Mic 2:1–13, see Ehud Ben Zvi, *Micah*, FOTL 21b (Grand Rapids: Eerdmans, 2000), 41–70.

whole offers a word of peril to Assyria and particularly to Nineveh and its inhabitants, and a word of hope and consolation to Judah who has long endured the injustices and oppression of Assyria, Judah's enemy nation. Historically, Assyria ruled by brute force and gained power in the region by exacting heavy tributes, deporting entire populations of people, and permitting no compromise or repudiation of treaties. Assyria became known as the lion of the ancient Near East. Assyria's leaders were fearless: Tiglath-pileser III (745–727 BCE) conquered Israel; Sargon II (721–705 BCE) and Sennacherib (705–681 BCE) made Judah a vassal state; and Ashurbanipal (668–627 BCE) devastated Thebes in Egypt and burned Babylon. When Ashurbanipal dies in 627 BCE, coalitions of Medes and Babylonians sought revenge against Assyria. In 612 BCE the armies of these countries took Nineveh by force and destroyed it. With the destruction of Nineveh came the eventual collapse of the Assyrian Empire. The woe in Nah 3:1–7 and the promise in Nah 1:12–15 were written in such a way so as to capture the sentiments and events of Nahum's day.

In Nah 1:12–15, the promise opens with a prophetic messenger formula "Thus says the Lord" which lends authority to the text. Judah receives good news (vv. 12–13); the Assyrians receive ominous news (vv. 14–15). Verse 14 is a specific address to the king of Assyria. To liberate the Judahites, God promises to destroy the Assyrian ruler, Ashurbanipal, his lineage, and his gods. The Assyrians and their king will be humiliated; their trusted gods will come to nothing.

Nahum 3:1–7 shifts the picture from promise to woe.[15] Featuring a variety of literary techniques, Nah 3:1–7 describes the imminent and the inevitable ruin of Nineveh, the city of bloodshed whose nakedness will be exposed to the nations. Nineveh will be made to suffer at the hands of its enemy nations because of the city's (and nation's) many crimes. The woe in verses 1–3 conveys a sense of warning regarding an impending invasion by an enemy nation. Marvin Sweeney notes that:

> The initial woe address implicitly levels an accusation against Nineveh. By referring to it as "city of bloodshed, utterly deceitful, full of booty—no end to the plunder." Insofar as the "woe" statement is an address form, the prophet thereby effectively accuses Nineveh of murder, dishonesty, and theft.[16]

---

[15] On the use of הוי in this passage, Duane L Christensen notes that "though *hoy* is the common cry of mourning heard in funeral processions it no longer represents lamentation for the dead in prophetic usage, particularly in this context. An ominous cry of 'woe' ... which presents Nineveh as 'the city of bloodshed' ... functions at the same time as an ironic announcement of the certain death that Nineveh faces." See Christensen, *Nahum*, AB 24F (New Haven: Yale University Press), 334.

[16] Sweeney, "Nahum," *Twelve Prophets*, 442.

The images in verses 2–3 capture the gruesomeness of warfare as a conquering army rushes through the streets of Nineveh, eventually overtaking it. Verses 4–7 list the reasons for Nineveh's downfall and the profound humiliation it will experience at the hand of God.[17]

GENRE, FUNCTION, AND INTENTION OF NAH 1:12–15 AND 3:1–7. The promise and woe in the book of Nahum serve to advance the book's overarching theme, namely, that one nation is not to lift up a sword against another nation, and if such a situation does occur, then the conquering nation will endure grave consequences from Israel's God who is sovereign over all.

Through the use of these two genres, the literati composers of Nah 1:12–15 and 3:1–7 reveal to their readers that Judah's earlier suffering and loss were divinely orchestrated (1:12); that Israel's God was responsible for liberating Judah from its yoke and bonds;[18] and that any people who oppresses another people will not be victorious. They will be a people forgotten, cut off, destined for the grave, and considered worthless. A powerful people, once feared, will be put to shame, treated with contempt, and brought low without any comfort. The story of the demise and fall of Nineveh, the city of bloodshed, becomes a symbol of depravity and the poster child for the strength of God's power.

For those who would have read Nah 1:12–15 and 3:1–7 in postexilic times, the promise and the woe function as an instruction on God's sovereign power. This God will not tolerate apostasy, idolatry, injustice of any kind, and especially the inordinate use of power and politics by one people used to suppress another people. The God of Israel will act on behalf of the oppressed to level the playing field in an attempt to establish peace among the nations (cf. Isa 2:1–5; Mic 4:1–5). The passages also function to remind the Judahites and Israelites who are reestablishing their community that even though they live under the threat from other nations, they also live, ultimately, under divine promise which is being fulfilled in their midst.

For contemporary readers and rereaders of Nah 1:12–15 and 3:1–7, the texts point out the folly of the assertion of human power over others, and that the quest for supremacy ultimately leads to he demise of a people and a nation. Furthermore, even though a people and a nation may experience oppression at the hands of another, such an experience will not be one that lasts forever. Liberation will come in time—a divine promise made and a prophetic word that will come to pass, all symbolized by the demise of the great and powerful "Nineveh."

---

[17] For further discussion on the rich imagery in Nah 3:1–7, see ibid. 442–44 and Michael H. Floyd, "Nahum," in *Minor Prophets, Part 2*, FOTL 22 (Grand Rapids: Eerdmans, 2000), 69–70.

[18] The oppressor who had Judah in yoke and bonds may refer to either Assyria that opposed Israel with the rod and staff (see Isa 10:5–34) or to Babylon (see Jer 27–28).

THE BOOK OF ZECHARIAH (ZECH 7:1–9:8)[19]

The superscription of the book of Zechariah indicates that the book was set in the second and fourth years of the reign of King Darius of Persia (522–486 BCE). Similar to the historical times of Haggai, this timeframe is when the construction of the second Temple had begun. The book presents an account of Zechariah's visions concerning the significance of the temple's reconstruction and points to a time when the corrupt shepherds, that is, the Persian monarchs, will be removed so that Israel's God can become sovereign over all nations, and indeed, over the entire cosmos.

The book of Zechariah contains both words of woe and words of promise.[20] In Zech 7:1–9:8, the interplay between woe and promise becomes apparent. Zech 7:1–14 can be divided into two units: verses 1–7 and verses 8–14. In verses 1–7, Zechariah poses a question about mourning and practicing abstinence that has been practiced for many years past. The response that God gives to Zechariah is a reminder that past fasts were self-centered and self-serving. Carol L. Meyers and Eric M. Meyers rightly observe that:

> The prophetic answer redirects the question. It is not a matter of should you or shouldn't you fast. Rather, the issue is one of recognizing what that fasting and its complement, the feasting, have accomplished in the seventy years. At this critical moment, with local authority and quasi-autonomy being reestablished, and with the seventy years of destruction nearly at an end, the emphasis on awareness of continuity with the preexilic state offers support and encouragement to those for whom self-rule is without the revival of a Davidic monarchy might be difficult to conceptualize and accept. The prophet thus reminds them that they have been behaving in certain public ways, to their own benefit in sustaining community identity, even without dynastic rule or temple focus. The people had inaugurated fasts in response to certain events. Yahweh had not commanded the people to fast nor would he tell them to stop fasting: God was not the beneficiary of such acts.[21]

Verses 8–14 are largely a retrospective message of woe that recalls the plight of those who have acted unjustly in the past. First a word of divine advice is offered (vv. 8–10) followed by a divine statement of Judah's disobedience and God's punitive action against the unruly people. These two messages set the stage for the promises that follow in Zech 8:1–23.

---

[19] With Marvin Sweeney, I read Zech 7:1–14:21 as a literary unit that contains the "Pronouncements of Zechariah of which Zech 7:1–9:8 is a part." See Sweeney, "Zechariah," *Twelve Prophets*, 634–36.
[20] See, e.g., Zech 9:9–15; 10:3–12; 13:7–9 for additional words of promise.
[21] See Carol L. Meyers and Eric M. Meyers *Haggai, Zechariah 1–8*, AB 25B (New Haven: Yale University Press, 2004), 394.

Zechariah 8:1–23 features several promises. These promises make certain God's ultimate promise which is to restore God's relationship with Jerusalem and Judah characterized by: (1) God's return to Zion and dwelling in the midst of Jerusalem (v. 3); (2) the return of the full flourishing of life and community to Jerusalem's streets (vv. 4–5); (3) a divine recommitment to covenant on the part of God and all people inclusive of all who have been exiled and scattered and not just those who have and will be resettled in the land (vv. 7–8); (4) the flourishing of the land which will produce an abundance for the people to enjoy (v. 12); and (5) the transformation of the people from being a curse among the nations to being a blessing among them (v. 13). All of this good fortune is promised to God's people as long as they live in right relationship with their God and especially with one another (vv. 16–17). Fasting will turn into feasting (vv. 18–19), and many peoples from many nations will come to seek the God of Israel, the Lord of hosts, who dwells, once again, in Jerusalem (vv. 20–23). Within the book as a whole, the promises of restoration offer hope and set the stage for later additional divine pledges and promises.[22]

The tone quickly changes in Zech 9:1–8. Words of promise give way to words of peril. These verses are a judgment upon Israel's enemy nations who will experience God's wrath. The news is ominous for Israel's neighboring nations but good for Israel. Israel's God will once again come to Israel's aid against injustice (v. 8).

GENRE, FUNCTION, AND INTENTION OF ZECH 7:1–9:8. For the literati who composed Zech 7:1–9:8, the genres of woe and promise served as an instruction to help inform their postexilic readers of the text about how they should live their lives. The texts also offer an instruction on the fullness of what was divinely promised which included not only the rebuilding of the Temple but also the restoration of Jerusalem, the land, covenant, and even the people themselves. Through the use of promise, the composers of the text are able to assure their readers that God's presence is among them and that God's intentions are being communicated through the prophet whose word is to be taken authoritatively. For those reading Zech 8:1–17 in postexilic times, the promises contained in these verses should become the motivating factor to live a life of justice and righteousness as proscribed in verses 16–17. The promise of restoration also communicates to them God's desire for "a new day" when divine chastisement and punishment will be an experience of the past and not become an experience of this new community being reconstituted. For contemporary readers and rereaders of Zech 7:1–9:8, the recalling of past experiences serve as a warning of dire consequences when one does not live in right relationship with God and with one another. The promises, however, shed light on how wondrous life can

---

[22] See, e.g., Zech 9:9–17 and 10:1–12.

be when a people, a community heeds the ways of God who longs to bless them abundantly.[23]

Comforting Promises

Having considered sample passages that contain both the woe and promise genre, focus now shifts again but this time to comforting promises. Within the Book of the Twelve, a series of promises complement the series of woes. These promises offer readers then and now a sense of hope while revealing the ultimate vision of the Divine that is for the restoration and transformation of all life on the planet. As a genre, the promises served as reminders of God's fidelity to the human condition and became sources of hope in the midst of trials and traumas. For later readers and rereaders of the texts, the promises continue to be a source of hope while challenging people to remember that the source of all life continues to be present even when that Presence is least felt or experienced. We have only to wait for our efforts to be brought to completion and the Divine promise to be brought to fruition "on that day."

The Book of Hosea (Hos 1:10–11; 14:4–7)

The rise of the Assyrian Empire in the mid-eighth century is the historical backdrop to the book of Hosea. The text reflects the time following the death of Jeroboam II and the days just prior to the Assyrian assault in 735–732 BCE. The book's primary focus is on the religious state of affairs of Israel and Judah. The text also reveals that life during the mid-eighth century BCE was fraught with idolatry, apostasy, and a myriad of transgressions.

The book of Hosea features two promises. The first one, Hos 1:10–11, appears between two judgment speeches against Israel (1:2–9 and 2:1–13). Here the countless or measureless "sand of the sea" is a common image for abundance in the Old Testament (see, e.g., Gen 41:49; Josh 11:4; Judg 7:12; 1 Sam 13:5; 1 Kgs 4:20).[24] The second promise occurs toward the end of the book in Hos 14:4–7 and is situated between a divine plea (14:1–3), a divine confession (14:8), and the book's epilogue (14:9).

In the context of the book of Hosea as a whole, the first promise functions as a word of hope and a reminder to the Israelites that all of the impending disasters they are about to experience on account of their apostasy, idolatry, and waywardness will not be the final lot of the community. Israel's God will not break covenant. Israel's and God's estrangement from each other will eventually be reversed, and someday a new kingdom will emerge, one that combines both

---

[23] For an excellent synchronic discussion on Zech 9:1–8, see Paul L. Reddit, *Zechariah 9–14*, IECOT (Stuttgart: Kohlhammer, 2012).
[24] See J. Andrew Dearman, *The Book of Hosea*, NICOT (Grand Rapids: Eerdmans), 104.

the northern kingdom Israel and the southern kingdom Judah. Covenant renewal will happen.

The second promise, Hos 14:4–7, gives the people of the day a reason to return to God (14:1–3) and assures the people of God's tender love for them and God's compassion that will become the impetus for their healing. Despite all of the people's transgressions heard throughout the book of Hosea, God's people are still desirable to their God and worthy of their God's enduring healing, restorative love. Thus, these two promises are words of hope for people who are soon to lose everything and serve as a word of encouragement to return to their God, which is one of the book's central themes.

GENRE, FUNCTION, AND INTENTION OF HOS 1:10–11 AND 14:4–7. Through the use of these two promises, the literati who composed the book of Hosea reveal to their readers the importance of remembering God's steadfast love despite human waywardness. For later readers and rereaders of the text in postexilic times and down through the centuries into contemporary times, these two promises reveal who Israel's God was and is: the sustainer, nurturer, and transformer of life who offers hope to all, who remains faithful to all, and who heals and restores not only human life but also the natural world.

THE BOOK OF JOEL (JOEL 2:18–32)

Most scholars date the composition of the book of Joel to postexilic times, a period that involved many challenges and struggles for the returnees of the exile who were now reconstituting their life in Judah. The book of Joel reflects two important events in the life of the community at this time: (1) the threat to the land by the invasion of the locust (1:2–20) and (2) the threat to the community itself by enemy invasion (2:1–14). The rest of the text records God's response to the people (Joel 2:15–20); offers a word of reassurance to both nature and the people (Joel 2:21–3:8); and records the prophet's call to the nations to gather for judgment because Israel's God is about to carry out the divine promise to restore the land and the nation (Joel 3:9–21).

Joel 2:18–32, part of two larger units (2:15–20 and 2:21–3:8) is a promise in response to a divine call to have the people return (2:12–14) and the prophet's call to lament (2:15–17). The promise describes all the wonderful things that God will do on behalf of the people, the land, the animals, and the fauna. The grand promise is compelling that ends with the intended outpouring of God's Spirit upon all flesh and the salvation of all who call upon God's name (2:28–32).

GENRE, FUNCTION, AND INTENTION OF JOEL 2:18–32. In the context of the book of Joel as a whole, the genre of promise found in Joel 2:18–32 centers the people on and in their God despite the threat of locusts and enemy nations. For those literati who composed the text, this promise served as a means to bolster the spirit and will of the postexilic community and to reveal to them that in spite of all threats, their God was in their midst and would respond positively to their efforts of lament. The promise also teaches the value of remaining faithful to God who in turn will remain faithful to the people. For the postexilic community reading this text, the promise offers a foundation for their lives, a reason to return to their God, and a hope for future days. The promise also reveals God's graciousness and benevolence toward them—the faithful remnant—and the natural world, both living under the threat of invasion. For contemporary readers and rereaders of Joel 2:18–32, the promise functions as a reminder that even in the midst of terrifying threats to one's life and livelihood, God's promise of sustainability and ongoing transformation of life through God's Spirit remains constant.

THE BOOK OF ZEPHANIAH (ZEPH 3:14–20)

The book of Zephaniah reflects the time of the Babylonian crisis just prior to the fall of Jerusalem in 587 BCE. The overall tone of the book is foreboding with its proclamation of judgment and imminent disasters (1:2–2:15), its statement of reproach against Jerusalem (3:1–7), and its statement of impending punishment and eventual purification of both the nations and God's people (3:8–13). Yet, the book is not without a vision of hope, a word of promise (3:14–20).

The last part of the book of Zephaniah is a promise (3:14–20) that functions as a word of hope, salvation, and restoration, to a people on the brink of exile who are about to lose their land, their kingdom, their temple, and their God's Holy City, Jerusalem. The God who condemned Judah and who is about to make the Judahites suffer at the hands of an enemy nation, the Babylonians, will in time remove disaster from among the people, will deal with the Judahites' oppressors, and will return the people to their land and restore their fortunes. The promise foreshadows the end of the Babylonian exile and the return of the Judahites to their land.

GENRE, FUNCTION, AND INTENTION OF ZEPH 3:14–20. For the literati composers of Zeph 3:14–20, this genre of promise functioned to remind their community that divine chastisement and purification have as their ultimate purpose the restoration of a people, one to another, and a people's restoration to their God and to the land. The promise becomes the impetus for praising God who has restored the people to their land and who waits to give further blessing and victory to the postexilic community that is so loved by God. For the postexilic community reading Zeph 3:14–20, this promise is a testament to God's word already being fulfilled in their lived experience. This promise bolsters their confidence in God, reassures them of God's presence, and reminds them of God's protective love. For contemporary readers and rereaders of the text, the promise functions as a word of hope for all who have endured suffering and trauma. Better days are on the horizon because the God of all remains in the midst of all and will continue to act positively on their behalf.[25]

THE BOOK OF HAGGAI (HAG 2:10–19; 2:20–23)

According to its superscription, the book of Haggai is set in 520 BCE, the second year of the reign of King Darius. This year marks the construction of the second Temple in Jerusalem begun under Zerubbabel ben Shealtiel, governor of Judah, and Joshua ben Jehozadak, the high priest. The central focus of the book is the building of the temple that the prophet Haggai insists is God's will. Two significant promises that appear in the text are 2:10–19 and 2:20–23, among others. These promises constitute the third and final part of the book. Haggai 2:10–19 describes God's promise of fecundity to the land. Haggai 2:20–23 describes God's promise of kingship to Zerubbabel. In the context of the book as a whole, these two promises function as the conclusion to the book. Hope is the prophet's final word. Furthermore, the prophet is the one who, acting in accord with God, has the task of bringing good news. Here the recipients of this good news are the community members themselves (2:19) and Zerubbabel (2:23). Finally, these two promises delivered by Haggai further attest to the dialogic relationship that God has with Haggai who acts in service if God's word (1:1–2:9).

GENRE, FUNCTION, AND INTENTION OF HAG 2:10–19 AND 2:20–23. For the literati who used the genre of promise, Hag 2:10–19 and 2:20–23 enabled them to communicate to the postexilic community that the prophet Haggai was indeed doing and saying all that God had commanded him to do and say with respect to the rebuilding of the Temple. These texts help to prove to the people that God's word was divinely revealed to Haggai and is thus reliable, and that the rebuilding of the Temple was divinely ordained. For those reading these texts in postexilic times, these two promises function to confirm God's active role in the rebuilding of the Temple and that, in fact, this second Temple is an edifice divinely willed and divinely inspired. The texts offer a word of hope: not only will the temple be rebuilt but also the monarchy will be reestablished someday as well. Both promises serve to move the Temple restoration project forward. The promises also help to garner support from the community for this building project. For contemporary readers and rereaders of these two texts, the promises function to show that God's word can be a source of inspiration to move persons

---

[25] For an excellent study on the book of Zephaniah, see Adele Berlin, *Zephaniah*, AB 25 (New Haven: Yale University Press, 2007). Berlin notes that Zeph 3:14–20, the last section of the book, "marks a reversal of previous parts.... God the destructive warrior is now the protector; the searching out for purposes of punishment turns into the gathering in for renewal. Fortunes are restored" (p. 148).

and a community forward, and that the spirit of God remains active, restorative, and transformative independent of religious and political institutions.

CONCLUSION

Within the Book of the Twelve, the genres of woe and promise play a significant role in the books in which they appear and in the life of the communities who read and reread these texts in different contexts down through the ages. Each woe and promise adds to the overall theme and intention of the various prophetic books, and each woe and promise when heard in different contexts offers insights into the ways and vision of God and what the divine hope is for all people. Together, the woe and promise genres provide a window into the dynamism of the human-divine relationship that existed in ancient Israel and that continues to exist today. Seeing the woe and promise genres and texts through the lens of the new form criticism allows readers and rereaders of the text to appreciate and critique the times that the texts reflect, to see the ways in which these texts functioned in different communities that read and reread them, and to discover how these ancient texts can continue to take on a life of their own in new contexts so that they can inform, instruct, challenge, and nourish the lives of those who encounter their messages today.

Finally, reading these texts from the perspective of the new form criticism also reminds readers that the biblical text is theologically, politically, historically, and ideologically conditioned. Thus, the work of the new prophet is to reread the biblical text, especially the prophetic texts, not only in dialogue with the newer methods of biblical inquiry but also in dialogue with the many communities that continue to read and reread these texts in new contexts. The genres of woe and promise, when heard in new contexts, offer the possibility of helping communities today to articulate a new social ethic for the full flourishing of all life on the planet. These two genres also beckon communities today to live in right relationship with one another and with the Divine Source of all life whose Spirit waits to inform, inspire, and transform. Like the communities of old, many human and nonhuman communities today have lived through and will continue to live through crises and traumas, especially natural disasters, military conflicts, and wars. Furthermore, many communities are now faced with having to redefine life in relation to the main crisis facing the planet today—global climate change. Thus, the prophetic woe genre remains ever important but so does the word of promise that provides hope and vision for all if only we humans, we readers and rereaders of the biblical text, are willing to ponder those texts of promise and make choices that lead to their fulfillment.

6

Twelve (and More) Anonyms: A Biblical Book without Authors

Erhard S. Gerstenberger

PRELIMINARIES

Research in various text-groups and topics of the Book of the Twelve over the past decades has sufficiently made clear, that the bulk of texts is of redactional origin and that most of the biographical information about assumed authors is of little historical weight. Thus superscriptions ostensibly giving family genealogies of prophetic preachers and/or references to their contemporaneous kings clearly come from retrospective organizers of the literary heritage. And "biographical" narration, as presumably found in Amos 7, Hos 1–3, and Jonah quite likely contains very few brute facts which could be used to reconstruct the life and mission of any of the "minor" prophets. In fact, even the best known "greater" messenger of Yahweh, Jeremiah, comes along as a largely fictitious figure whose historical profile remains in the dark. In the case of the Twelve we also must concede the possibility that at least two of them, Obadiah and Malachi, seem not to represent real persons at all but the generic titles "servant of Yahweh" and "my messenger," respectively.

Given this overall picture of the state of our knowledge we should seriously consider letting go of that nineteenth century mania to interpret prophetic words in intimate connection only with their presumed authors. Ferdinand Deist, among others, long ago proposed a necessary "paradigm switch" in Old

Testament research.[1] The former model imagined prophetic books with "authors," gradually revised and edited until they formed a "canonical" body of literature to provide general readers with written information. This may be a misleading preconception that does justice neither to the quality and purpose of ancient traditions nor to insights gained in our times concerning the genesis and use of literature in other cultural epochs. Alternatively, what could be more plausible than considering the bulk of biographical information within the Twelve as a very last redactional step to organize this considerable assemblage of quite different texts? We would then consequently try to understand the growth of this particular tradition in terms of an anonymous assemblage of compositions intended for communal use rather than private reading.

CLUSTERS OF COLLECTED GENRES

According to modern insights prophetic words rarely reached their literary embedding in isolation (Jer 26:18 may be just a quotation from a collection of prophetic sayings). Rather, possibly authentic words have been put into writing in anonymous groupings either in sentential, proverbial sequence or, more frequently, in the form of smaller compositions. Therefore, focusing on the material contained in the Book of the Twelve and considering those penultimate stages of its genesis before the final biographical order became dominant, we certainly are dealing not so much with individual prophetic pronouncements but with all sorts of compositional clusters (cf., e.g., Hos 1–3; Amos 3–4; Mic 6–7; Zeph 1–2; Zech 9 + 12 + Mal 1). This means to say: Our focus at the moment is not on the original collection of prophetic words, but on that stage of tradition which immediately precedes that a-historical subdivision of a larger mass of material into "biographically" oriented prophetic books. There seem to have existed clusters of divine communications, perhaps independent from each other *in* time and location, largely anonymous or at least not explicitly and arbitrarily attributed to named individuals. To recognize the nature and purpose of such unnamed collections of sayings would greatly enhance our evaluation of the final Book of the Twelve.

The variety of preserved genres within those early collections surely is surprising. We find narrative passages and a great variety of poetic ones. There are legal forms and all kinds of didactic speeches. Most of the literary clusters are concerned with faith communities like Israel, Judah, the habitants of Jerusalem or their respective adversaries. Nearly all of them derive their right to exist and

---

[1] Ferdinand E. Deist, "The Prophets: Are We Heading for a Paradigm Switch?" in *Prophet und Prophetenbuch: Festschrift für Otto Kaiser zum 65. Geburtstag*, ed. Volkmar Fritz, Karl-Friedrich Pohlmann, and Hans-Christoph Schmitt, BZAW 185 (Berlin: de Gruyter, 1989), 1–18. Cf. Martti Nissinen, "The Historical Dilemma of Biblical Prophetic Studies," in *Prophecy in the Book of Jeremiah*, ed. Hans M. Barstad and Reinhard G. Kratz, BZAW 388 (Berlin: de Gruyter, 2009), 103–20.

to go forth into the public from Yahweh, the Lord of the said congregations. Only a few explicitly employ an anonymous or vaguely identified prophetic speaker as an intermediary of divine communication. Legitimizing formulas like "Yahweh's murmur," "thus speaks Yahweh," and "the word of Yahweh came to …" are not consistently applied and certainly come from different theological backgrounds betraying varied conceptions of prophetic communication.[2] They are to be cautiously evaluated. The best procedure, it occurs to me, is to abstain from biographical interpretation at this stage and analyze forms, genres and intentions of the small compositions of kerygmatic words in their own rights. The presupposition previously in vogue in Old Testament scholarship, that the books of the Hebrew Bible were written for a general, literate readership, can no longer claim unquestioned validity. Within the Twelve references or even implicit hints to reading (instead of hearing!) prophetic words are so scarce and incidental that they can be ignored (e.g., Hab 2:2). As a rule, the smaller collections give us spoken messages directed to communities, not to individuals.

DIRECT ADDRESS OF COMMUNITY (ACCUSATION, EXHORTATION, CONTESTS)

It always has been a basic endeavor of form criticism to study the linguistic articulations of (presumably) anonymous Old Testament literature in order to understand its rootage in ancient life-situations. This interpretative principle is still valid in our case, even if we concede that we are working with an advanced stage of prophetic tradition. No longer are we dealing with the original moment of prophetic preaching, as if the text of a given cluster of sayings were the protocol of one person's single day's performance in a given historical situation. On the contrary, the small collections of discourses already present the results of extended accumulative and compositional labor of some figure other than the original speaker. These unknown redactors, scribes or compositors must have had a vital interest in preserving, interpreting, modifying, enlarging and "editing" messages coming from Yahweh and going to those congregations which are being addressed. The recipients are imagined and portrayed as "listeners," not as "readers" of the Word of God, as any close study of any of the small collections of words within the Twelve will demonstrate. "Listening," of course, may imply the public reading of a sacred text, as in Neh 8:1–6 (which at the same time refers to continuous translation and interpretation of the divine discourse, vv. 7–8), Exod 24:7, Deut 29:23–28 (note the "we" response of the congregation in v. 28), and Deut 31:9–11. Our "editors," we may conclude, have been functionaries of Yahweh-worshiping communities, not only selecting and collecting texts, but also modifying and producing them for the edification of such groups of believers. The modes of speech employed vary considerably, but

---

[2] A comprehensive up-to-date study of these formulaic expressions would be desirable. See the relevant entries in *TDOT* and WIBILEX (www.bibelwissenschaft.de/wibilex/).

in general, as we will see immediately, they fit into the homiletical and catechetical kinds of allocution. To specify all this we need to take up some examples.

INVECTIVES AGAINST THE COMMUNITY (AMOS 3–6)

A good number of small prophetic word-collections are of an accusatory and condemning kind, sometimes akin to legal speech forms directed against suspects and convicts. For example, Amos 3–6 is a vivid composition of dozens of divine oracles against the "house of Israel," alternatively called "house of Jacob (e.g., Amos 3:13) and "house of Joseph" (Amos 5:6; 6:6), geographically identified by frequent mentioning of "Samaria," "Bet-El," and "Gilgal" as the northern kingdom. The human speaker of these oracles is not revealed, neither by name nor by an authorial "I," with the faint possible exception of Amos 5:1.[3] Overall, Yahweh is chiding his people for "not knowing to do right" and resorting to "violence" and "robbery" (Amos 3:10), for "oppressing the poor" and "crushing the needy" (Amos 4:1), for living in luxury by exploiting plain people and bending the law (Amos 5:10–13; 6:4–6), for feigning religious correctness and staging ostentatious cultic ceremonies camouflaging social transgressions (Amos 5:21–24). The outcome of all these deviations from the right path will be catastrophic for the addressed community (Amos 3:11; 4:2–3; 5:2–7; 5:16–17; 5:27; 6:7–8; 6:9–10; 6:11–14). The whole collection seems to be a well-composed entity.[4] Why and for what purposes did the collectors write it down?

To answer this question we have to try to recognize the collectors' intentions in selecting, commenting and assembling the words of Yahweh. Assuming that original prophetic sayings have been concise and very specifically spoken into determined contexts the generalizing statements of Amos 3:1–2, in fact, must be the work of an editorial mind. The introductory formula "Hear this word" may be the normal incipit of a prophetic utterance, pointing only to one following saying (cf. Amos 4:1; 5:1). But the editor takes pains to define theologically the recipients of the message. He not only calls upon those "Israelites" who, for example, live at Samaria or Bet-El, or who betrayed their allegiance to Yahweh. But he also makes a sweeping outreach into the history of election: "Hear this word that Yahweh has spoken against you, O People of Israel, against the whole family [*kal-hammišpaḥah*; better: "all the folks"] that I brought out of the land of Egypt" (Amos 3:1). The collector/compositor molds a plain announcement of the word of Yahweh into a programmatic designation of partnership with the

---

[3] According to Jeremias (*Der Prophet Amos*, ATD 24.2 [Göttingen: Vandenhoeck & Ruprecht, 1995], 63), Amos 5:1 alone makes chs. 5–6 the discourse of the prophet (in distinction to God speaking in chs. 3–4), ignoring frequent introductory formulas and first person speech of Yahweh.

[4] Cf. Jeremias, *Amos*, XVI–XXI; 30–93. But is it really an "artistic" (p. XIX) or rather a liturgical composition?

God of old. And the first divine statement, without revelation formula, serves as a headline for the whole redactional unit in Amos 3–6:

> Only you have I known, of all the people [*mišpeḥot*] of the earth, therefore, I will punish you for all your iniquities. (Amos 3:2)[5]

The wording is not exactly Deuteronomistic, but the spirit and content of the announcement certainly are (cf. Deut 7). The assemblage of oracles and sayings is to testify to the special relationship of Israel with Yahweh and the responsibility of the people to keep strictly to ethical and cultic obligations of the elected people. More restricted original meanings of the sayings against violence, robbery, oppression, injustice now have to be understood in the light of this opening declaration. The collector makes two more basic statements before citing verbatim oracles to the community. He first justifies the pronouncements of any and all messengers of Yahweh, and thus gives a firm base to his texts (Amos 3:7–8—God shares his plans with the prophets!); and secondly, he summons international observers to witness the evil doings of Samaria (Amos 3:9). Only then is the first more or less concrete oracle launched against the people (Amos 3:10–11), to be followed by Amos 3:12 + 15 and 4:1–3. According to Jeremias the inserted verses in Amos 3:13–14 appear to be a Deuteronomistic interpretation of the function of prophecy throughout the history of Israel and a special denunciation of the apostasies of Bet-El (cf. 1 Kgs 12:25–33).[6]

To single out neatly all the authentic prophetic sayings in the small collection is not our task here. Suffice it to point out a few more vestiges of secondary reworkings. Amos 4:6–11 sticks to the same pattern of five-fold pedagogical punishments, applied in the hope of Israel's return, as we can find in Lev 26:14–32 and 1 Kgs 8:33–34, 35–36, 37–40; cf. Deut 28:20–44. There is not a trace of genuine "prophetic" discourse in these words. Rather, we have elements of Deuteronomistic preaching. Jeremias justly states: "The line of reasoning found in Amos 4:6–13 is oriented towards a liturgy of repentance used in the exilic community."[7]

There are more peculiarities in the small collection Amos 3–6 which might hint at additions of nonprophetic but community-directed catechetical speech. Amos 5:2 is designated in verse 1 as a "lamentation," and later on seems to be followed by three mourning cries (Amos 5:18–20; 6:1–3; and 6:4–7; cf. 5:16–17) reminiscent of funeral wailings. What could be the prophetic message in this form of speech? The book of Ezekiel uses lamentations extensively. The meaning in prophetic contexts could be a special emphasis on unavoidable doom. But was this intention an outright concern of divine messengers? Also in Amos 5 we find

---

[5] Bible translations are according to the NRSV. However, the name Yahweh (Zebaoth) has been consistently retained.

[6] Jeremias, *Amos*, 43. He classifies the terminology as belonging to "worship language."

[7] Ibid., 52; see also his extensive treatment of the passage on pp. 49–56.

instructional forms of discourse (i.e., Amos 5:4–7; 5:14–15). Exhortations to "seek me and live" (Amos 5:4), "Seek Yahweh and live" (Amos 5:6), "Seek good and not evil, that you may live" (Amos 5:14), and "hate evil and love good" (Amos 5:15) really belong to the repertoire of teachers, wise men and women, who try to bring young people onto the right path in life. Did the collector introduce this peculiar mode of addressing communities in order to counteract a little those harsh prophetic indictments? (See the next paragraph.) And lastly, two of the three enigmatic hymn-fragments found in the book of Amos (Amos 4:13; 5:8–9; 9:5–6) are included in our four chapters. They pose special problems and will be treated separately below.

The most burning issue now is to find plausible localizations for the use of these diverse forms of speech, especially the accusations of breaking norms and committing sins, as well as the announcements of concomitant castigations or retributions. As already stated, one of the deeply moving theological problems in Judah and among the deportees of the sixth century BCE was the question: Why did God permit our destruction at the hands of the Babylonians?[8] There were people who maintained a defensive attitude against Yahweh (cf. Pss 44; 89), but others firmly argued that the people and their leaders had accumulated so much guilt by apostasies from and breakings of the covenant with their God that he had had no choice but to deliver his people into the hands of their enemies (cf. 2 Kgs 23:25–27; Ps 106; Neh 9, etc.). This paradigm is the very heart of Deuteronomistic preaching (cf. Deut 1–4; 27–28; 29–31; Josh 23–24; Judg 2:6–23; 2 Kgs 17:7–23; Jer 10; 18, etc.). The theological program of sin-punishment-supplication-forgiveness was very likely enacted in worship ceremonies by recitations of the relevant prophetic/divine words and communal responses. And which ceremonial occasions can we imagine to have offered the liturgical setting for these rituals?

This mood of sin and repentance seems to correspond most closely to the days of "fasting" and "mourning" mentioned , for example, in Zech 7:1–6; 8:18. These commemorations of the catastrophe of Judah had become a habit in the sixth century BCE. Quite often Old Testament scholars link with them the book of Lamentations. It would be perfectly plausible also to think of rituals of mourning and rehabilitation to have been performed on such days. Other possibilities include regular readings of Torah, that is, worship services of the community on Sabbath days or at festive events in the religious calendar. Nehemiah 8:2–8 and Deut 31:9–11 mention different opportunities to proclaim the words of Torah. Imaginably so, the liturgical enactment of breaking the covenant and restoring a sound relationship with Yahweh could be corollary events in Torah worship. Zechariah 14:16–19 and Neh 10:1–40 are also

---

[8] Amos purportedly preached in the eighth century in northern state of Israel. Even if references to that situation in the collector's composition are authentic they were charged with Judaic experiences in later transmission.

interesting in this regard. The first passage fixes the Feast of Booths (cf. Deut 31:10) as the appropriate day when the formerly hostile nations may participate in worshipping Yahweh thus reversing the prophetic verdict against the nations. The second text is undated in terms of calendric determination, but it testifies, like other witnesses, especially in Deuteronomistic literature, to a covenant renewal ceremony, which probably was part of regular Jewish ritual. Such renewal of the religious alliance possibly implied commemoration of crises, and the anonymous collections of relevant literary compositions may well have served as matrixes for such liturgies.

INSTRUCTIONS AND PRAYER OF MEMBERS (MIC 6–7)

The present book of Micah is personalized only by the late superscription Mic 1:1 and the equally young verbatim quotation of Mic 3:12 in Jer 26:18. Otherwise there is no reference to the name and birthplace of this particular figure to which the "book" is attributed. There are only some personal pronouns of the first person singular indicating a prophetic or homiletic speaker (Mic 1:8; 2:11; 3:1; 3:8; 7:7). We may safely assume, for this reason, that the smaller collections of the present literary unit have been brought together anonymously.

What are the subunits of the "book"? Experts are, as is good custom in scholarship, divided in their opinion. And, in fact, there are no hard and clear structuring signals in the corpus of this writing. Following Rainer Kessler we may recognize overlapping and partially contradicting principles of composition, but assume as a possible solution and mainly for thematic reasons that the partition into Mic 1–3; 4–5; 6–7 may come close to the delineation of earlier collections.[9] The last section may well be the youngest part of the final product, as it shows some characteristics that reflect the Persian period.[10] There are notable differences in the rhetorical set-up over against Amos 3–6, to be sure, but the basic situation of a divine voice addressing a community remains identical. The speaker often and quite naturally is Yahweh himself (cf. Mic 6:3–5; 6:9–13), calling on his people directly without human mediation. Still, the mediator is there, hidden between the lines, coming to the fore somewhat timidly, as in Mic 6:8; 7:5, 7. In most cases the immediate respondent to the summons of Yahweh is the addressed congregation, who reply in various ways. There is the answer of each member in Mic 6:6–7, in the first person singular ("With what shall I come before Yahweh"; v. 6). Next, the assembly as a whole responds in the first person singular (Mic 7:1), and another time, it is the same community, but personified as the city of Jerusalem rebutting her female enemy, that is, a rivaling power (Mic 7:8–10). At the very end of the little collection the congregation even speaks out in the first person plural (Mic 7:19–20), a very

---

[9] Rainer Kessler, *Micha*, HKAT (Freiburg: Herder, 1999), 40; 41–47.
[10] Ibid., 47; cf. his detailed exegesis op. cit. 255–312.

special mode of discourse we will consider more closely below. In other words, the traditional pattern of prophetic speech is all but given up in this part of the Twelve. The only formula of divine legitimation, downgraded several degrees, is Mic 6:1a ("Hear, what Yahweh says"; LXX also forcefully interjects "Word of Yahweh").[11] Instead, the forms of discourse used in Mic 6–7 are plainly dialogical instead of revelatory, controversial and instructional instead of doctrinal, liturgical and ceremonial instead of literary.

Judging from the speech forms alone, then, we already get the impression of being in the midst of an early Judaic worship service in which the fate of the surviving community is being debated. A closer look at the contents of charges, confessions, instructions and prayers, as well as their theological backgrounds confirms this notion. An unnamed speaker calls upon the assembly (Mic 6:1a; imperative plural) to stand up in court and listen to Yahweh's charges of aberrancy against his "people" (Mic 6:3-5). The jury is composed of the mountains around (Mic 6:1b, 2; cf. Amos 3:9). That the plaintiff is rhetorically asking about his own faults ("What have I done to you?" Mic 6:3a) is a refined model of juridic-theological strategy (cf. Jer 2:4–9; Isa 1:2–9; Ps 50). It heightens suspense in expectation of the outcome. And it brings with it a good many ancient Near Eastern theological conceptualizations of the near-equality between God and humanity (cf. Gen 32:23–33; Ps 8:6–9; Job 9; 42:1–9, etc.). The enumeration of God's salvific actions in history (Mic 6:4–5) obviously builds on the Pentateuchal writings and the book of Joshua. The effect of the divine sermon is the community's uncertainty of how to serve their God correctly (Mic 6:6–7). The same problem of the comparative value of sacrifices (even of the firstborn son! v. 7) over against "obedience to the Torah" is also ventilated in a number of other Old Testament texts (cf. Gen 22:1–19; Isa 1:10–17; Pss 40:7–11; 50:7–23; 51:17–19; 119). This problem could become a matter of concern only after the Torah had been assembled and become the norm of Jewish life which, probably occurred in the fifth century BCE (Nehemiah; Ezra).

A new round of indictment and punishment takes up the rest of Mic 6, namely verses 9–16. The notion is that Yahweh cries out loudly his accusations of social ills over the city (of Jerusalem? vv. 9–12) continuing with punitive measures like those encountered in Amos or, for that matter, in the curses against disloyal covenant partners in Deuteronomy and Leviticus (Mic 6:13-16; cf. Deut 28:15–44 and Lev 26:14–39). Interestingly enough, the deviations of kings Omri and Ahab of the northern state of Israel are mentioned as abhorrent examples (Mic 6:16), rather late if the passage was formed in the Persian Period. Now, this fact does not warrant an ancient date of the text in question. Rather, it testifies to the knowledge of historical traditions on the part of the composers of our cluster (cf. 1 Kgs 18:1–22:40). Micah 7 begins with a communal lament (vv. 1–2), which assumes accusatory (or penitent?) overtones (vv. 2–4; note the

---

[11] Cf. Mic 4:4, 6; 5:9: These verses still have strong word-formulas.

denunciation of evil-doers in plural forms) and abruptly turns into a sapiential exhortation not to trust anybody in chaotic times (vv. 5–6). The speaker is drawing on standard depictions of a society falling into pieces. Closest human relations in family and friendship no longer function (cf. Exod 21:15, 17; 1 Sam 2:25; Ps 27:10; Prov 10:1; 15:5, 20; 19:26; 20:20; Ezek 22:7). The confessional statement Mic 7:7 falls in line with those first person self-references of an unnamed proclaimer already mentioned above (Mic 1:8; 2:11; 3:1, 8), the closest parallel being Mic 3:8. The leading voice in both cases positions itself over against the indicted community. Is this an indication of an internal rift in the faith-community (cf. Isa 65–66)? Or does the collector simply present a model of steadfastness that should be followed by the congregation?

The rest of chapter 7 (Mic 7:8–20), as is widely accepted, contains a number of elements of or reference to a communal liturgy of repentance, including the concomitant assurances of being saved and rehabilitated. As already indicated, this speech which overcomes lament by a confession of sin (Mic 7:8–9) must be, because of the reconstruction of her walls and her homages in verses 11–12, the exclamation of the city of Jerusalem. She will "rise from her fall" (v. 8), she will be completely vindicated and revenged (v. 10), even brought to a new glory (vv. 11–12; 16–17). There are no explicit indications of speakers, and no quotation formulas in Mic 7:8–20. This may be in itself a characteristic of liturgical authenticity. Speakers and modes of discourse change, that much is clear. After the declamation of Jerusalem (Mic 7:8–10) a liturgist talks to her (vv. 11–13), that is, to the assembly of worshippers, bringing the news of her restoration. The city will be rebuilt, she will flourish, and all the nations will flock to her and pay tribute while the rest of the world falls into ruins. From verse 14 on we have prayer language. The unmarked transition is particularly awkward for a literary text. In terms of liturgical composition markers are less necessary. The brute imperative "shepherd your people" (v. 14), lacking an addressee, can only refer to Yahweh himself. A vast extension of territory into the region east of the Jordan (v. 14) is asked for. The other nations are to be subdued (v. 16–17). The supplicants go unnamed and untagged; the two suffixes of the first person plural in verses 15 and 17 suggest that the great congregation may be speaking the prayer, but both instances are not completely warranted textually, in contrast to those suffixes in verses 19–20.

The concluding part of the liturgical composition (Mic 7:18–20) is a hymnic prayer, this time very clearly sung by the community. The opening line eulogizes the incomparable, the greatest God of Israel, pointedly playing on the name of Micah (v. 18aα: Hebrew: *mî 'ēl kāmôkā*). That same God will wipe out transgressions and establish a renewed relationship with his people:

> He will again have compassion upon us; he will tread our iniquities under foot.
> You will cast our sins into the depths of the sea. (Mic 7:19)

Here is the proof for the communal "we" intoning the hymn. The change from neutral third person allocation of God to direct address praise is in the Hebrew text, but is not supported by ancient translations. They, in turn, grant second person direct address to Yahweh only in verse 20, then in accordance with the Hebrew text.

A preliminary evaluation of Mic 6–7 in regard to its genres and purposes is in order. Forms of speech, literary structures, contents and theological implications give reason to consider the small collection a compilation of texts to be used, that is, read or recited, in ceremonies of the emerging Jewish community of the Persian period.[12] When the biographical interpretation of the Book of the Twelve is left aside—and there are practically no good reasons to claim personal authorship for the large majority of the material assembled in the Twelve—and if the theory of private reading habits in pre-Hellenistic times is discarded, the only plausible explanation of an aggregation of such texts is that of an archive or hand-book for ceremonial use in determined local faith-communities of Yahwistic provenance. The process of collecting, reworking and augmenting earlier and partially oral traditions may have taken several centuries, let us say from 600 until 300 BCE. Before the final division into twelve booklets took place we may expect that cultic functionaries in Israel (prophets, scribes, Levites, cultic singers, healers etc.) would, in execution of their professional functions, bring into writing texts that they had inherited from their forebears. The newly developing community of Yahweh-adherents after 587 BCE was the decisive ecclesiological body to produce and peruse these texts at varied cultic-ritual occasions. The loss of political independence, of a native dynasty, and, for some time, of proper national temple services made a new formation of religious and social institutions necessary, and this traumatizing loss had a great impact also on the cultic celebrations which were being performed, adopted and freshly created for this new community.

HOPE FOR THE FUTURE (ZECH 12–14)

The first part of the "book of Zechariah" (Zech 1–8) is most conspicuously engaged in giving exact dates for some divine words communicated to the prophet (cf. Zech 1:1; 1:7; 7:1; etc.; and likewise in the book of Haggai). Day, month, year of the Persian royal calendar are adduced. Nowhere else in the Twelve do we find a similar effort to historicize prophetic activity (although the said individual datings formally do not constitute a "book of Zechariah"). The latest attempts at biographical specificity, we may conclude, are the most precise and forceful ones, but they probably still may be secondary to the material of Zech 1–8. The remaining words now contained in "Zechariah" (Zech 9–14) are

---

[12] Erhard S. Gerstenberger, *Israel in der Perserzeit: 5. und 4. Jahrhundert v. Chr.*, Biblische Enzyklopädie 8 (Stuttgart: Kohlhammer, 2005), 238–46.

certainly additions or independent little collections, the redactional history of which remains in the dark. Different signals of literary structure also in this case overlap. Thus, for example, Zech 9:1 and 12:1 (cf. Mal 1:1) bear the autonomous superscription of *maśśā'*, while themes and motifs within the running texts suggest quite different attributions and interconnections.[13]

The last three chapters of Zechariah (Zech 12–14) may serve as another example of a possible anonymous collection of prophetic words. They are rather alien to the type of speech found in Amos or Micah. Sure enough, Yahweh is the principal agent and speaker. The addressees are still Jerusalem or the faith-community, but they are rarely, if at all, addressed directly in the second person. Zechariah 14:5 has two verb forms in the second person plural, but they are textually dubious. The only "I" of a human speaker also occurs in the same phrase. Furthermore, there are occasional direct addresses, for example, in Zech 14:1. In fact, Yahweh presents himself in the first person singular, almost without introductory ado or mediation (cf. only Zech 12:2–4; 13:2; 13:7; 13:9) taking the word abruptly and majestically (cf. Zech 12:2, 6, 9; 14:2). Or he is referred to in neutral third person singular forms, as a narrator points out his actions (Zech 14:3–9). The discourse on the whole is more explicative than dialogical. There seems to be a large distance between the speaker (reader) of the words and his audience. Their reaction is referred to once: "The clans of Judah shall say to themselves: 'The inhabitants of Jerusalem have strength through Yahweh Zebaoth, their God'" (Zech 12:5). This is a positive response to the drama announced in Zech 12:2–4.

The contents of Zech 12–14, although unfolded in several steps and with changing emphases (due to literary growth and/or liturgical necessities), are intimately connected with the main formal elements of the collection. Formulaic expressions point to a "day" in the future, which will bring the decision for the better (Zech 12:3, 4, 6, 8, 9, 11; 13:1, 2, 4; 14:1, 4, 6, 8, 9, 20, a total of fifteen references). Speculations about the origin of such formal elements are in vain. The collector either found them in the tradition or made them a dominant structural pattern in his work (or both). Be that as it may, Zech 12–14 focuses on that particular day of doom and liberation, which will bring heavy sufferings to Jerusalem (Zech 13:7–9: loss of two thirds of the population; 13:10–14: general mourning; 14:2: conquest, rape, exile), but these sufferings are at the same time the starting point of the utter defeat of all enemies (12:2–4, 6–8; 14:6–11, 12–19) and, obviously, a time of bliss and security for Jerusalem (12:7–8; 14:8, 10–11, 20–21). The central assertion in this dramatic scenery apparently is Zech 14:9:

> Yahweh will become king over all the earth; on that day Yahweh will be [the only?] one and his name [the only?] one.

---

[13] Wilhelm Rudolph, *Haggai, Sacharja 1–8, Sacharja 9–14, Maleachi*, KAT 13.4 (Gütersloh: Mohn, 1976), 159–64.

The famous passage Deut 6:4, Israel's prime confession, comes to mind: "Hear, O Israel: Yahweh is our God, Yahweh alone." And there is a thematic affinity to the Yahweh-kingship psalms (Pss 47; 93; 95–99) on the one hand and a number of prophetic announcements of the reign of Yahweh on the other hand. All these texts bear witness to an eschatological expectation which had come up in nascent Judaism by contact with Iranian-Babylonian conceptions of a day of final judgment for the whole world.[14] Other manifestations of such eschatological and later apocalyptic thinking in ancient Israel can be found, for example, in Isa 24–27; 60–62; Zeph 1–2; Zech 1:7–6:8; Jer 30–31; Ezek 36, et cetera. Eschatological and apocalyptical proclamation is considerably different from traditional prophetic speech as encountered in Hosea, Amos and Micah, although some end-of-time conceptions also have crept into their "Books" (cf. Hos 14:1–8; Amos 9:11–15; Mic 4–5).

Other intricate and very interesting details of Zech 12–14 cannot be discussed here. One particularity, however, still should draw our attention. Foreign and hostile nations that had oppressed the people of God will be terribly punished (Zech 12:2–4, 6; 14:12–15), but the survivors of Yahweh's campaign to revenge and save Israel, and their descendants "shall go up year after year to worship the King, Yahweh Zebaoth, and … keep the festival of booths" (Zech 14:16). This very idea of all nations being obliged to adore Yahweh on Mount Zion, also present in so many Psalms and other prophetic passages, is further specified, in a prose commentary to verse 16: "If any of the families of the earth do not go up to Jerusalem to worship the King, Yahweh Zebaoth, there will be no rain upon them" (Zech 14:17). A further elaboration explicitly includes Egypt into the circle of nations under such obligation (Zech 14:18–19). The significance of these verses lies not only in its emphasis on the universal reign of Yahweh and the claim of global dominance but also in the unique gravity they place on the Feast of Booths (cf. Deut 31:10). Isaiah 2:2–4 only mentions pilgrimages of nations to the Holy Mount to receive their share in Torah instruction without explicitly referring to the autumn festival. Could the threefold appearance of the Feast of Booths in Zech 14:16–20 signal a liturgical use of this text at this ceremonial occasion?

That question takes us back to the main issue we are pursuing: How can we possibly get to determine the origin and purpose of Zech 12–14 at its precanonic stage? Why have these eschatological texts been put together in the first place? The vivid scenery of one mediatory voice calling out a message of God is no longer present in our collection. A listening audience being directly challenged is all but missing (cf. the remnants in Zech 12:5; 14:1, 5). The text only partially comes in poetic lines (Zech 12:1; 14:1–16). The larger part is set in careful prose

---

[14] Erhard S. Gerstenberger, "Persian-Empire Spirituality and the Genesis of Prophetic Books," in *The Production of Prophecy: Constructing Prophecy and Prophets in Yehud*, ed. Diana V. Edelman and Ehud Ben Zvi, Bible World (London: Equinox, 2009), 111–30.

(Zech 12:2–13:6; 14:17–20). It looks like an originally written composition, destined to be proclaimed by *public* reading. Longer, enumerative sequences of detailed cases or ideas like Zech 12:10–14; 13:1–6; 14:12–15, 16–19 reinforce the impression of having before us an authentic literary piece of work. Excluding private readership, however, which other purpose can we assume than public recitation of the script? Public performance, on the other hand, needs a plausible recurring or else a ritual occasion. No writer in ancient times, to our knowledge, would take the liberty to read out his collected works as if standing at the corner of Hyde Park in London. Jeremiah 26 and 36, if they reflect some prophetic usage, presuppose a customary ceremonial, not a unique incident. The natural recurring opportunity to recite written instructions for a community of believers in Yahweh would be a regular assembly of members, like the one mirrored in Neh 8:2–8. There Torah is recited for six hours with all the paraphernalia of an early synagogue meeting. It should pose no problem for us to assume that small prophetic and eschatological collections originated in the context of Jewish congregational gatherings of a homiletical and catechetical nature. Sinagogal Sabbath worship including both of these components must have begun somewhere in exilic or post-exilic times. Such worship certainly offered, besides Torah recitations at great festivals, a good opportunity for such corollary prophetic readings. Of course, one should not insist on Torah reading exclusively, but in any case Torah looms large in some of the small collections of the Twelve (cf. Mic 6:8; Zech 1:2–6; 7:7–14; 8:16; Mal 2:3–9; 3:5–24). The "Orientation" (a much more adequate translation of Torah than "Law") of Yahweh had become the backbone of faith and community life.

WE-RESPONSES AND ADORATION

We have already touched upon passages in the Twelve, which ostensibly introduce a first person plural voice in the midst of and as a response to divine oracles. Furthermore, there are a good number of real hymnic passages apparently evoked by prophetic/divine communication.[15] The first phenomenon is well known also from the psalms, especially by communal laments and petitions. There are in the Old Testament Psalter fifty-three poems of different genres that show first person plural phrases, among them are some containing extensive passages (Pss 46; 47; 48; 79; 80; 90; 95; 100; 115; 124; 136; 147). Others contain smaller portions of collective speech (Pss 8; 33; 44; 60; 66; 74; 75; 85; 103; 106; 108; 118; 122; 123; 144). Psalm experts like Josef Scharbert and

---

[15] Erhard S. Gerstenberger, "Psalms in the Book of the Twelve: How Misplaced Are They?" in *Thematic Threads in the Book of the Twelve*, ed. Paul L. Reddit and Aaron Schart, BZAW 325 (Berlin: de Gruyter, 2003), 72–89.

Klaus Seybold[16] agree that for the most part the examples of "we"-discourse in the Psalter are not rhetorical or stylistic devices but authentic group voices reflecting the participation of a community in psalm singing. The same conclusion is appropriate in the case of the Book of the Twelve, based on the recognition of a number of hymnic poems representing authentic parts of liturgies of the Jewish community of old. The second type of "insertion," that is, hymnic poems, is treated concomitantly below but with less attention because I have already dealt with them elsewhere (see note 15).

"We"-speech of the addressed or participating congregation occurs more than once in the Twelve.

- Hos 6:1–3 could constitute that penitential prayer demanded in the prophetic threat of Hos 5:15, although the classical phrase "We have sinned/erred" is missing. Instead, the community calls out: "Come, let us return to Yahweh, / for it is he who has torn, and he will heal us" (Hos 6:1).
- In Hos 14:1–3 the prophetic voice suggests a similar "return" to Yahweh and puts the words into the mouth of the community (vv. 1–2): "Take away all guilt: / accept that which is good, and we will offer the fruit of our lips."
- In Joel after a long summons to lament and repent (Joel 1:2–18) a single voice, perhaps that of the liturgist, prays in the first person singular: "To you, O Yahweh, I cry" (Joel 1:19–20). In the same vein there is a second round of announcing doom and calling for repentance (Joel 2:1–17a).
- Again a prayer of and for the congregation is suggested: "Let them say: 'Spare your people, O Yahweh / and do not make your heritage a mockery'" (Joel 2:17b). Thereafter, the text states at length the gracious response of God and his promises for the people (Joel 2:18–27).

It is quite clear in the two cases of quoted prayer in Joel that such short specimens do not correspond to real liturgical procedures. But the scribes, authors or redactors of the written version of divine words were conscious of the correct ritual sequence. By indicating the adequate spot for a communal prayer they betray their involvement with the living liturgy and also suggest what should be the content of the proposed intervention of the whole congregation.

---

[16] Josef Scharbert, "Das 'Wir' in den Psalmen auf dem Hintergrund altorientalischen Betens," in *Freude an der Weisung des Herrn: Beiträge zur Theologie der Psalmen, Festgabe zum 70, Geburtstag von Heinrich Gross*, ed. Ernst Haag and Frank-Lothar Hossfeld (Stuttgart: Katholisches Bibelwerk, 1986), 297–324; Klaus Seybold, "Das 'Wir' in den Asaph-Psalmen: Spezifische Probleme einer Psalmgruppe," in *Neue Wege der Psalmenforschung*, ed. Klaus Seybold and Erich Zenger, HBS 1 (Freiburg: Herder, 1994), 143–55.

- The book of Amos does not contain prayers or "we"-discourse of the community, but it includes some seemingly erratic fragments of a hymn to Yahweh (Amos 4:13; 5:8-9; 9:5-6) that have stirred much debate in scholarship.[17] To our literary eyes they seem displaced but they possibly make good sense in a liturgical context allowing for alternating voices and the participation of the audience. The hymns in Amos highlight God's creative powers—not a bad theological topic for a communal response.
- The only occurrence of a first person plural form in Obadiah is of little avail for our research (Obad 1: "We have heard "; cf. the parallel text Jer 49:14).

The book of Micah has several communal responses inserted in their literary contexts.

- Mic 1:3-4 is a theophanic hymn.
- Mic 2:4 quotes a lamentation.
- Mic 4:2 (= Isa 2:3) is a self-summons to worship.
- Three times we find the community reacting directly, through each individual member, and therefore using the first person singular: Mic 6:6-7; 7:1-2; 7:8-10.
- Four passages are genuine "we"-statements of the worshipping congregation: Mic 4:5; 4:14; 5:4-5; 7:18-20.
- The concluding prayer Mic 7:14-20 is of particular importance for our study, as pointed out before. It is a strong manifestation of the influential role congregational worship had in the production, formation and performance of prophetic texts.

All these texts are strong indications for the affinity of the written version of Micah's early collection to the life and worship of the faith-community.[18]

Continuing the brief overview over the smaller collections in the Twelve, we come to the books of Nahum and Habakkuk. There are no express "we"-passages in these writings. Nevertheless, evidence for liturgical use of part or all of the texts is overwhelming.

- Nah 1:2-15 reveals the remains of an acrostic hymn (especially in vv. 2-8) with secondary additions and modifications.

---

[17] E.g., Aaron Schart (*Die Entstehung des Zwölfprophetenbuchs*, BZAW 260 [Berlin: de Gruyter, 1998], 234-51) who laudably includes in his discussion also the hymnic parts of Nahum and Habakkuk admitting their use in worship ceremonies (p. 247).

[18] Kessler (*Micha*, 234) attributes three we-passages (why omitting Mic 4:14?) to the "whole of the community."

- The "I" of a prophet, preacher, teacher, congregational leader or some such functionary, Habakkuk.
- Hab 1 consists of laments to God (vv. 2–4, 12–17) and chastising divine responses (vv. 5–11).
- Hab 2 is another dialogue between a watcher or guard of the community and Yahweh, describing in general terms the rotten state of a society dominated by violence and greed.
- Hab 3 poses as a theophanic hymn, explicitly designated by a (later) superscription as "A prayer of the prophet Habakkuk according to Shigionoth" (Hab 3:1)[19] whose performance is described by a cult-technical subscription, "To the leader: with stringed instruments" (Hab 3:19b), thus proving directly its provenance from Israelite worship ceremonies.

Zephaniah mostly consists of unilateral divine announcement centering around that ominous "day of wrath, anguish, ruin, devastation, darkness, gloom etc." (e.g., Zeph 1:15–16). Biographical dates of the mediator / preacher and formulas of legitimation are quite immaterial for our prehistorization collector.[20]

- He notably puts an outright communal hymn at the end of his collection (Zeph 3:14–18).[21]
- This hymn is followed by an oracle of assurance (Zeph 3:19–20).

Even in times of despair the praise of Yahweh may be a liturgical necessity. It anticipates thanksgiving for the salvation Yahweh will bring about.[22]

Haggai and Zech 1–8 belong together by virtue of their speech patterns (prose-poetry alternation), their dating of individual sayings according to Persian chronology, and their concern for such themes as temple, priesthood and messianism. The legitimizing formula "the Word of Yahweh came to ..." in this block of writing is prominent among all the other revelatory expressions. In Hag 1:1; 1:3; 2:1; 2:10; 2:20 introductions to oracles each mention Haggai by name.

---

[19] At least the name Habakkuk—a unique attribution of a psalm—is a last minute addition following the period of small collections.
[20] There are only a few formulas inserted: "Yahweh's murmur"—Zeph 1:2, 3, 10; 2:9; 3:8—and one final: "Yahweh has spoken" (Zeph 3:20).
[21] Erhard S. Gerstenberger, "Der Hymnus der Befreiung im Zefanjabuch," in *Der Tag wird kommen: Ein interkontextuelles Gespräch über das Buch des Propheten Zefanja*, ed. Walter Dietrich and Milton Schwantes, SBS 170 (Stuttgart: Katholisches Bibelwerk, 1996), 102–12.
[22] Erhard S. Gerstenberger, "Praise in the Realm of Death: The Dynamics of Hymn-Singing in Ancient Near Eastern Lament Ceremony," in *Lamentations in Ancient and Contemporary Cultural Contexts*, ed. Nancy C. Lee and Carleen Mandolfo, SBLSymS 43 (Atlanta: Society of Biblical Literature, 2008), 115–24.

Similarly in the introductions to oracles in Zech 1:1; 1:7; 6:9; 7:1; 7:4; 7:8; 8:1; 8:18[23] explicitly mention Zechariah. Audience or congregation is vividly addressed at times, but there are no liturgical texts put into their mouths. Nevertheless, the material may have served as pericopes in worship agendas.

COMMUNAL AND LITURGICAL ORIGIN AND USE OF PROPHETIC WORDS

We have to draw now some succinct conclusions inspired by the above observations and suppositions.

- The traditional author-reader paradigm of understanding prophetic collections is no longer tenable. It should be replaced by a community-ritual model of interpretation.
- Evidence for this approach comes among other factors from the anonymous collections of divine communications preceding the edition of the final, canonic Book of the Twelve.
- Prophetic speech in its various forms (announcements of doom; indictments; laments; oracles of salvation; exhortations; etc.) has been read or recited in appropriate rituals.
- One of the prime impulses for including rituals of accusation, repentance, pardon into communal worship has been the traumatic experience of defeat and exile among the Judahites.
- Messianic preaching apparently has developed independently and may be a later branch of prophecy in Israel sparked by contacts with Zoroastrian religion.
- Agents of prophetic worship services were Yahweh, his spokesman or spokeswoman, the assembly (congregation), the enemies (nations), possibly also instrumentalists and choirs.
- Biblical tradition has preserved only the verbal parts of liturgies possibly modified by some selective, descriptive, interpretive motivations. There is no full coverage of worship agendas.
- The Twelve are comparable to the collections of the Major Prophets, although each of them has characteristics of its own. Closest affinity of the Twelve is with Isaiah.
- The trial-repentance-rehabilitation sequence is one basic liturgical setup visible in the Twelve. In conclusion the congregation (choir?) apparently sang hymns of praise.

---

[23] The largest part of the cycle of visions (Zech 1:8–6:8) has a different formulaic pattern, including the dialogue with the angel-interpreter. Zechariah 1:7 does not fit this visionary scheme, it must have been imposed secondarily.

- Educational discourse in Judean worship services is related to wisdom tradition and Torah instruction. It may have been part of the regular cult or of special meetings (cf. Ps 119).
- Eschatological preaching in the Twelve seems to have been more formalized (as evident in the frequent use of such formulas as "the days are coming," etc.) than the former types of liturgy. Uncertain Messianic expectations were a characteristic part of it (as evident in Haggai and Zechariah).
- The anonymous prophetic collections on the whole betray an exclusive faith (in spite of Mic 4:5) in Yahweh. Their homiletical and catechetical discourses are typical for ancient Jewish identity.

7

Form and Eschatology in the Book of the Twelve Prophets

Marvin A. Sweeney

I

The Book of the Twelve Prophets presents unique challenges to form-critical readers of the prophetic literature because it comprises twelve discrete formal prophetic works, each with its own superscription or literary introduction that identifies the prophet to whom the work is attributed.[1] The Book of the Twelve

---

[1] For discussion of the Book of the Twelve Prophets, see my *The Twelve Prophets*, Berit Olam (Collegeville, MN: Liturgical Press, 2000), esp. 1:xv–xlii; *The Prophetic Literature*, IBT (Nashville: Abingdon, 2005), 165–214. See also Rainer Albertz, James D. Nogalski, and Jakob Wöhrle, eds., *Perspectives on the Formation of the Book of the Twelve: Methodological Foundations—Redactional Processes—Historical Insights*, BZAW 433 (Berlin: de Gruyter, 2012); Ehud Ben Zvi, "Twelve Prophetic Books or 'the Twelve': A Few Preliminary Considerations," in *Forming Prophetic Literature: Essays on Isaiah and the Twelve in Honor of J. D. W. Watts*, ed. James W. Watts and Paul R. House, JSOTSup 255 (Sheffield: Sheffield Academic, 1996), 125–56; Barry Alan Jones, *The Formation of the Book of the Twelve: A Study in Text and Canon*, SBLDS 149 (Atlanta: Scholars Press, 1995); Jason T. LeCureux, *The Thematic Unity of the Book of the Twelve*, Hebrew Bible Monographs 10 (Sheffield: Sheffield Phoenix, 2012); James D. Nogalski and Marvin A. Sweeney, eds. *Reading and Hearing the Book of the Twelve*, SBLSym 15 (Atlanta: Society of Biblical Literature, 2000); James D. Nogalski, *Literary Precursors to the Book of the Twelve*, BZAW 117 (Berlin: de Gruyter, 1993); Nogalski, *Redactional Processes in the Book of the Twelve*, BZAW 118 (Berlin: de Gruyter, 1993); Nogalski, *The Book of the Twelve*, 2 vols., HSBC (Macon, GA: Smyth & Helwys,

Prophets is therefore also known as the Minor Prophets due to the relatively shorter length of its twelve constituent prophetic works when compared to the larger prophetic works of Isaiah, Jeremiah, and Ezekiel. The manuscript traditions of Judaism and Christianity generally present the Twelve Prophets as a single work called *têrê 'āśār*, "the Twelve," in Hebrew Masoretic manuscripts, *ton dodekaprophetōn*, "the Twelve Prophets," in Greek Septuagint manuscripts, and *duodecim prophetarum*, "Twelve Prophets," in Latin Vulgate manuscripts. The Latin term *prophetae minores*, "Minor Prophets," first appears in Latin Patristic sources, such as Augustine's *City of God*. Although they are grouped as a single work in Christian tradition, they are counted as twelve separate books among the thirty-nine Old Testament books of Protestant tradition and the forty-six Old Testament books of Roman Catholic tradition. Judaism counts them only as one book among the twenty-four books of the Tanakh, although scribal practice calls for a space of three lines between each of the twelve prophets in contrast to the four lines normally left between biblical books (b. B. Bat. 13b). Selections from the Twelve Prophets (with the exception of Nahum, Zephaniah, and Haggai) are read as both weekly and festival *Haphtarot* in Jewish practice.[2] Passages from the Twelve Prophets are likewise quoted throughout the New Testament.

The composite nature of the Book of the Twelve Prophets complicates attempts to understand its formal character and its eschatological perspective, particularly because each of its constituent works is a discrete book with its own literary form, purported historical setting, and hermeneutical perspective. Is the Book of the Twelve Prophets a single, discrete formal unit with its own generic character? Or is it a collection or compilation of twelve discrete formal units, each with its own generic character? In fact, the answer to *both* of these questions appears to be "yes." And what implications does the apparently composite character of the Book of the Twelve Prophets have for understanding the generic character of the prophetic book?

The issue is further complicated by the fact that the order of the twelve prophetic books (and sometimes their chapters divisions) differs markedly in the various traditions. Although early Patristic tradition displays a variety of orders, modern readers of the Septuagint tradition ultimately settled on the following order:

2011); Paul L. Redditt and Aaron Schart, eds. *Thematic Threads in the Book of the Twelve*, BZAW 325 (Berlin: de Gruyter, 2003).

[2] See Michael Fishbane, *Haftarot*, JPS Bible Commentary (Philadelphia: Jewish Publication Society, 2002), passim.

THE *DODEKAPROPHETON*: THE TWELVE PROPHETS
(SEPTUAGINT ORDER)

I. Hosea	Hosea 1–12
II. Amos	Amos 1–9
III. Micah	Micah 1–7
IV. Joel	Joel 1–3
V. Obadiah	Obadiah
VI. Jonah	Jonah 1–4
VII. Nahum	Nahum 1–3
VIII. Habakkuk	Habakkuk 1–3
IX. Zephaniah	Zephaniah 1–3
X. Haggai	Haggai 1–2
XI. Zechariah	Zechariah 1–14
XII. Malachi	Malachi 1–4

Similar problems appear in relation to the Masoretic tradition. Although Qumran and Judean Desert manuscripts generally presuppose a pre-Masoretic form of the book, at least one Cave 4 manuscript of the Book of the Twelve presupposes an order in which Jonah follows Malachi.[3] Likewise, Talmudic tradition appears to be aware of the Septuagint order of the books (b. B. Bat. 14b), which should come as no surprise since the Septuagint was originally a Jewish version of the Bible. Nevertheless, the Masoretic tradition displays its own distinctive order of books:

THE *TERE ASAR*: THE BOOK OF THE TWELVE PROPHETS
(MASORETIC VERSION)

I. Hosea	Hosea 1–12
II. Joel	Joel 1–4
III. Amos	Amos 1–9
IV. Obadiah	Obadiah
V. Jonah	Jonah 1–4
VI. Micah	Micah 1–7
VII. Nahum	Nahum 1–3
VIII. Habakkuk	Habakkuk 1–3
IX. Zephaniah	Zephaniah 1–3
X. Haggai	Haggai 1–2
XI. Zechariah	Zechariah 1–14
XII. Malachi	Malachi 1–3

Interpreters generally attempt to argue that the order of the twelve prophetic books is determined by a principle of historical progression,

---

[3] For full discussion of the textual traditions of the Book of the Twelve, including LXX and the Qumran manuscripts, see Jones, *Formation of the Book of the Twelve*.

particularly in relation to the LXX order of books since Hosea, Amos, and Micah are all mid- to late eighth-century prophets; Nahum, Habakkuk, and Zephaniah are all seventh-century prophets; and Haggai, Zechariah, and Malachi are all Persian-period prophets.[4] Such a claim does not hold up to closer examination, however, because Joel, Obadiah, and Jonah are all ascribed to ninth-century figures. Joel's reference to the Valley of Jehoshaphat in Joel 4:21 (=NRSV 3:21) suggests the defeat of Ammon, Moab, and Edom by the ninth-century Judean King Jehoshaphat (r. 873–949 BCE; see 2 Chr 20). Obadiah is traditionally identified as the servant of the ninth-century Israelite King Ahab (r. 869–950 BCE) who hid the prophets of YHWH in the time of Elijah (1 Kgs 18). Jonah is identified in 2 Kgs 14:25 as a prophet prior to the reign of King Jeroboam ben Joash (r. 786–746 BCE). And Malachi is likewise associated with the ninth-century prophet Elijah in Mal 3:1, 23–24 (=NRSV 3:1; 4:5–6), although Malachi himself (insofar as his identity as an individual prophet is questioned) may be placed in the Persian period. Chronological problems emerge even among the other prophets. Amos dates to the mid-eighth century whereas Hosea dates to the latter portion of the eighth century. Zephaniah dates to the early reign of Josiah (r. 640–609 BCE); Nahum dates to the fall of Nineveh in 612 BCE; and Habakkuk dates to the Babylonian subjugation of Judah in 605 BCE. When these factors are considered, it becomes clear that a strict chronological principle does not determine the order of the Twelve Prophets in either the Masoretic or the Septuagint versions of the book.

Consideration of the contents of each of the twelve prophetic books and their respective orders in the Septuagint and Masoretic versions of the Book of the Twelve does point to the principles underlying the organization of each. Ironically, both orders point to the respective eschatological perspectives of each version as well, insofar as both versions are fundamentally concerned with the destructions of northern Israel, Judah, and Jerusalem, and the ultimate restoration of all three.

The LXX version begins with the three prophetic books that focus on the downfall of northern Israel and its implications for Judah and Jerusalem. Hosea condemns the northern Jehu dynasty for its alliance with Assyria and Egypt and calls for the reunification of Israel and Judah under Davidic rule. Amos condemns the Jehu dynasty for its failure to meet the needs of the poor, and likewise calls for the restoration of Davidic rule over the north. Micah begins with a critique of the northern Israel monarchy for instigating the events that led to the Assyrian invasion of the land, but he also condemns the Judean house of David on similar grounds. The following prophets then focus on Jerusalem and Judah. Joel looks to the day of YHWH when YHWH will deliver Jerusalem from the threat posed by the nations. Obadiah also invokes the day of YHWH in

---

[4] See my essay, "Sequence and Interpretation in the Book of the Twelve," in Nogalski and Sweeney, *Reading and Hearing*, 49–64.

positing Edom's downfall and ultimate submission to Jerusalem. Jonah raises questions about YHWH's mercy to Nineveh, particularly since Nineveh will ultimately destroy his native Israel. Nahum celebrates the downfall of Nineveh the oppressor of Israel and Judah. Habakkuk asks YHWH why Jerusalem is subjugated to the Chaldeans (Babylonians), but looks forward to YHWH's defeat of the oppressor. Zephaniah invokes the day of YHWH to call for a return of Jerusalem and Judah to YHWH. Haggai calls for the restoration of the Jerusalem Temple and the house of David. Zechariah points to the restoration of the Jerusalem Temple as the beginning of the process in which the nations will ultimately recognize YHWH at Zion. Finally, Malachi calls upon its readers to maintain the covenant until the manifestation of YHWH's presence on the day of YHWH. Altogether, the LXX sequence of books points to an interest in examining the downfall of northern Israel and its implications for understanding the downfall and ultimate restoration of Jerusalem and the Temple at the center of Israel and the world.

The Masoretic version likewise begins with Hosea and his condemnation of northern Israel and hopes for the reunification of Israel and Judah under Davidic rule, but it then turns directly to Joel with its concern for YHWH's defense of Jerusalem on the day of YHWH. Such a move points to a primary concern with the fate and restoration of Jerusalem from the outset of the book. Amos then follows with its condemnation of Israel and call for the restoration of Davidic rule over the north. Obadiah then turns to the condemnation of Edom on the day of YHWH and its ultimate submission to YHWH at Jerusalem. Jonah once again raises the question of YHWH's mercy to Nineveh, and Micah follows by portraying the land of Israel under Assyrian assault while positing the ultimate rise of a Davidic monarch to overthrow the oppressor. Nahum celebrates the downfall of the oppressive Assyrian capital. Habakkuk laments the rise of a new Babylonian oppressor, but looks forward to the time when YHWH will overthrow this new enemy. Zephaniah cites the day of YHWH once again to call on the people to return to YHWH, and ironically points to the Babylonian destruction of the city even though the book is set in the time of Josiah. Haggai again calls for the rebuilding of the Jerusalem Temple and the restoration of the house of David. Zechariah again envisions the restoration of the Temple as the beginning of the process in which Jews and later the nations will recognize YHWH's sovereignty at the Jerusalem Temple. Again, Malachi calls upon its readers to observe the covenant with YHWH until the day of YHWH when YHWH will act. Although the Masoretic version employs the same books as the Septuagint version of the Book of the Twelve, its focus is on the city of Jerusalem, its own experience of judgment, and its role in the world once that judgment is completed and the city and Temple are restored.

II

Both the LXX and the Masoretic versions of the Book of the Twelve display their own distinctive formal characters and eschatological concerns, but the perspectives of each of the individual books must also be considered.

The book of Hosea is the first of the twelve prophets in both the Masoretic and Septuagint sequences.[5] The superscription for the book in Hos 1:1 places the prophet in the reigns of the late-eighth century Judean monarchs, Uzziah (783–742 BCE), Jotham (742–735 BCE), Ahaz (735–715 BCE), and Hezekiah (715–687/6 BCE) as well as in the reign of the northern Israelite king, Jeroboam ben Joash (786–746 BCE). Ironically, the superscription does not mention Jeroboam's successors, although all of them overlapped with the above-mentioned Judean kings. Given Hosea's calls for the overthrow of the Jehu dynasty, of which Jeroboam was the fourth monarch, it is possible that Hosea was compelled to leave northern Israel to seek refuge in the south where his book was finally written and edited. Alternatively, either the prophet or his work may have come south in the aftermath of northern Israel's destruction by the Assyrians in 722/1 BCE

Hosea's eschatological perspective is determined by his calls for the overthrow of the ruling dynasty of northern Israel throughout the book and the statements envisioning Israel's return to righteous Davidic rule in the days to come (Hos 3:4–5). Many interpreters presume that Hosea is concerned with idolatry in Israel, particularly since he accuses his wife Gomer of adultery and employs her as a metaphor for Israel's adultery against YHWH. But close attention to Hosea's literary form, language and oracles indicates that Hosea's understanding of such idolatry is tied up with northern Israel's alliance with Assyria to open a trade passage to Egypt (Hos 12:1–2). Indeed, the literary form of the book indicates that it is organized to present Hosea's call for Israel's return to YHWH:[6]

---

[5] For discussion of Hosea, see esp. Sweeney, *The Twelve Prophets*, 1:1–144; Ehud Ben Zvi, *Hosea*, FOTL 21A (Grand Rapids: Eerdmans, 2005); G. I. Davies, *Hosea*, NCeB (Grand Rapids: Eerdmans, 1992); Francis Landy, *Hosea*, Readings (Sheffield: Sheffield Academic, 1995); A. A. MacIntosh, *Hosea*, ICC (Edinburgh: T&T Clark, 1997); Hans Walter Wolff, *Hosea*, Hermeneia (Philadelphia: Fortress, 1974).

[6] Sweeney, *Prophetic Literature*, 175.

Hosea's Call for Israel's Return to YHWH (Hos 1–14)

I. Superscription — 1:1
II. Main Body of the Book: Appeal for Israel's Return — 1:2–14:9
   A. Narrative account of YHWH's instructions to Hosea to marry a harlot and give their children symbolic names — 1:2–2:2
   B. Hosea's speeches to Israel — 2:3–14:9
      1. Hosea's appeal to his children for their mother's return — 2:3–3:5
      2. YHWH's basic charges against Israel: Abandonment of YHWH — 4:1–19
      3. Specification of YHWH's charges against Israel — 5:1–14:1
      4. Appeal for Israel's return to YHWH — 14:2–9
III. Concluding Exhortation concerning YHWH's Righteousness — 14:10

The initial narrative concerning Hosea's marriage to Gomer bat Diblaim and the birth of their three children makes it clear that Hosea is concerned with the ruling house of Jehu and Israel's relationship with YHWH. The narrative indicates that YHWH instructs Hosea to marry a wife of harlotry, and he marries Gomer in compliance with YHWH's instruction. The metaphor draws upon the tradition of Israel's or Bat Zion's marriage to YHWH in the prophetic tradition which is often employed to portray Israel's abandonment of YHWH (Jer 2; Ezek 16; 20) or Bat Zion's return or restoration to YHWH (Isa 49–54; Zeph 3:14–20).[7] Readers cannot possibly know if Gomer was actually a prostitute or anything of the like, but the book portrays her as such in order to make a point about its view of the Jehu dynasty. The names of the three children born to Gomer and Hosea then characterize his concerns. The first son, Jezreel, is named after the city of Jezreel where the Jehu dynasty came to power when Jehu, the founder of the dynasty, assassinated Omride King Jehoram ben Ahab of Israel and established his own dynastic line over Israel in place of the Omride dynasty (2 Kgs 9–10). The daughter born to Gomer and Hosea is named Lo-ruḥamah, which means "no mercy" in Hebrew, and refers to YHWH's refusal to show mercy to Israel on account of its purported abandonment of YHWH. Finally, the second son born to Gomer and Hosea is named Lo-ammi, which means "not my people" in Hebrew, and refers to YHWH's view that the covenant or "marriage" between YHWH and Israel is broken.

The basic appeal for Israel's return to YHWH appears in Hos 2:3–3:5 as the first element of Hosea's speeches to Israel that call for Israel's return and elaborate upon the reasons for the break-up in the first place. The appeal is metaphorically stated as YHWH's and Hosea's appeal to the children and to the

---

[7] Gerlinde Baumann, *Love and Violence: Marriage as Metaphor for the Relationship between YHWH and Israel in the Prophets* (Collegeville, MN: Liturgical Press, 2003), 85–104.

estranged wife, Israel or Gomer, to return to her husband. Although the passage begins with Hosea's appeals for the return of Gomer, YHWH's appeals to Israel emerge in the latter portions of the passage. References to Gomer's pursuit of other lovers or Israel's pursuit of Baalim, the fertility gods of Canaan, reinforce the notion that Hosea's complaints are essentially religious. But YHWH's instructions to Hosea to marry once again in Hos 3:1–3 followed by the statements that Israel will once again return to the rule of the house of David in Hos 3:4–5 points to Hosea's view that religious repentance and righteous political rule are coterminous. The use of the Hebrew term, *bĕ'aḥărît hayyāmîm*, "in the later days," simply refers to the future, not to the end of time as some presuppose.[8]

Hosea's complaint against the house of Jehu becomes clear throughout both YHWH's and Hosea's charges against Israel. YHWH's charges in Hos 4 focus on the religious dimensions, particularly the failure of the priests and prophets to teach the people properly concerning YHWH's will. Hosea's charges in Hos 5:1–14:1 likewise raise religious issues, but the character of Israel's rulers and the nation's relationship with Assyria becomes a key issue throughout. Hos 5:13–14 refers to Ephraim's (Israel's) sending of envoys to Assyria; Hos 7:11–12 refers to Israel's appeals to Egypt and Assyria; and Hos 12:1–2 refers to Israel's covenant with Assyria to carry oil to Egypt. Examination of ancient Near Eastern historical records confirms Hosea's concerns. When Jehu overthrew Jehoram, Israel was fighting a losing battle against the Arameans, but the house of Jehu ultimately defeated the Aramean threat. Although biblical records mention only Israel's victories over Aram under the Jehu monarchs (2 Kgs 13:1–5, 22–25; cf. 2 Kgs 10:32–33; 12:18–19), the Black Obelisk of the Assyrian monarch Shalmaneser III portrays Jehu's submission to Assyria[9] and the Assyrian monarch Adad Nirari III lists Joash the Samaritan (i.e., Jehoash ben Jehoahaz ben Jehu) as one of his tributaries.[10] Indeed, it was the Jehu dynasty's alliance with Assyria that ultimately checked the Aramean threat against Israel and enabled Jeroboam ben Joash, the fourth monarch of the Jehu line, to rule over a kingdom like that of Solomon that extended from Lebo-Hamath in the north to the Sea of the Aravah in the south in peace (2 Kgs 14:23–29). Hosea viewed such an alliance as abandonment of YHWH, particularly since Israel's ancestors had come from Aram, YHWH's prophet had led Israel from Egyptian slavery to the promised land, and Jacob had found his wives in Aram. For Hosea, Israel's return to YHWH entailed abandonment of its alliance with Assyria (and Egypt) and a return to its past relationships with Aram. Indeed, his final appeal for

---

[8] Simon J. De Vries, *From Old Revelation to New: A Tradition-Historical and Redaction-Critical Study of Temporal Transitions* (Grand Rapids: Eerdmans, 1995), 89–95.

[9] See *ANEP*, 351–355; *ANET*, 281.

[10] S. Page, "A Stele of Adad Nirari III and Nergal-ereš from Tell al Rimlah," *Iraq* 30 (1968): 139–53.

Israel to return to YHWH in Hos 14:2-9 notes that "Assyria will not save us," but that YHWH is ready to forgive all guilt when Israel returns. Indeed, Hosea's view of transformation calls for the overthrow of the Jehu dynasty and its policy of alliance with Assyria.

The book of Joel appears second in the Masoretic sequence of the Twelve Prophets and fourth in the Septuagint sequence.[11] The superscription of the book identifies the prophet only as Joel ben Pethuel, but it provides no information concerning historical setting. Interpreters generally view it as a post-exilic, proto-apocalyptic book, which is confirmed by its extensive references to earlier biblical literature. The reference to the Valley of Jehoshaphat in Joel 4:12 (=NRSV 3:12) refers to the ninth-century Judean monarch, although it draws on the account of Jehoshaphat's battle against the Ammonites and Moabites in 2 Chr 20:20-26. Nevertheless, the absence of historical setting, the metaphorical portrayal of Jerusalem's enemies as a locust plague, and the retrospective character of the reference to Jehoshaphat's victory contribute to a mythological portrayal of YHWH's deliverance of Jerusalem that can be read in relation to virtually any setting, past, present, and future. The call to turn plowshares into swords and pruning hooks into spears as YHWH's warriors prepare to repel the threat posed to Jerusalem recalls and reverses those by Isaiah (Isa 2:2-4) and Micah (Mic 4:1-5) for the nations to give up their weapons, stream to Zion, and learn YHWH's Torah or Instruction.

Joel's eschatological perspective is defined by its view of the Day of YHWH, viz., the day of deliverance when YHWH will defeat the forces of the nations that threaten Jerusalem. The literary form of the book indicates that it is formulated as an account of YHWH's response to Judah's appeals for relief from the threat of attackers, metaphorically portrayed as a locust plague like the locust plague that afflicted Egypt in the Exodus traditions (Exod 10:1-20)[12]:

---

[11] For discussion of Joel, see esp. Sweeney, *Twelve Prophets*, 1:145-187; John Barton, *Joel and Obadiah: A Commentary*, OTL (Louisville: Westminster John Knox, 2001); Richard J. Coggins, *Joel and Amos*, NCeB (Sheffield: Sheffield Academic, 2000); James L. Crenshaw, *Joel*, AB 24C (New York: Doubleday, 1995); Hans Walter Wolff, *Joel and Amos*, Hermeneia (Philadelphia: Fortress, 1977).

[12] Sweeney, *Prophetic Literature*, 181.

YHWH's Response to Judah's Appeals for Relief from Threat (Joel 1:1–4:21)

I. Superscription — 1:1
II. Body of the Book: YHWH's response to Judah's appeal — 1:2–4:21
   A. Prophet's call to communal complaint concerning the threat of the locust plague — 1:2–20
   B. Prophet's call to communal complaint concerning the threat of invasion — 2:1–14
   C. Prophet's announcement of YHWH's response to protect people from the threat — 2:15–4:21

Many interpreters maintain that the portents mentioned in Joel 3:4 in reference to the Day of YHWH, that is, the sun turned to darkness and moon turned to blood, indicate a fundamental transformation of creation that signals the end of time and the beginning of a new age. Such a view is unjustified, however, insofar as these features appear during the *Sharav* (Hebrew) or *Ḥamsin* (Arabic), a sirocco or strong, dry, desert wind, much like the Santa Ana winds of southern California, that appears in the Middle East at times of seasonal transition.[13] When the *Sharav* appears, it darkens the skies, blocks the sun, and makes the moon appear red due to the large quantities of blowing dust. In biblical tradition, the *Sharav* is known as the East Wind that manifests YHWH's power, as in Exod 14–15 when the wind splits the Red Sea allowing Israel to cross on dry land. Nevertheless, the Day of YHWH tradition in Joel points to YHWH's intervention in the world to redeem Jerusalem and Judah from threat.

The book of Amos appears as the third book of the Masoretic sequence and the second book of the Septuagint sequence.[14] Because of the prophet's concern with the rights of the poor, his condemnation of the Israelite monarchy and the Beth El sanctuary for trampling those rights, and the initial sequence of oracles concerning the nations in Amos 1:3–2:16, Amos is frequently viewed as the quintessential prophetic exemplar for universal social justice. Such a perspective is reinforced by his reference to the Day of YHWH in Amos 5:18–20, which is directed against those who would deny the poor, and his anticipation in Amos 9:11–15 of a future righteous Davidic monarch who would set the world aright.

The superscription of the book of Amos in Amos 1:1 identifies him as a "sheep breeder" from the Judean town of Tekoa during the reigns of King Jeroboam ben Joash of Israel (786–746 BCE) and King Uzziah ben Amaziah of Judah (783–742 BCE). The term "sheep breeder," Hebrew *nōqēd*, does not refer to a simple shepherd (Hebrew, *rōʿeh*) but to more highly placed figure, such as a king, chieftain, or officer, who functions as a sheep broker. Although this was a

---

[13] For discussion of the *Sharav*, see "Israel, Land of (Geographic Survey)," *EncJud* 9:189–90.
[14] For discussion of Amos, see Sweeney, *Twelve Prophets*, 1:189–276; Coggins, *Joel and Amos*; Shalom Paul, *Amos*, Hermeneia (Philadelphia: Fortress, 1991); Wolff, *Joel and Amos*.

period of security, prosperity, and wealth for northern Israel due to its alliance with Assyria, Judah was a vassal to Israel during this period and Amos apparently appeared at the northern Israelite Beth El temple to pay a portion of Judah's tribute to its northern Israelite suzerain. Throughout the book, Amos condemns northern Israel and the nations for acting contrary to YHWH's will, and calls upon its readers to seek YHWH. The formal literary structure of Amos indicates that the book is formulated as an exhortation to seek YHWH:[15]

Amos's Exhortation to Seek YHWH (Amos 1:1–9:15)

I. Introduction   1:1–2
    A. Superscription   1:1
    B. Motto: YHWH roars from Zion   1:2
II. Exhortation proper   1:3–9:15
    A. Oracles against the nations (culminating in northern Israel)   1:3–2:16
       1. Damascus/Aram   1:3–5
       2. Gaza/Philistia   1:6–8
       3. Tyre/Phoenicia   1:9–10
       4. Edom   1:11–12
       5. Ammon   1:13–15
       6. Moab   2:1–3
       7. Judah   2:4–5
       8. Israel   2:6–16
    B. Indictment of northern Israel   3:1–4:13
    C. Call for repentance of northern Israel   5:1–6:14
    D. Amos's vision reports: call for destruction of Beth El and rise of the house of David   7:1–9:15

Close attention to the form and contents of the book indicates that Amos acts and speaks as a Judean who would condemn northern Israel for its harsh treatment of Judah and call for the overthrow of King Jeroboam ben Joash. The initial motto for the book in Amos 1:2 portrays YHWH as a lion, the tribal symbol of Judah (see Gen 49:8–12), roaring from Zion and prompting the Carmel, the northern Israelite coastal range known for its fertility, to wither. The oracles concerning the nations target the various enemies of Israel who fought against Israel or who betrayed their alliances with Israel from the ninth and early eighth centuries. Although Amos's northern Israelite audience would have affirmed his condemnation of these nations for their past treachery against Israel, the culmination of the sequence with Israel reveals his rhetorical intent to

---

[15] Sweeney, *Prophetic Literature*, 184.

target Israel itself as his main concern.[16] The indictment of Israel (Amos 3–4) coupled with his exhortations for a return to YHWH (Amos 5–6) indicates his fundamental goal to bring Israel back to YHWH. The meaning of such a move becomes evident in the final sequence of five visions in Amos 7–9. The first four visions point to Amos's conviction that YHWH has shown him the divine intention to bring Israel down by visions of a locust plague, fire, a plumb line, and a basket of summer fruit. The brief narrative in Amos 7:10–17 indicates that Amos's understanding of YHWH's intent is the overthrow of King Jeroboam ben Joash and the destruction of the Beth El sanctuary, that is, the royal sanctuary of northern Israel. The final vision in Amos 9 then elaborates on this intention by portraying YHWH standing by the temple altar calling for the downfall of the capitals and thresholds that support the temple building itself. Although many interpreters maintain that Amos's call for the restoration of the fallen booth of David presupposes a postexilic setting when the house of David was defunct, Amos's Judean identity and Judah's vassal status to Israel indicate the prophet's object to restore Davidic rule over the north in order to reestablish the moral standing and economic well-being of the nation Israel.

The book of Obadiah is the fourth in the Masoretic order of the Twelve Prophets and the fifth in the Septuagint order.[17] The superscription in Obad 1 provides no indication of historical setting and identifies the work only as the vision of Obadiah. Traditional exegesis identifies Obadiah with the royal officer who assisted Elijah and protected the prophets of YHWH from the threat posed by King Ahab ben Omri of Israel and his Phoenician queen Jezebel (1 Kgs 18). Because of Obadiah's condemnation of Edom for its role in standing aside and thereby in enabling foreigners to overwhelm Jerusalem and to exile its inhabitants (cf. e.g., Ps 137; Isa 34:5–15; 63:1–6; Jer 49:7–22; Ezek 25:12–14; 35:2–15; Mal 1:2–5; Lam 4:21–22), modern interpreters date the book to the exilic or postexilic periods. The literary structure of the book points to its fundamental concern with condemning Edom for its actions against Jerusalem:[18]

---

[16] On the rhetorical characteristics and function of Amos, see now Karl Möller, *A Prophet in Debate: The Rhetoric of Persuasion in the Book of Amos*, JSOTSup 372 (Sheffield: Sheffield Academic, 2003).

[17] For discussion of Obadiah, see Sweeney, *Twelve Prophets*, 1:277–300; Barton, *Joel and Obadiah*; Ehud Ben Zvi, *A Historical-Critical Study of the Book of Obadiah*, BZAW 242 (Berlin: de Gruyter, 1996); Paul R. Raabe, *Obadiah*, AB 24D (New York: Doubleday, 1996); Hans Walter Wolff, *Obadiah and Jonah*, CC (Minneapolis: Augsburg, 1986).

[18] Sweeney, *Prophetic Literature*, 188.

Prophetic Announcement of Judgment against Edom (Obad 1–21)

I.	Superscription	1a
II.	Oracle concerning the condemnation of Edom	1b–21
	A. Prophetic messenger formula	1bα 1–5
	B. Oracle proper	1bα 6–21

Obadiah emphasizes the Day of YHWH as a day of judgment against Edom and the nations that threaten Jerusalem and oppose YHWH. Indeed, Obadiah employs the image of drinking from the cup of YHWH's judgment to illustrate its intent (Obad 15–16).

The book of Jonah is the fifth in the Masoretic sequence of the Twelve Prophets and sixth in the Septuagint sequence.[19] The book identifies the prophet as Jonah ben Amittai, who is mentioned in 2 Kgs 14:25 as the prophet who foresaw the restoration of Israel's territory under the reign of the ninth-century northern Israelite monarch Jeroboam ben Joash. The portrayal of Jonah in the book is fictitious, however, insofar as he is swallowed by a fish and prays to YHWH for deliverance. Overall, the literary form of Jonah is that of a Second Temple period novella that presents the narrative in order to examine the question of YHWH's mercy to Nineveh, the capital of the Assyrian empire that would one day destroy Jonah's home nation of Israel. The literary form of the book appears as follows:[20]

Narrative of YHWH's Mercy toward a Repentant Nineveh (Jonah 1–4)

I.	Jonah's attempt to flee from YHWH	1:1–2:1
	A. Jonah's attempt to flee YHWH's initial commission	1:1–3
	B. Jonah's encounter with the sailors during the storm	1:4–16
	C. Jonah's prayer to YHWH from the belly of the fish	2:1–11
II.	Encounter between YHWH and Jonah concerning YHWH's mercy toward a repentant Nineveh	3:1–4:11
	A. YHWH's renewed commission to Jonah and its outcome	3:1–10
	B. YHWH's assertion of the right to mercy in encounter with Jonah	4:1–11

---

[19] For discussion of Jonah, see Sweeney, *Twelve Prophets*, 1:301–334; Jack M. Sasson, *Jonah*, AB 24B (New York: Doubleday, 1990); Uriel Simon, *Jonah*, JPS Bible Commentary (Philadelphia: Jewish Publication Society, 1999); Phyllis Trible, "Jonah," *The New Interpreters Bible*, ed. L. E. Keck et al. (Nashville: Abingdon, 1996), 7:461–529; Wolff, *Obadiah and Jonah*.

[20] Sweeney, *Prophetic Literature*, 190.

Although many interpreters charge Jonah with petulance and animosity toward gentiles, the question of theodicy is a key concern in this book as it focuses on the questions of YHWH's mercy to the repentant. The narrative begins with Jonah's fleeing from YHWH who has commanded that he announce judgment against Nineveh. Although Jonah books passage on a ship, a storm threatens the ship and he is thrown overboard to placate YHWH. He is swallowed by a great fish and is vomited up on shore after praying for deliverance form YHWH. YHWH commissions him a second time to condemn Nineveh, but Nineveh repents when he does so and Jonah is angry because he claims that he knew that this would happen. The narrative quotes Exod 34:6–7 in Jonah 4:2 concerning YHWH's gracious and compassionate character to highlight its concern with the question of YHWH's mercy and righteousness. When Jonah swears that he wants to die (cf. Elijah in 1 Kgs 19:4), YHWH shades Jonah with a broom plant and then destroys it. YHWH asks Jonah if he grieves over the loss of the plant. When Jonah responds affirmatively, YHWH then asks rhetorically whether YHWH should not care about the lives of the one hundred and twenty thousand people who inhabit Nineveh. The book affirms repentance and YHWH's mercy, but YHWH's concluding question is left unanswered. It is then left to the reader to recognize that one day Nineveh will be responsible for the destruction of northern Israel.

The book of Micah is the sixth in the Masoretic sequence of the Twelve Prophets and third in the Septuagint sequence.[21] The superscription of the book in Mic 1:1 identifies Micah as a Moreshtite, that is, a resident of the town of Moreshet Gath in the Judean Shephelah (the border region between Judah and Philistia), during the reigns of the Judean monarchs Jotham (742–735 BCE), Ahaz (735–715 BCE), and Hezekiah. This makes Micah a contemporary of Isaiah ben Amoz, although it is mistaken to claim that both prophets represent the same viewpoint. Unlike the urbane Isaiah, Micah lives in the Judean countryside in a region that suffered the brunt of the Assyrian invasion of Judah in 701 BCE. As a result, he became a war refugee who was forced to flee to Jerusalem for refuge from Sennacherib's invading soldiers. He charges both the northern Israelite and Judean monarchies with incompetence and irresponsibility in making decisions to go to war with Assyria, particularly when the common people outside of Samaria and Jerusalem were the ones to pay the price when the Assyrians attacked. In his view, the downfall of Samaria emerges as a model for that of Jerusalem. Unlike Isaiah, Micah very clearly anticipates Jerusalem's destruction (Mic 3:12). Nevertheless, Micah views the present period of punishment as a means to prepare for Jerusalem's restoration and exaltation

---

[21] For discussion of Micah, see Sweeney, *The Twelve Prophets*, 2:337–416; Ehud Ben Zvi, *Micah*, FOTL 21B (Grand Rapids: Eerdmans, 2001); Mignon Jacobs, *The Conceptual Coherence of the Book of Micah*, JSOTSup 322 (Sheffield: Sheffield Academic, 2001); Hans Walter Wolff, *Micah*, CC (Minneapolis: Augsburg, 1990).

over the nations that once oppressed her. The formal literary structure of the book appears as follows:[22]

Micah's Announcement Concerning YHWH's Future Exaltation of Jerusalem at the Center of the Nations (Mic 1:1–7:20)

I. Superscription — 1:1
II. Announcement of YHWH's exaltation of Jerusalem proper — 1:2–7:20
    A. YHWH's punishment of Samaria as paradigm for Jerusalem — 1:2–16
    B. Process of punishment and restoration for Jerusalem: Babylonian exile, new Davidic monarch to punish oppressive nations — 2:1–5:14
        1. concerning the process of punishment — 2:1–13
        2. concerning YHWH's plans to punish and exalt Jerusalem — 3:1–5:14
    C. Appeal to Israel/Judah for return to YHWH — 6:1–16
    D. Liturgical psalm of confidence in YHWH — 7:1–20

In addition to his views concerning the coming destruction of Jerusalem, Micah's views concerning its future exaltation play an important role in defining the eschatological perspective of the book. Like Isaiah, Mic 4:1–5 presents a version of the famous vision in which the nations will stream to Zion to learn YHWH's Torah in the days to come (Hebrew, *bě'aḥărît hayyāmîm*, means "in the future"), resulting in an era of peace in which swords will be turned to plowshares and spears to pruning hooks. But Micah's understanding of this passage differs markedly from Isaiah's. Whereas Isaiah envisions the ultimate submission of Israel to YHWH by means of a foreign monarch, specifically King Cyrus of Persia (Isa 44:28; 45:1), Micah calls for the rise of a new Davidic monarch from Beth Lehem of Ephrath (Mic 5:1) who will ultimately defeat the nations that oppress Zion and Jacob.

The book of Nahum is the seventh book of both the Masoretic and Septuagint sequences of the Twelve Prophets.[23] The superscription in Nah 1:1 identifies the book as a pronouncement on Nineveh and the book of the prophet Nahum the Elkoshite. A prophetic "pronouncement" (Hebrew, *maśśā'*), sometimes incorrectly translated as "burden," identifies YHWH's actions in the human world. Although the superscription provides no indication of historical setting, the basic theme of the book is the downfall of Nineveh, the capital of the Assyrian empire, to Babylonian and Medean forces in 612 BCE. Some note the

---

[22] Sweeney, *Prophetic Literature*, 194.
[23] For discussion of Nahum, see Sweeney, *Twelve Prophets*, 2:417–449; Michael H. Floyd, *Minor Prophets, Part 2*, FOTL 22 (Grand Rapids: Eerdmans, 2000); Klaas Spronk, *Nahum* HCOT (Kampen: Kok Pharos, 1997).

reference to the fall of Thebes (No-Amon) in 663 BCE (Nah 3:8–10), but the fate of Thebes only serves as a confirmation of YHWH's power to bring down Nineveh. The formal literary structure of the book appears as the prophet's disputation or argument that YHWH is the true power in the world:[24]

Nahum's Argument that YHWH is the True Power of the World (Nah 1:1–3:19)

I. Superscription   1:1
II. Massa' Proper: Refutation of Contention that YHWH is Powerless   1:2–3:19
    A. Address to Judah and Assyria challenging their low estimation of YHWH   1:2–10
    B. Address to Judah asserting that the end of Assyrian oppression is an act of YHWH   1:11–2:1
    C. Address to Nineveh and the Assyrian king asserting that the fall of Nineveh is an act of YHWH   2:2–3:19

Although some interpreters decry the violence of the book or charge that it represents Judean hostility to gentiles, such views miss an important point, viz., the book of Nahum celebrates the downfall of an oppressor as an act of YHWH's power and justice in the world. Insofar as Nah 1:2 cites the litany of YHWH's characteristics in Exod 34:6–7 with a special emphasis on YHWH's justice, Nahum calls for a comparative reading with Jonah.

The book of Habakkuk is the eighth book in both the Masoretic and Septuagint sequences of the Twelve Prophets.[25] The superscription in Hab 1:1 identifies the book simply as the pronouncement (Hebrew, *maśśā'*) of Habakkuk the prophet, and the second superscription in Hab 3:1 refers simply to the prayer of Habakkuk the prophet. Although the superscriptions provide no historical information, the reference to the rise of the Chaldeans (Hebrew, *kaśdîm*) indicates that the book presupposes the neo-Babylonian subjugation of Judah in 605 BCE. Although many interpreters mistakenly argue that the book is designed to condemn Judah, close analysis of the literary form and content of the book indicates that it is a reflection on theodicy insofar as it defends YHWH's righteousness and power by arguing that YHWH was the one who brought the neo-Babylonian oppressors to Judah and that YHWH will also ultimately deliver Judah from the oppressor. The literary form of the book appears as follows:[26]

---

[24] Sweeney, *Prophetic Literature*, 197.
[25] For discussion of Habakkuk, see Sweeney, *Twelve Prophets*, 451–490; Floyd, *Minor Prophets*; Robert D. Haak, *Habakkuk*, VTSup 44 (Leiden: Brill, 1992).
[26] Sweeney, *Prophetic Literature*, 198.

Habakkuk's Oracle and Prayer Concerning YHWH's Righteousness (Hab 1:1–3:19)

I. Habakkuk's Oracle: Dialogue concerning YHWH's righteousness — 1:1–2:20
   A. Superscription — 1:1
   B. Massa' proper — 1:2–2:20
      1. Habakkuk's initial complaint to YHWH concerning oppression of righteous by wicked — 1:2–4
      2. YHWH's response: I brought the Chaldeans — 1:5–11
      3. Habakkuk's second complaint: why tolerate evil? — 1:12–17
      4. Report of YHWH's response: oppressor will fall — 2:1–20
II. Prayer of Habakkuk: Petition for YHWH to act — 3:1–19
   A. Superscription — 3:1
   B. Prayer proper: YHWH will act — 3:2–19a
   C. Instructions for the Choirmaster — 3:19b

Habakkuk's eschatological perspective is defined first of all in the prophetic pronouncement of Hab 1:2–2:20 in which the prophet engages in dialog with YHWH concerning the emergence of the evil Chaldeans to power over Judah. YHWH claims to be the one responsible for bringing the Chaldeans and maintains that it is a great work never before seen. Although YHWH's purpose in bringing the Chaldeans is never quite clear, the pronouncement is clear in maintaining that the oppressive Chaldeans will ultimately fall when they have swallowed more than they can handle. The concluding prayer in Hab 3 appears as a psalm that envisions YHWH's mythological assault against the wicked much like the defeat of Pharaoh and Egypt at the Red Sea (Exod 15) or Sisera and his army in the time of Deborah (Judg 5).

The book of Zephaniah is the ninth in both the Masoretic and Septuagint sequences of the Twelve Prophets.[27] Although the superscription of the book places Zephaniah in the reign of King Josiah ben Amon of Judah (640–609 BCE), its placement after Habakkuk and the rise of Babylon and before Haggai and the call for rebuilding the Temple prompts readers to see the coming Babylonian destruction of Jerusalem as a major concern. Such a reading is only inferred by its placement, however, and the book is formulated as an exhortation to seek YHWH in the time of King Josiah's program of religious reform and national restoration (see 1 Kgs 22–23):[28]

---

[27] For discussion of Zephaniah, see Sweeney, *Twelve Prophets*, 491–526; idem, *Zephaniah*, Hermeneia (Minneapolis: Fortress, 2003); Ehud Ben Zvi, *A Historical Critical Study of the Book of Zephaniah*, BZAW 198 (Berlin: de Gruyter, 1991); Floyd, *Minor Prophets*; J. Vlaardingerbroek, *Zephaniah*, HCOT (Leuven: Peeters, 1999).
[28] Sweeney, *Prophetic Literature*, 200.

Zephaniah's Exhortation to Seek YHWH (Zeph 1:1–3:20)

I.	Superscription	1:1
II.	Body of Book: Exhortation to seek YHWH	1:2–3:20
	A. Announcement of the Day of YHWH against Baal worshippers	1:2–18
	B. Exhortation to seek YHWH	2:1–3:20
	1. Exhortation proper	2:1–3
	2. Substantiation: YHWH's actions	2:4–3:20
	a. Basis for exhortation: destruction of Philistine cities	2:4
	b. Punishment of nations	2:5–15
	c. Restoration of Jerusalem	3:1–20

A key element in assessing Zephaniah's eschatological perspectives is the use of the Day of YHWH theme, particularly in Zeph 1:2–18. The Day of YHWH is employed here as a motif that is tied to the sacrificial liturgy of the Jerusalem Temple that signals YHWH's intentions to bring punishment to those who continue to venerate foreign gods. The exhortational element of the book in Zeph 2–3 then calls upon the audience to return to YHWH before it is too late and substantiates its call by pointing to YHWH's punishment of the nations hostile to Judah during Josiah's reign, offerings brought to YHWH from Cush (Ethiopia), and the restoration of Bat Zion to her husband YHWH. Although such themes were well at home in Josiah's reform, which envisioned the return of exiles from Assyria and Egypt, the book would later be read as a vision of Zion's restoration following the Babylonian exile.

The book of Haggai is the tenth book in both the Masoretic and Septuagint sequences of the Twelve Prophets.[29] The book is composed in narrative form, and its chronological formulas in Hag 1:1; 2:1, 18, 20 date Haggai's oracles to an approximately three-month period during the second year of the reign of King Darius of Persia. This would be approximately 520 BCE, the year that construction on the Second Temple in Jerusalem commenced. Overall, the literary form of the book indicates that Haggai's oracles are designed to convince its reading audience that they should build the Temple in order to fulfill YHWH's will:[30]

---

[29] For discussion of Haggai, see Sweeney, *Twelve Prophets*, 2:527–57; Floyd, *Minor Prophets*; Carol L. Meyers and Eric M. Meyers, *Haggai and Zechariah 1–8*, AB 25B (New York: Doubleday, 1987); David L. Petersen, *Haggai and Zechariah 1–8: A Commentary*, OTL (Philadelphia: Westminster, 1984); Paul L. Redditt, *Haggai, Zechariah, Malachi*, NCeB (Grand Rapids: Eerdmans, 1995); Hans Walter Wolff, *Haggai*, CC (Minneapolis: Augsburg, 1988).

[30] Sweeney, *Prophetic Literature*, 201.

Narrative Concerning Haggai's Oracles to Rebuild the Temple and Recognize Zerubbabel as YHWH's Regent (Hag 1–2)

I. Narrative concerning compliance with YHWH's instruction to build Temple — 1:1–15a
II. Narrative concerning future glory of Jerusalem Temple — 1:15b–2:9
III. Narrative concerning purity of land and establishment of Zerubbabel as YHWH's regent — 2:10–23

Haggai's eschatological perspective is defined in part by his view that the land of Israel suffers drought because the Temple has not yet been rebuilt. As a result, the offerings presented by the people at the altar are impure and unacceptable to YHWH. He envisions that YHWH will shake the heavens and the earth, which will prompt the nations of the world to recognize YHWH's sovereignty and to bring offerings to YHWH when the Temple is built. A messianic perspective also plays a role insofar as Haggai maintains that Zerubbabel ben Shealtiel, the grandson of King Jehoiachin ben Jehoiakim of Judah, will serve as YHWH's "signet ring" or regent in the world once "the throne of the nations," that is, the Persian empire, is overthrown. Such a move would signal the resumption of the rule of the house of David over Judah on behalf of YHWH, insofar as the royal signet ring symbolized royal authority in the ancient world.

The book of Zechariah is the eleventh book in the Masoretic and Septuagint sequences of the book of the Twelve.[31] The book focuses on the significance of the restoration of the Jerusalem Temple, and the various chronological statements in Zech 1:1; 1:7; and 7:1 place the book in the second and fourth years of the reign of King Darius of Persia, that is, 520 and 518 BCE, coinciding with the beginning of Temple construction in 520–515 BCE. The superscription of the book in Zech 1:1 identifies the prophet as Zechariah ben Berechiah ben Iddo. Insofar as Ezra 5:1 and 6:14 identify him as Zechariah bar Iddo, scholars have speculated about problems in the transmission of his name. But Isa 8:1–4 identifies a Zechariah ben Yeberechiah (a variant of the name Berechiah) as a witness to Isaiah's prophecies and the birth of his son, which together with the many intertextual references to Isaiah throughout the book indicates a deliberate effort to present Zechariah as the witness to Isaiah and the arbiter of his message. Overall, the book of Zechariah presents the prophet's visions concerning the significance of the rebuilding of the Temple in Jerusalem, including the restoration of the Temple priesthood and the recognition of

---

[31] For discussion of Zechariah, see Sweeney, *Twelve Prophets*, 2:559–709; Edgar Conrad, *Zechariah*, Readings (Sheffield: Sheffield Academic, 1999); Floyd, *Minor Prophets*; Meyers and Meyers, *Haggai, Zechariah 1–8*; Meyers and Meyers, *Zechariah 9–14*, AB 25C (New York: Doubleday, 1993); Petersen, *Haggai and Zechariah 1–8*; Petersen, *Zechariah 9–14 and Malachi: A Commentary*, OTL (Louisville: Westminster John Knox, 1995); Redditt, *Haggai, Zechariah, Malachi*.

YHWH at the Jerusalem Temple by the nations of the world. Such a view builds upon Isaiah's visions of restoration insofar as Zechariah envisions the overthrow of gentile rule as the nations recognize YHWH's sovereignty.

Modern critical discussion of the literary form of Zechariah posits that the authentic oracles of the prophet appear in Zech 1–8 but that Zech 9–14 (or 9–11 and 12–14) represent the proto-apocalyptic work or works of a later writer or writers. Earlier scholars tended to date Zech 9–14 to the Hellenistic age on the mistaken argument that the itinerary of the king and the reference to the Greek in Zech 9 presupposed Alexander the Great's conquest of the Near East in 333–332 BCE, but contemporary scholars tend to opt for the Persian period as the setting for the composition of these chapters. Despite the compositional history of the book, however, it is meant to be read as a single work in which the account of Zechariah's visions concerning the building of the Temple in Zech 1:7–6:15 provide the foundation for understanding the account of Zechariah's oracles which portray the world-wide recognition of YHWH's sovereignty at the Temple in Zech 7–14. The literary form of the book then appears as follows:[32]

Account of Zechariah's Visions and Oracles Concerning the Significance of the Restoration of Jerusalem (Zech 1:1–14:21)

I.	Introduction to the Book: YHWH's initial word to Zechariah	1:1–6
II.	Narrative presentation of YHWH's later words to Zechariah: visions and oracles	1:7–14:21
	A. Visions	1:7–6:15
	1. Divine horses: YHWH's anger against nations and plan to restore Jerusalem and Temple	1:7–17
	2. Four horns: restoration of Temple altar; scattering of Israel and punishment of nations	2:1–4
	3. City with walls of fire: restoration of Jerusalem	2:5–17
	4. Ordination of Joshua ben Jehozadak	3:1–10
	5. Menorah and two olive shoots: Zerubbabel and foundation stone	4:1–14
	6. Flying scroll: justice for land from Temple	5:1–4
	7. Woman in ephah basket: iniquity sent to Shinar/Babylon	5:5–11
	8. Four chariots proclaim crowning of Joshua ben Jehozadak	6:1–15

---

[32] Sweeney, *Prophetic Literature*, 204–5.

B.	Oracles	7:1–14:21
	1. Question concerning continued mourning for the Temple	7:1–7
	2. Answer: YHWH wants rejoicing and righteous action for restoration of Temple	7:8–14:21
	a. Call for righteous action	7:8–14
	b. Summation of former prophets: call for righteous action	8:1–17
	c. Zechariah's report of YHWH's oracles concerning restoration of Zion as holy center for the world	8:18–14:21

The eschatological perspective of the book of Zechariah presupposes that the time for Israel's and Judah's punishment is past and that the time of restoration—to be inaugurated by the reestablishment of the Jerusalem Temple—is at hand. The eight visions of the prophet, who is himself a Zadokite priest charged with holy service at the sanctuary, are guided by an angelic figure who conveys YHWH's words to Zechariah. As in Ezekiel and Daniel, such a guide plays an important role in characterizing the book as a heavenly revelation of YHWH's presence and plans for the future of the nation of Israel/Judah, the nations at large, and even creation itself. Each of the visions in Zech 1:7–6:15 takes up some aspect of the reestablishment of the Temple, including the gathering of horsemen at the site of the Temple, the construction of the altar, measuring lines for the city, the ordination of Joshua ben Jehozadak as High Priest, the Menorah or Lamp Stand structure, the reading of the Torah scroll from the Temple entry, the removal of impurity from the Temple, and the seating of the priest on the throne, as actions that portend YHWH's efforts to reestablish divine presence and sovereignty in the world. The account of the prophet's oracles in Zech 7–14 then lays out the means by which YHWH's presence and sovereignty are to be manifested in the world when the Temple is reestablished. The initial narratives in Zech 7:1–7; 7:8–14; and 8:1–17 question continued mourning for the Temple and call for righteous action to reinstitute the sanctity of the Temple in the midst of the land. Two oracular blocks in Zech 9–11 and 12–14, each introduced as a *maśśā'* or prophetic pronouncement of YHWH, then lay out the process by which YHWH's presence and sovereignty are to be manifested. Zechariah 9–11 anticipates the return of a new monarch who will overthrow the three shepherds, that is, the Persian kings Cyrus, Cambyses, and Darius, who have failed to manifest YHWH's purposes in the world. Zechariah 12–14 then describes YHWH's apocalyptic victories, first in Jerusalem and then over the nations of the world, that will see the reestablishment of the house of David and the recognition of YHWH by the nations at the Jerusalem Temple during the festival of Sukkot.

Finally, the book of Malachi is the twelfth book in both the Masoretic and Septuagint sequences of the Twelve Prophets.[33] The superscription of the book in Mal 1:1 identifies it as a *maśśā'* or a prophetic pronouncement of YHWH's word to Israel through Malachi, but interpreters are divided as to whether or not Malachi is a proper name or simply a Hebrew term that designates the prophet as "my messenger" or "my angel" (cf. Mal 3:1). Most interpreters date the book to the late-fifth century, that is, the period immediately prior to the reforms of Nehemiah in the latter fifth century and early fourth century, due to the apparent neglect of the Temple and the need to organize the Jewish community of early Persian-period Jerusalem. Indeed, the literary form of the book indicates that it is a series of disputation or argumentative speeches that are designed to call upon the priest and people to show proper reverence for YHWH, specifically by doing justice, ensuring the sanctity of the Temple offerings, and observing YHWH's Torah:[34]

Parenetic Address to Priests and People calling for Proper Reverence for YHWH (Mal 1:1–3:24)

I. Superscription — 1:11
II. Body of the Book: Parenetic Address Proper — 1:2–3:24
   A. First disputation: YHWH loves the people — 1:2–5
   B. Second disputation: People and Priests have Mishandled Cultic Matters — 1:6–2:16
   C. Third disputation: Justice will be done on the Day of YHWH — 2:17–3:5
   D. Fourth disputation: Call for proper treatment of YHWH's tithes — 3:6–12
   E. Fifth disputation: YHWH's justice will be realized on Day of YHWH — 3:13–21
   F. Concluding summation: observe YHWH's Torah — 3:22–24

The eschatological agenda of Malachi focuses especially on reestablishing the Temple as the holy center of Israel and creation at large on the Day of YHWH. By focusing on "my messenger" (Hebrew, *mal'ākî*) as the means by which YHWH's will is made known, Malachi draws on the Pentateuchal tradition in Exod 23:23–26 in which YHWH promises to send an angel before Israel to guide them into the promised land and ensure their observance of divine Torah. Malachi concludes by invoking both Moses as a reminder of the need to observe

---

[33] For discussion of Malachi, see Sweeney, *The Twelve Prophets*, 711–52; Floyd, *Minor Prophets*; Andrew E. Hill, *Malachi*, AB 25D (New York: Doubleday, 1995); Petersen, *Zechariah 9–14 and Malachi*; Redditt, *Haggai, Zechariah, Malachi*.
[34] Sweeney, *Prophetic Literature*, 207–8.

YHWH's Torah and Elijah as the figure who will inaugurate the Day of YHWH when YHWH's sanctity will be restored.

III

The Book of the Twelve Prophets clearly appears in at least two distinct forms, each with its own unique order of books and distinctive hermeneutical perspective. In addition, each form of the Book of the Twelve comprises the same twelve discrete prophetic books, each with its own individual formal characteristics and unique set of concerns. When we consider the generic character of the Book of the Twelve Prophets as a prophetic book, two important issues emerge.

The first is the two-fold (or more) formal character of the book. Past form-critical scholarship typically based its analysis of biblical books on the Masoretic form of the text. But recent advances in text-critical scholarship have moved well beyond the past practice of viewing textual versions of biblical works, such as the Septuagint, Targums, or the Peshitta, simply as sources for allegedly improved readings of individual passages in the Bible, toward a new view of versional editions of books as formal and literary works, with their own distinctive hermeneutical perspectives. Arie van der Kooij's study of Isa 23 in both its Masoretic and Septuagint forms demonstrates how each text form construes the chapter, viz., the Masoretic text construes Isa 23 as a condemnation of the Phoenician city of Tyre, whereas the Septuagint version of the text construes Isa 23 as a condemnation of the Phoenician city of Carthage.[35]

In the case of Jeremiah, the issue becomes even more complex when we recognize that the book does indeed appear in two very different forms, the longer Masoretic Hebrew form of the text and the shorter and very differently arranged Septuagint Greek version. Indeed, the discovery of 4QJer^b among the Dead Sea Scrolls indicates that there was a Hebrew *Vorlage* for the Septuagint form of the text and that both proto-Masoretic and proto-"Septuagint" forms of the texts therefore coexisted at Qumran without apparent problem.[36] Shelley Long's recent Claremont dissertation therefore examines the portrayal of Zedekiah in the Masoretic and Septuagint versions of the book and concludes that they represent very different understandings of Judah's last sitting monarch.[37] The proto-Septuagint version of the book employs the *Prophetenerzählung* genre to portray Zedekiah as a self-assured and despicable

---

[35] Arie van der Kooij, *The Oracle of Tyre: The Septuagint of Isaiah 23 as Version and Vision*, VTSup 61 (Leiden: Brill, 1998).

[36] Emanuel Tov, "Jeremiah," in Eugene Ulrich et al, *Qumran Cave 4. X. The Prophets*, DJD 15 (Oxford: Clarendon, 1997), 145–205, esp. 171–76.

[37] Shelley L. Long, "The Last King(s) of Judah: Zedekiah and Sedekias in the Hebrew and Old Greek Versions of Jeremiah 37(44)–40(47):6" (Ph.D. Dissertation; Claremont Graduate University, 2014).

monarch who deliberately revolted against Babylon and arrested Jeremiah, whereas the later proto-Masoretic version of the book employs the *Exemplum* to portray him as a more sympathetic character who was unprepared for his role as king and subsequently was overwhelmed by the events of his day. In both cases, scholars may question whether the Masoretic or Septuagint versions of Isaiah and Jeremiah each constitute the same book.

Similar conclusions might be drawn concerning the Masoretic and Septuagint forms of books, such as Daniel, Esther, and Psalms, insofar as each version has a somewhat different set of contents as the Septuagint forms of the text are expanded in relation to the Masoretic forms. Such observations indicate that we cannot simply speak of one form of the Book of the Twelve Prophets; there are indeed two distinctive forms of the book and alternative orders of the books at Qumran and among the Greek manuscripts of the Bible indicate that even more distinctive forms of the Book of the Twelve Prophets are extant.

The second issue is the composite character of the Book of the Twelve Prophets. Past form-critical scholarship characteristically analyzed the forms of the individual prophetic works that constituted the Book of the Twelve without asking about the formal or generic character of the whole. Such practice was due in large measure to the predominantly Protestant character of modern biblical scholarship through most of the twentieth century and the Protestant practice of reading the Twelve as twelve discrete "Minor" Prophets. But with the emergence of Jewish scholars in the field and the Jewish practice of reading the Twelve as one book as well as the growing role that reception history plays in exegesis, insofar as Christian tradition also identified the Twelve Prophets as the Dodekapropheton and the like, the practice must be reconsidered. As the above discussion indicates, the Book of the Twelve Prophets is a composite work comprised of twelve individual prophetic works as well as a single work, in various forms, in its own right. But such a phenomenon is hardly unique in biblical scholarship. It is well known that the book of Psalms comprises five discrete hymnic books in Pss 1–41; 42–72; 73–89; 90–106; and 107–150, each comprising a distinctive set of hymnic compositions and each with its own hymnic conclusion.[38] No one has yet successfully explained the rationale behind this arrangement, although some claim that is analogous to the five books of the Torah. And no one has yet fully examined the form-critical issues that arise from having one and five books of Psalms simultaneously. Similar questions might be raised about Proverbs and its various constituent compositions ascribed to Solomon (Prov 1–9; 10–24; 25–29); Agur ben Jakeh (Prov 30); and Lemuel, King of Massa (Prov 31). And we might further observe that the Septuagint and Peshitta forms of the book of Psalms differ markedly from the Masoretic form of the book insofar as the Septuagint version of Psalms includes Ps 151 and the

---

[38] See esp. Gerald H. Wilson, *The Editing of the Hebrew Psalter*, SBLDS 76 (Chico, CA: Scholars Press, 1981).

Peshitta version of Psalms includes Pss 151–155. Such observations also point to the multifaceted character of the book of Psalms and raise the question; indeed, as in the Book of the Twelve, we have multiple distinctive forms of the same book.

It would seem, then, that the example of the Book of the Twelve Prophets and the other works cited here point to a need to consider both multiple, distinctive forms of the same book, each with its own set of formal features and hermeneutical perspectives, and composite books that are simultaneously a single literary work and a compilation of multiple literary works. Future form-critical scholarship must be prepared to take account of both of these phenomena. For the time being, form-critical scholars must content themselves with the most basic generic definition of a prophetic book, viz., a prophetic book is the literary presentation of the words of a prophet and/or the events of the prophet's career. Apart from those basic and typical characteristics, prophetic works may vary widely in form.[39]

---

[39] I am indebted to my Research Assistant, Dr. Pamela Nourse, Ph.D. student in Hebrew Bible at the Claremont School of Theology, for her careful reading of my manuscript. Any errors that remain are my own.

8

Where *Are* the Prophets in the Book of the Twelve?

James D. Nogalski

INTRODUCTION

In 1921, Karl Budde published an article that begins with an astute observation and then offers a flawed explanation for the phenomenon he observes.[1] He observes that the Book of the Twelve offers very few biographical or autobiographical accounts of the prophets in comparison to the other prophetic books. Budde contends that these elements were systematically removed from the Book of the Twelve by an editorial process. This proposal has received virtually no followers because of its shortcomings. Nevertheless, his initial observation is correct, though it has not been given enough consideration in discussions of the redaction of the Book of the Twelve. It is at this point that the discussion can benefit from the insights of new form criticism (or as I would prefer to call it, a more mature form criticism). I will therefore summarize Budde's article and offer a critique before offering another proposal as a step toward explaining Budde's initial observation that takes account of some of the insights of new form criticism.

---

[1] Karl Budde, "Eine Folgenschwere Redaktion des Zwölfprophetenbuch," *ZAW* 39 (1921): 218–29.

Synopsis of Budde's "Eine Folgenschewere Redaktion des Zwölfprophentenbuch"

Karl Budde argues that traces of redaction can be found in the Book of the Twelve which changed the character of the scroll by eliminating narrative elements that would have provided more information about the prophet. Budde begins with a description of the problem of determining anything definitive regarding the prophets in the Book of the Twelve. The biggest problem, according to Budde, is the chaotic state in which the books have been transmitted:

> But more than individual vocabulary, the problem belongs to the chaotic condition of the transmission of the books as such: the undifferentiated and untraceable stringing together of word to word, saying to saying, and speech to speech; the complete lack of that which New Testament studies tends to label as contextualization. Consequently, with a few exceptions, the prophet never gains form and personality. He remains a scheme, and his words sound to our ear as though coming from empty space.[2]

Budde's arguments are based upon an investigation of texts in the Book of the Twelve, and in particular he deals with Hos 1 and 3, the book of Amos, and Mic 3.

Hosea 1 and 3 provide the only personal experience—according to Budde—in the book of Hosea. Budde argues that the metaphors of Hos 2 represent an insertion and that the beginning of Hos 3 ("go again") attached directly to Hos 1 before the addition of Hos 2. Moreover, Hos 2 does not continue Hos 1.[3] And yet, argues Budde, even chapter 3 does not follow well on chapter 1 since it contains no indication of the prophet's discovery of his wife's infidelity. Hosea 1 has nothing to say about the infidelity of Hosea's wife. The births of the children all concern the children as metaphors for the people and have *nothing* to do with the sin of the wife. Further, the report character of chapter 1 has changed with chapter 3 where the prophet speaks in the first person, but he has never been introduced. For this reason, Budde argues that a narrative must have continued that is no longer present which introduced the

---

[2] Budde, "Folgenschwere Redaktion," 218: "Aber noch mehr als der Wortlaut im einzelnen trägt die Schuld doch der chaotische Überlieferungszustand der Bücher als socher; die unterschiedlose und einhaltslose Ancinanderreihung von Wort an Wort, Spruch an Spruch, Rede an Rede, das völlige Fehlen dessen, was man in der Neutestamentliche Wissenschaft mit "Verumständigung" zu bezeichnen pflegt. Dadurch kommt es, von Teilausnahmen abgesehen, überhaupt nicht dazu, dass der Prophet Gestalt und Persönlichkeit gewinnt; er bleibt ein Schemen, und wie aus dem leeren Raume klingen seine Worte an unser Ohr."

[3] Budde, "Folgenschwere Redaktion," 219.

prophetic speech and explained how he came to know that his wife was unfaithful. If this were the only time such contextualization is mutilated, according to Budde, we could overlook the problem, but this mutilation is characteristic of other texts in the Book of the Twelve.[4]

Amos offers a second case for Budde. He argues that the prophetic narrative in Amos 7:10-17 offers an exception to the Book of the Twelve's lack of biographical detail, but also because its *insertion* into the vision cycle provides a context by which to interpret the visions.[5] Nevertheless, he notes that not only does 7:10-17 interrupt the third and fourth vision, but 7:10-17 also represents a fragmentary narrative. It assumes one knows who Amos is; it neither introduces him, nor explains why he was in Bethel. It does not indicate what happened to the letter that Amaziah sent to Jeroboam, and it does not tell the end of the story: what happened to Amos after Amaziah told Amos to leave the kingdom? If one removes 7:10-17, again according to Budde, not only does one have a better connection between the first four visions, but isolating 7:10-17 underscores that it is a fragmentary narrative. Budde explains this missing material by arguing that the narrative fragment represents the only remaining episode of a narrative collection of the appearance of Amos in the northern kingdom. Budde believes this narrative was kept because it "concludes" with a YHWH speech. The only other first person speech of the prophet in Amos appears in the five visions, but there the prophet only serves as a vehicle by which YHWH speeches are conveyed. For Budde, 7:10-17 would have originally been part of a narrative collection that opened the book, but a collection of which only 7:10-17 remains.[6]

The third case study presented by Budde of a shortened biographical narrative comes in Mic 3:1ff, where the prophet speaks for the only time in the book.[7] This use of "I" in Mic 3:1 has no clear connection to the preceding material according to Budde. For Budde (who believes 2:12-13 is a later addition), the material immediately preceding 3:1 (2:6-11) is a unit that requires

---

[4] Ibid., 221.

[5] Ibid., 221-22.

[6] Budde thinks that an early version of the superscription (1:1) would have introduced this narrative collection and the book, but 7:10-17 was kept and moved to its current location following the third vision report because of the pronouncement against Jeroboam in the third vision (7:9) that is also reported in the narrative (7:11). Budde begins with a false premise that the narrative *must* have existed in a collection that we still have (Budde, "Folgenschwere Redaktion," 221). Whatever source the narrative came from could just have well contained other material, oracular and/or narratives. It need not have been part of the current collection.

[7] According to Budde, "Folgenschwere Redaktion," 222. Budde apparently does not consider the 1cs pronouns in Mic 1:8-9 to be those of the prophet. By way of contrast, see Jakob Wöhrle, *Die frühen Sammlungen des Zwölfprophetenbuches: Entstehung und Komposition*, BZAW 360 (Berlin: de Gruyter, 2006), 139-46.

a narrative account wherein the prophet's enemies would have responded to the prophetic attack in 2:6–11. Budde assumes that a narrative, now lost, would have recounted the resistance Micah received (along the lines of Amos 7:10–17). The prophet would have then responded to those charges beginning in 3:1 ("And I said").[8] For Budde, unless one is willing to obliterate this first person common singular reference and replace it with something else, then one is forced to conclude that the unknown cause for this prophet's speech has broken away from the preserved prophetic response in 3:1.[9] In other words, for Budde the narrative account that motivates the prophet's speech has been removed and all that remains is the YHWH speech which the prophet proclaims.

Budde explains these narrative removals by arguing that the narrative data needed to understand the original setting has been deleted. He considers these three cases definitive for his model that narrative material concerning the prophet and the causes for speeches have been systematically removed from the writings in the Book of the Twelve. He also mentions, however, several other texts whose contextualizations are missing: Hab 1:5–11; Joel 2; Zeph 1.[10] Budde concludes that this fragmentary character cannot be accidental, but represents a thoroughgoing redactional process whose goal was to eliminate everything except YHWH speeches in order to create a more holy book.[11] He dates the redactional activity to the third or fourth century BCE at the time when battles were underway concerning which books constituted the canon, when the Samaritans only accepted the Torah, but he also thinks there were debates about the prophets and the canon between the (precursors to) the Sadducees and the Pharisees.[12]

A "NEW FORM-CRITICAL" RESPONSE TO BUDDE

One must first differentiate between Budde's observations and his solution. His proposal that a massive redaction of the entire Book of the Twelve sought to

---

[8] See his fuller treatment in Karl Budde, "Micha 2 und 3," *ZAW* 38 (1919–1920): 2–22, especially pages 6–7.

[9] The majority of commentators since Budde take 3:1 to be a response to 2:11 including Wilhelm Rudolph, *Micha—Nahum—Habakuk—Zephanja*, KAT 13.3 (Gütersloh: Mohn, 1975), 68–69; and Hans Walter Wolff, *Micah*, trans. Gary Stansell, CC (Minneapolis: Augsburg, 1990), 95–96; James L. Mays, *Micah*, OTL (London: SCM, 1976), 77–78 (though Mays does not think the two sayings necessarily come from a single speech but were redacted together by the compilers of Mic 1–3); and Francis I. Anderson and David Noel Freedman, *Micah*, AB 24E (New York; Doubleday, 2000), 349. See the more complete listing of opinions in John Willis, "A Note on ואמר in Micah 3:1," *ZAW* 80 (1968): 50–54.

[10] Budde, "Folgenschwere Redaktion," 223–224.

[11] Ibid., 225.

[12] Ibid., 226.

remove all human elements from the text has failed to receive any scholarly support in the more than ninety years since he wrote the article, although a few do acknowledge his arguments for a missing narrative make sense for Mic 3:1.[13] His arguments rest upon models of canon consciousness that are deemed anachronistic today, and with good reason. The so-called Samaritan schism which he describes is far too reductionist an explanation for a complex social, political, and religious phenomenon than his suggestion of a theological discussion about which books to consider holy takes into account.[14]

Nevertheless, Budde's basic observation deserves further consideration than it has received. The Book of the Twelve constantly requires the reader to provide explanations for abrupt changes of speaker and addressee. Often, texts appear to juxtapose disparate units with little notice to the reader, and Budde is certainly correct that the Twelve contains little in the way of contextualization of speeches, biographic accounts, or autobiographical narratives. In fact, only five of the Twelve mention the father's name and only three of the Twelve mention the hometown of the prophet. So, what would account for this phenomenon? If it is not part of an editorial process of deletions, but is part of the character of the text, how does one account for this characteristic?

Elements of the discussion surrounding new form criticism can illuminate the question at hand. New form criticism as practiced in this volume both critiques and extends the form-critical project.[15] Two elements of this discussion in particular offer a helpful lens by which to approach the question of the missing prophets in the Book of the Twelve, namely the idea of the relational aspects of form and the impact of forms as rhetorical elements within texts.

Martin Buss distinguishes five different models of form with the first three having roots that date back to Greek philosophy, including worldly forms as impure reflections of heavenly forms, forms sharing an essential structure, the particularist view of individual forms as belonging to a primary level of reality that sees associations between these forms as accidents arising from the purpose of those making the connections.[16] Buss refers to the fourth approach to forms as

---

[13] Budde is followed by a number of commentators concerning a missing narrative in Mic 3:1, including: Johannes Lindblom, *Micha, literarisch untersucht*, Acta Academiae Aboensis, Ser. Umaniora 6.2 (Abo: Akademi University, 1929), 69; Artur Weiser, *Die Propheten Hosea, Joel, Amos, Obadja, Jona, Micha*, ATD 24 (Göttingen, Vandenhoeck & Ruprecht), 1985), 254; Allen, *Books of Joel, Obadiah, Jonah, and Micah*, 305.
[14] See the recent work of Gary Knoppers, *Jews and Samaritans: The Origins and History of their Early Relations* (Oxford: Oxford University Press, 2013).
[15] See Colin M. Toffelmire, "Form Criticism," in *Dictionary of the Old Testament: Prophets*, ed. Mark J. Boda and J. Gordon McConville (Downers Grove, IL: InterVarsity and IVP Academic, 2012), 257–71.
[16] Martin J. Buss, "Form Criticism: An Introduction," in *The Changing Shape of Form Criticism: A Relational Approach* (Sheffield: Sheffield Phoenix, 2010), 98–101. Buss associates the first category with Plato, the second with Aristotle, and the third he argues for a line

"relationism." This view "regards a pattern as a system of relations that are an intrinsic part of reality" that manifests "both particularity and generality."[17] A fifth approach, skepticism, recognizes that neither particularity nor generality are absolute, and therefore both deserve to be doubted (as opposed to the fourth group which affirms both). Buss argues that the fourth, relational, model represents the best option available to scholars in the humanities at this point.[18] As will be noted below, recurring patterns in prophetic literature extend beyond individual speeches to include patterns of composition and collection that should also be evaluated.

In new form criticism, form elements are investigated not so much for their ability to shed light upon a presumed sociological setting, but for other reasons.[19] For example, taking his cue from Klaus Berger, James Bruckner, applies new form criticism to legal texts by adapting Berger's claim that "the 'forms' of form-critical scholarship be understood as rhetorical elements of the text."[20] Form criticism has "established categories and a critical matrix" for recurring patterns within texts which new form criticism evaluates as part of the text's rhetoric.[21]

The "forms" may therefore also help us to recognize implied logic within a text. Typically, prophetic forms have provided the major focus for understanding prophetic books on the level of individual pericopes, and recognition of genre categories can provide the reader with valuable resources for following the logic and/or the tenor of smaller sections of prophetic texts. Judgment oracles typically contain an accusation and a verdict with the latter frequently marked by the transitional word "therefore." The evocation of funerary laments alerts the reader to the somber tone of what follows when the text begins with "woe to those." The announcement that "the Lord showed me"

---

of thought from Democritus and Epicurus in ancient Greece to William of Ockham in the fourteenth century that had a lasting impact into the nineteenth century.
[17] Ibid., 99.
[18] Ibid., 100.
[19] Martin J. Buss, "The Idea of Sitz im Leben," in *The Changing Shape of Form Criticism: A Relational Approach*, HMB 18 (Sheffield: Sheffield Phoenix, 2010), 33–38. In this succinct essay, Buss describes the problematic nature of the assumptions of Gunkel with regard to the *Sitz im Leben* and genre. For example Buss, recognizes recurring cultural responses to the great events of life (death, marriage, sickness, etc), but the genres related to these occasions produce genre variants in too many ways to associate them absolutely with specific settings and practices.
[20] James K. Bruckner, *Implied Law in the Abraham Narrative: A Literary and Theological Analysis*, LHBOTS 335 (Sheffield: Sheffield Academic, 2001), 60. Bruckner draws upon the work of Klaus Berger, "Rhetorical Criticism, New Form Criticism, and New Testament Hermeneutics," in *Rhetoric and the New Testament: Essays from the 1992 Heidelberg Conference*, JSNT 90 (Sheffield: Sheffield Academic, 1993).
[21] Bruckner, *Implied Law in the Abraham Narrative*, 59.

alerts the reader to a prophetic vision report, and creates expectations for what follows.

Yet, other forms deserve to be considered as part of a discussion on the nature of prophetic books, especially in the Book of the Twelve. These elements concern the forms reflected in the text that have an impact on how the text came to be and what they are intending to convey rhetorically. These forms concern groupings of texts beyond the individual pericopes, but short of the entire prophetic writing. Within the individual writings of the Twelve, several patterns emerge (which are also shared with other prophetic writings). These patterns point to groupings of texts that exhibit the kinds of generalist and particularist relationships that constitute forms according to the relational definition of Buss. At the same time, the nature of these forms deserves reflection upon how they function rhetorically when reading prophetic literature.

AN ALTERNATIVE PROPOSAL

In my opinion, Budde's proposal has reversed the order of how the divine character came to dominate the material in the Twelve. The biographical material was not excised from the corpus; rather, it was never selected for inclusion. The individual writings are not interested in the life of the prophet because the prophet's message—the word from YHWH comprising the writing—is the key to the structure, rhetoric, and collection of material. Two factors account for the lack of biographical material better than a redactional process that removed these elements: (1) the nature of the collections that are incorporated into the individual writings and (2) the repurposing of source material in new contexts. The collections within the Book of the Twelve have a history that needs to be considered carefully.[22] In most cases, the individual writings contain significant blocks of material that were *not written* first for the Book of the Twelve. In some cases, this means that an individual writing found its shape primarily through a literary process that did not have the entire Book of the Twelve in view. Nevertheless, some of the writings resonate more fully within their literary context, which suggests that the material in the book has been adapted for its context in the Book of the Twelve. The reuse of source material in new and expanding contexts offers a better model in these instances. To clarify these materials, it is important to consider the terminology we use regarding the material found in prophetic books and then to ask about the character of that material relative to the writings in the Book of the Twelve.

---

[22] Here I differ from some practitioners of new form criticism who seek to limit the discussion of the implications of form solely to the final form of the text. The question of a text's presumed prehistory, while necessarily containing speculation, may offer plausible rationale for explaining both the coherence of a text and its points of disjuncture. See Odil Hannes Steck, *The Prophetic Books and their Theological Witness*, trans. James D. Nogalski (St. Louis: Chalice, 2000), 17–114.

Several terms require clarification to complete this task. These terms (headings, anthologies, source blocks, and shorter editorial comments) can be used to classify how books and portions of books within the Book of the Twelve reflect the types of material contained within them.

HEADINGS

Superscriptions and incipits typically introduce a collection of some sort, but it is not always clear that the headings reflect an entire book. Exceptions include the incipit of Jonah and the chronicled introductions of Haggai (1:1, 15; 2:1, 10, 20) and Zechariah (1:1, 7; 7:1).[23]

Some headings inside a book do not present biographical elements. Rather, these sections either provide markers to the reader or they represent the beginnings of smaller collections that have been unified at some point in the development of the corpus. Examples include headings (1) whose similarity suggests a rhetorical purpose within smaller collections, (2) formulaic elements that unite a composition, and (3) non-specific superscriptions.[24]

(1) Headings exhibiting a rhetorical purpose designed to focus disparate material include the beginnings of collections in Amos 3:1; 4:1; 5:1; and 6:1. These headings share much in common (hear this [word]), but they also indicate different addressees (sons of Israel, cows of Bashan, house of Israel, those at ease in Zion). As a side note, the plural imperative "hear" appears fourteeen times in the Book of the Twelve, but thirteen of these are in Hosea, Amos, and Micah. The remaining instance begins the book of Joel (between Hosea and Amos).

(2) Headings involving formulaic elements that attempt to unify a series of statements can be seen in the woe oracles of Hab 2. Here, a series of statements

---

[23] For distinctions between incipits and superscriptions, see John D.W. Watts, "Superscriptions and Incipits in the Book of the Twelve," in *Reading and Hearing the Book of the Twelve*, ed. James D. Nogalski and Marvin A. Sweeney, SBLSymS 15 (Atlanta: Society of Biblical Literature), 110–24. Superscriptions are titles that appear at the top of books, psalms, or portions of books while incipits are sentences that begin narratives.

[24] It should also not go unnoticed that most of the superscriptions in the Book of the Twelve relate to neighboring writings in some way and most are interpreted as introductions to the writings which they begin. For example, Joel's superscription is closer to Hos 1:1 than to any other superscription. Nahum and Habakkuk both use משא and a form of חזה. Haggai and Zechariah share a chronicled form; while Zech 9:1; 12:1; and Mal 1:1 all three begin with the same words (משא דבר־יהוה), unattested elsewhere. Hosea, Amos, Micah, and Zephaniah begin with superscriptions that mention kings of Judah and Israel, and three of those four also contain word-event formulas. Given that these four likely formed a book of four at one point in the development of the larger corpus, this similarity originally would have involved writings that were transmitted on the same scroll. See James D. Nogalski, *The Book of the Twelve: Hosea–Jonah*, SHBC (Macon, GA: Smyth & Helwys, 2011), 5–6.

about the wicked draw upon a form attested elsewhere. This form is recognizable by the use of "woe" (2:6, 9, 12, 15, 19) followed by a description of a group targeted for judgment.

(3) Finally, thematic sections within a book can be marked by headings of collections or episodes. Here, one can mention the dated appearances included in the vignettes of Haggai (1:1, 15; 2:1, 10, 20), the similar dates introducing the major sections of Zech 1–8 (1:1; 1:7; 7:1) that mirror those of Haggai, and the otherwise unattested headings (משא דבר יהוה) that set off the final sections of Deutero-Zechariah (9:1; 12:1) and that mimic the heading of Mal 1:1.

In most instances headings of the individual writings represent the source of most of the biographical information we supposedly know about the prophet. The collection's origins are (usually) otherwise unknown. Most scholarship *assumes* that the information in these headings generally reflects historical connections to a prophetic figure's sayings or writings. I see no compelling reason to doubt this is the case, but that does not mean that the superscription always introduced the book as we now have it.

In all likelihood, some portion of the book contains material associated with a prophet of the name mentioned in the superscription through some kind of traditioning process: Hosea, Joel, Amos, Micah, Nahum, Habakkuk, Zephaniah, Haggai, and Zechariah all have superscriptions which the majority of scholarly treatments have concluded are associated with actual prophetic figures. Obadiah, Jonah, and Malachi represent at least partial exceptions to this general tendency. A number of scholars have posited that Obadiah and Malachi are pseudonyms, and that the collections were given a name by which to associate the otherwise anonymous material contained in the collection. The case is particularly strong for Obadiah given that the opening quarter of the book is essentially a modified version of the Edom oracles from the book of Jeremiah.[25] Malachi contains a number of disputations, but a number of scholars have argued that the name Malachi comes from YHWH's reference to "my messenger" (מלאכי) in Mal 3:1.[26] Jonah's genre and content have long been treated as a fictional narrative written in the late Persian or early Hellenistic period based upon the eighth century prophetic figure from the northern

---

[25] See Hans Walter Wolff, *Obadiah and Jonah*, trans. Margaret Kohl, CC (Minneapolis: Augsburg, 1986), 38–40; Paul R. Raabe, *Obadiah*, AB 24D (New York: Doubleday, 1996), 22–31; Jörg Jeremias, *Die Propheten Joel, Obadja, Jona, Micha*, ATD 24.3 (Göttingen: Vandenhoeck & Ruprecht, 2007), 63–65; and Jeremias, "Zur Theologie Obadjas: Die Auslegung von Jer 49,7–16 durch Obadja," in *Die Unwiderstehliche Wahrheit: Studien zur Alttestamentlichen Prophetie*, ed. Rüdiger Lux and Ernst-Joachim Waschke (Leipzig: Evangelische Verlagsanstalt, 2006), 269–82.
[26] See Helmut Utzschneider, *Künder oder Schreiber? Eine These zum Problem der 'Schriftprophetie' auf Grund von Maleachi 1,6–2,9*, BEATAJ 19 (Frankfurt: Lang, 1989), 18–20; and Andrew E. Hill, *Malachi*, AB 25D (New York: Doubleday, 1998), 15–18.

kingdom mentioned in 2 Kgs 14:25.[27] Nevertheless, prophetic superscriptions suggest some kind of collection process was involved that provided the names of twelve different prophetic figures, whether these names were preserved or created by the collection process.

ANTHOLOGIES AND SMALL COLLECTIONS

A number of passages in the Book of the Twelve can best be characterized as anthologies, or collections of sayings. No writing in the Book of the Twelve consists entirely of oracular anthologies, but seven of the twelve contain sections that are best classified with this designation.

In most cases, these anthologies contain sayings, oracles, and short speeches ascribed to a particular prophet either directly (as in Haggai and Zech 7–8) or indirectly based upon a superscription in another part of the book (as in Hos 4–10, 12–13 and Amos 3–6). Such passages include much of Hos 4–10; 12–13; Amos 3–6; Mic 1–3; 4–5; 6–7; Nah 2–3; Zeph 1–3; Haggai; Zech 7–8. Very few of these passages contain prophetic narratives or even self-references to the prophet, but that is likely due to the nature of the collections as sayings and short speeches. These anthologies may be classified in different ways, but they often display some kind of recognizable organizational pattern involving themes and/or catchwords. It is the organization of these sayings that provide coherence and unity to that writing, not the inherent integrity of the content of a single composition.

Some of the anthologies can be classified as sayings and oracles regarding particular topics whose origins are claimed explicitly (Zech 7–8) or are unknown (Zech 14). The former contains seven introductory formulas (7:1, 8; 8:1, 9, 14, 18, 20) and relates to the encouragement of the community of Judah *and Bethel*, ostensibly in the midst of the temple building project.[28] Zechariah 14 has a series of sayings that are characterized by the presence of seven "on that day sayings" (14:1, 6, 8, 9, 13, 20, 21).[29]

---

[27] Wolff, *Obadiah and Jonah*, 81, 98–99; Jeremias, *Die Propheten*, 83.

[28] The chapters begin with a question posed to the prophet from a delegation from Bethel (Zech 7:1–3) regarding whether to continue the ceremonial fasts. His response concerning the fasts does not come until the end of the collection (8:19), thus essentially forming a frame around the entire unit. See discussions in James D. Nogalski, *The Book of the Twelve: Micah–Malachi*, SHBC (Macon, GA: Smyth & Helwys, 2011), 885–87, 897–98.

[29] Not all of these formulas introduce new sayings and some sayings do not exhibit the formula, but all deal with statements about what will happen on the coming day of YHWH when YHWH will intervene on behalf of Judah and Jerusalem. See discussion in Nogalski, *Micah–Malachi*, 969–81. A series of up to eleven units are arranged in five thematic blocks that, together, provide both some sense of cohesion and thematic progression.

Some anthologies of sayings and oracles are ascribed to a prophet by virtue of their location. These oracular units frequently show thematic arrangements, but the lack of concrete historical connections often makes dating individual units quite difficult. Nevertheless, scholars have *generally* deemed some collections to be earlier than others. They are often attributed to the prophet or the prophet's close associates (major portions of Hos 4–10; Amos 3–6; and Mic 1–3). Most of these collections, however, include signs that later hands have also added material. Conversely, there are other anthologies which scholars suggest were arranged and incorporated into the book in which they now reside long after the lifetime of the prophet associated with that book (e.g., Mic 4–5; and 6–7). These passages have the appearance of collections (with their own thematic arrangements) that likely entered Micah at different times, but they are designed to be read *as though* they present material from the prophet of the book, and the prophet's time. Micah 6–7 deal with what will happen from the time of Hezekiah to the destruction of Jerusalem and beyond and respond to the judgment of Mic 1–3 (with the change in orientation marked by the formula that introduces the anthology in 6:1: "hear that which YHWH is saying"). Chapters 4–5 of Micah, which sit precisely in the middle of the Book of the Twelve, deal with issues in the distant future (i.e., after Jerusalem's destruction) and in that respect have more in common with Zechariah 14 than with Mic 1–3.[30]

SOURCE BLOCKS

Source blocks are longer compositions that were not originally delivered or written with other building blocks of the book, but which now appear in a prophetic writing with those other elements. The extent of editing on these source blocks varies from the simple placement alongside another source to transitional elements creatively interposed to provide guidance to the reader. Source blocks can be used as the building material for the book/passage (Zech 9–14, Malachi, Habakkuk, and Joel) or used to enhance the meaning of existing collections/narratives (Nah 1; Hab 3; Jonah 2). Source blocks can be evaluated for their purposes when they were first composed as an independent element and for their function within their final literary context.

SOURCE BLOCKS USED AS THE BUILDING MATERIAL FOR THE BOOK/PASSAGE

---

[30] Note that the formula at the beginning of 4:1 sets this expectation for the reader: "And it will happen in the end of the days." Hence, Jerusalem's fate with Babylon plays a prominent role (4:9–10). While Assyria is mentioned (5:5–6), the reference to eight shepherds who will deliver "us" (Judah) by the sword refers to the kings of Judah who shepherd the country from Hezekiah to the fall of Jerusalem (Hezekiah, Manasseh, Amon, Josiah, Jehoahaz, Jehoiakim, Jehoiachin, Zedekiah). See Nogalski, *Micah–Malachi*, 563–65. In other words, the reference to the Assyrian threat really addresses the postexilic community.

Several source blocks have been used to create a prophetic writing or a major section within a prophetic writing. Writings compiled using such source blocks include: Malachi, Zech 9–14, Habakkuk, Obadiah, and Joel.[31] Zechariah 9–14 are best categorized as a thematic arrangement of compositions (and an anthology) secondarily associated with a prophetic figure already part of the larger scroll. This association, however, only comes by inference since the superscriptions of Zech 9:1 and 12:1 do not mention the name of the prophet. The core of the material in Zech 9–13 consists of longer units joined together thematically and linked with a series of shepherd materials.[32] Zechariah 9–11 begins with a threat from the nations (9:1–8) but transitions to the relationship of Ephraim and Judah (10–11). Zechariah 12–14 focuses on the nations and Judah/Jerusalem. Zechariah 14 reads like an anthology of Day of YHWH material, but it is also linked thematically to Zech 13 by the shepherd materials in Zech 13:7–9.

Malachi contains a series of six disputations, most of which document interpriestly concerns (or debates between priests and Levites). The Jerusalem cult plays a prominent role in these source blocks. The original conclusion to the disputations (3:16–21) reflects a narrative account of a response to the disputations involving a group of "those fearing YHWH."[33]

Habakkuk contains two different superscriptions (1:1; 3:1) that both mention "Habakkuk the prophet," though Hab 3:19b also functions as a subscription containing elements typically found in psalm superscriptions. It mentions the leader and stringed instruments (see especially Pss 4:1; 6:1; 54:1; 55:1; 61:1; 67:1; 76:1). Habakkuk 3 also shows undeniable signs of cultic use (the director mentioned in the subscription; the musical notation in the superscription; the reference to the stringed instruments in the subscription; the three-fold use of selah, which otherwise only appears as a note to the musicians in the Psalter). Habakkuk 1–2 also show signs of the dovetailing of sources, along with editorial glosses associating the wicked one in the woe oracles with Babylon.

Habakkuk thus utilizes four different sources.[34] (1) Chapter 1 contains a prophetic complaint (1:2–4, 12–13) about the prosperity of the wicked that ends with a narrative report of the prophet's decision to wait for a response in 2:1–3 (though he has already received one in 1:5–11 in the final form). (2) A

---

[31] Partial writings that draw upon source blocks include Hos 1–3; Nah 1; and Jonah 2, which are discussed in the next section below.

[32] See the description by Paul L. Redditt, "Israel's Shepherds: Hope and Pessimism in Zechariah 9–14," *CBQ* 51 (1989): 631–42; and James D. Nogalski, "Zechariah 13.7–9 as a Transitional Text: An Appreciation and Re-Evaluation of the Work of Rex Mason," in *Bringing out the Treasure: Inner Biblical Allusion in Zechariah 9–14*, ed. Mark J. Boda and Michael H. Floyd, JSOTSup 370 (Sheffield: Sheffield Academic, 2003), 292–304.

[33] See Nogalski, *Micah–Malachi*, 1061–65.

[34] See James D. Nogalski, *Redactional Processes in the Book of the Twelve*, BZAW 218 (Berlin: de Gruyter, 1993), 129–81.

preexisting oracular pronouncement is addressed to a group in which YHWH announces the coming of the Babylonians (1:5–11). This unit now serves as the "response" to part one of the individual complaint (1:2–4), and Babylonian commentary (1:14–17) follows the second part of the complaint (1:12–13). (3) A collection of woe oracles (2:4–15), expanded with editorial commentary assuming Babylon as the wicked one. (4) Chapter 3 contains a prayer, a theophany, and prophetic commentary (3:16–19) declaring YHWH's ability to defeat the enemy and the prophet's need to wait for deliverance until after the time of judgment has come. Each of these source blocks plays a role in the logical flow of Habakkuk, but each stands out from its context. The imposition of Babylon commentary helps connect the sources, but also provides the context for presuming the enemy in Hab 3 should be interpreted as Babylon, though Hab 3 never specifically names Babylon.

Joel exemplifies the most complex of the writings composed primarily of source blocks. The combination of sources and citations (in the form of quotes, allusions, echoes) suggests that sources with cultic overtones (or settings) are creatively adapted for some rhetorical purpose that is didactic in nature. The cultic overtones come in the form of a communal call to lament at the temple (1:2–18).[35] This call to lament culminates in a call to repent at the temple (2:12–17) and this call precedes promises that reverse the destruction *if* the people repent (2:18–27). These lamentation elements are disrupted and extended by citations and two other sources. These sources contain a prophetic intercession (1:19–20) at the end of the first call to lament (1:2–18) and a day of YHWH poem (2:1–11) that is framed by citations of Zephaniah and Malachi concerning the day of YHWH. The latter half of Joel extends the promises, chronologically and substantively. Joel 3:1 dates its action to the time *after* the promises of Joel 2:18–27 and Joel 4:1 dates itself to the same time as 3:1. The promises of Joel 3:1–5 and 4:1–21 should also be seen as source blocks. The latter exhibits essentially the same technique of citation as found in chapters 1–2, with the citations coming from the Twelve; Exod 34:6–7; and reversing the devastation imagery of Joel 1–2.[36]

Joel 4:1–21 is itself a composite source block with an introduction (4:1–3) and three other units that restate the themes of 4:1–3 in chiastic order.[37] Joel 4:3

---

[35] The variety of threats presumed herein keeps open the possibility that this material is itself a compilation, but the fact that the various threats all can be tied to the covenant curse material of Deut 28 makes it likely that this material was composed as a literary actualization of the covenant curse, not that it resulted from actual events. The situation of multiple threats leads to a call to communal repentance at the temple (Joel 2:12–17). See discussions in James D. Nogalski, "'Presumptions of Covenant' in Joel," in *Covenant in the Persian Period: From Genesis to Chronicles*, ed. Gary Knoppers and Richard Bautch (Winona Lake, IN: Eisenbrauns, 2015).

[36] See Nogalski, *Hosea–Jonah*, 220–21.

[37] See ibid., 243–51.

deals with the slavery of Judah by the nations and 4:4–8 represents an existing poem with its own integrity about the punishment of specific nations for enslaving Judeans. Joel 4:2 deals with judgment in the valley of Jehoshaphat, a theme mirrored in 4:9–17 which also deals with YHWH's judgment in the valley of Jehoshaphat (4:12). Joel 4:9–17 has also been expanded by a citation of Amos 1:2 and it reverses a text in Micah or Isaiah (cf. Joel 4:10 with Mic 4:3 and Isa 2:4). Joel 4:1 introduces the larger unit with the restoration of Judah and Jerusalem and 4:18–21 returns to this theme but also contains a doublet to Amos 9:13 and reverses the imagery of Joel 1–2. Hence, the final component pieces of Joel 4 combine a day of YHWH text with a reversal of Isa 2 (or Mic 4) and with citations of the beginning and end of Amos while at the same time reversing the curse of Joel 1–2.

Joel 3:1–5 is a very debated passage in redactional models regarding the point at which it enters the corpus, but even this text contains allusions to texts in the Twelve (Joel 3:5 quotes Obad 17; and Joel 3:4 uses the language of Mal 3:23 in referring to the "great and terrible day of YHWH"). The simplest explanation for these combinations of Joel's diverse text units combined with unifying elements and allusions to other texts, in my opinion, is not a rolling corpus, but a compositional style wherein a scribal prophet artfully combines preexisting texts with citations to other writings.[38]

The close connection between several of these texts and cultic activities suggests: (1) knowledge of cultic service, (2) access to cultic compositions, and (3) education in biblical texts. More work needs to be done to explain these elements, but I understand their presence to be quite compatible with some of the recent models on scribal education in which lengthy training in prophetic texts was required of scribes.[39] The training would have almost certainly included training in the texts and traditions that prophetic tradents were responsible for transmitting.

SOURCE BLOCKS USED TO ENHANCE MEANING OF AN EXISTING COLLECTION

In addition to source blocks used to build prophetic texts, evidence suggests that source blocks were also used to enhance the meaning of existing

---

[38] For a recent example of a rolling corpus model for Joel, see the work of Jakob Wöhrle, *Die frühen Sammlungen*, 387–435. Wöhrle isolates five redactional layers in Joel, plus isolated additions. For Wöhrle, all but the *Grundschicht* (and the isolated additions) are associated with redactional expansions of the developing multivolume corpus that transcend the individual writings.

[39] Note especially the works of Karel van der Toorn, *Scribal Culture and the Making of the Hebrew Bible* (Cambridge: Harvard University Press, 2007); David M. Carr, *Writing on the Tablet of the Heart: Origins of Scripture and Literature* (Oxford: Oxford University Press, 2005); and David M. Carr, *The Formation of the Hebrew Bible: A New Reconstruction* (Oxford: Oxford University Press, 2011).

collections/narratives (e.g., Nah 1; Hab 3; and Jonah 2 in their respective contexts).

Nahum 1 contains a theophany that is attached to the front of a thematically arranged anthology of anti-Assyrian poems, which has its own structure.[40] Largely lacking from the early anthology is a clear sense of the role of YHWH, a shortcoming that is addressed in Nah 1 with the theological affirmations that God will defeat God's enemies. The "logical" implication for the editor who placed the theophany at the beginning is that YHWH would make sure that Assyria would ultimately suffer for the wickedness it inflicted upon Judah.

A similar function is played by the addition of the theophany in Hab 3, except that this time the enemy is Babylon rather than Assyria. A number of scholars have posited a link between the addition of the theophany in Nah 1 and the theophany of Hab 3. It would make sense that those who incorporated Nahum into the corpus of the Twelve would have paired it with Habakkuk so that these two writings together would deal with the rise and fall of both Assyria and Babylon respectively.[41]

The late narrative of Jonah also has a poem inserted by an editor (or used by the narrative's author) which, in all likelihood, existed separately from the Jonah narrative in which it now resides.[42] The psalm's relationship to the cult is clear from its genre (individual thanksgiving song), its statements about the importance of the temple (2:5, 8), and its reflection of a thanksgiving ceremony (2:9–10).

INTERTWINING OF SOURCE BLOCKS

Some writings appear as though portions of the writings involve multiple sources that have been intertwined with one another (Habakkuk, Obadiah). As already mentioned, Hab 1 dovetails two sources, one being essentially an individual complaint song one might find in the psalter just as readily as in a prophetic writing (1:2–4, 13–14; 2:1–3) and the other represents an oracular warning of the impending attack of the Babylonians (1:5–12). A Babylonian commentary

---

[40] See James D. Nogalski, "The Redactional Shaping of Nahum 1 for the Book of the Twelve," in *Among the Prophets: Language, Image and Structure in the Prophetic Writings*, ed. Philip R. Davies and David J. A. Clines, JSOTSup 144 (Sheffield: JSOT Press, 1993), 193–202; see also Brevard S. Childs, *Introduction to the Old Testament as Scripture* (Philadelphia: Fortress, 1979), 454.

[41] James D. Nogalski, "One Book and Twelve Books: The Nature of the Redactional Work and the Implications of Cultic Source Material in the Book of the Twelve," in *Two Sides of a Coin: Juxtaposing Views on Interpreting the Book of the Twelve/the Twelve Prophetic Books*, ed. Ehud Ben Zvi and James D. Nogalski (Piscataway, NJ: Gorgias, 2009), 27–28, 30–39.

[42] For a rehearsal of various forms of this widely held view, and those of its opponents, see the discussions in Wolff, *Obadiah and Jonah*, 128–32; and Jeremias, *Die Propheten*, 78, 90–93.

(1:15–17) expands the second part of the complaint based upon the message of 1:5–12. Habakkuk 2 expands an existing woe oracle collection (or composition) with interpretive material associating the evil one with Babylon. Habakkuk 3 contains a poetic composition combining a theophanic victory song (3:3–15) with a prophetic "prayer" (3:1–2, 16–19).[43] This preexisting source material contains both its own superscription and subscription that attest to its independence despite the fact that it functions thematically quite well as the ending to Habakkuk, probably as the result of the prophetic prayer composed for its location.

Obadiah presents two very different compositions which look as though they have been dovetailed together so that the end of 1–14 + 15b overlaps with 15a + 16–21. Obadiah is quite complex in that Obad 1–5 essentially parallels a collection of anti-Edom sayings (Jer 49:14–16, 9) and 6–7 and 8–9 seem to extend reflections upon the entire block of sayings in Jer 49:7–22. The quick changes between the sayings also provide Obadiah with the characteristics of an anthology where these short sayings follow upon one another and lead to a series of accusations against Edom in 10–14 before a final pronouncement of judgment (15b). The latter part of Obad 15a + 16–21 also shows signs of expansion, though the question of when and why it was expanded elicits a number of responses.[44]

Zechariah 1:2–6 contains the summary of a prophetic sermon and the people's response. The theme and date of this sermon introduce Zech 1–8, but it also provides important information for Haggai. By explicitly recounting the repentance of the people at the conclusion of this sermon (1:6), the book of Zechariah opens differently than any other book in the Twelve. Just as importantly, the fact that this repentance is dated in the eighth month of the second year of Darius, puts this action prior to the last dated speeches of Haggai.

---

[43] A fairly typical interpretation of the origins of the independent hymn can be found in Theodore Hiebert, *God of My Victory: The Ancient Hymn in Habakkuk 3*, HSM 38 (Atlanta: Scholars Press, 1986), 81–128. Nogalski describes the literary form of Habakkuk as resulting from a combination of source blocks arranged for a rhetorical purpose and linked by transitional comments: Nogalski, *Micah–Malachi*, 649–52. By contrast, Wöhrle argues for a more gradual development into the book whose literary horizons include the book of Habakkuk alone and incorporation into the developing multivolume corpus with little additional editing: Jakob Wöhrle, *Der Abschluss des Zwolfprophetenbuches Buchübergreifende Redaktionsprozesse in den späten Sammlungen*, BZAW 389 (Berlin: de Gruyter, 2006), 311–23. Wöhrle argues that the liturgical elements of the psalm represent its latest pieces while its earliest portions focused only on the battle against the wicked. The Babylonian association, so Wöhrle, comes in with the remainder of the Babylonian supplements but only affects the third chapter by the insertion of 3:16b, 17.

[44] For an entry into the complicated literary divisions of Obadiah, see the discussions in Wolff, *Obadiah and Jonah*, 21–22; Jeremias, *Die Propheten*, 57–59, 62–65; Rudolph, *Haggai, Sacharja 1–8, Sacharja 9–14, Maleachi*, 295–96; Nogalski, *Hosea–Jonah*, 368–76.

Chronologically, the overlapping of the dating systems in Haggai and Zechariah also accounts for a gap in Haggai. Before Hag 2:10, it is not clear that the people were convinced of Haggai's entreaties to rebuild the temple. The previous date formula in Hag 2:1 comes in the seventh month while 2:10 articulates twenty-fourth day of the ninth month and refers to the day when the temple foundation stone (2:15) was laid. Zechariah 1:2–6 comes in between these two dates and indicates that the prophet's speech resulted in the turning of the people to YHWH.

LONGER COMPOSITIONS

Some writings contain what appear to be longer compositions: the OAN of Amos 1–2 (though it was likely updated at least once); the visions of Amos and Zechariah (with insertions added for the book); the Jonah narrative (probably prior to the inclusion of the thanksgiving hymn); and the disputations of Malachi (which appear to have been edited to some degree for its location at the end of the corpus).

Vision reports in Amos and Zechariah could be compared with the visions of Ezekiel to note the relative lack of contextualization in the two vision collections compared to those of Ezekiel. The vision of Ezek 1 contains a contextual note at the opening of the book, dating the vision to a specific day (Ezek 1:1), and several other references in that chapter to the visionary event (Ezek 1:15, 27–28) extend the vision throughout the chapter. Further, this vision reappears in other parts of the book through a series of cross-references (Ezek 10:15, 20; 43:3). In at least one other vision, the context is provided as well (11:1–2). By contrast, no such contextualization appears in the five visions of Amos (7:1–3, 4–6, 7–9; 8:1–3; 9:1–4). Nevertheless, the prophet uses first person language when describing the visions, and the reader naturally associates this figure with the eighth century prophet of the book. This association, however, concerns chronology more than biography. The only contextual clue in the vision reports of Zechariah appears in 1:7, but that date formula is generally considered a redactional element (along with 1:1; 7:1) added for the creation of the book.[45] No direct information about the prophet is provided in the visions of

---

[45] This statement is not to deny the presence of other clues to dating such as the mention of Joshua and Zerubbabel, but in those instances, the text assumes the readers know their identity, they do not provide the information. See Marvin A. Sweeney, *The Twelve Prophets, Volume Two: Micah, Nahum, Habakkuk, Zephaniah, Haggai, Zechariah, Malachi*, Berit Olam (Collegeville, MN: Liturgical Press, 2000), 573; Mark J. Boda, "Zechariah: Master Mason or Penitential Prophet?" in *Yahwism after the Exile: Perspectives on Israelite Religion in the Persian Period*, ed. Rainer Albertz and Bob Becking, Studies in Theology and Religion 5 (Assen: Van Gorcum, 2003), 46–49; and John Kessler, "Tradition, Continuity and Covenant in the Book of Haggai: An Alternative Voice from the Early Persian Period," in

Amos or Zechariah. That does not mean that the vision reports have no rhetorical aims, only that their function is not oriented toward the prophet.

The sequence of the visions of Amos is crucial. Two groups of paired visions escalate the threat against Israel even as the objects of the visions become less severe. The first two visions of Amos represent imminent threats (locusts, shower of fire), but the prophet successfully intercedes for Israel following each one (7:3, 6). The third and fourth visions appear far less devastating at first glance (a lump of tin and a basket of summer fruit), but neither of these contains prophetic intercession. Rather, immediately after the third vision, one finds instead of intercession, the expulsion of Amos by Amaziah in 7:10–17, the narrative fragment noted by Budde. The narrative of 7:10–17 is immediately followed by the fourth vision of the summer fruit (קיץ) that announces "the end" (הקץ) has arrived. What follows in 8:4–14 represents a series of sayings that reprise the themes and phrases of the collection of Amos before turning to the fifth and final vision (9:1–4) in which the prophet is a spectator to YHWH's destruction of Israel. Clearly, the visions have been expanded by two sources, a narrative fragment and a theological summary of the words of Amos that reads like an anthology, but may well be a composition designed for its purpose in the book.

The eight visions of Zechariah—like those of Amos—share similar stylistic and formal elements with one another. The thematic progression of the eight visions represents less of an escalation than a program, a depiction of what temple life should look like in the late sixth century. These visions begin with YHWH's decision to restore Jerusalem, to reign in the nations, and then discuss the extension of Jerusalem, the restoration of Joshua, the combination of Joshua and Zerubbabel, a scroll of accusation, the removal of guilt from the land, and the patrol of the four chariots and horses.

SHORTER EDITORIAL COMMENTS AND ADDITIONS

I conclude with a few notes about smaller editorial additions. Such insertions will always be more controversial and consensus on a particular addition will thus be harder to achieve. These shorter additions include diverse types of material whose function also needs to be considered:

1. parenthetical comments to clarify or explain the immediate context (Obad 7bβ)[46]
2. parenthetical comments to evoke other texts (Hag 2:17,19aβ evoking Amos 4 and Joel 1[47]; Nah 1:3a evoking Exod 34:7[48])

Tradition in Transition: Haggai and Zechariah 1–8 in the Trajectory of Hebrew Theology, ed. Mark J. Boda and Michael H. Floyd, LHBOTS 475 (New York: T&T Clark, 2008), 1–39.

[46] James D. Nogalski, "Obad 7: Textual Corruption or Politically Charged Metaphor?" *ZAW* 110 (1998): 67–71.

3. *Fortschreibungen* and insertions (e.g., the addition of an oracle on Zerubbabel to the visions that is widely recognized in Zech 4:6aβ–10a[49]). These additions to existing units generally update material for immediate contexts, but they can also pick up language from elsewhere in the Twelve (e.g., the use of Mic 4:6–7 in the redactional ending of Zeph 3:19–20[50]). Such continuations are less common in the Book of the Twelve than in other prophetic books like Jeremiah and Ezekiel, but they are present.
4. promissory endings—often several promises joined together so that they share characteristics with anthologies (Amos 9:7–15; Zeph 3:8–20; Mic 4:1–5:8 [Eng. 4:1–5:9]; 7:8–20).

The first two types often cause debate because of their size, but their presence can hardly be doubted. Anyone who has studied the differences between the LXX and MT versions of Jeremiah quickly realizes that small insertions constitute a significant number of the differences in these texts. Anyone who has looked at the great Isaiah scroll from Qumran can see where scribal additions appear between lines and in the margins. One can easily imagine how small parenthetical comments like these could make it into a scroll the next time the scroll was copied. In the Book of the Twelve, one also finds such parenthetical comments used to evoke other texts.

The insertions and *Fortschreibungen* have to be evaluated contextually. It is not uncommon to find explanations for insertions related to material in another part of a corpus. In the Book of the Twelve, the task becomes more complicated because the corpus can include other writings in the collection, and texts can cite other texts from outside the Twelve.[51]

The promissory endings added to many of the writings have long been considered as additions to the core of several of the individual collections (e.g., Amos 9:7–15; Zeph 3:9–20; Mic 4–5; 7:8–20). Often, the promissory endings themselves appear to be the result of more than one level of editorial activity. Analyzing these endings is complicated by the anthological character of the

---

[47] James D. Nogalski, *Literary Precursors to the Book of the Twelve*, BZAW 217 (Berlin: de Gruyter, 1993), 226–29.

[48] James D. Nogalski, *Redactional Processes*, 104–11; Nogalski, *Micah–Malachi*, 605–6.

[49] E.g., Wöhrle, *Die frühen Sammlungen*, 337–41; Sweeney, *Twelve Prophets*, 2: 607–12. Both scholars see the verses as secondary, but motivated by different portions of the broader context.

[50] Nogalski, *Literary Precursors*, 204–9.

[51] Hence, Joel 4:16 and 4:18 contain citations of the beginning and end of Amos (1:2; 9:13), the next writing in the MT order of the Twelve while Zephaniah contains three sets of allusions to Gen 1–11 to frame the Zephaniah collection in cosmic terms. See James D. Nogalski, "Zephaniah's Use of Genesis 1–11," *HBAI* 2 (2013): 1–23.

promises in a number of cases (e.g., the number of units in Zech 7–8 and 14 or the addition of Zech 3:18–20 to an existing set of promises discussed above).

Conclusions

The character of the writings in the Book of the Twelve reflects different editorial techniques and settings that must continue to be evaluated *both* within an individual writing *and* across the corpus. The character of the core material collected does *not* focus upon the prophet as person. There are no large scale prophetic narrative collections; in fact, there are no prophetic narratives apart from Jonah, Amos 7:10–17, and Hos 1 and 3.

There is evidence that some books combined smaller collections with editorial material designed to unify the writing in some way (Amos; Micah; Hosea; Zephaniah). Other writings appear to have begun as individual anthologies or compositions but have been repurposed for another literary context (Nah 2–3, the sources of Habakkuk, Joel, and Malachi). Some collections within writings appear to represent thematic compilations of short vignettes or sayings (Haggai; Zech 14; and Hos 4–10, 12–13).

The combination of these source blocks and anthologies generally offers a better starting point for understanding the shape of the individual writings than does the assumption of a rolling corpus model that figures prominently in some of the recent redactional treatments.

Contrary to Budde, the character of the collections and their sources simply shows no interest in the person of the prophet. The prophetic figures disappear behind the function of the collections associated with them whose purpose is to present the message of YHWH.

Significantly, the function of the source texts that are involved in the compilation and framing of the writings reflect more cultic associations than biographical material. Joel and Malachi focus heavily upon reforming the cult (both its worshipers and its personnel). Haggai and Zechariah focus on temple construction and its leadership. Cultic poems play prominent roles in Nahum, Habakkuk, and Jonah. The role of the nations in relationship to the temple or Zion comes up frequently (Joel 4; Obadiah; Mic 4; Nah 2:1; Zech 1–2; 8; and 14; Malachi). This cultic flavor has been underappreciated in prophetic studies and it requires more consideration in the development of the Twelve since it probably sheds more light upon the process of editing than the biographies of the prophets.

9

A Deafening Call to Silence: The Rhetorical "End" of Human Address to the Deity in the Book of the Twelve

Mark J. Boda

INTRODUCTION

During the past two decades we have witnessed a veritable explosion of research on the Book of the Twelve, not only on the individual books, but also on the corpus as a whole.[1] This present article builds on the foundation of recent scholarship investigating the shape of the Twelve as a literary unit. Scholarship on the Twelve was dominated in an earlier phase by developmental interest (especially redaction critical approaches),[2] but there has always been interest in literary design or at least emphases of the final literary form of the corpus.[3]

---

[1] With thanks to the rich conversation at the Barton College's Center for Religious Studies, Colloquy 2012 hosted by Rodney Werline, where the ideas for this paper were first presented. An earlier version of this paper served as my Presidential Address to the Canadian Society of Biblical Studies (2014).

[2] E.g., James D. Nogalski, *Literary Precursors to the Book of the Twelve*, BZAW 217 (Berlin: de Gruyter, 1993); James D. Nogalski, *Redactional Processes in the Book of the Twelve*, BZAW 218 (Berlin: de Gruyter, 1993); Aaron Schart, *Die Entstehung des Zwölfprophetenbuchs*, BZAW 260 (Berlin: de Gruyter, 1998); Jakob Wöhrle, *Die Frühen Sammlungen des Zwölfprophetenbuches: Entstehung und Komposition*, BZAW 360 (Berlin: de Gruyter, 2006); Jakob Wöhrle, *Der Abschluss Des Zwölfprophetenbuches: Buchübergreifende Redaktionsprozesse in den Späten Sammlungen*, BZAW 389 (Berlin: de Gruyter, 2008).

[3] E.g., Paul R. House, *The Unity of the Twelve*, BLS 27, JSOTSup 97 (Sheffield: Almond Press, 1990); Terence Collins, *The Mantle of Elijah: The Redaction Criticism of the Prophetical*

The present article investigates those instances in the Book of the Twelve where human voices address Yahweh. The analysis will first look at how these voices function within the individual prophetic books within the Twelve before looking at patterns that can be discerned in the various types of voices and shifts in the overall shape of the Book of the Twelve.

While the main focus will be on those instances in the Twelve where direct human address to the deity is employed, indirect human address to the deity will also be considered. Recent study of the Psalter has revealed the regular appearance of indirect human address alongside direct human address in compositions which appear to be functioning as prayer within the life of the biblical community.[4] In this way God not only hears but overhears human address and in both cases these function as address to the deity.

Past research has consistently noted that when these voices appear in the text they reflect an oral form-critical setting that predates the literary form of the prophetic book, placing the accent on a setting apart from the book.[5] When related to the book in which they are found, they have often been used as evidence for redactional development of the book.[6] Without dismissing such

---

Books, BibSem 20 (Sheffield: Sheffield Academic, 1993); James Nogalski and Marvin A. Sweeney, eds., *Reading and Hearing the Book of the Twelve*, SymS 15 (Atlanta: Society of Biblical Literature, 2000); Jason LeCureux, *The Thematic Unity of the Book of the Twelve: The Call to Return and the Nature of the Minor Prophets*, HBM 10 (Sheffield: Sheffield Phoenix, 2012).

[4] See Mark J. Boda, "'Varied and Resplendid Riches': Exploring the Breadth and Depth of Worship in the Psalter," in *Rediscovering Worship: Past, Present, Future*, ed. Wendy Porter, McMaster New Testament Series (Eugene, OR: Wipf & Stock, 2015), 61–82; cf. Gerald T. Sheppard, "'Enemies' and the Politics of Prayer in the Book of Psalms," in *The Bible and the Politics of Exegesis: Essays in Honor of Norman K. Gottwald on His Sixty-Fifth Birthday*, ed. David Jobling, Peggy L. Day, and Gerald T. Sheppard (Cleveland: Pilgrim, 1991), 61–82; W. Derek Suderman, "Prayers Heard and Overheard: Shifting Address and Methodological Matrices in Psalms Scholarship" (Ph.D. diss., University of St. Michael's College, 2007); W. Derek Suderman, "Are Individual Complaint Psalms Really Prayers? Recognizing Social Address as Characteristic of Individual Complaints," in *The Bible as a Human Witness to Divine Revelation: Hearing the Word of God through Historically Dissimilar Traditions*, ed. Randall Heskett and Brian Irwin, LHBOTS 469 (New York: T&T Clark International, 2010), 153–70.

[5] See my earlier Mark J. Boda, "From Complaint to Contrition: Peering through the Liturgical Window of Jer 14,1–15,4," *ZAW* 113 (2001): 186–97. In the Twelve this has been one key focus of research on the Doxologies in Amos, see Friedrich Horst, "Die Doxologien im Amosbuch," *ZAW* 47 (1929): 45–54; James L. Crenshaw, *Hymnic Affirmation of Divine Justice: The Doxologies of Amos and Related Texts in the Old Testament*, SBLDS 24 (Missoula, MT: Scholars Press, 1975).

[6] Again using the example of the Doxologies in Amos, see K. Koch, "Die Rolle der Hymnische Abschnitte in der Komposition des Amos-Buches," *ZAW* 86 (1974): 504–37; Jörg Jeremias, *Der Prophet Amos*, ATD 24.2 (Göttingen: Vandenhoeck & Ruprecht, 1995),

reflection as irrelevant, the present article focuses on the role of these forms within the rhetoric of the prophetic book in which they are found. Thus instead of *Sitz im Leben*, the focus will be on *Sitz im Buch* or *Sitz in der Literatur*. This setting will be considered for each of the "books" of the Twelve as found in the Hebrew Masoretic tradition before considering a general trend in the rhetorical shape of the Masoretic Twelve in relation to the phenomenon of human address to the deity.

Hosea

The book of Hosea contains four instances where a human voice addresses the deity.[7] We first hear such a voice in 2:25 (Eng. 23) in Yahweh's depiction of the ideal future when people and God experience normative relationship.[8] In this verse Yahweh cites the future covenantal declarations of both deity ("you are my people") and people ("my God").[9] In contrast, later in the book at 8:2 Yahweh again cites the voice of the people,[10] but this time it is the words of the present generation who are described in 8:1, 3 as having "transgressed my covenant and rebelled against my law ... rejected the good" (8:1, 3) and thus were inappropriately crying out to Yahweh with the claims: "My God" and "we, Israel, know you."[11] The climactic and most hopeful moment in the book comes

---

57–58; Jörg Jeremias, *The Book of Amos: A Commentary*, trans. Douglas W. Stott, OTL (Louisville: Westminster John Knox, 1998), 78.

[7] See Graham I. Davies, *Hosea*, OTG (Sheffield: Sheffield Academic, 1993), 71–75, who notes the way Hosea takes up "the language of public worship" even in formulating his oracles, especially noting the close association between Hosea and Psalms 80–81. Hosea 6:1–3 contains an echo of public liturgy; cf. Graham I. Davies, *Hosea*, NCB (London: Marshall Pickering, 1992), 150–52.

[8] On this collection of sayings in 2:18–25 (Eng. vv. 16–23), their cohesion as a unit and relationship to the surrounding prophetic material see Hans Walter Wolff, *Dodekapropheton 1, Hosea*, BKAT (Neukirchen: Neukirchener Verlag, 1961), 57; Hans Walter Wolff, *Hosea*, Hermeneia (Philadelphia: Fortress, 1974), 47. The unit functions "to elucidate the era of salvation" noted in 2:9, 17 (Eng. 7, 15).

[9] Notice how prior to 2:25 (Eng. 23) in 2:22 (Eng. 20) the vocabulary of "knowing" (ידע) is used in connection with the coming day of covenant renewal (cf. 2:20 [Eng. 18]; and note the repeated phrase "in that day" (בַּיּוֹם הַהוּא) in 2:18, 20, 23 [Eng. 16, 18, 21]).

[10] Davies, *Hosea*, 23, links this to "the public prayers of Hosea's day" (p. 23), noting that it is "probably citing phrases from two separate compositions" (p. 70, noting Wolff, *Hosea*), in particular because of the juxtaposition of the first common singular suffix on "my God" and the first common plural pronoun in "we Israel know thee" (Davies, *Hosea*, 198).

[11] The juxtaposition of "my God" and "we, Israel, know you" in 8:2 which may be suggestive of the amalgamation of two originally separate compositions (Davies, *Hosea*, 198; noting Wolff, *Hosea*) or the role of representative speakers in such declarations. See Duane A. Garrett, *Hosea, Joel*, NAC 19a (Nashville: Broadman & Holman, 1997), 181, for the view that "Israel" constitutes a third statement. On the meaning of "knowing" (ידע) in

in the final chapter, as the prophet calls the community to return to Yahweh by declaring the words cited in 14:3b–4 (Eng. 2b–3):

> Bear away all iniquity.
> Take goodness
> that we may present bulls (sacrifice),[12] that is, our lips.
> Assyria will not save us;
> we will not ride on horses
> nor will we say again: "Our God," to the work of our hands
> for in you the orphan finds mercy.

The initial three lines (14:3b [Eng. 2b]) are foundational for the penitential expression in the final four (14:4 [Eng. v. 3]).[13] The people are to request God's grace that will enable them to present their words in verse 4 (Eng. v. 3) as a sacrifice to God. In their repentance they eschew reliance on imperial (Assyria, horses) and idolatrous resources, as well as abuse of the vulnerable (orphan). Reference to "our God" echoes the earlier references to "my God" in the expressions found in 2:25 (Eng. v. 23) and 8:2.[14] Yahweh's response to prayer is expressed immediately as he promises to "heal their apostasy" and "love them freely," through blessing them (14:5–8 [Eng. vv. 4–7]), finally addressing them directly in verse 8 by emphasizing that he is the source of their harvest.[15] Hosea 14:2–8 (Eng. vv. 1–7) clarifies the role for human response in the future scenario of covenant relationship depicted in 2:25 (Eng. v. 23).[16]

Hosea see Mark J. Boda, *A Severe Mercy: Sin and Its Remedy in the Old Testament*, Siphrut: Literature and Theology of the Hebrew Scriptures 1 (Winona Lake, IN: Eisenbrauns, 2009), 298.

[12] OG and Peshitta suggest an original פְּרִי (fruit), thus, "that we may present the fruit of our lips." L is the more difficult reading.

[13] See James M. Trotter, *Reading Hosea in Achaemenid Yehud*, JSOTSup 328 (Sheffield: Sheffield Academic, 2001), 214–15, who divides 14:2–8 (Eng. 1–7) into three sections: Call to Repentance (14:2–3a [Eng. 1–2a]), Confession of Guilt (14:3b–4 [Eng. 2b–3]), Promise of Reconciliation (14:5–8 [Eng. 4–7]). Garrett, *Hosea, Joel*, 269, refers to this as "a liturgy of repentance."

[14] Notice, however, the use of the first common singular and first common plural in the two sayings of 8:2, see n. 11 above.

[15] Contra Trotter, *Reading Hosea in Achaemenid Yehud*, 215, who argues that the experience of reading Hosea leads the reader to not merely expect "a simplistic direct correspondence ... between repentance and salvation" but to rather merely look to "the complete, sovereign freedom of God." The flow of this passage encourages correspondence between penitential expression and salvation, as Garrett, *Hosea, Joel*, 270, notes: "repentance is essential to Hosea's theology ... no restoration is possible without repentance."

[16] Cf. Davies, *Hosea*, 299. The basis for the penitential agenda can be discerned in the call to repentance in 6:1–3, which appears to have failed in the present, but will be successful for a future community; see Boda, *Severe Mercy*, 300, 303.

One other voice addresses Yahweh in the book of Hosea and this occurs in 9:14a ("O Yahweh, what will you give?"). It appears to be the voice of the prophet, expressing his concern over God's severe judgment of Ephraim.

Yahweh's citation of human address to the deity in the book of Hosea thus highlights the deep contrast between the hypocrisy of the present generation (8:2) and the intimacy of the future ideal generation (2:25 [Eng. v. 23]). In both cases it is Yahweh who cites the words of these contrastive generations. The prophet, however, provides two other forms of voicing. The first is related to the judgment of the present generation, as the prophet registers his protest in the midst of the severe punishment articulated by Yahweh throughout chapter 9 (9:14). In the end the prophet projects a way forward, whether before or after the judgment, as he provides words for the community to express their penitence and thus open the way for Yahweh's healing love and blessing (14:3–4 [Eng. vv. 2–3]).[17] In both cases the prophet functions mediatorially, challenging both covenant partners, whether Yahweh (9:14) or the people (14:3b–4 [Eng. vv. 2b–3]). At regular intervals throughout the book of Hosea readers encounter short articulations of human address to the deity. These articulations are carefully mediated through the divine or prophetic voice and shape the religious response of the reader, focusing attention on covenant relationship (my/our God).[18] Verbal response to the deity appears to play a key role in the restoration of the covenant relationship (2:25 [Eng. v. 23]; 14:3b–4 [Eng. vv. 2b–3]), but 8:2 shows how verbal response must be expressed within a broader constellation of penitential response.[19]

Joel

At four places in the book of Joel one encounters a human voice addressing the deity.[20] The first voice is found in 1:15a in the phrase "Alas for the day!" This is

---

[17] See Gerald Morris, *Prophecy, Poetry and Hosea*, JSOTSup 219 (Sheffield: Sheffield Academic, 1996), 115, who notes the close relationship between the resolution of Hosea in 14:2–9 and motifs in the first three chapters. Thus, 2:25 (Eng. v. 23) foreshadows the climactic guidance of 14:3–4 (Eng. vv. 2–3).

[18] For the covenantal character of this relationship see Wolff, *Dodekapropheton 1, Hosea*, 68–69; Wolff, *Hosea*, 55.

[19] Note also 6:1–3 which encourages a penitential response from the people in a liturgical-like piece; cf. Boda, *Severe Mercy*, 299–300.

[20] See David Allan Hubbard, *Joel and Amos: An Introduction and Commentary*, TOTC (Downers Grove, IL: InterVarsity Press, 1989), 28–29; G. Ogden, "Joel 4 and Prophetic Responses to National Laments," *JSOT* 26 (1983): 97–106, for the close connection between Joel and Judah's liturgical literature.

the cry which is to be voiced by the priests at the solemn assembly on the day of fasting (1:13–14).[21]

The opening word of 1:15 (אֲהָהּ, Alas) is one that occurs at the outset of cries directed to a deity or heavenly figure (Josh 7:7; Judg 6:22; Jer 1:6; 4:10; 14:13; 32:17; Ezek 4:14; 9:8; 11:13; 21:5), but in those cases the term is followed immediately by the name of the person addressed in the vocative.[22] Second Kings 3:10 is similar to the use of this term in Joel 1:15, cases where אֲהָהּ is followed by the causal particle כִּי, even though in Joel 1:15 the phrase לַיּוֹם is found immediately following אֲהָהּ. It is this presence of לַיּוֹם after אֲהָהּ that leads us to conclude that this is part of some form of liturgical response to the exhortation to cry for help from Yahweh. The nearly identical collocation is found in Ezek 30:2–3 where the shortened form (הָהּ, Alas) is used and followed by לְיוֹם and then by כִּי־קָרוֹב יוֹם as here in Joel 1:15.[23] The short phrase הָהּ לַיּוֹם in Ezek 30:2–3 appears to be the content of the lament commanded by the preceding imperative הֵילִילוּ (wail) and the כִּי clause which then follows provides the reason for the exhortation as is the case in Isa 13:6; Zeph 1:7; Obad 12–15; cf. Jer 30:7. Thus, we at least have a short piece of material that was to be used by the priests on the day of fasting ("Alas for the day").[24]

There is some debate over whether what follows in 1:16–20 is also all part of the prayer response or whether some of it (particularly 1:16–18) is a continuation of the reason for the prayer introduced by כִּי in 1:15.[25] On analogy with Jer 14:2–6 it is possible that 1:16–18 is part of a prophetic liturgy which represents an initial description of the present predicament which lays the foundation for the direct address to the deity in 1:19–20:[26]

---

[21] See the superb discussion of the function of the words found in 1:15–18 in Eliyahu Assis, *The Book of Joel: A Prophet between Calamity and Hope*, LHBOTS 581 (New York: Bloomsbury, 2013), 106–11.

[22] Cf. Judg 11:35; 2 Kgs 6:5, 15 where addressed to a human.

[23] See Hans Walter Wolff, *Dodekapropheton 2, Joel und Amos*, BKAT (Neukirchen-Vluyn: Neukirchener Verlag, 1969), 25; Hans Walter Wolff, *Joel and Amos: A Commentary on the Books of the Prophets Joel and Amos*, trans. Samuel Dean McBride, Hermeneia (Philadelphia: Fortress, 1977), 23.

[24] See also Hubbard, *Joel and Amos*, 55, although v. 15b cannot be part of this cry. For the use of a short particle to typify mourning see Amos 5:16.

[25] See Assis, *Book of Joel*, 111, and various views cited there. For the view that 1:15–20 contains fragments of laments see e.g., Richard J. Coggins, *Joel and Amos*, NCB (Sheffield: Sheffield Academic, 2000), 33; Wolff, *Dodekapropheton 2, Joel und Amos*, 24; Wolff, *Joel and Amos*, 22; Garrett, *Hosea, Joel*, 327–28. Coggins sees in the "jerky style" evidence either of oral fragments or a "deliberate literary device to express the incoherence of the lamenters" (p. 33).

[26] See Hubbard, *Joel and Amos*, 53, for vv. 15–16 as communal lament. The direct prayer to the deity comes in Jer 14:7–9 in the 1cp. Cf. Boda, "Complaint."

> To you, O Yahweh, I cry out
> because fire has consumed grazing places of the wilderness
> and a flame has scorched all the trees of the field.
> In addition animals of the field pant for you
> because the stream beds of water have dried up
> and fire consumes the grazing places of the wilderness.

There is no question that 1:19–20 represents human address to the deity, and the use of the first person for the first time in the book increases the rhetorical effect.[27] However, the identity of the one who did or was to speak these words in first person is not clear. Although Jer 14 may suggest the prophet is interceding for the people in first person speech since a message is delivered (presumably through the prophet) to the people in what follows in Jer 14:10–12, it is also possible that the intercessory speech which follows the description of the present predicament was delivered by another leadership figure in the liturgy, possibly a priestly figure. Thus, the voice is either that of a prophetic figure interceding for the community, or the voice represents words being given to the priests to cry out to Yahweh.

As with the short phrase in 1:15a ("Alas, for the day!"), 1:19–20 focuses on highlighting for the deity the deplorable circumstances and not expressing any particular request.[28]

The second instance of human address to the deity comes in Joel 2:17. This address also follows a series of imperatives which appear to be delivered (at least predominantly) to the priests, those who would be responsible for consecrating a fast, proclaiming a solemn assembly, as well as gathering, sanctifying and assembling the community (2:15–16). The priests are clearly identified at the outset of 2:17 as they are called to weep in the temple precincts and are given the words to cry to Yahweh:[29]

> Look compassionately, O Yahweh, on your people
> and do not make your inheritance into a reproach,

---

[27] Coggins, *Joel and Amos*, 3.

[28] The lack of a request leads Assis to reject this as human address to the deity and instead see it as "the words of the prophet, who turns to God and seeks to justify his appeal in the eyes of the people" (Assis, *Book of Joel*, 115, note also 116). However, there is no claim that this is all that would be declared on a fasting day and certainly a key component of such a day is the articulation of the difficult circumstances (see John Barton, *Joel and Obadiah: A Commentary*, OTL [Louisville: Westminster John Knox, 2001], 58–63). For a lament in the face of a predicament that begins with אֲהָהּ and is lacking a request, see Josh 7:7–9.

[29] See Ezek 8:16 for the vestibule (אוּלָם) as a place for addressing the deity; cf. Assis, *Book of Joel*, 151. On the contrast between the actions in Ezek 8:16 and Joel 2:17 see Wolff, *Dodekapropheton 2, Joel und Amos*, 61; Wolff, *Joel and Amos*, 51.

for nations to rule over them.³⁰
Why should they say among the peoples:
'Where is their God?'

This prayer does contain a clear request (formulated both positively and negatively) and is addressed to the deity directly. The request and vocative is followed by a reason clause which focuses on Yahweh's fame among the nations.

Here then the priests are given the human address to direct towards Yahweh and it is a cry for God's mercy. This section that outlines the priestly call for a solemn assembly and provides the priests' prayer on behalf of the people is preceded by a clear call to a deep repentance by the people (2:12–14).³¹ No record of this repentance is provided, but then neither is there any record that the priests uttered their prayer for God's grace which follows. What does follow in 2:18–19 is a record of Yahweh's response, suggesting that in the literary gap between 2:17 and 2:18 something has occurred that has prompted this divine shift. Since the prophetic voice calls for both penitence from the people in 2:12–14 and a cry for mercy from the priests in 2:17, there is no reason to suggest that the prayer of the priests is somehow an inappropriate response to the call to repentance. Taking the call for repentance in the traditional sense, this prayer constitutes a cry for mercy from the priests that would follow a penitential expression from the people. The reason for this priestly cry for mercy can be discerned even in the call to repentance in 2:14 which reminds the reader of the deity's sovereign freedom in relation to forgiveness: "Who knows whether he may turn and relent and leave a blessing behind him?" As one can see in texts like Exod 33:19, repentance is not a guarantor of a shift in the predicament.³²

The final instance in Joel where a human addresses the deity comes in 3:11b in a short prayer in which the prophet calls God to bring down his mighty ones to do battle against the nations in the Valley of Jehoshaphat in the future.

The two main instances where humans address Yahweh in the book of Joel come at major junctures within the first half of the book and are thus in climactic points in the development of its structure. The first appears at the end of the initial phase of the book, one that calls the various entities to a day of fasting and prayer in relation to a great plague afflicting the land (ch. 1). The second appears at the end of the second phase of the book (2:1–17), one that reveals how the plague that afflicts the land is indicative of a much larger affliction that is

---

³⁰ See Wolff, *Dodekapropheton 2, Joel und Amos*, 44, 61; Wolff, *Joel and Amos*, 39, 52; Garrett, *Hosea, Joel*, 349–50, for this translation; cf. משׁל ב in Gen 1:18; 3:16; 4:7; 24:2; 45:8, 26; Isa 3:12.

³¹ On the contentious issue of whether repentance in Joel refers to a turning from moral failure see Boda, *Severe Mercy*, 306–7; contra recently Assis, *Book of Joel*, 140–41.

³² See Mark J. Boda, "Penitential Innovations in the Book of the Twelve," in *On Stone and Scroll: A Festschrift for Graham Davies*, ed. Brian A. Mastin, Katharine J. Dell, and James K. Aitken, BZAW 420 (Berlin: de Gruyter, 2011), 291–308.

approaching on the day of Yahweh.³³ This larger concern demands not only a cry to God for help, but also a deep repentance. The human address to Yahweh is a cry for grace in the midst of the predicament and the second of these appears to be accepted by Yahweh who transforms the people's situation.

The human address in 1:15a and 19–20 cries directly to Yahweh and focuses attention on the magnitude of the distress, but makes no precise demands on Yahweh to act. The human address in 2:17 also cries directly to Yahweh, but now makes specific requests (look compassionately, do not make a reproach) and focuses on the threat to the honor of Yahweh among the nations.

As with Hosea, Joel provides normative human address to be used by members of the community to address the deity. For the readers of this prophetic book these words are reminders that the deity is open to hearing the verbal response of the community. This is first seen in the words which articulate the terrible conditions of a natural disaster (1:15–20), but then in the words articulated in the midst of a much more severe national crisis which prompts seeking the mercy of the deity for a penitent community. As Assis has noted, "the prophet simulates both a prayer and God's response, thereby seeking to convince the people that this course of action would be beneficial."³⁴

AMOS

Direct human address to the deity occurs on only two occasions in the book of Amos, in two successive vision reports in chapter 7. In both cases Yahweh presents to the prophet a vision of an approaching divine judgment in the form of a natural disaster: the first a plague of locusts (7:1) and the second a mighty fire (7:4).³⁵ In both cases (7:3, 5) Yahweh responds to the prayer by "relenting" (נחם niphal) and announcing לֹא תִהְיֶה ("it will not come to pass"). The intercessory prayer of the prophet is nearly identical, both employing the same reason for God to not follow through with the discipline envisioned, while utilizing a different imperative: forgive (v. 3) and stop (v. 5).³⁶

---

³³ See Hubbard, *Joel and Amos*, 64, who sees 2:17 as the "climax" of 1:1–2:17 and the "turning point" in the book. Cf. Assis, *Book of Joel*, 65, 70.
³⁴ Assis, *Book of Joel*, 164.
³⁵ On the vision report form see Mark J. Boda, "Writing the Vision: Zechariah within the Visionary Traditions of the Hebrew Bible," in *Reading Dream and Vision Reports in the Hebrew Bible*, ed. Lena-Sofia Tiemeyer and Elizabeth Hayes, LHBOTS 584 (London: T&T Clark, 2014), 101–18.
³⁶ Hubbard, *Joel and Amos*, 222, attributes the difference in wording to the fact that the reemergence of divine punishment in the second vision revealed that his intercession did not result in forgiveness but only a stay of execution and so he capitulates to Yahweh and merely asks for him to stay again. If this is true then one can discern a rhetorical shift in the series of visions from request for forgiveness to request for cessation to no request.

3. אֲדֹנָי יהוה סְלַח־נָא מִי יָקוּם יַעֲקֹב כִּי קָטֹן הוּא
3. O Lord Yahweh, forgive, how can Jacob stand because he is small.

5. אֲדֹנָי יהוה חֲדַל־נָא מִי יָקוּם יַעֲקֹב כִּי קָטֹן הוּא
5. O Lord Yahweh, stop, how can Jacob stand because he is small.

There is one final vision report in Amos 7 (vv. 7–9). In this case, however, the vision of total destruction does not prompt an intercessory prayer by the prophet. In contrast to the visions of discipline directed against what appears to be the agricultural territory of Israel in 7:1–6 after which Amos protests (possibly related to Amos' background as a farmer, cf. Amos 1:1; 7:14–15), the final vision focusing on urban destruction is accepted by the prophet. The reason for the lack of prophetic protest may be related to the fact that the discipline envisioned is directed at what are considered illicit cult centres in the northern kingdom ("high places of Isaac … sanctuaries of Israel") and the royal patron of these cult sites ("the house of Jeroboam"). But it also may be because Yahweh makes clear that there is no longer room for forgiving or stopping when he declares: לֹא־אוֹסִיף עוֹד עֲבוֹר לוֹ ("I will no longer pass over him," see Amos 8:2; cf. Mic 7:18; Prov 19:11).[37] This acceptance of divine discipline against the urban royal cult centres is then furthered in the interchange which follows immediately in Amos 7:10–17 between the priest Amaziah at Bethel and Amos the prophet, an interchange which ends with Amos' prediction of the demise of the family of Amaziah.[38] The vision reports which follow in chapters 8 and 9 also do not prompt any prophetic protest.

The two prophetic protests at the outset of chapter 7 represent a stream of theodicy within the book of Amos, one that challenges God's justice in bringing destruction on the land by appeal to the vulnerability of Israel. Here we see a key role played by the prophetic figure, one with access to the deity who can challenge the actions of the deity. At the same time the silencing of the prophetic

---

[37] See Coggins, *Joel and Amos*, 141, who suggests "pass by" in "the sense of overlooking wrong doing." Wolff, *Dodekapropheton 2, Joel und Amos*, 339; Wolff, *Joel and Amos*, 294, notes that the use of לֹא־אוֹסִיף עוֹד assumes a connection with the first two vision reports of ch. 7, and thus is explicitly rejecting prophetic intervention. Contra Hubbard, *Joel and Amos*, 215, who attributes the lack of prophetic intercession to "the undeniable evidence of a plumb-line against a crooked wall" which "has convinced the prophet that the time of mercy had passed."

[38] Also note the use of measuring device language in both the vision of 7:7–9 (אֲנָךְ) and the prophetic word of 7:17 (חֶלֶק, חֶבֶל). See Wolff, *Dodekapropheton 2, Joel und Amos*, 339–40; Wolff, *Joel and Amos*, 294–95, for the original connection between 7:1–8 and 8:1–2 (possibly also 9:1–4) and the distinction of 7:10–17. Nevertheless he shows that 7:10–17 was inserted between 7:7–8 and 8:1–2 because "these texts interpret each other." The present form of ch. 7–8, however does weave these units together as a rhetorical unit.

protest signals for the reader the basis for Yahweh's action and thus subtly justifies the deity's actions.

This stream of theodicy within Amos needs to be set against the backdrop of another stream that can be discerned,[39] which is formulated in indirect human address to the deity, reflective of Israelite liturgical traditions.[40] Fragments of praise punctuate the text of Amos at three junctures within the book: 4:13; 5:8–9; and 9:5–6.

All share a common focus on the creational activities of Yahweh and contain the phrase "Yahweh … is his name." The Doxology in 4:13 follows a prophetic message which rehearses Yahweh's failed attempts to prompt repentance from the people through disciplinary actions ending with the climactic warning: "Prepare to meet your God, O Israel." It is followed by the declaration of a dirge over fallen virgin Israel in 5:1–2. The doxology in Amos 9:5–6 follows the first phase of the severe declaration of judgment in chapter 9, and immediately after the divine declaration: "I will set my eyes against them for calamity and not for prosperity," thus at a key juncture in the flow of the chapter. The placement of 5:8–9 appears to be in the middle of a description of those purveyors of injustice (5:7, 10–13) who are related to Bethel (5:6) and will experience the brunt of Yahweh's destruction of this illicit sanctuary city.[41] In each case where the doxological fragments appear in Amos there is reference in the context to a divine disciplinary destruction related to the sanctuary at Bethel (see 4:4–5; 5:5–6; 9:1). The doxologies represent a stream of theodicy within Amos, one that focuses on God's right as creator to bring judgment upon the land due to illicit worship and unjust actions. Using a form of praise in the third person contrasts the employment of lament in the first person. There is also irony in the use of praise in relation to the destruction of a sanctuary like Bethel which was created to foster worship. The doxologies not only justify God but reveal his ability to accomplish what he has warned.

While explanations have been suggested for the original role of such doxologies in the liturgical use of prophetic messages or even books, the present

---

[39] For review of recent scholarship on the Doxologies in Amos see Graham R. Hamborg, *Still Selling the Righteous: A Redaction-Critical Investigation of Reasons for Judgment in Amos 2:6–16*, LHBOTS 555 (New York: T&T Clark, 2012), 79–81. Some see Amos 1:2 as another fragment connected with these Doxologies; cf. Koch, "Die Rolle," 504–37.

[40] See e.g., Tchavdar S. Hadjiev, *The Composition and Redaction of the Book of Amos*, BZAW 393 (Berlin: de Gruyter, 2009), 136, for connection to the cultic use of the book of Amos, but also for the role of the doxologies as a "hymnic superstructure" for the book.

[41] 5:8–9 is the most awkwardly placed, coming as it does in the middle of a section with integrity in 5:7, 10–13, see Coggins, *Joel and Amos*, 125. However, see Jan de Waard, "Chiastic Structure of Amos 5:1–17," *VT* 27 (1977): 170–77, for the view that Amos 5:8–9 is placed at the center of a chiastic structure; cf. M. Daniel Carroll R., *Amos—The Prophet and His Oracles: Research on the Book of Amos* (Louisville: Westminster John Knox, 2002), 222.

article is concerned with their *Sitz im Buch*, that is, their role within the book of Amos. While it is not clear that the doxologies are each at key structural transitions within the book,[42] Möller has noted how they are rhetorically important within their respective contexts and Marks has highlighted their role within the book "at moments of exceptional severity, as though to solemnize the words of divine judgment."[43] Auld notes how the doxologies "reinforce the message of their contexts."[44] What may be overlooked in this discussion of the role of the doxologies within the book and their respective sections is careful attention to their relationship to the protest prayers of the prophet in the vision reports of chapter 7. Here we see how praise and prayer, hymn and lament, are intertwined in a prophetic section to justify God's actions, revealing God's power, grace, and justice, as such human address to or about the deity is declared or withheld.

JONAH

The book of Jonah contains three instances where humans address the deity directly. The first comes in Jonah 1:14 as the gentile sailors cry out to Yahweh as they are about to throw Jonah into the sea:

> Please, Yahweh,
> do not let us perish on account of this man's life
> and do not place upon us innocent blood;
> for You, O Yahweh, have done as You have pleased.

This prayer is addressed directly to Yahweh using the covenant name of Israel's God, passionately requesting release from any bloodguilt related to the potential drowning of Jonah.[45] The prayer ends with a declaration of the justice of Yahweh's actions towards his prophet Jonah. One should not miss the irony of the gentile sailors crying (קרא) to the Israelite God Yahweh when Jonah had

---

[42] Cf. Koch, "Die Rolle."
[43] Karl Möller, *A Prophet in Debate: The Rhetoric of Persuasion in the Book of Amos*, JSOTSup 372 (Sheffield: Sheffield Academic, 2003), 62–64; Herbert Marks, "The Twelve Prophets," in *The Literary Guide to the Bible*, ed. Robert Alter and Frank Kermode (Cambridge: Belknap, 1987), 218. Also see the work of Thomas Edward McComiskey, "The Hymnic Elements of the Prophecy of Amos: A Study of Form-Critical Methodology," *JETS* 30 (1987): 139–57.
[44] A. Graeme Auld, *Amos*, OTG (Sheffield: JSOT Press, 1986), 76.
[45] See the use of אָנָּה at the opening of a prayerful cry for help: 2 Kgs 20:3//Isa 38:3; Ps 116:4, 16; Dan 9:4; Neh 1:5, 11; cf. Hans Walter Wolff, *Dodekapropheton 3, Obadja und Jona*, BKAT (Neukirchen-Vluyn: Neukirchener Verlag, 1977), 96; Hans Walter Wolff, *Obadiah and Jonah: A Commentary*, CC (Minneapolis: Augsburg, 1986), 119.

failed to do so earlier (see Jonah 1:6).⁴⁶ The immediately following verse in 1:15 reveals God's answer to their prayer in the report that the sea calmed. This answer prompts the response of the gentile sailors depicted in 1:16: they feared Yahweh, but then offered a sacrifice (זבח זֶבַח) to Yahweh and made vows (נדר נֶדֶר). The prayer, the deity's answer and the sailors' response in 1:14–16 signal the closure of the first major episode of the book of Jonah (1:1–16), just prior to the transitional verse in 2:1 (Eng. 1:17) which will shift Jonah from the danger of the deep to the safety of the fish.

This short prayer and response of thanks by the gentile sailors is paralleled by the extensive prayer found on the lips of Jonah in 2:3–10 (Eng. vv. 2–9). This prayer reflects an individual thanksgiving psalm,⁴⁷ depicting not only the prayer of Jonah in his distress (2:3, 5, 8 [Eng. 2, 4, 7]), but also expressing thanksgiving and the intention to sacrifice (זבח) and pay (שׁלם *piel*) a vow (נֶדֶר), utilizing language which parallels the actions of the gentiles after their prayer in 1:16.⁴⁸ By introducing this prayer of thanksgiving with the verb פלל *hitpaʿel* the one(s) responsible for the book of Jonah signal that here thanksgiving functions as a request for full restoration from the sea to dry land.⁴⁹ The psalm in Jonah 2 is a mixture of direct and indirect human address to the deity, matching patterns found in the Psalter.⁵⁰ The psalm brings closure to the second major episode of the book of Jonah, just prior to the transitional verse in 2:11 (Eng. v. 10) which

---

⁴⁶ James Limburg, *Jonah: A Commentary*, OTL (Louisville: Westminster John Knox, 1993), 55.

⁴⁷ See Limburg, *Jonah*, 63, who identifies the phrases of the psalm in Jonah 2 which are also found in the Psalter, and shows the similarity in form between Jonah 2 and Ps 30. Psalms of thanksgiving include Pss 18; 30; 32; 34; 40:1–10; 66:13–20; 92; 116; 118; 138.

⁴⁸ Limburg, *Jonah*, 58. While Wolff is correct that the reference to the temple suggests a psalm that would find its home originally on dry land ("the formal language of the temple"), the fact that the psalm speaks of his deliverance is entirely appropriate for one who has been rescued from death in the water to the safety of the fish's belly; Wolff, *Dodekapropheton 3, Obadja und Jona*, 104; Wolff, *Obadiah and Jonah*, 129. Contra Wolff, *Dodekapropheton 3, Obadja und Jona*, 108–9; Wolff, *Obadiah and Jonah*, 133, who argues that the belly of the fish is the distress. Differences that Wolff, *Dodekapropheton 3, Obadja und Jona*, 104–5; Wolff, *Obadiah and Jonah*, 129, notes between the psalm and the rest of the book of Jonah are not surprising and indicate that the psalm may have been drawn from the liturgical collection of the temple, but this does not mean that the psalm was not chosen purposefully for this very spot in the narrative.

⁴⁹ Elsewhere פלל *hithpaʿel* followed by אֶל is always used for a prayer of request.

⁵⁰ See Limburg, *Jonah*, 65–66. Limburg sees the use of third person speech as an indication of liturgy with third person addressed to the congregation, he concludes that Jonah 2 assumes "the presence of a living congregation and thus point to the use of the psalms and of the entire book of Jonah in the context of a gathered community" (p. 66). However, third person speech may also be understood as indirect speech to the deity, even though the use of prayer forms invite religious affection towards Yahweh by those who read or hear the book of Jonah.

will shift Jonah from the safety of the fish to the new opportunity for obedience on dry land.

No direct address to the deity is found in Jonah 3. However, the king of Nineveh calls his citizens to "call (קרא) on God earnestly" even as they repent from their evil and violence (3:8). The response of the Ninevites prompts God to relent. There is though a deep contrast between Jonah 2 and Jonah 3. Jonah 2 gives much voice to the human address to God, filling the majority of the chapter, while Jonah 3 only makes reference to the human address to God of the Ninevites with no actual words spoken directly to God. Jonah 2 does depict the fact that Jonah prayed to Yahweh for help, but never cites his prayer directly, emphasizing instead the thanksgiving and intention to fulfill a vow to Yahweh. In Jonah 3 the prayer of the Ninevites is not recited and there is no confident expectation that the penitential rites would have an effect on the deity, only a hope (3:9): "Who knows, God may turn and relent and withdraw his burning anger so that we will not perish?"

It is the prayer and response of the Ninevites in chapter 3 which prompt the final series of human address to the deity in the closing chapter (4:2–3, 8–9). In his prayer to Yahweh Jonah now questions God's justice even though he knows it is based on the character credo which lies at the core of Israelite faith. The irony is thick as the angry prophet asks Yahweh to take his life, a fate that was all but sealed in the opening chapter and from which Yahweh had saved him. Furthermore, while the gentile sailors cried to Yahweh to save their lives and not hold them accountable for Jonah's death in 1:14, now Jonah, who sees himself as accountable for the gentile Ninevites' lives, cries to Yahweh to take his life.[51] The book closes then with theodicy as the prophet inappropriately challenges Yahweh's justice. The other prayers in the book are used at key transitions and serve to intertwine the fates of Jonah and the gentiles he encounters and to set up the climactic interchange between God and prophet at the end of the book.

MICAH

Human address to the deity only occurs at one point in the book of Micah in the final pericope of the book (7:14–20) which contains direct address in 7:14, 17b–20, a response from the deity in 7:15 and possibly indirect address in 7:16–17a.[52]

---

[51] The opening words of Jonah's prayer in 4:2 (אָנָּה יהוה) are the same as those of the sailors in 1:14; Limburg, *Jonah*, 89.

[52] Prior to this closing prayer, one finds a testimony not unlike many found in the book of Psalms (7:7–13). Some see 7:7 as the closing verse of 7:1–7 with 7:8–10 as the speech of Lady Zion to Lady Nineveh followed by a prophetic address to Zion in 7:11–13; cf. James Nogalski, *The Book of the Twelve: Hosea–Jonah*, SHBC (Macon, GA: Smyth & Helwys, 2011), 585. Sweeney sees 7:7 as the introduction to 7:7–20 (Marvin A. Sweeney, *The Twelve Prophets*, 2 vols., Berit Olam [Collegeville, MN: Liturgical Press, 2000], 408). Waltke sees 7:7 as playing a janus function in both 7:1–7 and 7:7–20 (Bruce K. Waltke, *A*

This human address to the deity begins by calling upon God to take up his role as royal shepherd of the people and instill fear once again in the nations of the earth (7:14, 16–17). The supplicant expresses wonder over God's forgiving character which will ensure compassion, truth and covenant faithfulness for the people (7:18–20).

These are the final words of the book of Micah, those that are left ringing in the ears of the readers, providing hope for a community experiencing life under imperial hegemony. It is testimony of faith in Yahweh, cry for Yahweh's leadership and expression of sincere repentance based firmly in the gracious character of Yahweh that brings the book to a close. In 7:18–20 Sweeney finds "the rhetorical goal of the book."[53] Nogalski notes how these words represent "a lengthy pause in the meta-narrative of the Book of the Twelve" and function "as a liturgical response from the prophet and the people, whose hope lies in YHWH's character as a God of compassion and forgiveness."[54] For the readers of the Book of the Twelve they represent but another milestone along the literary journey which prompts religious response through verbal expression.

Habakkuk

The book of Habakkuk is dominated by direct address to the deity.[55] The book is divided into two major sections, chapters 1–2 and chapter 3, the first focusing according to Nogalski on "theodicy" and the second on "theophany."[56] The two sections employ different forms of direct address to the deity.[57] The book begins in 1:2–4 with a cry of lament, utilizing the classic questions of lament ("how long

---

Commentary on Micah [Grand Rapids: Eerdmans, 2006], 430; cf. Philip Peter Jenson, *Obadiah, Jonah, Micah: A Theological Commentary*, LHBOTS 496 [New York: T&T Clark, 2008], 179, who calls 7:7 a transition verse). The speech of Lady Zion broaches the subject of theodicy, admitting sin and accepting the disciplinary action of Yahweh against the supplicant while expecting that eventually Yahweh would exercise justice on her behalf and release her from the crucible of judgment (7:9–10). Uncertain is the precise relationship between this testimony and the human address to the deity in 7:14–20, although Jenson argues that all the elements in 7:8–20 can be found in psalms of lament (Jenson, *Obadiah, Jonah, Micah*, 183) and Hillers treats 7:8–20 as a liturgy (Delbert R. Hillers, *Micah: A Commentary on the Book of the Prophet Micah*, Hermeneia [Philadelphia: Fortress, 1984], 85).

[53] Sweeney, *Twelve*, 413.
[54] Nogalski, *Micah–Malachi*, 592–94.
[55] See Sweeney, *Twelve*, 456, and Nogalski, *Micah–Malachi*, 645–46, for discussion over and defense of Habakkuk as cultic prophet; cf. Jörg Jeremias, *Kultprophetie und Gerichtsverkündigung in der Späten Königszeit Israels* (Neukirchen-Vluyn: Neukirchener Verlag, 1970), 55–127.
[56] Nogalski, *Micah–Malachi*, 654.
[57] See Marvin A. Sweeney, "Structure, Genre, and Intent in the Book of Habakkuk," *VT* 41 (1991): 63–83, for the structure of Habakkuk.

... why"), articulating the predicament of the distress, but all along challenging Yahweh for his lack of action in the midst of serious injustice.[58] A second challenge to God comes in 1:12–17, again employing the questions of lament ("why" in 1:13), but raising the issue of theodicy, whether God is justified in utilizing wicked entities to exact judgment.[59] The book ends in chapter 3 with a lengthy composition echoing the psalms and containing material which speaks about Yahweh in the third person (3:3–8a, 16–19a) alongside material which speaks directly to Yahweh in second person (3:2, 8b–15).[60] Although one can discern elements of the genre of theophany report in the composition, the passage represents prayer as the psalmist expresses trust in Yahweh (3:16–19a), but also calls upon Yahweh to act mercifully (3:2).[61] The two sections of theodicy and theophany express different modes of human address to the deity. Akin to the book of Job, in 2:1–4 the prophet stands ready for reproof from the deity and is told by the deity to prepare to record a vision even as he is given a message for the righteous to live faithfully through the devastation that is about to come. The call to silence then at the end of chapter 2 and prior to the visionary prayer of chapter 3 stands at a key transition in the book.[62] The prayer in chapter 3 thus

---

[58] See Nogalski, *Micah–Malachi*, 659, for connections to the lament tradition of the Psalter and to the prophetic confrontation traditions of Job and Jeremiah.

[59] On the original unity of the two complaint sections in ch. 1 and their original connection to the vision report in 2:4–5, see Nogalski, *Micah–Malachi*, 650–51, who sees the complaints/vision report as focused on theodicy regarding the prosperity of the wicked which was then applied by editors to the Babylonian issue. For a more unified view of composition see Sweeney, *Twelve*, 457–58, 479.

[60] Nogalski, *Micah–Malachi*, 687, sees in the shift from second to third person, a shift from prayer to the deity to recounting to those listening, but this does not take into account the role of third person address within prayer forms throughout the Psalter.

[61] See Sweeney, *Twelve*, 480, 482. Nogalski, *Micah–Malachi*, 679, refers to this as "a theophany report put into the framework of a prayer and a prophetic affirmation of trust." He thus sees it as functioning as "both a vision and a prayer" in which "the prophet 'sees' what YHWH will do in the future and petitions for mercy" (p. 689). See further John E. Anderson, "Awaiting an Answered Prayer: The Development and Reinterpretation of Habakkuk 3 in Its Contexts," *ZAW* 123 (2011): 57–71.

[62] See Nogalski, *Micah–Malachi*, 659: "After the initial cry in 1:2, the prophet's complaint changes to expressions of concern over the enemy attack until he is effectively silenced by YHWH's response to be quiet (2:20). Much like Job, when the prophet speaks in Hab 3, he does not confront YHWH with the same bravado as at the beginning." Nogalski though does note that 2:20 relates first to the contrast between YHWH and the powerless idols of 2:18–19, before noting that "The demand for silence marks a significant juncture in the book, recounting YHWH's temple presence that deserves obeisance from all the world and admonishing anyone who would challenge him—a subtle warning to the prophetic character—that the time for questioning has ended," Nogalski, *Micah–Malachi*, 674.

reflects a shift from prophetic theodicy to trust in response to divine theophany, which concludes the book.

Human address to the deity is thus key to the book of Habakkuk which brings together two streams of human address seen in previous books: the prophetic protest of lament seen in Hosea and especially Amos and Jonah as well as a concluding testimony declaring trust in Yahweh mixed with a direct address to Yahweh for help seen at the conclusion of Micah. The flow of Habakkuk and especially the placement of 2:20 and its call to silence, suggests a key shift in the role of human address to the deity not only in the book of Habakkuk, but as we will soon see in the book of the Twelve as a whole.

ZEPHANIAH–MALACHI

With the close of Habakkuk there is a paucity of direct human address to the deity in the remainder of the Book of the Twelve.[63] Human address to the deity is absent from Zephaniah and Haggai completely. Zechariah 1:6b probably reflects the idiom of the exilic penitential prayer tradition,[64] but is cast in third person as a declaration of Yahweh's justice in bringing discipline upon the people. Throughout the vision-oracle section of 1:7–6:15 the autobiographical prophetic figure does interact with heavenly figures, but in nearly every case this interaction entails the prophetic figure seeking to understand the details or significance of the visions. In one of the vision reports the prophet interacts with the deity (2:4 [Eng. 1:21]) but this is only to seek an interpretation of elements in the vision. This stands in stark contrast to the role of the prophet in the earlier vision reports of Amos where the prophet personally challenges the deity's intended disciplinary action (see above). Such a challenge does occur at one point in the vision reports of Zechariah in 1:12, but it is a heavenly messenger of Yahweh rather than the prophet who laments the enduring predicament of Jerusalem, employing the classic question of Hebrew disorientation psalms: "how long?" An opportunity for direct human address to the deity arises in Zech 7 as the contingent from Bethel approaches the temple site to "entreat the favour of God" (7:1), but 7:2 makes clear that they do this by "speaking to the priests and prophets." There is an indirect human address to the deity in Zech 11:5b: "Blessed be Yahweh, for I have become rich!," but this inappropriate declaration by the abusive owners of the sheep in 11:4–16 is certainly not regarded as normative speech. In Malachi direct human address to the deity returns, in every case cited by the deity (1:2, 5, 6, 7; 2:14, 17; 3:7, 8, 13). In

---

[63] As noted by Daniel F. O'Kennedy, "Prayer in the Post-Exilic Prophetic Books of Haggai, Zechariah and Malachi," *Scriptura* 113.1 (2014): 1–13.

[64] Mark J. Boda, "Zechariah: Master Mason or Penitential Prophet?" in *Yahwism after the Exile: Perspectives on Israelite Religion in the Persian Era*, ed. Bob Becking and Rainer Albertz, Studies in Theology and Religion 5 (Assen: van Gorcum, 2003), 49–69.

nearly every case these words of the people represent a challenge to the deity which is then refuted by Yahweh. Questions of theodicy are undermined consistently. The only time normative human address is employed is in 1:5 which cites indirect human address about Yahweh ("Yahweh be magnified beyond the border of Israel"), words which Yahweh says will be the response of those who see him accomplish what he has promised in relation to Edom. Interestingly, near the end of Malachi the depiction of those who respond appropriately to the message of the prophet ("those who feared Yahweh"), do speak words, but do so to one another (3:16). Yahweh is depicted as overhearing this speech and responding ("Yahweh gave attention and heard").

Thus beginning with Zephaniah and continuing through to the end of the Twelve there is a paucity of direct human address to the deity and when human address is cited in all cases except one it reflects the words of the people and is clearly identified as inappropriate.

Why does human address to the deity drop off significantly after Habakkuk? The reason for this can be traced to a repeated form which appears in the second half of the book of the Twelve. Habakkuk, Zephaniah, and Zechariah all contain calls for people to be silent before Yahweh (see chart: Calls to Silence).[65]

The call in Hab 2:20 comes at the end of a section that most likely has in view the injustice of an imperial entity, while the call in Zeph 1:7 comes in the midst of a chapter focused on offenders among the people of Judah, even though more universal entities may also be in view. Zechariah 2:17 [Eng. v. 13] comes

---

[65] For reflection on the role of the call to silence within the Twelve and its respective books see especially Nogalski, *Micah–Malachi*, 653, 675; Sweeney, *Twelve*, 477; Rüdiger Lux, "'Still Alles Fleisch vor Jhwh ...': Das Schweigegebot im Dodekapropheton und Sein Besonderer Ort im Zyklus der Nachtgesichte des Sacharja," *Leqach* 6 (2005): 99–113; Aaron Schart, "Deathly Silence and Apocalyptic Noise: Observations on the Soundscape of the Book of the Twelve," *Verbum et Ecclesia* 31 (2010): Article #383; Aaron Schart, "Totenstille und Endknall: Ein Beitrag zur Analyse der Soundscape des Zwölfprophetenbuchs," in *Sprachen–Bilder–Klänge: Dimensionen der Theologie im Alten Testament und in Seinem Umfeld; Festschrift für Rüdiger Bartelmus zu Seinem 65. Geburtstag*, ed. C. Karrer-Grube, et al., AOAT 30 (Münster: Ugarit-Verlag, 2009), 257–74. The call to silence is also found in Amos 6:10; 8:3, but this refers to its use within the funeral cult rather than temple cult; cf. Lux, "Still Alles Fleisch," 110. Also see Schart who distinguishes between the Amos references and those in Habakkuk, Zephaniah, and Zechariah, noting especially the similar elements: placement of the interjection in first position, common reference to "the location, 'before (the face of) YHWH,'" and inclusion of an explanation of the manner in which Yahweh is present. Schart highlights the use of these calls to silence as "a very fitting frame around the deepest cut in the narrative structure of the Book of the Twelve," reflective of "redactional activity." He sees this silence before Yahweh as "the appropriate attitude for coping with the painful punishment that YHWH has imposed on God's people" and in this draws in not only the three uses in Habakkuk, Zephaniah and Zechariah (which suggest the downfall of Babylon and Judah), but also Amos 6:9 and 8:3 which refer to the downfall of the northern kingdom.

at the end of a section celebrating God's punishment of the foreign nations and the return of people and God to Jerusalem. With Hab 2:20 there is a call for silence among the nations, allowing for one final and climactic expression of direct and indirect human address to Yahweh in Hab 3 from the prophet. Zephaniah 1:7, however, brings all human address, now even the people of God due to their disobedience, to a stop. What is interesting is that even with the announcement of the punishment of the imperial agent(s) in Zech 2, all humanity, whether within or outside the people of God are told to remain silent.

Thus, the final direct human speech to the deity which challenges the deity appears in Hab 1–2 and, following this, there are three calls to silence. After this point we do hear a final declaration of praise related to the appearance of God (Hab 3), but the focus is now on trust in Yahweh rather than challenge (cf. Hab 2:1–4; Zeph 3:8). When a challenge is allowed in Zech 1 it is on the lips of a heavenly messenger who is authorized to speak in such a way.

Calls to Silence	
ויהוה בְּהֵיכַל קָדְשׁוֹ הַס מִפָּנָיו כָּל־הָאָרֶץ	Hab 2:20
הַס מִפְּנֵי אֲדֹנָי יהוה כִּי קָרוֹב יוֹם יהוה כִּי־הֵכִין יהוה זֶבַח הִקְדִּישׁ קְרֻאָיו	Zeph 1:7
הַס כָּל־בָּשָׂר מִפְּנֵי יהוה כִּי נֵעוֹר מִמְּעוֹן קָדְשׁוֹ	Zech 2:17

The rationale for the silencing of human agents beginning with Hab 2:20 can be discerned at two key intervals in the Book of the Twelve. It is first encountered in Mic 3:7, as the prophet looks to a time when the evil deeds of the leaders of Israel will result in God no longer answering (ענה) their cry (זעק). Micah 3:12 associates this day with the destruction of Zion.[66] The second key passage is Zech 7:13–14a. Embedded within 7:11–14, a prophetic sermon which reviews the history of Judah's stubborn refusal to respond to Yahweh's prophetic calls to repentance which led to the destruction of land and exile of the people.

> And just as he called [קרא suffix conjugation] and they would not listen [שמע suffix conjugation], so they are calling [קרא prefix conjugation] and I will not listen [שמע prefix conjugation], and I am scattering them with a storm wind [סער prefix conjugation] among all the nations which they do not know.

The use of the prefix conjugations is a powerful rhetorical technique which enables the present hearers of Zechariah's sermon to relive the message of the earlier prophets.[67] The reason for the silencing of human address is the enduring

---

[66] See Mark J. Boda, "Babylon in the Book of the Twelve," *HBAI* 3 (2014): 225–48.
[67] See Mark J. Boda, "When God's Voice Breaks Through: Shifts in Revelatory Rhetoric in Zechariah 1–8," in *History, Memory, Hebrew Scriptures: A Festschrift for Ehud Ben Zvi*, ed. Ian Douglas Wilson and Diana V. Edelman (Winona Lake, IN: Eisenbrauns, 2015), 169–86.

sin of the people and their lack of response to Yahweh's message to the people. This disqualifies both cries for help as well as theodicy.[68]

One might expect that with the restoration this silencing of human address may have been removed.[69] The Book of the Twelve does create an expectation that a key ideal of the restoration will be that God will answer the call of his people (even as he answered the prayer of the heavenly messenger in Zech 1:12–13):

Joel 3:5 [Eng. 2:32]	whoever calls [קרא] on the name of Yahweh will be delivered
Micah 7:7	as for me I will watch expectantly for Yahweh, I will wait for the God of my salvation, my God will hear [שמע] me
Zeph 3:9	for then I will give to the peoples purified lips, that all of them may call [קרא] on the name of Yahweh to serve him shoulder to shoulder
Zech 10:6	for I am Yahweh their God and I will answer [ענה] them
Zech 13:9	they will call [קרא] on my name and I will answer [ענה] them[70]

But this expectation of a renewal of human address to deity for help lies in the future and this future lies beyond the time of the "restoration" vision of Zechariah. Zechariah 1–8 reveals that there are enduring problems with social injustice within the community of Yehud which has delayed the restoration and with this any hoped for restoration of human address to the deity.[71] Only a true

---

[68] Note the contrast between Zeph 1:7 and Joel 1:14–15 both of which provide a reason clause related to the nearness of the day of Yahweh. But yet Joel 1:14–15 calls for a verbal response seeking God's intervention and Zeph 1:7 calls for silence. Note also Zech 2:17 and Joel 3:1–5 (Eng. 2:28–32): both refer to "all flesh" and yet Joel refers to calling on the name of Yahweh while Zech 2:17 refers to silence.

[69] Nogalski has noted how the Calls to Silence appear at the beginning (Hab 2:20) and end (or better potential end, Zech 2:17) of the destruction of Jerusalem; Nogalski, *Micah–Malachi*, 635, 675. But the call to silence remains in Zech 2:17 and in light of the disappointing ending to Zechariah (chs. 7–14), the mode of silence remains.

[70] Zechariah 10–14 does encourage a request to Yahweh for help (10:1), but this request assumes a turning from reliance upon idols and diviners. Zechariah 12:10–13:1 looks to a day when penitential mourning is prompted by a divine gift of "the spirit of grace and supplication."

[71] Seen especially in the shift from suffix conjugation in v. 13 to prefix conjugation and from third person description of the past generation, to first person speech with its immediacy of message to the present generation; cf. Boda, "When God's Voice Breaks Through."

penitential response (Zech 7–8) will make possible a renewal of the human address (זעק/קרא) that will prompt divine response (שמע/ענה).

Habakkuk–Zephaniah link the calls to silence prayers for help and theodicy to the discipline associated with the destruction of Jerusalem and exile, and Zechariah links the calls to silence prayers for help even in the hoped for initial restoration, Malachi makes clear that theodicy is also deemed inappropriate in the initial restoration and possibly always. Yahweh consistently refutes any attempts to question God's actions, motives or character. But the lack of actual human address to the deity for help in the final section of the Book of the Twelve, suggests that even prayer for help is deemed inappropriate until penitential response is forthcoming.

Conclusion

All books in the Twelve from Hosea to Habakkuk which are addressed on the surface to Israelite audiences (thus not Obadiah and Nahum) contain prayers directed to Yahweh either directly or indirectly. They have various functions ranging from prophets providing normative speech for the people to address Yahweh (repentance, relational renewal, cry for salvation) to prophets challenging God through theodicy. Prayer seems to play a key function in each of the books, being placed at key junctures in the rhetorical flow of the books. One can discern certain general trends, but hardly trends that would suggest common origins for the prayer traditions within these books. These trends do, however, highlight for the reader the importance of human address to the deity in the reading of prophetic books and shape an expectation that human address is normative for the readers, whether in the form of repentance, relational renewal, or cry for salvation. Prophetic figures are regularly depicted challenging God through theodicy.

However human address to the deity ceases as the reader crosses into the section of the Twelve most often associated with the punishment of Israel and Judah, that is, Habakkuk and Zephaniah. In these two books we find exhortations to human silence before the deity, beginning near the end of Habakkuk, then in Zephaniah, and these exhortations coincide with the silencing of human address to the deity, whether prayers for help or theodicy. One might expect that human address to the deity would reemerge in the books often associated with "restoration" (Haggai–Malachi), but this is not the case.[72] Not only is there a lack of human address to the deity, but there is an additional exhortation to human silence in the midst of Zech 1–8. It appears that this series

---

[72] There is one voice that is encouraged to speak in this latter phase of the Book of the Twelve, that is, the voice of Daughter of Zion as seen in the series of *Aufrufe zur Freude* in Zeph 3:14–20; Zech 2:11, 14–15 (Eng. 7, 10–11); 9:9–10. See Boda, "Babylon in the Book of the Twelve."

of exhortations share a common origin and redactional strategy related to the latter portion of the Book of the Twelve.

The expectation of a restored community calling upon God and being answered by him, reveals the enduring significance of human address to the deity found throughout the first half of the Book of the Twelve. Such human address to the deity in the first half of the Twelve provides examples of the potential forms of address that will be used by the restoration community. Not surprisingly strewn throughout the first half of the Book of the Twelve are not only prayer forms, but references to a people who either call upon Yahweh or who are answered by Yahweh (Joel 2:19; cf. 2:13–14, 17; Jonah 1:6, 14; 2:2; 3:8). But the final form of the Book of the Twelve reminds the audience that human address to the deity for help is disallowed until there is a penitential response, and most likely theodicy is deemed completely inappropriate.[73] In the end the silence is deafening as the Twelve awaits the penitential response of its audience (Zech 7–8) accompanied by a divine work (Zech 12:10–14).

---

[73] See similar trends in Isaiah and Jeremiah; cf. Mark J. Boda, "'Uttering Precious Rather Than Worthless Words': Divine Patience and Impatience with Lament in Isaiah and Jeremiah," in *Why? How Long? Studies on Voice(s) of Lamentation Rooted in Biblical Hebrew Poetry*, ed. LeAnn Snow Flesher, Carol Dempsey, and Mark J. Boda, LHBOTS 552 (London: Continuum, 2014), 83–99.

10

The Book of Amos as "Prophetic Fiction": Describing the Genre of a Written Work that Reinvigorates Older Oral Speech Forms

Tim Bulkeley

Here I will propose that describing the prophetic books as "prophetic fictions" draws together much previous consideration of these books. It also accurately describes their content and form and reflects what is most distinctive about this genre as we find it in the Hebrew Bible. Having situated what is meant by the genre description "prophetic fiction" I will try to show how this language can help us understand the works themselves, focusing in particular on an outline reading of Amos 1–3.

APPROACHES TO THE GENRE OF THE PROPHETIC BOOKS

While the nature of the genre 'prophetic book' has been till recently little discussed some older assumptions do not accurately describe the contents. Suggestions that these works are "presentations" of a prophet may offer a way to read the works better.

Form-critical study of the prophets in the twentieth century was by and large conceived of as a kind of literary archaeology, driven by the desire to uncover an "authentic" stratum of the prophet's own words.[1] This means that

---

[1] See e.g., the opening to: Marvin A Sweeney, "Formation and Form," in *Old Testament Interpretation: Past, Present And Future*, ed. Karl May (Nashville: Abingdon, 1995), 113–26; Michael H. Floyd, "Basic Trends in the Form-Critical Study of Prophetic Texts," in *The*

more attention was focused on the smallest speech units that could be identified. The typical form, implied function, and *Sitz im Leben* of each has therefore been the subject of significant study and debate. Until recently the genre of the works themselves, as wholes, had been less considered. By and large, form-critics were not interested in whole books, and the scholars who were focused on the final form were less concerned with questions of genre than they perhaps should have been.

Yet as Neujahr recently noted in his consideration of the genre of Akkadian *ex eventu* texts:

> Whenever an ancient text is found and published for the first time, the question of that text's genre is actively engaged. In truth, any time any text is read by any reader, questions of genre are wrestled with and, at least provisionally, decided upon.[2]

Yet to a surprising degree this question was not overtly posed of the prophetic books of the Hebrew Bible, scholars were content largely to assume, rather than to discuss, the genre(s) of the works. Some assumed them to be collections of sayings. Indeed the superscriptions of Jeremiah and Amos *dibrê PN* could suggest this (Amos 1:1; Jer 1:1) and clearly they and the other books classed as "prophets" do contain many "sayings," and these comprise the largest sort of material in the books. On this view, the book of Jonah is quite different, with its focus on narrative rather than speeches. It has to be seen as an exception, and presumably misplaced among the prophetic books. However, there is significant material of other genres in most of these books, notably stories and songs, and the evidence of the superscriptions is not clear cut. While as we have seen two books begin *dibrê PN* (Amos, Jeremiah) and the superscriptions of six more speak of the *dᵉvar yhwh* (Hosea, Joel, Zephaniah, Micah, Haggai, Zechariah, cf. Jonah) which might also be seen as suggesting that they are collections of sayings, three call themselves *massā' PN* (Nahum, Habakkuk, Malachi) here strikingly *massā'* is singular so apparently the whole book was seen as one speech. The superscriptions of two other books talk only of visions *ḥăzôn* (Isaiah, Obadiah), and two have the standard opening of narrative texts *vayəhî* (Ezekiel, Jonah for narrative works that begin this way cf. Joshua, Judges, Ruth, 1 Samuel, 2 Samuel, Esther). Though the case of Jonah is complicated as the

---

Changing Face of Form Criticism for the Twenty-First Century, ed. Marvin Alan Sweeney and Ehud Ben Zvi (Grand Rapids: Eerdmans, 2003), 298–311.

[2] Matthew Neujahr, *Predicting the Past in the Ancient Near East: Mantic Historiography in Ancient Mesopotamia, Judah, and the Mediterranean World*, BJS 354 (Providence: Brown Judaic Studies, 2012), 103.

formula continues into a standard prophetic word formula which we expect to introduce a report of a prophetic word, a genre typical of the prophetic books.[3]

A more old-fashioned alternative way of understanding the genre of prophetic books saw them as in some sense biographical material. This approach is often typified in Skinner's work on Jeremiah.[4] Indeed, long after the naïve biographical approach ceased to be common, works appear with an interest in the person of Jeremiah and this book is perhaps the most amenable to such a reading.[5] However, except for Jonah the books actually contain little narrative,[6] and few, if any, are arranged chronologically. In Jeremiah and Ezekiel this non-chronological arrangement seems deliberate as dates are given but they move backwards and forwards in time with no apparent pattern as we progress through the text. Indeed Haggai's chronological arrangement seems atypical.[7] In other cases while the book might conceivably be arranged chronologically, such an arrangement is not indicated to the reader by the text itself. Also some of the books are anonymous or pseudonymous (Malachi?) which makes presenting them as "biographies" difficult.

The commentary series *Forms of Old Testament Literature* has been, as the opening words of the series description suggest, in many ways a summary of what form criticism has achieved in its traditional modes:

> The Forms of the Old Testament Literature (FOTL) is a series of volumes that seeks to present, according to a standard outline and methodology, a form-critical analysis of every book or unit of the Old Testament (Hebrew Bible).[8]

Yet it is particularly in this series also that outlines of the beginnings of new styles of form-critical study begin to emerge clearly. Concerning the key issue this paper addresses, in his 1996 *Isaiah* volume Sweeney offered a step towards defining the genre of these books: "The Prophetic Book is the literary presentation of the sayings of a particular prophet."[9] In the Micah commentary of 2000 Ben Zvi offers the more complex (but closely related):

---

[3] Marvin A Sweeney, *Isaiah 1–39: With an Introduction to Prophetic Literature*, FOTL 16 (Grand Rapids: Eerdmans, 1996), 19.
[4] John Skinner, *Prophecy and Religion: Studies in the Life of Jeremiah* (Cambridge: Cambridge University Press, 1922).
[5] Though carefully limited to the literary presentation of the prophetic persona Timothy Polk, *The Prophetic Persona: Jeremiah and the Language of Self*, JSOTSup 32 (Sheffield: JSOT Press, 1985) provides a striking example.
[6] See below.
[7] David L Petersen, *Haggai and Zechariah 1–8: A Commentary*, OTL (Philadelphia: Westminster, 1984), 32–33.
[8] The quotation comes from the publisher's website for the series http://www.eerdmans.com/Products/CategoryCenter.aspx?CategoryId=SE!FOTL.
[9] Sweeney, *Isaiah 1–39*, 16.

A "prophetic book" is a book that claims an association with the figure of a prophet of the past, in this case Micah, and that is presented to its readership as YHWH's word.[10]

I see these definitions as related, since in each case the description includes the element that such a book "presents" a prophet or their sayings. I will argue below that this notion of presentation is crucial to understanding the nature of "prophetic books." Thus while older (usually unexamined) genre descriptions do not reflect the phenomenon accurately we have in this newer work a pointer towards a more helpful understanding.

Forerunners and Clues

This section will consider two approaches to the issue that though they are similar to the "presentation of a prophet" approach predate it, and may also help us to sharpen the idea.

Peter Ackroyd's IOSOT paper a quarter of a century earlier offers the closest predecessor of this approach.[11] His major goal was to promote a more holistic approach to the study of the prophetic literature, a move that at that time was just beginning to impact other areas of Old Testament study. So he challenged: "the assumption ... that it is possible to consider Isa. i–xxxix as a book separate from the whole in which it is now contained."[12] So, although his paper was tightly focused on Isa 1–12, it is nevertheless significant for consideration of the *Gattung* of prophetic books as wholes. One of his goals in the paper was to show how the structure of this section of the book "provides a presentation of a prophetic figure and validates his authority in a particular manner."[13]

He notes that these chapters, indeed most prophetic books, contain little information about the prophet, and contrasts this with the typical introduction to a modern commentary.[14] In 1–12 such information as is provided on this topic, rather than serving (what in modern terms we might call) biographical ends, serves to authenticate the prophet's commission.[15] He presents the subsections of 1–12 leading to the conclusion that:

---

[10] Ehud Ben Zvi, *Micah*, FOTL 21b (Grand Rapids, Eerdmans, 2000), 4.
[11] Peter Ackroyd, "Isaiah I–XII: Presentation of a Prophet," in *Congress Volume Gottingen 1977*, VTSup 29 (Leiden: Brill, 1978), 16–48.
[12] Ibid., the quotation is from the opening page.
[13] Ibid., 29.
[14] Compare my comparative review of two Amos commentaries: Tim Bulkeley, "The Long and the Short of It: Two Recent Commentaries on the Book of Amos," *JSOT* 16, 51 (1991): 119–21.
[15] Ackroyd, "Isaiah I–XII," 40–41.

There are points at which a good case can be made out for genuine Isaianic sayings; but it is everywhere clear that the words of the prophet have been ordered and amplified to bring them into relationship with subsequent situations. It is not my intention to try to sort out either the genuine from the non-genuine, or the possible situations ... to which this or that passage may belong, or in which reapplication has been made. I am concerned rather to observe how, in these twelve chapters as they now stand, there is a presentation of the prophet.[16]

Some of Ackroyd's ideas that are particularly significant for the genre identification suggested in this paper were already present in Baltzer's work *Die Biographie der Propheten*, published a couple of years earlier. In this Baltzer sought to present the prophetic books as "ideal biographies" a *Gattung* he saw as developing from the career biographies of Egyptian functionaries. This form was concerned to present the subject's title and family background, their call and installation (including details of time, place, and witnesses etc.) and their area of competence (*Zuständigkeitsbereich*) shown through incidents showing their fitness to the task and examples illustrative of their role, concluding with notice of their successor or sometimes their death.[17] These features distinguish such ancient "biographies" not only from modern biography with its concern for the personality of the subject but also from common understandings of the nature of the prophetic books: "As far as *Gattung* is concerned, biography is to be differentiated from mere oracle-assemblage and, conversely, from annals or historical writing."[18] Thus if one takes Baltzer's stress on the typicality rather than individuality of the subject seriously his "ideal biography" begins to sound rather like Ackroyd, Sweeney and ben Zvi's "presentation of a prophet" approach, as long as the word "prophet" is not understood to stand in for the particularity of a prophetic person. However, Baltzer's genre designation was not much taken up, perhaps because the "biographical" approach epitomised in the English-speaking world by John Skinner's Cunningham lectures from 1920 had been rendered so thoroughly outmoded by form- and redaction-critical studies.

COGNATE LITERATURES

One might expect that investigating prophetic literature from surrounding cultures would throw light on the nature of the biblical prophetic books,

---

[16] Ibid., 44.
[17] Klaus Baltzer, *Die Biographie der Propheten* (Neukirchen-Vluyn: Neukirchener Verlag, 1975), particularly 19–38.
[18] Ibid., 194.

however, if claims that Israelite prophetic books are unique[19] may be somewhat exaggerated, these works are considerably more highly developed than the examples we have from Israel's neighbors. The Egyptian Twelfth Dynasty work "Prophecy of Neferti" (ca. 1990–1780 BCE) contains what scholars interpret as an *ex eventu* history of the future in a connected narrative, rather than a collection of somewhat independent pieces. Thus it is more like the visions of apocalyptic literature than the prophetic books of the Hebrew Bible. The Mari texts, though from a similar period seem closer to biblical prophetic books, yet Petersen summarises a consideration of them as analogues of prophetic books somewhat negatively:

> The Mari texts, though in an archive, betray no attempt to create a collection associated with an individual. Also, there is no evidence of later additions or reflections as one finds in Israelite prophetic literature.[20]

Perhaps the closest parallels to the prophetic books of the Hebrew Bible come from the Neo-Assyrian texts which are much closer in time to the books that concern us:

> One feature of the Neo-Asyrian texts is particularly striking: more than one oracle is present on a tablet. One tablet from Nineveh includes five oracles, all apparently attributed to the same prophet. Moreover the middle oracle seems to have been placed there because of its central importance for the overall sequence, namely, the basis for a covenant between the god Assur and the royal house of Assyria.[21]

This is, to date, the closest parallel to the biblical prophetic books, it shares with them a (possibly deliberate) placing of oracles in a sequence and with an ordering that seems to present a theological message related to a covenant with a divinity. What it does not have are elements that suggest a "presentation of the prophet." Yet this seems to be a most striking feature of (at least some of) the Israelite works.

The "Literary Image" of the Prophet

The description "presentation of a prophet" is perhaps somewhat open ended, and it may be sharpened by looking at the phenomenon of literary prophecy. While Hebrew prophecy is presented (both in the prophetic books and

---

[19] See e.g., Ronald E. Clements, "Prophecy as Literature: a Reappraisal," in *Old Testament Prophecy: From Oracles to Canon* (Louisville: Westminster John Knox, 1996), 203.
[20] David L. Petersen, *The Prophetic Literature: An Introduction* (Louisville: Westminster John Knox, 2002), 17.
[21] Petersen, *Prophetic Literature*, 17–18.

elsewhere) as an oral phenomenon, the prophetic books are literary works. Thus we might sharpen "presentation of a prophet" to "literary image of a prophet."

So, Steck's guide to studying the prophetic books at the turn of the century, *The Prophetic Books and Their Theological Witness*, provides both another approach similar to those already presented, and takes us a step further. He summarised the main tendency of twentieth century studies of the prophetic books saying:

> The interest concentrates upon isolated literary layers, but especially upon the original beginnings of the transmission, whether one seeks it with the prophet or in a later period. Behind this situation stands the self-evident assumption that a prophetic book is nothing more than the simple recording of sayings of the prophet for whom the book is named or the sayings of later anonymous prophets. Apparently, this assumption is justified by texts like Isaiah 8:16–18 and 30:8, or by scenes of prophetic appearance (like Isaiah 7–8; Jeremiah 7 and 26) or by the picture of transmission in Jeremiah 36. Additionally, one acknowledges varying numbers of isolated additions or actualizing individual continuations of these recordings along the broader path of transmission.[22]

He then questions the reliability of the detail of such diachronic studies, pointing to the diversity of conclusions which they produce,[23] and suggests that:

> The actual situation is different. A prophetic writing presents a literary image of a prophet, perhaps even in constitutive association with a series of prophetic writings. This literary image stands before the aesthetically oriented search for the image of a brilliant, creative, original prophetic personality. This literary image stands in front of the kerygmatically oriented search for the image of a theologically innovative preacher figure.[24]

He went on to suggest that this was a weakness of the current form-critical approaches to the prophetic writings:

> Form criticism only appears to open the door directly to the words of proclamation of this figure. The view of the prophet as speaker that dominated in the era of form criticism can no longer serve as the starting point for the question. The received location of prophetic messages in descriptions (!) of speaking situations is primarily not a speaking situation that can be immediately reconstructed. Instead, the received location is a book. We only possess the book, and only the book is the ground upon which we can pose our questions.[25]

---

[22] Odil Hannes Steck, *The Prophetic Books and Their Theological Witness*, trans. James D. Nogalski (St Louis: Chalice, 2000), 8.
[23] Steck, *Theological Witness*, 9; cf. for example my remarks in a comparative book review: Bulkeley, "The Long and the Short of It." (See n. 14 above.)
[24] Steck, *Theological Witness*, 9.
[25] Ibid., 9.

Thus the form criticism of the late twentieth century missed two critical elements:

> Like the prophetic book itself, this prophetic image that the book presents has received little attention. This image could look quite different from the original prophet.[26]

That is, Steck recognised a need for a closer examination of the actual books, which suggests to me a rethinking of assumptions about their genre(s) and in particular of the "prophetic image" which these books project, what he earlier identified as "a literary image of a prophet." He also draws attention to the irony that while what we have is a literary phenomenon, what this literary phenomenon presents is presented significantly as an oral phenomenon. We have a literary presentation of a prophet who speaks.

To be meaningful to readers of a later time, a "presentation" of a prophet is likely to do more than just recount their words as they were delivered. The words would presumably be adapted and reworked or added to, just as the redaction critics claim.[27] Indeed we might go further, unless we wish to ascribe to the writers of prophetic books a kind of historiographical interest hardly attested before the modern period, there is little *necessary* relationship between these presentations and the prophets who may have inspired them.[28]

This lack of necessary connection between the works and the historical people who may have been their starting points suggests a further sharpening of the description. It also points to another way in which Baltzer's talk of "career biographies" fails to reflect the works we are examining. In this connection Alter's talk of fictionalized history and historicized fiction will be useful.

Prophetic Fictions

While talk of a "literary image" of a prophet bears quite a strong resemblance to Baltzer's career biographies, it does not (as his term "career biography" might suggest) imply a biographical interest. Such a genre description seems summed up in the term "prophetic fiction." The term was once used by Crenshaw to describe the book of Jonah, but in the light of the suggestions and arguments above seems appropriate to describe most or even all of the prophetic books of the Hebrew Bible.[29] Such a work presents prophetic figures and their preaching,

---

[26] Ibid., 9.
[27] This remains true even if the conclusions these critics reach are too varied and uncertain to themselves provide a firm footing for a reconstruction of the history of the production of any particular prophetic book.
[28] Steck, *Theological Witness*, 9.
[29] James L. Crenshaw, *Prophetic Conflict: Its Effect Upon Israelite Religion* (Berlin: de Gruyter, 1971), 64–65.

with a possible but not a necessary connection to any historic prophets who may be identified. By this descriptor "prophetic fiction" I intend the word "fiction," not to imply the opposite of "factual," but rather as Alter used it in *The Art of Biblical Narrative* to underline the creativity of the writers, and to detach investigation of their works from an overriding concern for the historicity of the events (including speeches) they recount.[30]

Between the form and the contents of the prophetic books there is a disconnect which has often been noted, but perhaps not fully exploited to enhance our understanding of their nature. These works come to us as "books," that is written works with more or less stable contents,[31] yet within this written form they present oral phenomena. The prophets in these books are presented most often as speaking, while there are very few mentions of their words being written (pretty much limited to Isa 8:1; 30:8; Jer 36; Hab 2:2). Indeed, unlike the accounts of prophetic figures in the narrative texts of the former prophets, their actions are relatively seldom recounted.

Prophetic books are in the form of bounded written texts. These texts are unlike the records of single oracles, or collections of a very small number of oracles of which we have examples from nearby cultures. Yet the written texts of the prophetic books present prophets as speakers. As mentioned above they are only rarely associated with written texts. This discrepancy between form and contents (the form of a written text describing a person who speaks) can be understood in terms of an understanding of their genre as "prophetic fiction" without necessarily implying any connection to a prior oral phenomenon.

The possible place of oral performance in the history of the development of prophetic texts is much discussed. We have moved from an easy uncritical assumption of original oral performance of prophetic speech through its recording to collection in the works we now have to a certain degree of scepticism about this supposed history. My point is not to enter this debate, but rather that regardless of the possible histories of the development of prophetic texts or phenomena the prophetic books we have present prophets as speakers. Whether or not there were such people as prophets who spoke "words" like those recorded in the books this is how the writers of the books envisage prophets.

In the light of this it may be useful here to note that whether in the historicized fiction of Genesis, or the fictionalized history (to use Alter's

---

[30] Robert Alter, *The Art of Biblical Narrative* (New York: Basic Books, 1983), ch. 2 particularly p. 26.
[31] The variety of textual traditions even in its most extreme form (found perhaps in the two editions of the book of Jeremiah, typified in critical editions of the MT and LXX texts) does not invalidate this, though it may point to and hint at a fluidity to these written forms.

descriptions)³² of Samuel–Kings or Chronicles, one of the main (and arguably the primary) means used by the writers of biblical Hebrew narrative is to present the direct speech of the character.³³ Description, whether of people or events, is sparse, and although contrast and comparison between characters is an effective tool, it is not frequent. This feature is strong in all biblical Hebrew narrative texts and in marked distinction to most other narrative traditions. Indeed in biblical Hebrew narratives narration is sparse compared with speech.³⁴ In this respect the prophetic books may be considered as some sort of extreme case within a biblical Hebrew narrative spectrum. For many of these books do contain some description of actions, and also of the speech or thoughts (often presented in the regular prose narratives of the Hebrew Bible as saying to oneself) of other characters.

Most strikingly there is an interplay of first person divine speech with speech about YHWH. So in Amos 5:4–6 the unit begins with YHWH in the first person: "Seek me and live ..." reported by either the narrator or by Amos (as seen by the introduction: "For thus says the LORD to the house of Israel"), which then moves into direct speech by the prophet about YHWH: "Seek the LORD and live, or he will break out ..." We also find traces of a prophet's opponents' or hearers' reactions embedded in the prophet's speeches. For example "who say to their husbands, 'Bring something to drink!' (4:1) or "you who rejoice in Lo-debar, who say, 'Have we not by our own strength taken Karnaim for ourselves?'" (6:13). Through such implied dialogue, many of the features most commonly used to present ("characterize") the actors of biblical narrative texts are also available to readers of the prophetic books. Finding such characterization outside the works traditionally thought of as narrative is not unique, for example Jacobsen suggests:

> In the Psalter, as in biblical narrative, direct discourse also functions to portray the character of those whose speech is quoted: the psalmist, the enemies, God, and the congregation. Just as in biblical narrative, in the Psalter the different characters speak with different motives, with different degrees of truthfulness,

---

³² Alter, *Art of Biblical Narrative*, 23–46.
³³ Ibid., ch. 4; John A. Beck, *God as Storyteller: Seeking Meaning in Biblical Narrative* (St. Louis: Chalice, 2008), 39–42; Adele Berlin, *Poetics and Interpretation of Biblical Narrative* (Winona Lake, IN: Eisenbrauns, 1994), 64–66.
³⁴ Alter, *The Art of Biblical Narrative*, ch. 6; Jan Fokkelman, *Reading Biblical Narrative: An Introduction Guide* (Louisville: Westminster John Knox, 1999), 69; David M. Gunn and Danna Nolan Fewell, *Narrative in the Hebrew Bible*, Oxford Bible (New York: Oxford University Press, 1993), 57.

from different perspectives, with different faith perspectives, and with different authority.[35]

Jacobsen's words apply with equal force to the prophets as to the psalms.

Inevitably, as with any genre descriptor, the term "prophetic fiction" fits some works more closely than others. Jonah is at one end of such a spectrum, with Amos, Jeremiah, Ezekiel nearer that end, while books like Joel, Obadiah, and Zephaniah provide little personification of the prophets to whom the words are attributed. Yet even here, for example in Obadiah, an attribution precedes the divine speech(es). Whilst Obadiah (servant of Yah) may well be a descriptor rather than an individual's name (though examples of the name are attested in 1 Chron 3:21, 12:10; Ezra 8:9 and Neh 10:6, 12:25) it functions here to attach the "vision" to a human person and the messenger formulae in 1, 2, 4, 8, and 18 present this "person" as a prophet. Even in overtly narrative texts the degree of characterisation varies between those that are richly and deeply complex to those barely identified by their function.

The case of Isaiah is interesting. The presence of the character of the prophet seems to recede as the book progresses. In the early chapters the character of Isaiah is strongly present, not only in the introductions 1:1; 2:1; 13:1 but the use of his name on thirteen other occasions in chapters 1–39 (7:3; 20:2–3; and particularly in the narrative section: 37:2, 5–6, 21; 38:1, 4, 21; 39:3, 5, 8). In the section of the book which begins at chapter 40 while Isaiah is not mentioned an "I" who speaks is identified, and in some sense (as in Jeremiah) the experiences of this prophet are part of the message. In this section of the book, however, it is difficult to distinguish the "I" of the prophet from that of another character "the servant of YHWH." This phenomenon is reminiscent of the difficulty of distinguishing the prophetic "I" from the divine "I" in these books more generally. In the final section into which the book is commonly divided (56–66) the prophet recedes further and this section might be listed with the works that least strongly reflect the description "prophetic fiction."

Interestingly the translation panel of one modern English translation seems to view these books in a similar way. The *Contemporary English Version* (translated by the American Bible Society) renders most of the superscriptions "I am [name of prophet]"[36] (Isa 1:1; Jer 1:1; Ezek 1:1; Hos 1:1; Joel 1:1;[37] Mic 1:1; Nah 1:1;

---

[35] Rolf A. Jacobsen, *Many Are Saying: The Function of Direct Discourse in the Hebrew Psalter* (London: T&T Clark, 2004), 18.

[36] Except Jeremiah which reads "My name is Jeremiah" (Zechariah reads "I am the prophet Zechariah," an oddity since the Hebrew is close to Haggai see the footnote below.)

[37] The exceptions are Obadiah: "The Lord God gave Obadiah a message" as is Jonah: "One day the Lord told Jonah"; Haggai: "On the first day of the sixth month of the second year"; these books reflect rather different wording in the Hebrew which may explain their difference.

Hab 1:1; Zeph 1:1). Whether their rendering was a conscious or unconscious recognition of the nature of the books is unclear as no notes were provided to explain the translation.

The genre description "prophetic fiction" offers several useful features, besides describing well the content that we actually find in prophetic books. Fictional biography (such as the works that retell the life of some past figure) displays a concern both for the past (the writers of such works most often are concerned that their imaginations be controlled by the possible or likely events and speech of the time portrayed) and for the writer's present (these past lives are retold because they seem to have some enduring or present significance). This double concern seems to reflect the nature of prophetic books. Even the more sceptical of redaction critics usually ascribe some of the sayings to the prophet to whom the book ascribes them, at least some kernel of some sayings. They also suggest that the words have been edited for relevance in the redactor's time.

It may be felt that "prophetic fiction" over stresses the coherence of these works, which only half a century ago were believed to lack almost any coherence beyond the level of local speech units.[38] Yet many studies today either assume or argue for such coherence, in the case of the "Minor Prophets" sometimes even beyond the level of individual books.[39]

Interestingly while most previous descriptions of the genre "prophetic book" present Jonah merely as an outlier or exception, those presented here, from Ackroyd, Sweeney, and ben Zvi's "presentation" to my "prophetic fiction" (with the exception of Baltzer's "career biography," for few of its characteristic features are present in Jonah), must see Jonah as in some sense an extreme (even perhaps parodic) yet typical case. Some features of that book are extreme, most strikingly the near absence of oracular speeches of the prophet. However there are many words addressed to God and Jonah's longest speech in the book is the psalm in chapter two. Yet other prophetic books contain psalms or parts of psalms (e.g., Isa 38:9–20; the "hymnic fragments" in Amos 1:2; 4:13; 5:8–9; 9:5–6; Nah 1:2–8; Hab 3), so in this Jonah is extreme, but not atypical. The book of Jonah focuses on one incident, again this is not atypical, other books have a similar narrow focus. Still others contain narrative about the prophet and the

---

[38] E.g., Gerhard von Rad, "Origin of the Concept of the Day of Yahweh," *JSS* 4 (1959): 105, could write: "the individual speech units in Amos are in thematic respects in no way attuned to each other."

[39] See Tim Bulkeley, "Cohesion, Rhetorical Purpose and the Poetics of Coherence in Amos 3," *Australian Biblical Review* 47 (1999): 16–28; Tim Bulkeley, "Amos 7,1–8,3: Cohesion and Generic Dissonance," *ZAW* 121 (2009): 515–28 for attempts to demonstrate the coherence of parts of the book of Amos; and Tim Bulkeley, "L'Auteur Est Mort, But Won't Lie Down: Inventing Authors While Reading Amos," *Colloq.* 43.1 (2011): 59–70 for a presentation of some of the ideas expressed here.

reception of their speech, or concerning their interactions with God, like those we find in Jonah.[40]

The genre description "prophetic fiction," as understood above, accurately describes the contents of the prophetic books (even including Jonah) and is only a small extension of earlier ways of describing the genre, but does it also offer practical help in reading the works so described?

READING AMOS 1–3 AS PROPHETIC FICTION

Having briefly presented the idea of describing the genre of the prophetic books as "prophetic fictions" let me now show how this description might fit, and indeed assist us to read, the opening chapters of the book of Amos.[41]

The book opens, as most do, with a superscription (1:1). In the case of Amos this presents the "words" of a prophet, named Amos who was identified with herders from Tekoa. Whatever our current inability to assess the meaning of this information with confidence, it presumably provided the intended hearers with a social setting for the prophet. The "words" are next specified as ones which "he saw." The verb $ḥāzāh$ is strongly associated with prophecy, and effectively suggests the "words" were understood to be divinely inspired prophetic speeches. The target of these speeches is broadly identified as "Israel" and they are situated in time past: "in the days of King Uzziah of Judah and in the days of King Jeroboam son of Joash of Israel." This form of dating to me suggests, not a claim to immediacy but rather, some distance between the teller and the events or speech to be narrated. In the case of Amos the time is further specified as "two years before the earthquake," suggesting a relatively short period of activity for the prophet being presented.

The phrasing and contents of this superscription suggest a teller distanced from Amos in time who will present his "words" (divinely inspired prophetic speeches) and their audience. The next verse is a brief poetic fragment that is not directly linked, through its contents, to its surrounding texts. It seems to serve as an epigraph, perhaps to summarise or (since this is often the function of poetic texts embedded in narrative)[42] to celebrate the prophet's message. The introductory "he said" seems to refer back to Amos, yet in the first line "YHWH roars from Zion" and the speaker seems perhaps not to be Amos but the narrator of the superscription. This fits with the suggestion that this verse serves to celebrate (in advance) the ministry of a prophet whose "words" served to

---

[40] This material is most prominent in Jeremiah but is also found in other prophetic books including Isaiah and Ezekiel as well as Amos and Hosea.
[41] This book seems a fitting test case as it is often presented in introductory courses as the typical prophetic book.
[42] Fokkelman, *Reading Biblical Narrative*, ch. 10.

communicate YHWH's roar, indeed were YHWH's words (according to the shared prophetic ideology).

After this brief introduction, in verse 3, the account of Amos's preaching begins. The first speech is two chapters long and contains eight oracles linked to one another by shared formulae and content, with the last two more different from the rest than the six are from each other. The common opening formula: "For three transgressions of [name of a city or a people], and for four, I will not revoke it, because ..." is followed by accusation(s) and judgement. The first six concern neighbouring polities: 1:3–5, Damascus; 1:6–8, Gaza; 1:9–10, Tyre; 1:11–12, Edom; 1:13–15, the Ammonites; 1:1–3, Moab. In each case the crime is some sort of brutality in war, several times the victims of the atrocity are Israelites. When cities are the named targets they seem to stand as representatives. Thus though Gaza is introduced (1:6) Ashdod, Askelon and Ekron are included in the judgment (1:8). After this excoriation of neighbouring polities the speaker turns to first Judah (2:4–5) and finally Israel in the longest and by far the most developed speech (2:6–16). This sequence, with the greater detail and focus on the last item, leads most commentators to imagine a rhetoric in which the prophet's hearers respond at first with enthusiasm, as their neighbours are condemned for their crimes, reaching a peak of perhaps surprised approval when Judah joins those in the dock, setting them up for the shock of the final condemnation of Israel.[43]

During this final oracle of the series the address changes. In verses 6–8 those who are spoken about are identified in the third person plural. In verse 9 the audience are addressed directly in the second person plural, "you." This direct address continues until verse 13, though in verse 14–16 (where the judgement pronounced in verse 13 is spelled out in verbal pictures) the pronouns again become third person, but this time singular (as a "he" pictured for "your" consideration). Although second person pronouns have not been used in the book before 2:10 their identity has been suggested by the superscription: "against/concerning Israel." The addressees are the ancestors of the presumed hearers of the work (who are identified by most redaction critical studies as "Israelites" in the Persian period),[44] and indeed the (physical or spiritual) ancestors of the actual audiences of the canonized work once it becomes "Scripture."

How are the audience in the implied narrative world (Amos's Israelite hearers) or indeed the actual (implied) hearers to be expected to react? Surely such a strong attack, even if prepared by the careful and effective rhetorical

---

[43] See e.g., Shalom Paul, *A Commentary on the Book of Amos*, Hermeneia (Minneapolis: Fortress, 1991), 76 and the references there.

[44] E.g., the books of Ezra and Nehemiah use "Israel" regularly to refer to the residents of Yehud of whom the writer approves especially those who had "returned from the exile," by contrast the term *yehuday* is used less often.

strategy of 1:3–2:5, must provoke questions about the speaker's authority and/or message!

Chapter 3 is a unit; it begins with a strong formula: "Hear this word," and ends with the formula: "YHWH's oracle" which is followed by a repetition of the opening formula: "Hear this word" in 4:1. The chapter is expressed in ways that defend Amos's identity as a prophet who must proclaim a message of warning and destruction.[45] Rhetorical and linguistic features (such as the 'excessive' use of messenger formulae in vv. 9–15, or the effect of the questions in vv. 3–8) work together with the meaning expressed to underline that Amos is commissioned as a divine spokesperson, and must proclaim God's message of woe, not weal. Thus in a "prophetic fiction" the speech(es) assembled in chapter 3, reply to Amos's audience's presumed response to the preceding oracle series and to the potentially similar response by the implied audience of the book.

This may raise the question of whether the completeness of the destruction suggested by the imagery in verse 12 could really motivate the "prophet's" audience to change. Is a future near total national destruction really a stronger motivator than the preceding stripping of strongholds and plundering of citadels? However, for the writer of the account of Amos's message this might serve that purpose for their audience. Since the audience of the book knows the destruction of Samaria as a fact of past history. Note the fact that the third person subjects of verse 12 are named as "the children of Israel who live in Samaria" and not merely "Israel" might help suggest this double view, as in narrative naming is often significant of perspective.[46]

Conclusion

The genre of the book of Amos taken as an example of a prophetic book is a "prophetic fiction." The work presents the message (and to some extent the person and "story") of Amos to hearers of a later time. Thinking of the book this way allows us to read it in ways that permit the flow of sections (as well as the individual sections themselves) to make sense. This was illustrated by presenting a brief reading of the first three chapters. It was earlier argued that this genre description accurately describes the content and form of the book. Therefore I suggest that naming the genre of prophetic books as "prophetic fiction" is both accurate and helpful, though like most such descriptors it fits some examples more closely than others. It also allows us to draw together elements of the study of the book from redaction- and form-critical approaches and to understand them in the light of the literary paradigm of fictionalized history or historicized fiction.

---

[45] Bulkeley, "Cohesion, Rhetorical Purpose"; Yehoshua Gitay, "A Study of Amos's Art of Speech: A Rhetorical Analysis of Amos 3:1–15," *CBQ* 42 (1980): 293–309.

[46] Berlin, *Poetics and Interpretation of Biblical Narrative*, 59–61.

11

Sitz im What? Context and the Prophetic Book of Obadiah

Colin M. Toffelmire

INTRODUCTION

Among Hermann Gunkel's many influential proposals, his understanding of *Sitz im Leben* has been both fruitful and frustrating. The notion that a text-type, or genre (*Gattung*) is related in some important way to a context or situation was and is a vitally important insight for the analysis of texts (whether biblical or otherwise). Yet, questions abound. What is meant by "situation" or "context," and what is the nature of the relationship between a text and its "situation"?[1] While theory and practice related to *Sitz im Leben* have been topics of significant discussion in biblical studies (and especially Old Testament/Hebrew Bible studies), parallel discussions have also proceeded in other disciplines, and these discussions have the potential to inform and revitalize the conversation about context and situation in biblical studies. My focus here will be on the question of context from the perspective of modern functional linguistics, and more specifically the perspective of Systemic Functional Linguistics (SFL) as practiced by Ruqaiya Hasan and Michael Halliday (among others). I will begin by exploring the question of context and *Sitz im Leben* generally, and then I will provide an overview of context and register (or text-type) from the perspective of

---

[1] To say nothing of the added difficulties of understanding the nature of "genre" itself, and the relationship between individual instances of text and broader or more abstract categories of text-type/genre.

SFL. Using the book of Obadiah as an example I will then present a preliminary attempt at what SFL calls a "register analysis" of the text, as well as a summary description of the book's linguistic context, which SFL calls the "context of situation," as an example of the potential of SFL as a helpful point of contact for biblical form criticism generally, and for theory and practice related to situation and context particularly.[2]

SITZ IM LEBEN AND CONTEXT OF SITUATION

Hermann Gunkel's theories related to text-type were adopted widely among Old Testament/Hebrew Bible scholars. The exacting application of the notion of *Sitz im Leben* related to form criticism found in Wolff's work serves as an excellent example of the method. Wolff suggests that the *Sitz im Leben* of the first part of Obadiah is "an assurance proclaimed by the prophet during lament ceremonies held in the ruins of the Jerusalem sanctuary during the exilic period."[3] This, thus, involves a decidedly particular social location in postexilic Yehud. What is more, this specific social location is an historical reconstruction. Based, in part, on these conclusions Wolff suggests that verses 15a, 16, 17, 18, and 21 also fit this social context, but that verses 19, 20, and 17b are later literary additions, from ca. 400 BCE or later.[4] This is entirely consistent with Gunkel's understanding of the *Sitz im Leben* as the original oral setting for a given text.[5] It is also consistent with Gunkel's focus on the social location of theorized original oral substrata, and not on book-level context.[6] Relation to the underlying social situation of sub-units of a given prophetic book is, thus, one of the hallmarks of *Sitz im Leben* in the context of classic form criticism.

---

[2] According to Raabe, Obadiah serves as a helpful *précis* for much that is common in the prophetic literature due to its typicality and to its short length. Paul R. Raabe, *Obadiah: A New Translation with Introduction and Commentary*, AB 24D (New York: Doubleday, 1996), 3.

[3] Hans Walter Wolff, *Obadiah and Jonah: A Commentary*, trans. Margaret Kohl, CC (Minneapolis: Augsburg, 1986), 63, cf. 19.

[4] Wolff, *Obadiah and Jonah*, 63–64.

[5] Hermann Gunkel, "The Prophets as Writers and Poets," in *Prophecy in Israel*, ed. David L. Peterson (Philadelphia: Fortress, 1987), 22–73. Cf. also Claus Westermann, *Basic Forms of Prophetic Speech*, trans. Hugh C. White (Louisville: Westminster John Knox, 1991), 68.

[6] Gunkel, "Prophets as Writers and Poets." As a point of clarification, the focus on original oral situation is not myopic in classical form critical work. Form critics also paid significant attention to the development of the religious tradition, and to ongoing contexts in which a given form continued to maintain its relevance. Classical form critics were thus interested in both the *Sitz im Leben* of the original, oral prophecy, and in the ongoing situations (which may have differed in various ways from that original situation) in which the oracle may have been maintained. See, for example, Sigmund Mowinckel, *The Spirit and the Word: Prophecy and Tradition in Ancient Israel*, trans. K.C. Hanson (Minneapolis: Fortress, 2002), 7.

Gunkel also proposed that a determinative relationship existed between genre and text production in ancient Israel.[7] In a sense this is the keystone to Gunkel's use of form criticism. Because both he and those who were later to make use of form criticism were chiefly interested in the reconstruction of the history of the religion of ancient Israel, fixing the relationship between a given form (and thus the oral sub-strata of a prophetic text) and its social context was quite necessary.[8] If one could imagine flexibility either in terms of the form itself or in terms of the relationship of a form to a given social situation, form criticism would cease to be a functional tool for precise historical reconstruction. The addition of elements of flexibility undercuts, in a fashion, the purpose of the underlying project itself.

Since Gunkel's day, and since the heyday of the form-critical project (the early- to mid-twentieth century) both these, and other, elements of form criticism have been challenged. This has led to the problematization of the entire concept of *Sitz im Leben*, and of the relationship between social situation and genre. Knierim, for example, has criticized both the focus on the relationship between *Sitz im Leben* and genre, and the notion of foundationally oral genres.[9] In fact he has gone so far as to suggest that "'setting,' in the sense biblical form criticism has understood it cannot be regarded indispensably as one of the factors that constitute genres. Not if genre is understood as a *linguistic* phenomenon."[10] This suggests a significant, or even complete, divorce between the analysis of genre in the biblical literature and an understanding of social situation. If this state of affairs is to be accepted, no further conversation regarding *Sitz im Leben*, or anything like it, need be pursued.

However, as Becking has noted, Knierim's intense minimalism regarding social context may be something of an overreaction.[11] This is not to say that Becking himself accepts the account of *Sitz im Leben* provided by classic form

---

[7] Gunkel, "Prophets as Writers and Poets."

[8] For more see my discussion of the relationship between the history of tradition and *Sitz im Leben* in Colin M. Toffelmire, "Form Criticism," in Mark J. Boda and J. Gordon McConville, *Dictionary of the Old Testament: Prophets* (Downers Grove, IL: InterVarsity and IVP Academic, 2012), 257–71. The discussion here is closely related to my argument in the previous article.

[9] Rolf Knierim, "Old Testament Form Criticism Reconsidered," *Int* 27 (1973): 435–68.

[10] Ibid., 441. Knierim quite intentionally differentiates his definition of "linguistic" from the sociological concerns that underpin Gunkel's understanding of *Sitz im Leben*, which, as we will see, also means a rather sharp point of departure between my understanding of language and linguistics and Knierim's.

[11] Bob Becking, "Nehemiah 9 and the Problematic Concept of Context (Sitz Im Leben)," in *Changing Face of Form Criticism for the Twenty-First Century*, ed. Marvin A. Sweeney and Ehud Ben Zvi (Grand Rapids: Eerdmans, 2003), 262. Cf. Mark J. Boda, *Praying the Tradition: The Origin and Use of Tradition in Nehemiah 9*, BZAW 277 (Berlin: de Gruyter, 1999).

critics, but he does suggest that the concept remains useful if applied appropriately. In his analysis of Boda's form-critical comments on Nehemiah, Becking notes that this work "implies that the relation between a *Gattung* and its language is not always exclusive."[12] That is to say, there is a kind of fluidity or flexibility between the specific language of an individual text and the expected features generally associated with the genre that text is thought to represent. Instead of concluding that there is no relationship between genre and context, this suggests that genres may have a degree of flexibility in terms of their contextual background. Just as history writing involves the narration (and not exact recollection) of the past, Becking suggests that *Sitz im Leben* is a "representation of the past" that has a heuristic usefulness. The question at hand for Becking is whether and to what degree does a *Sitz im Leben* help to elucidate the text in question and overall history in general.[13]

For Becking this indicates a variety of potential originating dates that might be suggested by a given text.[14] *Sitz im Leben* thus remains a tool for recovering the original situation(s) of a given passage. But, Becking's suggestion that context forms a heuristic function may also allow us to think in terms of different points of reception by reading communities.[15] In either case we neither need accept a wooden and unyielding relationship between a genre and its social context, nor reject the existence of any such relationship at all. There is a good deal of middle ground available, and we should seize it.

The concept of context has not been rejected by newer iterations of form criticism, but it has undergone a significant shift from a focus on originally oral sub-units to final literary forms. This has involved a concomitant shift away from referring to a *Sitz im Leben*, a phrase which has retained the connotation of a focus on oral sub-strata, to referring to a *Sitz im Buch* or *Sitz in der Literatur*.[16] This is due to the suggestion that prophetic books (and other kinds of biblical literature) are more than just records of existing oral prophecies, but are instead distinct artefacts, created by individuals and communities who were interested in both preservation and creation.[17] Kim describes this difference in perspective by asking what the critic should have in mind when considering the idea of setting. "Is it the setting of the very event (e.g., the specific date, hour, and locale of the prophet's preaching), or that of the author, transmitter, redactor, or manuscript

---

[12] Becking, "Nehemiah 9," 257.
[13] Ibid., 264.
[14] Ibid., 264.
[15] See, for example, Ehud Ben Zvi, *Micah*, FOTL 21b (Grand Rapids: Eerdmans, 2000).
[16] See, for example, Boda's article in this volume.
[17] Mark E. Biddle, "Obadiah–Jonah–Micah in Canonical Context: The Nature of Prophetic Literature and Hermeneutics," *Int* 61 (2007): 154–66.

copyist that should be the target?"[18] Like Becking, Kim suggests not the attempt to recover the specific historical context of the creation of some unit of a given text, but focuses on the correlation between likely or plausible functions of a given text (in its final form) and theorized settings in the past.[19]

Biddle suggests that the textual features of the Old Testament/Hebrew Bible documents as we have them actually "permit and even exemplify the transposition of literarily fixed material onto new situations."[20] This is a helpful way of conceptualizing the possibilities of exploring context with relation to the final form of a given text, but I wonder if Biddle does not draw too sharp a dichotomy between an historical fixedness related to oral precursors, and a situational fluidity related to a final literary product. The SFL concept of context of situation, which I will describe in full below, suggests that any given text (whether oral or textual) includes situational encoding. It packs the social situation that it needs in its language, as it were, and thus can be planted and replanted in new material situations according to fit and to need. This is in keeping with Becking's and Kim's proposals.[21] In fact, it reframes the nature of Kim's question, quoted above, regarding which context should be the focus of attention. Any of Kim's options become viable possibilities if we see social context as an encoded feature of any given text.

Given all of this, I propose that some account of social context remains both possible and necessary to new iterations of the form-critical project. What is more, to acknowledge the continued importance of a relationship between social context and genre need not stand in tension with the examination of other contexts and their relationships to the genres of biblical literature (e.g., *Sitz im Buch, Sitz in der Literatur*), nor with a focus on the final form of a given text. Ben Zvi has noted that a "systemic approach to these books [i.e., prophetic books] shows a non-random distribution of important traits."[22] Given this suggestion that the prophetic books themselves evince discernable genre features, it follows from related research in the field of linguistics that prophetic books as genres of communication relate to some set of social situations.[23]

---

[18] Hyun Chul Paul Kim, "Form Criticism in Dialogue with Other Criticisms: Building the Multidimensional Structures of Texts and Concepts," in Sweeney and Ben Zvi, *Changing Face of Form Criticism*, 85–104.
[19] Ibid.
[20] Biddle, "Obadiah–Jonah–Micah in Canonical Context," 155.
[21] Ehud Ben Zvi has also done extensive work on various contexts of reception for biblical books from the perspective of final-form analysis. See, for instance, Ben Zvi, *Micah*; Ehud Ben Zvi, *Signs of Jonah: Reading and Rereading in Ancient Yehud*, LHBOTS 367 (Sheffield: Sheffield Academic, 2003).
[22] Ehud Ben Zvi, "Reconstructing the Intellectual Discourse of Ancient Yehud," *SR* 39 (2010): 7–23.
[23] I will expand upon this further below. There are, of course, those who continue to suggest that this focus on the prophetic book over and against individual oracles is

With a discussion of the creation and maintenance of prophetic literature (qua literature), we are back to discussions of social institutions, which were a significant part of the original conversation surrounding *Sitz im Leben*.[24] But, a key difference between Gunkel's account of *Sitz im Leben* and the examination of social situation that I am proposing involves a turn from excavation to interpretation. Here I follow Buss, who makes use of the concept of social situation to describe the nature of a given text, and as an interpretive tool, and not as a way of seeing behind the text to an earlier stratum.[25] To this end we still require some account of the *Sitz im Leben* of the prophetic literature, though not merely for the purpose of unearthing theoretical oral precursors.

A tool that I suggest can help to fulfill this necessity is register analysis, and the concept of context of situation. Register analysis is a sub-set of linguistic discourse analysis, related especially to functional linguistic theories. I will focus here on the account of register and context proposed by researchers in the sub-field of Systemic Functional Linguistics (SFL).[26] To this end a brief exploration of SFL and some definition of the terms "register" and "context of situation" is warranted.[27]

SFL is a functional theory of language, and thus argues strongly that language is intrinsically communicative, and that the evolution of human language is tied to the function of human language.[28] Language is, consequently, intrinsically social. In fact Halliday and other SFL theorists describe language as

---

artificial, and obscures the meaning of the parts that make up the whole. See, for instance, Robert P. Carroll, "Poets Not Prophets: A Response to 'Prophets through the Looking Glass,'" in *The Prophets: A Sheffield Reader*, ed. Philip R. Davies (Sheffield: Sheffield Academic, 1996), 43–49. Floyd has provided an able challenge to this contention. See, Michael H. Floyd, "'Write the Revelation!' (Hab 2:2): Re-Imagining the Cultural History of Prophecy," in *Writings and Speech in Israelite and Ancient Near Eastern Prophecy*, ed. Ehud Ben Zvi and Michael H. Floyd (Atlanta: Society of Biblical Literature, 2000), 103–143.

[24] For a discussion of prophecy as social institution see, Martti Nissinen, "How Prophecy Became Literature," *SJOT* 19 (2005): 153–72. Cf. also Floyd in this volume.

[25] Martin J. Buss, *The Changing Shape of Form Criticism: A Relational Approach*, ed. Nickie M. Stipe (Sheffield: Sheffield Phoenix, 2010), 48, 148.

[26] Note that the content of this section is drawn to a significant degree from Colin M. Toffelmire, "Orienting the Event: Register and the Day of YHWH in the Prophetic Book of Joel" (PhD diss., McMaster Divinity College, 2014), 65–80. Other accounts of register exist to be sure. See, for instance Teun A. van Dijk, *Discourse and Context: A Socio-Cognitive Approach* (Cambridge: Cambridge University Press, 2008).

[27] A complete exploration of the theory of language presented by SFL is far beyond the capacity of this paper. For accessible presentations of the basic theory see, M. A. K. Halliday, *An Introduction to Functional Grammar* (London: E. Arnold, 1985), xiii–xxxv; M. A. K. Halliday, *Language as Social Semiotic: The Social Interpretation of Language and Meaning* (London: Edward Arnold, 1978).

[28] M. A. K. Halliday and Ruqaiya Hasan, "Text and Context: Aspects of Language in a Social-Semiotic Perspective," *Sophia Linguistica* 6 (1980): 4–91.

a "socio-semiotic," or a communicative sub-system of a given society's or culture's meaning making system.[29] Given that language is social and communicative, SFL theorists suggest that all instances of linguistic communication are related to and even encode some kind of social situation. There is no de-contextualized communication, and therefore context is not merely an *ad hoc* tool to be used to clarify ambiguous phrasing. Some theory of context and the relationship between context and text is necessary. Hasan argues that context deserves the same degree of systematic attention as that given to grammar, semantics, and other strata of the language system.[30] An analysis of the register of a given text using the categories and methods provided by SFL (modified as necessary for classical Hebrew) offers the potential to illuminate elements of the social situation, or context of situation in SFL parlance, of a text.

While even an overview of SFL register theory is beyond this paper, I will outline briefly the categories and steps involved. SFL theorists refer to three high-level categories when examining linguistic register, the field, the tenor, and the mode of the text. Field refers to ideational and logical components of the text, including participants, arena (location and time), and verbal processes and transitivity structure. Tenor refers to the interpersonal dynamics of the text, including participant relations (modality) and any process sharing features. Mode refers to the texture of the text, to the way in which language is deployed as a communicative tool, including identity and similarity chains, and the medium and channel of the text. The composite result of an analysis of a text based on these features is a description of the register, or linguistic genre, of the text in question. A description of register can then be used to suggest a likely or plausible context of situation (social situation) to which it corresponds.

This context of situation is not a description of the actual historical and material situation of a text, though historical and cultural location are important factors. SFL theorists suggest four sub-categories of "context" that can provide helpful precision to our discussion of *Sitz im Leben* in a biblical text: context of situation, context of text (co-text), context of culture, and material situational setting. Let me move through these types of context in reverse order, beginning with material situational setting.

The material situational setting of an utterance refers to the actual physical environment of a communicative act. This material setting exists on a cline between more and less relevant to the communicative act in question, depending

---

[29] M. A. K. Halliday, *Explorations in the Functions of Language* (London: Edward Arnold, 1973), 74.

[30] Ruqaiya Hasan, "Speaking with Reference to Context," in *Text and Context in Functional Linguistics*, ed. Mohsen Ghadessy (Amsterdam: John Benjamins, 1999), 219–328. Ruqaiya Hasan, "Wherefore Context? The Place of Context in the System and Process of Language," in *Grammar and Discourse Proceedings of the International Conference on Discourse Analysis*, ed. S. Z. Ren et al. (Macau: University of Macau, 2001), 3.

on the nature of that act. In the case of oral communication, the material situational setting can be of significant importance, particularly if the interlocutors in the discourse incorporate deictic reference or depend on non-verbal forms of communication (pointing, gesturing, etc.). At the other end of the scale, a highly textualized instance of communication may depend very little or almost not at all on the material situational setting. I am writing this paragraph using a computer, but the type of computer is not an essential component of the communicative experience for the reader—the degree of physical and temporal distance is too great for that material element to matter.

Context of culture refers to the broader sociocultural frame of reference for a communicative act. This might include a great many variables, such as class, language, historical context, geographical location, and so on. Context of culture tends to be described at a high level of abstraction and, according to Hasan, refers to "an organization of all possible features of all possible situations in all their possible permunations, where 'possible' means socially recognizable."[31] Context of text, or co-text, refers to intertextual and intratextual relations, or to the way in which a given communicative act is internally self-referential or to the way it refers (explicitly or implicitly) to other texts.

Context of situation, which is what concerns us here, refers to the social situation of a given communicative act. This may or may not include features of the material situational setting, but refers to those elements of a situation relevant to the communicative act in a given text. Normally discussions related to context of situation in SFL research involve the observation of a situation and the identification of the ways in which that setting predicts (in probabilistic terms) the likely linguistic register. In the case of analyses of ancient texts we are working to apply this logic in reverse, describing the register of a text in order to suggest a likely or plausible context of situation.

Some brief comments regarding the relationships between context of culture, co-text, and context of situation are also necessary. Because context of culture and context of situation are given different names, the temptation may be to think of them as different things, or as belonging to different categories. Instead they should be considered the same essential phenomenon seen from different perspectives and described using different degrees of abstraction. Context of culture and context of situation are points at either end of a cline of linguistic context. Context of culture is an abstraction of all of contexts of situation that are real or possible within some identifiable set. Context of situation is the instantiation of this system of real or possible situations, or the social situation of some given text within the set of all possible or real texts in a given culture. My description of co-text above refers to both intratextual and

---

[31] Ruqaiya Hasan, "The Place of Context in a Systemic Functional Model," in *Continuum Companion to Systemic Functional Linguistics*, ed. M. A. K. Halliday and Jonathan J. Webster (London: Continuum, 2009), 166–89.

intertextual points of connection. This is related to the continuum between context of situation and context of culture, the former being related to intratextual connections and the latter related to intertextual connections.

A description of the social context of a given text, what SFL refers to as context of situation, is closely analogous to the form-critical concept of *Sitz im Leben*. In fact, this is not a coincidental relationship, but the two ways of describing context have a common intellectual heritage. The theoretical account of context of SFL arises out of the work of Firth, who was Halliday's teacher and who explored the relationship between language and context in his work. Firth's ideas regarding language and social situation were strongly influenced by his friend and colleague Bronislaw Malinowski, the renowned anthropologist. It was Malinowski who proposed that social context was intrinsically linked to linguistic communication, and who coined the term "context of situation." One of Malinowski's other academic contacts was the famed Egyptologist Alan Gardiner, who appears to have been influential in the development of Malinowski's theories of language and social context. As Buss has noted, Gardiner studied and worked in Berlin at the same time that Hermann Gunkel was developing his theories of form and context, and would certainly have been cognizant of developments in the field of biblical studies.[32] There is, therefore, an organic relationship between the concept of *Sitz im Leben* in biblical studies and the concept of context of situation as described by SFL.

Not only is there a meaningful connection between these two accounts of the relationship between register or genre and social situation, but there are also important points of divergence between the classic notion of *Sitz im Leben* and SFL's description of context of situation, which are important to recent developments in form-critical research. Those elements of Gunkel's use of *Sitz im Leben* which have been most roundly and forcefully criticized—the focus on oral sub-strata, and a rigid association between form and social institution—were not elements that developed in the SFL account of register. What is more, SFL focuses significant attention on the text itself as the object of analysis, and describes language as a system abstracted from instances of text.[33] This is therefore an analytical perspective consistent with the final-form analysis that is featured in at least some versions of new form criticism.

Systemic Functional Linguistics can therefore offer helpful tools and theoretical perspectives to contribute to a description of the social situations that are related to biblical literature. It offers developed methodological tools and a useful set of terms and categories for the description of both register and context

---

[32] Buss, *Changing Shape*, 153–56.
[33] Halliday, *Language as Social Semiotic*, 4–5. Note that in linguistics the term "text" refers to any identifiable unit of linguistic communications, whatever its medium or channel (oral/written, phonic/graphic). For our purposes this will, of course, refer to the graphic texts of the prophetic literature.

of situation, categories and analysis that are analogous to form criticism's focus on genres and *Sitz im Leben*. What is more, the account of context provided by SFL provides some helpful distinctions related to various types of context explored by biblical scholars. For instance, *Sitz in der Literatur* or *Sitz im Buch* could be considered a type of co-textual analysis, examining the context of text of a given piece of biblical literature. This might involve the exploration of intratextual relationships, issues of textual cohesion, and questions related to genre and sub-genre in a given text, or perhaps the examination of intertextual relationships and the comparison of genre or sub-genre relationships between biblical books. This is consequently distinct from, but vitally related to, context of situation, which we could feasibly refer to using the term *Sitz im Leben*, given all of the necessary caveats implied by the discussion above. Biblical scholars need not import technical terminology from SFL, but the distinctions between types of context, and the emphasis that all types of context are analytically important are tremendously valuable insights.[34] Of course, even though importing another discipline's jargon can be an onerous process which sometimes obscures insights for readers who are not accustomed to that cognate discipline, it is also notable that SFL has developed an extensive body of research and an analytical process and language for the description of register and context, both of which can be helpful for biblical researchers. In my analysis below I will attempt to sail between the Scylla of obscure jargon and the

---

[34] And this is to say nothing of SFL's long history of practical textual analysis from these theoretical perspectives. Also of import is the ongoing interdisciplinary interaction between biblical scholarship and theoretical linguistics (esp. linguistic discourse analysis). See, for instance, Robert D. Holmstedt, "The Typological Classification of the Hebrew of Genesis: Subject-Verb or Verb-Subject?" *JHS* 11 (2011): Article 14; Robert D. Holmstedt and Andrew R. Jones, "The Pronoun in Tripartite Verbless Clauses in Biblical Hebrew: Resumption for Left-Dislocation of Pronominal Copula?" *JSS* 59 (2014): 53–89; C. H. J. van der Merwe, "Biblical Exegesis, Cognitive Linguistics and Hypertext," in *Congress Volume Leiden 2004* (Leiden: Brill, 2006), 255–80; C. H. J. van der Merwe, "A Cognitive Linguistic Perspective on Hinneh in the Pentateuch, Joshua, Judges, and Ruth," *HS* 48 (2007): 101–140; Cynthia L. Miller-Naudé and C. H. J. van der Merwe, "הִנֵּה and Mirativity in Biblical Hebrew," *HS* 52 (2011): 53–81; Stanley E. Porter, "Studying Ancient Languages from a Modern Linguistic Perspective: Essential Terms and Terminology," *Filologia neotestamentaria* 2 (1989): 147–72; Stanley E. Porter, review of "Linguistics and Biblical Interpretation," ed. Edgar J Bakker, *JSNT* (1990): 124; Stanley E. Porter, "Grammar as Interpretation: Greek Literature in Its Linguistic Contexts," *JSNT* (2001): 125; Stanley E. Porter, "Matthew and Mark: The Contribution of Recent Linguistic Thought," in *Mark and Matthew I: Comparative Readings* (Tübingen: Mohr Siebeck, 2011), 97–119; Aaron Sherwood, "Paul's Imprisonment as the Glory of the Ethnē: A Discourse Analysis of Ephesians 3:1–13," *BBR* 22 (2012): 97–111; Andrew Todd, "The Interaction of Talk and Text: Re-Contextualizing Biblical Interpretation," *Practical Theology* 6 (2013): 69–85.

Charybdis of oversimplification in order to leverage the SFL account of register and context of situation in a register analysis of the prophetic book of Obadiah.

REGISTER ANALYSIS OF OBADIAH

A complete analysis of the register of Obadiah would depend first upon a fully-orbed discourse analysis of the text. Because this is beyond our scope here, what I offer instead are some preliminary comments on the register of the prophetic book. This analysis will cover the three categories noted above in my exploration of SFL: field, tenor, and mode. In the analysis of field I will briefly identify the discourse participants, and will then explore the discourse arena (including time and location), and transitivity structure in the book. In the analysis of tenor I will focus on participant relations, and especially on modality and grammatical person. Finally, in the analysis of mode I will focus on channel and medium and, to a lesser degree, on the role of intertextuality in an analysis of the register of Obadiah. I will conclude this analysis of register with an overview of the Context of Situation for the prophetic book of Obadiah.

FIELD

The book of Obadiah contains a relatively small number of discourse participants. These include: Edom/Esau, YHWH, the prophetic voice, the divine messenger (v. 1), those who participate in the destruction of Jerusalem (vv. 11–14), the nations (vv. 16–21), and of course, Judah/Jacob.[35] Of these, the principal discourse participants (i.e., those upon which the greatest focus rests) are Edom/Esau, YHWH, the prophetic voice, the nations, and Jacob/Judah.

The book of Obadiah contains thirteen instances of second person reference (three second person pronouns, ten pronominal suffixes), all of which refer to Edom/Esau. This suggests that, on the surface at least, the semantic Addressee of the book is Edom. And yet, there seems little if any likelihood that the prophetic book is meant to be read by the people of Edom.[36] The instances of second person address do not suggest action that the Addressees should take, or

---

[35] I have noted in my analysis of the register of the book of Joel that participants often group together into participant sets in the prophetic literature. These groupings are accomplished by means of semantic chains related to textual coherence, and thus to the mode of the text. Because I am not providing here a full analysis of the mode of Obadiah (for reasons of both space and relevance), some of this work related to the grouping or relatedness of discourse participants has been done "behind the scenes" as it were. Thus, in some instances, I will refer to a participant (e.g., Judah) and include under this title various specific discourse participants that may be represented in some way other than an actual instance of the lexeme (e.g., pronominal reference, or metaphorical reference).

[36] Daniel I. Block, *Obadiah: The Kingship Belongs to Yhwh*, Hearing the Message of Scripture 27 (Grand Rapids: Zondervan, 2013), 30–31.

could take on their own behalf, which suggests to the reader that the semantic Addressees play some other role in the discourse. Throughout the book, references to Esau/Edom point to a brotherly conflict and to the horror of fratricide.[37] Assis argues forcefully that this creates a focus in the book on election theology.[38] In prophetic theology Edom's attempts to occupy Israelite/Judahite territory was seen as an attempt to "reverse the situation and restore the birthright to Esau."[39] This is dramatically exacerbated by the fall of Jerusalem and the consequent theological crisis for the survivors. Anti-Edom polemic is "designed to extirpate from the people's consciousness the view that God had abandoned them and had chosen another people in their place."[40]

Patterns of transitivity related to Edom in the book of Obadiah bear out Assis's observation. The as-yet unnamed Addressees of verses 2–5 are the recipients of all verbal action, functioning as semantic Goal. When Edom/Esau is finally named explicitly in verse 6 this pattern continues. Here both "Esau" and "his treasures" function as Subject/Goal of passive verbal clauses. The semantic Actors in these clauses in verse 6 remain unspecified, but in verse 7 the "people of your covenant," and the "people of your peace" function as Subject/Actor in their respective clauses, and appear to be agents of the suffering of Edom.[41] In verse 8 YHWH is the referent of the clitic Subject/Actor of the verb אבד, and "the wise of Edom and understanding from mount Esau" function as Complement/Goal. Again, Edom or its co-referents receive the action of the verb. The clitic Subject/Actor of the opening clause of verse 9 is not identified, but the Complement/Goal of the clause is "the warriors of Teman," which is a clear reference to Edom (cf. Gen 36:11; Ezek 25:13).[42] Also in verse 9 "the people of mount Esau" function as Subject/Goal of the passive verb כרת. Following this in verse 10 the book once again refers to Edom/Esau in the second person where the second person object suffix functions as

---

[37] Block, *Obadiah*, 51–52, 73; Robert B. Robinson, "Levels of Naturalization in Obadiah," *JSOT* (1988): 83–97.

[38] Elie Assis, "Why Edom? On the Hostility Towards Jacob's Brother in Prophetic Sources," *VT* 56 (2006): 11.

[39] Ibid., 12.

[40] Ibid., 17.

[41] I have not noted the final two clauses in this verse, as these are a famous interpretive crux in the book. I tend to think that לַחְמְךָ should be understood as Nogalski suggests, a metaphor that functions as the Complement/Goal of the clause ("they have placed your bread beneath you as a trap"). In any case the rerendering of לַחְמְךָ as a substantival participle ("the ones eating your bread") as in many modern English translations, seems rather unlikely syntactically. Cf. Graham I. Davies, "New Solution to a Crux in Obadiah 7," *VT* 27 (1977): 484–87; James Nogalski, "Obadiah 7: Textual Corruption or Politically Charged Metaphor?" *ZAW* 110 (1998): 67–71.

[42] See also *HALOT*.

Complement/Goal, and Edom is the clitic Subject/Goal of the second person masculine singular passive נִכְרַתָּ.

A significant shift in this pattern of passivity takes place in verse 12, where Edom now functions as semantic Actor in each verbal clause. But, here where Edom takes the role of semantic Actor, each jussive form is successively negated, indicating that the action taken by Edom is uniformly condemned. This pattern holds throughout this sub-section of the book, until verse 15.

In verse 15 the Addressees of the book (coreferential with Edom) once again receive verbal action. Verse 15 acts as the bridge between the preceding section describing Edom's action ("as it was done"/"your deeds will return") and the following section describing YHWH's response ("it will be done to you"/"upon your head"). Verse 16 is something of an enigma, with its shift from singular to plural Addressee. Wolff sees this as indicative of two different forms, and thus of two different oracles.[43] Nogalski, however, suggests that the plural Addressees are the actual Addressees of the book, because the nations are addressed in the singular in the preceding verse.[44] This is potentially problematic, given that the other verbal forms, the Subjects of which are clearly the nations, are also in the plural. Also, there is no need to equate the Addressees of verse 15 with the nations if we understand Edom as simply a subset of the nations, experiencing the destruction they suffer. Thus it appears reasonable to assume that the second person singular references are reserved for Edom in particular, and the plural references to the nations, of which Edom is one. The latter of these solutions is preferable. Here the nations are briefly referred to, though readers must assume that Edom belongs to this broader category as well.

In the following verses, right up until the end of the book, a switch occurs in which Edom or its territories begin more and more to return to the earlier pattern of receiving verbal action (vv. 18, 19, 21). In fact, though there are certainly references to Edom in this final section of the book, they are much fewer than in the earlier sections and of much less import. Focus on Edom is reduced as it receives the consequences of its actions.

YHWH, the second of our key discourse participants, is identified as speaker in the various clauses where he functions as semantic Actor. In verse 1 we find the standard prophetic messenger formula, and here YHWH functions as Subject/Actor. This formula appears to cover the remainder of the prophetic book, suggesting that the entire prophetic book of Obadiah is an extended projection of the words of YHWH given to his prophet. Thus where we find first person singular verbal forms, the Subject in those cases must be YHWH (vv. 1, 2, 4, 8). Considering these references along with explicit references to YHWH as

---

[43] Wolff, *Obadiah and Jonah*, 37.
[44] James Nogalski, *The Book of the Twelve: Hosea–Jonah*, SHBC (Macon, GA: Smyth & Helwys, 2011), 388–89. Cf. Block who reads this as a reference to Judah. Block, *Obadiah*, 87.

a discourse participant (vv. 1, 4, 8, 15, 18, 21), it is clear that YHWH as a participant functions almost exclusively in the role of Subject/Actor in the book of Obadiah. The exceptions to this are found in verses 1, 15, and 21. In verse 1 YHWH is, in one instance, the Complement of the verb ("we have heard from YHWH") indicating the source of revelation (YHWH is the initiator of the message). In verse 15 the divine name modifies יוֹם, indicating the specific nature of the day that is coming (the day of YHWH). And in verse 21 YHWH functions as the Object/Goal of the equative verb, in this case indicating that YHWH is the possessor of the kingdom. It is clear, then, that even in those cases in which YHWH is not the semantic Actor, he controls and directs the action of the discourse completely. He is never acted upon in the way that Edom is.

The voice and person of the prophet are all but absent from the book of Obadiah. Block suggests that YHWH is the "true rhetor" of the book, demonstrated by the use of both the messenger formula and the נְאֻם־יְהוָה formula.[45] Obadiah is mentioned only in the opening clause, and then the divine voice overrides the voice of the prophet completely. Obadiah as a discourse participant never resurfaces.[46]

The participants in the destruction of Edom (vv. 5–7) and the nations (vv. 15–16) perform supportive roles. The former are never identified clearly. While these destroyers function as Subject/Actor in their respective clauses, the fact that they are never clearly named coupled with the declaration of YHWH in verse 8 that he is responsible for the destruction of Edom suggests that these participants are included for connotative and not denotative effect. The focus here is not on the identity of the supposed allies, but on their terrible betrayal, which emphasizes the unfaithfulness of Edom to Judah. The nations in verse 15–16 are not essential to the unfolding events of Obadiah. The coming day of YHWH, which is against all the nations, will encompass Edom in its destruction. Thus when we read of the nations drinking and being destroyed in verse 16, where the nations function as Subject/Actor in that succession of clauses, it is necessary to understand Edom as an implied member of that set. The destroyers of Judah take into and upon themselves their deserved destruction—they are the semantic authors of their deserved demise.

The collection of participants that are co-referential with Jacob tend to be recipients of verbal action, where they are present. Conceivably the first person plural clitic Subject/Actor of the verb שָׁמַעְנוּ (v. 1) is coreferential with Jacob, or at least with the implied readership of the book, but this is difficult to say with

---

[45] Block, *Obadiah*, 28, 37.
[46] Davis suggests that, beginning with Ezekiel, the turn toward textualized prophecy creates a shift away from the authority of the prophet and towards the authority of the prophetic word, thus the absence of the prophetic persona from later prophetic books (like Obadiah). Ellen F. Davis, *Swallowing the Scroll: Textuality and the Dynamics of Discourse in Ezekiel's Prophecy*, BLS 21 (Sheffield: Almond Press, 1989).

certainty. Clear references to Jacob begin in verse 10, and in that sub-section (vv. 10–14) coreferential participants function either as Complement/Goal or as Adjunct/Circumstantial (e.g., as part of a prepositional phrase). This changes, however, in the final sub-section of the book (vv. 15–21), as Jacob moves into the active role of Subject/Actor in verses 17–21.[47]

There is an observable relationship between the transitivity structure of the book of Obadiah in relation to the sets of participants noted above. First, there is an inverse relationship between Edom and Judah as discourse participants. Where Edom functions as semantic Actor, Judah tends to be found in receiving or supporting semantic roles (esp. vv. 11–14). Where Judah functions as semantic Actor, Edom tends to receive the verbal action (esp. vv. 17–21). However, this is not a simple process of inversion. In verses 2–10 Edom functions mostly in the role of Complement/Goal or Subject/Goal. But, as I will note below in the discussion of time in the book, the events described in these verses occur more or less at the same time as events described in verses 15–21. It is only in verses 11–14, then, where we find Edom as Actor in any significant way. And yet, even here this role of Actor is consistently found in negated volitional clauses. And so action taken by Edom is uniformly negative (more on this in the Tenor section below). The real principle Actor in the discourse is YHWH, even though he is found as Subject/Actor only a few times. But the actions taken by YHWH are key actions, and events related to YHWH are key events, which bring about the inversion of verses 15–16, and thus the active semantic role of Israel/Jacob in verses 17–21.

The next step in the analysis of register in Obadiah is what SFL theorists refer to as "arena," including elements of time and location. There is a degree of vagueness related to arena that is simultaneously frustrating and fascinating. As Robinson has noted, "Obadiah pointedly does nothing to fix his vision in a specific temporal or spatial frame which demands to be taken as the necessary context for interpreting the vision."[48] I will begin by exploring the description of time in Obadiah, and move from there to a description of location.

There are three essential timeframes referred to in Obadiah: the past, the near/immediate future, and the consequent future.[49] Verses 2–10 describe the near/immediate future, verses 11–14 describe the past, verses 15–16 describe

---

[47] Note that I am including the various subregions in the outward expansion in vv. 19–21 as coextensive with Jacob.
[48] Robinson, "Levels of Naturalization in Obadiah," 89.
[49] Robinson's contention that events in Obadiah do not fix easily "on the familiar continuum of past to future" is something of an overstatement. While precision may be difficult, it is possible to describe time in Obadiah in relative terms. Robinson's agnosticism here may be related to his understanding of the biblical Hebrew verbal system, which appears to include "tense" as a category Robinson, "Levels of Naturalization in Obadiah," 90.

the near/immediate future, and verses 17–21 describe the consequent future. In my description I will move in chronological, and not discourse, order.

That verses 11–14 describe a past situation is generally agreed upon, though a wide variety of explanations are provided. The crux of the problem is the repeated use of jussive verb forms, which are, of course, closely related to *yiqtol* or "imperfect" verb forms both morphologically and semantically. If one were to accept the traditional (and still widely held) view that Hebrew grammaticalizes tense, and that the *yiqtol* form suggests non-past time, it becomes difficult to reconcile the content of these verses (which appear to describe the destruction of Jerusalem) with clusters of *qatal* forms that appear to describe a time following that destruction. However, if we accept one of a variety of aspect-primary views of the Hebrew verbal system this difficulty dissipates.[50] Here the succession of jussive verbs is used to indicate a modal nuance (discussed below), but do not indicate specific time reference. The time of verses 11–14 must be gleaned from other contextual clues. Verse 10 indicates that violence against Jacob has the result of the destruction of the Addressees (Edom).[51] That violence must, consequently, be an event that precedes the coming destruction. Thus verses 11–14 refer to the past event of Edom's transgression against Israel, which is also the logical precursor to current and coming events for Edom.

Verses 2–10 describe the betrayal and destruction of Edom. Locating this portion of the discourse is more difficult. Nogalski argues that the use of *qatal* forms in this section suggests a past event, specifically the invasion of Nabonidus or the Nabateans.[52] However, the conditional phrases of verses 4–5 and the use of *yiqtol* forms in verses 4, 5, 7, 9, and 10 problematize this suggestion. It may be that this is a reference to a recent event in the past, but it is more likely, particularly given the use of אִם in verses 4–5, that an event in the near future is anticipated.

Verses 15–17 clearly refer to a future event, a fact marked by the use of קָרוֹב. These verses refer to a coming time of destruction and judgment identified as the day of YHWH. This also bolsters my suggestion that verses 2–10 describe a near future event, as those verses, like verses 15–16, appear to describe judgment as a consequence of Edom's betrayal of Israel. The destruction threatened in verses 2–10 appears, therefore, to parallel the destruction threatened in verses 15–16, and these may well be references to the same coming event.

---

[50] See, for example, John A. Cook, *Time and the Biblical Hebrew Verb: The Expression of Tense, Aspect, and Modality in Biblical Hebrew*, LSAWS 7 (Winona Lake, IN: Eisenbrauns, 2012); Yoshinobu Endo, *The Verbal System of Classical Hebrew in the Joseph Story: An Approach from Discourse Analysis* (Assen: Van Gorcum, 1996); Bruce K. Waltke and Michael Patrick O'Connor, *An Introduction to Biblical Hebrew Syntax* (Winona Lake, IN: Eisenbrauns, 1990).

[51] Reading מִן with a causative nuance here. Cf. Waltke and O'Connor, *An Introduction to Biblical Hebrew Syntax*, 11.2.11d.

[52] Note his use of "tense" categories. Nogalski, *Book of the Twelve: Hosea–Jonah*, 385.

Finally, verses 18–21 describe the future results of the destruction of Edom and the nations, which is the securing and expansion of the traditional boundaries of Israel. Given the description of Jacob as a participant in the destruction of Esau in verses 17–18, there appears to be some degree of temporal overlap between the day of YHWH and the resulting repossession of the land. These may be one and the same event, but there is some sense that a distinction is warranted. Note particularly the use of וְהָיָה at the opening of verse 18, which arguably marks a transition out of verses 15–17 and into verses 18–21. And yet, there is a strong overlap in subject matter between verse 17 and verse 18, which binds all of verses 15–21 together. Whatever the specific temporal structure of this sub-section, it is fair to suggest that both the day of YHWH and the reclamation of the land are described as future events from the perspective of the discourse as a whole.

The temporal circumstances of the book describe the past event of Edom's betrayal of Israel, including the past event of the destruction of Jerusalem by invaders, the near future event of YHWH's day and a time of retribution against Edom for that betrayal, and the consequent reclamation and extension of Israelite territory. As Ben Zvi has noted, the heavy interplay between past and future, and the near absence of a discernible "present" is a common feature of prophetic books. He suggests that the significance of the discourse present may actually increase when it is referentially absent from the text.[53] Obadiah is concerned with what was (the betrayal and destruction) and what will be (YHWH's coming retribution), but makes no particular note of what is. This focus on an imminent End may be related, as Buss suggests, to a negative view of the present.[54] The present is a situation from which the readers of Obadiah desire to be delivered.

There are four areas or locations that are of importance in the book of Obadiah: Jerusalem, Edom, locations associated with exile, and Judah/Israel (including its surrounding territory). Jerusalem is referred to specifically only twice in the book (vv. 11, 20), but is also related to the descriptions of destruction throughout verses 11–14. Jerusalem is the locus of the destruction of the people of YHWH, which is related to the betrayal perpetrated by Edom. Edom as a location is described especially in verses 2–10, and here location is used ironically to underscore the consequences of Edom's betrayal. Edom as a region is described as mountainous (note repeated references to mount Esau in verses 8, 9, 19, 21) and remote. While this would normally denote safety from invasion, the various metaphorical descriptions of verses 3–4 invert this expectation so that Edom's expected security is no barrier to YHWH's vengeance.

---

[53] Ben Zvi, "Reconstructing the Intellectual Discourse of Ancient Yehud," 11.
[54] Martin J. Buss, *Toward Understanding the Hebrew Canon: A Form-Critical Approach* (Sheffield: Sheffield Phoenix, 2013), 41.

Note also the opposition between "mount Esau" and "mount Zion." In the past-time portions of the book Jerusalem (Zion) is a place of destruction and betrayal, but in the future-time portions of the book this changes so that mount Esau, the supposed place of refuge, is destroyed and mount Zion, the past place of destruction, is a place of refuge and safety (vv. 19 and 21 especially).

In verses 15–21 we encounter the post-day of YHWH depiction of Israel, which appears to be a reestablishment and expansion of the Davidic kingdom.[55] This is a fascinating reconstruction in terms of space for several reasons. First, as Assis has noted the expansion of the kingdom does not only overcome and encompass Edom, but also expands into area never really occupied by the Edomites (the northern regions).[56] Occupation of Edomite space brings a sense of the now total security of reconstructed Israel,[57] but this reconstruction goes beyond traditional borders. It is a reclamation marked by dramatic overabundance for returning Israel. Thus, while there is a degree to which the return of land is related to the indictment against Edom, it involves more than simply regaining what was taken or enacting vengeance against the betrayers. Second, references to returnees from exile in relation to the expansion of the boundaries of the land suggest an opposition between external space (the place of oppression and exile) and internal space (the place of safety). This also focuses the reader/hearer's attention on the expansion of that strongly positive internal space.[58] Those who are distant will return home.

Block notes the fronted circumstantial clause that opens verse 17, which move us from a focus on YHWH's wrath against Edom to Zion as a place of safety and blessing.[59] To be sure there are still references to the destruction of Edom following this phrase, but the focus of attention from this point until the end of the book is on Zion and its surrounding regions as reclaimed space. Note also the ever-expanding sphere of Israel's new sovereignty. Not only does this highlight the extended borders of the post-Day kingdom, this also drives home the centrality of Zion. It is with Zion that the description of the reclaimed kingdom begins (v. 17) and ends (v. 21).

TENOR

My examination of the tenor of Obadiah will focus especially on the question of participant relations. To this end I will examine modality in the book, as well as the use of grammatical person (which is related to a degree to the discussion of transitivity above). These elements highlight the strong disjunction between

---

[55] Nogalski, *Book of the Twelve: Hosea–Jonah*, 391.
[56] Assis, "Why Edom?" 5–6.
[57] Block, *Obadiah*, 93
[58] I have noted a similar polarity between negative external space and positive internal space in the prophetic book of Joel. See Toffelmire, "Orienting the Event," 234–38.
[59] Block, *Obadiah*, 89.

virtual and real Addressees of the book of Obadiah, and help to give a sense of the book's message.

Given its small size, the book of Obadiah has a surprising prevalence of volitional forms. Of the seventy-four verbs in the book eleven are (arguably)[60] jussive, one is cohortative, and one is imperative, making a total of thirteen volitives (17.5 percent of the total verbs in the book). The imperative form and cohortative form appear in verse 1 with the command to the nations to rise up against Edom. In verse 4 the conditional particle plus jussive are used to suggest that were Edom to "soar like an eagle" this would avail for nothing. In verse 10 the speaking voice intones "for violence [against] your brother let shame cover you," which is also directed toward Edom. In verses 11–14 we find a string of eight jussives, all of which are negated and all of which are directed, again, toward Edom. The final jussive in the book is found in verse 16, where the nations are told to "drink continually." Though 17.5 percent of the verbal clauses in the book of Obadiah are presented as commands or exhortations of some kind, every single one is directed at either the nations or Edom, who are the virtual Addressees of the discourse, and none are directed at the actual readers/hearers of the book. There is a strong point of discontinuity here.

With all of these volitive forms one would expect that a command or instruction might actually be given at some point, but this is not the case. The suggestions of verses 4, 10, and 16 function rhetorically, signalling that it is YHWH's will that truly matters here. The negated jussives of verses 11–14 perform a condemnatory function, identifying the actions that Edom should not have taken. There is no sense that some kind of reparation or repentance is possible, there is merely indictment. This leads us to ask what the real readers/hearers of the book are meant to glean from these virtual instructions. No commands are directed toward the real Addressees; there is nothing for them to "do" as it were.

Patterns of grammatical person reinforce this impression. Throughout the book YHWH is found in the first person, second person Address is reserved for Edom or the nations, and Jacob/Israel is referred to consistently in the third person. Given the assumption that the true Addressees of the book are occupants of Jerusalem and environs in post-exilic Yehud, what can be concluded about the fact that this group of people is nowhere addressed directly in the book?

Both these patterns of volitive forms and grammatical person paint a clear picture of the relative power relationships at play in this discourse. YHWH, who speaks, instructs, and acts (cf. the analysis of transitivity above) holds all of the power. The Edomites and the nations, who might appear from the perspective of the people of Yehud to hold great power, are represented as ultimately

---

[60] Of these five are clearly identifiable on morphological grounds, and the remaining six are indistinguishable from *yiqtol* forms, but are marked as jussives by the use of the modifier אל, and by their immediate proximity to morphologically clear jussive forms.

powerless. Their actions are rendered meaningless, or they are commanded by YHWH to perform. Even though these participants are addressed again and again throughout the book the connotation of this language is condemnatory. The real Addressees of the book, who would presumably identify with references to Jacob/Israel, are either onlookers or secondary participants. They listen to the condemnation of Edom (vv. 2–10), they recall Edom's betrayal (vv. 11–14), they hear of YHWH's coming day of vengeance (vv. 15–16), and they listen as Edom's destruction heralds the rebirth of Israel (vv. 17–21). To be sure the house of Jacob is fire and the house of Joseph flame, but notice that even here all of the action is couched in the third person. Though it is the people of Jacob and Joseph who listen and appropriate the book, they are not directly addressed. This underscores the impression that YHWH, who speaks in the first person, is the true actor, and maintains true power throughout.

MODE

With reference to the mode of discourse, two issues are of particular interest. First, I will explore the channel and medium of the text. Second, I will examine intertextual ties to other pieces of biblical literature. Both of these elements underscore the meaningfully, but not exclusively, textual nature of the book of Obadiah as a communicative act.

In her account of medium Ruqaiya Hasan provides a helpful distinction between medium and channel. Describing channel Hasan says the "term refers to the modality through which the addressee comes in contact with the speaker's message—do the messages travel on air as sound waves, or are they apprehended as graven images, some form of graphic writing? The first channel I will call phonic, the second graphic."[61] This is related to, but distinct from, "medium" which "refers to the patterning of words themselves," and relates to a cline between "spoken" and "written."[62] The value of this distinction between channel and medium is that it allows one to distinguish between texts that appear in the phonic channel but have language patterns that more closely relate to writtenness (e.g., a paper delivered at an academic conference), or the opposite, a text that is in the graphic channel, but the spoken medium (e.g., a script for a play). Channel and medium are also related to the concept of process sharing, or turn-taking in linguistic communication. Texts that appear in a

---

[61] Hasan, *Text and Context*, 34.

[62] One of the more valuable axes of analysis for distinguishing between written and spoken medium is, unfortunately, unavailable to analysts of ancient texts. This is the distinction between grammatical complexity and lexical density (i.e., number of lexical items per clause). SFL research has demonstrated that, by and large, spoken language is more grammatically complex, while written language is more lexically dense. Halliday and Hasan, *Text and Context*, 34–35.

graphic channel and/or written medium have a reduced capacity for process sharing, which is to say, they are more intrinsically monologic.

The channel of the book of Obadiah is, of course, graphic. The medium of Obadiah is, perhaps, a slightly more complex affair. The book appears, in some way, to represent itself as being associated with the "vision" of some individual named "Obadiah." This raises the complex question of orality and textuality in the prophetic literature. A full examination of this issue is beyond the scope of our work here, but some tentative comments can be made.[63] There is nothing in this text to indicate any type of process sharing. There is no answering voice presented that might respond to or address the concerns of the principal speaking voice (i.e., the prophet/YHWH). This suggests a significant degree of writtenness. However, as Ben Zvi has noted, the maintenance and sacralisation of a text in a preliterate culture would almost certainly necessitate some kind of oral recitation.[64] And, Obadiah as a book would lend itself to interesting oral recitation. It is short, well-crafted, and its message is relatively straight-forward. This appears, consequently, to be a book in graphic channel and a primarily written medium, with potential for oral recitation.[65]

The other aspect of the mode of discourse of Obadiah that I will note here is the use of intertextual references in the book. As Block has noted, Obadiah is a profoundly intertextual book.[66] He suggests that readers and hearers of the book would be expected to note points of dependence and overlap with other prophetic literature. Wolff has suggested that Obadiah is, in some sense, a commentary on Joel 3 and on Amos 9.[67] And, of course, it has been widely

---

[63] For a fuller discussion of the questions at hand see the various essays in Ehud Ben Zvi and Michael H. Floyd, eds., *Writings and Speech in Israelite and Ancient Near Eastern Prophecy* (Atlanta: Society of Biblical Literature, 2000), esp. Floyd's essay in that volume. On the broader question of orality and literacy see also: Albert Bates Lord, Stephen A. Mitchell, and Gregory Nagy, *The Singer of Tales* (Cambridge: Harvard University Press, 2000); Susan Niditch, *Oral World and Written Word*, LAI (Louisville: Westminister John Knox, 1996); Walter J. Ong and John Hartley, *Orality and Literacy: The Technologizing of the Word*, 3rd ed. (London: Routledge, 2012).

[64] Ehud Ben Zvi, "Introduction: Writings, Speeches, and the Prophetic Books: Setting an Agenda," in Ben Zvi and Floyd, *Writings and Speech in Israelite and Ancient Near Eastern Prophecy*, 1–29.

[65] This is consistent with Biddle's suggestion that the shape of the prophetic books offers clues to the nature of prophecy in a point of transition from "revelation to exegesis." Biddle, "Obadiah–Jonah–Micah in Canonical Context," 155. It is something of an oversimplification to apply this statement to all of the prophetic literature simply due to its graphic nature, but this statement does appear to apply in large measure to Obadiah.

[66] Block, *Obadiah*, 38, 40–41.

[67] Wolff, *Obadiah and Jonah*, 17. Regarding connections to Amos 9, see also Nogalski, *Book of the Twelve: Hosea–Jonah*, 372.

observed that Obad 1–9 parallels Jer 49:7–11 closely.[68] Additionally, readers of this book would do well to be acquainted with the Jacob narratives in Genesis. This raises any number of interesting interpretive questions and questions related to direction of dependence, but setting those issues aside, this significant intertextuality suggests both a highly literate and literarily engaged author(s) and a highly literate and literarily engaged readership. Also, features like extensive intra- and intertextuality facilitate what Ben Zvi has called "multivocal" exegesis; readings of these texts are not finalizable because they are designed to be unfinalizable. The chain of connections never really reaches an end.[69]

Given all of these observations regarding the field, tenor, and mode of discourse in the book of Obadiah, what can be said regarding the social context, or context of situation represented by the book? The field of discourse suggests that the locus of action and event in the book lies with YHWH. Where Edom is active, its action is condemned, and where Israel is active, it works to enact YHWH's existing action. The book also presents YHWH as the speaking voice. The prophet is all but absent, and there is no sense of tension or discontinuity between the voice of YHWH and the voice of the prophet.[70] The past in the book refers to a time of destruction, perpetrated by the treacherous Edomites, and the future in the book refers to a time of YHWH's imminent intervention, and the consequential rectification of Israel's downtrodden status. There is no reference to a discourse present, which suggests that for readers the temporal context of the book exists in that "present" between past destruction and future restoration. Jerusalem, or more accurately Zion, is the locus of that restoration, just as it was the locus of destruction, and blessing expands outward in the reestablishment and extension of the traditional kingdom.

The book contains many volitional forms, but no actual commands or instructions. There is nothing for the real Addressees to "do," as it were. YHWH is generally referred to in the first person, Edom in the second, and Israel in the third (with some exceptions, of course). The virtual Addressees of the book, the Edomites, are not meant to hear its message, and were they to hear it, it would avail them nothing. The real Addressees of the book, the people of postexilic Yehud, are not instructed to act, but are told that their salvation will be accomplished by YHWH (though they will participate in that triumph).

The text is presented in graphic channel and written mode. There are no instances of process sharing (virtual or otherwise), and the text proceeds as a monologue. Nobody does or can answer the voice of YHWH. This textuality is reinforced by the many intertextual references in this small book. It has been created by someone with a high degree of knowledge of other sacred literature,

---

[68] Nogalski, *Book of the Twelve: Hosea–Jonah*, 367; Biddle, "Obadiah–Jonah–Micah in Canonical Context," 162.
[69] Ben Zvi, "Reconstructing the Intellectual Discourse of Ancient Yehud," 11.
[70] Compared, for instance, to Joel or Jeremiah.

and ideal readers of the book must have a similarly strong knowledge of Hebrew sacred literature.

In terms of social context these elements of the register of Obadiah suggest first the presence of at least some individuals who are highly literate. The ideal reader of this text would have a strong knowledge of a wide variety of texts and traditions. This does not preclude the possibility of non-literate or semiliterate readers or hearers. The absence of a distinct prophetic voice and the emphasis on YHWH as principal speaker and actor (based on both transitivity structure and interpersonal representation in the text) downplays the function of the reader of the text so that he/she becomes simply a vessel for YHWH's textualized word. References to Edom suggest the ongoing presence of (or at least a strong memory of the presence of) a treacherous neighbour. In the initial historical context of the book this may have been Edom itself,[71] but could simply be a reference to the classic exemplar of brotherly betrayal.[72] This, coupled with the description of time in the book, suggests a situation in which the ideal readers/hearers of the book recall a time of betrayal and destruction, and look forward to an as yet unrealized time of vindication and triumph. Just as the destruction of the past took place in and around Jerusalem, so the coming vindication will be focused first on mount Zion, and will move outward from there. The book looks forward to a future time in which the national boundaries of an idealized past will be regained.

While there is a degree of historical specificity to certain elements of this description of the context of situation of Obadiah, it is also notable that this situation is not historically fixed, but is continually reapplicable. Certain factors encourage this reapplicability. First, while the book almost certainly refers to an historical event (or set of historical events) in its focus on Edom as a national enemy, Edom is also a general enough entity in the text (particularly because of the etiological/metaphorical association with Esau) that one can imagine later reading communities referring to treacherous enemies as metaphorical "Edoms." Second, as Davis has noted, writtenness affects situation. Written texts are "less situationally concrete and more internally specific."[73] That is to say, such a text is not tied to some specific material situational setting (to borrow an SFL phrase) but is situationally flexible and reapplicable.[74] This limited reapplicability is a component of the context of situation for Obadiah.

---

[71] Cf. Block, *Obadiah*, 24–25, 27.

[72] Cf. Nogalski, *Book of the Twelve: Hosea–Jonah*, 385.

[73] Davis, *Swallowing the Scroll*, 31.

[74] On the question of context of situation and material situational context see Carmel Cloran, "Context, Material Situation and Text," in *Text and Context in Functional Linguistics*, ed. Mohsen Ghadessy (Amsterdam: John Benjamins, 1999), 177–218.

Conclusion

Context of situation as a theoretical concept is notably similar to and dissimilar from the traditional account of social context, *Sitz im Leben*, that has dominated biblical form criticism for decades. It shares a similar focus on the relationship between genres of text (or registers) and some identifiable social context, including a focus on the importance of patterns in language for exploring that underlying social context. Yet, where most accounts of *Sitz im Leben* have focused heavily on a fixed relationship between genre and situation, and on the primacy of supposed underlying oral genres, context of situation allows for a degree of flexibility in the text/register/context relationship, speaking in terms of probabilistic relationships and not deterministic relationships, and explores the language of the text as it is found. Such a shift allows for continued focus on social context in the analysis of genres of biblical literature while taking seriously critiques of *Sitz im Leben* that have been advanced in recent years.

My register analysis of Obadiah and the accompanying proposals regarding context of situation demonstrate, in an admittedly cursory way, how such an analysis might proceed and the kinds of results that it might provide. I do not argue that SFL nomenclature is a necessity for biblical scholars who wish to pursue the question of social context and genre, but given that SFL has been developing theories and methods related to this question, and drawn from a common intellectual heritage, it seems to me that the tools of SFL register and context analysis can be of significant use to the future of form criticism.

12

The Non-Israelite Nations in Zephaniah: Conceptual Coherence and the Relationship of the Parts to the Whole

D. C. Timmer

INTRODUCTION

Studies have long attributed different parts of Zephaniah to different authors and settings in order to resolve perceived tensions in the book. W. L. Holladay focused on vocabulary, grammar, and cognitive dissonance as part of a larger argument that eliminated (among other things) any positive future for non-Israelites from the book's original form.[1] More recently, T. S. Hadjiev reached similar conclusions primarily on the basis of the tension created by affirmations of the nations' future well-being in contexts that stress their destruction.[2]

New form criticism, with its strong interest in the text as a communicative whole, takes a very different tack.[3] Rather than separating a prophetic book into disparate bits, each of which is consistent (in terms of vocabulary, imagery,

---

[1] William L. Holladay, "Reading Zephaniah with a Concordance: Suggestions for a Redaction History," *JBL* 120 (2001): 671–84.
[2] Tchavdar S. Hadjiev, "Survival, Conversion and Restoration: Reflections on the Redaction History of the Book of Zephaniah," *VT* 61 (2011): 570–81.
[3] Anthony F. Campbell, "Form Criticism's Future," in *The Changing Face of Form Criticism for the Twenty-First Century*, ed. Marvin A. Sweeney and Ehud Ben Zvi (Grand Rapids: Eerdmans, 2003), 24.

perspective, etc.) and/or coherent (in terms of semantics or content) as a unit, new form-critical approaches, especially those focused on conceptual criticism, retain the methodological priority of the text as we have it.[4] On that basis the reader pursues integration of the text's surface features and underlying concepts without premature recourse to diachronic solutions that depend on the text's fundamental heterogeneity.

This study will heuristically explore the usefulness of an approach focused on conceptual coherence by examining the two texts in Zephaniah judged most problematic for the coherence of the book's treatment of the nations, 2:11 and 3:9. The formal and material aspects of each passage will be studied in their immediate contexts, as part of Zephaniah's presentation of the non-Israelite nations, and in relation to the book as a whole.

THEORY AND METHOD

It will be helpful to elaborate a few theoretical bases and their methodological implications before turning to our task. The first of these is the distinction between coherence, which refers to the integrity a text's semantics or overall message, and cohesion, which refers to the harmony of surface-level features like vocabulary, grammar, syntax, and so on.[5] Semantic or conceptual 'cohesion' entails not merely the absence of contradiction, but also the presence of meaning-producing interrelations of various sections of text with one another. Put differently, coherence refers to an "infratextual conceptual system" in the text that is replicated in the mind of the reader. This "conceptual system" embodies the semantic consistency and wholeness of the text.[6] On this understanding it is not problematic if a single text includes more than one

---

[4] See E. Ben Zvi, "The Prophetic Book: A Key Form of Prophetic Literature," in *The Changing Face of Form Criticism for the Twenty-First Century*, ed. M. A. Sweeney and E. Ben Zvi (Grand Rapids: Eerdmans, 2003), 276–97.

[5] "In a narrower sense, coherence is separate from grammatical cohesion and specifically signifies the semantic meaning and the cohesion of the basic interconnection of the meanings of the text, its content/semantic and cognitive structure. Semantic coherence can be represented as a sequence of propositions that form a constellation of abstract concepts and connected relations." Hadumod Bussmann, *Routledge Dictionary of Language and Linguistics*, trans. and ed. Gregory P. Trauth and Kerstin Kazzazi (London: Routledge, 1996), 198. The distinction between cohesion as a textual or linguistic phenomenon and coherence as a mental phenomenon in the mind of the reader is widely accepted but need not be stressed here; see T. Sanders and H. Pander Maat, "Cohesion and Coherence: Linguistic Approaches," in *Encyclopedia of Language and Linguistics*, 2nd ed. (London: Elsevier, 2006), 592; Ellen J. van Wolde, "The Creation of Coherence," *Semeia* 81 (1998): 159–74.

[6] See W. W. Lee, *Punishment and Forgiveness in Israel's Migratory Campaign* (Grand Rapids: Eerdmans, 2003), 47.

perspective on a subject as long as there exists a unifying conceptual basis that accommodates the particularities of the various occurrences of the subject in the text.

With this distinction made, we can articulate the working hypothesis that semantic coherence is more important for the text as a communicative tool than surface-level cohesion. James Barr put it in slightly different terms when he wrote, "The linguistic bearer of the theological statement is usually the sentence and the still larger literary complex and not the word or the morphological and syntactical mechanisms."[7] This means that the interpreter must attempt to understand a literary text as a coherent unity before having recourse to diachronic or other explanations to account for its dynamics, difficulties, and perceived contradictions.[8]

The border between coherence and incoherence is not a precise one. The relation between the two is best viewed as a continuous spectrum, and the location of a given text's semantic content on the spectrum depends directly on the interpretative framework of the interpreter. Direct contradiction, involving contradictory statements of the same entity in the same setting, is perhaps the clearest example of incoherence. However, problematic texts are rarely, if ever, reducible to neatly packed logical statements. In most cases, one or more factors complicate the discourse and impede the conclusion that the text is incoherent. For example, in studies of Israelite prophetic literature some consider the punishment of specific nations in some cases and of the 'nations' in general in other cases such a sharp difference that the two perspectives are thought to be incoherent, and so must be attributed to different authors or redactors.[9] Others doubt that this difference constitutes incoherence, and argue that such changes in perspective and reference can coexist within one author's mind or within one text.[10]

Finally, it is important to note that incohesion at the level of individual terms (*Numeruswechsel*, changes in verbal tense/aspect, etc.) cannot overwhelm semantic coherence. Indeed, Eve-Marie Becker, reflecting the opinion of many linguists, argues that even if a text lacks cohesion on linguistic and text-

---

[7] James Barr, *The Semantics of Biblical Language* (Oxford: Oxford University Press, 1961), 269.

[8] Lee, *Punishment and Forgiveness*, 54. The significance of this point is brought to bear on biblical interpretation in Francis Landy "Three Sides of a Coin: In Conversation with Ben Zvi and Nogalski, 'Two Sides of a Coin,'" *JHebS* 10 (2010): article 11, esp. 9–10, 13–14, 16–17.

[9] E.g., Jakob Wöhrle, *Der Abschluss des Zwölfprophetenbuches: Buchübergreifende Redaktionsprozesse in den späten Sammlungen*, BZAW 389 (Berlin: de Gruyter, 2008), 19, 161–64, 279–81, 351–54.

[10] E.g., David L. Petersen, "Israel and the Nations in the Later Latter Prophets," in *Constructs of Prophecy in the Former and Latter Prophets and Other Texts*, ed. Lester L. Grabbe and Martti Nissinen, ANEM 4 (Atlanta: Society of Biblical Literature, 2011), 157–64

grammatical grounds, the reader can still profitably pursue its coherence.[11] Moreover, it is this very pursuit that will bring into view the cognitive-linguistic or hermeneutical means by which the reader apprehends the concepts expressed by the text. It is with this heuristic method and orientation that we now turn to the Zephaniah's most striking texts on the nations.

Zeph 2:11: Particular Nations Punished, "All the Coastlands Worship"

Zephaniah's first announcement of a positive future for some among the nations appears abruptly in a series of oracles of varied form that addresses nations to Israel's west, east, south, and north.[12] This careful selection of nations based on their location vis-à-vis Judah recalls the global perspective with which the book began (e.g., 1:2–3, now with the obvious exception of Judah).[13] The effect of this representative selection is to introduce "the nations," *pars pro toto*, as a group that is guilty of misdeeds in the past and will therefore be punished in the future. This monochromatic presentation of the nations will not continue unchanged throughout the section, as we will see.[14]

2:5–7

The first oracle, the only woe-oracle in the collection, is directed against the Philistines (note the mention of the Philistine pentapolis in 2:4).

> Woe to the inhabitants of the seacoast, the nation of the Cherethites! The word of YHWH is against you, O Canaan, land of the Philistines; I will destroy you

---

[11] E.-M. Becker, "Was ist 'Kohärenz'? Ein Beitrag zur Präzisierung eines exegetischen Leitkriteriums," *ZNW* 94 (2003): 97–121.

[12] So, correctly, Heinz-Dieter Neef, "Vom Gottesgericht zum universalen Heil: Komposition und Redaktion des Zefanjabuches," *ZAW* 111 (1999): 536. At the same time, there may be a focus on Assyria and her allies. Adele Berlin, "Zephaniah's Oracles against the Nations and an Israelite Cultural Myth," in *Fortunate the Eyes That See: Essays in Honor of David Noel Freedman*, ed. Astrid B. Beck et al. (Grand Rapids: Eerdmans, 1995), 176–77, points out Egypt's curious absence.

[13] Given that only four nations need to be mentioned for the author to construct a universal perspective based on the points of the compass, and that other nations who were Judah's enemies (past or present) are omitted from the list (e.g., Edom), it is unlikely that the list is meant to be comprehensive.

[14] On the level of semantics, the four nations in 2:5–13 are comparable to "the nations," i.e., a non-exhaustive reference to non-Israelites that allows for the existence of other non-Israelites who either are not guilty of the same crimes or who will not suffer the same punishment. Such a distinction requires that the two groups of non-Israelites be characterized in distinct ways so that their different fates can be accounted for (otherwise the text risks incoherence).

so that there will be no inhabitant! The coastland will be pastures, with caves for shepherds and folds for flocks. The coastland will be for the remnant of the house of Judah; they will pasture on it. In the houses of Ashkelon they will lie down at evening, for YHWH their God will intervene for them and restore their fortunes.

The oracle announces that the Mediterranean coast will be emptied of its inhabitants (2:5d), and will subsequently be used as pastureland. While no reason is given for this punishment, the subsequent shift in imagery from literal pastureland for flocks in 2:6 to metaphorical lands upon which the Judean remnant itself will graze in 2:7 makes it most likely that this destruction is a reprisal for Philistine aggression against Judah.[15]

The oracle's closing line, "for YHWH their God will intervene for them, and return their captivity/restore their fortunes," is ambiguous. Not only is there textual uncertainty regarding שבותם (Qere שביתם), but both statements are generic rather than precise.[16] The unusual mention of Canaan in 2:5, which presents what was Philistine territory (even in this oracle) in terms evocative of the territory that Israel was to possess long ago by means of military endeavors which were simultaneously punishment of the land's inhabitants, arguably colors the restoration/return referred to here with shades drawn from Israel's initial settlement in Canaan.[17]

2:8–10

The second oracle, against Moab and Ammon (2:8–10), includes no announcement of woe but begins by immediately specifying the guilty parties' offences: they have taunted, reviled, and boasted against YHWH's people and their territory (2:8).[18]

---

[15] This is probably clearest from the references to "houses," which never shelter sheep (the reference to Canaan may also evoke the idea of the remnant inhabiting homes they did not build, as in the entry into Canaan, Deut 6:10).

[16] The versions represent both senses (captivity, fortunes), Anthony Gelston, ed., *The Twelve Minor Prophets*, BHQ 13 (Stuttgart: Deutsche Bibelgesellschaft, 2010), *127–28. See in more detail Marvin Sweeney, *Zephaniah: A Commentary*, Hermeneia (Minneapolis: Fortress, 2003), 131–32.

[17] Berlin, "Zephaniah's Oracles," 178. The Book of Joshua does not list the seacoast among the territories conquered; cf. Richard S. Hess, *Joshua*, TOTC (Downers Grove, IL: Inter-Varsity Press, 1996), 241–42.

[18] Moab's cooperation with Assyria as one of her vassals may lie behind to the arrogance and scorn mentioned here; cf. Moab's presence among those who paid tribute to Sennacherib per his account of the siege of Jerusalem, "Sennacherib's Siege of Jerusalem," translated by M. Cogan (*COS* 2.119B: 302–303). Ammon's standing around this time is hinted at by the fact that it submitted large vassal payments to Assurbanipal.

> "I have heard the taunting of Moab and the insults of the sons of Ammon with which they have taunted my people and become arrogant against their territory. Therefore as surely I live," declares YHWH of hosts, the God of Israel, "Surely Moab will be like Sodom, and the sons of Ammon like Gomorrah—a place possessed by nettles and salt pits, a perpetual desolation. The remnant of my people will plunder them, and the remainder of my nation will inherit them. This they will have in return for their pride, because they have taunted and become arrogant against the people of YHWH of hosts."

The destruction announced in this oracle seems more complete than in 2:5–7, where only the inhabitants were affected, and is guaranteed by a divine oath (2:9a). Moabite and Ammonite territories will be made like Sodom and Gomorrah, "possessed only by nettles and salt pits" and are foreseen as perpetually desolate. This oracle also differs from the first by assigning to Judah's remnant an active role in plundering and possessing Moab and Ammon. The oracle seems to close in 2:10 with a clear echo of two of the terms used to specify the offences of Moab and Ammon at the opening of the oracle (חרף, *piel*; גדל, *hiphil*, 2:8).

The end of the oracle cannot be so easily identified, however, especially because of the presence of an unspecified pronominal referent ("them") in the first clause of 2:11:

> YHWH will be terrifying to them, for he will starve all the gods of the earth, and all the coastlands of the nations will bow down to him, everyone from its own place.

If the reference is to Moab and Ammon, YHWH's actions against them are part of a larger divine intervention that will "famish all the gods of the earth," while a cataphoric reference would have in view "all the gods of the earth." Determining the referent in question will clarify the sense of 2:11 as well as its relation to the seemingly complete oracle in 2:8–10.

2:11

It should not escape notice that the ambiguous pronominal reference in the opening clause of 2:11 arguably presupposes a close connection of the statement to its context.[19] If it is a redactional addition that was intended to qualify the context's emphasis on universal judgment, reference to entities in 2:10 would render it so tightly integrated that it could hardly be identified as such on lexical or syntactic grounds. The shift from third-person to first-person grammar for YHWH is of very limited value as a redactional trace, since the same shift is widespread in prophetic utterances across the Hebrew Bible, including 2:5–7

---

[19] *Pace* Hadjiev, "Survival," 574, who claims that it is "completely isolated from its context both formally and thematically."

and 2:8–10. Holladay's observations that 2:10–11 are in prose, and that the nations are there referred to in general rather than specific terms, are likewise not sufficient grounds on which to conclude, as he does, that "these two verses are secondary."[20]

The possibility remains, of course, that the redaction was smoothly integrated on the formal level (i.e., cohesion is evident), and so can be identified only because of the semantic tension it creates within the section by pointing in a direction precisely opposite that of the universal judgment announced by the four oracles against the nations (i.e., coherence is compromised).[21] The central question is thus whether this verse coheres semantically with its context and with the rest of the book.[22]

It is beyond doubt that 2:11 is the first time in the book that the nations are associated positively with YHWH (i.e., as his worshippers rather than those who fall under his judgment). However, Judah's own fate in the book also includes an abrupt shift from judgment to deliverance. Ben Zvi describes the development of the Judah-theme as the movement from an initial guilty condition (status A) through punishment (status non-A) to an ideal condition (status B).[23] The fact that the characterization and fates of Judah and the nations are both developed in essentially the same way encourages the reader to consider the nations (not only in 2:11 but throughout the book) alongside, and indeed in relation to, Judah.

Such a bifocal reading, taking the themes of Judah and the nations in parallel or at least in relation to one another, highlights a consistent emphasis on religious identity as distinct from nationality. Consider the oracles in 1:2–3, 17–18 that bracket the announcement of Judah's judgment in 1:4–16. The book's

---

[20] Holladay, "Reading Zephaniah," 678. The argument of Arvid S. Kapelrud, *The Message of the Prophet Zephaniah: Morphology and Ideas* (Oslo: Universitetsforlaget, 1975), 34, that 2:10–11 is late because of its "prose form" and sermonic tone should similarly be rejected until clear distinctions between prose and poetry are offered (and shown to very likely involve redactional activity), and until sermonic discourse is similarly proven to derive from one author/redactor and conclusively denied to another.

[21] This semantic dynamism seems to be the primary basis for Hadjiev's conclusion that 2:11 is a redactional addition: he calls "the idea of the nations' conversion to Yahweh" an "alien idea" that is in "tension" with the context's emphasis on judgment ("Survival," 574).

[22] It is also plausible to view 2:10–11 as foreshadowing the plot's denouement, as Paul R. House suggests, *Zephaniah: A Prophetic Drama*, BLS 16, JSOTSup 69 (Sheffield: Almond Press, 1988), 67. On Neef's logic ("Vom Gottesgericht") it seems inevitable that any future perspective (he singles out 2:7, 9 along with 2:10–11) using converted perfective verbs or imperfective forms (as do those verses) would be judged salvation-historical, but it is far from clear that such thinking must be consigned to the post-exilic period.

[23] Ehud Ben Zvi, "Understanding the Message of the Tripartite Prophetic Books," *ResQ* 35 (1993): 93–100.

opening lines (after the incipit) are inevitably the first information the reader receives, and their emphasis on the universal scope of the coming judgment does more than simply impress—it establishes a conceptual context for understanding what follows.[24] The scope of the hyperbolic prediction in 1:3 shares with the primordial flood its nature as retribution against sin, but also exceeds that of the deluge by including aquatic life in its scope:

> "I will completely remove all things from the face of the earth!" declares YHWH. "I will remove man and beast, I will remove the birds of the sky and the fish of the sea, and the ruins along with the wicked. I will cut off man from the face of the earth," declares YHWH.

Whether the phrase "the ruins along with the wicked" in 1:3 is original or not, the description of the coming judgment as judgment for sin is explicit in 1:17, and corresponds well to the focus on humanity at the beginning and end of the chapter.[25] The reference to אדם in 1:17 echoes the same term in 1:3, and is followed immediately by its undoing: human bodies disintegrate like the dust (עפר) from which they are formed (cf. Gen 2:7) because of sin (כי ליהוה חטאו) (Zeph 1:17). Zephaniah 1 thus contributes to the reader's understanding of Judah, the nations, and their interrelation an initial universal framework within which all subsequent material relating to either one should be placed. Perhaps most salient for our discussion is the allocation of divine judgment along moral, rather than national, lines.

This distinction is further developed in the following pericope (2:1–3), which announces the possibility that some within Judah might escape the punishment just described. The title of "undesired nation," given to Judah in 2:1, makes the point bluntly but effectively.[26] Despite her descent from Jacob, the presence of the Davidic monarch (1:1) and many other distinguishing characteristics, Judah's moral/spiritual condition takes precedence over other identifying factors in relation to its ultimate destiny. Only the possibility of escape is mentioned (אולי), and this slim hope is presented not to "sinners" or to some group that might more easily be tied to such a fate (and, of course, not to all Judahites on the basis of their belonging to Judah), but to the "humble" who perform YHWH's ordinances. While this raises questions of theodicy that will not detain us here, it

---

[24] *HALOT* emends the text to do away with all hiphil forms of סוף, being here and Jer 8:13; see the longer discussion in Sweeney, *Zephaniah*, 59–62.
[25] On the phrase והמכשלות את־הרשעים in 1:2, see Gelston, *Twelve Prophets*, *126, and Domenique Barthélemy, *Critique textuelle de l'Ancien Testament*, 4 vols., OBO 50.1-4 (Göttingen: Vandenhoeck & Ruprecht, 1982–2005), 3:882.
[26] "Undesired nations" is the most probable meaning although the syntax of לא־נכסף may be incomplete, and Roberts is right to compare it with "unpitied nation" (לא־רחמה) in Hos 1:6; J. J. M. Roberts, *Nahum, Habakkuk, and Zephaniah*, OTL (Louisville: Westminster John Knox, 1991), 187.

is significant for this study that this section of Judahite society can be distinguished from the idol-worshipping, syncretistic, apostate Judahites mentioned in 1:4–6. In other words, 2:3 distinguishes between Judahites on the basis of their performance or rejection of YHWH's will.

If we now return to 2:11 with these examples of religious distinctions within a single, nationally-defined group in mind, it becomes clear that 2:11 has nearly the same relation to 2:5–10 as does 2:1–3 to 1:2–18. Much as YHWH will come in judgment to destroy especially Judahite sinners in 1:2–18 but may also "hide" those Judeans who seek righteousness and humility, so alongside his coming judgment against nations all around Judah, YHWH will intervene in such a way as to realize (not merely make possible) a radically new relationship between some non-Israelites and the God of Israel while destroying others.

The nature of YHWH's actions against "all the gods of the earth" is cryptically described as starvation in 2:11.[27] The phrase נורא על with gods other than YHWH as the indirect object sheds light on the nature of the conflict behind the intervention, since it consistently affirms Yahweh's superiority to other gods (cf. 1 Chr 16:25 // Ps 96:4; Ps 89:7). Since other uses of the phrase do not include any actions against human beings, and because 2:11b explicitly mentions deities, "them" in 2:11a is most likely cataphoric, and so does not refer in the first place to Moab and Ammon. Consequently, 2:11 is less a "summary-appraisal" of 2:8–10 (so Floyd[28]) than it is a complementary and contrasting image of deliverance. At the same time, since the deities associated with Moab and Ammon surely figure among "all the gods of the earth, YHWH's action is not without consequence for Moab and Ammon."

Despite a lack of clarity regarding the nature of this divine intervention and its effects in the supernatural realm, its outcomes in human terms are clear. YHWH's demonstrated superiority to all other gods incites non-Israelites to worship him, wherever and whoever they are.[29] While Marvin Sweeney takes the subject of the verb וישתחוו in 2:11 to be "all the gods of the earth" and so speaks of *their* "submission" to the God of Israel, it is more likely that non-

---

[27] While רזה in the Piel means to let wither or shrivel, the MT as it stands attests the Qal, which has the sense "dwindle" (transitive); cf. Ludwig Koehler and Walter Baumgartner, *The Hebrew and Aramaic Lexicon of the Old Testament*, trans. and ed. M. E. J. Richardson, 2 vols., study edition (Leiden: Brill 2001), 1209. At bottom the semantic difference is quite small: if Yahweh starves them (so Roberts, *Nahum, Habakkuk, and Zephaniah*, 201–2), these gods are hardly better off than if he destroyed them outright. The Greek, Latin, and Syriac versions have a future tense/imperfect aspect verb, which suits well the *waw*-imperfect-consecutive syntax that follows the verb here.

[28] Michael H. Floyd, *Minor Prophets Part 2*, FOTL 22 (Grand Rapids: Eerdmans, 2000), 223.

[29] Not only is there no evidence of compulsion in the nations' response in the very similar scenario presented in 3:9, but there is always an element of acquiescence in the *hishtaphel* of חוה; cf. especially H.-P. Stähli, "חוה," *TLOT* 1:398–401.

Israelites are in view.[30] Note, first, that the only other occurrence in the Hebrew Bible of the phrase "all the coastlands of the nations" in Gen 10:5 refers to human beings, not to deities. The syntagm is particularly striking in the Genesis context for its inclusion of all humanity, as after the deluge "all the coastlands of the nations were separated into their lands, each one according to his language." Second, not only the phrase, but also the key term "coastlands" (אי) is consistently restricted to places (coastlands, Isa 11:11; perhaps Ps 97:11) or people (Est 1:10; Ps 72:10; Isa 20:6; note the parallel use of איים and גוים in Isa 40:15),[31] and never refers to deities.[32] There is thus no precedent for understanding this phrase as a reference to various deities, and the alternative proposed here is plausible even if it involves a sharp semantic contrast (which has precedents earlier in Zephaniah as well as a strong parallel in 3:9).

2:12

The third oracle against the nations, in 2:12, should perhaps be classified otherwise due to what is arguably a retrospective orientation. As Floyd and others have noted, 2:12 is without verbal-syntactic connections to its immediate context, and so without a clear grammatical tense.[33] Since there is little historical evidence for a fall of Cushites later than the seventh century, the fall of Thebes as the center of Cushite power in 664/663 is the most visible candidate, after which Assurbanipal returned rulers from Sais to power.[34] It is probably best, therefore, to take 2:12 as a statement regarding one of the nations, to the effect that YHWH has already begun his campaign against the nations.[35]

---

[30] Sweeney, *Zephaniah*, 142.
[31] Jer 31:10 has גוים (as a human audience) in parallel with איים ממרחק.
[32] Little changes if the gods are in fact in view, since those who worshipped them would see them vanquished by YHWH and be forced to recognize his unique status.
[33] Floyd, *Minor Prophets Part 2*, 226. The connections that do exist, גם in 2:12 and ו on a perfective form in 2:13, of course establish that 2:12 is connected to its context, but the nature of these connections is not dependent on verbal (and thus chronological or aspectual) continuity.
[34] Nicolas Grimal, *A History of Ancient Egypt*, trans. I. Shaw (Oxford: Blackwell, 1992), 352; Roberts, *Nahum, Habakkuk, and Zephaniah*, 202; Michael H. Floyd, *Minor Prophets, Part 2*, FOTL 22 (Grand Rapids: Eerdmans, 2000), 212–13; Marc Van De Mieroop, *A History of Ancient Egypt*, Blackwell History of the Ancient World (Chichester: Wiley-Blackwell, 2011), 293. This renders unnecessary the arguments advanced by R. W. Anderson Jr. for a Cushite presence in Syria-Palestine, "Zephaniah ben Cushi and Cush of Benjamin: Traces of Cushite Presence in Syria-Palestine," in *The Pitcher is Broken: Memorial Essays for Gösta W. Ahlström*, ed. Steven W. Holloway and Lowell K. Handy, JSOTSup 190 (Sheffield: Sheffield Academic, 1995), 45–70.
[35] It is less clear that there is a specifically Judahite aspect that would partially account for its fall. Cushites figure in a variety of roles in the Hebrew Bible, ranging from positive (e.g., "the Cushite" who spoke in favor of David, 2 Sam 18) to negative (the Cushites who

2:13–15

The fall of the Cushites as (probably) a *fait accompli* is particularly effective as a preface to the last oracle against a foreign nation, this one focused on Assyria, until recently Judah's most dangerous and proximate enemy.

> He will stretch out his hand against the north and destroy Assyria, and he will make Nineveh a desolation, parched like the wilderness. Flocks will lie down in her midst, all kinds of beasts; both the owl and the hedgehog will lodge in the capitals of her pillars, a voice will sing in the windows. Desolation will be on the threshold, for he will lay bare the cedar beams. This is the exultant city which dwells securely, who says in her heart, "I am, and there is no one besides me." What a desolation she has become, a lair for beasts! Everyone who passes by her will hiss and wave his hand.

The imagery used to portray Assyria's destruction is quite similar to that used for the destruction of the Philistine coast in 2:5–7, although wild animals rather than livestock will meander among its ruins (probably because of the references to its lack of water, 2:13) and although various aspects are elaborated or developed. Similarly, the reasons for Assyria's fate are comparable to those alleged against Moab and Ammon, although Assyria's self-image is underlined more clearly by the use of a citation and the mention of her incomparability (2:15).

Assyrian pride and self-confidence are amply documented in the empire's self-description. A prophecy addressed to Assurbanipal, king of Assyria from 668–627, puts the king in control of the destinies of other nations:

> [Mullis]su has said: [You shall reig]n over [the king]s of the countries! You shall show them their boundaries; you shall determine the [ro]ads they take![36]

The reign of Assurbanipal (ca. 668–627) saw widespread use of leonine imagery to amplify the king's power and splendor, and as contemporaneous with Zephaniah's setting may have affected some of the choices of imagery here (e.g., the territory overrun by wild beasts).[37] Whatever its correlation with a particular

---

participated in Shishak's raid on Jerusalem, 1 Kgs 14:25–28; 2 Chr 12:1–11). It is possible, but not necessary, that this statement is made in light of past Cushite aggression like that recorded in 2 Chr 14:9–15.

[36] Martti Nissinen, "A Report of Prophecies: Mullissu-kabtat to Assurbanipal," in *Prophets and Prophecy in the Ancient Near East*, ed. Martti Nissinen, Peter Machinist, WAW 12 (Atlanta: Society of Biblical Literature, 2003), 127.

[37] Cf. G. H. Johnston, "Nahum's Rhetorical Allusions to the Neo-Assyrian Lion Motif," *BSac* 158 (2001): 287–307, who cites Assurbanipal's statement that favorable climatic conditions had apparently expanded the hunting grounds available to lions in parts of Assyria, so that his extensive lion hunts were part of his divinely-authorized role as the deliverer of his people (299–300); cf. Daniel D. Luckenbill, *Ancient Records of Assyria and Babylonia* (Weisbaden: Harrassowitz, 1968), 224. See further Frederick M. Fales, *Guerre et*

historical setting, the emphasis on Assyria's hubris and autonomy make clear the reasons for the divine pronouncement of judgment.

SUMMARY

While diverse in terms of their literary forms, the oracles against foreign nations in 2:5–10, 13–15, and the statement in 2:12 present "the nations" as (on occasion) the enemies of Judah and as (always) opposed to YHWH her God.[38] While the theological significance of Assyria's pride and the similarly-motivated boasts of Moab and Ammon is clear, one would be hard pressed to imagine a significantly different rationale for the judgments against Cush and the Philistines.

The relation of 2:11 to this otherwise homogeneous section can be described as follows. First, it appears in the middle of the sequence that addresses four nations in each of the cardinal directions vis-à-vis Judah. The integration of 2:11 in its context both syntactically (via the possibility that its initial pronominal reference includes Moab and Ammon, at least indirectly by means of their gods) and semantically (via the same sphere of reference, i.e., the nations) favors the conclusion that future divine intervention will include both punishment and transformation for the nations. Second, this judgment-deliverance pair with respect to the nations finds a precedent and analogue in the material on Judah in 1:4–2:3.

If 2:11 is taken as the source of semantic incoherence in 2:5–13, the same judgment must apply to the various descriptions of deliverance for Judah (including 2:1–3). This is hardly tenable, however. First, it presupposes the semantic incoherence of a judgment-deliverance pair that is patient of several plausible explanations (e.g., that those judged are not those delivered; that those delivered are sometimes those who are transformed through judgment, etc.). Second, the same paradox is very common elsewhere in the Hebrew Bible, including one or two passages to which Zephaniah refers: the flood, from which eight persons did in fact escape (cf. 1:2–3), and Sodom and Gomorrah, from which four persons were able to escape (cf. 2:8–10).[39] Third, the use of remnant-

---

paix en Assyrie: Religion et impérialisme, Les Conférences de l'École Pratique des Hautes Études (Paris: Cerf, 2010), 69–94, and Steven W. Holloway, *Assur is King! Assur is King! Religion in the Exercise of Power in the Neo-Assyrian Empire*, CHANE 10 (Leiden: Brill, 2002).

[38] The explanation of Ehud Ben Zvi, *A Historical-Critical Study of The Book of Zephaniah*, BZAW 198 (Berlin: de Gruyter, 1991), 334, is helpful: "the real source of trouble for the Ammonites and Moabites can only be that they failed to recognize that YHWH is not a god but God. Therefore they could not but fail to take into account the logical inference from the 'fact' that YHWH = God of Israel = God, and consequently they dared to taunt Israel, and by implication, no other than God."

[39] The conceptual proximity of the remnant that left Sodom is accentuated by the mention of Moab and Ammon in the oracle in Zeph 2:8–10; cf. Gen 19:36–38.

language in Zephaniah for those Judahites who survive or escape judgment removes all doubt that a Judean author was able of imagining such a distinction within his own nation.[40] The fact that this language occurs in the section under investigation (שארית בית יהודה in 2:7; שארית עמי and יתר גויי [Qere][41] in 2:9) makes it very difficult to argue against its applicability to the nations.[42] Finally, the same judgment-deliverance pair appears a second time in the treatment of the nations in 3:8–9, a passage to which we now turn.

ZEPH 3:9: "NATIONS AND KINGDOMS" PUNISHED, "PEOPLES" TRANSFORMED

After the oracle against Assyria in 2:13–15, Zephaniah addresses a woe oracle against Judah (3:1–8).[43] The presence of such an oracle at this point in the book is itself surprising, since in a "normal" tripartite prophetic book, oracles against the nations would normally be followed by an oracle of salvation for Israel.[44] Instead, this section brings the focus back to Judah once more, rather like 2:1–3.

The section's relation to the nations-theme is intriguing. On the one hand, as the first woe oracle against Judah, it suggests a connection with the preceding woe-oracle against the Philistine pentapolis in 2:5–7. On the other hand, it affirms that YHWH has attempted to sensitize Judah to his leading by punishing other nations for their own failings, but to no avail (3:6–7). This brings to prominence the relation of Judah to the nations, and while YHWH has seen fit

---

[40] In Zephaniah, when "remnant" governs the meaning of "people," (i.e., when יתר and שארית are in construct with "house of Judah/my people"), the setting is clearly future due to temporal indicators such as והיה (2:7) or imperfective verbal forms (תהיה, 2:9). By contrast, "my people" by itself (e.g., 2:8; similarly "the people of YHWH of hosts," 2:10) most naturally refers to the historical Judah that Moab and Ammon have reproached in the past, and these elements are the subject of simple perfective verbs. Cf. further Silvio S. Apóstolo, "On the Elusiveness and Malleability of 'Israel,'" *JHebS* 6 (2006): article 7; Ehud Ben Zvi, "Inclusion in and Exclusion from Israel as Conveyed by the Use of the Term 'Israel' in Post-Monarchic Biblical Texts," in *The Pitcher is Broken: Memorial Essays for Gösta W. Ahlström*, ed. Steven W. Holloway and Lowell K. Handy, JSOTSup 190 (Sheffield: Sheffield Academic, 1995), 95–149.
[41] The Qere of MT is supported by the Old Greek, Vulgate, and Syriac; cf. Gelston, *Twelve Minor Prophets*, 106, *128.
[42] See Donn M. Morgan, "Remnant," in *Dictionary of the Old Testament: Prophets*, ed. M. J. Boda and J. Gordon McConville (Downers Grove, IL: Inter-Varsity and IVP Academic, 2012), 658–64.
[43] Floyd sees the oracle ending after 3:7 (*Minor Prophets*, 229–31). Here I include 3:8 both because woe oracles sometimes include punishments (of which there is none prior to 3:8), and because our focus on 3:9 requires us to include it regardless.
[44] Ben Zvi, "Understanding the Message," 98.

to begin with punishment against the nations for their sins, Judah (having failed to learn from what she observed) now faces the same unpleasant prospect.⁴⁵

The past judgment of the nations will continue, however, before Judah reaches any turning point (3:8). While it is not impossible that the "nations" and "kingdoms" in 3:8 would include Judah, the clear distinction between them everywhere else in the book strongly favors seeing non-Israelite entities as the focus of divine wrath here.⁴⁶ Nevertheless, the connection between 3:1–7 and 3:8 links the fate of Judah to that of the nations, while the connection of 3:8 to 3:9 links the judgment of the nations to their deliverance. Both these connections invite further examination.⁴⁷

The focus of 3:9 is a diverse body of non-Israelites called "peoples" (עמים).⁴⁸ This group is first the object of one transformation made by YHWH, and then becomes the subject of various verbs that manifest the results of that change. YHWH's words describe the transformation thus: "I will give peoples a pure lip." The expression "pure lip" is very rare (Job 33:3 only; cf. also Pss 15:3; 24:4; Prov 10:8, 11, 32; Isa 33:15), although parallel concepts are attested several times. Most relevant among these parallels are Hos 2:17, which speaks of removing Baal's name from unfaithful Israel (cf. Zeph 1:4–6), and Isa 6:5, which

---

⁴⁵ The fact that judgment begins with the nations may also explain why Zephaniah presents their deliverance first (in terms of textual order). The first clear affirmation of deliverance for some of Judah appears in 3:11–13 (or perhaps in 3:10), following two clear affirmations of renewal and restoration of relationship with YHWH for the nations in 2:11; 3:9.

⁴⁶ Many other pieces of data point in the same direction. Until this point in the book עם (sg.) has generally been used to refer to Israel (with a contextual qualifier; one exception is "people of Canaan" in 1:11), and the plural appears here for the first time. The term גוי has also been used in the singular of national Israel (2:1), of other nations (the Philistines, 2:5; Nineveh, 2:14), or of the remnant of Israel (2:9, with יתר). The plural גוים, as with עמים, has been used only of non-Israelite groups (2:11; 3:6).

⁴⁷ Hadjiev does not take account of these themes' potential interrelation, and affirms of 3:9, 10 that "they seem to talk in the same breath about two completely different things— the transformation of the nations (v. 9) and the return of dispersed Judeans (v. 10)" ("Survival," 574). His assertion that the two concepts are distinct is doubtless valid, but he does not seem to consider the possibility that two distinct facts, which are not mutually contradictory in any case, might be both interrelated and part of a larger, polychrome whole.

⁴⁸ The emendation of "peoples" to "my people" proposed by J. Vlaardingerbroek, *Zephaniah*, Historical Commentary on the Old Testament (Leuven: Peeters, 1999), 195, is without textual evidence and surmises that the MT's reading can be explained by a later scribe's belief that Judah's judgment was "a judgment upon the world." It should be rejected since the earliest attestations of the text preserve the plural, as does LXX. Further, Hubert Irsigler, *Zefanja*, HThKAT (Freiburg: Herder, 2002), 369, points out that the corresponding term "nations" in 3:6, 8 is also anarthrous and that a plural referent in 3:9a is presupposed by "they all" in 3:9b.

speaks of a cleansing from sin via a coal from the altar that focuses on the lips (plural).⁴⁹ These two references' focus on proximity to the divine made possible by purification parallels Zephaniah's focus on proximity to YHWH brought about by the day of YHWH, and in all three cases purification is a prerequisite for the positive roles (i.e., various sorts of divine service) that follow.⁵⁰ Finally, a good case can be made that ברר is not primarily cultic but moral or ethical when paired with heart or hands: Irsigler's contention that it "versteht sich im Sinne einer umfassenden sittlich-religiösen Läuterung" is well founded.⁵¹

Turning to the results of this transformation on these "peoples," the phrase "call on YHWH's name" (with a variety of prepositions) can describe various types of communication with YHWH, but in light of 2:11 the most reasonable interpretation is to see this as expressive of a new relationship with YHWH.⁵² This is confirmed by the following expression "serve YHWH," which is frequently contrasted with serving other gods, less often in a cultic setting than more generally.⁵³ Zephaniah 3:9 thus presents the "giving of a pure lip to peoples" as an event that creates among non-Israelites who formerly worshipped other gods a unified group that submits to YHWH and serves him harmoniously.⁵⁴

It is not clear whether non-Israelite entities are still in view in 3:10. Gärtner has recently adopted this view (i.e. that a non-Israelite pilgrimage is in view in 3:10), and not without reason.⁵⁵ First, the difference in deixis between 3:8, 11–12 (second-person) and 3:9–10 (third-person) suggests that 3:9–10 share the same subject. Further, the pilgrimage mentioned in 3:10 is not without precedent

---

⁴⁹ Ben Zvi's protest, *Zephaniah*, 224–25, that the singular "lip" in Zeph 3:9 cannot be equivalent to the plural "lips" elsewhere seems unnecessary; note Ps 22:4; Isa 28:11 (in construct with a plural adjective) and the Qere for Prov 16:27, where one lip as part of the mouth is comprehensible. It is metonymy for speech in Gen 11:1; Job 12:20; Isa 33:19 (in construct with a plural adjective); and Ezek 3:5, 6 (in construct with a plural adjective).
⁵⁰ Greg A. King, "The Day of the Lord in Zephaniah," *BSac* 152 (1995), 16–32 (27), notes that darkness, cloud, thick darkness in Zeph 1:15 also appear in the description of the Sinai theophany in Deut 4:11; 5:22–23, and that the only other collocation is in Joel's description of the Day of YHWH (Joel 2:2).
⁵¹ Irsigler, *Zefanja*, 374.
⁵² F. L. Hossfeld and E.-M. Kindl, "קרא," *TDOT* 13:113. In light of Zephaniah's penchant for moving backward through Genesis, Gen 4:26 is an interesting cotext.
⁵³ Helmer Ringgren, "עבד," *TDOT* 10:384–87.
⁵⁴ Essentially the creation of a remnant among the nations, as suggested by Martin Beck, "Das Tag YHWHs-Verständnis von Zephanja iii," *VT* 58 (2008): 175.
⁵⁵ Judith Gärtner, "Jerusalem—City of God for Israel and for the Nations in Zeph 3:8, 9–10, 11–13," in *Perspectives on the Formation of the Book of the Twelve. Methodological Foundations—Redactional Processes—Historical Insights*, ed. Rainer Albertz, James Nogalski, and Jakob Wöhrle, BZAW 433 (Berlin: de Gruyter, 2012), 269–83, esp. 275–77; so also Marvin A. Sweeney, "A Form-Critical Reassessment of the Book of Zephaniah," *CBQ* 53 (1991): 402, and Sweeney, *Zephaniah*, 185–86.

elsewhere in the Hebrew Bible, whether for non-Israelites (the Egyptians bring a מנחה in Isa 19:21) or for a portion of Judah (Zeph 3:11).[56] Third, uses of פוץ in Gen 10:18; 11:4, 8, 9 (where all human people groups are in view) share with Zeph 3:10 the elements of language and opposition of those who were scattered to YHWH's purposes.[57]

However, several objections can be raised against this understanding of בת־ פוצי, most notably the possibility that expatriated Judahites had fled to Cush following Esarhaddon's alliance with the Saites and Ashurbanipal's attestation that Manasseh sent soldiers there to defeat Taharqa.[58] There are also other biblical texts which presume the presence of Israelites/Judahites in Egypt (e.g., Isa 11:11).[59] For these reasons, and because 3:10 would add very little to our understanding of the nations based on 3:9, we will leave it aside in our study of non-Israelite groups here.

SUMMARY

Zephaniah 3:9 conceives of a time when God pours out his wrath on "all the earth." As part of this complex action, he creates among non-Israelites who formerly worshipped other gods a group that submits to him and serves him. The fact that elsewhere in Zephaniah the nations meet with destruction, and the clear introduction of the remnant concept to describe similar dynamics within Judah, allow us to conclude that Zephaniah also foresees the creation of another remnant, this one among the nations.[60]

CONCLUSIONS

Does the transformation of (some from among) the nations into worshippers of YHWH fit smoothly into Zephaniah? While some have tried to identify 2:11 and

---

[56] Sweeney, *Zephaniah*, 185, explores additional links between Zeph 3:8b–10 and Isa 18–19.
[57] Cf. Mark Brett, "Reading the Bible in the Context of Methodological Pluralism: The Undermining of Ethnic Exclusivism in Genesis," in *Rethinking Contexts, Rereading* Texts, ed. M. Daniel Carroll R. (Sheffield: Sheffield Academic, 2000), 48–74.
[58] "Campaigns against Egypt, Syria, and Palestine," translated by A. L. Oppenheim (*ANET* 294–97), 294.
[59] See John D. W. Watts, *Isaiah 1–33*, WBC 24 (Waco, TX: Word, 1985), 179, Rodney S. Sadler Jr., *Can A Cushite Change His Skin? An Examination of Race, Ethnicity, and Othering in the Hebrew Bible*, LHBOTS 425 (London: T&T Clark, 2005), 46–49, 73–78, and Dan'el Kahn, "Judean Auxiliaries in Egypt's Wars against Kush," *JAOS* 127 (2007): 507–16.
[60] This is also suggested by Beck, "Das Tag YHWHs-Verständnis," 17. This holds regardless of which group is in view in 3:10. If Israelites are in view in 3:10, 3:9 and 3:10 reflect numerous similarities. If non-Israelites are in view in 3:9–10, the same is true of the relation of 3:9–10 to 3:11–13.

3:9 as redactional additions (i.e., as elements extraneous to their contexts, especially on the level of semantics) on the basis of grammatical or syntactical differences, such arguments are not convincing.[61] Others judge 2:11 and 3:9 to be the work of a single redactor (e.g., Hadjiev) and identify them as redactional additions primarily because a transformation of the nations seems hard to integrate in the overall presentation of one or the other context.[62]

THE ACTORS: WORLD, JUDAH, AND THE NATIONS

The approach taken here has aimed at a more comprehensive interpretation that, while not neglecting cohesion at the surface level, has focused on the degree to which these two texts cohere with the book of Zephaniah as a whole. This approach highlighted several related themes in Zephaniah, which can be described as a series of concentric circles. The largest circle is the world as a whole (and all humanity in particular): characterized as sinful, all humanity is threatened by the coming divine judgment.

At the center of this largest circle is the smallest circle, representing Judah.[63] Judah is first identified as a particular target of divine retribution and is eventually separated into a remnant and a majority. The majority disappears from view, while the remnant is ultimately delivered and takes its place as the

---

[61] Holladay's suggested redaction history for 3:1–13 consists of numerous facets, all of which must be convincing as individual emendations for the whole to be convincing ("Reading Zephaniah"). Such multiplication of probability vastly reduces the chances of producing a convincing overall argument, however. As Landy explains ("Three Sides of a Coin," 17 n. 52), "a proposal with two-thirds (2/3) probability will decrease to four-ninths (4/9) at the second stage and to only 16 in 81 chances of being correct in the third stage." See in more detail Joshua A. Berman, "A Response: Three Points of Methodology," *JHebS* 10 (2010): article 9, 42–49, esp. 43–44: if a conclusion rests on multiple factors, "we must compute the likelihood of each factor, and multiply them, for a final determination of probability" (43).

[62] Hadjiev, "Survival," 579, makes the interesting observation that both 2:11 and 3:9 present the salvation of the nations in the context of their sinful speech (implicit in 3:9, explicit in 2:8, 10) and in relation to Cush (2:12; 3:10). The very different characterizations of Cush (destroyed in 2:12; the source of YHWH worshippers in 3:10) makes any neat comparison difficult, but the presence of the same elements in both passages suggests both their compatibility and the feasibility of considering the nations in conjunction with Judah.

[63] Putting Judah at the center, even if the nations are concentric, underlines Judah's primacy as YHWH's partner as well as its primacy in Zephaniah as the one group whom "all the peoples of the earth" admire (3:20). Judah's primacy also appears from the fact that the nations' destruction in 3:6–7 was meant to instruct Judah. The announcement of the nations' deliverance before that of Judah may be explained by the fact that they fall under judgment before Judah does.

object of admiration among a generic human audience, enjoying YHWH's reign, protection, and affection.

A third circle, concentric with Judah but larger, includes all the non-Israelite nations.[64] Like Judah, the nations are judged for their sins (whether against Judah or against YHWH), and again like Judah, some from among the nations are made into worshippers of YHWH. The rest of the nations disappear from view rather silently.

THE PLOT: BIFURCATION

The movement of Zephaniah thus begins with the largest circle, passes through the nations and concludes with Judah, whose remnant appears at the end of the book as the group admired by "all the peoples of the earth" (3:20). The movement from the outside of the circle to its center bisects both smaller circles along the way, so that part of the nations and part of Judah are associated with deliverance while their other sections are associated with judgment and destruction.

THE DENOUEMENT (OR NOT?)

Is this picture a coherent one? If one adopts a monochrome characterization of the nations (as always and only opposed to YHWH), and in particular if one supposes that the nations cannot undergo a spiritual-moral transformation, Zephaniah as it stands is indeed incoherent with respect to the nations. As has been pointed out, however, the presentation of Judah stands or falls with that of the nations, since the two themes exhibit the same dynamics of bisection and identification or creation of a remnant. More pointedly, there is no inherent incoherence in a chronologically demarcated shift that sees an initial group subsequently divided into two parts. The same is true for the dynamics according to which these two groups have radically different fates, since their primary characteristics are not merely different but diametrically opposed.

With respect to the nations-theme itself, incoherence would be present if the *same* group were the recipient of two diametrically opposed fates for one and the *same* reason. Imagine, for example, "Babylon and Nebuchadnezzar her king" being foreseen as worshippers of YHWH *and* the victims of his fury for the sole reason that they are Babylonian.[65] The characterization of the nations in Zephaniah is hardly monochromatic, however. Those whom YHWH destroys are arrogant, autonomous, and never show the least interest in YHWH. The

---

[64] The concentricity of Judah and the nations underlines the ultimately secondary nature of national appurtenance, since Judah is one nation among others.

[65] Because prophetic discourse is so consistently non-literal, such a description might well allow for the salvation-through-judgment that 2:1–3 seems to contemplate with respect to Judah, but for the sake of a clear argument, such complexities can be left aside.

characterization of those among the nations who are associated with YHWH apart from judgment is radically different, and clearly imagines them leaving behind their gods (2:11) and worshiping (2:11) and serving (3:9) YHWH as a unified group.

The transformation of some non-Israelites into worshipers of YHWH in Zeph 2:11; 3:9 doubtless constitutes a complex, dynamic conception of the nations in the mind of the author(s). It seems easier, however, to elaborate a dynamic nations-theme than to arrive at a simple redactional explanation that possesses sufficient probability, particularly because all such explanations involve multiple hypotheses each of which reduces the probability of the whole. The various points of connection between the dynamic nations-theme sketched above and the rest of the book further suggest that arguments for the excision of 2:11 and 3:9 have not given sufficient attention to the interrelation of the nations-theme to the rest of the book, and that doing so uncovers new possibilities for understanding the relation of Zephaniah's parts to the whole.

13

Form Criticism in Haggai, Zechariah, and Malachi: From Oral Sayings to Literature

Paul L. Redditt

INTRODUCTION

The method of biblical studies known as form criticism arose as an attempt to recover early (ideally original) forms of biblical materials, in the case of speeches by the prophets hopefully their *ipsissima verba*. It sought to recover those messages without the accoutrements of the redactors and others who reemployed, modified, and situated them within literary strata or documents. It was (and remains) a useful, if limited tool.[1] Form critics have worked effectively in isolating sayings of prophets from later accretions, especially when they used

---

[1] For descriptions of the method, see Claus Westermann, *Basic Forms of Prophetic Speech*, trans. Hugh Clayton White (Philadelphia: Westminster, 1957); Gene M. Tucker, *Form Criticism of the Old Testament* (Philadelphia: Fortress, 1971); W. Eugene March, "Prophecy," *Old Testament Form Criticism*, ed. John H. Hayes, TUMSR 2 (San Antonio: Trinity University Press, 1974), 141–77; Daniel J. Harrington, S.J., *Interpreting the Old Testament; A Practical Guide* (Wilmington, DE: Michael Glazier, 1981), 69–82; John Barton, *Reading the Old Testament* (Philadelphia: Westminster, 1984), 30–44; Odil Hannes Steck, *Old Testament Exegesis: A Guide to the Methodology*, trans. James D. Nogalski, RBS 33 (Atlanta: Scholars Press, 1995), 99–125; Marvin A. Sweeney, "Form Criticism," *To Each Its Own Meaning*, rev. ed. (Louisville: Westminster John Knox, 1999), 90–104; and Steven L. McKenzie, *How to Read the Bible* (Oxford: Oxford University Press, 2005), 67–89.

other methods in conjunction. In the booklet[2] of Amos, for example, form critics isolated a number of passages that appear to derive (more or less) from the prophet himself. Of course, those critics worked on the presupposition that Amos did not record them; someone else remembered and wrote them down, a crucial presupposition indeed. The opening and closing sections, Amos 1–2 and 7–9, contain sayings widely considered not authentic to Amos,[3] and the conclusion of Amos 9:11–15 *presupposes* and looks back on a fallen "booth of David" (either the monarchy or Jerusalem or both in 586). It is clear, therefore, that sayings attributed to Amos arose over time beginning with Amos and attracted supplementation until the time of the exile and later. The key to this whole literary (not oral) process, of course, was the work of scribes, who recorded, arranged, and even disseminated the sayings of the prophets for posterity, albeit with their own, often successive, additions.

One (but not the only) very fruitful line of investigation in studying this process has posited successive layers of additions often tied to discernible, previously exiting collections lying behind the Twelve: that is, a Book of the Four (Hosea, Amos, Micah, and Zephaniah), and what may be called a Book of the Three (Haggai, Zechariah, and Malachi), and a Book of the Two (Nahum and Habakkuk).[4] In other words, the originally oral sayings of the prophets contained

---

[2] I will call the individual works within the Twelve "booklets" to emphasize their brevity. Hosea and Zechariah are the only two containing more than ten chapters, and Amos has nine. Obadiah on the other extreme runs only twenty-one verses. A rough comparison of their overall length may be obtained by determining the number of pages taken up by all of them in *Biblia Hebraica Stuttgartensia* and comparing that total with the pages taken up by the other three Latter Prophets: Isaiah runs 104 pages, Jeremiah 115, Ezekiel 84, and the Twelve 95.

[3] Jörg Jeremias, *The Book of Amos*, OTL (Louisville: Westminster John Knox, 1998), 6. Jeremias argues that the oracles against Tyre and Edom (1:9–10 and 11–12, see pp. 29–31) and the one against Judah (2:4–5, "with its characteristically Deuteronomistic terminology," p. 44) date from a time after Amos. For an accurate, but disdaining analysis of form and redaction critical interpretations of Amos, see R. Reed Lessing, *Amos*, CC (Saint Louis: Concordia, 2009), 21–29. He endorses rhetorical analysis (pp. 29–37), which clearly also has its rightful place among the tools at the disposal of the student of the Bible.

[4] See, among others, James D. Nogalski, *Literary Precursors to the Book of the Twelve*, BZAW 217 (Berlin: de Gruyter, 1993) and *Redactional Processes in the Book of the Twelve*, BZAW 218 (Berlin: de Gruyter, 1993); Aaron Schart, *Die Entstehung der Zwölfprophetenbuchs* (Berlin: de Gruyter, 1998); and articles in James W. Watts and Paul R. House, eds., *Forming Prophetic Literature: Essays on Isaiah and the Twelve*, JSOTSup 235 (Sheffield: Sheffield Academic, 1996); James D. Nogalski and Marvin A. Sweeney, eds. *Reading and Hearing the Book of the Twelve*, SBLSym 15 (Atlanta: Society of Biblical Literature, 2000); Paul L. Redditt and Aaron Schart, eds., *Thematic Threads in the Book of the Twelve*, BZAW 325 (Berlin: de Gruyter, 2003); and Rainer Albertz, James D. Nogalski, and Jacob Wöhrle, eds., *Perspectives on the Formation of the Book of the Twelve*, BZAW 433 (Berlin: de Gruyter, 2012).

in the Book of the Twelve seem to have undergone a lengthy period of growth in which those sayings were elaborated *over time* (i.e., through successive editions or redactions), first in small collections (for example, the sayings of Amos and Hosea moved south and were reapplied there and supplemented first with the redacted sayings of Micah and then of Zephaniah), then in these two-to-four-booklet collections, then in an overall Book of the Twelve, which also incorporated Joel, Obadiah, and Jonah. Finally the Book of the Twelve became part of an emerging canon of Law and Prophets (see Mal 4:4–6 [MT: 3:19–24]).

The purpose of this essay is not to flesh out this theory of the growth of the Twelve; that work has been done and is background for this study. (See footnote 4.) The purpose of this essay, instead, is to highlight what has happened to the method of form criticism in those and other studies. If the focus therein has shifted from the structure, locus, and contents of the original sayings of the prophets to understanding their meaning(s) in their various places in a growing body of literature, what role does form criticism still play? The answer simply is that form criticism still provides the baseline and many of the categories for such studies. In so doing, it remains essential. This essay, therefore, will address how scholars still employ form criticism in studying the Book of the Twelve, and it will do so by focusing on the last three collections or booklets in the Twelve, Haggai, Zechariah, and Malachi.[5]

Aside from Haggai–Zechariah 1–8, the best case can be made for a previously existing "Book of the Four" (Hosea/Amos/Micah/Zephaniah) which Christoph Levin ("Das 'Vierprophetenbuch': Ein exegetischer Nachruf," *ZAW* 123 [2011]: 221) called a "Forschungskonsensus," though he unsuccessfully attacked it. The idea of a Book of the Three (Haggai, Zechariah, Malachi) recognizes not only the interconnected dating scheme in Haggai/Zech 1–8, but very similar superscriptions and inner borrowing between Zech 9–14 and Malachi. On Nahum/Habakkuk, see Duane L. Christensen, *Nahum*, AB 24F (New Haven: Yale University Press, 2009), 4, and earlier "The Book of Nahum: A History of Interpretation," in Watts and House, *Forming Prophetic Literature*, 192–94. A debate over this way of reading the Twelve appears in Ehud Ben Zvi and James D. Nogalski, *Two Sides of a Coin: Juxtaposing Views on Interpreting the Book of the Twelve / the Twelve Prophetic Books*, Analecta Gorgiana 201 (Piscataway, NJ: Gorgias, 2009).

[5] For an extensive bibliography on Haggai and Zechariah, readers are directed to Mark J. Boda, *Haggai and Zechariah Research: A Bibliographical Survey*, Tools for Biblical Study (Leiden: DEO, 2003). Special mention must be made here of three classic American commentaries on Haggai–Malachi: Carol L. Meyers and Eric M. Meyers, *Haggai, Zechariah 1–8* and *Zechariah 9–14*, AB25C (New York: Doubleday, 1993); Andrew T. Hill *Malachi*, AB25D (New York: Doubleday); and David L. Petersen, *Haggai and Zechariah 1–8* OTL (Philadelphia: Westminster, 1984) and *Zechariah 9–14 and Malachi*, OTL (Louisville: Westminster John Knox, 1995). They remain foundational in the study of the Twelve. This article, however, will deal often with specific articles and monographs or this author's own work.

THE USE OF FORM CRITICISM IN STUDYING HAGGAI

A comparison/contrast of two commentaries will demonstrate some of the recent changes in the use of form criticism in connection with Haggai in particular and the Book of the Twelve in general. The first commentary is by Hans Walter Wolff.[6] After introducing the early post-exilic period and the man, booklet, and message of Haggai, Wolff treats the booklet one section at a time: 1:1-14, 1:15a + 2:15-19, 1:15b-2:9, 2:1-10 + 14, and 2:20-23. Four excurses on special topics are included at the ends of discussions where such excurses add needed detail. In treating each section, Wolff first discusses the Hebrew text with a series of notes. Next he analyses the form or structure and the setting. (Form criticism, after all, was concerned with the relationships among the structure, the setting, and the contents of a passage.) He then discusses/explains each verse, and he concludes with a discussion of the pericope's purpose and thrust.

The second commentary is by Tim Meadowcraft. It focuses on the nature and location of meaning in the act of reading.[7] In doing so, Meadowcraft is interested in narrative and imagination in Haggai. The overall picture that emerges is more important than the individual genres; the artistry of the prophet, something by no means ignored by form critics, is highlighted. The *booklet* of Haggai is valued as a *written* work, which records the words of the prophet and more. The placement of the sayings, that is, the flow of the narrative/argument within the booklet, is noted. These two studies reflect changes in the approach to the Twelve and to Haggai in particular and to Haggai/Zechariah/Malachi in general. In readings like Meadowcraft's those three collections are valued as literary creations, and those works, not the recovered original oral sayings of the prophets, was deemed that which was important.[8]

Despite such developments, the form-critical study of Haggai and other prophetic books is still appropriate. It can enable a modern reader to "hear" traditional prophetic voices behind the work of the editor. It is not, however, sufficient as the sole or even necessarily the primary method of study of the prophets. What follows, then, is a review of a number of genres of prophetic

---

[6] Hans Walter Wolff, *Haggai*, trans. Margaret Kohl, CC (Minneapolis: Augsburg, 1988). The original German edition was published in 1986.

[7] Tim Meadowcroft, *Haggai*, Readings: A New Commentary (Sheffield: Sheffield Academic, 2006), 3.

[8] It is worth pointing out in this connection that one of the early leaders in reading the Twelve as a volume edited to be read as one work Paul R. House (*The Unity of the Twelve*, JSOTSup 97 [Sheffield: Almond Press, 1990], 240-41) reminded readers that the "implied" author was YHWH. Indeed, the superscriptions and other headings in Hag 1:3, 7; 2:1, 10, 20, 23; Zech 1:1, 2, 7; 2:6; the dialogue that is Zech 3; 6:9; 7:1, 8; 8:1, 2, 3, 4, 7, 11, 14, 18, 20, 23; 9:1; 11:4, 13, 15; 12:1; 13:1, 2; 14:8; Mal 3:7, 13, 17; 4:1, 3 (MT 3:19-21) say so explicitly, and other passages are cast as speeches of God to the prophets.

speech as isolated through form criticism, genres still visible behind later written, edited, and literarily manipulated versions of those speeches.

The prophet Haggai spoke four times that are reported in the booklet bearing his name: first in "the second year of King Darius" (superscription found in Hag 1:1) or 520, in the sixth month (roughly August/September) on the first day of the month; second (Hag 1:15b–2:1) on the twenty-first day of the seventh month in the second year or 519; then (Hag 2:10) in the seventh month of that same year on the twenty-fourth day; and finally in the fourth year or 517 (Hag 2:20) on the same day. The booklet of Zechariah likewise gives three dates for that prophet's speeches in Zech 1:1, 7, and 7:1. These particular *date formulae* are unique among the Nebiim in that they set the activities of the two prophets in the context of foreign rulers, whereas the superscriptions of the books of Isaiah, Jeremiah, Ezekiel, Hosea, Amos, Micah, and Zephaniah set their namesakes during the reigns of Judean kings. (The booklets of Hosea and Amos also add the names Israelite kings, reflecting the place where their namesakes flourished.) These date formulae demarcate divisions within Haggai and Zech 1–8, and also redactionally link the two as contemporaries. They also mark the major divisions in both booklets, dividing their contents under different headings. They are clearly literary and not verbal markers. That is, they constitute a written genre, not an oral one.[9] They disappear after Zech 7:1, no longer demarcating divisions within the Haggai-Zechariah-Malachi corpus.[10] Other types of headings do appear later, and they will be dealt with in place.

After date formulae the second genre that one encounters in Haggai is the *prophetic narrative* in 1:1b–15a. Such narratives could be biographical (as here) or autobiographical (as Isa 6:1–13). Readers should remember, however, that the terms "biographical" and "autobiographical" are descriptive. Simply because a life narrative is written in the first as opposed to the third person does not prove that the narrative *is* autobiographical, let alone true. The 1987 American bestseller *Zen and the Art of Motorcycle Maintenance*[11] offers a contemporary example of this point. It has been called fictionalized autobiography, biography, and a long, discursive essay. It can even be seen as a novel written in the first person singular. It tells of a father and son who travel cross-country by motorcycle one

---

[9] See, for example, Janet E. Tollington, *Tradition and Innovation in Haggai and Zechariah 1–8*, JSOTSup 150 (Sheffield: Sheffield Academic, 1993), 11.

[10] Richard A. Taylor in Richard A. Taylor and E. Ray Clendenen, *Haggai, Malachi*, NAC 21A (Nashville: Broadman & Holman, 2004), 59–66, recognizes the vacillation between first and third person portions of Haggai and explains that vacillation as possibly a natural consequence of Haggai's messages being copied by his secretary. On doctrinal grounds, however, he insists that it reports the *ipsissima verba* of Haggai. A *confessional* (not a scholarly) response to Taylor could run thus: the words were inspired regardless of how many or few of them Haggai spoke. In any case, rightly or wrongly, critical scholars do not settle such issue on the basis of an appeal to faith.

[11] Robert Pirsig, *Zen and the Art of Motorcycle Maintenance* (New York: HarperCollins, 1974).

summer, but it also forays into Zen Buddhist-based philosophical musings. Despite its title, it is not a manual about motorcycle maintenance, and it, like all narratives, is only a partial account of what the characters did. Some details were recounted; many were omitted. Some details may be pure fiction.

To return to form criticism of the Hebrew Bible, if early form critics thought they could deduce the *Sitz im Leben* of writings, they were very adept and very selective in what they chose as determinative of genre, and (probably) were occasionally wrong. Contemporary students of Haggai, therefore, may feel freed from the necessity of demonstrating the original setting for what Haggai did and said, unless by doing so the result yields useful information not otherwise obtainable. They may even focus instead (or in addition) on the place/function of Haggai in the Twelve.

In any case Hag 1:1b–15a summarizes or epitomizes the preaching of Haggai in verses 4–11, 13b. The rest (Hag 1:2–3 and most of 12–15a) is the surrounding narrative that situates the sayings. An earlier collection in the Twelve, Habakkuk, by contrast has not one contextualizing verse other than the reference in Hab 1:6 to the Chaldeans, whom God would raise to punish all nations. If taken as authentic prophecy and not prophecy after the fact, that verse implies a date for the original version of Habakkuk before the Babylonian destruction of Nineveh in 605 BCE. Even so, the "Prayer of Habakkuk" with which the booklet closes balances the partial alphabetic acrostic with which the sayings attributed to Nahum opens, and connects those two booklets redactionally.[12] It is not difficult for readers to reconstruct the context of Hab 3 based on what they know about the last days of Judah and Jerusalem from Kings, Chronicles, and ancient Near Eastern texts. It anticipates a Babylonian attack on the city and envisions the city's survival. As part of a document that lived on into the exile, that expectation turned into a hope for Zion's renewal.

Unlike Hab 1:1b–15a, however, Hag 1:1, 15a locate the action reported at a specific time. The words in between take the form of an exchange between God and the people, mediated through Haggai. In the process the author employs a direct address by God to the prophet (1:2), an introductory formula (1:3), a rhetorical question (1:4), a command and accusation from God (1:5–6), a command from God via Haggai to rebuild the temple (1:8), an accusation explaining divine punishment (1:9) followed by the announcement of the ensuing result based on disobedience (1:10–11). Finally, the last part of the narrative framework (vv. 12–15a) contains a short saying of assurance: "I am with you, oracle of YHWH" (in v. 13).[13]

---

[12] See Duane L. Christensen, *Nahum*, AB 24F (New Haven: Yale University Press, 2009), 4.

[13] The terms "command" and "accusation" are sometimes used as technical terms for genres.

A third genre (or perhaps just a literary device) one encounters in Haggai is the *rhetorical question* (see 1:4, and also 2:3, 19), which was designed to force an audience and the reader to face an issue and render a judgment. In 1:4 the question was whether the time had come to rebuild the temple in Jerusalem, and in 2:3 the questions concerned the blatant differences between the grandeur of the first temple (which, perhaps, the oldest residents in Persian Yehud could actually remember, and about which everyone no doubt had heard) and the plainness of the building being erected on the same site. Perhaps some/most of the stones for the altar and temple were still in the vicinity, but the skill to rebuild a grand temple and the laborers to do the work were in short supply. Haggai commanded the builders to work and to let God take care of beautifying the structure. The overall narrative assures the reader that members of Haggai's audience obeyed.

John Kessler points to what in Hag 2:6–9 he calls the "generalization" and "focalization" of this overall passage. In doing so he notes both its similarities to and differences from Ezek 38–39, Joel 4 (Eng. 3), and Zech 14. For example, who are the "nations" and where will the great battle take place? Some of the details differ from text to text. Zechariah 14, moreover, speaks specifically of an earthquake.[14] Kessler defines "focalization" as "the highlighting of certain details of a theme or tradition."[15] That is, the commonalties among the traditions are tailored to the prophet's particular situation and perspective. Kessler then situates the message of Haggai squarely in Jerusalem soon after the events of 520 BCE to which the superscription attributes the saying.

Fourth, the reader of Haggai encounters descriptions of the practice of consulting priests on a matter of pollution. That is, worshipers wondered whether persons were polluted (and thus unqualified to bring sacrifices) for having done X. The answer to such a question is called a *torah*, a teaching. Readers of the Hebrew Bible encounter them regularly in the Torah or Pentateuch, but elsewhere also. In this literary casting of the work and words of Haggai, the question/answer torah dialogue is followed by a secondary application. Still, one need not imagine worshippers physically seeking out a priest to whom to pose the question. That familiar action, a crowd gathering to hear a prophet—Haggai—is called to mind for the reader literarily.

Fifth, a reader encounters in Hag 2:20–23 a complex message, form-critically speaking. On the one hand it constitutes a message of *doom against foreign nations* (2:21), in this case Persia, whose overthrow Haggai predicts. In verse 21 God, speaking to the prophet in the first person singular, instructs Haggai to deliver the message to Zerubbabel, but readers are allowed to "eavesdrop" in the written version. There is no report of its being delivered to the people orally.

---

[14] John Kessler, *The Book of Haggai; Prophecy and Society in Early Persian Yehud*, VT Sup 91 (Leiden: Brill, 2002), 190–91.
[15] Ibid., 192–94.

Indeed, there is such mystery surrounding Zerubbabel one may even wonder whether the message was delivered to him. Regardless, the message is one of punishment/destruction against the "throne of the kingdoms" and of salvation for Yehud. In 521, the intended object of that destruction could only have been the rulership over Jerusalem of the Persian king himself, Darius I. The previous year Darius had fought his way to the throne of Persia. He, of course, claimed legitimacy, a claim which might have been accurate, but whose accuracy was ultimately immaterial to Haggai. The prophet dared to proclaim that God would overthrow Darius. That prediction might have been foolhardy (the prophet might have been arrested or worse), but times were dire.

Sixth, however, Hag 2:20–23 also contains a *prophecy of salvation*, which genre scholars usually say articulated an "indication of the situation," a "prediction of salvation," and a "concluding characterization."[16] Verses 20–23 articulate the expectation that God would make the Davidide Zerubbabel into God's signet ring. Regardless of whether the saying was ever delivered orally, Hag 2:20–23 is literary in that it reworked/reversed a prediction of Jeremiah (in Jer 22:24–30) forecasting the demise of (Je)Coniah: namely, though King Coniah (called Jehoiachin in Kings and Chronicles) was the signet (signature) ring of God, worn on God's right hand, God would yank him off and throw him away into Babylon. Haggai 2:23 recasts the prediction of Jehoiachin's doom into a positive saying for Zerubbabel.

That new saying, however, raises an abiding question concerning the prophets: how does one distinguish a true prophet from a false one? Deuteronomy 20:18–22 addresses directly that very issue. One criterion it adduces is whether the prediction came true. If the answer did not come before one had to act, a second admonition was to heed prophets predicting evil rather than good. It was too easy to say what people wanted to hear, so few would make up prophecies of destruction. By those criteria, Haggai appears hard to call. On the one hand, he demanded work on and offerings for the temple, a demand people already strapped financially might not want to hear. On the other hand, his prediction concerning Zerubbabel did not pan out. Neither Zerubbabel nor any other Yehudite king ever reoccupied the throne of David. Even the hope for such a king waned after a while and rarely appears later in the Hebrew Bible. (See the discussion of Zech 9–14 below.) It seems clear, however, that the tradition-bearers responsible for preserving Haggai considered him a true prophet.

---

[16] See March, "Prophecy," 162. He (p. 163) and others also speak of a similar genre: an oracle of salvation, which promises divine intervention, states the results, and declares God's purpose for intervening; and an oracle of salvation, introduced by the formula "fear not."

THE USE OF FORM CRITICISM IN STUDYING ZECHARIAH 1–8

Zechariah 1–8 continues Haggai redactionally, employing the same introductory superscription with date formulae. (See the discussion above.) It features several genres not attested in Haggai, however. The first passage (Zech 1:1–6) is a redactional hodge-podge. It opens with a superscription (v. 1), a historical retrospect (v. 2), a prophetic warning and *admonition* (or command) to return to YHWH (vv. 3–4a), a summary of the preaching of the preexilic prophets (Hosea through Zephaniah, v. 4b), the drawing of an object lesson from the historical experience of the preexilic community (vv. 5–6a), and a report of the effectiveness of that preaching (v. 6b).[17] Such a composite was characteristic of Haggai as well. It sets the context for what follows in Zech 1:7–6:15 (a series of eight visions) and Zech 7:1–8:23 (a mixed bag of genres). The superscriptions for Zech 9–11 and 12–14, however, are quite short, and Zech 9 continues the motif of king. (See below on Zech 9–14.) Still Zech 9–14 abandons the visions and the context of 520–515. Nothing in Zech 1:1–6 intimates the subject matter of those last six chapters. It appears, then, that Zech 9–14 grew incrementally onto Zech 1–8 to address the failure of those prophecies to come true.

Edgar W. Conrad, by contrast, dissents from the typical critical view that separates chapters 1–8 from 9–14 and offers a reading of Zechariah in its entirety. He makes quite clear, however, that his is an interpretive reading, one that deals with the text as received. His approach is a deliberate attempt to read the booklet *as if* it had been written by Zechariah, and for that purpose Conrad lays aside the issues that form and other critical reading strategies emphasize.[18] In so doing, he deliberately flattens out, if not ignores, the growth that is discernible behind Zech 1–14 through the use of both form and redaction criticism, and he runs the danger of missing or at least downplaying the inner tensions and dynamics of the redacted whole.

Clearly, the most extensively used and most notable genre in Zech 1–6 is the *vision*.[19] Simply stated a "vision" (or an "audition" if a prophet reported only what he heard or even a "vision with audition" if he did both) reports what a prophet saw (and/or heard). These visions were introduced with a description of the prophet's circumstances (see Zech 1:7). They describe some or all of the prophets actions or state of mind (see Zech 4:1), employed visionary language (I looked, I saw), described actions he and others took during the reception of the vision or that occurred during its course (see Zech 1:8; 2:4; 5:7–8), and ended with a clear conclusion (Zech 6:8). Zechariah 1:7–6:15 contains eight visions with auditions, all involving descriptions of what Zechariah saw and

---

[17] Paul L. Redditt, *Haggai, Zechariah, Malachi* NCeB (Grand Rapids: Eerdmans, 1995), 49.
[18] Edgar W. Conrad, *Zechariah*, RNBC (Sheffield: Sheffield Academic, 1999). In fact, his analysis of the text varies little from mine.
[19] See Zoltán Rokay, *Die Nachtgesichte des Propheten Sacharja* (Frankfurt: Lang, 2011).

conversations between the prophet and an interpreting angel: 1:7–17, 1:18–22 (MT 2:1–4), 2:1–3 (MT 2:5–7), 3:1–10, 4:1–14, 5:1–4, 5:5–11, and 6:1–8.[20] Scholars sometimes argue that originally the booklet contained only seven visions, with Zech 3:1–10 being added later and Zech 4 having undergone one or even two expansions.[21] It is such anomalies in the structure that draw attention here, since they suggest growth in the text. For example, Zech 4 may have consisted of verses 1–6aα plus verses 10b–13. That vision consists of a prediction of what scholars often call a diarchy: the high priest and a Davidide. Both are called "anointed ones." Verses 11 and 12 perhaps state and repeat the same question for emphasis rather than constituting an expansion. Verses 13 and 14 interpret the vision: the post-exilic community would have two leaders, one a priest (Joshua), and the other a local ruler (Zerubbabel).

With regard to the meaning of the vision, the following points seem pertinent. The nomination of the high priest as a leader (whether a ruler or not) would have been obvious in the postexilic period, but the inclusion of Zerubbabel as a ruler most likely was the critical point. The booklet of Haggai as redacted emphasized his role too. Whether he returned in 539 (Sheshbazzar alone is mentioned in Ezra 1, though Zerubbabel and Joshua are both mentioned in Ezra 2:2), which seems likely, may be left open to studies on Ezra/Nehemiah. What happened to Zerubbabel and the hope for a new king remains debated. What is important here is the action of both Haggai and Zechariah in promoting him as the new David.[22] It would appear, therefore, that Haggai and Zechariah, aware of the Davidic background of Zerubbabel,

---

[20] See, for example, Klaus Seybold, *Bilder zum Tempelbau: Die Visionen der Propheten Sacharja*, Stuttgarter Bibelstudien 70 (Stuttgart: KBW, 1974), 16–17, and Karl Elliger, *Das Buch der zwölf kleinen Propheten*, ATD 25 (Göttingen: Vandenhoeck and Ruprecht, 1982), 2.103, 119–22.

[21] See, for example, David J. Clark and Howard A. Hatton, *A Handbook on Haggai, Zechariah, and Malachi* (New York: United Bible Societies, 2002), 132; Meyers and Meyers, *Haggai, Zechariah 1–8*, 228–59, who treat vv. 6b–10a as an insert, as do Petersen, *Haggai and Zechariah 1–8*, 214–37 and many other critical commentators.

[22] On that issue readers might read Wolter H. Rose, *Zemah and Zerubbabel: Messianic Expectations in the Early Postexilic Period*, JSOTSup 304 (Sheffield: Sheffield Academic, 2000). Rose reads the conflicting opinions of scholars concerning the identity of the one called "*Zemah*" as a result of a failure to recognize that *Zemah* was another name for Zerubbabel. His solution is debatable, like all scholarly conclusions, but that issue will not be pursued further here because it does not belong to the realm of form criticism. It does show, however, that form-critical considerations may well impinge heavily on other issues of interpretation. See also Paul L. Redditt, "The King in Haggai–Zechariah 1–8 and the Book of Twelve, *Tradition in Transition: Haggai and Zechariah 1–8 in the Trajectory of Hebrew Theology*, ed. Mark J. Boda and Michael H. Floyd, LHBOTS 475 (London: T&T Clark, 2008), 56–82. Most if not all of the articles in that volume pertain to the subject of intertextuality between Haggai/Zechariah 1–8 and other texts. See also Mark J. Boda, *Haggai, Zechariah*, NIVAC (Grand Rapids: Zondervan, 2004).

were prepared to back him as the future ruler. Antonios Finitsis goes so far as to describe the perspective of Zech 1–6 as "restorative eschatology," because it was peculiar to the sociohistorical developments pertaining to the restoration of the Second Temple.[23] Joshua the high priest might have seemed tainted by his years/birth in Babylon to some members of the community in Yehud. Thus Zech 3 was added to emphasize that God had cleansed him of that filth (Zech 3:4–5). This line of reasoning demonstrates the continuing use of form criticism in connection with historical reconstruction and redaction criticism.

While the visions of Zech 1–8 comprise the majority of those chapters, other genres appear as well. Staying within the visionary section of the booklet (1:7–6:15), one first encounters an admonition (Zech 2:6–12; MT 2:10–16), ending with a psalm-like command for silence (Zech 2:13; MT 2:17). It is placed redactionally after the vision of an angel measuring for a wall of fire to surround and protect the city. Then after the last vision one encounters an admonition that combines instructions (Zech 6:9–12) with a prophecy of salvation (Zech 6:13–15).

Zechariah 7–8, however, begins with a new superscription (see above) and moves its readers from the visionary realm into a collection of diverse, short sayings. They consist of the following: first, a narrative introduction in Zech 7:1–3 in which messengers from Bethel (a city traditionally belonging to Ephraim, but after the fall of Israel to Assyria belonging to Judah and in the post-exilic period to Yehud) came to the priests at the temple, asked a question, and received a *priestly torah* or instruction. Their question was whether to continue the practice of mourning (the destruction of the temple?) in the fifth month (see 2 Kgs 24:13). Zechariah 7:4–7 gives God's reply through the prophet Zechariah to both parties. It over-answers their question, however. They asked only about the fifth month. The answer in Zech 7:14 dealt with fasts in the fifth and seventh months. The second answer to the question appears in Zech 8:18–21. In effect it says: "No, discontinue all four fasts in the calendar: those in the fourth, fifth, seventh, and tenth months." In these verses God's answer to the question is introduced with a lengthy superscription combining both a narrative transition to the question, namely "The word of YHWH came to me, saying …"), and the introductory phrase "Thus says YHWH." In verses 18–19 the prophet gives the priestly instruction that four fasts (those of the fourth, fifth, seventh, and tenth months) should be turned into feasts. The passage then gives way (vv. 21–23) to the prediction that "many peoples and strong nations" will come to Jerusalem to seek YHWH.[24]

---

[23] Antonios Finitsis, *Visions and Eschatology: A Socio-Historical Analysis of Zechariah 1–6*, 79 (London: T&T Clark, 2011), 168. Though he does not investigate Haggai, it is difficult to see why that same description would not apply to Haggai as well.

[24] Zech 14:16–17 repeats that theme, perhaps taking it from Zech 8:21–23, but darkly suggests that some people would not come. Experience had kept a "dear school."

That answer, however, is introduced by the formula "The word of YHWH came to me, saying ...." That same slight variation (the use of the first as opposed to third person) appears also in Zech 8:1, which introduces a collection of ten sayings introduced by the phrase "Thus says the Lord of Hosts."[25] Zechariah 8:1 and 18, therefore, introduce two subunits, one with seven sayings (8:1-17) and the other (8:18-23, the original answer to the question in 7:1-3) with three. They provide the answer to a question posed by representatives of the people in Bethel (recorded in Zech 7:1-3), whose question was not really answered in between. Thus a question-and-answer tradition (7:1-3 + 8:18-23) was used to frame the two sets of sayings in between. Within that large framework Zech 7:4-7 plus 7:8-14 form one set of sayings, and then Zech 8:1-17 plus 8:18-23 make another. That set contains ten redactionally connected words of God by the prophet Zechariah. Shades of Moses!

Zechariah 7:8-14 was mentioned above as an addition, and it too deserves closer inspection. It records a prophetic saying, introduced by the typical prophetic introduction: "thus says YHWH" (v. 9a). The rest of verses 9 and 10 also proclaims the quintessential prophetic message concerning justice: do not cheat or favor the rich over the poor at court; show kindness and covenantal fidelity to each other; do not plot/devise evil.[26] Verse 12 sounds like a motif out of Deuteronomy and perhaps even the Deuteronomistic history in Joshua through 2 Kings. Verse 13 reads like Isa 1:15 and Jer 7:13-15. This article is not the place to look into the history of those texts; it is sufficient to note that such talk was "in the air" already in the early post-exilic period. What is important here is that this passage is the same kind of literary composite readers encounter in Hag 1. It might contain bits and excerpts from the prophet Zechariah, but it is a literary composition concocted by a redactor in the history of the rise of Haggai/Zechariah, apparently before Zech 9-14 was attached.

With the work of Michael R. Stead the study of intertextuality in Zech 1-8 reached a state of full maturity. Stead argued that the "former prophets" alluded to in Zech 1-8 included the book of Jeremiah in a form closer to the MT than the LXX text of that prophet, a rather complete book of Ezekiel that included parts of Ezek 40-48 and 38-39, parts of Isa 1-55 and possibly 56-66, Job 1-2, and Joel 1-2. For Stead Zech 1-2 predicts what YHWH was about to do (return to a restored Jerusalem); Zech 3-4 + 6:9-15 says the restoration will occur through the priesthood, the temple, and the Davidic line; Zech 5:1-6:8 spells out the implications and consequences of YHWH's return; and Zech 7-9 spells out

---

[25] Zech 8:2, 4, 7, 9, 14, 19, 20, and 21. The tenth occurrence is in 8:3, which omits "of Hosts." Whether the omission was original and deliberate is unclear.

[26] Compare Mic 6:8. There is no proof that Zechariah had that passage in view, though he or a redactor of the Twelve might have. Regardless, the same understanding of justice was common to both texts.

God's renewed covenant.[27] Stead does not abandon form criticism in his work, but he does move beyond it.

THE USE OF FORM CRITICISM IN STUDYING ZECH 9–14

Scholars routinely (though not universally) attribute Zech 9–14 to a different hand than that or those responsible for Zech 1–8 or Haggai–Zech 1–8. They do not, however, agree upon the identity or background of that hand. Raymond F. Person, for example, argues that "Second Zechariah" was edited by the Deuteronomic School responsible for the "Deuteronomic History" (Joshua through 2 Kings) and the book of Jeremiah.[28] Paul D. Hanson, by contrast, situated the chapters within a group of "disenfranchised visionaries" that flourished between 520 and 420.[29] Nicholas Ho Fai Tai speaks of four different time frames and places for the chapters. According to him Zech 9:1–11:3 arose soon after the incursion of Alexander in Palestine as a reaction to that event (i.e., ca 331); Zech 11:4–16 arose as a continuation of that thinking among a group that contested the accuracy of that assessment; 12:1–13:6 arose among persons familiar with Ezek 36–39; and Zech 14 laid out the dimension of the forthcoming day of YHWH. The four pieces were assembled by scribes who shared the theology of Jeremiah and Ezekiel.[30] Still, the close connection between the hope for Zerubbabel in Haggai–Zech 1–8 and the hope for a future king in Zech 9 seem too obvious to ignore as the genesis of Zech 9–14. Nor (as argued above) is there any reason to look later than ca. 400 BCE for the date of the entire collection.[31] Readers of this essay will note, moreover, that in much recent scholarship the *Sitz im Leben* has become a literate group, that is, a group of scribes. The connection among the sections, moreover, is redactional, one in fact that has received extensive attention.

---

[27] Michael R. Stead, *The Intertextuality of Zechariah 1–8*, LHBOTS 506 (London: T&T Clark, 2009), 13–14.
[28] Raymond F. Person, *Second Zechariah and the Deuteronomic School*, JSOTSup 167 (Sheffield: Sheffield Academic, 1993), 24–37. The rest of the monograph works out the particulars of that conclusion.
[29] Paul D. Hanson, *The Dawn of Apocalyptic* (Philadelphia: Fortress, 1975), 409.
[30] Nicholas Ho Fai Tai, *Prophetie als Schriftauslegung in Sacharja 9–14*, Calwer Theologische Monographien 17 (Stuttgart: Calwer, 1996), summary on pp. 285–90.
[31] Walter Harrelson, "The Celebration of the Feast of Booths according to Zechariah xiv 16–21, in *Religions in Antiquity. Essays in Memory of Erwin Ramsdell Goodenough*, ed. Jacob Neusner, Supplements to *Numen*, XIV (Leiden: Brill, 1968), 88. The oft-held date of ca. 330 (or later) rests upon the mistaken view that Zech 9:1–8 had in view Alexander's incursion along the Mediterranean coast. For a detailed refutation of that view, see Byron G. Curtis, *Up the Steep and Stony Road*, AcBib 25 (Atlanta: Society of Biblical Literature, 2006), 172–82.

The genres themselves likewise are complex and intermingled. Still, it is possible to detect predictions of disaster or doom against Judah and Jerusalem (10:2–3a; 12:1–2; 13:2–6, 7–9a; 14:1–2, 12–15, 17–19) and prophecies of salvation (9:1–7, 8, 11–13, 14–15, 16–17; 10:3b–12; 12:3–9; 12:10–13:1;[32] 14:3–11, 16, 20–21[33]) as well as a *hymn*-like call to rejoice (9:9–10), a call to *lament* (11:1–3), an *allegory* based on two passages in Ezekiel (11:4–16), and a *woe oracle* (11:17).[34] Such a mixture suggests extensive redactional work, that is, writing and combining/rewriting. It is unlike passages in Amos, for example, where some oral sayings alone are preserved, albeit in an edited form, or in Hag 1, where the words of the prophet were reported in a narrative context. It is unclear how much, if any, of Zech 9–14 was presented orally, though that possibility cannot be ruled out. Nor is it clear who added those chapters. What the reader of Zech 9–14 deals with preeminently is written prophecy. Old oral genres are reused in written compositions.

That insight guides a contemporary reading of Zech 9. That chapter responds to the unfulfilled hope for a Davidic ruler expressed in Haggai and Zech 1–8, and restates it after whatever happened to Zerubbabel precluded his playing the role the two prophets predicted for him.[35] Since no other clearly post-exilic passage expresses hope for a new David (i.e., that hope took a back seat in projections of the future), the earlier after the time of Haggai and Zechariah one dates these verses the better. Zechariah 9:9–10 serves as the fulcrum of Zech 9 and anticipates a peaceful, non-combative king. He is described as "righteous and liberated" (or "saved"[36]) and as "humble and riding on a colt," not as a victorious warrior as is sometimes argued.[37] A date of 500

---

[32] Form critically Zech 12:10–13:1 is peculiar. Verse 10 sets forth God's coming blessing (a spirit of compassion), which will have the effect of making people repent of their sins (vv. 11–14), leading to the cleansing of the people of Jerusalem and Judah from their sins (13:1).

[33] Some passages contain threats against Judah's enemies, which makes them predictions of good for Judah. In addition, scholars sometimes distinguish what may be called subtypes of positive sayings: a prophecy of salvation, an oracle of salvation, and a prophecy of salvation. See March, "Prophecy," 162–64.

[34] Recently scholars have preferred the translation "alas" over "woe," and sometimes they also call the genre an "alas oracle."

[35] Rose (*Zemah and Zerubbabel*, 21–22 and throughout) disagrees that Zerubbabel was the *Zemah* or "Shoot" expected in Zech and argues instead that Zemah was someone else. See also Henning G. Reventlow, *Die Propheten Haggai, Sacharja und Maleachi*, ATD, 25.2, rev. ed. (Göttingen: Vandenhoeck & Ruprecht, 1993), 54; and Nurmela Risto, *Prophets in Dialogue. Inner-Biblical Allusions in Zechariah 1–8 and 9–14* (Åbo: Åbo Akademi University, 1996), 65.

[36] See Meyers and Meyers, *Zechariah 9–14*, 4.

[37] On the translation see Paul L. Redditt, *Zechariah 9–14*, IECOT (Stuttgart: Kohlhammer, 2012), 33, 35.

BCE or soon thereafter for those verses seems warranted.[38] Indeed, Zech 9 as a whole probably arose that early since it appears to be a written addendum to a written text concerning hopes for Zerubbabel that were alive ca. 520. Form-critically verses 9–10 call upon "daughter Zion" to rejoice, as a psalm might.[39]

Zechariah 9:1–7 consists of a montage of predictions of disaster against the neighbors surrounding the traditional territory ruled by David and Solomon, but the verses serve as a prequel to the prediction or promise in verse 8 that God would make of God's house "a garrison."[40] That is God would fortify it against all would-be conquerors. Hence, verses 1–8 function as prophecies of salvation, a function long noted by form critics. The motif of God's fighting to protect Jerusalem appears again in Zech 12:1–8 and Zech 14.

Zechariah 9:11–17 is likewise comprised of smaller pieces. First, verses 11–13 constitute a collage. Verse 11 is a promise of salvation, promising that God would rescue "prisoners" (exiles taken from Jerusalem/Judah by the Babylonians) from the "waterless pit" (Babylon). Why? God would do so because God stood in a covenant relationship with both the city and the exiles. Verse 12 is a command for the exiles to return, but it appeals to the promises of Deutero-Isaiah that God would set the prisoners free.[41] Verse 13 then uses the image of a Divine Archer/Warrior, who would use Judah as a bow and Ephraim (probably the whole northern kingdom) as an arrow. The last half of the verse makes the

---

[38] Richard Steiner ("Four Inner-Biblical Interpretations of Genesis 49:10: On the Lexical and Syntactic Ambiguities of עד as Reflected in the Prophecies of Nathan, Ahijah, Ezekiel, and Zechariah," *JBL* 132 [2013], 52–53) finds the suggestion "plausible," but suggests that the hope continued another decade or so into the first decade of the fifth century, i.e., during the lifetime of Zerubbabel's daughter.

[39] Anthony R. Petterson (*Behold Your King: The Hope for the House of David in the Book of Zechariah*, LHBOTS 513 [London: T&T Clark, 2009], 210–12) mounts an impressive but flawed argument that the coming king anticipated after Zerubbabel's disappearance in Zech 9:9–10 reappears in 13:7–9. There, however, God is punishing the shepherd and the people who followed him. The shepherd is neither a hero nor a virtuous sacrificial victim as Pettersen thinks.

[40] See Redditt, *Zechariah 9–14*, 42–43.

[41] Readers should remember that the accounts of 49,000+ exiles returning to Jerusalem under Sheshbazzar (Ezra 1:8) or Zerubbabel and Joshua (Ezra 2:2, 64–66 and Neh 7:62–65) probably exceeded the total population of Yehud at the end of the Persian period and well into the Greek period. Charles E. Carter (*The Emergence of Yehud in the Persian Period; A Social and Demographic Study*, JSOTSup 294 [Sheffield: Sheffield Academic, 1999], 201–2) in fact arrived at population estimates for all of Yehud at the lower figures of 13,350 by 450 BC and 20,650 (i.e., less than half the number of Returnees alone reported in Ezra 2 // Neh 7) by 331. Similarly, a recent estimate of the population of post-exilic Jerusalem (Oded Lipschits, "Achaemenid Imperial Policy and the Status of Jerusalem," *Judah and Judeans in the Persian Period*, ed. Oded Lipschits and Manfred Oeming [Winona Lake, IN: Eisenbrauns, 2006], 32) sets it no higher than about 1500 as late as the end of the Persian period.

same type of promise: God would rouse the sons of Zion and wield them like a sword.[42] Verses 14–17 continue the motif of God as the Divine Warrior, wreaking havoc on God's enemies and restoring the early post-exilic community. This collage of borrowed images and motifs looks bookish, and not like orally-delivered prophetic speeches.

Zechariah 10 also illustrates the use and reuse or reinterpretation of older sayings. Zechariah 10:1 + 3b–5, 6–10 constitutes two prophecies of salvation. Zechariah 10:1 is often understood as an exhortation, but the verb שאלו should be read as a *qal*, perfect, third masculine plural and should be translated "They asked."[43] Its continuation in verse 3b explains why they did so: "YHWH of hosts cares for his flock, the house of Judah." Verses 4–5 talk about people who belong to that flock. Zechariah 10:6–10 turns its attention to the house of Joseph (the northern tribes) by means of a simple redactional move in verse 6: "I (YHWH) will strengthen the house of Judah, and the house of Joseph I will save." Like the English translation just given, the Hebrew sentence places the clauses "house of Judah" and "house of Joseph" back to back in the middle of the sentence; the verbs on either side open and close it. The rest of the passage specifies Ephraim (v. 7) and Gilead (v. 10), that is, not just the tribes north of Judah, but the tribes in Transjordan as well. Zechariah 10:11 also exhibits knowledge of the traditions of the exodus, regardless of whether it knows the book of Exodus. Zechariah 10:2–3a, however, stands out from its context because it blames "shepherds" for the ills of Judah. The verse is a proverbial "bolt out of the blue" in Zech 10, but it anticipates a series of additional modifications to the hope of Zech 10. Zechariah 11–13 actually abandons hope for the reunion of Judah and Israel, for a Davidic king, and for a dutiful priesthood. The preoccupation with people called "shepherds" in Zech 11:4–16 and a scathing condemnation of one shepherd called "God's associate" in Zech 13:7–9 articulate the redactor's concern. The "merchants" introduced in Zech 11:4–16 (see discussion below), moreover, are condemned again at the very end of Zech 14, and the Davidides, priests, and some or all prophets come in for denunciation as well (Zech 12:10–13:6). It appears, therefore, that Zech 10:2–3a, form-critically classifiable as an indictment with punishment, is the redactional piece tying together Zech 9 and 10 with Zech 11–14. Its use is highly literary and stunningly effective.[44]

---

[42] The reference to Greece is widely understood as an addition, partly because it overloads the line of poetry in which it appears. In any case, it need not be, and probably is not a reference to Alexander as scholars (especially earlier ones) often claim. The Ionians had raided the cities of the eastern Mediterranean as early as 738.

[43] The *qal* perfect, third masculine plural form appears in Josh 9:14 and Ps 122:6 as שָׁאֲלוּ, but the imperative form is שַׁאֲלוּ, the pointing in the MT.

[44] Paul L. Redditt, "Redactional Connectors in Zechariah 9–14," *Perspectives on the Formation of the Book of the Twelve*, ed. Rainer Albertz, James D. Nogalski, Jakob Wöhrle, BZAW 433 (Berlin: de Gruyter, 2012), 216–17.

Structurally, Zech 11 stands at the center of Zech 9–14 as a whole, a position I argued in 1989 and one Katrina J. A. Larkin adopted.[45] I further argue here that the chapters grew incrementally: Zech 9 (around Zech 9:9–10), then Zech 10:1 + 3b–12, then Zech 11–14, with Zech 11 serving as the centerpiece or as the fulcrum on which all six chapters pivot. In addition, as seen in the paragraph above, Zech 10:2–3a was written by that same redactor to weld together Zech 9–10 and 11–14. This argument employs form criticism in the analysis of the chapters, but treats the chapters as a collection that grew in stages. Some scholars argue that Zech 14 was added after Zech 9–13 took shape, but it too shows interest in the villains of Zech 11:4–16, the "merchants," and makes one last condemnation of them (Zech 14:21b, another redactional addition).

Zechariah 11:1–3 and Zech 13:7–9 join Zech 10:2–3a as the primary redactional seams.[46] The literary nature of Zech 11:1–3 can be demonstrated by means of a diagram that shows the intertextual bases of the three verses.

Isa 10:33–34	Destruction of trees of Lebanon	Zech 11:1
Isa 2:13–15	Trees of Lebanon and Bashan	Zech 11:1–2
Jer 25:34	Call to Lament ("Wail....")	Zech 11:2
Jer 25:36	Wailing of the shepherds	Zech 11:3
Jer 25:36–37	Despoiling of something belonging to shepherds	Zech 11:3
Jer 25:38	Lions leave their covert or roar	Zech 11:3[47]

To what genre, however, does Zech 11:4–16 belong? It has been called a "sign-enactment report" or a "parable." There is widespread agreement, moreover, that the passage constitutes a reuse and a modification of two prophetic narratives of symbolic acts in Ezekiel: Zech 11:7–16 // Ezek 37:15–23 and Zech 11:16 // Ezek 34:3–4. Functionally, it describes the postexilic situation experienced by postexilic Yehud from the redactor's perspective: Persian officials ruling through Davidides and Yehudite priests. It is tied to Zech 9–10 by means of Zech 11:1–3, a taunt song against the "Shepherds" (Jewish and other leaders of Yehud). It concludes with a curse against the Worthless Shepherd (most likely the High Priest).[48] Zech 13:7 returns to that motif as part of a redactional

---

[45] Katrina J. A. Larkin, *The Eschatology of Second Zechariah; A Study of the Formation of a Mantological Wisdom Anthology*, CBET 6 (Kampen: Kok Pharos, 1994), 45.

[46] See Redditt, *Zechariah 9–14*, 24–26.

[47] This example was carefully, even selectively chosen. Nurmela (*Prophets in Dialogue*) finds sure to possible to probable allusions in Zech 9–14 to other texts in fifty-seven cases, and borrowing from other texts in seven. It is not necessary to agree with him completely to recognize the similarities between texts and the difficulty in assessing both the number and the direction of prophetic texts in dialogue.

[48] Nurmela, *Prophets in Dialogue*, 88.

conclusion to Zech 11–13. Zechariah 13:9, moreover, dialogues with Mal 3:2b–3.[49]

Against the background just painted, Zech 12:1–9 and Zech 14:1–21 constitute predictions of God's salvation, which are themselves comprised of smaller, reworked units. Zechariah 12:10–13:6, however, makes the case against the indigenous leadership of Yehud: the Davidides (who do not rule!), the priests (who especially were implicated in Zech 11), and false prophets. Zechariah 12:10–14, however, is a prophecy of salvation in the form of God's promise to bless the guilty on the condition that they repent of their bad conduct.

THE USE OF FORM CRITICISM IN STUDYING MALACHI

In the booklet of Malachi it is possible, as in Haggai and Zech 1–8, to find sayings that appear to have been delivered orally and that belong to a specific genre. In particular Mal 1:2–5, 1:6–2:9, 2:10–16, 2:17–3:5, 3:6–12, and 3:13–15 are typically classified as *trial speeches* or *disputes*.[50] Those passages, however, reveal elaboration or expansion in places. The most obvious place is Mal 2:1–9. Like Mal 1:6–14 those verses are explicitly addressed to priests. The passage is called "this command" (Heb. *mitsvah*). Actually, no command per se is given, but the command implied throughout Mal 1:6–2:9 is this: "You shall not profane the name of God." (See similarly Lev 21:6, which, however, speaks of priests in the third person.) If writers are sometimes guilty of writing run-on sentences, Malachi is guilty of writing a run-on dialogue in 1:6–2:9. Time after time the people's hypothetical response is given and refuted. Then God says, "If you ...," threatens the people, and gives the people's response. This dialogical structure provides the prophet all the freedom he needs to explore his subjects in more than one direction and a redactor the setting to continue that development.

Malachi 3:16–18, on the other hand, is a short narrative that reports the actions of certain obedient persons, but Mal 4:1–3 (MT 3:19–21) constitutes a prophecy of salvation in which God discloses the future blessing of those people. Those verses form an appropriate conclusion to the six trial speeches, but do not themselves constitute the end of Malachi. Three more verses, Mal 4:4–6 (MT 3:22–24 suddenly mention Moses and Elijah. The first "postscript is a command to remember/obey the statutes of God given at Mount Horeb. Moses is mentioned only four other places in the Latter Prophets: Isaiah (63:11–12),

---

[49] See below the discussion of the relationship between Mal 1:14b and Zech 14:9, 16–17.

[50] See, for example, Aaron Schart, *Die Entstehung des Zwölfprophetenbuchs*, BZAW 260 (Berlin: de Gruyter, 1998), 291–93; E. Ray Clendenen in Richard A. Taylor and E. Ray Clendenen, *Haggai, Malachi*, NAC 21a (Nashville: Broadman & Holman), 227; Beth Glazier-McDonald, *Malachi, the Divine Messenger*, SBLDS 98 (Atlanta: Scholars Press, 1987), 21; Theodor Lescow, *Das Buch Maleachi*, AzT (Stuttgart: Calwer, 1993), 12. These four scholars cover various pairings: German and English, Jewish and Christian, critical and traditional.

Jeremiah (15:1) and the Twelve (Mic 6:4).⁵¹ Elijah is mentioned nowhere else in the Latter Prophets, but it seems clear that here Elijah represents at least the former prophets and quite possibly even the Nebiim. It is quite probable, therefore, that those verses were added when the Torah and the Nebiim were combined.⁵²

Recently scholars have paid attention to intertextuality between Malachi and still other passages. One such text is Mal 1:14b, which announces the kingship of God. Malachi 1:5 and 11 announce the greatness of God among the nations, but in Mal 1:18 God renounces impure sacrifices and does so on the grounds that God was a great king. That claim appears nowhere else in Malachi, but it stands at the very heart of Zech 14 in verses 9a and 16–17. However, the motif of the oneness of God that appears in Zech 14:9b appears nowhere else in Zechariah and appears to draw upon Mal 1:14.⁵³ In other words, when Zech 9–14 and Malachi were placed next to each other, a redactor tied them together in both directions.

HAGGAI, ZECHARIAH, AND MALACHI AS THE CLOSING SECTION OF THE TWELVE

One more recent development should be mentioned. The relationships between Haggai and Zech 1–8, between those two collections and Zech 9–14, and among Haggai, Zechariah, and Malachi have long been the subject of literary, form, and redaction-critical studies. More recently, scholars have proposed that Haggai–Malachi constituted the closing section of the Book of the Twelve, edited to be read as one volume.⁵⁴ That argument, however, is not based on form-critical, but redactional critical and other considerations. Form criticism per se is interested primarily, and some would say exclusively, in the original oral form of prophetic speech. What these and other recent studies have shown is not simply that originally oral materials in Haggai through Malachi were changed and elaborated in transmission, but also that Zech 9–14 seems to have been generated through written additions to Haggai–Zech 1–8 and occasional

---

⁵¹ The mention of Aaron *and Miriam* in Mic 6:4 makes it appear likely that a redactor of Micah was aware of traditions about both of them in the Torah.

⁵² See, for example, Lescow, *Maleachi*, 174, and Hill, *Malachi*, 364–66. Dissenting voices include Glazier-McDonald, *Malachi*, 262–64, and Clendenen, *Haggai, Malachi*, 455. Julia M. O'Brien (*Priest and Levite in Malachi*, SBLDS 121 [Atlanta: Scholars Press, 1990], 81–82) specifically argues form-critically that the genre employed, namely the *rîb* or covenant lawsuit, accounts adequately for all alleged irregularities, in particular in Mal 1:11, 2:12, 3:22, and 3:23–24.

⁵³ See the excursus and discussion in Redditt, *Zechariah 9–14*, 142–144.

⁵⁴ See studies referenced in footnote 4, especially Steck (*Abschluss*), who argues that the Twelve dialogued with Isaiah.

dialogue with the Twelve as a whole and with other literature, especially Isaiah, Jeremiah, and Ezekiel, but also Exodus, Psalms, and possibly others as well.

Conclusion

The result of this study is not that form criticism on the Book of the Twelve in general and on Haggai through Malachi in particular is dead or even dying. In fact, it stands with textual, source, and redaction criticism as a foundational method in the study of the Twelve. What has happened in recent decades is that scholars have become interested in the whole history of the traditions, from their oral, preliterary stage to their latest redactional stage—and indeed, though not discussed here, in the reading of the traditions/books in later biblical literature, in the New Testament, and in Rabbinic circles. Scholars have also borrowed methods or strategies from various other disciplines. The study of biblical texts runs from the earliest oral stage to its meaning for readers today.

14

A New Form-Critical Approach to Zechariah's Crowning of the High Priest Joshua and the Identity of "Shoot" (Zechariah 6:9–15)

Anthony R. Petterson

Zechariah 6:9–15 contains many interpretative challenges: Is it a report of a prophetic sign-action, or an oracle connected to the previous or earlier vision reports? How many crowns are involved? Why are some of the names of the returned exiles different in verse 10 and verse 14? Is the priest of verse 13 a second figure or a further description of Shoot? How many thrones are there? And perhaps most crucially, who is Shoot (צֶמַח) in verse 12?[1] There are currently two competing views concerning the identity of Shoot which relate to the overall interpretation of this passage. The first identifies Shoot as Zerubbabel and understands the passage to be addressing the political arrangements in Yehud and garnering support for the temple-rebuilding project. The second identifies Shoot as a future Davidic figure, beyond Zerubbabel and beyond the reconstruction of the temple, who will play a pivotal role in the coming of Yahweh's kingdom. In this instance the passage functions to look beyond the reconstruction of Zerubbabel's temple to a future act of Yahweh. Most studies over the last decade fall firmly on one side or the other and often are explicit in their rejection of the alternative. This present study seeks to understand why this is the case.

Unsurprisingly, decisions that are made about these challenging interpretative issues, including the identity of Shoot, depend to a large extent on the

---

[1] Since "Shoot" is a proper noun (Zech 6:12), I use it without the definite article.

methodological approach adopted and presuppositions about the nature and compositional history of the text. One of the significant developments in the shift towards the "new form criticism" is the focus on the final form of the text and its authorship, readership, and audience (its social location). While some elements of the reconstruction of social location can be just as speculative as the earlier form-critical reconstructions of *Sitze im Leben*,[2] there are also important and less speculative issues that become evident when a prophetic book is read from this perspective. Three of these issues are coherence, inner-biblical exegesis, and intention. I will show how these issues come to the fore with a new form-critical approach and then evaluate from this perspective interpretations of this passage published in the last decade to explore why they are so polarized.

THE NEW FORM CRITICISM AND SOCIAL LOCATION

Robert Gordon has well documented the shift in the study of the prophets during the 1970s, where rather than looking behind the text to reconstruct the history of Israel and its social institutions, or to recover the "historical" prophet and the preliterary origins of prophetic texts, there was a shift to apply approaches from the wider study of literature to the final form of the biblical books.[3] One of the effects of this shift for form-critical studies was a move from studying and classifying genres so as to reconstruct the *Sitze im Leben* of the prophets, towards reconstructing the social locations in which the prophetic books themselves were written.[4] In addition, the concern to appreciate the social locations of the books grounds the subsequent reading of them in history, unlike some literary readings

---

[2] See Hyun Chul Paul Kim, "Form Criticism in Dialogue with Other Criticisms: Building the Multidimensional Structures of Texts and Concepts," in *The Changing Face of Form Criticism for the Twenty-First Century*, ed. Marvin A. Sweeney and Ehud Ben Zvi (Grand Rapids: Eerdmans, 2003), 96: "our reconstruction of the setting of the final stage of a text may still be no more than mere conjecture."

[3] R. P. Gordon, "A Story of Two Paradigm Shifts," in *"This Place is Too Small for Us": The Israelite Prophets in Recent Scholarship*, ed. R. P. Gordon (Winona Lake, IN: Eisenbrauns, 1995), 3–26.

[4] Reflected in the introduction of Ehud Ben Zvi, *Hosea*, FOTL 21A (Grand Rapids: Eerdmans, 2005), 5–6: "To be sure, it is most likely that written sources underlie the present book. It is also likely that the present book is the end result of some redactional processes. This being said, the book of Hosea—that is, this particular instance of YHWH's word—is a book that is presented to its intended readers as a unit, and that asks them to approach it as such and carries particular meanings as such.... There is no indication that the intended readership of the book was asked to divide it into potential sources, read each of them separately and then reconstruct the possible redactional processes that led to the book in its present form. There is no reason to assume that any historical (ancient) community read the book in such a manner. Accordingly, a historical commentary on the BOOK of Hosea ... has to deal with the book as a whole and, of course, as a written document to be read and reread, again and again."

that exclude the author(s) and any discernible intention that they might have in their writing, and focus only on reception.⁵

There are a number of fruitful products of this shift within form-critical studies. First, the focus on social location in the production of the prophetic books and the reception community to whom the books were read and reread supports the inference that the individual prophetic books are coherent, both internally and against the wider cultural and intellectual environment in which they were read.⁶ This approach contrasts with those that see the prophetic books as more of a haphazard collection of disparate prophetic material, where apparent incoherence gives rise to theories about different authors and redactional layers without really questioning how such an incoherent work would be received by its reception community. Admittedly, an approach that presumes internal and external coherence of the final form of a book is a particular challenge for the book of Zechariah which for the last two centuries has been treated for the most part as at least two separate books with different authors and different social settings.⁷ Many see these parts standing at least in tension or at most in contradiction to each other. Yet a new form-critical approach will prefer an interpretation that explains the final form of the text as it stands rather than one that involves emending the text and reconstructing editorial changes.

The coherence of the prophetic books in their reception community entails other subsidiary points. It means that to the extent that authors and their reception community share their "theological viewpoints," there is direct access to these viewpoints through the books themselves. It follows, therefore, that reconstructing these theological viewpoints or thought worlds is not such a speculative enterprise because it is reconstructed from the books that we actually have (from the world "of the text," so to speak, unlike the earlier form-critical project that sought to reconstruct the world "behind the text").⁸ Furthermore, one of the key components of this theology which has a crucial bearing on the

---

⁵ A point made by Kim, "Dialogue," 96: "giving up on the historicity of a text implies ahistoricism."
⁶ So Colin M. Toffelmire, "Form Criticism," in *Dictionary of the Old Testament: Prophets*, ed. Mark J. Boda and J. Gordon McConville (Downers Grove, IL: InterVarsity and IVP Academic, 2012), 266: "New form critics begin their investigations with the assumption that these texts are coherent and have been skillfully collected, edited and transmitted." While Ehud Ben Zvi ("The Prophetic Book: A Key Form of Prophetic Literature," in Sweeney and Ben Zvi, *Changing Face of Form Criticism*, 289) seems happy with some measure of internal incoherence, he still argues that "the world of these books could not stand in a flagrant contradiction with the world of knowledge and the theological viewpoints shared by authorship and primary readership and rereadership."
⁷ For a recent treatment of the history of scholarship on the division of Zech 9–14, see Byron G. Curtis, *Up the Steep and Stony Road: The Book of Zechariah in Social Location Trajectory Analysis*, AcBib 25 (Atlanta: Society of Biblical Literature, 2006), 118–23.
⁸ See Toffelmire, "Form Criticism," 266.

interpretative task is the central claim of each of the prophetic books to speak the word of God.⁹ The literature itself presents Yahweh transcending and governing the created order and through his powerful word proclaimed by his prophets bringing history to its appointed purpose (see, e.g., Isa 45:18–25; 55:8–13). A significant consequence of this view of God (shared by the authorship, readership, and audience to a greater or lesser extent), is that it is difficult to see how prophecies that were understood to have supposedly "failed" would continue to be viewed as authoritative by the reception community and passed from generation to generation. Gordon comments on "the problem of unfulfilled prophecy":

> ...society's familiarity with, and expectations of, the prophet figure are of crucial importance, and on at least two different levels. First, the success or failure of the claimed prophet relates closely to his fulfilling the prophetic stereotype as this is perceived by the society in which he operates.... If a prophet does not conform in some way to the popular conception of a prophet his credibility will diminish. Secondly, the social expectation that produced the formulation of the prophetic role in Israelite society should be a datum in the modern scholar's investigation of prophecy in Israel.¹⁰

This is a significant issue with respect to Zech 6:9–15 and any hope it expresses for Zerubbabel, since all are agreed that Zerubbabel did not usher in the promised restoration and at the same time, in verse 15 the prophet stakes his authority on his oracle coming to pass (cf. Zech 2:13, 15 [Eng. 2:9, 11]; 4:9).¹¹ This demands an explanation since, as Michael Floyd asks:

> How could predictions that did not happen become the basis for predicting something that will happen? If the reconfiguration of monarchial Judah as imperial Yehud did not really amount to a restoration, wouldn't this completely discredit the very idea of "restoration" rather than foster hope in an even more glorious one? How could unkept divine promises fan the flames of even more ardent faith in divine promises?¹²

---

⁹ Ben Zvi, "Prophetic Book," 282.
¹⁰ Gordon, "Paradigm," 21–22; cf. John Van Seters, "Prophetic Orality in the Context of the Ancient Near East: A Response to Culley, Crenshaw, and Davies," in *Writings and Speech in Israelite and Ancient Near Eastern Prophecy*, ed. Ehud Ben Zvi and Michael H. Floyd, SBLSym 10 (Atlanta: Society of Biblical Literature, 2000), 88: "Those groups whose oracular collections were confirmed by the final outcome of events were the ones who survived, and the others were then false and perished."
¹¹ That it is perceived as a problem is seen in the fact that from the time of Wellhausen, many scholars who have identified Zerubbabel as Shoot have sought to solve it by proposing that an earlier version of this passage was edited. See further, Anthony R. Petterson, *Behold Your King: The Hope for the House of David in the Book of Zechariah*, LHBOTS, 513 (New York: T&T Clark, 2009), 15–16.
¹² Michael H. Floyd, "Was Prophetic Hope Born of Disappointment? The Case of Zechariah," in *Utopia and Dystopia in Prophetic Literature*, ed. Ehud Ben Zvi (Göttingen:

A second product of the shift to read the prophetic books in view of their social locations is the recognition that they are not to be read in isolation since the books themselves quote, allude to, and echo earlier authoritative texts, prophetic and otherwise.[13] Indeed, the book of Zechariah sets itself in the stream of the "earlier prophets" (cf. 1:4; 7:12). The corollary of this is that prophetic books are to be read against this wider textual background and this trend is seen in the growing interest in the inner-biblical exegesis or intertextuality of the prophets.[14] For Zech 6:9–15 this is important for there are several words, ideas and phrases that cannot really be understood (including the word Shoot [צֶמַח]) without taking this wider textual background into account.[15]

Third, the shift to study the final form of prophetic books in view of their social location raises the important question of the intention of the author of the book and what they wanted to achieve among readers and hearers of their book. This focus shares a key feature of rhetorical criticism and contrasts with some approaches to the prophets that seem to assume that the books are doing little more than recording the prophets' words for posterity.[16] Marvin Sweeney captures this contrast between the concerns of classical form criticism with the new form criticism:

> ...the prophetic message was not read exclusively as an archival chronicle of past prophetic speeches delivered to an earlier Israelite or Judean community.

Vandenhoeck & Ruprecht, 2006), 269. See also Robert C. Kashow, "Zechariah 1–8 as a Theological Explanation for the Failure of Prophecy in Haggai 2:20–23," *JTS* 64 (2013): 389.

[13] So Toffelmire, "Form Criticism," 267.

[14] For the book of Zechariah, see Rex A. Mason, *Preaching the Tradition: Homily and Hermeneutics After the Exile* (Cambridge: Cambridge University Press, 1990); Janet E. Tollington, *Tradition and Innovation in Haggai and Zechariah 1–8*, JSOTSup 150 (Sheffield: JSOT Press, 1993); Katrina J. A. Larkin, *The Eschatology of Second Zechariah: A Study of the Formation of a Mantological Wisdom Anthology*, CBET, 6 (Kampen: Kok Pharos, 1994); Risto Nurmela, *Prophets in Dialogue: Inner-Biblical Allusions in Zechariah 1–8 and 9–14* (Åbo: Åbo Akademi University, 1996); Michael R. Stead, *The Intertextuality of Zechariah 1–8*, LHBOTS 506 (New York: T&T Clark, 2009).

[15] This raises an issue with which there is little scholarly consensus, namely the provenance of the prophetic (and other biblical) books. However, inner-biblical exegesis may help to resolve some of these debates if the direction of influence can be determined, since appeal to non-existent prophetic works, explicit in the case of Zechariah, would make no sense to Zechariah's audience. See Stead, *Intertextuality*, 43.

[16] Thomas Renz, *The Rhetorical Function of the Book of Ezekiel*, VTSup 76 (Leiden: Brill, 2002), 13, notes one of the differences between form and rhetorical criticism is that "the unity and coherence of a rhetorical unit is to be found not in the uniformity of its structure, but in the unity of its rhetorical situation. Thus, the boundaries of a rhetorical unit can be identical with the boundaries of a form-critical unit, but they can also extend over several form-critical units."

> Rather, the prophetic literature was preserved, transmitted, supplemented, and
> reformulated because later writers and communities believed that it addressed
> them and their situations respectively.[17]

Sweeney writes this in the introduction to his commentary on Isaiah in the *Forms of the Old Testament Literature Series*, the format of which includes a discussion of "Intention" for each of the units, that is, what it is trying to do amongst those who read it. This raises another key issue for my purposes—who is the audience? Regarding Isaiah, Sweeney addresses intention with respect to the "7th-century edition of the book," the "6th-century edition," and the "final form" from the Persian empire in the fifth century.[18] This in itself shows Sweeney's belief that different audiences will hear the same text differently. It is my contention that one of the reasons that the interpretation of Zech 6:9–15 is so polarized amongst interpreters today is because like Isaiah, interpreters each have a different audience in mind and hence conceive of different intentions for the passage. This is due in no small part to the lack of consensus about the relationship of the book of Zechariah to its parts.[19]

The current thinking on the redaction of the Book of the Twelve is that Haggai and Zech 1–8 were composed for the dedication of the temple in 515 BC and existed together before they were added to the Book of Four (Hosea, Amos, Micah, and Zephaniah), which had been edited also in the early postexilic period with reference to the kings of Israel and Judah.[20] There is less clarity about when the other books entered the collection, but it seems that Nahum, Habakkuk, Jonah, and Malachi were placed with a view to chronology, and Joel and Obadiah were placed with a view to themes and linguistic elements. At present there is no consensus on when and how Zech 9–14 was incorporated into the larger collection. Some contend that Malachi originally followed Zech 1–8, and 9–14 was inserted later.[21] Others, that Malachi was added after Zech 9–14 had been

---

[17] Marvin A. Sweeney, *Isaiah 1–39 with an Introduction to Prophetic Literature*, FOTL 16 (Grand Rapids: Eerdmans, 1996), 12.

[18] Ibid., 61.

[19] Michael H. Floyd, "Zechariah and Changing Views of Second Temple Judaism in Recent Commentaries," *Religious Studies Review* 25 (1999): 262. "It is odd that no recent commentaries have attempted to grasp either the ideational concept or the sociohistorical context forming the matrix for the book as a whole, particularly in view of the way in which commentators have come to approach 9–14."

[20] James D. Nogalski, *The Book of the Twelve: Micah–Malachi*, SHBC (Macon, GA: Smyth & Helwys, 2011), 493–96.

[21] E.g., James D. Nogalski, *Literary Precursors to the Book of the Twelve*, BZAW 217 (Berlin: de Gruyter, 1993), 53–56.

added to 1–8.[22] Sweeney identifies the consequences of dividing Zechariah in this way:

> …the current consensus is based on redaction-critical considerations that are designed to identify and to isolate early or original literary units, but that do not address the question as to how those units might work together to create a rhetorically coherent text that is designed to communicate with its reading or listening audience.[23]

Decisions about the composition and redaction of the book of Zechariah have obvious bearing on how the audience (or audiences) of the book of Zechariah are conceived of and in turn this can dramatically influence the way that its parts are read.[24] This will be illustrated with reference to Zech 6:9–15.

READINGS IDENTIFYING SHOOT AS ZERUBBABEL

Having identified several key issues that arise when the social location of the readership and audience are taken into account (internal and external coherence, inner-biblical exegesis, and intention), I will now explore these in dialogue with representative interpretations of this passage published in the last decade.[25] I will begin with interpretations that consider Shoot to be Zerubbabel and then deal with those that believe that Shoot is a future Davidic figure beyond Zerubbabel.

Michael Stead seeks to read Zech 6:9–15 against its "intertexts," of which he identifies two key "sets."[26] The first set is from Jeremiah. In Jer 22:30, three things are removed from king Jehoiachin (כִּסֵּא, מֹשֵׁל, and יָשַׁב), and these are now given to "the Branch" in Zech 6:13 as a reversal of the earlier judgment. Similarly, just as Jehoiachin lost his "honor" (הָדָר) in Jer 22:18, Shoot will bear "honor" (הוֹד) in Zech 6:13. Stead understands Jer 23:5 as "a promise that the Davidic line will

---

[22] E.g., Aaron Schart, "Reconstructing the Redaction History of the Twelve Prophets: Problems and Models," in *Reading and Hearing the Book of the Twelve*, ed. James D. Nogalski and Marvin A. Sweeney (Atlanta: Society of Biblical Literature, 2000), 42.

[23] Marvin A. Sweeney, "Zechariah's Debate with Isaiah," in Sweeney and Ben Zvi, *Changing Face of Form Criticism*, 338. Similarly, Floyd, "Changing Views," 262: "For whatever reason, interpreters seem reluctant to confront the fact that the editors who put the prophetic corpus in its canonical form regarded all fourteen chapters of Zechariah as constituting a distinct prophetic book. This block of text is separated from Haggai and Malachi in the same way that all other prophetic books are demarcated, with a superscription or introduction identifying the prophet for whom the book is named."

[24] Floyd, "Changing Views," 262.

[25] There have been several other treatments of Zechariah published in this time, but I have not dealt with those published at a more popular level. I have surveyed interpretations prior to this more broadly in Petterson, *Behold Your King*, 13–45. For my own treatment of this passage, see *Behold Your King*, 100–120.

[26] Stead, *Intertextuality*, 137.

endure, notwithstanding the fact that Jehoiachin and his children will be excluded from it," and this is what is being activated in Zech 6:9–15.[27] There are also references to Jer 33 with "the Branch" "branching out" (Zech 6:12; cf. Jer 33:15) and "the Branch" working in parallel with a priest (cf. Jer 33:17–18).[28] The second intertext that connects with the temple building in verses 12–13 is 2 Sam 7. Stead notes the striking parallel in expression between 2 Sam 7:13 and Zech 6:13.[29] He summarises: "the significance of the promises in 2 Sam 7 is that they establish that the temple building role was intrinsic to the promises which inaugurated the Davidic line."[30] Stead further notes the way that Cyrus is called God's "anointed" because of his role in rebuilding the temple in Isa 44:28–45:1, and five kings in 2 Chronicles who are given an unqualified positive assessment have a key part to play in rebuilding or restoring the temple.[31]

Having established these intertexts, Stead seeks to understand "how this double allusion should be understood with reference to its sixth-century BCE context."[32] He argues:

> Zerubbabel is the "Branch" of Zech 6:12–13 precisely because he is a "messianic" figure who rebuilt the "house" of Yahweh and through whom the "house" of David was re-established.... Zerubbabel is given the title "Branch" precisely because he is a Son-of-David-temple-builder (i.e., *a* messiah).[33]

Hence, Stead asserts there is no "Zerubbabel problem" since the expectations for Zerubbabel to build the temple were met.[34] The temple that "the Branch" will build is not an eschatological temple, but the temple that is the focus elsewhere in Zech 1–8. The crown will be placed in the temple (v. 14) after it has been built, not before.[35]

Stead then seeks to establish his interpretation with reference to the historical (sociological) context, arguing that Zerubbabel was present in Jerusalem in 520 BCE for the refounding of the temple, absent when the sign-act occurred (possibly in Persia as part of a delegation to Darius), and then present again in 515 BCE

---

[27] Ibid., 138.
[28] Ibid., 139.
[29] Ibid., 140.
[30] Ibid., 140.
[31] These are Asa (15:18); Joash (24:4–14); Jotham (27:1–4); Hezekiah (29:1–11, 35–36); Josiah (34:1–8). Stead, *Intertextuality*, 141.
[32] Ibid., 142.
[33] Ibid., 143. Stead deliberately distinguishes between "a messiah" (a ruling son of David) and "The Messiah" (the final figure at the end of time who would bring salvation). Crucially, he believes that Jer 23 is "not necessarily describing 'The Messiah' ... but a restoration of the Davidic line" (p. 144).
[34] Ibid., 145. A similar treatment is offered by Floyd, "Prophetic Hope," 284: "Thus there are no failed prophecies here."
[35] Stead, *Intertextuality*, 155.

when the temple was completed.³⁶ Stead understands the crowning of Joshua as part of his commissioning for his role as high priest.³⁷ The other crown symbolizes the future "crowning" of (the absent) Zerubbabel.³⁸ Hence: "The dual crowning thus anticipates the time when the 'Branch' will have built the temple, and the high priest will be administering it."³⁹

Stead certainly enriches an appreciation of this passage through a discussion of its intertexts. Yet like others, Stead reads 6:9–15 solely in reference to the period from 520–515 BC, and not in view of the book of Zechariah as a whole.⁴⁰ He has a reduced view of what is promised to Shoot in verse 13, presumably to seek coherence with what Zerubbabel actually accomplished. Rather than "bear majesty," and "sit and rule on his throne," Stead argues the "Branch" will simply "sit on his seat and rule."⁴¹ Stead is certainly correct to note that the things Zerubbabel did achieve were very significant, namely rebuilding the temple and reestablishing the Davidic line in Jerusalem. However, there is arguably a wider Davidic dynasty tradition that presents a strong hope for a future individual king (to reverse Stead's phraseology, not "a messiah," but "*the* Messiah") who is central to the coming of Yahweh's kingdom (e.g., Isa 9:6–7; 11:1–10; 16:4–5; Ezek 21:26–27; 37:21–25; Hos 3:5; Mic 4:8–5:6 [Eng. 4:8–5:5]; Amos 9:11–15; cf. Zech 3:8).⁴² This wider hope is what is captured in Jeremiah's use of the term "Shoot," who is explicitly a wise and just Davidic king who will reign in the land and in whose days Judah will be saved. Similarly, in Zech 3:8–10, the coming of Shoot is said to usher in an age comparable to that of Solomon (cf. 1 Kgs 5:5 [Eng. 4:25]). Zerubbabel certainly did not realize these expectations. To make this cohere, Stead considerably underplays the force of the Jeremiah intertexts. Furthermore, he does not address how this passage would be heard by the audience of the book,

---

³⁶ Ibid., 151.
³⁷ Rather than sitting on a "throne," Stead translates כִּסֵּא as "seat," so the priest in v. 13 sits on his own seat, like Eli in 1 Sam 1:9.
³⁸ Stead, *Intertextuality*, 155.
³⁹ Ibid., 155.
⁴⁰ Ibid., 40–41. This observation is also made by Marvin A. Sweeney, "Review: The Intertextuality of Zechariah 1–8," *JSS* 56 (2011): 416. "Like many modern critics, he [Stead] presupposes that Zech 1–8 must be viewed as a discrete diachronic unit within the book of Zechariah which he then dates to the late sixth century BCE. But recent work on the synchronic form of the book of Zechariah as a whole by Edgar Conrad and the present reviewer has some diachronic implications for the classical critical reading of Zechariah."
⁴¹ Stead, *Intertextuality*, 187.
⁴² See Anthony R. Petterson, "The Shape of the Davidic Hope Across the Book of the Twelve," *JSOT* 35 (2010): 225–46.

for whom the temple had been completed.⁴³ While Zerubbabel may have come to mind to those who witnessed Zechariah's sign-action and heard his oracle about Shoot when it was delivered, the reality is that Zerubbabel is not named as Shoot in the passage, nor in Zech 3:8, which sets the coming of the Shoot into an eschatological timeframe with the phrase "in that day" (v. 10).⁴⁴ This demands another interpretation by those who read the final form of the book after the completion of the temple, especially since the hopes associated with Shoot were not realized.

Antonios Finitsis considers this passage to be an "oracle" and seeks to read it against a reconstructed social location, which he develops from chapters 1–6. He argues that there are two crowns involved since verse 13 "clearly refers to two persons."⁴⁵ One crown is set on the head of the high priest as a coronation which "points to the elevated position of the high priest in the post-exilic community." Because the one crowned "shall build the temple" and "bear royal honour," Finitsis believes that the original form of the text had Zerubbabel being crowned and this was later edited out when it never took place.⁴⁶ The priest standing by the throne of the king, implies a lesser status for the priest (contrary to what Finitsis states earlier?), but the dual leadership arrangement enables each to keep the other in check, particularly to avoid mistakes in the past when the king abused his power with no other authority to keep him in check.⁴⁷ Nevertheless, there will be a cooperative leadership arrangement with a "peaceful understanding between the two."

Finitsis believes that צמח has messianic connotations on account of its background in Jeremiah.⁴⁸ He states: "The fact that the temple got built but Zerubbabel never came to the throne proves the prophet's failure."⁴⁹ Finitsis is not troubled that there are elements in the presentation that do not cohere, since "it is typical of the biblical text to allow loose ends to stand."⁵⁰ Yet one wonders how Zechariah's prophecy was received as prophetic scripture if this were the case, especially since it does not cohere with the popular expectations of a prophet, nor

---

⁴³ The temple was completed in the sixth year of Darius according to Ezra 6:14–15. That the book comes from after the temple is completed is inferred from the way that the temple seems to be functioning in Zechariah's sign action in Zech 11:13.

⁴⁴ See further, Petterson, *Behold Your King*, 98–100.

⁴⁵ Antonios Finitsis, *Visions and Eschatology: A Socio-Historical Analysis of Zechariah 1–6*, LSTS 79 (London: T&T Clark, 2011), 133.

⁴⁶ Ibid., 134.

⁴⁷ Ibid., 135.

⁴⁸ Ibid., 130–31. The "messianic connotations [of צמח] in Isaiah and Jeremiah" are discussed only in relation to Zech 3:10 in a footnote.

⁴⁹ Ibid., 121–22. He is here referring to the prophet Haggai, but the same must be true of Zechariah.

⁵⁰ Ibid., 134–35.

with Zechariah's own claim in 6:15.[51] The social context Finitsis constructs is:

> ...a period of change and both prophets [Haggai and Zechariah] tried to shape a new and cohesive cultic community around the newly rebuilt temple in Jerusalem.... The two prophets wished to show that the future was possible. That is why they identified the leaders of the community as the people responsible for ushering in the new era. Their argument was that the future will follow the present if only people would be bold enough to discern and accept it.[52]

For Finitsis, the night visions evince what he calls "restoration eschatology" where for Zechariah the eschaton is brought into the present, or very close to the present. This construal is based solely on Zech 1–6 (and Haggai) and he does not seek to read these chapters in relation to the rest of the book where there is clearly a more distant horizon in view. Yet even in Zech 1–6 there are a number of elements that look beyond Zechariah's day. These include Yahweh's return to Jerusalem in glory to bring prosperity and peace (2:5–9 [Eng. 2:1–4]; 2:14 [Eng. 2:10]), the removal of the iniquity of the land (Zech 5), and the judgment and incorporation of the nations (2:10, 15 [Eng. 2:6, 11]; 6:8).[53] Zechariah's hope for Shoot sits more coherently alongside these elements.

In James Nogalski's recent commentary on the Twelve, he understands Zech 6:9–15 to be an oracle that relates to the fourth and fifth visions. Three leaders from among the returned exiles are to go to the house of Josiah (one of the Judeans already living in the land) with a collection of silver and gold. They are to make crowns (plural) which will be placed on the head of Joshua. Since there is only one person crowned, Nogalski suggests:

> ...this oracle originally referenced both Zerubbabel and Joshua as recipients of the crowns, but subsequent political events prompted the removal of direct references to Zerubbabel...this action suggests a deliberate attempt in the text's redactional history to downplay Zerubbabel's role as political leader who might threaten the Persian king Darius.[54]

For Nogalski, since the high priest is crowned and the mysterious "branch" is only credited with reconstructing the temple, it implies power was to be shared between them. Branch will build the temple and is described with royal attributes in verse 13. Since Joshua stands by his side, branch "must be identified as Zerubbabel, the descendant of Davidic kings."[55] Yet he is never called "king" and is not mentioned

---

[51] See the earlier comments of Robert Gordon.
[52] Finitsis, *Visions and Eschatology*, 135–36.
[53] I have engaged with Finitsis's thesis more thoroughly in Anthony R. Petterson, "The Eschatology of Zechariah's Night Visions," in *'I Lifted My Eyes and Saw': Reading Dream and Vision Reports in the Hebrew Bible*, ed. Lena-Sophia Tiemeyer and Elizabeth R. Hayes (London: T&T Clark, 2014), 119–34.
[54] Nogalski, *Micah–Malachi*, 880.
[55] Ibid., 881.

by name—his role was deliberately downplayed over time. The crowns are a symbol of the exiles ("those who are far off") coming to help in the reconstitution of the temple.[56]

Nogalski understands 6:9–15 working along with the fourth and fifth visions to regulate the ruling structures of the community where "the political power vested in Zerubbabel is placed on a par with that of the high priest and the religious power of the country."[57] There are limits placed on the governor, with an officially sanctioned place for religious authority (the high priest). Yet, the claims made for Zerubbabel as "the branch" probably posed a threat to the Persian king Darius. If Zerubbabel had plans to reinstitute the Davidic monarchy, or if the expectations of Zechariah and Haggai made it look this way, Darius may have removed him from power. Nogalski believes: "The prophet's hope either went unrealized, meaning Zerubbabel's role was downplayed, Zerubbabel himself was not interested in pursuing a larger role, or Zerubbabel attempted to lead a rebellion but was quickly removed. At any rate, the political power of David's descendant never appears to have achieved the status Zechariah envisioned."[58] This raises again the issue of coherence in the wider environment.

Intriguingly, Nogalski suggests that the original oracle has been reworked for the final form of the book. In a sidebar he says: "It is thus suggestive that someone has downplayed the role of Zerubbabel in the book by removing direct references to him as the branch, while still leaving an expectation of a 'branch' to come."[59] Here Nogalski seems to suggest that a final-form readership might read the passage to refer to a future figure, but he unfortunately does not say any more than this. In terms of the passage's rhetorical intent, Nogalski only draws out its implications for an audience in Zechariah's day before the completion of the temple. He states that the report of those returning with gifts to build the temple would have rallied those who had become discouraged "to build the temple, to reconstitute the community as God's people, and to reinstitute worship at YHWH's house."[60] This is clearly a message that predates the completion of the temple and the final form of the book.

Robert Kashow deals with Zech 6:9–15 in an article that seeks to explain "the failure of prophecy in Hag 2:20–23." He argues that Haggai's prophecy should be read in the light of Zech 1–8, where conditionality is added to the promises concerning the "Davidic heir." Hence, the promises concerning Zerubbabel in the final form of Haggai and Zechariah should be understood as not being fulfilled

---

[56] Nogalski (ibid.) believes that there is no satisfactory text-critical explanation for the different names between verses 10 and 14. Either the intention is to refer to the same four people, or two of the people responsible for making the crowns were not responsible for its care and storage in the temple.
[57] Ibid., 882.
[58] Ibid., 883.
[59] Ibid., 881.
[60] Ibid., 883.

since the condition of obedience by the Judahites was not met.⁶¹

The sign-action in Zech 6 is key for Kashow's thesis. He suggests there are two crowns—one for the head of Joshua and the other (although not specified) is for the head of the Branch when he arrives (the expectation is that it would be imminent). Zechariah's sign-action indicates that the role of Joshua will be to govern the affairs of the temple (cf. Zech 3:7) and the role of the Branch will be to rule "in Davidic fashion."⁶² Kashow notes the contingency in Zech 6:15b and translates it: "And it will come to fruition, *if you all genuinely obey* the voice of the Lord your God." For Kashow, this indicates that the conditionality in Zech 3:8 also attaches to the promise of the imminent arrival of the Davidic heir. He concludes:

> Understanding Haggai in the light of the editorial shaping of Zechariah 1–8—i.e. in accord with the way the post-exilic Judahites would have read this text post-Zerubbabel—communicates that the ascendancy of Zerubbabel and the fullness of restoration associated with Zerubbabel's ascendancy was a *conditional* promise and ultimately never occurred on account of covenantal disobedience to YHWH.⁶³

This quote supports my wider argument that reading Zech 1–8 (and Haggai) from a new form-critical perspective highlights the problem of "the failure of prophecy" if Zerubbabel is identified as Shoot. Kashow's thesis at first appears to resolve "the failure of prophecy," but a closer investigation of the relevant passages does not support his proposal, and it creates other difficulties.

Kashow admits there is no conditionality in Haggai, and that the conditionality in Zech 3:8 does not attach to the Davidic heir, but to the priesthood. His thesis hinges on Zech 6:15b, but here it is not clear exactly what the conditionality attaches to. Kashow asserts that it is "the full restoration spoken of in Hag. 2:20–3, Zech. 3:7–10, and Zech. 6:9–15," but this is not obvious.⁶⁴ If it is the case, it poses another difficulty in that Zechariah stakes his prophetic credentials on it coming to pass: "And you will know that Yahweh of hosts has sent me to you." What would this mean for a final-form audience for whom it had not materialized? Were they to disregard the prophet? Significantly, this same prophet authentication statement is attached to the construction of the temple in Zech 4:9 and this is exactly what is in view at the beginning of 6:15:

---

⁶¹ In a couple of footnotes, Kashow, "Theological Explanation," 396, 398, states that he is assuming that Zerubbabel is Branch and that his thesis also holds for those who those who consider Branch an indefinite future figure. However, there is no problem of a "failure of prophecy" for those who hold the latter view. Furthermore, his thesis poses other problems if Branch is a future figure, which I identify below.
⁶² Ibid., 398.
⁶³ Ibid., 403. Italics original.
⁶⁴ Ibid., 400.

And the ones who are far off shall come and build in the temple of the LORD. And you will know that Yahweh of hosts has sent me to you. And it will come to pass if you diligently obey the voice of Yahweh your God.

In view of the final-form audience for whom the temple building was completed, the conditionality is more naturally understood as attaching to the temple completion and functions to authenticate Zechariah and indicate that other elements of his prophecy (such as the coming of Shoot) will be fulfilled. Furthermore, in Hag 1:12–15, the people obey the voice of God and work on the temple—this conditionality is portrayed as met. One would expect a clearer explanation for "the failure of prophecy" if it concerned Zerubbabel, especially given the magnitude of the expectations accompanying Shoot from this and earlier prophetic texts.

Another issue that Kashow does not discuss is the way that in both Zech 3 and 6:9–15, the stone given to Joshua (3:9) and the crown placed in the temple as a memorial (6:14) seem to indicate that Zechariah expected some distance of time before Shoot would come. Finally, Kashow's proposal creates the impression that Zechariah is saying that the kingdom of Yahweh will not be inaugurated until the people obey – it is all up to them. Yet there is a sense from passages like Jer 30–33 that "the full restoration" including the coming of Shoot (cf. Jer 30:9; 33:15), will be accomplished by God in spite of ongoing covenantal disobedience—God will ultimately do for his people what they are unable to do for themselves and circumcise their hearts so that they will obey in the new kingdom (Jer 31:33; cf. Deut 30:6). Certainly in the final form of the book, Zech 9–14 indicates that the work of Yahweh in "the full restoration" is primary.

READINGS IDENTIFYING SHOOT AS A FUTURE DAVIDIC FIGURE

Two further studies explicitly approach the book from a social location perspective and both conclude that Shoot is a future Davidic figure, those of Byron Curtis and Heiko Wenzel.[65] Both studies also seek to read the final form of Zechariah as a unity, though they configure this quite differently. Byron Curtis argues that there are two divergent social locations underlying Zech 1–8 and 9–14. Zechariah 1–8 comes from the center of Jerusalemite institutions in the early years of Darius the Great with a view to the temple completion. Zech 9–14 comes from a very different social location, still within the prophet's lifetime, but now the prophet is marginalized and found at the social periphery.[66]

Regarding the sign-action, Curtis believes that there are two crowns involved, perhaps one of silver and one of gold (cf. v. 11a). He suggests it is the silver one that is placed on the head of Joshua "signifying the perhaps-expanded duties of the

---

[65] Curtis, *Steep*; Heiko Wenzel, *Reading Zechariah with Zechariah 1:1–6 as the Introduction to the Entire Book*, CBET 59 (Leuven: Peeters, 2011).
[66] Curtis, *Steep*, 3–4.

high priest in a time without a Yehudean monarch."⁶⁷ The gold crown is held in reserve for the future *Zemah*. He suggests that there was no need to crown Zerubbabel since he had already been authorized as governor by the Persians and needed no coronation. Rather over-optimistically he states: "Once the understanding appears that *Zemah* is not Zerubbabel, but a future Davidide, many of the difficulties in 6:9–15 vanish."⁶⁸ For Curtis, the temple that *Zemah* will build is either an enlargement or renovation of Zerubbabel's temple, or otherwise the eschatological temple envisioned in places like Ezek 40–48.⁶⁹ He argues against reading *Zemah* as a priest-king, instead the priest is another figure with his own throne. Regarding הָעֲטָרֹת in verse 14, Curtis entertains reading it as either a plural, in which case both crowns are placed on display in the temple, or as a singular, in which case Joshua retains his crown and only the gold crown is placed in the temple.⁷⁰ The promise that "those who are far away" will come to build the temple could refer to exiles, or non-Israelites, or both and this again refers to the eschatological temple. Curtis concludes with what this sign action means:

> In social location analysis, Zechariah shows himself to be a loyal, but not an unconditional, supporter of the Yehudean restoration led by Zerubbabel and Joshua. He is also loyal to the Persian emperor, but is able to see beyond Persian domination to a time of Yehudean autonomy, when the *Zemah* will rule. Zerubbabel is not the *Zemah*; that role is given to a future figure. The high priest shall not bear royal responsibility, his is a lesser, though prominent, role. The closing exhortation implies a warning about the prospect of failure. Obedience to the prophetic message is in part the determining criterion for future fulfillment.⁷¹

While Curtis seeks to read Zechariah against the background of its social location, it is the social location of the author in two different settings which is in view, rather than the social location of the audience of the final form of the book. He argues that Haggai–Zech 1–8 was a composite unity before the completion of the temple which functioned with the intention to further encourage "the community so heavily engaged in the work of building."⁷² Zechariah 9–14 comes from a later time after the completion of the temple. He later summarizes his perspective:

> …in Zech 1–8 the author writes in order to bolster a nascent leader and to anticipate a messianic leadership. In Zech 9–11 the author writes to condemn a tyrannical leadership and to anticipate a messianic leadership. In Zech 12–14 the author writes to rebuke the house of David and to anticipate a divine

---

⁶⁷ Ibid., 145.
⁶⁸ Ibid., 146.
⁶⁹ Curtis is not clear what temple he has in mind until later: "the eschatological temple associated with the restoration of Davidic rule" (p. 147).
⁷⁰ Ibid., 147.
⁷¹ Ibid., 148.
⁷² Ibid., 112.

leadership. Thus, in respect the leadership theme, chs. 9–14 stand partly in continuity with chs. 1–8, and partly in discontinuity.⁷³

In this way, Curtis seeks to resolve what he sees as different emphases in the two parts of the book, but the question of the intention of the final form of the book for its readership is not really addressed.

Wenzel is concerned to read the book of Zechariah in its final form with the insights of Mikhail Bakhtin on dialogical orientation. This means that he is concerned with social location and audience since "the dialogical orientation of the word focuses on the relationship between [the book of] Zechariah and its audience."⁷⁴ For Wenzel, the audience of the entire book is essentially the same as the audience of the prophet. What is distinctive about his study is he argues that there is no real difference in perspective between the two parts of the book. Whereas many argue that Zech 1–8 has an imminent eschatology and 9–14 sets the coming of God's kingdom at more of a distance, Wenzel argues that from the perspective of the book as a whole, Zechariah announces "a time of waiting" from the beginning of the book. This is a time in which the leaders and people are called to renewed faithfulness to the Sinai covenant, which he contends the introduction to Zechariah (1:1–6) establishes. This is no different to the perspective of 9–14: "These chapters [9–14] do not introduce a time of waiting because the people did not obey (*pace* Moseman) or because the prophecies of Zech 1–6 had failed; rather, they elaborate on what the time of waiting will bring for the people."⁷⁵ Wenzel demonstrates this "time of waiting" in relation to Zech 3 and 4 and then reads Zech 6 from this perspective.⁷⁶

Zechariah 6:15 is one of Wenzel's case studies to demonstrate his thesis that the time of waiting calls for covenant obedience. He deals with this verse in the context of the sign-action of 6:9–15, which he believes has an important role in framing the night visions. It reveals "a time of waiting" before the complete fulfillment of Yahweh's promises.⁷⁷ He notes the absence of a direct object with "set on the head" (וְשַׂמְתָּ בְרֹאשׁ) in verse 11 and argues by comparison with Deut 1:13 that it refers to making Joshua (and subsequent high priests) leaders of the priesthood until Shoot comes. If Joshua was crowned, there is no indication that Joshua's (political) status changes. Like Zech 3:8, "it is a revelatory sign in the present, looking into the future."⁷⁸ He thinks it is more probable that there is only one crown because of the singular verb in 6:14. In this case the plural form refers to either the materials (gold and silver), several bands, or several layers. Regarding

---

⁷³ Ibid., 264.
⁷⁴ Wenzel, *Reading Zechariah*, 35–36.
⁷⁵ Ibid., 204.
⁷⁶ Ibid., 140. Also (p. 152): "In light of the shift from Zech 3:6–7 to 3:8–10, the word צמח refers to a future figure."
⁷⁷ Ibid., 142.
⁷⁸ Ibid., 148–49.

other issues he says: "A careful reading of the Hebrew text does not answer all of these questions in a satisfactory manner. Most of the attempts to solve the riddles, however, can be excluded on the basis of the text."[79] Against Rignell, he argues that verses 12–13 are not a reflection of the present time (referring to Joshua and Zerubbabel) and there is no indication that the subject changes between these verses. Indeed, the lack of an article on כֹּהֵן suggests it continues to refer to "the Branch" as a priest. Furthermore, if there was a separate priest reigning "on his (own) throne, one would expect יֵשֵׁב."[80] For Wenzel, the antecedents of שְׁנֵיהֶם in verse 13 are the high priest Joshua and his successors, and the Branch. It refers to two individuals and their roles. Since the crown will be stored away for the Branch when he comes, "It confirms that Zerubbabel is not the promised king."[81] Later he notes that the temple that the Branch will build is not the בֵּית, but the הֵיכָל: "Zerubbabel (and Joshua) will finish the former; but they should be well aware that the complete fulfillment of Yahweh's promises (concerning the היכל) awaits the arrival of the Branch."[82] Those who are far away (רְחוֹקִים) refer to Jews who still live in Babylon, of whom the individuals who provide silver and gold for the crown are representatives.

In this survey of recent interpretations, Wenzel comes closest to reading the book from a new form-critical perspective. He treats the book of Zechariah as a coherent whole, coming from the prophet Zechariah, but he does not make very much of any distinction between the prophet and his book, nor of identifying the book's origin and *Sitz im Leben*.[83] He is more interested in how the book portrays the audience and their relationship with Yahweh. He also believes it is coherent in its external environment with no evidence of failed expectations or dissonance.[84]

In terms of intention, the sign-action does several things according to Wenzel. It draws attention to the time of waiting once again and explicitly calls the people to obedience (v. 15). It also challenges those Jews in Babylon—will they return to the Promised Land? This is an intention that serves an audience after the completion of the temple and after Zerubbabel.

My own treatment of this passage seeks a coherent reading of it in the final form of the book, which addresses an audience after the temple reconstruction, an audience who realize that the completion of the temple has not brought about the restoration promised by the "earlier prophets."[85] The sign-action report records Zechariah making a crown and crowning the high priest Joshua in order to reiterate the hope for the future king of prophetic expectation, the Davidic Shoot,

---

[79] Ibid., 149.
[80] Ibid., 149.
[81] Ibid., 150.
[82] Ibid., 153.
[83] Ibid., 278.
[84] Ibid., 280.
[85] Petterson, *Behold Your King*, 100–120. More recently, Anthony R. Petterson, *Haggai, Zechariah, and Malachi*, ApOTC 25 (Nottingham: Apollos, 2015), 181–91.

who is associated with God's coming kingdom (e.g. Isa 11:1; Jer 23:5–6; 33:14–18; Ezek 17:3–6, 22–23; 21:26–27). Nowhere in this passage or elsewhere is Zerubbabel identified as Shoot, and this is the point—it looks to a king beyond him. The reason for crowning the high priest Joshua is not explicit, but perhaps against the background of Ezek 21:31–32 (Eng. 21:26–27) and Ps 89:39–41 (Eng. 89:38–40) where the rejection of the Davidic king at the exile involved a defiling of his crown, the crowning of the high priest sanctifies the crown so that it can be taken up in the future by its rightful heir. The word that accompanies this sign-action (6:12–13) establishes that Shoot when he comes will build the eschatological temple hoped for by the prophets (cf. Isa 2:2–3; Jer 3:16–18; Ezek 40–42; Mic 4:1–2; Hag 2:7–9). He will bear majesty and rule as Yahweh's co-regent and priest, issuing in a reign of peace (the ideas of Ps 110 seem to be reflected here). In the meantime, the crown will remain in Zerubbabel's temple as a memorial of the exiles and the hope that they have for his coming. Hence, in the final form of the book, the crowning of Joshua looks forward to the crowning of the Shoot and therefore to the coming king of Zech 9–14. The intention of the passage in its final form is to engender hope for its audience. It also validates Zechariah as a true prophet since his prophecy about the completion of the temple is realized, and it calls on its audience to continue in covenant obedience.

Summary and Conclusion

In this survey I have evaluated treatments of Zech 6:9–15 in terms of coherence (internal and external), inner-biblical exegesis, and intention, issues all raised by the new form-criticism. Despite the plea of Floyd at the end of the twentieth century for studies that read all fourteen chapters as a distinct prophetic book, reading the book of Zechariah in its final form and asking questions about how it functioned in its social location (authorship, readership and audience) is still not commonly done.[86] It is my contention that a major reason for the polarized views

---

[86] Floyd, "Changing Views," 262. Cf. Michael H. Floyd, *Minor Prophets: Part 2*, FOTL 22 (Grand Rapids: Eerdmans, 2000). One of the intriguing features of Floyd's own commentary is that he refers to readers of the various parts of the book, rather than readers of the book as a whole. For instance, in the "Intention" section of 4:1–14, he argues that it shows why "temple reconstruction deserves their full support" (p. 387), clearly referring to an audience prior to 515 BCE. Similarly, in the "Intention" section for 6:9–15 it is an audience prior to the completion of the temple: "If they will act in accord with the claim made by the sign, that only the royal temple can give this sacramental significance to Judah and its leadership, their assent will cause events to unfold in a way that confirms their faith" (p. 409). For a more recent treatment of this passage by Floyd along similar lines, see Floyd, "Prophetic Hope," 268–96. Floyd argues that this passage is to be read in light of the "compositional design and rhetorical aim" of 1:7–6:15 (p. 273). He identifies Shoot as Zerubbabel, but like Stead, downplays the full connotations associated with the Shoot and the Davidic dynasty tradition, so that Shoot is only a

of the identity of Shoot in Zech 6:9-15 is the different audiences of this passage envisaged by interpreters.[87]

This survey shows that interpretations that identify Shoot as Zerubbabel lack coherence on important issues (such as how the passage authenticated Zechariah as sent by Yahweh when Zerubbabel did not become king), in terms of inner-biblical exegesis they reduce the significance of the wider Davidic dynasty tradition found in other texts (Zerubbabel as *a* messiah, rather than *the* Messiah), and/or limit the intention of the passage to the audience of the prophet. At the same time, readings that identify Shoot as a future figure are not always clear on the audience of the passage and its intention.

I am not suggesting that the audience of the prophet is unimportant. Rather, my argument is that the final form of the book is addressed to a different audience and that the issues that this perspective raises need to be appreciated when reading the parts of the book.[88] At the same time, it is fascinating to see with regard to this passage the number of scholars who still seek to reconstruct the actual words (and actions) of the prophet, reflecting the concerns of classical form-criticism. Ultimately it is impossible to know if the intent of Zechariah when he performed this sign-action was different to how it is recorded in the book. In any case, his actual words and actions have been appropriated for a broader purpose in the final form of the book, as is the case for all the prophets.[89]

If the implications of the new form-criticism are taken seriously, readers of the final form of the book of Zechariah read it not simply as a chronicle of earlier times, but as a communication from an author who had an intention to do something among his readers. Furthermore these readers were all too conscious that Zerubbabel did not come near to exhausting the expectations of the Davidic

---

temple builder (p. 282): "The aim is obviously to gain support for Zerubbabel, but only with respect to the completion of the temple building." Note Serge Frolov, "Is the Narrator also Among the Prophets? Reading Zechariah Without Presuppositions," *BibInt* 13 (2005), 16: "What both Conrad and Floyd are offering is an intertextual reading of 'Deutero-Zechariah' against the backdrop of 'Proto-Zechariah' rather than an integrated reading of the book of Zechariah."

[87] Of course there are other factors. For instance, if one is unconvinced of the hope for a future Davidic king elsewhere, then one is unlikely to see it here, regardless of the audience being addressed.

[88] I recognize that this challenges prevailing approaches which interpret each part of the book in its own terms. Furthermore, I admit that the book of Zechariah is complex and it may lack coherence as many have concluded. However, if a coherent interpretation of the book as a whole can be found, and reading its parts in the light of the whole offers an enriched perspective, then perhaps the original grounds for dividing the book in the first place need to be questioned.

[89] On "appropriated discourse," see Nicholas Wolterstorff, *Divine Discourse: Philosophical Reflections on the Claim that God Speaks* (Cambridge: Cambridge University Press, 1995), 51–53. Thanks to my colleague Andrew Sloane for drawing my attention to this.

dynasty tradition found in the wider received literature (and in Zech 9–14). When Zech 6:9–15 is read from the perspective of its final-form audience, it continues to hold out the hope expressed elsewhere for a future Davidic king (cf. 9:9) who will build the temple of earlier prophetic expectation, a temple which is also envisioned at the end of the book where its holiness spills out to encompass Jerusalem and Judah (Zech 14:20–21). This is a much greater temple than what Zerubbabel built and is accompanied by a much grander vision than was achieved under him. The intention of Zech 6:9–15 in the final form of the book is to call its readers to an obedience that involves more than temple building, rather, to covenantal obedience to Yahweh.[90] At the same time, the passage continues to engender hope amongst the final-form audience for Yahweh's coming kingdom, just like the previous visions, and the book as a whole.[91]

---

[90] In calling for covenantal obedience, this passage functions like the call to repent in 1:1–6 and the call for obedience in chapters 7–8 (e.g., 7:9–10; 8:16–17). Yet this obedience is not what will bring in the kingdom, rather the people are to obey in view of its coming.

[91] Cf. Ehud Ben Zvi, "The Concept of Prophetic Books and Its Historical Setting," in *The Production of Prophecy: Constructing Prophecy and Prophets in Yehud*, ed. Diana V. Edelman and Ehud Ben Zvi (London: Equinox, 2009), 75. "The prophetic books are about hope." Cf. Mark J. Boda, "Messengers of Hope in Haggai–Malachi," *JSOT* 32 (2007): 113–31.

15

Goals and Processes of the "New" Form Criticism

Martin J. Buss

This collection of studies shows that current "form criticism" has a variety of concerns and thus includes a variety of procedures and assumptions. Past form criticism often acted as a branch of historical criticism, with an interest in reconstructing the oral background of texts. That approach was not antiquarian, to be sure, since many believed that oral expressions represent the dynamic character of life as a whole and of faith more specifically. The historicist phase of form criticism came to a close when scholars recognized that form-critical analysis is not very helpful for placing traditions in time and place. On the basis of the essays before us, it is now possible to gain a composite picture of at least some of the "new" form criticism.

    A basic feature of what has been called "form criticism" is its interest in the relations between language, thought, and life. Redditt mentions this characteristic, and it is exhibited systematically, for instance, in Gerstenberger's present contribution. Since relations are repeatable, form criticism has a general concern. In fact, "genres"—which are verbal patterns exhibiting the three aspects that have been mentioned—are treated in most of the essays. Sweeney, Nogalski, and Bulkeley deal with the genre of a prophetic book as a whole. More specifically, Tiemeyer describes patterning for vision reports, Dempsey for woes and promises, and Boda for human address to and a call for silence before Deity.

    Most genres that are reasonably broad in their scope transcend a single culture. Several contributors—including Floyd, Trotter, Gerstenberger, and Bulkeley—thus deal with more or less comparable formations in neighboring cultures. However, unlike much of earlier form criticism, little attention is paid here to non-neighboring cultures, although Gerstenberger and perhaps other contributors have done so elsewhere (of course, the essay format provides limits to what can be said). Among the human sciences, cognitive linguistics makes an appearance in the discussion of metaphor theory by Stovell.

The new form criticism focuses, at least first of all, on the text as it lies at hand, as Tiemeyer and Petterson explicitly emphasize. Since there may be tensions within the text as it stands, Timmer distinguishes between "cohesion" on the textual/linguistic level and conceptual "coherence" that recognizes "meaningful interrelations of various sections of the text." Both coherence and incoherence are interesting for synchronic reader-response views, but this standard is of limited value for historical criticism, which should be based primarily on allusions to known events and conditions. Most of the essays do add a diachronic perspective. Floyd, Tiemeyer, Nogalski, and Redditt explicitly defend that combination.

Earlier form criticism had widely assumed that early oral patterns were "pure" and rigid. In contrast, Stovell, Tiemeyer, Toffelmire, and Redditt, among others, point out that genres are usually fluid and often mixed. Indeed, according to relational theory—upon which I have reported, as is mentioned briefly by Nogalski—all actual relations require some looseness in order to be "relations." However, that same theory also holds that relations involve, at least partially, a theoretically meaningful connectivity, which in traditional rhetoric is called "aptness." This aspect interested Gunkel and his followers but is not overtly addressed in these essays.

In a partial contrast with Gunkel's use of the term *Sitz im Leben*, which referred to a normal context in life, some scholars have come to speak of a *Sitz in der Literatur*. Toffelmire points out that this relation can be described as "co-textual" and that a "context of situation" would be in addition to that. If "life context" is conceived in terms of dynamic human patterns that are in many ways continuous although varied, form-criticism has a trans-chronic and trans-geographic reach. Potential relevance for the present is, in fact, expressly indicated by Dempsey and Boda.

I have been asked to state clearly the position from which I operate. The following sketch represents succinctly what I have described and demonstrated elsewhere.

The special contribution of historical criticism lies in its focus on particularity. This supported the possibility of change during a period in which "modernity" came to be embraced as a positive value in contrast to stability. Generic criticism, which came to be called "form criticism," balanced this focus by attention to commonality between expressions in different places and times. Developments in the disciplines of biology and linguistics can serve as illustrations. At one time, they focused on standard forms, viewed as "essences." Then they became interested in evolutionary history. Now they deal heavily with relational processes, as Saussure famously argued for linguistics. This newer way recognizes that, while objects and events are particular, relations are general in the sense of being repeatable. Even attention to difference, as distinct from observing an isolated datum, implies a combination of these dimensions. What makes things "special" is a more or less unusual combination of features each of which can be shared.

A relational outlook is actually quite old and was present also in biblical literature. In fact, it is possible that human thinking and life oscillates between the poles of particularity and generality. In the twentieth century, however, a combined outlook received disciplined attention and developed a political aspect in social democracy, in which Gunkel participated.

In order to combine particularity with generality, Gunkel placed elements of the older essentialism together with elements of the more recent developmental perspective. Both kinds of elements were questionable, but their combination yielded a constructive understanding of the biblical text that resembled a relational approach. This had relevance also for the present, which was Gunkel's avowed aim. Differently, a number of biblical scholars after Gunkel treated his approach, labeled "form history," as a branch of "historical criticism" (a term that Gunkel had disliked). Specifically, they sought to use attention to literary forms as a basis for reconstructing a history that lies behind the biblical text, which Gunkel had left quite vague. Subsequently, however, both this speculative historical criticism and the elements of essentialism that were present in Gunkel's conception were recognized as questionable.

A number of participants in a "new" form criticism then followed Wolfgang Richter's interpretation of linguistics (e.g., he is mentioned by Stovell, n. 27). Apparently influenced by the predominantly historical interest of his scholarly heritage, however, he believed that particularity is primary. A more appropriate view in line with current linguistics is that a relatively small number of relations produce a great multitude of languages and even more of sentences. A language "system" that is used in a given society (mentioned by Stovell and Toffelmire) represents relations within an intermediate level of generality that stands between particular sentences and human language as such. Human language itself is a subset of a larger whole, without a completely clear boundary. There appear to be a few relative universals in language, but true universals are such as operate within our whole universe, especially so "action" in space-time. A possibly even larger relation is "receptivity," depending on one's theology. Because of its particularist emphasis, the adoption of Richter's conception had the effect of discouraging or at least not encouraging reflection, which is inherently general.

More reflective is a relational approach. In the study of literature, it involves attention to relations between language, thought, and an implied context, as Gunkel recognized. It can also be concerned with relations between elements of thought (coherence or dissonance, for relations need not be positive) and needs to consider throughout the relation of phenomena with the observer. For instance, in my 1969 study of the "prophetic word" of Hosea (one of the prophetic books under discussion), I largely avoided micro-historical issues in favor of a broader perspective and dealt with issues of literature, communication, terms (including symbols), and (dynamic) structure.[1] In regard to a limited topic, I observed that positive statements used direct address relatively often, while negative statements used indirect address relatively frequently (and were perhaps soon put in writing). Such a correlation has fairly obvious reasons, although randomness or mystery operates as well. In fact, while a particularist outlook tends to support either non-rational rebelliousness or unreasoned authority, the approach described recognizes partial reasonableness. This has theological implications: Is Deity totally irrational? I do not think so, nor does most of biblical literature.

Attention to relations is fundamental not only for understanding, but also for a possible relevance for another occasion. After all, the standard formula for analogy is a correspondence of relations: A is to B as C is to D. Just as the physical sciences always discuss particular phenomena in terms of their relations which have potential usefulness, so we need to proceed in the investigation of human expressions. For this purpose, we can draw on a preexisting knowledge of relations. Comparative study aids such knowledge. A gain in insight comes when we discover a previously unknown relation or combination of several. At the same time, it is important to realize that associations between objects and events are not rigid, for several relations operate together on any occasion, and sheer contingency appears to play a role. Any application of analogy must thus allow for the interplay of different relations. Historical, especially macro-historical, perspectives need to be taken into account, for they may show why one should now do things differently even when continuing a given relation, because the historical situation is different.

"Old" form criticism engendered a great deal of excitement. In part, it did so because of the historical implications that were drawn. In Hebrew Bible studies, they supported some traditional historical perspectives; in Christian Testament studies, they favored some quite non-traditional historical views. More importantly, however, "old" form criticism engendered excitement since it discussed important issues of meaning, such as the role of cult and the significance of a covenantal view. If issues of meaning continue to be prominent, the "new" form criticism can be exciting, too—perhaps by being both inspiring and disturbing.

These comments deal only with the goals and procedural principles of the essays. For all of these, I have pointed out the presence of significant principles. In regard to the essays' substantive contributions, I have found few, if any, that

---

[1] Martin J. Buss, *The Prophetic Word of Hosea: A Morphological Study*, BZAW 111 (Berlin: Töpelmann, 1969). Since then I have treated Hosea with regard to a number of issues beyond what can be mentioned here in *Toward Understanding the Hebrew Canon*, Hebrew Bible Monographs 61 (Sheffield: Sheffield Phoenix, 2013).

have a doubtful basis. Nevertheless, there are more issues that can be discussed, as is to be expected.

16

New Form Criticism and the Prophetic Literature: The Unfinished Agenda

Robert R. Wilson

Beginning roughly in the middle of the twentieth century, the classic form-critical approach to biblical literature began to undergo a number of transformations, a process which finally culminated in what this volume designates "new form criticism." Although it is not yet clear that "new form criticism" represents a new or even a coherent approach to biblical interpretation, it does seem to have certain tendencies, which in various ways are reflected in the essays contained in this volume. The essays themselves are complex, creative, and often quite provocative, but constraints of space prevent me from dealing with each of them in detail. Rather, in the essay that follows I will concentrate on the ways in which the new form criticism informs these studies of prophetic literature. By way of introduction, I will first indicate briefly why the older form-critical method was modified, and then I will try to indicate some of the major emphases of the new, revised version of the method. Finally, I will indicate areas in which the new form-critical approach requires further research and how some of the authors in this volume address the remaining issues. Like the volume itself, which focuses on the Book of the Twelve, I will confine my remarks to prophetic literature.

From its inception in the late nineteenth century, the form-critical method displayed some imprecision in explaining its focus and goals. Hermann Gunkel, who is usually credited with developing and popularizing the method, was interested initially in writing a history of ancient Israelite literature, a task which, in his view, required dealing both with Israel's oral literature and with the written literature that later grew from it. For Gunkel, this sort of study involved recovering the literary genres (*Gattungen*) that Israel employed, first at the oral level and then at the written one. The result of such an effort could then be called *Gattungsgeschichte* (the history of genres) or *Formgeschichte* (the history of literary forms), although Gunkel himself would eventually question the use of these labels.[1] Lying behind this description of the enterprise was Gunkel's belief that oral literature was somewhat formulaic and that oral genres would follow regular patterns. At this point he was probably being influenced by the new academic discipline of folklore studies, which began to be prominent in Germany in the late nineteenth century. In some cases the oral patterns were preserved when the material eventually reached written form. In these cases, a careful reading of Israelite written literature could allow a reconstruction of the oral originals. As part of the recovery of the original oral genres or forms, Gunkel also tried to recover the setting in the life of the people (*Sitz im Volksleben*) in which the oral material was used.

Gunkel formulated his form-critical program in an academic atmosphere that was heavily influenced by German Romanticism, so it is not surprising that he, and even more obviously some of his later students, accepted the tenets of the Romantic Movement without examining them. In particular, he believed that inspiration, whether artistic or religious, was rooted in a personal, almost mystical experience and that the recovery of that experience depended on getting as close as possible to the original event. As this idea was worked out later by his successors in the movement, this quest for origins caused biblical scholars to see the oral speech of inspired individuals to be superior to later written versions of the material, which was likely to be the uninspired elaboration of scholars. Similarly, the romantics saw poetry to be more inspired than prose, and the uneducated but inspired common people to be preferred to the educated but uninspired writers. As form criticism developed, there was in some circles so much energy expended trying to recover the oral, inspired material that the later written form of that material was undervalued or ignored. The effort at recovery sometimes did violence to the written text by stripping away as inauthentic the uninspired prose in order to reach the inspired oral, usually poetic, nugget that lay buried within. Genuine inspiration lay only within the small core, and in order to reach it, much of the surrounding text had to be removed. In

---

[1] For Gunkel's own brief description of his program, see Hermann Gunkel, "Israelite Literary History," in Hermann Gunkel, *Water for a Thirsty Land: Israelite Literature and Religion*, ed. K. C. Hanson, trans. A. K. Dallas and James Schaaf (Minneapolis: Fortress, 2001), 31–41. A brief history of the development of form criticism may be found in Antony F. Campbell, "Form Criticism's Future," in Sweeney and Ben Zvi, *Changing Face of Form Criticism*, 15–23.

theological terms, genuine revelation had to be recovered by removing all of the later uninspired additions and modifications.[2]

In fairness to Gunkel, it is important to note that he himself was not guilty of making some of the questionable methodological moves that routinely marked the work of later form critics. To be sure, Gunkel did feel that the narratives of Genesis, for example, originated in short, inspired tales produced by the common people and then circulated orally until they were later written down and elaborated by the uninspired authors of the biblical texts. However, his treatment of these materials in his commentary on Genesis by no means neglects the actual written text of the book. He tries to recover the oral originals, but he also analyzes the written text as the last stage of the book's literary history.[3]

Nevertheless, Gunkel's failure to elaborate his method clearly and to resolve ambiguities in his descriptions of it created problems which later generations of form critics were unable to resolve. For example, he failed to distinguish clearly between the German terms *Gattung*, usually translated "genre" and *Form*, "form" or "structure," and as a result created confusion about what scholars were supposed to be recovering or tracking. "Genre," as the term is used in English, usually refers to larger literary categories, such as "narrative," "oracular speech," "laments," and the like. On the other hand, "form" does not usually describe a category but the structure of a specific text. One term is quite general, while the other is very specific, although scholars often use the terms interchangeably, as do some of the authors in this volume. There is still some work to be done to clarify terms if form criticism is to continue to be used as an interpretive method.[4]

Furthermore, in practice form critics have had great difficulty recovering the settings of the literary genres, in part because Gunkel was unclear about whether the setting referred to the language used in the genre or to the social location in which the genre was actually used. The two are sometimes related, but not always. For example, Gunkel notes that the home of legal language is the law court, but the appearance of such language in a prophetic text does not necessarily mean that the prophets carried out their activities in legal settings, although some scholars have tried to advance this argument.[5] As a result of this looseness with which Gunkel referred to setting, there has been little agreement on questions of setting in form-critical analyses. The one exception has been the

---

[2] The role of the Romantic Movement in shaping form criticism has often been noted. See most recently Marvin A. Sweeney and Ehud Ben Zvi, "Introduction," in Sweeney and Ben Zvi, *Changing Face of Form Criticism*, 2–3.

[3] Hermann Gunkel, *Genesis*, trans. Mark E. Biddle (Macon, GA: Mercer University Press, 1997 [translated from the third German edition, 1910]).

[4] For a discussion of these two terms and their meanings, see Campbell, "Form Criticism's Future," 24–31; and Erhard Blum, *"Formgeschichte*—A Misleading Category?: Some Critical Remarks," in Sweeney and Ben Zvi, *Changing Face of Form Criticism*, 32–45.

[5] Gunkel, "Israelite Literary History," 33–34.

temple setting of the Psalms, although even here some literary forms in Psalms, such as the individual lament, were surely used on occasions of personal mourning and were not confined to the context of formal worship. In short, Gunkel's concept of setting was slippery, and determining the settings of literary forms has frustrated form critics for generations.

Finally, the description of distinct oral literary patterns has often been difficult and has led to scholarly disagreements. Many of the reconstructions contain little that is detailed enough to identify a given literary form clearly. For example, the ancestral narratives of Genesis were analyzed by Gunkel simply as *Sagen*, a label which basically means that the narratives were originally oral rather than written. At the written level, the narratives exhibit few distinctive formulaic patterns, and there is much formal variation in individual texts, so it is no surprise that the reconstructed oral forms are similarly diverse. In terms of literary form, form criticism has had its greatest success in analyzing Psalm patterns and wisdom genres, but even in this case a good bit of formal fluidity still exists.

The issue of the form criticism of prophetic texts is also a complicated one. Gunkel actually wrote very little about prophetic literature, but it is clear that he thought about the development of prophetic books in the same way that he did other types of Israelite literature. In his view, prophecy was originally an oral phenomenon, and each instance of prophecy began with the private, mystical experience of the prophet. After this experience had ended, the prophet delivered the revelation orally to an audience, although Gunkel is unclear about how the experience was transformed into an oral oracle. Eventually the oracles were written down, perhaps by members of the audience, but Gunkel is a bit vague about how this process eventually led to the prophetic books that we now have. He was also unclear about the setting of prophetic activity, which seems to have taken place in a number of different social locations, if the biblical narratives themselves are to be believed. Similarly, Gunkel did not try to describe a distinctive literary form associated with prophecy, either at the oral or written level, and he recognized that prophets used a great variety of speech forms in their work.[6]

Gunkel's preliminary remarks about prophetic literature were eventually expanded by Claus Westermann.[7] Westermann argued that the announcement of judgment was in fact the original oral prophetic literary form, but his description of the form had so few distinctive features that scholars quickly began

---

[6] Hermann Gunkel, *Die Propheten* (Göttingen: Vandenhoeck & Ruprecht, 1917), 1–31, 104–140; Hermann Gunkel, "The Prophets: Oral and Written," in *Water for a Thirsty Land*, 85–133.

[7] Claus Westermann, *Grundformen prophetischer Rede* (Munich: Kaiser, 1960; 2nd ed. 1964); English translation: *Basic Forms of Prophetic Speech*, trans. Hugh Clayton White (Philadelphia: Westminster, 1991).

to doubt the form's existence. Furthermore, there are few pure examples of the form, and the ones that do exist are found primarily in Deuteronomistic literature, thus raising the possibility that if the form did exist at the oral level it was not widespread. Furthermore, Westermann did little to clarify the problem of the setting of either prophetic speech or prophetic activity, although he implied a juridical setting for both, an idea that was eventually explored by others. Finally, he did not deal with prophetic promises at all, following the scholarly consensus of the time that salvation oracles in Israel were a late development.[8] Later form-critical scholarship attempted to refine Westermann's work, but for the most part efforts at reconstructing original oracle forms failed to convince the majority of scholars, and attempts to deal with the question of setting led mostly to frustration.

It is against these scholarly developments that the main emphases of the "new form criticism" must be understood. Although the designation "new form criticism" suggests that the practitioners of the approach see themselves in continuity with the classic form-critical method, so much of Gunkel's original program has been jettisoned that observers might wonder why the traditional terminology is used at all. Although the new form critics exhibit a good bit of variation in their approaches, most of them share some obvious similarities. First, there is a tendency for the new form critics who study prophecy to give up Gunkel's quest for oral material that might lie beneath the surviving biblical text. They do this in varying degrees. In its most extreme form, this disinterest in the oral original denies that oral oracles ever existed, a point of view that dovetails nicely with minimalist claims that prophecy as it is described in the biblical text never existed at all. More moderate is the claim that oral prophecy probably existed in Israel but that scholars can no longer reconstruct its characteristics and certainly cannot recover its oral literary forms with any certainty. In either case, many new form critics believe that recovery of the oral level is irrelevant to the interpretive task.[9]

---

[8] Westermann eventually took up the question of promise oracles in his *Prophetic Oracles of Salvation in the Old Testament*, trans. Keith Crim (Louisville: Westminster John Knox, 1991). For an early critical analysis of Westermann's work, see Robert R. Wilson, "Form-Critical Investigation of the Prophetic Literature: The Present Situation," SBLSP 1973, 1:100–27. A more recent critique may be found in David L. Petersen, "The Basic Forms of Prophetic Literature," in Sweeney and Ben Zvi, *Changing Face of Form Criticism*, 269–75.

[9] For a brief summary of the perspectives of the new form critics, see Michael H. Floyd's article in this volume, pp. 17–18. Earlier treatments may be found in Sweeney and Ben Zvi, "Introduction," 3–5; and Campbell, "Form Criticism's Future," 24–27. For the extreme view that Israelite prophets did not exist or that their words can no longer be recovered, see, among others, Robert P. Carroll, "Poets Not Prophets," *JSOT* 27 (1983): 25–31. More moderate, but still denying that oral prophecy can be recovered, is Philip R. Davies, "'Pen of Iron, Point of Diamond' (Jer. 17:1): Prophecy as Writing," in *Writings and*

Second, just as many of the new form critics dispense with the quest for oral literary forms, so also many of them do not attach any importance to the traditional effort to reconstruct the original setting of prophetic speech or activity. For the scholars who deny the existence of prophets and prophecy, the disinterest in setting is an obvious corollary of their belief. For the more moderate scholars who believe that there was a setting for early prophetic activity, the exercise of reflecting on setting is so fruitless that it pays no interpretive dividends.

Third, rather than focusing their attention on what precedes the biblical text as we now have it, the new form critics begin and end their investigations with the text itself. This means that for the new form critics, literary forms are in fact descriptions of the actual features of specific texts in all of their particularity. The interest of classic form criticism in typical literary patterns has been replaced by a focus on individual texts that for the most part do not contain much in the way of patterns. It is at this point that observers might wonder how the new form criticism differs from a purely literary approach, like the sensitive readings of Robert Alter, the holistic approach of Moshe Greenberg and others, or even the various canonical approaches inspired by the work of Brevard Childs.

Fourth, just as the minimalist historians date the writing of Israel's history to the exilic period or later, so also the new form critics locate the formation of Israelite prophetic literature in the exilic and early post exilic periods and attribute prophetic compositions from those periods to the work of anonymous scribal elites. According to most new form critics, the work of shaping prophetic texts began in the exile, in Babylon, but was finished by scribes in Israel after the return.[10]

Finally, some of the new form critics have recently argued that the aim of literary analysis should be the study of whole prophetic books, and that the creation of such books was the aim of the scribes that wrote them. In short, the books as we have them are not simply the result of agglomeration and mild editing over time but have been intentionally crafted by the scribes to reflect their own interests. Taking this process one step farther, in recent years there has been an additional concern with describing how books were gathered together in groups by the scribes and shaped so as to be unified expressions of their creators' views. Examples of this scholarly interest may be found in recent studies of how

---

Speech in Israelite and Ancient Near Eastern Prophecy, ed. Ehud Ben Zvi and Michael H. Floyd (Atlanta: Society of Biblical Literature, 2000), 65–81.

[10] For a discussion of exilic and postexilic dates for the formation of prophetic books, see Michael H. Floyd, "Basic Trends in the Form-Critical Study of Prophetic Texts," in Sweeney and Ben Zvi, *Changing Face of Form Criticism*, 298–311. For efforts at reconstructing this process in greater detail, see the essays contained in Diana V. Edelman and Ehud Ben Zvi, eds., *The Production of Prophecy: Constructing Prophecy and Prophets in Yehud* (London: Equinox, 2009).

the Torah was formed and how the individual books making up the Book of the Twelve were finally brought into a unified literary whole.[11]

Each of these developments reflected in the new form criticism raises new scholarly issues which deserve further investigation. The omission of a consideration of possible oral origins from the study of prophetic literature may be understandable in the light of the controverted history of efforts to reconstruct oral material, but this omission does raise a number of problems. In the first place, comparative evidence from contemporary prophecy studies and from the ancient Near East suggests that prophecy as a religious phenomenon is initially oral in character everywhere it appears. This evidence also suggests that prophets exhibit stereotypical behavior, including patterned actions and speech.[12] In theory, then, oral prophecy in Israel should be a subject worth exploring, if there were some way to do it. In the second place, to ignore the oral stage of the prophetic process in Israel is to risk removing the prophet from the history of Israelite prophetic literature, thereby creating some major authority issues.[13] As a religious phenomenon, prophecy is of interest to a contemporary audience or to later readers only if the prophet in question actually received a divine revelation. Later readers of Amos would not be interested in the book if they did not believe that a genuine prophet was the source of what it contains. In short, the authority of prophetic writings seems to depend on the existence of a prophet who actually existed or who was thought to have actually existed, no matter how fictionalized later biographies of the prophet might be. If prophecy in Israel really began with late scribal literary productions, then the scribes either had to convince their audience that a genuine historical prophet existed in the past or that the scribes themselves did what they did as a result of divine inspiration. Both of these claims have been advanced in recent scholarship, but the whole question requires further study.[14] Finally, it is worth noting that oral prophecy not only enters the scholarly discussion when the beginning of a text's

---

[11] See in particular Ehud Ben Zvi, "The Prophetic Book: A Key Form of Prophetic Literature," in Sweeney and Ben Zvi, *Changing Face of Form Criticism*, 276–97.

[12] See most recently Martti Nissinen, "Since When Do Prophets Write?," in Kristin De Troyer et al., eds., *In the Footsteps of Sherlock Holmes: Studies in the Biblical Text in Honour of Anneli Aejmelaeus* (Leuven: Peeters, 2014), 585–606.

[13] This problem is recognized and discussed in Michael H. Floyd's article in the volume, p. 17–36.

[14] For preliminary discussions of this problem, see Hans M. Barstad, "What Prophets Do: Reflections on Past Reality in the Book of Jeremiah," in Hans M. Barstad and Reinhard G. Kratz, eds., *Prophecy in the Book of Jeremiah*, BZAW 388 (Berlin: De Gruyter, 2009), 10–32; and Stuart Weeks, "Jeremiah as a Prophetic Book," in Barstad and Kratz, *Prophecy in the Book of Jeremiah*, 265–74. It is interesting to note that even Ehud Ben Zvi, who advocates focusing on whole prophetic books, stresses that the books identify their subject matter as coming from a single prophet, whom the scribes supply with a fictitious biography. See his discussion in "Prophetic Book," 284.

history is being considered, but also after the text has been fixed in writing. Written texts are often reoralized in order to pass them on to illiterate audiences. Thus written texts do not seem to have existed only in written form after their creation, but they became oral again under certain conditions. This phenomenon of alternation between the written and the oral has been noted in several recent scholarly studies and requires more elaboration.[15]

Given the neglect of oral prophecy by the new form critics, it would seem reasonable to conclude that they would also not be interested in the question of the setting of prophetic material. Although this is true in some cases, in fact what seems to be happening is that the question of setting is now being explored in connection with the circumstances of the text's final writing rather than in connection with a hypothetical reconstruction of the circumstances of the material's origin. Historical reconstruction is still required, although the focus of scholarly inquiry is now the exilic and postexilic periods rather than earlier periods in Israelite history. Fortunately for these recent efforts to understand more clearly the dynamics of literary production in the Neo-Babylonian and Persian periods, there are now new resources for understanding the problems facing the Judean community in exile. However, this new material has not yet been studied in detail.[16]

Because the new form critics have shifted the focus of their attention to the exilic and postexilic periods and to scribal activities in those periods, there has been much new research on scribal activity in Israel.[17] In general, scholarship on prophetic books has attributed their creation to scribal elites, probably associated with the palace or the temple, although both of these suggested venues seem improbable during the exile itself, and a royal setting seems unlikely after the exile. The attribution of prophetic books to scribes therefore seems to make sense, but it leaves unanswered such crucial questions as who the scribes were and why they were interested in producing prophetic books. If they were not concerned simply to pass along earlier prophetic stories and oracles, then they must have had other purposes in mind. When the new form critics have

---

[15] This phenomenon has been noted particularly in recent studies of Jer 36. See initially Susan Niditch, *Oral World and Written Word* (Louisville: Westminster John Knox, 1996), 104–5; and the more detailed exploration of the idea in Joachim Schaper, "On Writing and Reciting in Jeremiah 36," in Barstad and Kratz, eds., *Prophecy in the Book of Jeremiah*, 137–47.

[16] For the most recent discussions of Judean communities in exile, see Laurie E. Pearce, "Continuity and Normality in Sources Relating to the Judean Exile," *HBAI* 3 (2014): 163–84. The cuneiform texts on which this article is based have now been published in Laurie Pearce and Cornelia Wunsch, *Documents of Judean Exiles and West Semites in Babylonia in the Collection of David Sofer* (Bethesda, MD: CDL, 2014).

[17] See particularly William M. Schniedewind, *How the Bible Became a Book* (Cambridge: Cambridge University Press, 2004); and Karel van der Toorn, *Scribal Culture and the Making of the Hebrew Bible* (Cambridge: Harvard University Press, 2007).

explored the question of scribal interests and intentions at all, they have come up with a variety of hypotheses, and to date there is no scholarly agreement in sight. The most specific suggestion is also the narrowest: The scribes represented the interests of their employers, primarily the government and/or the temple. However, this explanation seems inadequate, given the fact that the prophetic literature does not seem particularly interested in or supportive of either the government or the temple. It is therefore likely that scribal interests, whatever they were, are being viewed too narrowly. To be sure, it is certainly possible that the scribes represented the interests of the temple, but they could have represented the interests of other groups as well. They may also have simply represented their own idiosyncratic opinions. Recent studies of text production and scribal activity at Qumran also suggest another possibility. Scribes may have participated in larger groups and shaped the texts that they eventually wrote on the basis of oral conversations with other scribes. In this case it is possible that the prophetic books as we have them were the results of oral interpretive activity grounded in earlier texts or traditions. In such cases, the scribes may have exercised some creativity as they dealt with their inherited material, but they may have finally claimed authority for what they did because of their belief in the divine inspiration of their source material rather than in the divine inspiration of their own activities.[18] However that may be, if the new form critics continue to attribute prophetic writings to scribes, then they need to engage in a more thorough investigation of scribalism than has been undertaken so far.

Finally, scholarly study of collections of texts such as the Book of the Twelve is certainly important and has produced some interesting results already, but a number of questions remain to be answered. How thorough was scribal editing across the whole collection? Why are individual books set in different time periods and cultural settings? How was this large collection intended to function at the oral level when it was read to an audience? Would subtle editorial links have been noticeable to a listening audience? What were the interests of the scribes who created the collection? Do the varying orders of the books in different traditions suggest different purposes in the minds of the scribes who

---

[18] For a criticism of recent research on scribes as being unduly narrow in understanding the scribal office, see Michael H. Floyd, "'Write the Revelation' (Hab 2:2): Re-imagining the Cultural History of Prophecy," in Philip R. Davies and Thomas Römer, eds., *Writing the Bible: Scribes, Scribalism and Script* (Durham: Acumen, 2013), 103–43. On the independence of scribes, see Walter J. Houston, "The Scribe and His Class: Ben Sira on Rich and Poor," in Davies and Römer, eds., *Writing the Bible*, 108–23. For an introduction to scribal activity at Qumran, see Mladen Popović, "Qumran as Scroll Storehouse in Times of Crisis? A Comparative Perspective on Judean Manuscript Collections," *JSJ* 43 (2012): 551–94; and Sarianna Metso, *The Serekh Texts* (London: T&T Clark, 2007), 63–71.

created them?[19] Clearly much more work needs to be done on book collections of this sort.

Seen against this background, it is clear that all of the authors who have contributed to this volume are aware in varying degrees of both the perspectives of the new form criticism and the problems that remain. As a whole, the authors share the major claim of new form criticism that interpretation should focus on the final form of the texts as we now have them. There is little interest in these essays in recovering earlier literary levels and certainly not in reconstructing earlier oral forms. However, when analyzing individual texts, the authors apply various methods of reading, few of which resemble the focus of classic form criticism on formulaic literary patterns. Exceptions appear in the studies of Michael Floyd, James Trotter, and Lena-Sofia Tiemeyer. Floyd discusses the tradition of lists in the ancient Near East and suggests that such lists might have influenced the literary formation of prophetic oracles.[20] Like other contributors, he uses data from another field to understand the biblical text, so in this sense he is not simply doing a close reading of the biblical material. Trotter's contribution is an interesting study of the *rîb* or lawsuit form, which classic form critics sometimes thought to be at the heart of prophetic speech. Trotter accepts the Persian period dating of the prophetic books, and using comparative material from the legal realm in Mesopotamia, asks whether or not the audience at the time of the texts' creation would have recognized the legal allusions. His negative answer would not please classic form critics, but his approach to the problem would certainly be recognizable to them. He is talking about literary forms and allusions in a particular setting, which is a very form-critical enterprise, although the setting with which he deals is the matrix of the reception of the text and not the matrix of its hypothetical point of origin.[21] Tiemeyer's careful study also investigates a traditional form-critical issue by analyzing the use of vision reports in Amos and Zechariah to see whether or not the latter depends on the former, thus blending an interest in a traditional literary form with the question of resonance within the Book of the Twelve. Her negative conclusions are a useful reminder of the complexity of the editorial history of the Twelve.

Other essays do not explore literary structure as much as they pay attention to contents, themes, and motifs. In this category would be Beth M. Stovell's literary study of textual allusions in the Book of the Twelve. In this essay ancient Near Eastern comparative material is not used, but there is heavy use of contemporary literary studies of metaphor to better understand the biblical text. Carol J. Dempsey too studies content and analyzes the language of weal and woe in the Book of the Twelve, a major departure from the classic form-critical

---

[19] The last question is prompted by the discussion of the variations in the exemplars of the Twelve in Sweeney's essay in this volume, pp. 137–61.
[20] See above, Michael H. Floyd, pp. 21–31.
[21] See above James M. Trotter, pp. 63–74.

tendency to remove salvation oracles as a later addition. Marvin A. Sweeney studies eschatological motifs in the Twelve, although his essay is well aware of structural issues. D. C. Timmer examines the way that literary units in Zephaniah relate to each other.

In addition to focusing their studies on the prophetic texts as they stand, some of the contributors to this volume seem to be uncomfortable with the tendency of new form critics to ignore the presumed oral roots of the prophetic books and with their denial that the prophetic books have a recoverable literary history. The authors in this volume handle these concerns in different ways. Floyd calls attention to the danger of losing sight of an original prophet and maintains that the prophetic books have a prehistory, even though it may not be recoverable.[22] More often, the authors pass over the issue of oral origins and contextualize the prophetic literature in the assumed period of its creation. Trotter takes this approach, as does Colin M. Toffelmire, who suggests the use of Systemic Functional Linguistics to study the setting of Obadiah.[23]

A somewhat different approach is taken by James B. Nogalski and Mark J. Boda. Nogalski recognizes the relatively late date of the Book of the Twelve in its present form, but he argues that the figure of the prophet has been eliminated in these books, thus in effect dehistoricizing and decontextualizing the literature. This would seem to make the setting less important than a classic form critic would suppose, but it is important to note that most of the books included in the Twelve still include historical references. Boda also points to the fact that the Book of the Twelve lacks the references to human addresses to God that one might expect. This situation too might be understood as both a dehistoricizing editorial move and an effort to make the Twelve reflect issues appropriate to the time of the collection's compilation.[24]

Finally, Tim Bulkeley recognizes the existence of historiographic material in the prophets, but he claims that such references are fictional. This is certainly a plausible argument, and such fictional accounts probably exist in prophetic books not included in the Twelve. However, to admit the existence of fictional material leaves unanswered the question of whether or not actual prophets were associated with the Book of the Twelve. The likelihood of fictional biographical material and the occasional absence of specific references to prophets in the Book of the Twelve are also accurately noted by Erhard S. Gerstenberger and Paul L. Redditt. Both of these authors do, however, reconstruct a history of the development of prophetic literature contained in this larger collection. Both thus in a sense restore the notion of history to the prophetic material now contained in the Book of the Twelve, even though their account differs greatly from that supplied by earlier form critics.

---

[22] See above Floyd, pp. 17–21.
[23] See above Trotter, pp. 64–65.
[24] In contrast to Boda's position, note Erhard S. Gerstenberger's claim above, p. 119–36.

It appears, then, that the authors that are represented in this volume exhibit the major characteristics of the new form criticism, but many of them are also aware of the problems that the new approach raises, and some of the essays attempt to address these problems, at least obliquely. However, the fact remains that additional research still needs to be done on some of the issues highlighted earlier in this essay. In particular, the issues surrounding exilic and postexilic scribal activity need to be explored to determine the settings in which Israel's scribes worked, the methods that they used, and the interests that caused them to write as they did. The authors in this volume touch on these issues and are certainly are aware of them, but many questions still need to be answered before the field can advance.

BIBLIOGRAPHY

Abma, Richtsje. *Bonds of Love: Methodic Studies of Prophetic Texts with Marriage Imagery, Isaiah 50:1–3 and 54:1–10, Hosea 1–3, Jeremiah 2–3*. SSN 40. Assen: Van Gorcum, 1999.

Achtemeier, Elizabeth. *Preaching from the Minor Prophets: Texts and Sermon Suggestions*. Grand Rapids: Eerdmans, 1998.

Ackroyd, Peter. "Isaiah I–XII: Presentation of a Prophet." Pages 16–48 in *Congress Volume Göttingen 1977*. VTSup 29. Leiden: Brill, 1978.

Albertz, Rainer, James D. Nogalski, and Jakob Wöhrle, eds. *Perspectives on the Formation of the Book of the Twelve: Methodological Foundations—Redactional Processes—Historical Insights*. BZAW 433. Berlin: de Gruyter, 2012.

Allen, Leslie C. *The Books of Joel, Obadiah, Jonah and Micah*. NICOT. Grand Rapids: Eerdmans, 1976.

Alter, Robert. *The Art of Biblical Narrative*. New York: Basic Books, 1983.

Anderson, Francis I., and David Noel Freedman. *Amos: A New Translation with Introduction and Commentary*. AB 24A. New York: Doubleday, 1989.

———. *Hosea: A New Translation with Introduction and Commentary*. AB 24. New York: Doubleday, 1980.

———. *Micah: A New Translation with Introduction and Commentary*. AB 24E. New York: Doubleday, 2000.

Anderson Jr., R. W. "Zephaniah ben Cushi and Cush of Benjamin: Traces of Cushite Presence in Syria-Palestine." Pages 45–70 in *The Pitcher is Broken: Memorial Essays for Gösta W. Ahlstrom*. Edited by Steven W. Holloway and Lowell K. Handy. JSOTSup 190. Sheffield: Sheffield Academic, 1995.

Anderson, John E. *"Awaiting an Answered Prayer: The Development and Reinterpretation of Habakkuk 3 in Its Contexts." ZAW* 123 (2011): 57–71.

Apóstolo, Silvio S. "On the Elusiveness and Malleability of 'Israel.'" *JHebS* 6 (2006): article 7.

Assis, Elie. *The Book of Joel: A Prophet between Calamity and Hope*. LHBOTS 581. New York: Bloomsbury, 2013.

———. "Why Edom? On the Hostility Towards Jacob's Brother in Prophetic Sources." *VT* 56 (2006): 1–20.

Auld, A. Graeme. *Amos*. OTG. Sheffield: JSOT Press, 1986.

———. "Prophets through the Looking Glass: Between Writings and Moses." *JSOT* 27 (1983): 27–42.

Bakhtin, M. M. *Speech Genres and Other Late Essays*. First edition. Edited by Michael Holquist. Translated by Michael Holquist and Caryl Emerson. University of Texas Press Slavic Series 8. Austin: University of Texas Press, 1986.

Balogh, Casbah. "Isaiah's Prophetic Instruction and the Disciples in Isaiah 8:16." *VT* 63 (2013): 1–18.
Baltzer, Klaus. *Die Biographie der Propheten*. Neukirchen-Vluyn: Neukirchener Verlag, 1975.
Barr, James. *The Semantics of Biblical Language*. Oxford: Oxford University Press, 1961.
Barstadt, Hans M. "What Prophets Do: Reflections on Past Reality in the Book of Jeremiah." Pages 10–32 in *Prophecy in the Book of Jeremiah*. Edited by Hans M. Barstadt and Reinhard G. Katz. Berlin: de Gruyter, 2009.
Barthélemy, Domenique. *Critique textuelle de l'Ancien Testament*. OBO 50.1–4. Göttingen: Vandenhoeck & Ruprecht, 1982–2005.
Barton, John. *Joel and Obadiah: A Commentary*. OTL. Louisville: Westminster John Knox, 2001.
———. *Reading the Old Testament*. Philadelphia: Westminster, 1984.
———. *The Theology of the Book of Amos*. OTT. New York: Cambridge University Press, 2012.
Bauks, Michaela, and Klaus Koenen, eds. "Das wissenschaftliche Bibellexikon im Internet (WiBiLex)." www.bibelwissenschaft.de/wibilex/.
Baumann, Gerline. *Love and Violence: Marriage as Metaphor for the Relationship between YHWH and Israel in the Prophetic Books*. Collegeville, MN: Liturgical Press, 2003.
Beck, John A. *God as Storyteller: Seeking Meaning in Biblical Narrative*. St. Louis: Chalice, 2008.
Beck, Martin. "Das Tag YHWHs-Verständnis von Zephanja iii." *VT* 58 (2008): 159–77.
Becking, Bob. "Nehemiah 9 and the Problematic Concept of Context (*Sitz im Leben*)." Pages 253–68 in *Changing Face of Form Criticism for the Twenty-First Century*. Edited by Marvin A. Sweeney and Ehud Ben Zvi. Grand Rapids: Eerdmans, 2003.
———. *Studies in Theology and Religion 5*. Assen: Van Gorcum, 2003.
Becker, E.-M. "Was ist 'Kohärenz'? Ein Beitrag zur Präzisierung eines exegetischen Leitkriteriums." *ZNW* 94 (2003): 97–121.
Behrens, Achim. *Prophetische Visionsschilderungen im Alten Testament: sprachliche Eigenarten, Funktion und Geschichte einer Gattung*. AOAT 292. Münster: Ugarit-Verlag, 2002.
Belknap, Robert E. *The List: The Uses and Pleasures of Cataloguing*. New Haven: Yale University Press, 2004.
Ben Zvi, Ehud. "The Concept of Prophetic Books and Its Historical Setting." Pages 73–95 in *The Production of Prophecy: Constructing Prophecy and Prophets in Yehud*. Edited by Diana V. Edelman and Ehud Ben Zvi. London: Equinox, 2009.
———. *A Historical-Critical Study of the Book of Obadiah*. BZAW 242. Berlin: de Gruyter, 1996.
———. *A Historical-Critical Study of the Book of Zephaniah*. BZAW 198. Berlin: de Gruyter, 1991.
———. *Hosea*. FOTL 21A. Grand Rapids: Eerdmans, 2005.
———. "Inclusion in and Exclusion from Israel as Conveyed by the Use of the Term 'Israel' in Post-Monarchic Biblical Texts." Pages 95–149 in *The Pitcher is Broken: Memorial Essays for Gösta W. Ahlström*. Edited by Steven W. Holloway and Lowell K. Handy. JSOTSup 190. Sheffield: Sheffield Academic, 1995.
———. "Introduction: Writings, Speeches, and the Prophetic Books: Setting an Agenda." Pages 1–29 in *Writings and Speech in Israelite and Ancient near Eastern Prophecy*. Edited by Ehud Ben Zvi and Michael H. Floyd. SymS 10. Atlanta: Society of Biblical Literature, 2000.

———. "Is the Twelve Hypothesis Likely from an Ancient Readers' Perspective?" Pages 53–90 in *Two Sides of A Coin: Juxtaposing Views on Interpreting the Book of the Twelve/The Twelve Prophetic Books*. Edited by Ehud Ben Zvi and James D. Nogalski. Analecta Gorgiana 201. Piscataway, NJ: Gorgias, 2009.

———. *Micah*. FOTL 21B. Grand Rapids: Eerdmans, 2000.

———. "Micah 1:2–16: Observations and Possible Implications." *JSOT* 77 (1998): 103–20.

———. "The Prophetic Book: A Key Form of Prophetic Literature." Pages 276–97 in *The Changing Face of Form Criticism for the Twenty-First Century*. Edited by Marvin A. Sweeney and Ehud Ben Zvi. Grand Rapids: Eerdmans, 2003.

———. "Reconstructing the Intellectual Discourse of Ancient Yehud." *SR* 39 (2010): 7–23.

———. *The Signs of Jonah: Reading and Rereading in Ancient Yehud*. JSOTSup 367. Sheffield: Sheffield Academic, 2003.

———. "Twelve Prophetic Books or 'the Twelve': A Few Preliminary Considerations." Pages 125–56 in *Forming Prophetic Literature: Essays on Isaiah and the Twelve in Honor of J. D. W. Watts*. Edited by James W. Watts and Paul R. House. JSOTSup 235. Sheffield: Sheffield Academic, 1996.

———. "Understanding the Message of the Tripartite Prophetic Books." *ResQ* 35 (1993): 93–100.

Ben Zvi, Ehud, and Michael H. Floyd, eds. *Writings and Speech in Israelite and Ancient Near Eastern Prophecy*. SymS 10. Atlanta: Society of Biblical Literature, 2000.

Ben Zvi, Ehud, and James D. Nogalski. *Two Sides of a Coin: Juxtaposing Views on Interpreting the Book of the Twelve/The Twelve Prophetic Books*. Analecta Gorgiana 201. Piscataway, NJ: Gorgias, 2009.

Berger, Klaus. "Rhetorical Criticism, New Form Criticism, and New Testament Hermeneutics." Pages 390–96 in *Rhetoric and the New Testament: Essays from the 1992 Heidelberg Conference*. Edited by Stanley E. Porter and Thomas H. Olbricht. JSNTSup 90. Sheffield: Sheffield Academic, 1993.

Bergler, Siegfried. "'Auf der Mauer—auf dem Altar': Noch einmal die Visionen des Amos." *VT* 50 (2000): 445–71.

Bergmann, Claudia D. *Childbirth as a Metaphor for Crisis: Evidence from the Ancient Near East, the Hebrew Bible, and 1QH XI, 1–18*. BZAW 382. Berlin: de Gruyter, 2008.

Berlin, Adele. *Poetics and Interpretation of Biblical Narrative*. Winona Lake, IN: Eisenbrauns, 1994.

———. *Zephaniah*. AB 25. New Haven: Yale University, 2007.

———. "Zephaniah's Oracles against the Nations and an Israelite Cultural Myth." Pages 175–84 in *Fortunate the Eyes That See: Essays in Honor of David Noel Freedman*. Edited by Astrid B. Beck et al. Grand Rapids: Eerdmans, 1995.

Berman, Joshua A. "A Response: Three Points of Methodology." *JHebS* 10 (2010): article 9, 42–49.

Biddle, Mark E. "Obadiah–Jonah–Micah in Canonical Context: The Nature of Prophetic Literature and Hermeneutics." *Int* 61 (2007): 154–66.

Block, Daniel I. *Obadiah: The Kingship Belongs to YHWH*. Hearing the Message of Scripture 27. Grand Rapids: Zondervan, 2013.

Boda, Mark J. "Babylon in the Book of the Twelve." *HBAI* 3 (2014): 225–48.

———. "From Complaint to Contrition: Peering through the Liturgical Window of Jer 14, 1–15, 4." *ZAW* 113 (2001): 186–97.
———. *Haggai and Zechariah Research: A Bibliographical Survey, Tools for Biblical Study.* Leiden: DEO, 2003.
———. *Haggai, Zechariah.* NIVAC. Grand Rapids: Zondervan, 2004.
———. "Messengers of Hope in Haggai–Malachi." *JSOT* 32 (2007): 113–31.
———. "Penitential Innovations in the Book of the Twelve," Pages 291–308 in *On Stone and Scroll: A Festschrift for Graham Davies.* Edited by Brian A. Mastin, Katharine J. Dell, and James K. Aitken. BZAW 420. Berlin: de Gruyter, 2011.
———. *Praying the Tradition: The Origin and Use of Tradition in Nehemiah 9.* BZAW 277. Berlin: de Gruyter, 1999.
———. *A Severe Mercy: Sin and Its Remedy in the Old Testament,* Siphrut: Literature and Theology of the Hebrew Scriptures 1. Winona Lake, IN: Eisenbrauns, 2009.
———. "'Uttering Precious Rather Than Worthless Words': Divine Patience and Impatience with Lament in Isaiah and Jeremiah." Pages 83–89 in *Why? How Long? Studies on Voice(s) of Lamentation Rooted in Biblical Hebrew Poetry.* Edited by LeAnn Snow Flesher, Carol Dempsey, and Mark J. Boda. LHBOTS 552. London: Continuum, 2014.
———. "'Varied and Resplendent Riches': Exploring the Breadth and Depth of Worship in the Psalter." Pages 61–82 in *Rediscovering Worship: Past, Present, Future.* Edited by Wendy Porter. McMaster New Testament Series. Eugene, OR: Wipf & Stock, 2015.
———. "When God's Voice Breaks Through: Shifts in Revelatory Rhetoric in Zechariah 1–8." In *History, Memory, Hebrew Scriptures: A Festschrift for Ehud Ben Zvi.* Edited by Ian Douglas Wilson and Diana V. Edelman. Winona Lake, IN: Eisenbrauns, 2015.
———. "Writing the Vision: Zechariah within the Visionary Traditions of the Hebrew Bible." Pages 101–18 in *'I Lifted My Eyes and Saw': Reading Dream and Vision Reports in the Hebrew Bible.* Edited by Elizabeth R. Hayes and Lena-Sofia Tiemeyer. LHBOTS 584. London: T&T Clark, 2014.
———. "Zechariah: Master Mason or Penitential Prophet?" Pages 49–69 in *Yahwism after the Exile: Perspectives on Israelite Religion in the Persian Era.* Edited by Bob Becking and Rainer Albertz. Studies in Theology and Religion 5. Assen: van Gorcum, 2003.
Boda, Mark J., Carol Dempsey, and LeAnn Snow Flesher, eds. *Daughter Zion: Her Portrait, Her Response.* AIL 13. Atlanta: Society of Biblical Literature, 2012.
Boer, Roland. *Bakhtin and Genre Theory in Biblical Studies.* SemeiaSt 63. Atlanta: Society of Biblical Literature, 2007.
Bos, James M. *Reconsidering the Date and Provenance of the Book of Hosea: The Case for Persian-Period Yehud.* LHBOTS 580. London: Bloomsbury, 2013.
Botterweck, G. Johannes, and Helmer Ringgren, eds. *Theological Dictionary of the Old Testament.* Translated by John T. Willis, et al. 15 vols. Grand Rapids: Eerdmans, 1974–2006.
Brett, Mark. "Reading the Bible in the Context of Methodological Pluralism: The Undermining of Ethnic Exclusivism in Genesis." Pages 48–74 in *Rethinking Contexts, Rereading Texts.* Edited by M. Daniel Carroll R. Sheffield: Sheffield Academic, 2000.
Bruckner, James K. *Implied Law in the Abraham Narrative: A Literary and Theological Analysis.* LHBOTS 335. Sheffield: Sheffield Academic, 2001.
Budde, Karl. "Eine folgenschwere Redaktion des Zwölfprophetenbuch." *ZAW* 39 (1921): 218–29.

———. "Micha 2 und 3." *ZAW* 38 (1920): 2–22.
Bulkeley, Tim. "Amos 7,1–8,3: Cohesion and Generic Dissonance." *ZAW* 121 (2009): 515–28.
———. "Cohesion, Rhetorical Purpose and the Poetics of Coherence in Amos 3." *ABR* 47 (1999): 16–28.
———. "L'auteur Est Mort, But Won't Lie Down: Inventing Authors While Reading Amos." *Colloq* 43:1 (2013): 59–70.
———. "The Long and the Short of It: Two Recent Commentaries on the Book of Amos." *JSOT* 16 (1991): 119–21.
Buss, Martin J. *The Changing Shape of Form Criticism: A Relational Approach.* Edited by Nickie M. Stipe. HBM 10. Sheffield: Sheffield Phoenix, 2010.
———. "Form Criticism: An Introduction." Pages 97–113 in *The Changing Shape of Form Criticism: A Relational Approach.* Sheffield: Sheffield Phoenix, 2010.
———. "The Idea of *Sitz im Leben.*" Pages 33–38 in *The Changing Shape of Form Criticism: A Relational Approach.* HBM 18. Sheffield: Sheffield Phoenix, 2010.
———. *The Prophetic Word of Hosea: A Morphological Study.* Berlin: de Gruyter, 1969.
———. *Toward Understanding the Hebrew Canon: A Form-Critical Approach.* Sheffield: Sheffield Phoenix, 2013.
Bussmann, Hadumod. *Routledge Dictionary of Language and Linguistics.* Translated by Gregory P. Trauth and Kerstin Kazzazi. London: Routledge, 1996.
Campbell, Antony F. "Form Criticism's Future." Pages 15–31 in *The Changing Face of Form Criticism for the Twenty-First Century.* Edited by Marvin A. Sweeney and Ehud Ben Zvi. Grand Rapids: Eerdmans, 2003.
Carr, David M. *The Formation of the Hebrew Bible: A New Reconstruction.* Oxford: Oxford University Press, 2011.
———. *Writing on the Tablet of the Heart: Origins of Scripture and Literature.* New York: Oxford University Press, 2005.
Carroll R., M. Daniel. *Amos—The Prophet and His Oracles: Research on the Book of Amos.* Louisville: Westminster John Knox, 2002.
Carroll, Robert P. "Inventing the Prophets." *IBS* 10 (1988): 24–36.
———. "Poets Not Prophets: A Response to 'Prophets through the Looking Glass'." Pages 43–49 in *The Prophets: A Sheffield Reader.* Edited by Philip R. Davies. Sheffield: Sheffield Academic, 1996.
———. "Prophecy and Society." Pages 203–25 in *The World of Ancient Israel: Social, Anthropological and Political Perspectives.* Edited by R. E. Clements. Cambridge: Cambridge University Press, 1989.
———. "Whose Prophet, Whose History? Troubling the Interpretive Community Again: Notes to a Response to T. W. Overholt's Critique." *JSOT* 48 (1990): 33–49.
Carter, Charles E. *The Emergence of Yehud in the Persian Period: A Social and Demographic Study.* JSOTSup 294. Sheffield: Sheffield Academic, 1999.
Carver, Terrell, and Jernej Pikalo. *Political Language and Metaphor: Interpreting and Changing the World.* Routledge Innovations in Political Theory. New York: Routledge, 2008.
Charteris-Black, J. *Corpus Approaches to Critical Metaphor Analysis.* New York: Palgrave Macmillan, 2004.
Childs, Brevard S. *Introduction to the Old Testament as Scripture.* Philadelphia: Fortress, 1979.

Christensen, Duane L. "The Book of Nahum: A History of Interpretation." Pages 192–94 in *Forming Prophetic Literature*. Edited by James W. Watts and Paul R. House. JSOTSup 235. Sheffield: Sheffield Academic, 1996.

———. *Nahum*. AB 24F. New Haven: Yale University Press, 2009.

Clark, David J., and Howard A. Hatton. *A Handbook on Haggai, Zechariah, and Malachi*. New York: United Bible Societies, 2002.

Clements, Ronald E. "Amos and the Politics of Israel." Pages 23–34 in *Old Testament Prophecy: From Oracles to Canon*. Louisville: Westminster John Knox, 1996.

———. "Prophecy as Literature: A Reappraisal." In *Old Testament Prophecy: From Oracles to Canon*. Louisville: Westminster John Knox, 1996.

Clendenen, E. Ray. *Haggai, Malachi*. NAC 21a. Nashville: Broadman & Holman, 2004.

Clifford, Richard J. "The Use of Hoy in the Prophets." *CBQ* 28 (1966): 458–64.

Clines, David J. A., and Philip R. Davies, eds. *Among the Prophets: Language, Image, and Structure in the Prophetic Writings*. JSOTSup144. Sheffield: Sheffield Academic, 1993.

Cloran, Carmel. "Context, Material Situation and Text." Pages 177–218 in *Text and Context in Functional Linguistics*. Edited by Mohsen Ghadessy. Amsterdam: John Benjamins, 1999.

Cogan, Michael D. "Sennacherib's Siege of Jerusalem." *COS 2.119B*: 302–3.

Coggins, Richard J. *Joel and Amos*. NCB. Sheffield: Sheffield Academic, 2000.

Collins, Terence. *The Mantle of Elijah: The Redaction Criticism of the Prophetical Books*. BibSem. Sheffield: Sheffield Academic, 1993.

Conrad, Edgar. *Zechariah*. RNBC. Sheffield: Sheffield Academic, 1999.

Cook, John A. *Time and the Biblical Hebrew Verb: The Expression of Tense, Aspect, and Modality in Biblical Hebrew*. LSAWS 7. Winona Lake, IN: Eisenbrauns, 2012.

Crenshaw, James L. *Hymnic Affirmation of Divine Justice: The Doxologies of Amos and Related Texts in the Old Testament*. SBLDS 24. Missoula, MT: Scholars Press, 1975.

———. *Joel*. AB 24C. New York: Doubleday, 1995.

———. *Prophetic Conflict: Its Effect Upon Israelite Religion*. Berlin: de Gruyter, 1971.

———. "Transmitting Prophecy across Generations." Pages 31–44 in *Writings and Speech in Israelite and Ancient Near Eastern Prophecy*. Edited by Ehud Ben Zvi and Michael H. Floyd. SymS 10. Atlanta: Society of Biblical Literature, 2000.

Curtis, Byron G. *Up the Steep and Stony Road: The Book of Zechariah in Social Location Trajectory Analysis*. AcBib 25. Leiden: Brill, 2006.

Dandamaev, M. A. "Achaemenid Mesopotamia: Traditions and Innovations." Pages 229–34 in *Continuity and Change*. Edited by Heleen Sancisi-Weerdenburg, Amelie Kuhrt, and Margaret Cool Root. Vol. 8 of *Achaemenid History*. Leiden: Nederlands Instituut voor het Nabije Oosten, 1994.

Dandamaev, M. A., Vladimir G. Lukonin, and Philip L. Kohl. *The Culture and Social Institutions of Ancient Iran*. Cambridge: Cambridge University Press, 1989.

Daniels, Dwight R. "Is there a "Prophetic Lawsuit" Genre." *ZAW* 99 (1987): 339–60.

Darr, Katheryn Pfisterer. "Like Warrior, Like Woman: Destruction and Deliverance in Isaiah 42:10–17." *CBQ* 49 (1987): 560–71.

Davies, Graham I. *Hosea*. OTG. Sheffield: Sheffield Academic, 1993.

———. *Hosea*. NCB. Grand Rapids: Eerdmans, 1992.

———. "New Solution to a Crux in Obadiah 7." *VT* 27 (1977): 484–87.

Davies, Philip R. "The Audiences of Prophetic Scrolls: Some Suggestions." Pages 48–62 in *Prophets and Paradigms: Essays in Honor of Gene M. Tucker*. Edited by Stephen Breck Reid. JSOTSup 229. Sheffield: Sheffield Academic, 1996.

———. "'Pen of Iron, Point of Diamond' [Jer 17:1]: Prophecy as Writing." Pages 65–81 in *Writings and Speech in Israelite and Ancient Near Eastern Prophecy*. Edited by Ehud Ben Zvi and Michael H. Floyd. SymS 10. Atlanta: Society of Biblical Literature, 2000.

———. "Why Do We Know about Amos?" Pages 55–72 in *The Production of Prophecy: Constructing Prophecy and Prophets in Yehud*. Edited by Diana V. Edelman and Ehud Ben Zvi. London: Equinox, 2009.

Davis, Ellen F. *Swallowing the Scroll: Textuality and the Dynamics of Discourse in Ezekiel's Prophecy*. BLS 21. Sheffield: Almond Press, 1989.

Dearman, J. Andrew. "My Servants the Scribes: Composition and Context in Jeremiah 36." *JBL* 109 (1990): 403–21.

———. *The Book of Hosea*. NICOT. Grand Rapids: Eerdmans, 2010.

Deist, Ferdinand E. "The Prophets. Are We Heading for a Paradigm Switch?" Pages 1–18 in *Prophet und Prophetenbuch: Festschrift für Otto Kaiser zum 65. Geburtstag*. Edited by Volkmar Fritz, Karl-Friedrich Pohlmann, and Hans-Christoph Schmitt. BZAW 185. Berlin: de Gruyter, 1989.

Delkurt, Holger. *Sacharjas Nachtgesichte: zur Aufnahme und Abwandlung prophetischer Traditionen*. BZAW 302. Berlin: de Gruyter, 2000.

Démare-Lafont, Sophie. "Judicial Decision-Making: Judges and Arbitrators." Pages 335–57 in *The Oxford Handbook of Cuneiform Culture*. Edited by Karen Radner and Eleanor Robson. Oxford: Oxford University Press, 2011.

De Roche, Michael. "Yahweh's Rîb against Israel: A Reassessment of the So-Called 'Prophetic Lawsuit' in the Preexilic Prophets." *JBL* 102 (1983): 563–74.

De Vries, Simon J. *From Old Revelation to New: A Tradition-Historical and Redaction-Critical Study of Temporal Transitions*. Grand Rapids: Eerdmans, 1995.

Dijk, Teun A. van. *Discourse and Context: A Socio-Cognitive Approach*. Cambridge: Cambridge University Press, 2008.

Donald, David Herbert. *Lincoln*. New York: Simon & Schuster, 1995.

Eco, Umberto. *The Infinity of Lists*. Translated by Alastair McEwen. New York: Rizzoli, 2009.

Elliger, Karl. *Das Buch der zwölf kleinen Propheten*. ATD 25. Göttingen: Vandenhoeck & Ruprecht, 1982.

Endo, Yoshinobu. *The Verbal System of Classical Hebrew in the Joseph Story: An Approach from Discourse Analysis*. SSN 32. Assen: van Gorcum, 1996.

Fales, Frederick M. *Guerre et paix en Assyrie: religion et impérialisme*. Les Conférences de l'École Pratique des Hautes Études. Paris: Cerf, 2010.

Fauconnier, Gilles, and Mark Turner. "Rethinking Metaphor." Pages 53–66 in *The Cambridge Handbook of Metaphor and Thought*. Edited by Raymond W. Gibbs. New York: Cambridge University Press, 2008.

———. *The Way We Think: Conceptual Blending and the Mind's Hidden Complexities*. New York: Basic Books, 2002.

Fensham, F. Charles. "The Marriage Metaphor in Hosea for the Covenant Relationship between the Lord and His People (Hos 1:2–9)." *JNSL* 12 (1984): 71–78.

Figulla, H. H. "Lawsuit concerning a Sacrilegious Theft at Erech." *Iraq* 13 (1951): 95–101.

Finitsis, Antonios. *Visions and Eschatology: A Socio-Historical Analysis of Zechariah 1–6.* LSTS 79. London: T&T Clark, 2011.

Fishbane, Michael. *Haftarot.* JPS Bible Commentary. Philadelphia: Jewish Publication Society, 2002.

Floyd, Michael H. "Basic Trends in the Form-Critical Study of Prophetic Texts." Pages 298–311 in *The Changing Face of Form Criticism for the Twenty-First Century.* Edited by Marvin A. Sweeney and Ehud Ben Zvi. Grand Rapids: Eerdmans, 2003.

———. "The *Maśśā'* as a Type of Prophetic Book." *JBL* 121 (2002): 401–22.

———. *Minor Prophets: Part 2.* FOTL 22. Grand Rapids: Eerdmans, 2000.

———. "The Production of Prophetic Books in the Early Second Temple Period." Pages 276–297 in *Prophets, Prophecy and Prophetic Texts in Second Temple Judaism.* Edited by Michael H. Floyd and Robert D. Haak. LHBOTS 427. New York: T&T Clark, 2006.

———. "Prophecy and Writing in Habakkuk 2,1–5." *ZAW* 105 (1993): 462–81.

———. "Was Prophetic Hope Born of Disappointment? The Case of Zechariah." In *Utopia and Dystopia in Prophetic Literature.* Publications of the Finnish Exegetical Society 92. Edited by Ehud Ben Zvi. Göttingen: Vandenhoeck & Ruprecht, 2006.

———. "'Write the Revelation!' (Hab 2:2): Re-Imagining the Cultural History of Prophecy." Pages 103–43 in *Writings and Speech in Israelite and Ancient Near Eastern Prophecy.* Edited by Ehud Ben Zvi and Michael H. Floyd. SymS 10. Atlanta: Society of Biblical Literature, 2000.

———. "Zechariah and Changing Views of Second Temple Judaism in Recent Commentaries." *RSR* 25 (1999): 257–63.

Fokkelman, Jan. *Reading Biblical Narrative: An Introduction Guide.* Louisville: Westminster John Knox, 1999.

Garrett, Duane A. *Hosea, Joel.* NAC. Nashville: Broadman & Holman, 1997.

Gärtner, Judith. "Jerusalem—City of God for Israel and for the Nations in Zeph 3:8, 9–10, 11–13." Pages 269–283 in *Perspectives on the Formation of the Book of the Twelve. Methodological Foundations—Redactional Processes—Historical Insights.* Edited by Rainer Albertz, James A. Nogalski, and Jakob Wöhrle. BZAW 433. Berlin: de Gruyter, 2012.

Gelston, Anthony. *The Twelve Minor Prophets.* BHQ 13. Stuttgart: Deutsche Bibelgesellschaft, 2010.

Gerstenberger, Erhard S. "Der Hymnus der Befreiung im Zefanjabuch." Pages 102–12 in *Der Tag wird kommen: Ein interkontextuelles Gespräch über das Buch des Propheten Zefanja.* Edited by Walter Dietrich and Milton Schwantes. SBS 170. Stuttgart: Katholisches Bibelwerk, 1996.

———. *Israel in der Perserzeit: 5. und 4. Jahrhundert v. Chr.* Biblische Enzyklopädie 8. Stuttgart: Kohlhammer, 2005.

———. "Persian-Empire Spirituality and the Genesis of Prophetic Books" Pages 111–30 in *The Production of Prophecy: Constructing Prophecy and Prophets in Yehud.* Edited by Diana V. Edelman and Ehud Ben Zvi. Bible World. London: Equinox, 2009.

———. "Praise in the Realm of Death: The Dynamics of Hymn-Singing in Ancient Near Eastern Lament Ceremony." Pages 115–24 in *Lamentations in Ancient and Contemporary Cultural Contexts.* Edited by Nancy C. Lee and Carleen Mandolfo. SymS 43. Atlanta: Society of Biblical Literature, 2008.

———. "Psalms in the Book of the Twelve: How Misplaced Are They?" Pages 72–89 in *Thematic Threads in the Book of the Twelve*. Edited by Paul L. Reddit and Aaron Schart. BZAW 325. Berlin: de Gruyter, 2003.

———. "The Woe-Oracles of the Prophets." *JBL* 81 (1962): 249–63.

Gese, Hartmut. "Komposition bei Amos." Pages 74–95 in *Congress Volume Vienna 1980*. Edited by John A. Emerton. VTSup 32. Leiden, Brill, 1981.

Gibbs, Raymond W. "Taking Metaphor Out of Our Heads and Putting It into the Cultural World." Pages 145–66 in *Metaphor in Cognitive Linguistics*. Edited by Raymond W. Gibbs and Gerard Steen. Current Issues in Linguistic Theory 4. Philadelphia: John Benjamins, 1999.

Gitay, Yehoshua. "A Study of Amos's Art of Speech: A Rhetorical Analysis of Amos 3:1–15." *CBQ* 42 (1980): 293–309.

Glazier-McDonald, Beth. *Malachi, the Divine Messenger*. SBLDS 98. Atlanta: Scholars Press, 1987.

Goody, Jack. *The Domestication of the Savage Mind*. Cambridge: Cambridge University Press, 1977.

Gordon, R. P. "A Story of Two Paradigm Shifts." Pages 3–26 in *"This Place is Too Small for Us": The Israelite Prophets in Recent Scholarship*. Edited by R. P. Gordon. Winona Lake, IN: Eisenbrauns, 1995.

Green, Barbara. *Mikhail Bakhtin and Biblical Scholarship: An Introduction*. SemeiaSt 38. Atlanta: Society of Biblical Literature, 2000.

Grimal, Nicolas. *A History of Ancient Egypt*. Translated by I. Shaw. Oxford: Blackwell, 1992.

Gunkel, Hermann. *The Legends of Genesis*. Translated by W. H. Carruth. Chicago: Open Court Publishing, 1901.

———. "The Prophets as Writers and Poets." Pages 22–73 in *Prophecy in Israel*. Edited by David. L. Peterson. Philadelphia: Fortress, 1987.

Gunn, David M., and Danna Nolan Fewell. *Narrative in the Hebrew Bible*. Oxford Bible. New York: Oxford University Press, 1993.

Haak, Robert D. *Habakkuk*. VTSup 44. Leiden: Brill, 1992.

Hadjiev, Tchavdar. *The Composition and Redaction of the Book of Amos*. BZAW 393. Berlin: de Gruyter, 2009.

———. "Survival, Conversion and Restoration: Reflections on the Redaction History of the Book of Zephaniah." *VT* 61 (2011): 570–81.

———. "Zephaniah and the 'Book of the Twelve' Hypothesis." Pages 325–38 in *Prophecy and Prophets in Ancient Israel: Proceedings of the Oxford Old Testament Seminar*. Edited by John Day. LHBOTS 531. New York: T&T Clark, 2010.

Hall, Gary Harlan. *Deuteronomy*. College Press NIV Commentary. Joplin, MO: College Press, 2000.

Halliday M. A. K. *Explorations in the Functions of Language*. London: Edward Arnold, 1973.

———. *An Introduction to Functional Grammar*. 2nd Edition. New York: Edward Arnold, 1985.

———. *Language as Social Semiotic: The Social Interpretation of Language and Meaning*. Baltimore: University Park Press, 1978.

Halliday, M. A. K., and Ruqaiya Hasan. *Cohesion in English*. London: Longman, 1976.

———. *Language, Context, and Text: Aspects of Language in a Social-Semiotic Perspective*. Geelong, Australia: Deakin University Press, 1985.

———. "Text and Context: Aspects of Language in a Social-Semiotic Perspective." *Sophia Linguistica* 6 (1980): 4–91.

Hanson, Paul D. *The Dawn of Apocalyptic*. Philadelphia: Fortress, 1975.

Harrelson, Walter. "The Celebration of the Feast of Booths according to Zechariah xiv 16–21." Pages 88–96 in *Religions in Antiquity: Essays in Memory of Erwin Ramsdell Goodenough*. Edited by Jacob Neusner. Supplements to Numen XIV. Leiden: Brill, 1968.

Harrington, Daniel, J., S.J. *Interpreting the Old Testament: A Practical Guide*. OTM 1. Wilmington: Michael Glazier, 1981.

Harvey, Julien. "Le 'Rîb-Pattern,' réquisitoire prophétique sur la rupture de l'alliance." *Bib* 43 (1962): 172–96.

Hasan, Ruqaiya. "The Place of Context in a Systemic Functional Model." Pages 166–89 in *Continuum Companion to Systemic Functional Linguistics*. Edited by M. A. K. Halliday and Jonathan J. Webster. London: Continuum, 2009.

———. "Speaking with Reference to Context." Pages 219–328 in *Text and Context in Functional Linguistics*. Edited by Mohsen Ghadessy. Amsterdam: John Benjamins, 1999.

———. "Wherefore Context? The Place of Context in the System and Process of Language." Pages 1–21 in *Grammar and Discourse Proceedings of the International Conference on Discourse Analysis*. Edited by Shaozeng Ren et al. Macau: University of Macau, 2001.

Hayes, John H. *Amos the Eighth-Century Prophet: His Times and His Preaching*. Nashville: Abingdon, 1988.

Hess, Richard S. *Joshua*. TOTC. Downers Grove, IL: Inter-Varsity Press, 1996.

Heinzmann, G. "Formgeschichtliche Untersuchung der prophetischen Visionsberichte." PhD diss., University of Heidelberg, 1978.

Hiebert, Theodore. *God of My Victory: The Ancient Hymn in Habakkuk 3*. HSM 38. Atlanta: Scholars Press, 1986.

Hilgert, Markus. "Von 'Listenwissenschaft' und 'epistemischen Dingen': Konzeptuelle Annäherungen an altorientalische Wissenspraktiken." *Journal for General Philosophy of Science* 40 (2009): 277–309.

Hill, Andrew E. *Malachi*. AB 25D. New York: Doubleday, 1995.

Hillers, Delbert R. *Micah*. Hermeneia. Philadelphia: Fortress, 1984.

Ho Fai Tai, Nicholas. *Prophetie als Schriftauslegung in Sacharja 9–14*. Calwer Theologische Monographien 17. Stuttgart: Calwer, 1996.

Holladay, William L. *A Commentary on the Book of the Prophet Jeremiah: Chapters 1–25*. Vol. 1 of *Jeremiah*. Hermeneia. Philadelphia: Fortress, 1986.

———. "Reading Zephaniah with a Concordance: Suggestions for a Redaction History." *JBL* 120 (2001): 671–84.

Holloway, Steven W. *Assur is King! Assur is King! Religion in the Exercise of Power in the Neo-Assyrian Empire*. CHANE 10. Leiden: Brill, 2002.

Holmstedt, Robert D. "The Typological Classification of the Hebrew of Genesis: Subject-Verb or Verb-Subject?" *JHebS* 11 (2011): Article 14.

Holmstedt, Robert D., and Andrew R. Jones. "The Pronoun in Tripartite Verbless Clauses in Biblical Hebrew: Resumption for Left-Dislocation of Pronominal Copula?" *JSS* 59 (2014): 53–89.

Holtz, Shalom E. *Neo-Babylonian Court Procedure*. CM 38. Leiden. Boston: Brill, 2009.

Horst, Friedrich. "Die Doxologien im Amosbuch." *ZAW* 47 (1929): 45–54.
———. "Die Visionsschilderungen der alttestamentlichen Propheten." *EvT* 20 (1960): 193–205.
Hossfeld, F. L., and E.-M. Kindl. "להק." *TDOT* 13:113.
House, Paul R. *The Unity of the Twelve.* BLS 27. JSOTSup 97. Sheffield: Almond Press, 1990.
———. *Zephaniah: A Prophetic Drama.* BLS 16. JSOTSup 69. Sheffield: Almond Press, 1988.
Hubbard, David Allan. *Joel and Amos: An Introduction and Commentary.* TOTC. Downers Grove, IL: InterVarsity Press, 1989.
Huffmon, Herbert B. "The Covenant Lawsuit in the Prophets." *JBL* 78 (1959): 285–95.
Hugenberger, Gordon Paul. *Marriage as a Covenant: A Study of Biblical Law and Ethics Governing Marriage, Developed from the Perspective of Malachi.* VTSup 52. Leiden: Brill, 1993.
Irsigler, Hubert. *Zefanja.* HThKAT. Freiburg: Herder, 2002.
Jacobs, Mignon. *The Conceptual Coherence of the Book of Micah.* JSOTSup 322. Sheffield: Sheffield Academic, 2001.
Jacobsen, Rolf A. *Many Are Saying: The Function of Direct Discourse in the Hebrew Psalter.* London: T&T Clark, 2004.
Janzen, J. Gerald. "Metaphor and Reality in Hosea 11." *Semeia* 24 (1982): 7–44.
Janzen, W. *Mourning Cry and Woe Oracle.* BZAW 125. Berlin: de Gruyter, 1972.
Jas, Remko. *Neo-Assyrian Judicial Procedures.* Helsinki: The Neo-Assyrian Text Corpus Project, 1996.
Jemielity, Thomas. *Satire and the Hebrew Prophets.* LCBI. Louisville: Westminster John Knox, 1992.
Jenson, Philip Peter. *Obadiah, Jonah, Micah: A Theological Commentary.* LHBOTS 496. New York: T&T Clark, 2008.
Jeremias, Christian. *Die Nachtgesichte des Sacharja: Untersuchungen zu ihrer Stellung im Zusammenhang der Visionsberichte im Alten Testament und zu ihrem Bildmaterial.* FRLANT 117. Göttingen: Vandenhoeck & Ruprecht, 1977.
Jeremias, Jörg. *The Book of Amos: A Commentary.* Translated by Douglas W. Scott. OTL. Louisville: Westminster John Knox, 1998.
———. *Der Prophet Amos.* ATD 24.2. Göttingen: Vandenhoeck & Ruprecht, 1995.
———. *Kultprophetie und Gerichtsverkündigung in Der Späten Königszeit Israels.* Neukirchen-Vluyn: Neukirchener Verlag, 1970.
———. "Zur Theologie Obadjas: die Auslegung von Jer 49,7–16 durch Obadja." Pages 269–82 in *Die unwiderstehliche Wahrheit: Studien zur alttestamentlichen Prophetie.* Edited by Rüdiger Lux and Ernst-Joachim Waschke. Leipzig: Evangelische Verlagsanstalt, 2006.
Johnston, G. H. "Nahum's Rhetorical Allusions to the Neo-Assyrian Lion Motif." *BSac* 158 (2001): 287–307.
Jones, Barry Alan. *The Formation of the Book of the Twelve: A Study in Text and Canon.* SBLDS 149. Atlanta: Scholars Press, 1995.
Jursa, Michael. *Neo-Babylonian Legal and Administrative Documents: Typology, Contents and Archives.* GMTR 1. Münster: Ugarit-Verlag, 2005.
Kahn, Dan'el. "Judean Auxiliaries in Egypt's Wars against Kush." *JAOS* 127 (2007): 507–16.

Kakkanattu, Joy Philip. *God's Enduring Love in the Book of Hosea: A Synchronic and Diachronic Analysis of Hosea 11,1–11*. FAT 2/14. Tübingen: Mohr Siebeck, 2006.

Kapelrud, Arvid S. *The Message of the Prophet Zephaniah: Morphology and Ideas*. Oslo: Universitetsforlaget, 1975.

Kashow, Robert C. "Zechariah 1–8 as a Theological Explanation for the Failure of Prophecy in Haggai 2:20–23." *JTS* 64 (2013): 385–403.

Keefe, Alice A. *Woman's Body and the Social Body in Hosea 1–2*. Gender, Culture, Theory 10. JSOTSup 338. Sheffield: Sheffield Academic, 2001.

Kelle, Brad E. *Hosea 2: Metaphor and Rhetoric in Historical Perspective*. AcBib 20. Leiden: Brill, 2005.

Kessler, Rainer. *Micha*. HKAT. Freiburg: Herder, 1999.

Kessler, John. "Tradition, Continuity and Covenant in the Book of Haggai: An Alternative Voice from the Early Persian Period." Pages 1–39 in *Tradition in Transition: Haggai and Zechariah 1–8 in the Trajectory of Hebrew Theology*. Edited by Mark J. Boda and Michael H. Floyd. LHBOTS 475. New York: T&T Clark, 2008.

———. *The Book of Haggai; Prophecy and Society in Early Persian Yehud*. VTSup 91. Leiden: Brill, 2002.

Kim, Hyun Chul Paul. "Form Criticism in Dialogue with Other Criticisms: Building the Multidimensional Structures of Texts and Concepts." Pages 85–104 in *The Changing Face of Form Criticism for the Twenty-First Century*. Edited by Marvin A. Sweeney and Ehud Ben Zvi. Grand Rapids: Eerdmans, 2003.

King, Greg A. "The Day of the Lord in Zephaniah." *BSac* 152 (1995): 16–32.

Kirk-Duggan, Cheryl A. "Demonized Children and Traumatized, Battered Wives: Daughter Zion as Biblical Metaphor of Domestic and Sexual Violence." Pages 243–68 in *Daughter Zion: Her Portrait, Her Response*. Edited by Mark J. Boda, Carol Dempsey, and LeAnn Snow Flesher. AIL. Atlanta: Society of Biblical Literature, 2012.

Knierim, Rolf. "Old Testament Form Criticism Reconsidered." *Int* 27 (1974): 435–68.

Knoppers, Gary. *Jews and Samaritans: The Origins and History of their Early Relations*. Oxford: Oxford University Press, 2013.

Koch, Klaus. "Die Rolle der Hymnische Abschnitte in der Komposition des Amos-Buches." *ZAW* 86 (1974): 504–37.

Koehler, Ludwig, and Walter Baumgartner. *The Hebrew and Aramaic Lexicon of the Old Testament*. Translated by M. E. J. Richardson. Leiden: Brill, 2001.

Kotzé, Zacharias. "A Cognitive Linguistic Approach to the Emotion of Anger in the Old Testament." *HTS* 60 (2004): 843–63.

Kovecses, Zoltan. *Metaphor in Culture: Universality and Variation*. Cambridge: Cambridge University Press, 2005.

Krecher, Joachim. "Kommentare." Pages 188–91 in *Reallexikon der Assyriologie und Vorderasiatischen Archäologie* 6. Edited by Erich Ebeling, Dietz Otto Edzard, and Michael P. Streck. Berlin: de Gruyter, 1980–83.

Kruger, Paul A. "A Cognitive Interpretation of the Emotion of Anger in the Hebrew Bible." *JNSL* 26 (2000): 181–93.

Kwakkel, Gert. "The Land in the Book of Hosea." Pages 169–81 in *The Land of Israel in Bible, History, and Theology: Studies in Honour of Ed Noort*. Edited by Jacques Ruiten Edward Noort and Jacobus Cornelis De Vos. VTSup 124. Leiden: Brill, 2009.

Kwasman, T. "Two Aramaic Legal Documents." *BSOAS* 63 (2000): 274–83.

Labat, René. *Commentaires Assyro-Babyloniens sur les Présages*. Bordeaux: Imprimerie Librairie de l'Université, 1933.

Lakoff, George. "Conceptual Metaphor: The Contemporary Theory of Metaphor." Pages 185–238 in *Cognitive Linguistics: Basic Readings*. Edited by Dirk Geeraerts. Cognitive Linguistics Research 34. Berlin: de Gruyter, 2006.

———. *Women, Fire, and Dangerous Things: What Categories Reveal About the Mind*. Chicago: University of Chicago Press, 1987.

Lakoff, George, and Mark Johnson. *Metaphors We Live By*. Chicago: University of Chicago Press, 1980.

———. *More Than Cool Reason: A Field Guide to Poetic Metaphor*. Chicago: University of Chicago Press, 1989.

Landy, Francis. *Hosea*. Readings, a New Biblical Commentary. Sheffield: Sheffield Academic, 1995.

———. "Three Sides of a Coin: In Conversation with Ben Zvi and Nogalski, 'Two Sides of a Coin.'" *JHebS* 10 (2010): article 11, 9–17.

Lange, Armin. "Interpretation als Offenbarung: Zum Verhältnis von Schriftauslegung und Offenbarung in apokalyptischer und nichtapokalyptischer Literatur." Pages 17–33 in *Wisdom and Apocalypticism in the Dead Sea Scrolls and in the Biblical Tradition*. Edited by F. García Martínez. BETL 168. Leuven: Peeters, 2003.

———. "Literary Prophecy and Oracle Collection: A Comparison between Judah and Greece in Persian Times." Pages 248–75 *Prophets, Prophecy and Prophetic Texts in Second Temple Judaism*. Edited by Michael H. Floyd and Robert D. Haak. LHBOTS 427. New York: T&T Clark, 2006.

———. *Vom prophetischen Wort zur prophetischen Tradition: Studien zur Traditions-und Redationsgeschichte innerprophetischer Konflikte in der Hebräischen Bibel*. FAT 34. Tübingen: Mohr Siebeck, 2002.

Larkin, Katrina J. A. *The Eschatology of Second Zechariah; A Study of the Formation of a Mantological Wisdom Anthology*. CBET 6. Kampen: Kok Pharos, 1994.

LeCureux, Jason T. *The Thematic Unity of the Book of the Twelve*. Hebrew Bible Monographs 10. Sheffield: Sheffield Phoenix, 2012.

Lee, W. W. *Punishment and Forgiveness in Israel's Migratory Campaign*. Grand Rapids: Eerdmans, 2003.

Lescow, Theodor. *Das Buch Maleachi: Texttheorie, Auslegung, Kanontheorie*. AzTh 75. Stuttgart: Calwer, 1993.

Lessing, R. Reed. *Amos*. ConcC. Saint Louis: Concordia, 2009.

Levin, Christoph. "Das 'Vierprophetenbuch': Ein exegetischer Nachruf." *ZAW* 123 (2011): 221–35.

Limburg, James. *Jonah: A Commentary*. OTL. Louisville: Westminster John Knox, 1993.

Lindblom, Johannes. *Micha, literarisch untersucht*. Acta Academiae Aboensis, Ser. Humaniora 6.2. Åbo: Åbo Akademi University, 1929.

Lipschits, Oded. "Achaemenid Imperial Policy and the Status of Jerusalem." In *Judah and Judeans in the Persian Period*. Edited by Oded Lipschits and Manfred Oeming. Winona Lake, IN: Eisenbrauns, 2006.

Long, Burke O. "Reports of Visions Among the Prophets." *JBL* 95 (1976): 353–65.

Long, Shelley L. "The Last King(s) of Judah: Zedekiah and Sedekias in the Hebrew and Old Greek Versions of Jeremiah 37(44)–40(47):6." PhD diss., Claremont Graduate University, 2014.

Longman III, Tremper. "Israelite Genres in Their Ancient Near Eastern Context." Pages 177–95 in *The Changing Face of Form Criticism for the Twenty-First Century*. Edited by Marvin A. Sweeney and Ehud Ben Zvi. Grand Rapids: Eerdmans, 2003.

Lord, Albert Bates. *The Singer of Tales*. Cambridge: Harvard University Press, 2000.

Luckenbill, Daniel D. *Ancient Records of Assyria and Babylonia*. Weisbaden: Harrassowitz, 1968.

Lundbom, Jack R. *Deuteronomy: A Commentary*. Grand Rapids: Eerdmans, 2013.

Lux, Rüdiger. "'Still Alles Fleisch vor Jhwh …': Das Schweigegebot im Dodekapropheton und Sein Besonderer Ort im Zyklus der Nachtgesichte des Sacharja." Pages 99–113 in *Leqach 6: Mitteilungen und Beiträge*. Edited by Forschungsstelle Judentum Theologische Fakultät, Leipzig. Leipzig: Thomas, 2005.

Macintosh, A. A. *Hosea: A Critical and Exegetical Commentary*. ICC. Edinburgh: T&T Clark, 1997.

Maier, Christl. *Daughter Zion, Mother Zion: Gender, Space, and the Sacred in Ancient Israel*. Minneapolis: Fortress, 2008.

Mandolfo, Carleen. *Daughter Zion Talks Back to the Prophets: A Dialogic Theology of the Book of Lamentations*. SemeiaSt 38. Atlanta: Society of Biblical Literature, 2007.

March, W. Eugene. "Prophecy." Pages 141–77 in *Old Testament Form Criticism*. Edited by John H. Hayes. TUMSR 2. San Antonio: Trinity University Press, 1974.

Marks, Herbert. "The Twelve Prophets." Pages 207-33 in *The Literary Guide to the Bible*. Edited by Robert Alter and Frank Kermode. Cambridge: Belknap, 1987.

Marrs, Rick R. "'Back to the Future': Zion in the Book of Micah." Pages 77–96 in *David and Zion: Biblical Studies in Honor of J. J. M. Roberts*. Edited by Bernard F. Batto and Kathryn L. Roberts. Winona Lake, IN: Eisenbrauns, 2004.

Mason, Rex A. *Preaching the Tradition: Homily and Hermeneutics After the Exile*. Cambridge: Cambridge University Press, 1990.

Mays, James Luther. *Amos: A Commentary*. OTL. London: SCM, 1969.

———. *Hosea: A Commentary*. OTL. Philadelphia: Westminster, 1969.

———. *Micah*. OTL. London: SCM, 1976.

McComiskey, Thomas Edward. "The Hymnic Elements of the Prophecy of Amos: A Study of Form-Critical Methodology." *JETS* 30 (1987): 139–57.

McKenzie, Steven L. "Exodus Typology in Hosea." *ResQ* 22 (1979): 100–108.

———. *How to Read the Bible*. Oxford: Oxford University Press, 2005.

Meadowcroft, Tim. *Haggai*. Readings: A New Commentary. Sheffield: Sheffield Academic, 2006.

Melugin, Roy Frank. "Muilenburg, Form Criticism, and Theological Exegesis." Pages 91–100 in *Encounter with the Text: Form and History in the Hebrew Bible*. Edited by Martin J. Buss. Philadelphia: Fortress, 1979.

———. "Prophetic Books and the Problem of Historical Reconstruction." Pages 63–78 in *Prophets and Paradigms: Essays in Honor of Gene M. Tucker*. Edited by Stephen Breck Reid. JSOTSup 229. Sheffield: Sheffield Academic, 1996.

———. "Recent Form Criticism Revisited in an Age of Reader Response." Pages 46–64 in *The Changing Face of Form Criticism for the Twenty-First Century*. Edited by Marvin A. Sweeney and Ehud Ben Zvi. Grand Rapids: Eerdmans, 2003.

Meyers, Carol L., and Eric M. Meyers. *Haggai, Zechariah 1–8*. AB 25B. New York: Doubleday, 1987. Repr. New Haven: Yale University Press, 2004.

———. *Zechariah 9–14*. AB 25C. New York: Doubleday, 1993.

Millar, William R. "A Bakhtinian Reading of Narrative Space and Its Relationship to Social Space." Pages 129–56 in *Constructions of Space I: Theory, Geography, and Narrative*. Edited by Jon L. Berquist and Claudia V. Camp. LHBOTS 481. New York: T&T Clark, 2007.

Miller-Naudé Cynthia L., and C. H. J. van der Merwe. "הִנֵּה and Mirativity in Biblical Hebrew." *HS* 52 (2011): 53–81.

Moberly, R. W. L. "'In God We Trust?' The Challenge of the Prophets." *ExAud* 24 (2008): 18–33.

Möller, Karl. *A Prophet in Debate: The Rhetoric of Persuasion in the Book of Amos*. JSOTSup 372. Sheffield: Sheffield Academic, 2003.

Morgan, Donn M. "Remnant." Pages 658–64 in *Dictionary of the Old Testament: Prophets*. Edited by Mark J. Boda and J. Gordon McConville. Downers Grove, IL: InterVarsity Press and IVP Academic, 2012.

Morris, Gerald. *Prophecy, Poetry and Hosea*. JSOTSup 219. Sheffield: Sheffield Academic, 1996.

Moughtin-Mumby, Sharon. *Sexual and Marital Metaphors in Hosea, Jeremiah, Isaiah and Ezekiel*. OTM. Oxford: Oxford University Press, 2008.

Mowinckel, Sigmund. *Prophecy and Tradition: The Prophetic Books in the Light of the Study of the Growth and History of the Tradition*. Oslo: Dybwad, 1946.

———. *The Spirit and the Word: Prophecy and Tradition in Ancient Israel*. Translated by K. C. Hanson. Minneapolis: Fortress, 2002.

Neef, Heinz-Dieter. "Vom Gottesgericht zum universalen Heil: Komposition und Redaktion des Zefanjabuches." *ZAW* 111 (1999): 530–46.

Neujahr, Matthew. *Predicting the Past in the Ancient Near East: Mantic Historiography in Ancient Mesopotamia, Judah, and the Mediterranean World*. BJS 354. Providence: Brown Judaic Studies, 2012.

Neusner, Jacob, Alan J. Avery-Peck, and William Scott Green, eds. *Encyclopedia of Judaism*. Vol. 9. 2nd Edition. Leiden: Brill, 2005.

Newsom, Carol A. "Bakhtin." Pages 20–27 in *Handbook of Postmodern Biblical Interpretation*. Edited by A. K. M Adam. Atlanta: Chalice, 2000.

Nielsen, Kirsten. *Yahweh as Prosecutor and Judge: An Investigation of the Prophetic Lawsuit*. JSOTSup 9. Sheffield: University of Sheffield Press, 1978.

Niditch, Susan. *The Symbolic Vision in Biblical Tradition*. HSM 30. Chico, CA: Scholars Press, 1980.

———. *Oral World and Written Word: Ancient Israelite Literature*. LAI. Louisville: Westminister John Knox, 1996.

Nissinen, Martti. "The Historical Dilemma of Biblical Prophetic Studies." Pages 103–20 in *Prophecy in the Book of Jeremiah*. Edited by Hans M. Barstad and Reinhard G. Kratz. BZAW 388. Berlin: de Gruyter, 2009.

———. "How Prophecy Became Literature." *SJOT* 19 (2005): 153–72.

———. "A Report of Prophecies: Mullissu-kabtat to Assurbanipal." In *Prophets and Prophecy in the Ancient Near East*. Edited by Martti Nissinen and Peter Machinist. WAW 12. Atlanta: Society of Biblical Literature, 2003.

———. "Spoken, Written, Quoted, and Invented: Orality and Writtenness in Ancient Near Eastern Prophecy." Pages 235–72 in *Writings and Speech in Israelite and Ancient*

Near Eastern Prophecy. Edited by Ehud Ben Zvi and Michael H. Floyd. SymS 10. Atlanta: Society of Biblical Literature, 2000.
Nissinen, Martti, and Peter Machinist, eds. *Prophets and Prophecy in the Ancient Near East*. WAW 12. Atlanta: Society of Biblical Literature, 2003.
Nogalski, James D. *The Book of the Twelve: Hosea–Jonah*. SHBC. Macon, GA: Smyth & Helwys, 2011.
———. *The Book of the Twelve: Micah–Malachi*. SHBC. Macon, GA: Smyth & Helwys, 2011.
———. *Literary Precursors to the Book of the Twelve*. BZAW 217. Berlin: de Gruyter, 1993.
———. "Obadiah 7: Textual Corruption or Politically Charged Metaphor?" *ZAW* 110 (1998): 67–71.
———. "One Book and Twelve Books: the Nature of the Redactional Work and the Implications of Cultic Source Material in the Book of the Twelve." Pages 11–46 in *Two Sides of a Coin: Juxtaposing Views on Interpreting the Book of the Twelve/the Twelve Prophetic Books*. Edited by Ehud Ben Zvi and James D. Nogalski. Analecta Gorgiana 201. Piscataway, NJ: Gorgias, 2009.
———. "'Presumptions of 'Covenant' in Joel." In *Covenant in the Persian Period: From Genesis to Chronicles*. Edited by Gary Knoppers and Richard Bautch. Winona Lake, IN: Eisenbrauns, 2015.
———. "Recurring Themes in the Book of the Twelve: Creating Points of Contact for a Theological Reading." *Int* 61 (2007): 125–36.
———. *Redactional Processes in the Book of the Twelve*. BZAW 218. Berlin: de Gruyter, 1993.
———. "The Redactional Shaping of Nahum 1 for the Book of the Twelve." Pages 193–202 in *Among the Prophets: Language, Image and Structure in the Prophetic Writings*. Edited by Philip R. Davies. JSOTSup 144. Sheffield: Sheffield Academic, 1993.
———. "Zechariah 13.7–9 as a Transitional Text: An Appreciation and Re-Evaluation of the Work of Rex Mason." Pages 292–304 in *Bringing out the Treasure: Inner Biblical Allusion in Zechariah 9–14*. Edited by Mark J. Boda and Michael H. Floyd. JSOTSup 370. Sheffield: Sheffield Academic, 2003.
———. "Zephaniah's Use of Genesis 1–11." *HBAI* 2 (2013): 351–72.
Nogalski, James, and Marvin A. Sweeney, eds. *Reading and Hearing the Book of the Twelve*. SymS 15. Atlanta: Society of Biblical Literature, 2000.
Nurmela, Risto. *Prophets in Dialogue: Inner-Biblical Allusions in Zechariah 1–8 and 9–14*. Åbo: Åbo Akademi University, 1996.
O'Brien, Julia M. *Priest and Levite in Malachi*. SBLDS 121. Atlanta: Scholars Press, 1990.
O'Kennedy, Daniel F. "Prayer in the Post-Exilic Prophetic Books of Haggai, Zechariah and Malachi," *Scriptura* 113 (2014): 1–13.
Odell, Margaret S. "Ezekiel Saw What He Said He Saw: Genres, Forms, and the Vision of Ezekiel 1." Pages 162–76 in *The Changing Face of Form Criticism for the Twenty-First Century*. Edited by Marvin A. Sweeney and Ehud Ben Zvi. Grand Rapids: Eerdmans, 2003.
Oelsner, Joachim, Bruce Wells, and Cornelia Wunsch. "Neo-Babylonian Period." Pages 911–74 in *A History of Ancient Near Eastern Law*. Edited by Raymond Westbrook and Gary M. Beckman. HdO 79. Leiden: Brill, 2003.
Ogden, G. "Joel 4 and Prophetic Responses to National Laments." *JSOT* 26 (1983): 97–106.
Ong, Walter J. *Orality and Literacy: The Technologizing of the Word*. London: Routledge, 2012.

Oppenheim, A. L., trans. "Campaigns against Egypt, Syria, and Palestine." Pages 294–97 in Pritchard, James B., ed. *The Ancient Near Eastern Texts Related to the Old Testament*. 3rd ed. Princeton: Princeton University Press, 1969.

Page, S. "A Stele of Adad Nirari III and Nergal-ereš from Tell al Rimlah." *Iraq* 30 (1968): 139–53.

Park, Aaron W. *The Book of Amos as Composed and Read in Antiquity*. StBibLit 37. New York: Lang, 2001.

Parpola, Simo. "International Law in the First Millennium." Pages 1045–66 in *A History of Ancient Near Eastern Law*. Edited by Raymond Westbrook and Gary M. Beckman. HdO 79. Leiden: Brill, 2003.

Paul, Shalom M. *A Commentary on the Book of Amos*. Hermeneia. Minneapolis: Fortress, 1991.

Person, Raymond F. *Second Zechariah and the Deuteronomic School*. JSOTSup 167. Sheffield: Sheffield Academic, 1993.

Petersen, David L. *Haggai and Zechariah 1–8: A Commentary*. OTL. Philadelphia: Westminster John Knox, 1984.

———. "Israel and the Nations in the Later Latter Prophets." Pages 157–64 in *Constructs of Prophecy in the Former and Latter Prophets and Other Texts*. Edited by Lester L. Grabbe and Martti Nissinen. ANEM 4. Atlanta: Society of Biblical Literature, 2011.

———. *The Prophetic Literature: An Introduction*. Louisville: Westminster John Knox, 2002.

———. *The Roles of Israel's Prophets*. JSOTSup 17. Sheffield: JSOT Press, 1981.

———. *Zechariah 9–14 and Malachi: A Commentary*. OTL. Louisville: Westminster John Knox, 1995.

Petterson, Anthony R. *Behold Your King: The Hope for the House of David in the Book of Zechariah*. LHBOTS 513. London: T&T Clark, 2009.

———. "The Eschatology of Zechariah's Night Visions." Pages 119–34 in *'I Lifted My Eyes and Saw': Reading Dream and Vision Reports in the Hebrew Bible*. Edited by Lena-Sofia Tiemeyer and Elizabeth R. Hayes. LHBOTS 584. London: T&T Clark, 2014.

———. *Haggai, Zechariah, and Malachi*. ApOTC 25. Nottingham: Apollos, 2015.

———. "The Shape of the Davidic Hope Across the Book of the Twelve." *JSOT* 35 (2010): 225–46.

Pirsig, Robert. *Zen and the Art of Motorcycle Maintenance*. New York: HarperCollins, 1974.

Polk, Timothy. *The Prophetic Persona: Jeremiah and the Language of Self*. JSOTSup 32. Sheffield: JSOT Press, 1985.

Porten, Bezalel. "Elephantine." Pages 861–81 in *A History of Ancient Near Eastern Law*. Edited by Raymond Westbrook and Gary M. Beckman. HdO 79. Leiden: Brill, 2003.

Porten, Bezalel, and Ada Yardeni. *Textbook of Aramaic Documents from Ancient Egypt: Contracts*. 4 vols. Winona Lake, IN: Eisenbrauns, 1989.

Porter, Stanley E. "Matthew and Mark: The Contribution of Recent Linguistic Thought." Pages 97–119 in *Mark and Matthew I: Comparative Readings*. WUNT 271. Tübingen: Mohr Siebeck, 2011.

———. "Studying Ancient Languages from a Modern Linguistic Perspective: Essential Terms and Terminology." *Filologia neotestamentaria* 2 (1989): 147–72.

———. Review of *Grammar as Interpretation: Greek Literature in Its Linguistic Contexts*. Edited by Egbert J. Bakker. *JSNT* (2001): 125.

———. Review of *Linguistics and Biblical Interpretation* by Peter Cotterell and Max Turner. *JSNT* 39 (1990): 124.
Pritchard, James B., ed. *The Ancient Near Eastern Texts Related to the Old Testament.* 3rd ed. Princeton: Princeton University Press, 1969.
———. *The Ancient Near East in Pictures Relating to the Old Testament.* 2nd ed. Princeton: Princeton University Press, 1994.
Pröbstle, Martin. Review of *Prophetische Visionsschilderngen im AltenTestament*, by Achim Behrens. *RBL* (2004). http://www.bookreviews.org/pdf/3984_4081.pdf.
Raabe, Paul R. *Obadiah.* AB 24D. New York: Doubleday, 1996.
Radine, Jason. *The Book of Amos in Emergent Judah.* FAT 2.45. Tübingen: Mohr Siebeck, 2010.
Reimers, Stephan. "Formgeschichte der profetischen Visionsberichte." PhD. diss., University of Hamburg, 1976.
Renaud, Bernard. *La formation du livre de Michée: Tradition et actualisation.* Paris: Gabalda, 1977.
Redditt, Paul L. *Haggai, Zechariah, Malachi.* NCeB. Grand Rapids: Eerdmans, 1995.
———. "Israel's Shepherds: Hope and Pessimism in Zechariah 9–14." *CBQ* 51 (1989): 631–42.
———. "The King in Haggai–Zechariah 1–8 and the Book of Twelve, Tradition in Transition: Haggai and Zechariah 1–8." Pages 56–82 in *Tradition in Transition: Haggai and Zechariah 1–8 in the Trajectory of Hebrew Theology.* Edited by Mark J. Boda and Michael H. Floyd. LHBOTS 475. London: T&T Clark, 2008.
———. "Redactional Connectors in Zechariah 9–14." Pages 206–17 in *Perspectives on the Formation of the Book of the Twelve.* Edited by Rainer Albertz, James D. Nogalski, and Jakob Wöhrle. BZAW 433. Berlin: de Gruyter, 2012.
———. *Zechariah 9–14.* IECOT. Stuttgart: Kohlhammer, 2012.
Redditt, Paul L., and Aaron Schart, eds. *Thematic Threads in the Book of the Twelve.* BZAW 325. Berlin: de Gruyter, 2003.
Renz, Thomas. *The Rhetorical Function of the Book of Ezekiel.* VTSup 76. Leiden: Brill, 2002.
Reventlow, Henning G. *Die Propheten Haggai, Sacharja und Maleachi.* ATD 25.2. Göttingen: Vandenhoeck & Ruprecht, 1993.
———. "Tradition und Aktualisierung in Sacharjas siebentem Nachtgesicht Sach 6,1–8." Pages 180–90 in *Alttestamentlicher Glaube und biblische Theologie: Festschrift für Horst Dietrich Preuß.* Edited by Jutta Hausmann and Hans-Jürgen Zobel. Stuttgart: Kohlhammer, 1992.
Riede, Peter. *Vom Erbarmen zum Gericht: Die Visionen des Amosbuches (Am 7–9*) und ihr literature- und traditionsgeschichtlicher Zusammenhang.* WMANT 120. Neukirchen-Vluyn: Neukirchener Verlag, 2008.
Ringgren, Helmer. "עבד." *TDOT* 10:384–87.
Roberts, J. J. M. *Nahum, Habakkuk, and Zephaniah.* OTL. Louisville: Westminster John Knox, 1991.
Robinson, Robert B. "Levels of Naturalization in Obadiah." *JSOT* 40 (1988): 83–97.
Rokay, Zoltán. *Die Nachtgesichte des Propheten Sacharja.* Frankfurt: Lang, 2012.
Rooker, Mark E. "The Use of the Old Testament in the Book of Hosea." *CTR* 7 (1993): 51–66.

Rösel, Martin. "Inscriptional Evidence and the Question of Genre." Pages 107–21 in *The Changing Face of Form Criticism for the Twenty-First Century*. Edited by Marvin A. Sweeney and Ehud Ben Zvi. Grand Rapids: Eerdmans, 2003.
Rose, Wolter H. *Zemah and Zerubbabel: Messianic Expectations in the Early Postexilic Period*. JSOTSup 304. Sheffield: Sheffield Academic, 2000.
Rudolph, Wilhelm. *Haggai, Sacharja 1–8, Sacharja 9–14, Maleachi*. KAT 13.4. Gütersloh: Mohn, 1976.
Sadler Jr., Rodney S. *Can A Cushite Change His Skin?: An Examination of Race, Ethnicity, and Othering in the Hebrew Bible*. LHBOTS 425. London: T&T Clark, 2005.
Sandburg, Carl. *Abraham Lincoln: The Prairie Years and the War Years*. New York: Harcourt Brace Jovanovich, 1970.
Sanders, T., and H. Pander Maat. "Cohesion and Coherence: Linguistic Approaches." Pages 591–5 in *Encyclopedia of Language and Linguistics*. Edited by Keith Brown et al. 2nd ed. London: Elsevier, 2006.
Sasson, Jack M. *Jonah*. AB 24B. New York: Doubleday, 1990.
Schaper, Joachim. "Exilic and Post-exilic Prophecy and the Orality/Literacy Problem." *VT* 55 (2005): 324–42.
———. "On Writing and Reciting in Jeremiah 36." Pages 137–47 in *Prophecy in the Book of Jeremiah*. Edited by Hans M. Barstad and Reinhard G. Katz. BZAW 388. Berlin: de Gruyter, 2009.
Scharbert, Josef. "Das ‚Wir' in den Psalmen auf dem Hintergrund altorientalischen Betens." Pages 297–324 in *Freude an der Weisung des Herrn: Beiträge zur Theologie der Psalmen: Festgabe zum 70, Geburtstag von Heinrich Gross*. Edited by Ernst Haag and Frank-Lothar Hossfeld. SBB 13. Stuttgart: Katholisches Bibelwerk, 1986.
Schart, Aaron. "Combining Prophetic Oracles in Mari Letters and Jeremiah 36." *JANESCU* 23 (1995): 75–93.
———. "Deathly Silence and Apocalyptic Noise: Observations on the Soundscape of the Book of the Twelve." *Verbum et Ecclesia* 31 (2010): Article #383 (5 pages).
———. *Die Entstehung des Zwölfprophetenbuchs*. BZAW 260. Berlin: de Gruyter, 1998.
———. "Reconstructing the Redaction History of the Twelve Prophets: Problems and Models." Pages 34–48 in *Reading and Hearing the Book of the Twelve*. Edited by James D. Nogalski and Marvin A. Sweeney. SymS 15. Atlanta: Society of Biblical Literature, 2000.
———. "Totenstille und Endknall: Ein Beitrag zur Analyse der Soundscape des Zwölfprophetenbuchs." Pages 257–74 in *Sprachen–Bilder–Klänge. Dimensionen der Theologie im Alten Testament und in Seinem Umfeld. Festschrift für Rüdiger Bartelmus zu Seinem 65. Geburtstag*. Edited by C. Karrer-Grube, et al. AOAT 30. Münster: Ugarit-Verlag, 2009.
Schniedewind, William M. *How the Bible Became a Book*. Cambridge: Cambridge University Press, 2004.
Schultz, Richard L. "The Ties That Bind: Intertextuality, the Identification of Verbal Parallels, and Reading Strategies in the Book of the Twelve." Pages 27–45 in *Thematic Threads in the Book of the Twelve*. Edited by Paul L. Redditt and Aaron Schart. BZAW 325. Berlin: de Gruyter, 2003.
Seybold, Klaus. *Bilder zum Tempelbau: Die Visionen der Propheten Sacharja*. SBS 70. Stuttgart: KBW, 1974.

———. "Das ‚Wir' in den Asaph-Psalmen: Spezifische Probleme einer Psalmgruppe." Pages 143–55 in *Neue Wege der Psalmenforschung*. Edited by Klaus Seybold and Erich Zenger. HBS 1. Freiburg: Herder, 1994.

Shaw, Charles S. *The Speeches of Micah: A Rhetorical-Historical Analysis*. JSOTSup 145. Sheffield: Sheffield Academic, 1993.

Sheppard, Gerald T. "'Enemies' and the Politics of Prayer in the Book of Psalms." Pages 61–82 in *The Bible and the Politics of Exegesis: Essays in Honor of Norman K. Gottwald on His Sixty-Fifth Birthday*. Edited by David Jobling, Peggy L. Day, and Gerald T. Sheppard. Cleveland: Pilgrim, 1991.

Sherwood, Aaron. "Paul's Imprisonment as the Glory of the Ethnē: A Discourse Analysis of Ephesians 3:1–13." *BBR* 22 (2012): 97–111.

Simon, Uriel. *Jonah*. JPS Bible Commentary. Philadelphia: Jewish Publication Society, 1999.

Sister, Moses. "Die Typen der prophetischen Visionen in der Bibel." *MGWJ* 78 (1934): 399–430.

Skinner, John. *Prophecy and Religion: Studies in the Life of Jeremiah*. Cambridge: Cambridge University Press, 1922.

Smith, Jonathan Z. "Sacred Persistence: Towards a Redescription of Canon." Pages 36–52 in *Imagining Religion: From Babylon to Jonestown*. Chicago: University of Chicago Press, 1982.

Smith, Neil, and Cindi Katz. "Grounding Metaphor: Toward a Spatialized Politics." Pages 66–81 in *Place and the Politics of Identity*. Edited by Michael Keith and Steve Pile. London: Routledge, 1993.

Soggin, J. Alberto. *The Prophet Amos: A Translation and Commentary*. Translated by John Bowden. OTL. London: SCM Press, 1987.

Soskice, Janet Martin. *Metaphor and Religious Language*. Oxford: Clarendon, 1985.

Spronk, Klaas. *Nahum*. HCOT. Kampen: Kok Pharos, 1997.

Stead, Michael R. "The Interrelationship between Vision and Oracle in Zechariah 1–6." Pages 149–68 in *'I Lifted My Eyes and Saw': Reading Dream and Vision Reports in the Hebrew Bible*. Edited by Elizabeth R. Hayes and Lena-Sofia Tiemeyer. LHBOTS 584. London: T&T Clark, 2014.

———. *The Intertextuality of Zechariah 1–8*. LHBOTS 506. London: T&T Clark, 2009.

Steck, Odil Hannes. *Old Testament Exegesis: A Guide to the Methodology*. Translated by James D. Nogalski. RBS 39. Atlanta: Scholars Press, 1998.

———. *The Prophetic Books and Their Theological Witness*. Translated by James D. Nogalski. St. Louis: Chalice, 2000. Translation of *Die Prophetenbücher und ihr theologisches Zeugnis: Wege der Nachfrage un Fährten zur Antwort*. Tübingen: Mohr Siebeck, 1996.

Stefanowitsch, Anatol, and Stefan Thomas Gries. *Corpus-Based Approaches to Metaphor and Metonymy*. Trends in Linguistics 171. Berlin: de Gruyter, 2006.

Steiner, Richard. "Four Inner-Biblical Interpretations of Genesis 49:10: On the Lexical and Syntactic Ambiguities of עד as Reflected in the Prophecies of Nathan, Ahijah, Ezekiel, and Zechariah." *JBL* 132 (2013): 52–53.

Stolper, Matthew W. "The Governor of Babylon and Across-the-River in 486 B.C." *JNES* 48.4 (1989): 283–305.

Stovell, Beth M. *Mapping Metaphorical Discourse in the Fourth Gospel: John's Eternal King*. LBS 5. Leiden: Brill, 2012.

---. *Minor Prophets I (Hosea–Micah)*. SGBC 21. Grand Rapids: Zondervan, forthcoming.

---. "Mother and Whore, Vine and Water: Rhetorical Violence and Comfort through the Blended Metaphors of Jeremiah." Paper presented at the Annual Meeting for the Society of Biblical Literature. Chicago, 17–20 November, 2012.

---. "Seeing the Kingdom of God, Seeing Eternal Life: Comparing Cohesion and Prominence in John 3 and the Apocryphal Gospels in Terms of Metaphor Use." Pages 439–67 in *The Language of the New Testament: Context, History and Development*. Edited by Stanley Porter and Andrew Pitts. LBS 6. Leiden: Brill, 2013.

---. "Yahweh as Shepherd-King in Ezekiel 34: Linguistic-Literary Analysis of Metaphors of Shepherding." In *Modeling Biblical Language: Papers from the McMaster Divinity College Linguistics Circle*. Edited by Stanley Porter, Christopher Land, and Gregory Fewster. LBS. Leiden: Brill, forthcoming.

Stuart, Douglas. *Hosea–Jonah*. WBC 31. Waco, TX: Word, 1987.

Suderman, W. Derek. "Are Individual Complaint Psalms Really Prayers?: Recognizing Social Address as Characteristic of Individual Complaints." Pages 153–70 in *The Bible as a Human Witness to Divine Revelation: Hearing the Word of God through Historically Dissimilar Traditions*. Edited by Randall Heskett and Brian Irwin. LHBOTS 469. New York: T&T Clark, 2010.

---. "Prayers Heard and Overheard: Shifting Address and Methodological Matrices in Psalms Scholarship" Ph.D. diss.: University of St. Michael's College, 2007.

Sweeney, Marvin A. *Form and Intertextuality in Prophetic and Apocalyptic Literature*. FAT 45. Tübingen: Mohr Siebeck, 2005.

---. "Form Criticism." Pages 90–104 in *To Each Its Own Meaning*. Edited by Steven L. McKenzie and Stephen R. Haynes. Louisville: Westminster John Knox, 1999.

---. "Formation and Form." Pages 113–26 in *Old Testament Interpretation: Past, Present And Future*. Edited by Karl May. Nashville: Abingdon, 1995.

---. *Isaiah 1–39 with an Introduction to Prophetic Literature*. FOTL 16. Grand Rapids: Eerdmans, 1996.

---. *King Josiah of Judah: The Lost Messiah of Israel*. New York: Oxford University Press, 2001.

---. "A Form-Critical Reassessment of the Book of Zephaniah." *CBQ* 53 (1991): 388–408.

---. *The Prophetic Literature*. IBT. Nashville: Abingdon, 2005.

---. Review of *The Intertextuality of Zechariah 1–8* by Michael R. Stead. *JSS* 56 (2011): 416.

---. "Sequence and Interpretation in the Book of the Twelve." Pages 49–64 in *Reading and Hearing the Book of the Twelve*. Edited by James D. Nogalski and Marvin A. Sweeney. SymS 15. Atlanta: Society of Biblical Literature, 2000.

---. *The Twelve Prophets*. 2 Volumes. Berit Olam. Collegeville, MN: Liturgical Press, 2000.

---. "Zechariah's Debate with Isaiah." Pages 335–50 in *The Changing Face of Form Criticism for the Twenty-First Century*. Edited by Marvin A. Sweeney and Ehud Ben Zvi. Grand Rapids: Eerdmans, 2003.

---. *Zephaniah*. Hermeneia. Minneapolis: Fortress, 2003.

Sweeney, Marvin A., and Ehud Ben Zvi. "Introduction." Pages 1–11 in *The Changing Face of Form Criticism for the Twenty-First Century*. Edited by Marvin A. Sweeney and Ehud Ben Zvi. Grand Rapids: Eerdmans, 2003.

Sykes, Seth. *Time and Space in Haggai–Zechariah 1–8: A Bakhtinian Analysis of a Prophetic Chronicle*. StBibLit 24. New York: Lang, 2002.

Taylor, Richard A., and E. Ray Clendenen. *Haggai, Malachi*. NAC 21A. Nashville: Broadman & Holman, 2004.

Theocharous, Myrto. *Lexical Dependence and Intertextual Allusion in the Septuagint of the Twelve Prophets: Studies in Hosea, Amos and Micah*. LHBOTS 570. New York: T&T Clark, 2012.

Tigay, Jeffrey H. *You Shall Have No Other Gods: Israelite Religion in the Light of Hebrew Inscriptions*. HSS 31. Atlanta: Scholars Press, 1986.

Tiemeyer, Lena-Sofia. "The Guilty Priesthood (Zech 3)." Pages 1–19 in *The Book of Zechariah and Its Influence*. Edited by Christopher M. Tuckett. Aldershot: Ashgate, 2003.

———. "The Polyvalence of Zechariah's Vision Report." Pages 16–29 in *'I Lifted My Eyes and Saw': Reading Dream and Vision Reports in the Hebrew Bible*. Edited by Elizabeth R. Hayes and Lena-Sofia Tiemeyer. LHBOTS 584. London: T&T Clark, 2014.

———. *Zechariah and His Visions: An Exegetical Study of Zechariah's Vision Report*. LHBOTS 605. London: T&T Clark, 2015.

Todd, Andrew. "The Interaction of Talk and Text: Re-Contextualizing Biblical Interpretation." *Practical Theology* 6 (2013): 69–85.

Toffelmire, Colin M. "Form Criticism." Pages 257–71 in *Dictionary of the Old Testament: Prophets*. Edited by Mark J. Boda and J. Gordon McConville. Downers Grove, IL: InterVarsity and IVP Academic, 2012.

———. "Orienting the Event: Register and the Day of Yhwh in the Prophetic Book of Joel." PhD diss.: McMaster Divinity College, 2014.

Tollington, Janet E. *Tradition and Innovation in Haggai and Zechariah 1–8*. JSOTSup 150. Sheffield: JSOT Press, 1993.

Tov, Emanuel. "Jeremiah." Pages 145–205 in *Qumran Cave 4. X. The Prophets*. Edited by Eugene Ulrich, et al. DJD 15. Oxford: Clarendon, 1997.

Trible, Phyllis. "Jonah." Pages 461–529 in vol. 7 of *The New Interpreters Bible*. Edited by Leander E. Keck. Nashville: Abingdon, 1996.

Trotter, James M. *Reading Hosea in Achaemenid Yehud*. JSOTSup 328. Sheffield: Sheffield Academic, 2001.

Tucker, Gene M. *Form Criticism of the Old Testament*. GBS. Philadelphia: Fortress, 1971.

Utzschneider, Helmut. *Künder oder Schreiber? Eine These zum Problem der 'Schriftprophetie' auf Grund von Maleachi 1,6–2,9*. BEATAJ 19. New York: Lang, 1989.

Van De Mieroop, Marc. *History of Ancient Egypt*. Blackwell History of the Ancient World. Chichester: Wiley-Blackwell, 2011.

Van der Kooij, Arie. *The Oracle of Tyre: The Septuagint of Isaiah 23 as Version and Vision*. VTSup 61. Leiden: Brill, 1998.

Van der Merwe, C. H. J. "Biblical Exegesis, Cognitive Linguistics and Hypertext." Pages 255–80 in *Congress Volume Leiden 2004*. Leiden: Brill, 2006.

———. "A Cognitive Linguistic Perspective on הִנֵּה in the Pentateuch, Joshua, Judges, and Ruth." *HS* 48 (2007): 101–40.

Van der Toorn, Karel. *Scribal Culture and the Making of the Hebrew Bible*. Cambridge: Harvard University Press, 2007.
Van Hecke, Pierre. *Metaphor in the Hebrew Bible*. BETL 187. Leuven: Peeters, 2005.
Van Seters, John. "Prophetic Orality in the Context of the Ancient Near East: A Response to Culley, Crenshaw, and Davies." Pages 51–89 in *Writings and Speech in Israelite and Ancient Near Eastern Prophecy*. Edited by Ehud Ben Zvi and Michael H. Floyd. SymS 10. Atlanta: Society of Biblical Literature, 2000.
Vlaardingerbroek, J. *Zephaniah*. HCOT. Leuven: Peeters, 1999.
Von Rad, Gerhard. "Origin of the Concept of the Day of Yahweh." *JSS* 4 (1959): 97–108.
Von Soden, Wolfram. *The Ancient Orient: An Introduction to the Study of the Ancient Near East*. Translated by Donald G. Schley. Grand Rapids: Eerdmans, 1994.
Waard, Jan de. "Chiastic Structure of Amos 5:1–17." *VT* 27 (1977): 170–77.
Wagenaar, Jan A. *Judgement and Salvation: The Composition and Redaction of Micah 2–5*. VTSup 85. Leiden: Brill, 2001.
Waltke, Bruce K. *A Commentary on Micah*. Grand Rapids: Eerdmans, 2007.
Waltke, Bruce K., and Michael Patrick O'Connor. *An Introduction to Biblical Hebrew Syntax*. Winona Lake, IN: Eisenbrauns, 1990.
Ward, James M. "The Eclipse the Prophet in Contemporary Prophetic Studies." *USQR* 41 (1988): 97–104.
Watts, John D. W. *Isaiah 1–33*. WBC 24. Waco, TX: Word, 1985.
———. "Superscriptions and Incipits in the Book of the Twelve." Pages 110–24 in *Reading and Hearing the Book of the Twelve*. Edited by James D. Nogalski and Marvin A. Sweeney. SymS 15. Atlanta: Society of Biblical Literature, 2000.
Watts, James W., and Paul R. House, eds. *Forming Prophetic Literature: Essays on Isaiah and the Twelve*. JSOTSup 235. Sheffield: Sheffield Academic, 1996.
Weinfeld, Moshe. *Deuteronomy and the Deuteronomic School*. Oxford: Clarendon, 1972; repr. Winona Lake, IN: Eisenbrauns, 1992.
Weiser, Artur. *Die Propheten Hosea, Joel, Amos, Obadja, Jona, Micha*. ATD 24. Göttingen: Vandenhoeck & Ruprecht, 1985.
Wenham, Gordon J. "The Date of Deuteronomy: Linch-Pin of Old Testament Criticism." *Themelios* 10 (1985): 15–20.
Wenzel, Heiko. *Reading Zechariah with Zechariah 1:1–6 as the Introduction to the Entire Book*. CBET 59. Leuven: Peeters, 2011.
Westermann, Claus. *Basic Forms of Prophetic Speech*. Translated by Hugh C. White. Louisville: Westminster John Knox, 1991.
Whitt, William D. "The Divorce of Yahweh and Asherah in Hos 2:4–7,12ff." *SJOT* 6 (1992): 31–67.
Williams, James G. "The Alas-Oracles of the Eighth Century Prophets." *HUCA* 38 (1967): 75–91.
Willis, John. "A Note on *wa'omar* in Micah 3:1." *ZAW* 80 (1968): 50–54.
Wilson, Gerald H. *The Editing of the Hebrew Psalter*. SBLDS 76. Chico: Scholars, 1981.
Wilson, Robert R. *Prophecy and Society in Ancient Israel*. Philadelphia: Fortress, 1980.
Wöhrle, Jakob. *Der Abschluss des Zwölfprophetenbuches Buchübergreifende Redaktionsprozesse in den späten Sammlungen*. BZAW 389. Berlin: de Gruyter, 2006.
———. *Die frühen Sammlungen des Zwölfprophetenbuches: Entstehung und Komposition*. BZAW 360. Berlin: de Gruyter, 2006.

Wolde, Ellen J. van. "The Creation of Coherence." *Semeia* 81 (1998): 159–74.
Wolff, Hans Walter. *Dodekapropheton 1, Hosea*. BKAT. Neukirchen: Neukirchener Verlag, 1961.
———. *Dodekapropheton 2, Joel und Amos*. BKAT. Neukirchen-Vluyn: Neukirchener Verlag, 1969.
———. *Dodekapropheton 3, Obadja und Jona*. BKAT. Neukirchen-Vluyn: Neukirchener Verlag, 1977.
———. *Haggai*. Translated by Margaret Kohl. CC. Minneapolis: Augsburg, 1988.
———. *Hosea*. Translated by Gary Stansell. Hermeneia. Philadelphia: Fortress, 1974
———. *Joel and Amos*. Translated by Waldemar Janzen, S. Dean McBride, Jr., and Charles A. Muenchow. Hermeneia. Philadelphia: Fortress, 1977.
———. *Micah: A Commentary*. Translated by Gary Stansell. CC. Minneapolis: Augsburg, 1990.
———. *Obadiah and Jonah*. Translated by Margaret Kohl. CC. Minneapolis: Augsburg, 1986.
Wolterstorff, Nicholas. *Divine Discourse: Philosophical Reflections on the Claim that God Speaks*. Cambridge: Cambridge University Press, 1995.
Wood, Joyce L. Rilett. *Amos in Song and Book Culture*. JSOTSup 337. Sheffield: Sheffield Academic, 2002.
Würthwein, Ernst. "Der Ursprung der prophetischen Gerichtsrede." *ZTK* 49 (1952): 1–16.
Yee, Gale A. *Poor Banished Children of Eve: Woman as Evil in the Hebrew Bible*. Minneapolis: Fortress, 2003.
Young, Liam Cole. "On Lists and Networks: An Archaeology of Form." Amodern 2: Network Archaeology, http://amodern.net/article/on-lists-and-networks/.
———. "Un-Black Boxing the List: Knowledge, Materiality, and Form." *Canadian Journal of Communication* 38 (2013): 497–516.

Ancient Sources Index

Hebrew Bible

Genesis, 213, 242, 254, 313
1–11, 181
1:18, 190
2:7, 252
3:16, 190
4:7, 190
4:26, 259
10:5, 254
10:18, 260
11:1, 259
11:4, 260
11:8, 260
11:9, 260
19:36–38, 256
22:1–19, 126
22:17, 51
24:2, 190
32:12, 51
32:23–33, 126
36:11, 232
41:49, 113
45:8, 190
45:26, 190
49:8–12, 147

Exodus, 284
10:1–20, 145
14–15, 146
15, 153
20:17, 106
21:15, 127
21:17, 127
22:26–27, 106
23:23–26, 158
24:7, 121
33:19, 190
34:6–7, 150, 152, 175
34:7, 180
34:24, 106

Leviticus
18:24–25, 107
21:6, 282
26:14–32, 123
26:14–39, 126

Numbers
21:27–30, 104

Deuteronomy, 59, 60, 276
1–4, 124
1:13, 300
4:11, 259
5:21, 106
5:22–23, 259
6:4, 130
6:10, 249
7, 123
18:22, 27
20:18–22, 272
27–28, 124
28, 59, 175
28:4, 59
28:11, 59
28:15–44, 126
28:20–44, 123
29–31, 124
29:23–28, 121
29:28, 121
30:6, 298
31:9–11, 121, 124
31:10, 125, 130

Joshua, 126, 206, 276–77
7:7, 188
7:7–9, 189
9:14, 280
11:4, 113
23–24, 124

Judges, 206
2:6–23, 124
5, 153
6:22, 188
7:12, 113
11:35, 188

Samuel–Kings, 214

1 Samuel, 206
1:9, 293
2:25, 127
4:21, 33
13:5, 113

2 Samuel, 206
7, 292
7:13, 292
18, 254
18:24–28, 22

1 Kings
4:20, 113
4:32, 104
5:5, 293
8:33–34, 123
8:35–36, 123
8:37–40, 123
12:25–33, 123
14:25–28, 255
14:27, 22
18, 140, 148
18:1–22:40, 126
19:4, 150
22, 80
22–23, 153
22:17, 77, 79–80
22:19–22, 77, 79–80

2 Kings, 276–77
3:10, 188
6:5, 188
6:15, 188
8:17–20, 22
9–10, 143
10:32–33, 144
12:18–19, 144
13:1–5, 144
13:22–25, 144
14:23–29, 144
14:25, 140, 149, 172
14:25–28, 101
15–17, 33
17:7–23, 124
20:3, 194
22, 75
23:25–27, 124
24:13, 275

Chronicles, 214

1 Chronicles
3:21, 215
12:10, 215
16:25, 253

2 Chronicles, 292
12:1–11, 255
14:9–15, 255
15:18, 292
20, 140
20:20–26, 145
24:4–14, 292
27:1–4, 292
29:1–11, 292
29:35–36, 292
30:1–12, 22
30:6–9, 23
34:1–8, 292

Ezra, 126, 218, 274
1, 274
1:8, 279
2, 279
2:2, 274, 279
2:64–66, 279
5:1, 155
6:14, 155
6:14–15, 294
8:9, 215

Nehemiah, 126, 218,
  224, 274
1:5, 194
1:11, 194
7, 279
7:62–65, 279
8:1–6, 121
8:2–8, 124, 131
8:7–8, 121
9, 124
10:1–40, 124
10:6, 215
12:25, 215
13:22, 22

Esther, 160, 206
1:10, 254
3:12–14, 23
8:9–10, 23

Job, 198
1–2, 276
9, 126
12:20, 259
33:3, 258
42:1–9, 126

Psalms, 160–61, 196,
  284
1–41, 160
4:1, 174
6:1, 174
8, 131
8:6–9, 126
15:3, 258
18, 195
22:4, 259
24:4, 258
27:10, 127
30, 195
32, 195
33, 131
34, 195
40:1–10, 195
40:7–11, 126
42–72, 160
44, 124, 131
46, 131
46:10, 104
47, 130, 131
48, 131
49:4, 104
50, 126
50:7–23, 126
51:17–19, 126
54:1, 174
60, 131
61:1, 174
66, 131
66:13–20, 195
67:1, 174

72:10, 254
73–89, 160
74, 131
75, 131
76:1, 174
78:2, 104
79, 131
80, 131
80–81, 185
85, 131
89, 124
89:39–41, 302
89:7, 253
90, 131
90–106, 160
92, 195
93, 130
95, 131
95–99, 130
96:4, 253
97:11, 254
100, 131
103, 131
106, 124, 131
107–150, 160
108, 131
110, 302
115, 131
116, 195
116:4, 194
116:16, 194
118, 131, 195
119, 126, 136
122, 131
122:6, 280
123, 131
124, 131
127:1, 22
136, 131
137, 148
138, 195
144, 131
147, 131
151, 160
151–155, 161

Proverbs, 25
1–9, 160
10–24, 160
10:1, 127
10:8, 258
10:11, 258
10:32, 258
15:5, 127
15:20, 127
16:27, 259
19:11, 192
19:26, 127
20:20, 127
25–29, 160
30, 160
31, 160

Canticles
3:3, 22
5:7, 22

Isaiah, 2, 22, 38, 44,
 135, 138, 145, 151,
 155, 160, 176, 181,
 204, 206, 215, 217,
 266, 269, 279, 282–
 83, 284, 290, 294
1–12, 208
1–39, 208, 215
1–55, 276
1:1, 215
1:2–9, 126
1:10–17, 126
1:15, 276
2, 101, 176
2:1–5, 110
2:1, 215
2:2–3, 302
2:2–4, 145
2:2–5, 56
2:3, 133
2:4, 176
2:13–15, 281
3:12, 190
4:2–4, 130

6, 75, 77, 79–80
6:1–13, 269
6:5, 258
7–8, 211
7:3, 215
7:8, 22
8:1, 213
8:1–4, 22, 155
8:16, 21
8:16–18, 211
9:6–7, 293
10:5–34, 110
10:33–34, 281
11:1, 302
11:1–10, 293
11:11, 254, 260
13:1, 215
13:6, 188
16:4–5, 293
16:14, 33
18–19, 260
19:21, 260
20:2–3, 215
20:6, 254
21:1–10, 77
21:6, 22
21:11–12, 22
21:16, 33
23, 159
24–27, 130
28:11, 259
30:8, 21, 211, 213
33:15, 258
33:19, 259
34:5–15, 148
37:2, 215
37:5–6, 215
37:21, 215
38:1, 215
38:3, 194
38:4, 215
38:9–20, 216
38:21, 215
39:3, 215
39:5, 215

39:8, 215
40, 215
40:9, 22
40:15, 254
41:27, 22
42, 44
44:28, 151
44:28–45:1, 292
45:1, 151
45:1–7, 108
45:18–25, 288
49–54, 143
52:7, 22
55:8–13, 288
56–66, 215, 276
60–62, 130
62:6, 22
63:1–6, 148
63:11–12, 282
65–66, 127

Jeremiah, 2, 21, 22,
   38, 45, 51, 80, 94,
   119, 138, 159, 160,
   171, 181, 198, 204,
   206–7, 213, 215, 217,
   242, 266, 269, 272,
   276–77, 283–84, 291,
   293–94, 341
1, 75, 80, 93, 95
1:1, 206, 215
1:6, 188
1:11, 93
1:11–12, 77, 93, 95
1:11–14, 77, 79
1:12, 93
1:13, 93, 95
1:13–14, 93–94
1:13–16, 77
1:13–19, 93, 95
1:14, 93–95
1:15, 94
1:15–16, 93–95
1:16, 94
1:17–19, 93–95
2, 45, 143

2:2–4, 65
2:2–3, 45
2:4–9, 45, 126
3:16–18, 302
4:5ff., 77
4:6–10, 95
4:10, 188
4:23–26, 81
6:17, 23
7, 211
7:13–15, 276
8:13, 252
10, 124
14, 184, 189
14:2–6, 188
14:7–9, 188
14:10–12, 189
14:13, 188
15:1, 283
18, 124
22:18, 291
22:24–30, 272
22:30, 291
23, 292
23:5, 10, 291
23:5–6, 302
23:21, 23
24, 75, 80, 93–94
24:1–2, 93
24:1–10, 77, 79, 93, 95
24:3, 93
24:4–10, 93
24:5–7, 94
24:8–10, 94
25:34, 281
25:36, 281
25:36–37, 281
25:38, 281
26, 131, 211
26:18, 120, 125
27–28, 110
29, 22
30–31, 130
30–33, 298
30:2, 21
30:7, 188

30:9, 298
31:10, 254
31:33, 298
32:17, 188
33, 292
33:14–18, 302
33:15, 292, 298
33:17–18, 292
33:15–18, 10
35:4, 22
36, 21, 24, 131, 213,
   318
38:21–22, 78
38:21–23, 81
49:7–11, 242
49:7–22, 148, 178
49:9, 178
49:14, 133
49:14–16, 178

Lamentations, 124
4:21–22, 148

Ezekiel, 38, 80–81,
   123, 138, 157, 179,
   181, 206–7, 215, 217,
   269, 277–78, 284
1, 75, 79, 179
1–3, 81
1:1, 179, 215
1:1–2:8, 80–81
1:15, 179
1:27–28, 179
2:9–3:9, 80–81
3:5, 259
3:6, 259
3:17, 23
4:14, 188
8–11, 75, 79
8:16, 189
9:8, 188
10:15, 179
10:20, 179
11:1–2, 179
11:13, 188
16, 143

Ancient Sources Index 351

17:3–6, 302
17:22–23, 302
21:5, 188
21:26–27, 293, 302
21:31–32, 302
22:7, 127
25:12–14, 148
25:13, 232
30, 101
30:2–3, 188
33:7, 23
34:3–4, 281
35:2–15, 148
36, 130
36–39, 277
37, 75
37:15–23, 281
37:21–25, 293
38–39, 271, 276
40–42, 302
40–48, 75, 79, 276, 299
43:3, 179

Daniel, 80, 157, 160
7, 75, 81
8, 75, 79
8–12, 81
9:4, 194
10, 75
10–12, 79
12, 75

Hosea, 38–41, 43–55, 57, 59, 60, 61, 64, 87, 99, 113, 114, 130, 139, 140–44, 164, 167, 170–71, 182, 185–87, 191, 199, 203, 206, 217, 233, 266–67, 269, 273, 286, 290, 307, 333
1, 6, 40, 49, 164, 182
1–2, 40, 52
1–3, 119, 120, 174

1–12, 139
1–14, 143
1:1, 142–43, 170, 215
1:2–9, 113
1:2–2:2, 143
1:2–14:9, 143
1:6, 252
1:10, 51
1:10–11, 99, 113, 114
2, 12, 40, 48–49, 50–54, 60–61, 73–74, 164
2:1–13, 113
2:3–14:9, 143
2:3–25, 3, 63, 65, 72, 74
2:3–3:5, 143
2:4, 49, 186
2:5, 49
2:8, 50
2:9, 185
2:14, 50
2:16–17, 50
2:17, 185, 258
2:18, 185
2:18–25, 185
2:20, 50, 185
2:22, 185
2:23, 185
2:23–24, 50
2:25, 50, 185–87
3, 6, 164, 182, 185
3:1–3, 144
3:4–5, 142, 144
3:5, 293
4, 73–74, 144
4–10, 172–73, 182
4:1–3, 3, 63, 65, 72, 74
4:1–19, 143
5:1–14:1, 143–44
5:13–14, 144
5:15, 132
6:1, 132
6:1–3, 132, 186–87
7:11–12, 144

8, 53
8:1, 185
8:2, 185–87
8:3, 185
9, 12, 48, 53–61, 187
9:1, 55–56
9:1–9, 55–57
9:1–17, 55
9:8, 23
9:9, 55, 57–58
9:10, 54–58
9:10–17, 55–56, 58
9:11, 53, 57–58
9:12, 53, 58
9:13, 53–54, 58
9:13–14, 56
9:14, 54, 58, 187
9:15, 54
9:16, 54, 58
9:17, 56
12–13, 172, 182
12:1–2, 142, 144
14:1–2, 132
14:1–3, 14, 132
14:1–8, 130
14:2–3, 186
14:2–8, 186
14:2–9, 143, 145, 187
14:3, 186
14:3–4, 186–87
14:4, 186
14:4–7, 99, 113–14
14:5–8, 186
14:9, 113
14:10, 143

Joel, 99, 114, 139–41, 145–46, 170–71, 173–75, 182, 187, 190–91, 206, 215, 231, 242, 267, 290
1, 180, 190, 276
1–2, 175, 176
1–3, 139
1–4, 139

1:1, 146, 215
1:1–2:17, 191
1:1–4:21, 146
1:2–18, 132, 175
1:2–20, 114, 146
1:2–4:21, 146
1:13–14, 188
1:14–15, 202
1:15, 187–89, 191
1:15–16, 188
1:15–18, 188
1:15–20, 191
1:16–18, 188
1:16–20, 188
1:19–20, 132, 175, 188–89, 191
2, 101, 166
2:1–17, 132
2:1–11, 175
2:1–14, 114, 146
2:1–17, 190
2:2, 259
2:12–14, 114, 190
2:12–17, 175
2:13–14, 204
2:14, 190
2:15–16, 189
2:15–17, 114
2:15–20, 114
2:15–4:21, 146
2:17, 132, 189–91, 204
2:18, 190
2:18–19, 190
2:18–27, 132, 175
2:18–32, 99, 114–15
2:19, 204
2:21–3:8, 114
2:28–32, 114
3, 241
3:1, 175
3:1–5, 175–76, 202
3:4, 146, 176
3:5, 176, 202
3:9–21, 114
3:11, 190
4, 176, 182, 271

4:1, 175–76
4:1–3, 175
4:1–21, 175
4:2, 176
4:3, 175
4:4–8, 176
4:9–17, 176
4:10, 176
4:12, 145, 176
4:16, 181
4:18, 181
4:18–21, 176
4:21, 140

Amos, 4, 60, 75–77, 80–81, 83, 85–86, 89, 90, 92–94, 99, 101, 124, 129–30, 133, 139–41, 146–47, 164, 170–71, 176, 179–82, 191–93, 206, 215, 217, 219, 266–67, 269, 290, 320
1–2, 179, 266
1–3, 205, 217
1–9, 139
1:1, 146–47, 165, 192, 206, 217
1:1–2, 147
1:1–3, 218
1:1–9:15, 147
1:2, 147, 176, 181, 193, 216
1:3, 218
1:3–5, 147, 218
1:3–2:5, 219
1:3–2:16, 102, 146–47
1:3–9:15, 147
1:6, 218
1:6–8, 147, 218
1:8, 218
1:9–10, 147, 218, 266
1:11–12, 147, 218, 266
1:13–15, 147, 218
2:1–3, 147
2:4–5, 147, 218, 266

2:6–8, 218
2:6–16, 147, 218
2:8, 101
2:9, 218
2:10, 218
2:13, 218
2:14–16, 218
3, 219
3–4, 120, 122, 148
3–6, 122–23, 125, 172, 173
3:1, 170
3:1–2, 122
3:1–4:13, 147
3:1–5:6, 102
3:2, 123
3:7–8, 123
3:8–9, 102
3:9, 123, 126
3:10, 122
3:10–11, 123
3:11, 122
3:12, 123, 219
3:13, 122
3:13–14, 123
3:15, 123
4, 180
4:1, 101–2, 122, 170, 219
4:1–7, 102
4:2–3, 122
4:3, 102
4:3–8, 219
4:4, 102
4:4–5, 193
4:4–7, 102
4:5–6, 102
4:6–11, 123
4:6–13, 123
4:7, 102
4:8, 102
4:8–10, 102
4:9–15, 219
4:11–14, 102
4:12–13, 102

4:13, 82, 124, 133, 193, 216
4:14, 102
5, 123, 191
5–6, 122, 148
5:1, 122–23, 170
5:1–2, 193
5:1–6:14, 147
5:2, 123
5:2–7, 122
5:4, 124
5:4–6, 214
5:4–7, 124
5:5–6, 193
5:6, 122, 124, 193
5:7, 193
5:7–12, 101
5:8–9, 124, 193, 216
5:8–9, 82, 133, 193
5:10–13, 122, 193
5:14, 124
5:14–15, 124
5:15, 124
5:16, 188
5:16–17, 122–23
5:18–20, 101–2, 123, 146
5:18–27, 99, 101–3
5:20, 101
5:21, 101
5:21–24, 101, 122
5:22, 101
5:23, 101
5:24, 101, 103
5:27, 122
6:1, 170
6:1–3, 123
6:1–6, 101
6:1–14, 99, 101–3
6:1–7, 102
6:4–6, 122
6:4–7, 102, 123
6:6, 122
6:7–8, 122
6:8, 102

6:9, 102, 200
6:9–10, 122
6:10, 200
6:11–14, 122
6:12, 103
6:14, 102
7, 119, 191–92, 194
7–8, 80, 92, 192
7–9, 75, 83, 85–86, 90, 95, 148, 266
7:1, 82, 83, 191
7:1–3, 75, 77, 80, 82, 93, 95, 179
7:1–6, 77, 79–80, 192
7:1–8, 88, 90, 192
7:1–9:10, 102
7:1–9:15, 147
7:2, 82, 95
7:3, 82, 86, 95, 180, 191–92
7:4, 82–83, 191
7:4–6, 75, 77, 80, 82, 93, 95, 179
7:5, 82, 191–92
7:6, 82, 86, 180
7:7, 82–83
7:7–8, 79, 87–89, 93, 95
7:7–9, 75, 77, 80, 82, 88–89, 179, 192
7:8, 82, 85, 88–89, 95
7:8–9, 88–89
7:9, 82–83, 86–89, 93, 95, 165
7:10–17, 6, 87, 148, 165–66, 180, 182, 192
7:11, 87, 165
7:14–15, 192
7:17, 87, 192
8, 87, 192
8:1, 82
8:1–2, 79, 87–90, 93, 192

8:1–3, 75, 77, 80, 82, 88–89, 179
8:2, 82–83, 85–86, 88–89, 192
8:2–3, 89
8:3, 82, 83, 86–89, 93, 200
8:4–14, 87–88, 180
8:9, 89
9, 89, 148, 192–93, 241
9:1, 82–83, 89, 193
9:1–4, 75, 77, 80, 83, 89–90, 95, 179–80, 192
9:4, 82
9:5–6, 82, 124, 133, 193, 216
9:7–10, 82
9:7–15, 82, 181
9:11–15, 82, 130, 146, 266, 293
9:13, 176, 181

Obadiah, 60, 119, 133, 139, 140–41, 148, 171, 174, 177–78, 182, 203, 206, 215, 221–22, 231–35, 237–38, 239, 241–44, 267, 290
1, 133, 148–49, 231, 233–34
1–5, 149, 178
1–9, 242
1–14, 178
1–21, 149
2, 233
2–5, 232
2–10, 235–37, 240
3–4, 237
4, 233–34, 236, 239
4–5, 236
5, 236
5–7, 234

6, 232
6–7, 178
7, 180, 232, 236
8, 232–34, 237
8–9, 178
9, 232, 236–37
10, 232, 235–36, 239
10–14, 178, 235
11, 237
11–14, 231, 235–37, 239, 240
12, 233
12–15, 188
15, 178, 222, 233–34
15–16, 149, 234–36, 240
15–17, 236–37
15–21, 235, 237–38
16, 222, 233–34, 239
16–21, 178, 231
17, 176, 222, 237–38
17–18, 237
17–21, 235–36, 240
18, 222, 233–34, 237
18–21, 237
19, 222, 233, 237–38
20, 222, 237
21, 222, 233–34, 237–38

Jonah, 119, 139–41, 149, 152, 171, 177, 179, 182, 194–95, 206–7, 212, 215–17, 267, 290
1–4, 139, 149
1:1–3, 149
1:1–16, 195
1:1–2:1, 149
1:4–16, 149
1:6, 195, 204
1:14, 194, 196, 204
1:14–16, 195
1:15, 195
1:16, 195

2, 173, 174, 177, 195, 196
2:1, 195
2:1–11, 149
2:2, 204
2:3, 195
2:3–10, 195
2:5, 177, 195
2:8, 177
2:9–10, 177
2:11, 195
3, 196
3:1–10, 149
3:1–4:11, 149
3:8, 196, 204
3:9, 196
4:1–11, 149
4:2, 150, 196
4:2–3, 196
4:8–9, 196

Micah, 31, 34–36, 39–41, 43–50, 52–53, 55, 57, 59, 60–61, 64, 99, 105–8, 125, 127, 129, 130, 133, 139, 140–41, 145, 150–51, 166, 170–71, 176, 182, 196–97, 199, 206–8, 225, 266–67, 269, 290
1, 12, 48–53, 60, 61
1–3, 105, 107, 125, 166, 172–73
1–7, 105, 107, 139
1:1, 31, 125, 150–51, 215
1:1–16, 8, 31
1:1–7:20, 151
1:2, 32
1:2–4, 32
1:2–7, 32, 107
1:2–7:20, 151
1:2–15, 33
1:2–16, 31–32, 151
1:3–4, 32, 133

1:5, 31–32
1:6–7, 32
1:6–15, 33
1:7, 50
1:8, 32, 125, 127
1:8–9, 165
1:8–16, 32, 107
1:9, 32
1:10–15, 32
1:12, 32
1:13, 31–32
1:14, 31–32
1:15, 31–33
1:16, 33
1:22, 31
2:1–2, 106
2:1–5, 106–8
2:1–5:14, 151
2:1–13, 99, 105–8, 151
2:2, 106
2:3, 106
2:3–5, 106
2:3–7, 106
2:4, 106, 133
2:5, 106
2:6, 106
2:6–11, 106–7, 165, 166
2:8, 106
2:8–9, 106
2:9, 106
2:9–11, 106
2:11, 125, 127, 166
2:12–13, 106–8, 165
3, 164
3:1, 6, 125, 127, 165, 167
3:1–4, 107
3:1–5:14, 151
3:5–7, 107
3:7, 201
3:8, 107, 125, 127
3:9–12, 107
3:12, 125, 150, 201
4, 4, 12, 44, 48, 53–54, 56–61, 136, 176, 182

Ancient Sources Index

4–5, 105, 107, 125, 130, 172–73, 181
4:1, 58, 173
4:1–2, 302
4:1–5, 32, 56, 59, 110, 145, 151
4:1–5:8, 181
4:1–5:14, 107
4:2, 58, 133
4:3, 58, 176
4:4, 54, 57, 58, 126
4:5, 133, 136
4:6, 126
4:6–7, 181
4:6–5:14, 107
4:6–7, 57, 59
4:7, 59
4:8, 59
4:8–5:6, 293
4:9, 44, 59
4:9–10, 44, 173
4:9–5:4, 57
4:10, 44, 54–55
4:11–12, 32
4:14, 133
5:1, 151
5:2, 44
5:4–5, 133
5:5–6, 173
5:7–9, 32
5:9, 126
6, 73, 74, 126
6–7, 105, 120, 125–26, 128, 172–73
6:1, 126, 173
6:1–8, 3, 63, 65, 72, 74
6:1–16, 151
6:2, 126
6:3, 126
6:3–5, 125–26
6:4, 283
6:4–5, 126
6:6, 125
6:6–7, 125–26, 133
6:7, 126

6:8, 125, 131, 276
6:9–12, 126
6:9–13, 125
6:9–16, 126
6:13–16, 126
6:16, 126
7, 126–27
7:1, 125
7:1–2, 126, 133
7:1–7, 196
7:1–20, 151
7:2–4, 126
7:5, 125
7:5–6, 127
7:7, 125, 127, 196–97, 202
7:7–13, 196
7:7–20, 196
7:8, 127
7:8–9, 127
7:8–10, 125, 127, 133, 196
7:8–20, 127, 181, 197
7:9–10, 197
7:10, 127
7:11–12, 127
7:11–13, 107, 127, 196
7:14, 127, 196–97
7:14–20, 133, 196–97
7:15, 127, 196
7:16–17, 32, 127, 196–97
7:17, 127
7:17–20, 196
7:18, 127, 192
7:18–20, 107, 127, 133, 197
7:19, 127
7:19–20, 125, 127
7:20, 128

Nahum, 99, 108, 133, 138–41, 151–52, 171, 177, 182, 203, 206, 266–67, 290

1, 173, 174, 177
1–3, 139
1:1, 151–52, 215
1:1–3:19, 152
1:2, 152
1:2–8, 133, 216
1:2–10, 152
1:2–15, 133
1:2–3:19, 152
1:3, 180
1:11–2:1, 152
1:12–13, 109
1:12–15, 108–10
1:14, 109
1:14–15, 109
1:12, 110
1:12–15, 99, 108
2–3, 172, 182
2:1, 22, 182
2:2–11, 77
2:2–3:19, 152
3:1–3, 77, 109
3:1–7, 99, 108–10
3:1–17, 108
3:2–3, 110
3:4–7, 110
3:8–10, 152

Habakkuk, 99, 103–4, 133, 139–41, 152–53, 171, 173–74, 177–78, 182, 197, 199, 200, 203, 206, 266, 267, 270, 290

1, 134, 177, 198
1–2, 174, 197, 201
1–3, 139
1:1, 152–53, 174, 216
1:1–15, 270
1:1–2:20, 153
1:1–3:19, 153
1:2, 198
1:2–4, 134, 153, 174–75, 177, 197
1:2–2:20, 153

1:5–11, 77, 134, 153, 166, 175
1:5–12, 178
1:6, 104, 270
1:12–13, 174–75
1:12–17, 134, 153, 198
1:13, 198
1:13–14, 177
1:14–17, 175
1:15–17, 178
2, 134, 170, 178, 198
2:1, 23
2:1–3, 174, 177
2:1–4, 198, 201
2:1–20, 153
2:2, 21, 22, 121, 213
2:2–5, 23
2:3–5, 23
2:4–5, 198
2:4–15, 175
2:6, 104, 171
2:6–8, 104
2:6–17, 104
2:6–20, 99, 103–5
2:9, 171
2:12, 171
2:12–14, 104
2:15, 171
2:15–17, 104
2:16, 104
2:18–19, 198
2:18–20, 104
2:19, 171
2:20, 2, 198–99, 200–202
3, 134, 153, 173–78, 197–98, 201, 216, 270
3:1, 134, 152–53, 174
3:1–2, 178
3:1–19, 153
3:2, 198
3:2–19, 153
3:3–8, 198
3:3–15, 178
3:8–15, 198

3:16–19, 175, 178, 198
3:17, 178
3:19, 134, 153, 174

Zephaniah, 9, 11, 13, 99, 115, 138–41, 153–54, 170–71, 175, 181–82, 199–200, 203, 206, 215, 245–46, 248, 254, 256–58, 261–63, 266–67, 269, 290
1, 166, 252
1–2, 120, 130
1–3, 139, 172
1:1, 154, 216, 252
1:1–3:20, 154
1:2, 134, 252
1:2–3, 248, 251, 256
1:2–18, 154, 253
1:2–2:15, 115
1:2–3:20, 154
1:3, 134, 252
1:4–6, 253, 258
1:4–16, 251
1:4–2:3, 256
1:7, 2, 104, 188, 200–202
1:10, 134
1:11, 258
1:14–18, 101
1:15, 259
1:15–16, 134
1:17, 252
1:17–18, 251
2–3, 154
2:1, 252, 258
2:1–3, 101, 154, 253, 256–57, 262
2:1–3:20, 154
2:3, 253
2:4, 154, 248
2:4–3:20, 154
2:5, 249, 258
2:5–7, 248, 250, 255, 257

2:5–10, 253, 256
2:5–13, 248, 256
2:5–15, 154
2:6, 249
2:7, 249, 251, 257
2:8, 249–50, 257, 261
2:8–10, 249–51, 253, 256
2:9, 134, 250–51, 257–58
2:10, 250, 257
2:10–11, 251
2:11, 13, 246, 248, 250–51, 253, 256, 258–63
2:12, 254–56, 261
2:13, 254–55
2:13–15, 255–57
2:14, 258
2:15, 255
3:1–7, 115, 258
3:1–8, 257
3:1–13, 261
3:1–20, 154
3:6, 258
3:6–7, 257, 261
3:7, 257
3:8, 134, 201, 257–59
3:8–9, 257
3:8–10, 260
3:8–13, 115
3:8–20, 181
3:9, 202, 246, 253–54, 257–63
3:9–10, 259–60
3:9–20, 181
3:10, 258–61
3:11, 260
3:11–12, 259
3:11–13, 258, 260
3:14–18, 134
3:14–20, 99, 115–16, 143, 203
3:19–20, 134, 181
3:20, 134, 261–62

Ancient Sources Index

Haggai, 4, 60, 99, 116,
128, 134, 136, 138–
41, 154–55, 170–72,
178–79, 182, 199,
203, 206–7, 215, 265,
267–78, 282–84,
290–91, 295–97, 299
1, 134, 276
1–2, 139, 155
1:1, 134, 154, 170–71,
269–70
1:1–14, 268
1:1–15, 155, 269–70
1:1–2:9, 116
1:2, 270
1:2–3, 270
1:3, 134, 268, 270
1:4, 270, 271
1:4–11, 270
1:5–6, 270
1:7, 135, 269
1:8, 270
1:9, 270
1:10, 171
1:10–11, 270
1:12–15, 270, 298
1:13, 270
1:15, 170–71, 268, 270
1:15–2:1, 269
1:15–2:9, 155, 268
2:1, 134, 154, 170–71,
179, 268
2:1–10, 268
2:3, 271
2:6–9, 271
2:7–9, 302
2:10, 134, 170, 179,
268–69
2:10–19, 99, 116
2:10–23, 155
2:14, 268
2:15, 179
2:15–19, 268
2:17, 180
2:18, 154

2:19, 116, 180, 271
2:20, 134, 154, 170–
71, 268–69
2:20–23, 99, 116, 268,
271–72, 296–97
2:21, 271
2:23, 116, 268

Zechariah, 4, 10, 26,
75–78, 80–81, 85, 90,
92–93, 96, 111, 128–
29, 135–36, 139–41,
155–57, 170–71, 173,
178–80, 182, 191,
199, 200–203, 206,
215, 265–69, 273–74,
276–78, 283, 285,
287–91, 293–303,
320, 328, 330
1, 201, 278–79
1–2, 182, 276
1–6, 75–76, 81, 83,
85–86, 92, 95, 202,
273, 275, 294–95,
297–98, 300
1–8, 128, 134, 156,
171, 178, 203, 267,
269, 273, 275–78,
282–83, 290–93,
296–300
1–14, 139, 273
1:1, 128, 135, 155,
170–71, 179, 268–69,
273
1:1–6, 26, 156, 273,
300, 304
1:1–14:21, 156
1:2, 268, 273
1:2–6, 131, 178–79
1:3–4, 273
1:4, 273, 289
1:5–6, 273
1:6, 178, 199, 273

1:7, 78, 128, 135, 155,
170–71, 179, 268,
273
1:7–17, 156, 274
1:7–6:15, 156–57, 199,
273, 275, 302
1:7–6:8, 130
1:7–14:21, 156
1:8, 75, 81, 83–84, 273
1:8–6
1:8–11, 90, 95
1:8–17, 79, 81, 84
1:8–6:8, 135
1:9–11, 84
1:9–15, 81
1:11, 90
1:12, 84–85, 94, 199
1:12–13, 90, 95, 202
1:12–14, 90
1:12–17, 95
1:13, 84, 86
1:14–16, 90
1:14–17, 84, 86, 90, 95
1:17, 90
1:18–22, 274
2, 201
2:1, 84
2:1–3, 252, 274
2:1–4, 79, 84, 90, 95,
156
2:2, 84
2:4, 84, 90, 199, 273
2:5–8, 84, 91, 95
2:5–9, 78, 84, 295
2:5–17, 156
2:6, 78, 84, 91, 268
2:6–12, 275
2:8, 78, 84–85, 91, 94–
95
2:9, 84, 86, 91, 95, 129
2:10, 295
2:10–17, 84
2:11, 203
2:13, 104, 275, 288
2:14, 295

2:14–15, 203
2:15, 288, 295, 301
2:17, 2, 200, 202
3, 268, 275, 298, 300
3–4, 276
3:1–5, 84, 91
3:1–7, 77
3:1–10, 84, 156, 274
3:4–5, 275
3:6–7, 84, 86, 91, 300
3:7, 297
3:7–10, 297
3:8, 91, 293–94, 297, 300
3:8–10, 86, 91, 293, 300
3:9, 13, 91, 298
3:10, 91, 294
3:18–20, 181
4, 95–96, 274, 300
4:1, 273
4:1–6, 91, 274
4:1–14, 79, 84, 156, 274, 302
4:2–3, 84
4:4–6, 84, 86
4:6–7, 95
4:6–10, 84, 86, 91, 96, 181, 274
4:8–10, 95
4:9, 288, 297
4:10–13, 274
4:10–14, 84, 91
4:11, 274
4:12, 274
4:13, 274
4:14, 81, 91, 96
5, 130, 295
5:1–2, 84, 91, 95
5:1–3, 91
5:1–4, 79, 84, 156, 274
5:1–6:8, 276
5:2, 84
5:3, 84–85, 91, 95
5:4, 84, 86, 91, 95
5:5–6, 85

5:5–11, 79, 85, 90, 95–96, 156, 274
5:6, 85
5:7–8, 273
5:8, 85
5:8–9, 85
5:10–11, 85
5:11, 81
6, 297, 300
6:1–3, 85
6:1–7, 92
6:1–8, 79, 85, 95, 274
6:1–15, 156
6:4–6, 85
6:6, 92
6:8, 81, 85–86, 92, 273, 295
6:9, 135, 268
6:9–12, 275
6:9–15, 9–10, 84, 276, 285, 288–93, 295–300, 302, 304
6:10, 285, 296
6:11, 298
6:12, 285, 292
6:12–13, 292, 301–2
6:13, 285, 291–95
6:13–15, 275
6:14, 285, 292, 296, 298–300
6:15, 288, 295, 297, 300
7, 199
7–8, 172, 181, 203, 204, 275, 304
7–9, 276
7–14, 156, 157, 202
7:1, 135, 155, 170–72, 179, 199, 268–69
7:1–3, 172, 275–76
7:1–6, 124
7:1–7, 111, 157
7:1–14, 99, 111
7:1–8:23, 273
7:1–9:8, 111–12
7:1–14:21, 111, 157

7:2, 199
7:4, 135
7:4–7, 275–76
7:7–14, 131
7:8, 172, 268
7:8–10, 111
7:8–14, 111, 157, 276
7:8–14:21, 157
7:9, 276
7:9–10, 304
7:10, 276
7:11–14, 201
7:12, 276, 289
7:13, 276
7:13–14, 201
7:14, 275
8, 111, 182, 276
8:1, 111, 135, 172, 268, 276
8:1–17, 99, 112, 157, 276
8:1–23, 111–12
8:2, 268, 276
8:3, 112, 268
8:4, 268, 276
8:4–5, 112
8:7, 268, 276
8:7–8, 112
8:9, 172, 276
8:11, 268
8:12, 112
8:13, 112
8:14, 172, 268, 276
8:16, 131
8:16–17, 112, 304
8:18, 124, 135, 172, 268, 276
8:18–14:21, 157
8:18–19, 112, 275
8:18–21, 275
8:18–23, 276
8:19, 276
8:20, 172, 268, 276
8:20–23, 99, 112
8:21, 276
8:21–23, 275

Ancient Sources Index

8:23, 268
9, 120, 156, 273, 277–81
9–10, 281
9–11, 156–57, 174, 273, 299
9–13, 174, 281
9–14, 4, 128, 156, 173–74, 267, 272–73, 276–78, 281, 283, 287, 290, 298, 300, 302, 304
9:1, 129, 170–71, 174, 268
9:1–7, 278–79
9:1–8, 99, 112–13, 174, 277, 279
9:1–11:3, 277
9:8, 112, 278
9:9, 304
9:9–10, 10, 203, 278–79, 281
9:9–15, 111
9:9–17, 112
9:11, 279
9:11–13, 278–79
9:11–17, 279
9:12, 279
9:13, 279
9:14–15, 278
9:14–17, 280
9:16–17, 278
9:9–10, 278
10, 280
10–11, 174
10–14, 202
10:1, 202, 280–81
10:1–12, 112
10:2–3, 278, 280–81
10:3, 280
10:3–5, 280
10:3–12, 111, 278, 281
10:4–5, 280
10:6, 202, 280
10:6–10, 280

10:7, 280
10:10, 280
10:11, 280
11, 281, 282, 300
11–13, 280, 282
11–14, 280–81
11:1, 281
11:1–2, 281
11:1–3, 278, 281
11:2, 281
11:3, 281
11:4, 268
11:4–16, 199, 277, 278, 280–81
11:5, 199
11:7–16, 281
11:13, 268, 294
11:15, 268
11:16, 281
11:17, 278
12, 120, 279
12–14, 128, 129–30, 156–57, 174, 273, 299
12:1, 129–30, 170–71, 174, 268–79
12:1–2, 278
12:1–8, 279
12:1–9, 282
12:2, 129
12:2–13:6, 131, 277
12:2–4, 129, 130
12:3, 129
12:3–9, 278
12:4, 129
12:5, 129–30
12:6, 129–30
12:6–8, 129
12:7–8, 129
12:8, 129
12:9, 129
12:10, 278
12:10–14, 131, 204, 282
12:10–13:1, 202, 278

12:10–13:6, 280, 282
12:11, 129
12:11–14, 278
13, 174, 301
13:1, 129, 268, 278
13:1–6, 131
13:2, 129, 268
13:2–6, 278
13:4, 129
13:7, 129, 281
13:7–9, 111, 129, 174, 278–81
13:9, 129, 202, 282
13:10–14, 129
14, 172, 174, 181–82, 271, 274, 277, 279–81, 283
14:1, 129, 130, 172
14:1–2, 278
14:1–16, 130
14:1–21, 282
14:2, 129
14:3–9, 129
14:4, 129
14:5, 129
14:6, 129, 172
14:6–11, 129
14:8, 129, 172, 268
14:9, 129, 172, 282–83
14:10–11, 129
14:12–15, 130–31, 278
14:12–19, 129
14:13, 172
14:16, 130, 278
14:16–17, 275, 282–83
14:16–19, 124, 131
14:16–20, 130
14:17, 130
14:17–19, 278
14:17–20, 131
14:18–19, 130
14:20, 129, 172
14:20–21, 129, 278, 304
14:21, 172, 281

Malachi, 4, 60, 65,
119, 139, 140–41,
158, 171, 173, 174–
75, 179, 182, 199,
203, 206–7, 265–69,
282–84, 290–91, 333
1, 120
1–3, 139
1–4, 139
1:1, 129, 158, 170–71
1:1–3:24, 158
1:2, 199
1:2–5, 148, 158, 282
1:2–3:24, 158
1:5, 199, 200, 283
1:6, 199
1:6–14, 282
1:6–2:9, 282
1:6–2:16, 158
1:7, 199
1:11, 158, 283
1:14, 282–83
1:17, 199
1:18, 283
2:1–9, 282
2:3–9, 131
2:10–16, 282
2:12, 283
2:14, 199
2:17–3:5, 158, 282
3:1, 140, 158, 171
3:2–3, 282
3:5–24, 131
3:6–12, 158, 282
3:7, 199, 268
3:8, 199
3:13, 199, 268
3:13–15, 282
3:13–21, 158
3:16, 200
3:16–21, 174
3:16–18, 282
3:17, 268
3:22, 283
3:22–24, 158
3:23, 176

3:23–24, 140, 283
4:1, 268
4:1–3, 282
4:3, 268
4:4–6, 267, 282

**Early Jewish
Literature**
4QJer[b], 159

b. baba Batra 14b, 139

Ben Sira, 28
24
24:32–33, 29
39:1–3, 28

**Ancient Near
Eastern/Greco-
Roman Sources**
A. 1121, 24
A. 2731, 24

AP 45, 71
AP 6, 71

ARM 26 no. 414:29–
42, 21, 22
ARM 26, no. 199, 24
ARM 26, no. 237, 24

Deir 'Alla, 24

Dēnu 7, 66
Dēnu 10, 66
Dēnu 11, 66

Herodotus, *Histories*
3.14, 70
Herodotus, *Histories*
3.91–92, 69

Julius Caeser, *The
Gallic Wars*, 19

Prophecy of Neferti,
210

SAA 9 3.2, i 27–ii 9,
22
SAA 9, no. 3, 25
SAA 9, no. 1, 24
SAA 9, no. 2, 24
SAA 9, no. 3, 24

TAD 7.2, 71
TAD 7.2, 71
TAD B7.1, 71
TAD B7.1–7.3, 71
TAD B7.2, 71
TAD B7.3, 71
TAD B8.6, 72
TAD B8.7, 72
TAD B8.8, 72

Modern Authors Index

Abma, Richtsje, 48, 323
Achtemeier, Elizabeth, 60, 323
Ackroyd, Peter, 208–9, 216, 323
Albertz, Rainer, 137, 266, 323
Allen, Leslie C., 167, 323
Alter, Robert, 12, 194, 212–14, 316, 323
Anderson, Francis I., 60, 166, 323
Anderson Jr., R. W., 254, 323
Anderson, John E., 87, 198, 323
Apóstolo, Silvio S., 257, 323
Assis, Elie., 323
Assis, Eliyahu, 188–91, 232, 238
Auld, A. Graeme, 20, 194, 323
Avery-Peck, Alan J., 337

Bakhtin, M. M., 41, 300, 323
Balogh, Casbah, 324
Baltzer, Klaus, 209, 212, 216, 324
Barr, James, 247, 324
Barstadt, Hans M., 20, 324, 317
Barthélemy, Domenique, 252, 324
Barton, John, 60, 145, 148, 183, 189, 265, 324
Bauks, Michaela, 324
Baumann, Gerline, 40, 48, 52, 143, 324
Baumgartner, Walter, 253, 334
Beck, John A., 214, 260, 324
Beck, Martin., 259, 324
Becker, Eve Marie, 247–48, 324
Becking, Bob, 223–25, 324
Behrens, Achim, 78, 80–81, 88, 93, 324
Belknap, Robert E., 26, 324
Ben Zvi, Ehud, 2–3, 12, 14, 17, 23, 29, 30–36, 46, 50, 53, 55–56, 60, 97–98,
100, 108, 137, 142, 148, 150, 153, 201, 207–8, 216, 224–25, 237, 241, 242, 246, 251, 256, 257, 259, 267, 286–88, 304, 313, 315–17, 324–25, 344
Berger, Klaus, 168, 325
Bergler, Siegfried, 88, 325
Bergmann, Claudia D., 44–45, 59, 325
Berlin, Adele, 116, 214, 219, 229, 248–49, 325
Berman, Joshua A., 261, 325
Biddle, Mark E., 224–25, 241–42, 325
Block, Daniel I., 231–34, 238, 241, 243, 325
Blum, Erhard, 313
Boda, Mark J., 2, 55, 75, 179, 184, 186, 187–88, 190–91, 199, 201–4, 223, 224, 267, 274, 304, 305–6, 321, 325–26
Boer, Roland, 326
Bos, James M., 19, 326
Botterweck, G. Johannes, 326
Brett, Mark, 260, 326
Bruckner, James K., 168, 326
Budde, Karl, 6, 163–67, 169, 180, 182, 326–27
Bulkeley, Tim, 11–12, 208, 211, 216, 219, 305, 321, 327
Buss, Martin J., 1, 15, 38, 53, 97, 167, 168–69, 226, 229, 237, 308, 327
Bussmann, Hadumod, 246, 327

Campbell, Antony F., 37–38, 46, 245, 312–13, 315, 327
Carl Sandburg, 20

Caroll, Robert P., 18
Carr, David M., 23, 176, 327
Carroll R., M. Daniel, 193, 327
Carroll, Robert P., 19, 20, 226, 315, 327
Carter, Charles E., 279, 327
Carver, Terrell, 42, 327
Charteris-Black, J., 42, 327
Childs, Brevard S., 177, 316, 327
Christensen, Duane L., 109, 267, 270, 328
Clark, David J., 142, 274, 319, 328
Clements, Ronald E., 88, 210, 328
Clendenen, E. Ray, 269, 282–83, 328, 344
Clifford, Richard J., 99, 328
Clines, David J. A., 328
Cloran, Carmel, 328
Cogan, Michael D., 328
Coggins, Richard J., 145–46, 188–89, 192–93, 328
Collins, Terence, 183, 328
Conrad, Edgar, 155, 273, 293, 303, 328
Cook, John A., 236, 328
Crenshaw, James L., 21–22, 145, 184, 212, 328
Curtis, Byron G., 277–87, 298–300, 328

Dandamaev, M. A., 69–71, 328
Daniels, Dwight R., 63–64, 328
Darr, Katheryn Pfisterer, 44, 328
Davies, Graham I., 25, 55, 142, 185–86, 232, 315, 328
Davies, Philip R., 19, 329
Davis, Ellen F., 234, 243, 329
De Roche, Michael, 63–64, 73, 74, 329
De Vries, Simon J., 144, 329
de Waard, Jan, 193
Dearman, J. Andrew, 23, 52, 113, 329
Deist, Ferdinand E., 17, 119–20, 329
Delkurt, Holger, 90, 329
Démare-Lafont, Sophie, 66, 329
Dempsey, Carol, 5, 55, 305–6, 320, 326
Dijk, Teun A. van, 329

Donald, David Herbert, 20, 329

Eco, Umberto, 26, 329
Edelman, Diana V., 316
Elliger, Karl, 274, 329
Endo, Yoshinobu, 236, 329

Fales, Frederick M., 255, 329
Fauconnier, Giles, 38, 42, 44
Fauconnier, Gilles, 329
Fensham, F. Charles, 48, 329
Fewell, Danna Nolan, 214, 331
Figulla, H. H., 68, 329
Finitsis, Antonios, 275, 294–95, 330
Fishbane, Michael, 138, 330
Flesher, LeAnn Snow, 326
Floyd, Michael H., 17–18, 22, 92, 98, 100, 110, 151–55, 158, 205, 226, 241, 253–54, 257, 288, 290–92, 302–3, 305–6, 315–17, 319–21, 330
Fokkelman, Jan, 214, 217, 330
Freedman, David Noel, 60, 87, 166, 323
Frolov, Serge, 303

Gardiner, Alan, 229
Garrett, Duane, 185–86, 188, 190, 330
Gärtner, Judith, 259, 330
Gelston, Anthony, 249, 252, 257, 330
Gerstenberger, Erhard, 6–9, 12, 99, 128, 130–31, 134, 305, 321, 330–31
Gese, Hartmut, 88, 331
Gibbs, Raymond W., 42, 331
Gitay, Yehoshua, 331
Glazier-McDonald, Beth, 282–83, 331
Goody, Jack, 26, 331
Gordon, R. P., 286, 288, 295, 331
Green, Barbara, 41, 331
Green, William Scott, 337
Greenberg, Moshe, 316
Gries, Stefan Thomas, 42, 342
Grimal, Nicolas, 254, 331
Gunkel, Hermann, 10, 14–15, 43, 64, 97, 168, 221–23, 226, 229, 306–7, 311–15, 331
Gunn, David M., 214, 331

Haak, Robert D., 152, 331
Hadjiev, Tchavdar, 47, 82, 88–90, 193, 245, 250–51, 258, 261, 331
Hall, Gary Harlan, 59, 331
Halliday, M.A.K., 37, 221, 226–27, 229, 240, 331–32
Hamborg, Graham R., 193
Hanson, Paul D., 277, 332
Harrelson, Walter, 277, 332
Harrington, Daniel, J., 265, 332
Hartley, John, 241
Harvey, Julien, 64, 332
Hasan, Ruqaiya, 37, 221, 226–28, 240, 331–32
Hatton, Howard A., 274, 328
Hayes, John H., 88–89, 191, 332
Heinzmann, G., 76, 332
Hess, Richard S., 249, 332
Hiebert, Theodore, 178, 332
Hilgert, Markus, 25, 332
Hill, Andrew E., 158, 171, 267, 283, 332
Hillers, Delbert R., 57, 197, 332
Ho Fai Tai, Nicholas, 277, 332
Holladay, William L., 94, 245, 251, 261, 332
Holloway, Steven W., 256, 332
Holmstedt, Robert D., 230, 332
Holtz, Shalom E., 67–69, 71, 72, 332
Horst, Friedrich, 77–78, 184, 333
Hossfeld, F.L., 259, 333
House, Paul R., 183, 251, 266–68, 333, 345
Houston, Walter J., 319
Hubbard, David Allan, 187–88, 191–92, 333
Huffmon, Herbert B., 64, 73, 333
Hugenberger, Gordon Paul, 40, 51, 333

Irsigler, Hubert, 258–59, 333

Jacobs, Mignon, 150, 333
Jacobsen, Rolf A., 214–15, 333
Janzen, J. Gerald, 48, 333

Janzen, W., 99, 333
Jas, Remko, 66, 333
Jemielity, Thomas, 58, 333
Jenson, Philip Peter, 197, 333
Jeremias, Christian, 76, 80, 333
Jeremias, Jörg, 87–88, 91, 122–23, 172, 177–78, 184–85, 197, 266, 333
Johnson, Mark, 38, 44, 335
Johnston, G. H., 255, 333
Jones, Andrew R., 230, 332
Jones, Barry Alan, 137, 139, 333
Jursa, Michael, 67, 333

Kahn, Dan'el, 260, 333
Kakkanattu, Joy Philip, 48, 334
Kapelrud, Arvid S., 251, 334
Kashow, Robert C., 289, 296–97, 298, 334
Katz, Cindi, 42, 342
Keefe, Alice A., 52, 334
Kelle, Brad E., 40, 49, 52–53, 334
Kermode, Frank, 194
Kessler, John, 179, 271, 334
Kessler, Rainer, 125, 133, 334
Kim, Hyun Chul Paul, 39, 41, 224, 225, 286, 287, 334
Kindl, E.-M., 259, 333
King, Greg A., 259, 334
Kirk-Duggan, Cheryl A., 55, 334
Knierim, Rolf, 223, 334
Knoppers, Gary, 167, 334
Koch, Klaus, 46, 184, 193–94, 334
Koehler, Ludwig, 253, 334
Koenen, Klaus, 324
Kohl, Philip L., 70–71, 328
Kotzé, Zacharais, 43, 334
Kövecses, Zoltan, 42, 334
Krecher, Joachim, 334
Kruger, Paul A., 43, 334
Kwakkel, Gert, 49, 51, 334
Kwasman, T., 69, 334

Labat, René, 25, 335
Lakoff, George, 38, 41, 44, 335
Landy, Francis, 142, 247, 261, 335

Lange, Armin, 21, 24–25, 29, 30, 335
Larkin, Katrina J.A., 281, 289, 335
LeCureux, Jason T., 137, 184, 335
Lee, W.W., 246–47, 335
Lescow, Theodor, 282–83, 335
Lessing, R. Reed, 266, 335
Levin, Christoph, 267, 335
Limburg, James, 195–96, 335
Lindblom, Johannes, 167, 335
Lipschits, Oded, 279, 335
Long, Burke O., 77–79, 335
Long, Shelley L., 159, 335
Longman III, Tremper, 39, 43, 45, 336
Lord, Albert Bates, 241, 336
Luckenbill, Daniel D., 255, 336
Lukonin, Vladimir G., 70–71
Lundbom, Jack R., 59, 336
Lux, Rüdiger, 200, 336

Maat, H. Pander, 246, 341
Macintosh, A. A., 54, 57, 336
Maier, Christl, 55, 336
Malinowski, Bronislaw, 229
Mandolfo, Carleen, 55, 336
March, W. Eugene, 265, 272, 278, 336
Marks, Herbert, 194, 336
Marrs, Rick R., 44, 336
Mason, Rex A., 289, 336
Mays, James Luther, 56–57, 86–87, 166, 336
McComiskey, Thomas Edward, 194, 336
McKenzie, Steven L., 60, 265, 336
Meadowcroft, Tim, 268, 336
Melugin, Roy Frank, 19, 38, 45–46, 336
Metso, Sarianna, 319
Meyers, Carol L., 111, 154–55, 267, 274, 278, 336
Meyers, Eric M., 111, 154, 155, 267, 274, 278, 336
Michael H. Floyd, 325
Millar, William R., 41, 337
Miller-Naudé, Cynthia L., 230, 337
Mitchell, Stephen A., 241
Moberly, R. W. L., 102, 337
Möller, Karl, 148, 194, 337

Morgan, Donn M., 257, 337
Morris, Gerald, 187, 337
Moseman, 300
Moughtin-Mumby, Sharon, 40, 337
Mowinckel, Sigmund, 21–22, 222, 337
Muilenburg, James, 11

Nagy, Gregory, 241
Neef, Heinz-Dieter, 248, 251, 337
Neujahr, Matthew, 34, 206, 337
Neusner, Jacob, 337
Newsom, Carol A., 41, 337
Niditch, Susan, 77–80, 88, 241, 318, 337
Nielsen, Kirsten, 64, 337
Nissinen, Martti, 19, 21, 22, 23, 24, 25, 120, 226, 255, 317, 337, 338
Nogalski, James, 2–3, 6–8, 12, 47, 137, 170, 172–75, 177–78, 180–81, 183–84, 196–98, 200, 202, 211, 232–33, 236, 238, 241–43, 266–67, 290–91, 295–96, 305–6, 321, 323, 325, 338
Nurmela, Risto, 338

O'Brien, Julia M., 65, 283, 338
O'Connor, Michael Patrick, 236, 345
O'Kennedy, Daniel F., 199, 338
Odell, Margaret S., 39, 338
Oelsner, Joachim, 67, 69, 338
Ogden, G., 187, 338
Ong, Walter J., 241, 338
Oppenheim, A. L., 260, 339
Overholt, Thomas, 20
Page, S., 144, 339
Park, Aaron W., 89, 339
Parpola, Simo, 66, 339
Paul, Shalom M., 89, 146, 339
Pearce, Laurie E., 318
Person, Raymond F., 277, 339
Petersen, David L., 21, 154–55, 158, 207, 210, 247, 267, 274, 315, 339
Petterson, Anthony R., 9–10, 14, 279, 288, 291, 293–95, 301, 339
Pikalo, Jernej, 42, 327
Pirsig, Robert, 269, 339
Polk, Timothy, 207, 339
Popović, Mladen, 319

Porten, Bezalel, 71, 72, 339
Porter, Stanley E., 230, 339
Pritchard, James B., 340
Pröbstle, Martin, 81, 340

Raabe, Paul R., 148, 171, 222, 340
Radine, Jason, 82, 88, 90, 340
Redditt, Paul L., 2–5, 113, 138, 154–55, 158, 174, 266, 273–74, 278–81, 283, 305–6, 321, 340
Reimers, Stephan, 78, 80, 340
Renaud, Bernard, 57, 59, 340
Renz, Thomas, 289, 340
Reventlow, Henning G., 92, 278, 340
Richter, Wolfgang, 46, 307
Riede, Peter, 88, 340
Rignell, 301
Ringgren, Helmer, 259, 326, 340
Risto, Nurmela, 278, 289
Roberts, J. J. M., 252–53, 340
Roberts, O. Palmer., 254
Robinson, Robert B., 232, 235, 340
Rokay, Zoltán, 273, 340
Rooker, Mark E., 60, 340
Rose, Wolter H., 91, 274, 278, 341
Rösel, Martin, 39, 341
Rudolph, Wilhelm, 129, 166, 178, 341

Sadler Jr., Rodney S., 260, 341
Sandburg, Carl, 20, 341
Sanders, T., 246, 341
Sasson, Jack M., 341
Schaper, Joachim, 22–23, 318, 341
Scharbert, Josef, 131–32, 341
Schart, Aaron, 3, 24, 133, 138, 183, 200, 266, 282, 291, 340–41
Schniedewind, William M., 23, 318, 341
Schultz, Richard L., 48
Seybold, Klaus, 132, 274, 341
Shaw, Charles S., 53, 59, 254, 342
Sheppard, Gerald T., 184, 342
Sherwood, Aaron, 230, 342
Simon, Uriel, 342
Sister, Moses, 76–77, 342

Skinner, John, 207, 209, 342
Smith, Jonathan Z., 342
Smith, Neil, 27, 42, 342
Soggin, J. Alberto, 87, 342
Soskice, Janet Martin, 42, 342
Spronk, Klaas, 151, 342
Stähli, H.-P., 253
Stead, Michael R., 75, 86, 276, 277, 289, 291–93, 302, 342
Steck, Odil Hannes, 18, 29, 169, 211–12, 265, 283, 342
Stefanowitsch, Anatol, 42, 342
Steiner, Richard, 279, 342
Stolper, Matthew W., 342
Stovell, Beth M., 11, 12, 40, 45–46, 51, 306–7, 320, 342
Stuart, Douglas, 56, 343
Suderman, W. Derek, 184, 343
Sweeney, Marvin A., 2, 12, 46–47, 55, 57, 60, 101, 106, 109, 111, 137, 142, 145, 146–58, 179, 181, 184, 196–98, 200, 205, 207, 209, 216, 249, 252–54, 259–60, 265–66, 289–91, 293, 305, 313, 315, 320–21, 338, 343–44
Sykes, Seth, 41, 344

Taylor, Richard A., 269, 282, 344
Theocharous, Myrto, 47, 344
Tiemeyer, Lena-Sofia, 4, 91, 96, 191, 305–6, 320, 344
Tigay, Jeffrey H., 52, 344
Timmer, Daniel, 9, 11, 13–14, 306, 321
Todd, Andrew, 230, 344
Toffelmire, Colin M., 11, 14, 17, 37, 98, 167, 223, 226, 238, 287, 289, 306, 307, 321, 344
Tollington, Janet E., 269, 289, 344
Tov, Emanuel, 159, 344
Trible, Phyllis, 149, 344
Trotter, James M., 3–5, 63, 73, 186, 305, 320–21, 344
Tucker, Gene M., 344
Turner, Mark, 38, 42, 44, 329

Utzschneider, Helmut, 171, 344

Van De Mieroop, Marc, 254, 344
van der Kooij, Arie, 159, 344
van der Merwe, C. H. J., 230, 337, 344
van der Toorn, Karel, 21, 22, 25, 176, 318, 345
van Dijk, Tuen A., 226
Van Hecke, Pierre, 42, 345
Van Seters, John, 288, 345
van Wolde, Ellen J., 246
Vlaardingerbroek, J., 153, 258, 345
Vladimir, Vladimir G., 328
von Rad, Gerhard, 216, 345
von Soden, Wolfram, 24–25, 28, 345

Waard, Jan de, 345
Wagenaar, Jan A., 50, 53, 56–57, 345
Waltke, Bruce K., 59, 196, 236, 345
Ward, James M., 18, 345
Watts, James W., 345
Watts, John D. W., 170, 260, 266–67, 345
Weeks, Stuart, 317
Weinfeld, Moshe, 46–47, 60, 345
Weiser, Artur, 167, 345
Wells, Bruce, 67, 338
Wenham, Gordon J., 59, 345
Wenzel, Heiko, 298, 300–301, 345
Westermann, Claus, 3, 63, 99, 222, 265, 314–15, 345
Whitt, William D., 53, 345
Williams, James G., 99, 345
Williamson, H. G. M., 20
Willis, John, 166, 345
Wilson, Gerald H., 1, 15, 21, 160, 345
Wilson, Robert R., 1, 315, 345
Wöhrle, Jakob, 88, 90, 165, 176, 178, 181, 183, 247, 266, 137, 323, 345
Wolde, Ellen J. van, 346
Wolff, Hans Walter, 53, 55–57, 59, 82, 87, 142, 145–46, 148–50, 154, 166, 172, 177–78, 185, 187–90, 192, 194–95, 222, 233, 241, 268, 346
Wolterstorff, Nicholas, 303, 346
Wood, Joyce L. Rilett, 89, 346
Wunsch, Cornelia, 67, 318, 338

Würthwein, Ernst, 64, 346

Yardeni, Ada, 71, 72, 339
Yee, Gale A., 52, 346
Young, Liam Cole, 26–27, 346

www.ingramcontent.com/pod-product-compliance
Lightning Source LLC
Chambersburg PA
CBHW020055020526
44112CB00031B/151